A Commentary
on the
Pauline Epistles

A Commentary
on the
Pauline Epistles

by Charles B. Williams

MOODY PRESS
CHICAGO

Printed in the United States of America

Contents

Contents

The First Letter to the Thessalonians

INTRODUCTION

1. *Paul the Pathfinder in Letters as Christian Literature.* James, the author of the Letter bearing his name, who seems to have written about the same time that Paul wrote his first Letters, is the only possible rival for this honor. But as Paul wrote thirteen Letters, whereas James wrote only one, the honor easily belongs to Paul as the pathfinder in the letter as Christian literature. As the Letters were written before the Gospels, he is the pathfinder of all Christian literature.

But he did not originate the letter as a form of literature. Cicero, about one hundred years before Paul, had made the letter an attractive form of Roman literature. His letters are now a permanent part of the great Latin literature. Pliny the Younger, who made Cicero his model, a little after Paul, also lends dignity to the letter as a form of literature, as his letters are recognized in the body of Greek literature. The Letters of Junius have come to be recognized as a valuable portion of English literature. The letter is also recognized in German, French, and Russian literatures.

The letter was a facile vehicle for Paul to express his views of important doctrines and teachings, about which the individual churches were in doubt, or of which they had hazy conceptions. For example, the second coming of Christ in the letters to the Thessalonians; the doctrine of salvation by grace through faith for the Christians in the provinces of Galatia and Asia (in Galatians and Ephesians), and the doctrine of the person and work of Christ as set forth in Colossians. The letter being a message directly from one person to another or others emphasizes the personal relation of the individual to God, and also personal relations among Christians. The letter became a facile tool in the solution of doctrinal problems in the early churches. Paul was the pathfinder led by the Spirit.

2. *The Origin of the Church in Thessalonica.* Thessalonica was the second city in Macedonia evangelized by Paul on his second mis-

sionary journey (Acts 17:4). The city was founded by Philip of
Macedon and named in honor of his daughter, whose birth occurred
on the day of one of his glorious victories. The city has continued
down to our times under the name Salonica.

So the church was founded by Paul, and converts of his preaching constituted its first members; some were Jews, but most were
pagans. Paul at first, as was his custom, preached in the synagogue,
but the Jews became enraged at his teachings and then he made the
home of Jason, a Greek, headquarters. Gentiles flocked to Jason's
home to hear the good news of salvation by faith based on the love
of God and the grace of Christ. So the Jews set up a campaign of
severe persecution against Paul and his missionary group as "those
who had turned the world upside down." They further accused
them of being traitors to Caesar for calling "Jesus another King."
But the good news prevailed and "not a few chief women" of the
city believed and many noted Greeks who had become proselytes
to Judaism. But the church there was mainly Gentilic in constituency.

3. *Occasion and Date of the First Letter to Them.* Under the
heat of fiery persecution by the Jews, Paul escaped to Athens where
he stopped on his way to Corinth, the capital of Greece (Achaia).
Not being able himself to return, he sent Timothy back to Thessalonica to ascertain their condition and to let them know how he was
praying for them in their persecutions (2:14, 17, 18; 3:1). While
Timothy was on his way to Thessalonica, Paul went on to Corinth
where Timothy soon rejoined him and reported the steadfastness of
the Thessalonian Christians and their beautiful fidelity to Paul and
his gospel (3:6-8). It is quite certain that he also reported their
misunderstanding of Paul's teaching on the parousia (Christ's return) and their grief over their lost loved ones.

4. *The Purpose.* The historical environment, the spirit of the
letter, as well as its diction and style, all point to Paul as the author,
so we deem it unnecessary to discuss the authorship of the letter.
Why did Paul write this his first letter—perhaps the first of all the
New Testament books written? (a) First of all, to let them know his
abiding love and interest for them; to pour out his heart's affection
for them. They were his spiritual children. He had become their

father through the fires of raging persecution and now they are heirs to that persecution. Because he fled for safety does not mean that he does not care for them, and has deserted them. (b) To encourage them bravely to endure these persecutions (3:4-4:8). He reminds them that he had told them in person that they might expect to suffer affliction for the sake of the gospel. (c) He also writes with a didactic purpose—to instruct them further concerning the parousia. From Timothy he had learned that they were grief-stricken over their deceased loved ones. They seem to have concluded from Paul's preaching when there that these loved ones could not share in the glories of the coming kingdom. So he assures them that they would "precede" the living at that time in sharing the glorious kingdom of the parousia (4:15).

5. *The Main Teachings.* (a) God is the Father. (b) Christ Jesus is the Messiah promised in the Old Testament. This was his first message after his conversion (Acts 9:20). In Thessalonica he preached it. "For three sabbaths he reasoned with them from the Scriptures—and alleging that this Jesus, whom I proclaim to you, is the Christ" (Acts 17;2, 3). As Messiah He is the Son of God (1:10). (c) The necessity of His sufferings and resurrection not emphasized but implied (1:10b). "Jesus who delivers us from the wrath to come." The verb *deliver* is a synonym of the verb *redeem* (Gal. 3:13). We know that Paul did emphasize the death and resurrection of Christ, because that was the theme of his first sermons at Thessalonica. "It behooved the Christ to suffer and rise again from the dead" (Acts 17:3). (See I Cor. 15:2-4.) He did not put special emphasis on the cross and resurrection in this letter because his first doctrinal purpose was to set the readers right as to the parousia. (d) Divine election is a basic teaching of his (1:4). "Knowing, brothers, beloved by God, that He has chosen you." This is the basis of his elaborate teaching on election in Romans 9; Ephesians 1:4, 11; 2:8, 10). (e) Faith, love, and hope, the immortal trio in Paul's scheme of thought, occur in this order in this first letter (1:3), since in this letter he is stressing the parousia as the object of hope, and so it is fitting to make hope the climax; in I Corinthians (13:13) love is the climax and "greatest," because it is the ethical, not the eschatological, which is at the front of the

screen. (f) Toil and industry in the social life are not only commended but commanded. "Study to be quiet, and practice attending to your own business and to work with your own hands" (4:11). (g) The parousia, the great doctrine of the letter, is the return of the Lord Jesus to gather His people to Himself at the end of the age. Paul emphasized it as the object of the believer's hope (1:3, 10), the goal for which he is "waiting." It is to be sudden and at a time when not expected (5:2, 3). Christians who have died will be raised first—then those remaining alive will be caught up, transformed, to meet the Lord in the air (4:16). Paul has no discussion as to details connected with the glorious event; no suggestion as to a thousand years of reign on earth before His people meet the Lord in the air. His supreme emphasis is on the fact, "The dead in Christ will rise first." This is to comfort the despondent Christians who are grieving over their lost loved ones. See comments later on 4:13-18.

OUTLINE

I. Salutation (1:1)
II. Personal Portion (1:2-3:13)
   1. His first preaching in Thessalonica (1:2-10)
   2. In sincerity and sufferings he labored among them (2:1-12)
   3. They enthusiastically received his message as God's Word (2:13-16)
   4. He desires to see them (2:17-20)
   5. He rejoices that Timothy could report their faith and love, and devotion to him (3:1-10)
   6. His prayer for them (3:11-13)
III. The Didactic Portion (4:1-5:24)
   1. Exhorts to moral living and sanctification (4:1-12)
   2. Comforts them concerning their deceased loved ones, who will share the blessings of Christ's second coming (4:13-5:11)
   3. He gives various exhortations: to respect their leaders, be at peace, be forgiving, helpful, rejoicing, prayerful, thankful, etc. (5:12-22)
IV. Conclusion: asks their prayers for him, greets them, and asks that the letter be read to all (5:25-28)

Chapter I

SALUTATION; HIS FIRST PREACHING AT THESSALONICA

Verse 1. Salutation. Silvanus and Timothy join the apostle in greeting the church. Silvanus (long form for Silas, Acts 15:40) was selected by Paul as his fellow worker on the second missionary journey—after Barnabas and he had separated. So Silvanus was with Paul when Thessalonica was evangelized and the church organized. Timothy also joined the party at Lystra (Acts 16:1). So both of them have personal recollections of the Thessalonians and so sent greetings. "To the church of the Thessalonians in God and the Lord Jesus Christ." This is the only time he addressed a church with a genitive of the people ("church of the Thessalonians"); usually it is to the saints or the church in or at such and such a place (Rom. 1:7: "To all God's beloved in Rome"); I Corinthians 1:2, and II Corinthians 1:1: "To the church of God . . . at Corinth." Galatians 1:2: "To all the churches of Galatia"; Ephesians 1:1: "To the saints who are also faithful in Christ Jesus"—no place given in oldest Manuscripts. Philippians 1:1: "To all the saints . . . at Philippi"; Colossians 1:2: "To the saints . . . at Colossae."

"In God our Father and the Lord Jesus Christ." "In union with God and the Father and the Lord Jesus Christ" (Williams). Deissmann, in his scholarly book, *In Christ,* shows conclusively that this is the meaning of this phrase in Paul. "Grace to you and peace." Grace, spiritual blessing; peace, health and happiness (general greeting of friends). Observe, the conjunction *and* connects God the Father and the Lord Jesus Christ in 1 and 2, which is a co-ordinate connection suggesting if not demanding the equality of Jesus Christ with the Father. See Philippians 2:6, where Paul asserts the equality of Christ with God. See Robertson (*Grammar, in loc.*) who confirms this interpretation.

THE APOSTLE'S FIRST PREACHING IN THESSALONICA AND HOW THE READERS WELCOMED HIS MESSAGE (1:2-10)

[2] We always thank God for you all as we continually mention you in our prayers, [3] for we can never for a moment before our God forget your energizing faith, your toiling love, and your enduring hope in our Lord Jesus Christ. [4] For we know, brothers so

beloved by God, that He has chosen you, ⁵ for our preaching of
the good news came to you not entirely in words but with power
and with the Holy Spirit and with absolute certainty (for you
know the kind of men we were among you for your own sakes).
⁶ And you followed the example set by us and by the Lord, because
you welcomed our message with a joy inspired by the Holy Spirit,
in spite of the painful persecutions it brought you, ⁷ so that you became examples to all the believers in Macedonia and Greece. ⁸ For
the message of the Lord has rung out from you, not only in Macedonia and Greece, but everywhere the report of your faith in God
has been told, so that we need never mention it. ⁹ For the people
themselves tell us what a welcome you gave us, and how you
turned from idols to the true God, to serve the God who lives on
and is real, ¹⁰ and to wait for the coming from heaven of His Son,
whom He raised from the dead, Jesus who delivers us from the
wrath to come.

Key words and phrases. Verses 2-3. "We give thanks to God
always for you all . . . in our prayers . . . remembering your work of
faith and labor of love and steadfastness of hope in our Lord Jesus
Christ." Three graces cherished by Paul as the groundwork of the
Christian life and character. Here "hope" is the climax of the three,
because he is emphasizing the future in this letter, explaining the
second coming of Christ more in detail. Really and logically, faith
and love precede hope. See I Corinthians 13:13 where love is the
climax, because the ethical is more in discussion than the eschatological.

Verses 4-5. "For we know, brothers beloved by God, that He
has chosen you." This is the first written intimation of Paul's belief in divine election. See Acts 13:48 for his first spoken word about
election: "As many as were ordained to eternal life believed." He
had just completed his first recorded sermon; they believed it, but
they had been ordained to eternal life (marked off as God's), and
yet they were free to accept or reject the gospel message. In Paul's
mind there is no conflict between God's foreordination and man's free
agency. The fifth verse links the preaching of the good news with
foreordination. "For our gospel came to you . . . in power and in
the Holy Spirit and absolute certainty." They had confidence in
Paul and Silas the preachers, so the Holy Spirit sealed the truth

on their hearts; they believed, for God had chosen them to eternal life. Yet God used human instrumentality to bring the foreordination to light in a profession of faith that fruited in toiling labor and steadfast hope.

Verses 6-8. The Thessalonians followed the examples set by Paul and Silas and Jesus in submitting to and patiently enduring persecution. Paul and Silas had just escaped from jail in Philippi, suffering for preaching the gospel. Jesus was persecuted by the Pharisees who incited other groups, Herodians and Sadducees, to join them in demanding His crucifixion. The Jews were persecuting Paul and Silas in Thessalonica, and early the Gentile neighbors persecuted the believers in that city. But they did not flinch. "They welcomed the message with joy inspired by the Holy Spirit, in spite of the painful persecutions it brought them." "So that you became an example to all the believers in Macedonia and in Greece." Examples of heroic faith that brooks no opposition!

Verses 9-10. "For the people themselves tell us what a welcome you gave us, and how you turned from idols to the true God." Paul in his early preaching there has emphasized giving up all idols for the true and living God. They had done it. They are now "serving" (slaves to) the living God of Abraham, Moses, and the prophets. He must have emphasized the "coming of the Son from Heaven," the second coming of Christ Jesus. They were "waiting for His [God's] Son from Heaven. Later some stopped work and were waiting for, expecting, His coming at any time (II Thess. 3:11). "Who rescues us from the wrath to come." Christ is the Redeemer who rescues us from the wrath of God at the final judgment. Because He died for us, we will not have to depart and eternally die (spiritual death, separation from God in Hell; Matt. 25:41; II Thess. 1:9).

Chapter II

In Sincerity and Suffering He Labored among Them; They Received His Message Enthusiastically (2:1-12)

For you know yourselves, brothers, that our visit to you was by no means a failure. 2 But, although we had just suffered and been insulted, as you remember, at Philippi, we again summoned courage by the help of God, in spite of the terrific strain, to tell you

God's good news. [3] For our appeal did not originate from a delusion or an impure motive; it was not made in fraud; [4] for since we have been so approved by God as to be entrusted with the good news, we are now telling it, not to please men but God, who proves and finds approved our hearts.

[5] Indeed, we never resorted to flattery, as you are well aware, nor to any pretext for making money; God is our witness. [6] We never sought praise from men, either from you or from anyone else; although as apostles we could have stood on our official dignity. [7] Instead we were little children among you; we were like a mother nursing her children. [8] Because we were yearning for you so tenderly, we were willing, not only to share with you God's good news, but to lay down our very lives too for you, all because you were so dearly loved by us. [9] You remember, brothers, our hard labor and toil. We kept up our habit of working night and day, in order not to be a burden to any of you when we preached to you. [10] You can testify, and God too, with what pure, upright, and irreproachable motives I dealt with you who believed; [11] for you know how, as a father deals with his children, we used to encourage you, cheer you on, and charge each of you [12] to live lives worthy of God who calls you into His kingdom and His glory.

Key words and phrases. Verses 1, 2. With renewed courage, after being beaten with rods and imprisoned at Philippi, Paul successfully preached the good news of God at Thessalonia. (See Acts 16:19-24.) "The good news of God." Several times in this chapter he calls the gospel "the good news of God." It is the good news of His love for sinners lost (John 3:16; Rom. 5:8; I John 4:9, 10). The good news also includes the plan of salvation through simple faith in Christ's death. It is the good news of God, because it originates with God as well as being the message of His love and mercy in salvation.

Verses 3, 4. Paul was approved by God to be His minister and entrusted with the good news of God. He preached, not to please men but to please God. No error or guile crept into his sermons. He felt that only God's message would please Him; so he preached nothing else.

Verses 5, 6. He used no flattery and had no greed for gain or glory. Glory means praise from men.

Verses 7, 8. He was gentle as a nurse or mother caring for her children. They were very dear to him; he was affectionately desirous of them. Therefore, he was willing, not only to share with them the good news of God but also his very life. He was a preacher who suffered for Christ and sacrificed himself for others.

Verses 9, 10. He worked night and day (with his hands), not to burden any of them (with compensation for his preaching). He pursued this course, even in Corinth (II Cor. 11:7). And yet he taught that the preacher has a right to compensation for his service (I Cor. 9:6-12). He calls God to witness "how holy, righteous, and irreproachable" were his motives in dealing with them.

Verses 11, 12. "Like a father deals with his children." He was their spiritual father and so encouraged them and charged them to live lives worthy of God, who calls them into His own kingdom and glory. He loved them as a father, and cheered and counseled them as a father. "Live lives worthy of God." Holy, devoted, sacrificial in praise of His love and mercy in salvation. "Who calls." An echo of the divine election (1:4). "Into His kingdom and glory." To be members of the kingdom doing God's will and as a reward His glory. This refers to the future enjoyment, by the saints, of God's splendid, magnificent presence forever. See Thayer.

He Thanks God That the Readers Accepted His Message as the Message of God; That They Bravely Suffered Persecution from Their Fellow Countrymen as Jewish Christians Did in Judea from Their Fellow Countrymen; Longs to See Them, His Joy and Crown and Hope and Glory
(2:13-20)

¹³ For another reason too, we, as far as we are concerned, are constantly giving thanks to God; that is, when you received the message you heard from us, you welcomed it not as the message of men but as the message of God, as it really is, which keeps on working in you who believe. ¹⁴ For you, brothers, followed the example of God's churches in Judea that are in union with Christ Jesus, for you too have suffered the same sort of ill-treatment at the hands of your fellow-countrymen as they did at the hands of the Jews, ¹⁵ who killed the Lord Jesus and persecuted the prophets

and us; and who continue to displease God and show themselves in opposition to all mankind, ¹⁶ by trying to keep us from speaking to the heathen, so that they may be saved, so as always to fill to the brim the cup of their sins. But at last God's wrath has come upon them.

¹⁷ Now we, brothers, on our part, when we were separated from you for a little while—in person but not in heart—were extremely eager and intensely longing to see you. ¹⁸ Because we did want to come to see you; I mean, that I myself, Paul, wanted again and again to come, but Satan prevented it. ¹⁹ For what is our hope or happiness or crown of boasting, except you, in the presence of our Lord Jesus Christ when He comes? ²⁰ You, indeed, are our glory and our joy.

Key words and phrases. Verse 13. "We thank God constantly for this." They accepted his message as "the word of God, not the word of men." He was so sincere and spiritually minded they recognized him as God's messenger. He gives God credit for their doing this and so thanks Him for it. Most of the *we's* in this letter are editorial, which is evident from Paul's own definition of it in verse 18, "I, Paul."

Verses 14-16. "They became imitators of the churches in Judea." Not only was there a church at Jerusalem but also other churches in Judea. Members in these churches joined the ranks of persecuted ones, "prophets and the Lord Jesus." And even Paul. He had to escape from Judea as the Jews were pursuing him (Acts 9:28-30). Now these Thessalonians are proving to be brave martyrs to the cause of Christ. Paul is thankful for it.

Verses 17-20. He assures them that his heart had been with them all the time in their suffering such treatment, though he was absent in body. "He had great desire to see them face to face." But Satan hindered him. Satan is responsible for placing insurmountable difficulties in the path of God's servants. He even brings on them physical diseases (II Cor. 12:7). Think of Job as an example of it. The readers, his converts and now consecrated martyrs to the faith, are his hope and joy and crown and glory. This is the reward of a faithful minister who has preached the Word of God and made genuine converts with this instrument.

Chapter III

HE SENDS TIMOTHY TO CHEER THEM; REJOICES OVER THE GOOD
NEWS TIMOTHY BRINGS BACK OF THEIR FAITH AND LOVE;
A PRAYER OF BENEDICTION (3:1-13)

So when I could not bear it any longer, I decided to be left behind in Athens alone. ² And so I sent my brother Timothy, God's
minister in the preaching of the good news of Christ, to strengthen
and encourage you in your faith, ³ so that none of you might
be deceived amid these difficulties. For you knew yourselves that
this is our appointed lot, ⁴ for when we were with you, we told
you beforehand that we were going to be pressed with difficulties,
and it took place, as you know. ⁵ That was why, when I could
bear it no longer, I sent to learn about your faith, for I was
afraid that the tempter had tempted you and our labor might be
lost.

⁶ But now, since Timothy has just come back to me from you,
and brought me good tidings of your faith and love, and told me
how kindly you remembered me and that you are longing to see
me as much as I am to see you, ⁷ this is the very reason, namely,
through your faith, brothers, that I have been encouraged about
you, in spite of all my distresses and crushing difficulties, ⁸ for
now I am really living, since you are standing firm in the Lord.
⁹ For how can I render God enough thanks for you, for all the joy
I have on account of you in the presence of our God, ¹⁰ as night
and day I continue to pray with deepest earnestness and keenest
eagerness that I may see your faces and round out to completeness what is lacking in your faith?

¹¹ Now may our God and Father Himself and our Lord Jesus
guide my way to you! ¹² May the Lord make you increase and
overflow in love for one another and for all men, as my love for
you does, ¹³ so that He may strengthen your hearts to be faultless
in purity in the sight of God, when our Lord Jesus comes back
with all His consecrated ones.

Key words and phrases. Verses 1-5. Paul under suspense about
the Thessalonians so that he could no longer bear it, decided to remain alone in Athens and send Timothy, half Greek and so capable
of understanding the Macedonians (Greeks) and God's minister for
telling the good news, to strengthen them in their faith and to

encourage them in bearing the persecution by their fellow citizens. He had told them when in Thessalonica first to expect opposition, but he was apprehensive that they would be caught unprepared to meet so heavy and crushing blows as were being hurled at them. Paul himself is under, and overwhelmed by, a covering of persecution and affliction. Such is the meaning of the verb *stego*, bear; he is covered with difficulties and dangers; can scarcely see out except by faith. Suspense as to the success of the issue in Thessalonica intensifies the gloom in the covering of sorrows. The readers are hard-pressed by opposition and affliction, the noun *thlipsis*, distress, affliction, is a picture of a wagon heavily loaded with iron, steel, or lead, until the wagon wheels are almost crushed beneath the load. So the believers there are being crushed down by the heavy load of hate and hostility and incriminations hurled upon them by their pagan neighbors for forsaking their native religion to accept the foreign faith of Christianity's crucified Founder. "You know that this is to be your lot." Paul warned them that this was the Christian's portion; a part of the divine plan and made a historical fact by social conditions. "They that will live godly must suffer persecution."

Paul says that he sent Timothy because he feared that the tempter, the Devil, might tempt them so severely that their faith might almost fail and his labor among them be in vain.

Verses 6-10. Timothy's report of their conquering faith over all opposition has comforted Paul's heart and made his faith triumphant. The readers not only triumphed over all opposition but they told Timothy how they longed to see him, and this cheered his sinking soul. "And now we [I] live, if [since] you stand fast in the Lord." He feels that it is well-nigh impossible for him to thank God enough for their triumphant faith and their abiding love for him. So he earnestly, night and day, prays that he may see them face to face and complete what may be lacking in their faith. Selfless prayer; not merely for his own joy in seeing them but their spiritual perfection (*katartisai*, literally knitting back the broken joints, broken by what they had to suffer).

Verses 11-13. His prayer and benediction for them. "May our God and Father Himself and our Lord Jesus direct our way to you."

Again he places the Father and the Lord Jesus on a par as the divine givers of the blessings requested. "Direct our way to you." Prays for a successful journey to Thessalonica. Note the blessings requested for the readers:

I. An Overflowing Love. Love for one another and for all men. "Increasing and abounding." Latter verb means, "overflowing." As the Nile overflows its banks to enrich all Egypt, so Christian love should overflow the banks of our own hearts and lives to enrich the lives of fellow Christians; yea, even the lives of "all men." To do so we must be evangelistic and active in missions. So were the Thessalonians (I Thess. 1:7-8). "The word of the Lord sounded forth from you in Macedonia and Greece."

II. The Result: "so that He may establish your hearts unblamable in holiness." Holiness is a matter of heart-establishing— hearts strong in love for all men. It is a product of the Lord Jesus. But the believer must be active not entirely passive to be holy. "Before our God and Father." The Father is the ultimate standard of true holiness (Matt. 5:48; I Peter 1:16).

III. "At the Coming of our Lord Jesus." His second coming a dynamic motive for attaining holiness and for executing the mission of the church in evangelization and missions. This was true in Paul's life. He urges others with an appeal to the same high motive for loving all men, for attaining holiness in God's sight and in accordance with His standard.

Chapter IV

SOME PRACTICAL EXHORTATIONS AS TO PERSONAL PURITY IN
SELECTING A WIFE; BROTHERLY LOVE; ATTENDING TO ONE'S
OWN BUSINESS; URGING OUR INFLUENCE ON OUTSIDERS
AS A COMPELLING MOTIVE; COMFORTING EXPLANA-
TIONS OF THE PRIVILEGES OF OUR DEPARTED
LOVED ONES; THE PRACTICAL EXHORTA-
TIONS (4:1-12)

Now, brothers, we ask and beg you, in the face of our union with the Lord Jesus, as you once received from us how you ought to live so as to please God—as indeed you are living—to continue to live this life better and better. ² For you are aware of the instructions which we gave you by the authority of the Lord Jesus.

3 For it is God's will that you should keep pure in person, that you should practice abstinence from sexual immorality, 4 that each man among you should learn to take his own wife out of pure and honorable motives, 5 not out of evil passions as the heathen do who do not know God; 6 that no one should do wrong and defraud his brother in this matter, because the Lord takes vengeance for all such things, as we told you before and solemnly warned you. 7 For God did not call us to a life of immorality, but to one of personal purity. 8 So whoever rejects this teaching is rejecting not man but God who continues to put His Spirit in you.

9 Now as to brotherly love, you have no need of anyone's writing you, for you have yourselves been taught by God to love one another, 10 as you are practicing it toward all the brothers all over Macedonia.

We beg you, brothers, to continue to live better and better; 11 also keep up your ambition to live quietly, to practice attending to your own business and to work with your own hands, as we directed you, 12 so that you may live influentially with the outsiders, and not be dependent on anybody.

Key words and phrases. Verses 1, 2. "Finally" (A.S.V.) His conclusion is lengthy. As the Spirit suggested new lines of thought as to moral living and as to the second coming of the Lord Jesus, he kept on writing to give them full instructions. "You learned from us [me] how you ought to live and to please God." When there he had instructed them in all these personal matters and they "are practicing them," but he is desirous that they live better and better. A Christian's life ought to be better each day than the day before. Progress in living is Paul's personal aspiration (Phil. 3:12-14), and he urges his converts to follow his example (Phil. 4:9).

Verses 3-6. Sexual purity urged; a first step to consecration and sanctification. Christians must not be like the heathen in selecting a wife. The prime motive must not be the satisfaction of the sex impulse. Sex capacity is given man as a means to an honorable end; not as an end in itself. It is a necessary basis of family life for the perpetuation of the race. So it "is the will of God" that a man take a wife, not to satisfy his passion but to carry out God's purpose in instituting the family for the perpetuation of the race. The

Greek word, *hagiasmos*, here, as in Romans 6:19, denotes "moral purity," and sexual purity is the basis of moral purity. Immorality, to Paul, is sexual uncleanness. It is the goal for the Christians' personal character and life—to be clean sexually. Hence his exhortation to the readers. Marriage is holy and a man must enter its holy state with pure motives; not to satisfy the sex passion of his lower nature but to do the will of God in perpetuating the race. "Wrong his brother in this matter." His brother may refer to another suitor whom the man in question defrauds of his best girl, his fiancée. Some think it means the father of the maiden, but this is improbable. At any rate, each man in selecting a wife ought to act on the square; act above sexual or economic motives. The editorial *we* is prominent in this section. Paul is fond of it, especially in the second Letter to the Corinthians and in this one. "For the Lord takes vengeance for all such things." The fear of divine punishment is urged as a motive, along with the positive motive of a beautiful moral character. "Disregards God who gives His Holy Spirit to you." Another motive is urged, the goodness of God in giving His Holy Spirit to help us maintain moral purity and lead us to consecration and sanctification.

Verses 9, 10. "Taught by God to love one another." How has God taught these heathen to love one another? By the teaching of conscience. Paul urges this moral revelation of God to the heathen as a ground for the heathen's responsibility for his sins (Rom. 1:18-20; 2:12a). "And indeed you do love all the brethren throughout Macedonia." Paul is a good practical psychologist. He always praises his readers if they have merit for such praise. This lays a good foundation for further exhortation. "But we exhort you, brethren, to do so more and more." Love is the only debt never fully paid (Rom. 13:8).

Verses 11, 12. Quiet living and honorable toiling by Christians exert an irresistible influence on outsiders. Paul teaches Christians to be industrious and attend to their own business, "that they may command the respect of outsiders." Such living has an irresistible influence on non-Christians. Personal independence is another end reached by such living. "Dependent on nobody." (See II Thess. 3:10-13 for further emphasis on this teaching.)

To Comfort Them He Urges the Priority Given, at the Parousia, to the Dead over Those Living Then (4:13-18)

13 Also we do not want you to have any misunderstanding, brothers, about those who are falling asleep, so as to keep you from grieving over them as others do who have no hope. 14 For if we believe that Jesus died and rose again, then through Jesus, God will bring back with Him those who have fallen asleep. 15 For on the Lord's own authority we say that those of us who may be left behind and are still living when the Lord comes back, will have no advantage at all over those who have fallen asleep. 16 For the Lord Himself, at the summons sounded by the archangel's call and by God's trumpet, will come down from heaven, and first of all the dead in union with Christ will rise, 17 then those of us who are still living will be caught up along with them on clouds in the air to meet the Lord, and so we shall be with the Lord forever. 18 So continue encouraging one another with this truth.

Key words and phrases. Verse 13. The readers were grieving over their deceased loved ones, because they had misunderstood Paul's preaching about the parousia. They understood that those still alive when Jesus came back would enter fully into the glories of His kingdom, but that the deceased Christians would suffer some sort of disadvantage as to their privileges in the kingdom. Paul is sympathetic and wishes to relieve this sorrow caused by a misunderstanding of his preaching. To misunderstand is the meaning of *agnoein*, rather than to be ignorant.

Verse 14. The resurrection of Christians based on the resurrection of Jesus. The "if" clause, "if we believe . . . ," is a logical condition practically equivalent to a causal clause, "Since we believe that Jesus died and rose again, in this manner [by death and resurrection] through Jesus as His medium God will bring those in fellowship [*sun*] with Him [Jesus], who have fallen asleep in death." This *thesis* is set forth in his classic on the resurrection (I Cor. 15; see verses 20-22). "But in fact Christ has been raised from the dead, the first fruits of those who have fallen asleep [in death]." As Adam brought death to the natural race, Christ by His resurrection has brought resurrection (spiritual and physical) to the spiritual race, those in fellowship with Him. So it is likely Paul's thought that "with Him" modifies "those who have fallen asleep," rather than "will bring," as in King James. See line of thought above.

Verse 15. "For on the Lord's own authority . . . By the word of the Lord." Paul is sure that his teaching on the parousia and accompanying events has been given to him by the Lord Himself. It is "inspired." The first thing to remember about it is that the dead in Christ will not occupy the last line in the procession of saints at the parousia; on the contrary, they will lead the procession. "We who are alive, who are left at the coming of the Lord." Does Paul think that he himself will live to see the parousia by saying "we who are alive?" If he did not actually believe it, he hoped it; this hope became a powerful motive to his activity and patience in suffering for Christ.

Verses 16, 17. The order of events accompanying the parousia: First, the parousia, the coming of the Lord Jesus Himself at the sounding of God's trumpet (i.e., at the time appointed by God). Second, the dead in fellowship with Christ will rise, taking priority over the living at that time. Third, those still alive on earth will be caught up on the clouds along with the risen dead to meet the Lord in the air. Fourth, in this manner (in this order and this spiritual state) to be forever with the Lord.

The place where the dead in Christ and living saints, caught up, will meet the Lord is "in the air." Whatever that means, it cannot be made to mean "on earth"—in Palestine or anywhere else. As to the exact place in the air does not matter to us; the heart of the message is "we shall be with the Lord, in fellowship with the Lord, and that forever." This is the meaning of *sun kurio*. This preposition expresses the most intimate human personal fellowship possible. *Pros* is used in John 1:1 to express a more intimate relation, that of the pre-existent Logos with God. He was "face to face with God." But Paul has given us the picture of the noblest fellowship of man with God, when he exclaims, "We shall be forever with the Lord." Not only in company with *(meta)* Him, but in intimate fellowship with Him. Forever we shall be His spiritual "chums."

"Even so . . . *and so*" (vv. 14, 17) express manner and not a conclusion, as King James and American Standard Version seem to make it mean. It describes the manner of life to be lived then, spiritual not physical; death being past, resurrection taking place and ushering in the spiritual order. Verse 17 possibly suggests the priority of the dead in Christ over the living at the parousia, as the spiritual heavenly kingdom is ushered in. (See I Cor. 15:43, 44, where Paul asserts the spiritual nature of the new order; even our bodies are to be "spiritual bodies.")

Verse 18. "Therefore comfort one another with these words." That is, with the blessed truths of hope expressed in these words. Because these things are true, let each one comfort the other that his loved ones asleep in Christ are sure to have the priority when the heavenly kingdom is ushered in at the parousia.

Chapter V

THE EXACT TIME OF THE PAROUSIA UNKNOWN. SO WE MUST AS
SONS OF LIGHT KEEP ALERT AND READY FOR IT; VARIOUS
EXHORTATIONS: TO ESTEEM SPIRITUAL LEADERS, BE AT
PEACE, ALWAYS BE JOYFUL, PRAYING, THANKFUL,
YIELDING TO THE SPIRIT, PROVING AND APPROV-
ING THE MESSAGES OF PREACHERS
(PROPHETS)

REMINDS THEM THAT THE EXACT TIME OF THE PAROUSIA IS
UNKNOWN; SO THEY MUST BE WATCHING AND
WAITING FOR IT (5:1-11)

But as to times and dates, brothers, you have no need of any-one's writing you, ² for you yourselves know perfectly well that the day of the Lord is coming like a thief in the night. ³ When people say, Such peace and security! then suddenly destruction falls upon them, like birth pains upon a woman who is about to become a mother, but they shall not escape, no, not at all. ⁴ But you, brothers, are not in darkness, so that that day, like a thief, should take you by surprise; ⁵ for you are all sons of the light and sons of the day. We do not belong to the night or the darkness. ⁶ So let us stop sleeping as others do, but let us stay awake and keep sober. ⁷ For those who sleep sleep at night and those who get drunk are drunken at night, ⁸ but let us who belong to the day keep sober, clothed with faith and love for a coat of mail and with the

hope of salvation for a helmet. ⁹ For God appointed us not to reap
His wrath but to gain salvation through our Lord Jesus Christ,
¹⁰ who died for us, so that whether we still live or sleep we may live
in fellowship with Him. ¹¹ So continue encouraging one another and
helping one another in character building.

Key words and phrases. Verses 1-3. The exact time of the
parousia not known. Paul had likely told them this when preaching
there. He may have used the illustration of how uncertain it is as
to the exact time when birth pangs may seize a woman with child in
the seventh, eighth, and ninth months. Also probably he has used
the illustration of how uncertain is the time when a thief comes
at night.

Verse 4. "But you, brothers, are not in darkness [ignorance],
so that that day should take you by surprise." This statement rather
proves that he had instructed them about the uncertainty of the
time of the parousia.

Verses 5-7. Christians are sons of the day and sons of the light.
Light is the symbol of knowledge and righteousness. In these verses
he seems to be stressing righteouness rather than knowledge. But
knowledge is very prominent. The readers are not in the darkness
of ignorance concerning the uncertainty of the exact time of the
parousia. Since we Christians are sons of light and sons of day we
must not sleep or be drunken as if we were sons of night and darkness. We must not give ourselves up to carousing and drinking, because we do not know but that the Lord is coming in a very short
time or exactly when He is coming.

Verse 8. "Let us . . . keep sober, clothed with faith and love
for a coat of mail and with the hope of salvation for a helmet."
Paul is warning the readers that they must not relax in strict living
merely because they are not to expect Christ to come immediately.
They must arm themselves against relaxing and committing the sins
of night and darkness, by putting on the breastplate of faith and
love and for a helmet the hope of salvation. The breastplate protects
the heart, the seat of the soul (Thayer). In this uncertainty about
the day of the Lord's second coming the heart must not be permitted
to relax and love grow cold. Notice he has changed the elements in
the breastplate when he later writes to the Ephesians (6:14). There

it is "the breastplate of righteousness." Here in the Letter to the Thessalonians he is stressing "faith and love," the graces that undergird righteousness, right-doing and living. "And the hope of salvation for a helmet." The word *hope* makes it certain that salvation is here used in the eschatological sense, as in Romans 13:11. That is, it is the final deliverance from all evil and from the wrath of God at the parousia; the salvation which includes the resurrection of the physical bodies of saints and their transformation into spiritual bodies (I Cor. 15:44-49). It includes "meeting the Lord in the air and being forever with the Lord" (I Thess. 4:17).

Verses 9, 10 give the reason for the apostle's exhortation in verse 8: "God appointed us not to reap His wrath, but to gain salvation [final] through our Lord Jesus Christ, who died for us so that whether we live or sleep we may live in fellowship with Him." Christ's death is the means of securing our completed (eschatological) salvation (at the parousia and resurrection). "Live or sleep" likely means "live on till the parousia or die before."

Verse 12. The logical conclusion, "therefore," is that their duty is to encourage one another and keep on building one another's character by patiently watching and waiting for the coming of the Lord.

PRACTICAL EXHORTATIONS: ESTEEM RELIGIOUS LEADERS, BE AT PEACE, WARN THE SHIRKERS IN THE CHURCH, CHEER THE FAINT-HEARTED, HELP THE WEAK, BE PATIENT, JOYFUL, PRAYERFUL, THANKFUL, FOLLOW THE SPIRIT, ETC.

(5:12-22)

¹² We beg you, brothers, to practice showing respect to those who labor among you, who are your leaders in the Lord's work, and who advise you; ¹³ continue to hold them in the highest esteem for the sake of the work they do. Practice living at peace with one another. ¹⁴ We beg you, brothers, continue to warn the shirkers, to cheer the faint-hearted, to hold up the weak, and to be patient with everybody. ¹⁵ Take care that none of you ever pays back evil for evil, but always keep looking for ways to show kindness to one another and everybody. ¹⁶ Always be joyful. ¹⁷ Never stop praying. ¹⁸ Make it a habit to give thanks for every-

thing, for this is God's will for you through Christ Jesus. [19] Stop stifling the Spirit. [20] Stop treating the messages of prophecy with contempt, [21] but continue to prove all things until you can approve them, and then hold on to what is good. [22] Continue to abstain from every sort of evil.

Key words and phrases. Verses 12-13a. Proper attitude toward religious leaders in a church. The readers are begged to love them and very highly esteem them. This attitude guarantees to the rank and file in the church the greatest good from preaching and teaching and warning by those over them. "For the work's sake." This esteem and love is not bestowed for personal motives, but for the sake of the work they are doing. It is God's work and it is for *all the church members,* for their spiritual growth and joy.

Verses 13b-15. Social duties. "Be at peace." Have no factions in the church. "Warn the shirkers." Literally the Greek word means those "out of line, out of order." They are not co-operating with those who are working in the church. This is the vast majority in most modern churches. *Warn* them of the greatness of such sinning, of their personal responsibility to Christ and His Church, of the fatal consequences to them if they persist in shirking their duties. "Encourage the fainthearted." People who lack courage to face life's battles and daily troubles. Cheer them and put courage in them. "Help the weak." Not only those who are weak physically (sick) but those weak morally and spiritually, and oftentimes weak materially (very poor). "Be patient with them all." Those that are strong morally and spiritually must be longsuffering with everybody, especially the morally weak and lazy and fainthearted. "See that none of you render evil for evil." Instead of giving "tit for tat," keep looking for ways to show kindness to one another and everybody. The same thought is in Romans 12:21, "Overcome evil with good."

Verses 16-22. Various personal duties. "Rejoice always." If anyone can, Christians can smile under all circumstances—always. "Pray constantly." Not on our knees but breathing the breath of prayer with every breath. "Give thanks in all circumstances." Yes, if a loved one has been taken away; if the crop has failed; if sickness puts you to bed. It might have been worse. So be thankful it is no worse. "This is the will of God." That is, not to complain but to submit and thank God. "Stop stifling the Spirit." The figure is that of putting out a fire. You stifle it by covering it up. The Spirit kindles fires of love and spiritual aspiration in our hearts; we must not put them out but let these fires move us to action and sacrifice for Christ and others. "Do not despise prophesying." Literally, "Stop treating as nothing the messages of prophets." These are New Testament prophets, and preachers should be these prophets; very many are real prophets of God, and Christians are warned not to set at nought the messages of these modern prophets. "Test everything; hold fast what is good." Primarily he warns each listener to prove every word spoken by the prophet (preacher) and if it is to be "approved," accept it and "hold it fast as good." As a general truth, however, the proposition is true. We should "prove all things and hold fast what is good." Not only sermons but "all things."

CONCLUSION: A PRAYER FOR THE COMPLETE CONSECRATION OF THE READERS; GOD WHO IS TRUSTWORTHY WILL GRANT THIS; ASKS FOR PRAYER FOR HIMSELF; GREET ONE AN-OTHER AS A HOLY FAMILY; HAVE THE LETTER READ TO ALL THE BROTHERS; BENEDICTION (5:23-28)

23 May God Himself who gave you peace, consecrate your whole being. May you be safely kept, spirit, soul, and body, so as to be blameless when our Lord Jesus Christ comes back. 24 He who calls you is trustworthy and He will do this. 25 Brothers, pray for us. 26 Greet all the brothers with a sacred kiss. 27 I solemnly charge you before the Lord to have this letter read to all the brothers. 28 The spiritual blessing of our Lord Jesus Christ be with you.

Key words and phrases. Verses 23-24. A prayer for complete consecration. Wholly *(holoteleis)*—literally, as a complete whole, your whole being. This whole being includes spirit, soul, and body. This is not a complete psychological description of a personality, for mind *(nous)* and heart *(kardia)* are left out. Nor is he trying to show that spirit and soul are distinct segments, or elements, in the personality. He is not teaching trichotomy over against dichot-omy. He is not concerned about psychology but is urging a *com-*

plete consecration. He feels that these three terms, spirit, soul, and body, include the whole being. *Soma* denotes the physical body, *Psuche* denotes the soul, the mind, the inner self, in relation to the body and all natural objects. *Pneuma* denotes the inner self in its spiritual relation to God; according to dichotomists, it is the soul functioning in spiritual activities; according to trichotomists, it is a separate segment, or element, of one's being; some believe that it is imparted to believers at regeneration (non-believers not having any spirit). This last view appears to us as unthinkable. It is better to think of man as a spiritual being, but sin has suppressed the spiritual nature and made the natural dominant till the Spirit regenerates.

The keeping is done by God. "He is trustworthy and will do it" (that is, keep spirit, soul, and body so as to be blameless, etc.).

Verse 25. "Pray for us [me]." Likely an editorial *us*. Might include Silvanus and Timothy who join Paul in greeting them (1:1).

Verse 26. "Greet all the brothers with a sacred kiss." This was practiced by early Christians to emphasize the brotherhood of Christians. The "kiss was holy." No natural tie or motive back of it.

Verse 27. He puts them under oath to have the letter read to all the brothers. Certainly all the members of the church in Thessalonica; perhaps all in the surrounding country.

Verse 28. Grace means spiritual blessing, including the power of the Spirit (Acts 1:8).

SERMON TOPICS SUGGESTED ON CHAPTER 5:

Proper Respect for Church Leaders (12-13);
Social Duties of Christians (14-15);
Ceaseless Christian Joy (16);
Ceaseless Prayer and Thanksgiving (17-18);
Proving Sermon Messages and Approving What
    Is True and Good (19-21).
A Prayer for Complete Consecration (23-24)

The Second Letter to the Thessalonians

INTRODUCTION

1. *The Occasion and Date.* While Paul, in Corinth on the second missionary journey, was having new converts—even Crispus the ruler of the synagogue (Acts 18:8-10)—news came to him that the Thessalonian Christians had received a misapprehension from his preaching there, or from his first letter to them, or possibly from some other source, that the messianic blessing had already begun. So they had stopped working and planning for the future, and the forces of disorder and disintegration had already set in.

We do not know with certainty how long it took for these misapprehensions to make themselves so serious as to make it necessary to notify Paul about it. Possibly three months after the first letter he received this news and wrote the second letter.

2. *The Purpose.* (a) The prime purpose was to correct these misapprehensions concerning the parousia. They inferred from his teachings, and possibly from the warning in I Thessalonians about its being sudden, that it must be imminent; so some thought there was no need to continue business or any work that looked toward the future. (b) His second aim is to insist on their preserving the proper social and moral order in the common relations of life in the city and surrounding country. (c) Closely linked with these two aims was the aim to encourage them to be courageous, faithful, and patient under persecution which is still being inflicted upon Christians there by their pagan neighbors.

3. *The Pauline Authorship.* It has been denied, or at least questioned, by some New Testament scholars, Spitta, Schmidt, McGiffert, and a few others. The three grounds on which they have denied or questioned it are (a) an imitation of the style of the first letter; (b) the eschatology is un-Pauline; (c) the personal relation of Paul to the church in Thessalonica is different; it is tender and loving in the first letter, harsh and commanding in the second.

Some claim that the emotional tone is different, joy prominent in the first letter, disappointment predominating in the second.

In reply we would say that the similarity of style is rather a proof of the Pauline authorship than of a spurious hand trying to imitate the style of the first letter. The eschatology is different from that in the first Letter in that it adds much to it in order to clear up misunderstandings of that in the first Letter. It is natural that his personal emotions should be different as he faces these serious changes in the readers. On the other hand, the external evidence must not be ignored, as these objectors do, which is stronger for the second Letter than for the first. It is quoted by Justin, Polycarp, Irenaeus, Clement of Alexandria, and Tertullian. It is found in the canons of Marcion and the Muratorian Fragment, and in Old Latin and Syriac versions. It is accepted as Pauline by Findlay, Denney, Peake, Moffatt, and most British scholars; by Robertson, Hayes, and most American scholars; by distinguished Germans and Frenchmen, Reuss, Godet, Weiss, Sabatier; Jülicher, Bousset, Zahn, Harnack, and others.

4. *The Main Teachings.* (a) His teaching on the parousia completed. (b) The Fatherhood of God and the Lordship of Jesus. (c) Persecution is a natural consequence of Christian loyalty and devotion (1:5). (d) Election from all eternity by divine grace (2:13). Emphasized more than in the first letter (1:4). (e) Christian living is social and moral. It is not mere assent to a creed but is the maintaining of clean living and upholding the social order with toil and co-operation.

OUTLINE

I. Greeting (1:1, 2)

II. The Apostle's Thanksgiving for Their Progress and His Comfort for Them in Their Persecution (1:3-12)

III. Their Misapprehension Concerning the Parousia Corrected (Chap. 2)
  1. The Parousia not imminent (2:1, 2)
  2. Some events must precede it, the coming of the man of lawlessness, the restraining power over him, etc. (2:3-12)
  3. He thanks God that it is the divine purpose to save and

sanctify them unto the obtaining of the glory of the parousia (2:13-15)
  4. Benediction (2:16-17)
IV. Conclusion (Chap. 3)
  1. Requests their prayers for his deliverance from evil plot-
  ters (3:1-3)
  2. He prays for them to be faithful and patient under persecution; is optimistic (3:4, 5)
  3. He exhorts busybodies to go to work, for workers only have
  have a right to eat (3:6-13)
  4. How to deal with the disobedient (3:14, 15)
  5. Another benediction (3:16)
  6. Autograph and greeting (3:17, 18)

INTERPRETATION

Chapter I

THE GREETING; THE APOSTLE'S THANKSGIVING FOR THEIR PROGRESS; COMFORTS THEM UNDER PERSECUTION

THE GREETING (1:1, 2)

This is the same as in the first Letter to the Thessalonians,
except he uses *"our* God and Father," instead of "God and Father."
Secondly, instead of the short form, "Grace to you and peace," as
in the first Letter, he adds "from God the Father and the Lord
Jesus Christ." These additions add nothing to the thought, except
to emphasize the source of grace and peace, which is easily implied.
See comments on first Letter (1:1, 2).

HIS THANKSGIVING AND COMFORT (1:3-12)

³ We always ought to be thanking God for you, brothers, as it is
right to do so, because your faith is growing so much and the love
of every one of you for one another is increasing ⁴ so that we are
always boasting of you among the churches of God for your patient
endurance and faith, in spite of your persecutions and crushing
sorrows which you are enduring. ⁵ This is a proof of God's righteous judgment, His aim being to let you show yourselves worthy
of His Kingdom, for which you are suffering; since, ⁶ indeed, it is
right for God to repay with crushing sorrows those who cause you

these crushing sorrows, [7] and to give rest to you who are being crushed with sorrows, along with us, at the unveiling of our Lord Jesus Christ from heaven, with His mighty angels [8] in a flame of fire, who will take vengeance on those who do not know God, that is, those who will not listen to the good news of our Lord Jesus. [9] These will receive the punishment of eternal destruction as exiles from the presence of the Lord and His glorious might, [10] when on that day He comes to be glorified in His consecrated ones and to be admired by all who believe in Him—because our testimony has been confidently accepted among you.

[11] With this in view we are always praying for you too, that our God may make you worthy of His call, and by His power fully satisfy your every desire for goodness, and complete every activity of your faith, [12] so that the name of our Lord Jesus may be glorified in you and you through union with Him, in accordance with the favor of our God and the Lord Jesus Christ.

Key words and phrases. Verses 3-4. He thanks God that their faith is growing abundantly and their love for one another increasing, and for their steadfastness in persecutions. Their faith, faith in Christ, is growing beyond measure *(huperauxanei)*. Their love each for the other is increasing. Because of such growth and development in the basic graces, faith and love, they have endurance or steadfastness *(hupomone)*. This last word means literally abiding or living under a burden. "Therefore, we boast of you in the churches of God for your steadfastness and faith in all your persecutions," etc. In these graces the church at Thessalonica furnishes a worthy example for other churches to follow, so Paul boasts of them in the other churches—to stimulate them to follow their example.

Note the phrase, churches of God. Paul emphasizes the local church (churches). It is the "church of God." God calls out *(ekkaleo)* those who constitute the church *(ekklesia)*. For a thorough research in this prominence given to the local church see Carroll, *The Ecclesia*.

Verses 5-10. God's justice in inflicting as punishment eternal destruction, with crushing sorrows, upon those who inflict crushing sorrows upon God's people. "This is evidence of the righteous

judgment of God." That is, the fact that He metes out to persecutors crushing sorrows as punishment on them who inflict crushing
sorrows on Christians. In verse 8 God is thus inflicting vengeance
upon these persecutors. Vengeance is not revenge or spite, but
retributive punishment which is justice. "That you may be made
worthy of the kingdom of God, for which you suffer" (v. 5). Persecution purifies the persecuted and helps "make them worthy of
the kingdom of God." One of God's ways of rewarding His own
who suffer for His kingdom.

"And to grant rest with us . . . when the Lord Jesus is revealed
from heaven." *Us* including Paul and all others who are not suffering the specific persecutions now being inflicted upon the Thessalonians. "Rest" is a prominent feature of the Christian's reward.
(See Heb. 4:9, "There remains a sabbath rest," etc. Rev. 14:13,
"rest from their labors," etc.)

"When the Lord Jesus is revealed from heaven with His mighty
angels in flaming fire." This is the parousia, the coming of Jesus
at the end of the age. He is coming with His mighty angels. So
says Jesus (Matt. 25:31). "In flaming fire." Fire is the symbol of
punishment to be meted out to the wicked—"those who do not obey
the gospel." (See Matt. 25:41; Rev. 20:14-15.) Paul seems to be
familiar with the early traditions as to Jesus' teaching. To obey the
gospel is to accept it by faith.

"Eternal destruction and exclusion [exile, Williams] from the
presence of the Lord." Of course, destruction could not literally be
"eternal." All hope of salvation is lost, and so the wicked are in
an eternal lost state. The lost state is eternal. The hope of having
fellowship with God is destroyed. They are in a state of eternal
exile. "To be glorified in His saints." At His second coming Christ
will be glorified—praised and exalted—by and in the splendor of
His saved and sanctified ones.

"Because our testimony to you was believed" (10c). The glorification of Christ on that day and that of His saints are both traced
to faith in Paul's testimony that Jesus is the Son of God and the
Saviour of sinners. (See I Thess. 1:10.)

Verses 11-12. Paul's Prayer for the Readers. "To this end,"

namely, the glorification of Christ at the parousia and also the glorification of His saints. "That our God may make you worthy of His call." See chapters 1 and 2 of Ephesians for the essence of God's call. "That we should be holy and blameless. . . . Destined us in love to be His sons through Jesus Christ. . . . Destined and appointed to live for the praise of His glory. . . . Created in Christ Jesus for good works." From these excerpts we see how high and holy is the goal involved in God's call. How can sinners saved by grace be made worthy of God's call to character so holy and destiny so high? Only God can make us worthy. Believers can work with God to achieve the result; but without God, all is failure. "And may fulfill [fully satisfy] your every good resolve and work of faith by His power." Again, God only can make our good resolutions come true. Also God can make the work of faith round out to completion. (See Phil. 2:12, 13.) So the apostle adds, "by His power." This comes through the indwelling Spirit (Eph. 3:16).

"So that the name of our Lord Jesus may be glorified in you, and you in Him." The result of being made worthy of God's call, of having our good resolutions come true, and our work of faith rounded out to completion, is that the name of Jesus our Lord may be glorified. The glorification of Christ is the noblest goal we Christians can reach in life. "Glorified in you." Christ is glorified in the lives and achievements of His followers, and only in this way can He be glorified in time and at the parousia. "And you in Him." A verb must be supplied. Naturally we look for one in the context: "And you glorified in Him," or "in union with Him." Not only will Christ be glorified, exalted, on that great day, but all His saints, through union with Him, if they have been worthy of God's call and have let Him fully satisfy their good resolutions and complete their work of faith, will be glorified with Him, exalted to His throne to sit with Him there in glory (Rev. 3:21).

"According to the grace of our God and the Lord Jesus Christ." Grace here means God's unmerited favor expressing itself in spiritual blessing. God and the Lord Jesus Christ are placed on a par as the givers of this unmerited favor and spiritual blessing. This grace is the measure of standard (*kata* with accusative. See Robertson, *Grammar, in loc.*) of the Christian's achievement of his good resolutions, the completion of the work of his faith, and the glorification of Christ and His saints at the parousia.

This prayer of the apostle is a good theme for a topical sermon.

Chapter II

THE PAROUSIA NOT IMMINENT SINCE OTHER EVENTS MUST
PRECEDE IT; AGAIN HE THANKS GOD FOR THEM; PLEADS
WITH THEM AND PRAYS FOR THEM

EVENTS THAT MUST PRECEDE THE PAROUSIA (2:1-12)

As to the coming of our Lord Jesus Christ and our final muster before Him, we beg you, brothers, [2] not to let your minds be easily unsettled or even be excited, whether by some message by the Spirit or by some saying or letter that is claimed as coming from me, saying that the day of the Lord is already here. [3] Do not let anybody at all deceive you about this, because that cannot take place until the great revolt occurs and the representative of lawlessness is uncovered, the one who is doomed to destruction, [4] the one who keep up his opposition and so far exalts himself above every so-called god or object of worship, that he actually takes his seat in the sanctuary of God, proclaiming himself to be God. [5] Do you not remember that while I was with you I used to tell you this? [6] So now you know the power that is holding him back, that he is to be unveiled at his own appointed time. [7] For the secret power of lawlessness is already at work, but only until he who is holding it back has been gotten out of the way. [8] Then the representative of lawlessness will be uncovered, and the Lord Jesus will destroy him with the breath of His mouth and put a stop to his operations by His appearance and coming; [9] that is, the representative of lawlessness, whose coming is in accordance with the working of Satan, with his plenitude of power and pretended signs and wonders, [10] and with a completely wicked deception for men who are on the way to destruction, because they refused to love the truth so as to be saved. [11] This is why God sends them a misleading influence till they actually believe what is false, [12] so that all who have refused to believe the truth but have chosen unrighteousness instead might be condemned.

Key words and phrases. In this paragraph we have the climax of Paul's apocalyptic teaching. In the first Letter to the Thessalonians we saw his first important apocalyptic teaching (4:13-5:11). Review the comments there. Here he is adding some features to his elementary apocalyptic teachings in the first Letter. There is no contradiction between the teaching in the first and second Letters; he is merely adding new materials here to correct their misunderstanding of what he wrote in the first Letter.

There is a historical background for Paul's apocalypse; found in its elements in the Old Testament itself (I Kings 21:13, Belial the basis of his man of lawlessness; II Samuel 22, David's deliverance from his great enemy.) The reference to Antiochus Epiphanes in Daniel 11:36 was recognized by Paul. For details Paul doubtless was familiar with the later Jewish apocalyptic writings, Enoch, Ascension of Moses, Sibylline Oracles, and so on. So he elaborated his doctrine of the Great Opponent and Man of Lawlessness, the Jews referring these preliminaries to the first coming of Messiah, while Paul, inspired by the Spirit, adds Christian teaching and makes them refer to the second coming. He sanely omits the wild speculations of the Jewish writers as to a definite historical program to be carried out prior to the parousia. Even in his major letters Paul refers to the parousia and apocalyptic principles (I Cor. 15; Rom. 8:11-15; II Cor. 5) and also in later letters (Phil. 3:20, 21; II Tim. 4:8).

Verses 1, 2. "Shaken from your mind, nor yet be troubled, either by spirit, or by word, or by epistle as from us" (A.S.V.). This mental disturbance on the part of the Thessalonian Christians is the occasion of Paul's developing his apocalyptic teaching, as found in this paragraph (2:1-12). According to the American Standard Version, here quoted, it is difficult to know what is meant by "spirit." Perhaps, only a mental disturbance caused either by some word from some other teacher, even by a letter someone wrote in Paul's name to throw these good people into excitement about the immediate coming of the Lord. Translating the word Spirit with a capital letter it would mean that they were disturbed by what the Spirit had said to them in Paul's first Letter (4:13-5:11), or by some other letter purporting to be from Paul. But the main thought, the important thing to remember, is that they are disturbed because they misunderstood what Paul has written or preached about the second coming of the Lord.

Verses 3-8. The key phrases are: "The man of lawlessness . . . the son of perdition . . . he who now restrains it or him." Who is the man of lawlessness, the son of perdition? These two phrases are synonymous. So who is the man of lawlessness (the better reading, not, *the man of sin)?*

Scholars are divided with two dominant interpretations: First, some outstanding Jewish opposition to Christianity. Secondly, Caligula or some other Roman emperor. The more probable view, judging from historical conditions and especially from Paul's high consideration of Roman government and his own Roman citizenship, is the first one. Then who is the restraining power? That would be the Roman government, heading up in Claudius who is emperor and trying to check the movement to deify the Roman emperor. For further discussion on these two views, see Peake, *A Critical Introduction to the New Testament* (Scribner's, 1910); Moffatt, *An Introduction to the Literature of the New Testament* (Scribner's, 1918); Zahn, *Introduction to the New Testament;* Williams, *Introduction to New Testament Literature;* the *International Critical Commentary;* the *Expositor's Greek Testament;* Hastings' *Dictionary of the Bible;* the *International Standard Biblical Encyclopedia.*

Perhaps, Paul's prediction was not literally fulfilled; that is, no individual Jewish opponent, claiming to be Messiah, actually seated himself in the temple of God and proclaimed himself to be God, and that a historical individual Roman authority restrained him and kept him in check. The permanent value of Paul's apocalypse is that a violent wave of crime and immorality usually precedes a great moral reformation or spiritual awakening. It was so in Europe when the great reformations broke forth in Germany, Switzerland, England. It was so in America when the great revival under Dwight L. Moody swept our country. Similar conditions preceded the great revivals of Torrey and Sunday. It may be that the terrific crime wave sweeping our country today is to be followed by a nationwide spiritual awakening that will shake our nation from hub to circumference, and make our nation a really Christian nation and prepare us for the national leadership which World War II seemed to thrust upon us.

"And the Lord Jesus will slay him with the breath of His mouth and destroy him by His appearing and His coming." To "slay with the breath of His mouth" is quoted from the Jewish apocalypse. There is no literal fulfillment of this as yet. It is to occur at "His appearing and coming [parousia]." The spiritual value of this great doctrine is the inspiration of Christ's people with conquering faith and triumphant hope.

Verses 9-12. Still while the years are going by and Christians are waiting for the parousia, the man of lawlessness is at work under the "working of Satan with all power" (A.S.V.); "with his plenitude of power" (Williams). He is empowered by Satan, who is not omnipotent as is God, but He gives the man of lawlessness plenitude of power so as to work pretended signs and wonders which resulted in "wicked deception for those who are to perish, because they refused to love the truth and so be saved." *Pretended* signs and wonders, literally signs and wonders of falsehood. This is a genitive of quality, so false signs, etc. Satan's agents can perform only false, pretended miracles. But he has power to deceive unbelievers and keep them from loving the truth and being saved. Because they are thus under the power of Satan, "God sends upon them a strong delusion, to make them believe what is false." God is not responsible for this delusion. The unbelievers allowed Satan to deceive them, so the delusion that God permits (*sends* only in this sense) is the natural result of their deception by Satan.

Let us give a brief summation of Paul's teaching about Satan. He uses the word Satan eight times (II Thess. 2:9; Rom. 16:20; I Cor. 5:5; II Cor. 2:11; 11:14; 12:7; I Tim. 1:20; 5:15). In this text (2:9) he is the archenemy of unbelievers and evildoers. In Romans 16:20 he is the archenemy of God who will crush him under the feet of true believers. In I Corinthians 5:5 he is to have the incestuous man in his hands to chastise. In II Corinthians he is the archdeceiver of men; so also in II Corinthians 11:14, where he shows himself as an angel of light. In II Corinthians 12:7 he brings disease on one of God's loyal workers (Paul), "the thorn in the flesh, a messenger of Satan." In I Timothy 1:20 he is leader of backsliders; the same in 5:15. In Ephesians 2:2 he calls him "the prince of the power of the air" who is inspiring and dominating "the sons of disobedience." So we may sum it up by saying, Satan is the archenemy of God and man, the leader of workers of evil, the one who chastises believers who yield to his devices, the one who (with God's permission) brings suffering on God's children, as Job and Paul. Possibly he is referred to as the evil one in Ephesians 6:17, the archenemy of Christians.

He Thanks God for Them; Prays for Them (13-17)

¹³ We ought always to be thanking God for you, brothers dearly loved by the Lord, because God chose you from the beginning for salvation through the Spirit's consecration of you and through your faith in the truth, ¹⁴ and to this end He called you by our preaching of the good news, so that you may obtain the glory of our Lord Jesus Christ.

¹⁵ So then, brothers, continue to stand firm and keep a tight grip on the teachings you have received from us, whether by word of mouth or by letter. ¹⁶ May our Lord Jesus Christ Himself and God our Father, who has loved us and graciously given us encouragement that is eternal, and a hope that is well-founded, ¹⁷ encourage your hearts and strengthen you in every good thing you do or say.

Key words and phrases. Verses 13-15. Thanking God for calling them to obtain salvation and the glory attending and following the parousia of the Lord Jesus. His thanksgiving is based on God's choosing them to be saved and to see the glory of the Lord Jesus. The verb *choose* is not the regular word Paul later uses in Romans and Ephesians *(eklego)*. Our word *election* comes from this verb, which means God's choice of us from all eternity. This verb in II Thessalonians *(haireo)* is likely synonymous with *eklego;* and yet he is emphasizing the effectual call through the preaching of the good news—"through our gospel . . . by belief in the truth." Paul had preached this good news there and they had believed it. God elects in eternity, He chooses effectually when sinners believe the good news preached. "Brethren beloved by the Lord." This is the basis of the eternal election and the effectual calling in the preaching of the good news. ' "God chose you from the beginning to be saved." Likely referring to the call or election in eternity (as in Eph. 1:5-9). "To be saved," or, "for salvation," must refer to the eschatological salvation at the parousia; "because," he adds, "so that you may obtain the glory of our Lord Jesus Christ." This glory is the glory attending His second coming (parousia). So this is another proof text for salvation in the eschatological sense. See Romans 13:11, for another text in this sense. "Through consecration by the Spirit." This is the process of being saved in preparation for the eschatological salvation (at the parousia). "And belief in the truth." Man must co-operate with God in working down to the finishing point our salvation (see Phil. 2:12, 13).

"So then, brethren, stand firm and keep a tight grip on the teachings you have received from us [me]." These are the teachings Paul gave in his preaching at first, then in his first letter, and now in this one. "Stand firm." Swerve not to the right or the left however much false teachers may try to disturb you.

Verses 16-17. A benediction prayer. "Our Lord Jesus Christ Himself and God our Father." Again Paul links Christ and the Father by the co-ordinate conjunction *and*, thus placing them on equality as the source of spiritual blessing. "Who has loved us." This verb refers only to God our Father. It is not to deny that Christ loves us too, but to emphasize the Father as the absolute source of redemptive love. "And has graciously given us encouragement that is eternal, and a hope that is well-founded." *Graciously* means by His unmerited favor. "Eternal," not temporary, encouragement—through these new teachings in this second letter, as well as those in the first letter. "Well-founded." Literally "good hope." It is hope based on Christ the expression of the Father's eternal love. Nothing can shake it (Rom. 8:38-39) or separate us from it. "Encourage your hearts and strengthen you in everything good you do or say." The first verb means either comfort or encourage; but likely the stronger meaning, encourage, here, as the verb *strengthen*, or *establish*, follows it. They need it for every good work and word. To be busy.

Chapter III

AGAIN HE PRAYS FOR THEM, AS HE ASKS THEM TO PRAY FOR HIM;
IS CONFIDENT OF THEIR RESPONSE AND OBEDIENCE; HOW TO
DEAL WITH IDLE SHIRKERS; HIS AUTOGRAPH AND
BENEDICTION

HIS PRAYER AND EXHORTATION AS TO HOW TO DEAL WITH SHIRKERS (3:1-13)

Finally, brothers, pray for us, that the message of the Lord may continue to spread and prove its glorious power as it did among you, ² and that we may be delivered from unprincipled and wicked men; for not all men have faith.

³ But the Lord is to be trusted, and He will give you strength and guard you from the evil one. ⁴ We have confidence in you through the Lord that you are now practicing the directions which we give you and that you will continue to do so. ⁵ May the Lord guide you into a realization of God's love for you and into a patient endurance like Christ's.

⁶ Now we charge you, brothers, on the authority of the Lord Jesus Christ, to hold yourselves aloof from any brother who is living as a shirker instead of following the teachings you received from us. ⁷ You know yourselves how you ought to follow my example; for I was not a shirker when I was with you; ⁸ I did not eat any man's bread without paying for it, but with toil and hard labor I worked night and day, in order not to be a burden to any of you. ⁹ Not that I have no right to be supported, but to make myself an example for you to follow. ¹⁰ For when I was with you, I gave you this direction, "If a person refuses to work, he must not be allowed to eat." ¹¹ But we are informed that some among you are living as shirkers, mere busybodies, instead of busy at work. ¹² Now on the authority of the Lord Jesus Christ we charge and exhort such persons to do their own work with quiet and eat their own bread. ¹³ But you, brothers, must never grow tired of doing right.

Key words and phrases. Verses 1-2. "Pray for us [me]." Paul is fond of the editorial *we*. He asks them to pray for two things for him: First, that "the message [word] of the Lord may speed on and triumph." Literally "run and be glorified." How Paul would have rejoiced if he could have put "the word of the Lord" on an airplane to cross oceans and continents in hours instead of days and weeks and months! Or, spoken it on the radio around the world in a few minutes! He longed for it to speed on, to run as fast as possible, to be glorified in being believed for the saving of thousands of souls. Secondly, "that we [I] may be delivered from wicked [unprincipled] and evil men." He knew the Judaizers were still watching a chance to have him executed for preaching a new gospel and tearing down old religions (Judaism and Emperor Worship). He felt that "more things are wrought by prayer than this world dreams of."

Verses 3-4. "And we have confidence in the Lord about you," because "the Lord is faithful [to be trusted], He will strengthen you and guard you from evil." His confidence is first in the trustworthiness of the Lord and then in the readers to do what he commands from the Lord. The things which Paul commands: Endure persecution, wait for the parousia in patience, stand firm and hold tight to his teachings at all points—as to treatment of shirkers, as to working with their hands, etc.

Verse 5. "May the Lord direct your hearts to the love of God and to the steadfastness of Christ." "To the love of God," means to the "realization of God's love": to realize how much and how unchangeably God loves them; to know that they lie "close to the heart of God." *Steadfastness* is rather *patient endurance* which Christ exhibited or which He inspires in those who trust Him.

Verses 6-8. He enjoins upon Christians that they work at some vocation and each one bear his burden of social and industrial life. "You ought to imitate us [me]." When in Thessalonica he toiled with his own hands that he might not be a burden to anyone.

Verse 9. "It was not because we [I] have not that right, but to give you in our conduct an example to imitate." He had a right to ask financial support from them, but he gave up his right to be an example of industry.

Verse 10. While in Thessalonica he gave this vocational order, "If anyone will not work, let him not eat." No healthy man or woman has any right to eat at the expense of his or her fellows. But he would hasten to say today, "Care for the sick and helpless dependents." (See I Tim. 5:9-16.)

Verses 11-13. Some in Thessalonica were so sure that Christ was coming in a few days, or weeks at most, that they had stopped all work or planning for the future. This was demoralizing in industry and all social affairs. But Christians are a part of society and must bear their own industrial burdens. They have no right to be idlers or busybodies. Such persons Paul commands and exhorts, and that "on the authority of the Lord Jesus Christ, to do their work in quietness and to earn their own living." " On the authority of the Lord Jesus Christ," means, not a specific example from Jesus' own earthly life, or a direct teaching of Jesus while on earth, but through his union with Christ the Spirit has shown him that quiet industry for self-support is proper for every healthy, normal man or woman, Christian as well as non-Christian.

VIOLATORS OF THESE ORDERS MUST BE ADMONISHED AS BROTHERS; BRIEF PRAYER FOR THEM, AUTOGRAPH, BENEDICTION (3:14-18)

Verses 14, 15. Members of the church who refused to follow these orders in this letter must not be regarded as enemies, but warned as brothers. The voluntary principle and moral suasion are the potent principles to follow in social and moral activities.

Verse 16. A short prayer. "Lord of peace" means the Lord who gives peace (obj. gen.). May He give you peace—peace among the individuals of the church.

Verses 17, 18. Autograph and benediction. Grace is spiritual blessing.

The Letter to the Galatians

INTRODUCTION

1. *Author and Date.* Paul the apostle is generally believed to be the author. Even Baur, the father of the most radical school of critics in Germany (of Tübingen University), conceded it. His followers likewise do. Even the most radical Dutch scholars follow suit. The date is the bone of contention. According to the South Galatian theory, which regards the churches of Galatia as consisting of the churches at Pisidian Antioch, Iconium, Lystra, and Derbe, the date is the winter of A.D. 54-55. The North Galatian theory regards the churches of Galatia as belonging to the ancient kingdom of Galatia, and places the date at A.D. 58, after I and II Corinthians and Romans. This is at the close of the third missionary journey. Bishop Lightfoot in his commentary on Galatians champions the North Galatian theory. Sir William Ramsay champions the South Galatian theory, and his arguments seem logical and convincing to us.

2. *Historical Situation.* The occasion which prompted the apostle to feel led by the Spirit to write this letter was a bitter controversy between him and the Judaizers. These were false teachers, Jewish, who sought to make all Christians Jews by compelling males to be circumcised and all, males and females, to keep the law of Moses as a condition to salvation. Their doctrine was contrary to Paul's experience in conversion. He knew that he was saved by trusting Jesus Christ as his personal Saviour and Lord. When he had the vision of the risen Christ, he was convinced that He was the Son of God and the Messiah promised in the Scriptures. So he surrendered to Him as such and the peace of God came into his soul.

3. *Purpose.* The apostle's purpose in writing this letter to these churches was to counteract this destructive propaganda against him and his gospel of faith which he preached and championed. They had denied that he was a genuine apostle, on the grounds that

he had not seen the Lord in person and had repudiated the law of Moses. So he writes to prove his apostleship by showing that he had a revelation of Christ and so had the right to preach the gospel of faith apart from keeping the law to be saved. However, he did not minimize the law; he regarded it as "God's tutor to lead men to Christ," and as God's standard of normal living after being saved by faith. In his two last chapters in Galatians he describes the high moral and spiritual life that results from being saved by faith, the logical fruiting of the Spirit.

OUTLINE

I. Greeting (1:1-5)
II. His Defense, Proving That He Is an Apostle Sent from God and Not by Man (1:6-2:14)
III. His Gospel of Salvation by Faith Proved to Be True (2:15-4:31)
IV. The High Moral Life of the Believer Saved by Faith, a Life That Is the Natural Fruiting of the Spirit (5:1-6:10)
V. The Conclusion (6:11-18)

Chapter I

GREETING; BEGINNING THE PROOF THAT HIS GOSPEL CAME BY REVELATION; GREETING (1:1-5)

This is Paul's most elaborate salutation. Under the spur of the Judaizers he feels that he must state his theme in his greeting. He sketches the defense of his apostleship:

> Paul, an apostle sent not from men nor by any man, but by Jesus Christ and God the Father who raised Him from the dead— ² and all the brothers who are here with me—to the churches of Galatia: ³ spiritual blessing and peace to you from God the Father and the Lord Jesus Christ, ⁴ who gave Himself for our sins, to save us from the present wicked world in accordance with the will of our God and Father; ⁵ to Him be glory forever and ever. Amen.

Key words and phrases. Verse 2. "The churches of Galatia." Notice, he does not say, "The church of Galatia." To Paul there is no state or national church. There were local churches of believers in Christ, banded together for the worship of God and Christ, and for work in the kingdom—evangelism and missions. The word *ecclesia,* church, occurs about 109 times in the New Testament; and in three senses, a little over 100 times in the local sense; once to signify the assembly of saints in Heaven, the rest to denote the Church as an institution (nearly all in Eph. and Col.). Here it denotes the local bodies of believers in Christ.

Verse 3. "Grace." This word occurs often in the New Testament. It has five senses: literally, favor; then unmerited favor (of God for lost sinners); spiritual blessing; spiritual gift or function; thanks. Here it is spiritual blessing (or power).

Verse 3. "Peace." This is the regular word for greeting among Jews and Gentiles; means health and prosperity to you, physical and material blessings be yours.

Verse 4. "The will of God." The determining purpose of the Supreme Being, the universal law of the moral and spiritual realm.

Verse 5. "Glory." This word likewise has several meanings: the splendid presence of God in Heaven; the goal of Christian pilgrims at last; "summation of the attributes of God" (Sanday, Rom. 6:4); praise. The last is the meaning here. "To whom be praise" (glory).

Basic Doctrines.

(1) The deity of Christ. In verse 3 "the Lord Jesus Christ" is connected with "God the Father" by the copula *and,* which, as Robertson maintains *(Greek Grammar)* asserts the deity of Christ. He is an equal partner with God the Father in dispensing grace and peace to believers.

(2) Salvation through the sacrificial death of Christ. "Who gave Himself for our sins, to save us," etc. (v. 4). This is a basic doctrine with Paul. Christ saves us from sin by becoming the sacrifice for sin. He saves us to life eternal by giving Himself to die for us (see 3:13; Rom. 3:26; II Cor. 5:21, etc.).

A great text with a brief sermon outline (3, 4):
I. Christ Making the Supreme Sacrifice—"Himself"
II. His Death Vicarious—"For Our Sins"
III. The Purpose of His Sacrificial Death—"To Save Us"

IV. This Plan of Salvation Part of God's Universal Will—"According to the Will of God."

The Apostle Astonished That the Galatians Are Falling for the False Teachings of the Judaizers (1:6-12)

⁶ I am astonished that you are beginning so soon to turn away from Him who called you by the favor of Christ, to a different good news, ⁷ which is not really another one; only there are certain people who are trying to unsettle you and want to turn the good news of Christ upside down. ⁸ But even if I or an angel from heaven preach a good news that is contrary to the one which I have already preached to you, a curse upon him! ⁹ As I have said it before, so now I say it again, if anybody is preaching to you a good news that is contrary to the one which you have already received, a curse upon him!

¹⁰ Am I now trying to win men's favor, or God's? Or, am I trying to be pleasing to men? If I were still trying to be pleasing to men, I would not be a slave of Christ at all. ¹¹ For I tell you, brothers, the good news which was preached by me is not a human message, ¹² for I did not get it from any man; I was not taught it, but I got it through a revelation given by Jesus Christ.

Key words and phrases. Verse 6. "So soon removing from Him [God]." Notice, Paul goes to the root of their backsliding to a false doctrine—removing, or turning away, from God. All lapses into false teaching start with spiritual delinquency. The heart gets cold from failure to pray and walk with God. First it is heart failure, then head failure; failing to understand the basic truths of the gospel and failure to cling to them. As the soul relaxes its hold on God, the mind slips from its mooring and false doctrines creep in and take possession.

Verse 7. "Gospel." Both the Greek and the Anglo-Saxon words mean "good news." The gospel is the message of good news—the good news of God's love and His plan of salvation by grace through faith in Christ. It is not the true gospel if you mix law with love and grace. The Judaizing gospel of law was not the real gospel, Paul proves in the letter to the Galatians.

Verses 8-9. "If I or an angel from heaven . . . if anyone preaches," etc. Paul uses two forms of conditional sentence; they have different meanings. The first one is only a supposed case in the future. "If I myself or an angel from heaven should in the future preach a gospel different," and so on. The second condition denotes a realized fact. "If anyone is actually preaching a different gospel." The Judaizers were at that very time doing that very thing. Paul did not assert that he or an angel was likely to do so. It is highly hyperbolical language.

Verse 12. "A revelation of Christ." Here he refers to his vision of Christ near Damascus, where Christ called him to be a believer, an apostle and a preacher. He means to assert that he received his call to be an apostle and a preacher of the true gospel by a revelation of Christ Himself. He was not a man-made apostle. His gospel he received from Christ Himself—at Damascus and in the Arabian wilderness as he communed with Christ "three years."

His Pre-conversion and Conversion Experiences Prove It.
(1:13-17)

[13] You have heard, indeed, of my former conduct as an adherent of the Jewish religion, how I kept on furiously persecuting the church of God, and tried to destroy it, [14] and how I outstripped many of my own age among my people in my devotion to the Jewish religion, because I surpassed all others in my zeal for the traditions handed down by my forefathers. [15] But when God, who had already set me apart from my birth, and had called me by His unmerited favor, [16] chose to unveil His Son in me, so that I preach the good news about Him among the heathen, at once, before I conferred with any human creatures, [17] and before I went up to Jerusalem to see those who had been apostles before me, I retired to Arabia, and afterwards returned to Damascus.

Key words and phrases. Verse 13. "The church of God." This church of God he persecuted. What church was it? It was likely the local church in Jerusalem. He calls it the "church of God" because he thinks of God as the ultimate Founder of the church through Christ His Son.

Verse 16. "To reveal His Son to me." The Greek reads, "to reveal His Son in me." At Damascus God did unveil His Son to Paul, showing him that Christ had risen from the dead and thus proved He is the Son of God. But the sphere of this unveiling of

Christ was in his heart and inner spirit. So it is a revelation to
Paul, to be sure, but to be more exact, it was a revelation in him.

HIS EARLY CHRISTIAN EXPERIENCE PROVES IT (1:18-24)

18 Then three years later I went up to Jerusalem to get acquainted with Cephas, but I spent only two weeks with him; 19 and not
another single one of the apostles did I see, except James, the
Lord's brother. 20 In writing you this, I swear before God, I am
telling you the solemn truth. 21 After that I went into the districts
of Syria and Cilicia. 22 But I was personally unknown to the Christian churches in Judea; 23 only they kept hearing people say, "Our
former persecutor is now preaching as good news the faith which
once he tried to destroy," 24 and they kept on praising God for me.

Key phrases. Verse 18. "To see Cephas." This Greek verb
means either to visit or to get acquainted with one. The purpose
of Paul in going to Jerusalem on this brief visit was merely to get
acquainted with Peter and hear of the work he was doing there
and in Judea. It was not to take orders from Peter and to receive
a commission from him as an apostle. There is no hint in this
phrase or in this visit that Peter conferred any authority on Paul
as an apostle and preacher.

Verse 22. "Churches of Christ in Judea." There were other
churches in Judea besides the church in Jerusalem. This phrase emphasizes the conclusion reached above about local churches. In
all these texts in Galatians Paul is talking about local churches.

A GREAT TEXT WITH SERMON OUTLINE (1:15, 16a)
THE CHAMPION PERSECUTOR CONVERTED

I. Paul a Persecutor of Christ and Christians—"I persecuted
the Church of God"

II. God Predestinated Him to Be Saved—"Chose to reveal His
Son in Me"

III. God Predestinated Him to Preach to the Heathen (v. 16a)

IV. Paul's Part, Trusting and Surrendering to Christ—"We have
believed in Jesus Christ" (2:16)

Chapter II

PROCEEDINGS OF THE JERUSALEM CONFERENCE PROVE PAUL'S APOSTLESHIP AND GOSPEL NOT HUMAN BUT DIVINE IN ORIGIN (2:1-10)

Then, fourteen years later, I again went up to Jerusalem, with Barnabas, and took Titus with me too. ²I went up under the guidance of a divine revelation. Now I laid before them the good news that I was in the habit of preaching among the heathen, but first I did so privately before the leaders, for fear that my course might be or might have been to no purpose. ³But they did not even try to compel my companion, Titus, although he was a Greek, to be circumcised—⁴they did not try it even for the sake of the false brothers who had been smuggled in, who stole in to spy out the freedom we enjoy in Christ Jesus, so as to make us slaves again. ⁵But we did not for a moment yield them submission, in order that the truth of the good news might prevail for you. ⁶Those who were looked upon as leaders—what they were makes no difference to me—God pays no attention to outward appearances—these leaders added nothing new to me. ⁷On the contrary, because they saw that I had been entrusted with the good news for the heathen, just as Peter had been entrusted with it for the Jews—⁸for He who had been at work in Peter for his apostleship to the Jews had been at work in me too for the apostleship to the heathen—⁹and because they recognized the favor God had shown me, James, Cephas, and John, the so-called pillar apostles, gave Barnabas and me the right hand of fellowship, with the understanding that we should go to the heathen and they to the Jews. ¹⁰Only they wanted us to remember the poor, the very thing that I was eager to do.

Key words and phrases. Verse 2. "I went up by revelation." That is, the apostle prayed and found the will of God in this perplexing problem of circumcision for Gentile believers. The Judaizers contended that Gentiles must be circumcised and keep the law of Moses, in order to be saved (Acts 15:1). This false doctrine was filtering into the churches of Galatia and unsettling the minds of the members of these churches. After praying for light upon the question, Paul felt impressed by the Spirit to go up to Jerusalem and have an understanding with the leaders—the pillar apostles,

Peter, James, and John—concerning this troublesome issue, which was threatening to divide all Christendom and defeat the advancing missionary programs among the Gentiles. Before he started for Jerusalem he knew that God had revealed His will to him. God had given him "the green light," so he went.

Verse 4. "The false brothers." This expression characterizes the extreme Judaizers who demanded circumcision of all Gentiles and the keeping of the law of Moses, in order to be saved. Were they Christians or not? Many were doubtless not regenerated and were deceived as to their religious status, while others had been regenerated but were merely deluded as to this question of circumcision.

Verse 9. "The pillar apostles." As the pillars support a huge building, Peter, James, and John "seemed" to the Christians in Jerusalem to be the undergirding pillars of the church. Paul minimized this high estimate of human leaders in the church. He said God did not pay any attention to external titles and trappings of men.

Verse 9. "The right hand of fellowship." Peter, James, and John, the pillar apostles, gave Barnabas and Paul the right hand of fellowship, after they had heard Paul explain his gospel of grace and faith, "apart from the works of the law." This means that they endorsed his gospel. Peter at that conference had made a speech in which he had endorsed the gospel of faith (Acts 15:9, 10). He asserts that God had shown him at Caesarea that "the hearts of Gentiles are purified by faith," just as the hearts of Jews were. So why, he asks, at the conference, should we put a yoke (the law) on the necks of Gentiles, a yoke that Jews were not able to bear? James also make a speech of endorsement (Acts 15:13-18) of Peter's views, which is also an endorsement of Paul's gospel. No speech of John is recorded, but he joined the other pillar apostles in giving the right hand of fellowship to Barnabas and Paul.

Basic Doctrines. (1) Justification, or salvation, by faith in Christ. This is the agreement reached between the two parties at the conference, the pillar apostles on the one hand, and Paul and Barnabas on the other, as representatives of the church at Antioch and Gentile Christianity. There is no schism between the Jewish group represented by the pillar apostles and the Gentile group represented by Paul and Barnabas. The plan of salvation is the same in both groups. Sinners of Jewish or Gentile stock are justified and purified by faith in Christ. No circumcision is required; no keeping of the law is demanded.

(2) "Fellowship of Christians" (v. 9). The Antioch group and the Jewish group of Christians, though having slight differences of opinion on some things, yet can give each other the right hand of fellowship and be brothers living and working in a beautiful spirit of unity and brotherhood. This is real Christianity—being tolerant toward each other as to minor differences but agreeing on the major doctrines and vital principles of the gospel, and living and working together in unity and "fellowship."

(3) "Liberty in Christ Jesus" (v. 4). Paul is exultant over the freedom believers enjoy in the gospel of grace and faith. They have no yoke of law chafing their necks. They are free from legalism and ceremonialism. They are free to trust wholly in Christ Jesus as Saviour and Lord. They are free to follow the Spirit's call to their inner spirits; free to follow Christ wherever the Spirit leads, without being enslaved by rites and ceremonies. But above all else they are free from the guilt and curse and power of sin. This thought is elaborated by the apostle in Romans 8:1-10.

THE PETRINE—PAULINE EPISODE AT ANTIOCH PROVES IT (2:11-14)

[11] Now when Cephas came to Antioch, I opposed him to his face, because he stood condemned. [12] For before the coming of certain people from James, he was in the habit of eating with heathen Christians, but after they came, he began to draw back and hold aloof from them, because he was afraid of the circumcision party. [13] The rest of the Jewish Christians, too, joined him in this pretense, so that even Barnabas was influenced to join them in their pretense. [14] But when I saw that they were not living up to the truth of the good news, I said to Cephas, and that before them all, "If you are living like a heathen and not like a Jew, although you are a Jew yourself, why do you try to make the heathen live like Jews?"

Key words and phrases. Verse 11. "Cephas." This is Peter's Aramaic name which means stone, rock. See John 1:42, where Jesus gave him this name. Then it was translated into Greek, Petros, then into English, Peter. I heard a distinguished Bible scholar once assert that this Cephas is not the apostle Peter. But scholars are practically unanimous in saying that Cephas is the same as Peter the apostle.

Verse 12. "Withdraw." This word means to draw back as if afraid of defilement from contact with another. The next step is "to separate from others"; that is, go into isolation and have nothing to do with others. This is what Cephas did at Antioch—after the Judaizers came he had nothing to do with Gentile Christians.

Verse 12. "Eating with." Eating with another in the East is the highest expression of sociability and friendship. Peter had that attitude toward the Gentile Christians at first but changed his attitude after the false teachers came. He did this because he was afraid of losing his prestige with the teachers from Jerusalem.

Verse 12. "Dissemble." The Greek word for this term is the word from which we get our English word hypocrisy. It means pretense, believing one thing but practicing the opposite; trying to make others think you are what you are not. Notice, it is Peter, the head apostle in Jerusalem, who is accused of this gross sin. He knew it was wrong for him to have nothing to do with Gentile Christians, yet he did it. It must be emphasized that his wrong course had a tremendous influence on others, on the rest of the Jewish Christians, and even on strong Barnabas, "a good man" (Acts 11:24) who "withdrew" and left his colleague, the peerless, conscientious Paul, to stand alone for the truth of the gospel in Antioch that day.

Verse 14. "Living like a Jew, or living like a Gentile." Living like a Jew means living like a circumcised man is expected to live, having no intimate association (as eating) with Gentiles. Living like a Gentile means not to be under these restrictions.

Paul's use of this episode. Why does he refer to this conflict with the head apostle at Jerusalem? Evidently it is to prove to the Galatians that he did not get his credentials as an apostle from Peter. He, Paul, had actually become a teacher of Peter instead of Peter teaching Paul. These Judaizers had likely told the Galatians that Paul was indebted to Peter and so was a man-made apostle. So Paul says to them, "Remember that instead of Peter teaching me I taught him."

JUSTIFICATION BY FAITH, THE CORE OF PAUL'S GOSPEL FIRST SET FORTH (2:15-21)

[15] We ourselves are Jews by birth and not heathen sinners, and yet, [16] because we know that a man does not come into right standing with God by doing what the law commands, but by simple trust in Christ, we too have trusted in Christ Jesus, in order to come into right standing with God by simple trust in Christ and not by doing what the law commands, because by doing what the law commands no man can come into right standing with God. [17] Now if, in our efforts to come into right standing with God through union with Christ, we have proved ourselves to be sinners like the heathen themselves, does that make Christ a party to our sin? Of course not. [18] For if I try to build again what I tore down, I really prove myself to be a wrongdoer. [19] For through the law I myself have become dead to the law, so that I may live for God. [20] I have been crucified with Christ, and I myself no longer live, but Christ is living in me; the life I now live as a mortal man I live by faith in the Son of God who loved me and gave Himself for me. [21] I never can nullify the unmerited favor of God. For if right standing with God could come through law, then Christ died for nothing.

Key words and phrases. Verses 15-17. "Justify." This verb, with the corresponding substantive, denotes coming into right standing with God. Literally the English word means "to make just." As Paul uses it it does not mean to make just, but to come into right standing with God and be regarded by Him as just or righteous. Abraham put his trust in God, and his trust was counted for him as righteousness. If the sinner puts his trust in Christ it is counted as righteousness—he is justified. The faith of a trusting sinner unites him with Christ, and because Christ is righteous this union with Christ permits God to regard the sinner thus trusting Christ as righteous or justified.

Verse 16. "Faith." This word has three meanings in the New

Testament: simple childlike trust or surrender to Christ as Saviour and Lord; conquering confidence in God, as used in Hebrews 11; by faith the heroes of old performed incredible feats; and last, it means a body of doctrines believed, as when Jude (3) wrote, "Contend for the faith once delivered to the saints." In Galatians it means trust that unites a believer to Christ—"justified by faith in Christ."

Verses 15, 17. "Sin . . . sinners." The Greek verb means "to miss the mark." The substantive has a kindred meaning, "missing the mark." Missing the mark of right and good set by God. The substantive has two meanings: abstractly, the sin-priniciple; concretely, a sin act. Sinners are those who miss God's mark; those who transgress the law.

Verses 16:20, 21. "Law." Law is used in two senses: the Mosaic codes and the moral law written in man's constitution (Rom. 2:14, 15). In Galatians it refers to the Mosaic codes.

A basic doctrine and a Pauline thought-form. (1) *Justification.* Justification by faith is the central theme of Galatians. It is the initial stage of the salvation process, which reaches from God's work of regeneration in the believer through sanctification to perfection at the parousia and the resurrection of the righteous. Justification denotes the state into which the believer comes when he trusts Christ as Saviour and Lord. He was not in right standing with God before he trusted Christ. Now he is. And he is "justified without the works of the law."

(2) *Mystic realism.* Used in 2:20. "I have been crucified with Christ; it is no longer I who live, but Christ who lives in me." This expression is used by theologians to denote the wholly personal relation between a believer and God. The human spirit and the Divine Spirit are in direct union with each other. Here Paul uses the thought-form to say that he was crucified with Christ. By faith he was with Him on the cross. This is mysticism. Because of his faith in Christ, what Christ did on the cross becomes the cause of a spiritual crucifixion in Paul; and because the dying Christ rose again, by this same faith, He lives in Paul. This is realism. So the whole process is mystic realism.

Two Great Texts with Sermon Outlines
Living the Higher Life (2:20a)

I. **Dying with Christ.** "I have been Crucified with Christ."
II. **The Living Christ Living in Believers.** "Christ lives in me."
III. **Faith in Christ the Conquering Power.** "By faith in the Son of God."

The World's Most Wonderful Lover (2:20b)

I. **A Divine Lover.** "The Son of God."
II. **A Lover of Individuals.** "Who loved *me.*"
III. **Making the Supreme Sacrifice.** "Gave *Himself.*"
IV. **A Substitutional Sacrifice.** *"For* me."

Illustration for either sermon: John Masefield in his poetic drama, "The Trial of Jesus," has Procula, wife of Pilate, concerned about Christ's crucifixion. She asks a soldier, "Is He dead?" "No." "Then where is He?" "Let loose in the world so that nothing can stop His truth." Yes, Christ was let loose in the world by His resurrection and ascension to live in the lives of consecrated Christians.

Argument from the Experience of the Galatians (3:1-9)

O senseless Galatians! Who has bewitched you, before whose very eyes Jesus Christ was pictured as the crucified One? ² I want to ask you only this one thing: Did you receive the Spirit by doing what the law commands, or by believing the message you heard? ³ Are you so senseless? Did you begin by the Spirit, but are now approaching perfection by fleshly means? ⁴ Have you suffered so much for nothing? If it really is for nothing. ⁵ Now when He supplies you with the Spirit and performs His wonder-works among you, does He do it because you do what the law commands, or because you believe the message that you heard— ⁶ just as "Abraham put his faith in God, and it was credited to him as right standing with God"?

⁷ So you see, it is the men of faith who are the real descendants of Abraham. ⁸ Because the Scripture foresaw that God would bring the heathen into right standing with Himself on condition of faith, He beforehand proclaimed the good news to Abraham in the promise, "It is through you that all the heathen will be blessed." ⁹ So the men of faith are blessed as partners with trusting Abraham.

Key words and phrases. Verse 1. "Foolish Galatians, who bewitched you?" The word *foolish* means not thinking, not considering the facts in the case. It expresses no disparagement of their intelligence, but of their failure to use their minds to weigh the doctrine presented them by the Judaizers. "Bewitch" means to charm, as the snake charms the bird so he cannot move as he would. As the snake has a complete charming power over his victim, so the Judaizers had charmed and put to sleep the minds of the Galatians.

Verse 1. *"Set forth . . . crucified."* The verb *set forth* expresses a graphic picturing, placarding, of Christ as crucified before the very eyes of the Galatians. Paul must have preached Christ crucified in the most vivid and vigorous language.

Verse 2. *"Receive the Spirit."* This is not regeneration but an after enduement of believers with the power of the Spirit—what Jesus promised the disciples in Acts 1:8.

Verse 3. *"Made perfect."* Used ironically by Paul. Did you Galatians begin your Christian lives by the Spirit and are now approaching perfection by fleshly means (circumcision)? Is that reasonable? No, never!

Verse 5. *"Working miracles."* In the early days of their experience they had received power to work miracles, perhaps, to heal the sick. Would they for a moment think they were empowered to do these miracles because they had been circumcised?

Verse 7. *"Children of Abraham."* Not the natural descendants of Abraham, like Ishmael, but the "men of faith," those who trust Christ as their Saviour, are the real children of Abraham; that is, the spiritual children of the "father of the faithful."

Verse 8. *"The Scripture . . . beforehand preached the gospel to Abraham."* The special promise that God made to Abraham that in him should "all the nations of the earth be blessed," is counted by Paul as the beginning of the preaching of the gospel.

THE LAW SATISFIED BY CHRIST'S REDEEMING DEATH (3:10-14)

10 For those who depend on what the law commands are under a curse, for the Scripture says, "Cursed be everyone who does not continue in all the commands that are written in the book of the law, to do them." 11 Now it is evident that through the law no

man is brought into right standing with God, for "The man in right standing with God will live by faith," [12] and the law has nothing to do with faith, but it says, "It is the man who does these things that will live by doing them." [13] Christ ransomed us from the curse of the law by becoming a curse for us—for the Scripture says, "Cursed be everyone who is hanged on a tree"—[14] that the blessing promised to Abraham might through Jesus Christ come to the heathen, so that through faith we might receive the promised Spirit.

Key words and phrases. Verse 13. *"The curse."* This is the penalty God pronounces on the transgressor of His law. The curse is death. "The soul that sinneth it shall die."

Verse 13. *"Redeemed."* This verb means to "buy off or out of." The picture is that of a prison in which sinners are shut up and held there by Satan. But Christ pays the ransom price and buys them out of prison, or from under the curse of the broken law. He does this by Himself becoming a curse for them or in their place. He bears the death penalty and thus pays the ransom price.

Verse 13. *"For."* This preposition *(huper)*, or the preposition *anti*, denotes in the place of, instead of (Thayer, *Lexicon*). See Robertson's *Grammar of the Greek New Testament, in loc.*

A Great Text with Sermon Outline (3:13, 14)

Christ's Death the Ransom Price to Set Us Free

I. All Men under the Curse of the Law (see Rom. 3:23)
II. Christ's Death the Ransom Price—"Becoming a Curse"
III. Extent of the Ransom—"to the Nations"
IV. The Blessing of the Ransom Appropriated by Faith in Christ verse 14, "Blessing of Abraham"; "promise of the Spirit."

The Historical Argument for Justification by Faith in Christ (3:15-22)

[15] Brothers, I am going to use a human illustration: Even a human contract, once it has been ratified, no one can annul or change. [16] Now the promises were made to Abraham and his descendant. It does not say, "and to your descendants," in the plural, but in the singular, "and to your descendant," that is, Christ. [17] I mean this: The law which was given four hundred and thirty years later

could not annul the contract which had already been ratified by God, so as to cancel the promise. [18] For if our inheritance depends on the law, it can no longer depend on the promise. But it was by promise that God so graciously bestowed it upon Abraham.

[19] Then what about the law? It was added later on to increase transgressions, until the descendant to whom the promise was made should come, enacted through the agency of angels in the person of an intermediary. [20] Though an intermediary implies more than one party, yet God is only one. [21] Is the law then contrary to God's promises? Of course not. For if a law had been given that was able to impart life, surely, then, right standing would have come through law. [22] But the Scripture pictures all mankind as prisoners of sin, so that the promised blessing through faith in Christ might be given to those who have faith.

Key words and phrases. Verses 15, ff. *"Covenant."* This word is referred by Paul to the promise which God made to Abraham (Gen. 15 and 17) that he should have a son (Isaac) whose descendants would be as numberless as the sands of the sea and the stars of the sky. This promise is compared to a human contract, an agreement between two parties. Here it is a solemn agreement between God and Abraham in which the central thought is the gracious promise of God for a future descendant (the Christ) in whom the nations should be blessed.

Verse 16. *"Seed."* The apostle plays upon the singular of this substantive. The promise said "seed" not "seeds." So it refers to an individual, and that individual is Christ.

Verse 17. *"Four hundred and thirty years after."* This is the key sentence in Paul's argument in this paragraph. The law was not given till four hundred and thirty years after the gracious promise had been made to Abraham that he should give to the world a child who should be the Messiah. How then could the law, not in existence, have anything to do with Abraham's justification, or with the covenant that God was making to be in effect for all the future? Then if it had nothing to do with Abraham's justification, why suppose that it can effect the justification of anyone today? And the agreement with Abraham cannot be annulled or changed any more than a human contract can be changed or canceled (except by consent of the two parties). Certainly neither God nor Abraham ever hinted at a change.

Verse 18. *"God gave it."* The verb *gave* here used is a strong verb; it means "graciously give." It was by God's grace that He gave it (the promise to Abraham). Paul sees in the transaction between God and Abraham then a prophecy of the gospel of grace. It was an unchangeable agreement which God was making for His plan of salvation for mankind in future generations.

Verses 19-22. *"Why the law added . . . because of transgressions?"* If the law has no part in saving mankind, then what service did it render? Certainly it was not God's purpose to increase transgressions by giving the law. And yet because of the giving of the law man's transgressions did increase. God's purpose was not only that the law should set up high moral standards for man to live by, but also to show men that they cannot perfectly keep it and thus save themselves. In this way the law drives men to despair and they cry out for God's mercy. The law is not "against the promises of God" (21), but it was not in God's plan for it "to make alive" or bring men "into right standing with God." Yet it helped to fulfill the promises of God as a "tutor" (24, 25) to bring men to Christ to teach and save them. Discussed in next paragraph.

The Law System Inferior to the Faith System (3:23-29)

²³ But before this faith came, we were kept locked up under the law, in preparation for the faith which was to be unveiled. ²⁴ So the law has been our attendant to lead to Christ, so that we might through faith obtain right standing with God. ²⁵ But now that this faith has come, we are no longer in charge of the attendant. ²⁶ For all of you are sons of God through faith in Christ Jesus. ²⁷ For all of you who have been baptized into union with Christ have clothed yourselves with Christ. ²⁸ There is no room for Jew or Greek, no room for slave or freeman, no room for male or female, for you are all one through union with Christ Jesus. ²⁹ And if you belong to Christ, then you are real descendants of Abraham, and heirs in accordance with the promise made to him.

Key words and phrases. Verses 24-25. *"The law our schoolmaster, or tutor."* Schoolmaster is not the meaning of this word *(paidagogos)*. Nor is our word tutor a perfect translation. According to the Greek custom the *paidagogos* was a slave attendant on a teacher, and the business of the slave attendant was to bring the pupils to the teacher, and after the teaching was over to take them back home. Thus the slave attendant had an important function as a helper to a teacher, but he was not a teacher or schoolmaster. So Paul conceives of the law system as a helper to bring men to Christ. It was God's method of preparing the world for the coming of Christ. The individual sinner too is prepared by the law to trust Christ, by showing him his helplessness to save himself and thus driving him in despair to Christ as the only Saviour. Paul knew this by his own experience. See Romans 7:24, 25, where in despair he cries out, "O wretched man that I am! who shall deliver me? . . . I thank God through Jesus Christ our Lord."

Verse 23. "The law system and the faith system." The words *law* and *faith* in this paragraph have an unusual meaning. Nowhere else are the words used as they are here. "Under the law" refers to the time when the Jews were under the law system as a preparative method for training them to receive the Messiah when He came; that is, for the superior faith system in the messianic period. This does not mean that there was no faith under the law system, for all the righteous believed in God and His promise of the coming Messiah in order to be saved, in those centuries before Christ. But the law system held the right of way and was prominent as a tutor, a subordinate attendant, in preparing for the higher faith system, and even to extend its sway to the Gentiles, even to all the nations.

Verse 25. "No longer under the law." This means that now we are under the faith system and do not have to consider the law as having any saving significance. We are beyond that stage in history and in an advanced stage of God's dealing with the lost world. The law still, properly preached, is a subordinate attendant to bring us to Christ as our Saviour.

Verse 26. "Children of God by faith in Christ." We are now enjoying a higher status, that of divine sonship through our trust in Christ as Saviour. Faith in Christ is the human condition on which the Spirit makes us children of God by a new birth.

Verse 27. "Baptized into Christ." This does not mean "baptismal regeneration," as claimed by some interpreters. It is Paul's vivid symbolism to picture to us what the Spirit does in the soul of the believer trusting in Christ. He dies to sin and to the world, he is buried with Christ (Rom. 6:4; Col. 2:12), as pictured in his baptism; he is raised with Him to "walk in a new life," he is a "new creation" (Gal. 6:15).

Verse 28. "All one in Christ." Paul rises to the highest summit in Christianity's supremacy over ethnic religions in his doctrine of a beautiful unity and equality in Christ. There is no room for racial, national and social distinctions when men put on Christ and clothe themselves with His spirit and ideals of love and unity and equality. All eternal marks of division and distinction are swept away by Christ and in Christ. When Chief Justice Charles Evan Hughes, the first Sunday after he arrived in Washington to take his seat on the Supreme Court bench, presented himself for membership in the First Baptist Church there, a Chinese laundryman was received with him. The pastor, as he received them, looked at the scene and remarked, "At the foot of the cross all men are equal." This is what Paul means when he says, "You are all one in Christ." This also means (v. 29) that such believers in Christ are the real (spiritual) descendants of Abraham.

A Great Text with Sermon Outline (3:24)

The Function of the Law in Relation to Salvation

I. It Does Not and Cannot Save (2:16; Rom. 3:20)

II. Properly Presented and Received It Prepares the Sinner for Christ to Save Him

III. It Shows the Sinner His Helplessness and Drives Him to Despair to Call on Christ (Rom. 7:24-25)

Chapter IV

The Superior Status of Believers, Sons and Heirs of God; Argument from the Experience of the Galatians; Argument from the Historical Allegory of Abraham's Two Sons, Isaac and Ishmael

THE SUPERIOR STATUS OF BELIEVERS (4:1-11)

I mean this: As long as the heir is under age he is not a whit better off than a slave, although he is heir of all the property, ² but he is under guardians and trustees until the time fixed by the father. ³ So when we were spiritually under age, we were slaves to the world's crude notions, ⁴ but when the proper time had come, God sent His Son, born of a woman, born subject to law, ⁵ to ransom those who were subject to law, so that we might be adopted as sons. ⁶ And because you are sons, God has sent the Spirit of His Son into your hearts, crying, "Abba," that is, "Father." ⁷ So you are no longer a slave, but a son; and if a son, then an heir by God's own act.

⁸ But at that former time, as you did not know the true God, you were slaves to gods that do not really exist, ⁹ but now, since you have come to know God, or rather have come to be known by Him, how can you turn back to your own crude notions, so weak and worthless, and wish to become slaves to them again? ¹⁰ You are observing days, months, seasons, years. ¹¹ I am beginning to fear that I have bestowed my labors on you for nothing.

Key words and phrases. Verse 1. "A child." The Greek word denotes even an unborn baby, then a child up to ten. Paul uses this illustration to show in what an immature state the Galatians were before they were converted to Christ.

Verse 2. "He is under tutors and governors." A better translation would be "guardians and trustees." The guardian looked after the conduct and business affairs, the trustee, especially the food, clothes, and other personal needs, of the child. Paul uses this helpless child to illustrate how helpless these pagans were before their conversion to Christ.

Verse 3. "The elements of the world." That is, as pagans they were slaves to idolatry and a low level of moral living, the *abc* of life and religion.

Verse 4. "The fullness of the time." The Jews divided history into two ages, the present or pre-messianic, the future or messianic. In this passage Paul means that the pre-messianic age is coming to a completion when God sent His Son to introduce the messianic age, in which the gospel of grace and faith is to be proclaimed that sinners may be saved by simple trust in Christ without the works of the law being necessary for their salvation. God picked the fitting time for the incarnation of His Son to bring redemption to mankind. The world had been prepared by the law system, so far as the Jews were concerned; the world was unified as never before into a great Roman Empire with roads penetrating the remote provinces of the empire, and Alexander the Great had spread the Greek language and culture over the whole Western world. It was the best time God could have selected for His Son to be born into the world.

Verse 5. "The adoption of sons." The glorious purpose of Christ's incarnation and redemption of men was that men might become sons of God. Notice, the apostle says they are "adopted as sons." Does he ignore regeneration? Is it not necessary? Surely, he recognized both regeneration and adoption. But they are two phases of the same great transaction. In Titus 3:5 he says He "saved us, not by works of righteousness which we have done, but by the washing of regeneration and the renewal of the Holy Spirit." In Galatians 6:15 the believer in Christ becomes "a new creation." Regeneration emphasizes the initial stage of the transaction of salvation; adoption looks toward a higher stage, the dignity and prestige and privileges of the children of God, as heirs and "joint-heirs with Christ."

Verse 6. "The Spirit of His Son." This is undoubtedly the Holy Spirit, not simply the disposition or spirit of Jesus. He calls the Holy Spirit "the Spirit of His Son," because Christ promised that the Paraclete would be "sent in His name" (John 14:26). The highest privilege of the sons of God is to have the Holy Spirit dwelling permanently in them; to be His temple (Rom. 8:9-11; I Cor. 6:19).

Verse 7. "No more a servant but a son." It is to be noticed here that Paul individualizes his readers. He addresses each one individually. Each one of you is a son and heir of God with all the prestige and privileges pertaining to this high relationship.

Verse 8. "Did service to those who were no gods." The Galatians were pagans and before conversion worshiped idols which Paul says are no gods at all. Then how can they think of dropping from the dignity of sons to the true God into the doom of idolaters?

Verse 10. "You observe days and months and seasons and

years." This sentence refers to their beginning to observe Jewish customs and feasts, some of them apparently going over to Judaism.

ARGUMENT FROM THEIR FIRST LOYALTY TO HIM (4:12-20)

12 I beg you, brothers, take my point of view, just as I took yours. You did me no injustice then. 13 And yet you know that it was because of an illness of mine that I preached the good news to you the first time, 14 but still you did not scorn the test my illness made of you, nor did you spurn me for it; on the contrary, you welcomed me as an angel of God, as Christ Jesus Himself. 15 Where is your self-congratulation? For I can testify that you would have torn out your very eyes, if you could, and have given them to me. 16 Have I then turned into an enemy to you, because I tell you the truth?

17 These men are paying you special attention, but not sincerely. They want to shut you off from me, so that you may keep on paying them special attention. 18 Now it is a fine thing to have special attention paid you, if it is done sincerely and unceasingly, and not only when I am with you. 19 O my dear children, I am suffering a mother's birth pangs for you again, until Christ is formed in you. 20 I wish I could be with you right now and change the tone of my speech, for I do not know which way to turn in your case.

Key words and phrases. Verse 12. "Be as I am, for I am as you are." Paul is here appealing to them to be as considerate of him as he was of them when he first preached to them and as he is now. "Be as I am" means take my point of view that one is saved by trusting Christ, "apart from the works of the law."

Verse 12. "Through infirmity of the flesh I preached to you at the first." This means that Paul was suffering a personal illness when he first visited them. The illness was either ophthalmia (so Lightfoot, *St. Paul's Epistle to the Galatians*, Macmillan, 1910; Expositor's Greek Testament; B. H. Carroll, *Interpretation of the English Bible*). Or malaria (so Ramsay, *A Historical Commentary on St. Paul's Epistle to the Galatians*, Putnam, 1900, and David Smith, *Life and Letters of Paul*, Doran, n.d.). Lightfoot's argument for ophthalmia, because they were willing to pluck out their own eyes for Paul, is not conclusive. This is a general adage to express one's supreme devotion to another. I feel that Ramsay's arguments for malaria are much weightier. Paul rushed up from the coast town of Perga to Pisidian Antioch in the hills, which would be sensible to do if he had malaria.

Verse 15. "Would have plucked out your eyes for me." As said above, this is an almost universal proverb for expressing supreme devotion of one for another.

Verse 18. "I travail in birth pangs for you till Christ be formed in you." Paul uses this figure of speech, a woman in birth pangs to bear a baby, to express his anguish and agony over the defection of the Galatians from the simple gospel of Christ. "O my dear Galatian children, I am in spiritual birth pangs for you, until Christ is really born in you!" It expresses doubt about some of them, but hope also that some of them are real children of God.

THE ARGUMENT CLINCHED BY AN ALLEGORICAL ILLUSTRATION
(4:21-31)

[21] Tell me, you who want to be subject to law, will you not listen to what the law says? [22] For the Scripture says that Abraham had two sons, one by a slave-girl, the other by a free woman. [23] But the child of the slave-girl was born in the ordinary course of nature, while the child of the free woman was born to fulfill the promise. [24] This is spoken as an allegory. For these women are two covenants, one coming from Mount Sinai, bearing children that are to be slaves; [25] that is, Hagar (and Hagar means Mount Sinai, in Arabia) and corresponds to the present Jerusalem, for Jerusalem is in slavery with her children. [26] But the Jerusalem that is above is free, and she is our mother. [27] For the Scripture says:

"Rejoice, you childless woman, who never bore a child;
Break forth into shouting, you who feel no birth pangs;
For the desolate woman has many children,
Even more than the married one."

[28] Now we, brothers, like Isaac, are children born to fulfill the promise. [29] But just as then the child born in the ordinary course of nature persecuted the one born by the power of the Spirit, so it is today. [30] But what does the Scripture say? "Drive off the slave-girl and her son, for the slave-girl's son shall never share the inheritance with the son of the free woman." [31] So, brothers, we are children, not of a slave-girl but of a free woman.

Key words and phrases. Verse 21. *"The law."* Law in this verse is neither the Mosaic nor the moral law, the usual meanings of the term. The quotation is from Genesis which does not contain the Mosaic codes. Here the word is used in a broader sense to include the whole Pentateuch, the five books of Moses. See Luke 24:44, where Jesus uses the term in this wider sense.

Verse 23. *"By promise."* Paul traces the gospel of grace and faith back to the promise of God to Abraham (Gen. 17). When he was one hundred years old (Sarah being ninety), God promised him that he should have a child by a supernatural birth; that is, this child should be "born by the Spirit." So are the children of God by faith; they are children of promise, children by the Holy Spirit.

Verse 24. *"Which things are an allegory."* This is the only allegory used by Paul in all his letters. What is an allegory? It is a story from everyday life, or history, as here, to illustrate and enforce spiritual truths. It differs from a parable in that the parable usually teaches only one great truth or principle, while an allegory expresses a truth in every part of it. As another has said, "It runs on all fours."

A Great Text in Chapter IV with Outline

The Preacher's Compassion for His People in Error (4:19)

I. The Cause of the People's Defection from Truth—flattering fallacies of false teachers. Judaizers are seducing the Galatians.

II. Comfort Needed by the Victims of False Teachers—love and sacrificial suffering by the preacher. Paul in birth pangs for them.

III. The Remedy for False Teaching—winsome warning and teaching the truth in love. See how Paul lovingly warns the Galatians and patiently teaches them.

Chapter V

The Higher Life of Believers; the Nature of Their Freedom; Bearing the Fruit of the Spirit; Freedom in Christ and Slavery to the Law Contrasted (5:1-12)

This is the freedom with which Christ has made us free. So

keep on standing in it, and stop letting your necks be fastened in the yoke of slavery again.

[2] Here is what I am saying to you: If you let yourselves be circumcised, Christ can do you no good. [3] I again insist that if any man lets himself be circumcised, he is under obligation to obey the whole law. [4] You people, whoever you are among you, who try to get into right standing with God through law have cut yourselves off from Christ, you have missed the way of God's favor. [5] For we, by the Spirit, are awaiting the hoped-for blessing which our right standing with God will bring us. [6] For in union with Christ Jesus neither circumcision nor the lack of it counts for anything; but only faith that is spurred on to action by love.

[7] You were running beautifully! Who was it that cut into your way and kept you from obeying the truth? [8] Such persuasion never came from Him who called you. [9] A little yeast will transform the whole dough. [10] By our union with the Lord I have confidence in you that you will take no other view of the matter. The man who is unsettling you will certainly pay the penalty for it, no matter who it turns out to be. [11] As for me, myself, brothers, if I am still preaching circumcision, why am I still being persecuted? In such a case the hindrance done by the cross has presumably ceased! [12] I almost wish that these men who are upsetting you would go all the way, and have themselves mutilated.

Key words and phrases. Verse 1. "With freedom Christ has made us free." The substantive "freedom or liberty" is likely in the instrumental case and should be translated as an Aramaic instrumental of emphasis: "with a genuine freedom He surely set us free." The freedom is positively proved as a fact of Christian experience.

Verse 1. "Stand in it." This verb is present imperative denoting continuous action. Paul exhorts the Galatians to continue to stand in this glorious freedom in Christ.

Verse 1. "Yoke of bondage." The yoke is the symbol of slavery; here it is slavery to the law.

Verse 2. "I Paul myself say." Paul considers himself as the outstanding champion of the freedom from the law by faith in Christ. Peter and James at the Jerusalem conference recognized it as true, but Paul is the stalwart champion of the doctrine.

Verse 2. "Christ shall profit you nothing." The law method and the faith method of justification are directly opposite to each other and exclude each other. Christ must do all the saving of a sinner or He cannot do it at all. It is not partly done by faith and partly by circumcision, or law. Keeping the law cannot supplement the work Christ does in the heart.

Verse 4. "You are fallen from grace." This does not mean that they had become children of God and now had completely lapsed so as to lose the salvation they once had. No; the apostle is contrasting the two methods of justification, the law method and the faith method. Whoever tries to be justified by the law method (as he calls it) has cut himself off from Christ and has fallen away from the grace method which justifies on condition of faith. The next verse (5) states that Paul and other believers look for the hope of right standing with God by the Spirit *on condition of faith.*

Verse 6. "Faith which worketh by love." Here Paul describes the nature of the faith that is effective in bringing the believer into union with Christ. It is not a merely intellectual faith; not a historical belief in an event, be it the crucifixion or resurrection of Christ. It is a vital heart trust, a personal commitment of oneself to Christ as Saviour (Rom. 10:9, 10); a faith which has the dynamic of love to Christ behind it and beneath it to produce action, to work for Christ and His program of salvation.

Verse 7. "Hinder you." This verb is a military term and pictures an enemy cutting a ditch across the road of a marching army to impede its march.

Verse 8. "This persuasion." The flattering speeches of the Judaizers to woo and win the Galatians to their false teachings is called "persuasion."

Verse 9. "Leaven." It is used for an evil influence.

Verse 10. "He that troubleth you shall bear his judgment." A universal moral principle in the government of God (see Gal. 6:7).

Verse 12. "I would they were even cut off." Likely it is not a wish that these false teachers should be cut off from Christ and lost forever, but that they might have themselves *mutilated physically.*

Two Great Texts and Sermon Outlines
Our Freedom in Christ (5:1)

I. What Is It? Negatively and Positively

II. Who Gave Us This Freedom? Our Emancipator: "Christ Set Us Free" (See John 8:36; Rom. 7:25)

III. How Was It Won? "By Faith" (vv. 5, 6)

IV. A Prize to Be Guarded—"Stand in It." "Eternal vigilance is the price of liberty."

The Faith That Saves (Gal. 5:6)

I. A Vital Faith—Linked with the Risen Christ (Gal. 2:20)

II. A Vigorous Faith—"Faith That Worketh"

III. Love Is Its Dynamic—"By Love"; Love to Christ and Men.

The Nature of Freedom in Christ (5:13-15)

For you, brothers, were called to freedom; only you must not let your freedom be an excuse for the gratification of your lower nature, but in love be slaves to one another. ¹⁴ For the whole law is summed up in one saying, "You must love your neighbor as you do yourself." ¹⁵ But if you continue to bite and eat one another, beware lest you are destroyed by one another."

Key words and phrases. Verse 13. "An occasion to the flesh." The word *occasion* is a military term and means a camping place, which becomes a sallying point from which an enemy dashes forth to surprise and capture the opposing army. So Paul conceives of our freedom as a possible camping ground, or sallying point, from which our *sarx*, lower nature, suddenly attacks and captures us. So he warns his readers.

Verse 13. "By love serve one another." The word *love* is here used instrumentally, and so love is the dynamic in the hearts of believers which motivates them to serve their fellow Christians. "Serve" is the strong Greek verb *douleuo*, to serve as a slave. Not as a bondslave but as a voluntary servant ready for even the most menial service, footwashing, plowing another's corn, bearing his burden of grief or sorrow.

Verse 14. "The law is fulfilled." It here means to sum up; love is the summary, the summing up of the whole law; to love your neighbor as you do yourself is the summing up of the whole moral law.

Verse 15. "Bite, devour, consume." These are words of the jungle, a picture of wild beasts biting and eating and consuming one another. Christians must beware of hate and let love be the master of life. Liberty in Christ does not mean license to sin but love to serve.

THE HIGHER LIFE OF SERVICE
THE PRODUCT OF THE SPIRIT (5:16-26)

[16] I mean this: Practice living by the Spirit and then by no means will you gratify the cravings of your lower nature. [17] For the cravings of the lower nature are just the opposite of those of the Spirit, and the cravings of the Spirit are just the opposite of those of the lower nature; these two are opposed to each other, so that you cannot do anything you please. [18] But if you are guided by the Spirit, you are not subject to the law. [19] Now the practices of the lower nature are clear enough: Sexual immorality, impurity, sensuality, [20] idolatry, sorcery, enmity, quarreling, jealousy, anger, intrigues, dissensions, party-spirit, [21] envy, drunkenness, carousing, and the like. I now warn you, as I have done before, that those who practice such things shall not be heirs of the kingdom of God. [22] But the product of the Spirit is love, joy, peace, patience, kindness, goodness, faithfulness, [23] gentleness, self-control. There is no law against such things. [24] And those who belong to Jesus the Christ have crucified the lower nature with its passions and evil cravings.

[25] If we live by the Spirit, let us also walk where the Spirit leads. [26] Let us stop being ambitious for honors, so challenging one another, envying one another.

Key words and phrases. Verse 16. "Flesh." Paul often uses this word, not a physical sense, but in an ethico-psychological sense, to denote the lower nature of man. It is that part of man—the moral ego—which drags him down; which prompts him to do wrong. (See Rom. 8 for same use.)

Verse 16f. "The lusts." This word here means the sinful desires originating in and overflowing the lower nature. The verb from the same root means to covet, or have an evil desire.

Verse 17. "Contrary to one another." The cravings of the lower nature are ethically the opposite of the wooings of the Spirit.

Verse 17. "You cannot do the things that you would." The will by the power of the Spirit must overcome the natural choices of the lower nature. So one's natural desires are not a safe guide to follow. However, we can do the things that we will to do, if we are empowered by the Spirit.

Verses 19, 24. "Works of the flesh . . . fruit of the Spirit." Notice, as Paul sets these two forces over against each other, he calls the product of the lower nature works, the product of the Spirit fruit. That is, the lower nature is merely a force, a power, which *works*, is active and never takes a vacation. But the Christian guided and governed by the Spirit is a living entity, a live personality, which bears fruit. Fruit grows on a living tree. The Christian is a living tree "planted by the rivers of water, which bears its fruit in due season." That tree is watered by the Spirit; not only watered but energized and dynamized by the Spirit (Acts 1:8). Notice, the product of the lower nature is a complex of works of various dark shades of sin; the product of the Spirit is a simplex of fruit. The nine qualities or traits flowing from the Spirit's presence and power in the believer constitute a unit; all of them work together in harmony. The works of the lower nature have no vital relation to each other; just a complex mixture of sinful desires and deeds.

Observe further, the desires and deeds of the lower nature are both individual and social. They are rooted in the individual but spread out and affect others in the group. Paul here enumerates only fifteen of these works, while in Romans 1:29-31 he names twenty-one. But in Galatians he adds, "and the like," a phrase which includes the remaining sins.

The nine traits which constitute the fruit of the Spirit are headed by love, the mightiest moral force in human life, and are closed by self-control, the climax of all victories. Alexander conquered the world but failed to conquer Alexander and died a drunken sot at thirty-three. The Christian can conquer Self by the power of the Spirit.

Verse 18. "If led by the Spirit . . . not under the law." This means that the Christian, if guided by the Spirit, does not have to follow literally the requirements of the law. He is under a higher law, the law of the Spirit, which often guides the Christian to "go the second mile"; to do more that the law requires. The Spirit inspires him with love, the mightiest force of life, and helps him live up to this higher law.

Verse 23. "Against such there is no law." No law forbids the practicing of love, joy, peace, patience, and all the rest of these noble qualities.

Verse 24. "Crucified the flesh." That is, the Christian must "kill" this lower nature, put it out of action, with its passions and sinful desires.

Verse 25. "If we live in the Spirit . . . walk in the Spirit." Better translated, "If we live by the Spirit, let us also walk by the Spirit." Paul is exhorting his readers to let their moral conduct (walk) be compatible with the inner spiritual life which the Spirit has generated in them.

SERMON OUTLINE ON A GREAT TEXT (5:22-23)

THE HIGHER LIFE BEARING GOLDEN FRUIT

I. Much Fruit *the Goal* of Christian Living (see John 15:2-8)
II. The Holy Spirit the Source and Power of Fruit-Bearing
III. The Unity of the Higher Life

These nine qualities blending to make a beautiful character and personality. The product of the Spirit is *fruit*, not fruits.

Chapter VI

CERTAIN CHRISTIAN DUTIES EMPHASIZED (6:1-10)

Brothers, if anybody is caught in the very act of doing wrong, you who are spiritual, in the spirit of gentleness, must set him right; each of you continuing to think of yourself, for you may be tempted too. ² Practice bearing one another's burdens, and in this way carry out the law of Christ. ³ For if anybody thinks he is somebody when really he is nobody, he deceives himself. ⁴ Everyone should test his own work until it stands the test, and then he will have ground for boasting with reference to himself alone and not with reference to someone else. ⁵ For everyone must carry his own load.

⁶ Those who are taught the truth should share all their goods with the man who teaches them. ⁷ Do not be deceived any more; God is not to be scoffed at. A person will reap just what he sows, whatever it is. ⁸ The person who sows to gratify his lower nature will reap destruction from that lower nature, and the person who sows to gratify his higher nature will reap eternal life from the Spirit. ⁹ Let us stop getting tired of doing good, for at the proper time we shall reap if we do not give up. ¹⁰ So then whenever we have an opportunity, let us practice doing good to everybody, but especially to the members of the family of faith.

Keys words and phrases. Verse 1. "Overtaken in a fault." This verb means not only taken but "foretaken." That is, before the results of his deed are known; or in the act, or soon after, he is caught. It is an extreme case Paul here supposes, and yet the spiritual Christians in the church should deal gently with the offender. The word fault implies falling by the wayside.

Verse 1. "Restore . . . in the spirit of meekness." Restore literally means to join up again the broken joints. As the delinquent fell he broke loose some joints, and these must be restored to their places. He must be put back where he was before the fall and given another chance. *Meekness* is better translated gentleness; tender consideration. This is the spirit to show toward the fallen, not self-complacency and scolding.

"Lest you be tempted." No Christian, however spiritual, is absolutely sin-proof in a world of moral miasma. Even preachers and deacons may be tempted and fall by the wayside.

Verse 2. "Bear one another's burden." The word for burden in verse 2 is *bare,* a weight attached to one; something that weighs him down, as cares, troubles, losses, disappointments. They come from external circumstances. The word for burden in verse 5 is *phortion,* a load which is a part of the individual, his personal responsibility. No one can carry that burden but the individual himself. But Paul exhorts us to help our fellows bear their external burdens due to circumstances and make life easier and happier for them.

"Fulfill the law of Christ." Law is used in a different sense from either the Mosaic or moral law. It means the manner of life

Christ lived, helping others, healing the sick, sympathizing with the sorrowing, cleansing lepers.

Verse 3. "Something . . . nothing, deceiveth himself." Even spiritual leaders are possibly warned by the apostle against too great self-confidence. They must not think they are somebody when they are nobody. This is deception of the grossest type.

Verse 4. "Prove his own work." The safe way for spiritual leaders, or for anyone is to test his own works until they stand approved. Then he may rejoice in his own spiritual achievements and not simply in another's.

Verses 6-8. "Sowing and reaping." The apostle is here giving instruction concerning the support of church leaders, pastors and teachers. The lay members of the churches who receive spiritual blessings from their pastors and teachers ought to share their material goods and thus support the church leaders, so they can "live on the gospel" (I Cor. 9:14), without being compelled to make tents or follow some other trade or vocation to make a living. This teaching in Galatians is more definitely emphasized in the first Letter to the church at Corinth.

He is here encouraging the lay members to obey this law of nature and grace—reaping what we sow. If we Christians use our material good for gratifying the cravings of the lower nature (flesh), we shall reap decay and destruction. If we sow our money in bonds and stocks, a tornado or panic may sweep it all away in the twinkling of an eye. If we sow it in the erection of beautiful buildings and a splendid home, a tornado or cyclone may destroy them. On the other hand, if we sow our money in the support of the churches and their ministries and missions, we shall reap a reward that enriches eternal life which is our present possession. Paul, however, does not mean that we can buy eternal life with our libral donations to the churches and their ministries. The Christian already possesses eternal life but his liberal gifts to God's churches will enrich the excellent quality of the eternal life he has. He will enjoy his religion more, God will be more real to him, and his experiences will be richer and riper. See Broadus, *Preparation and Delivery of Sermons;* Lightfoot, *Commentary on Galatians;* Burton, *Commentary;*

Carroll, *Interpretation of Bible,* for a similar interpretation of these verses.

Verses 9-10. "Weary in well doing . . . doing good to all men." To be weary is to get tired. Paul is exhorting his readers to stop getting tired of doing good, assuring them that they will reap a reward if they do not give up. He is likely thinking still of their sharing their goods with the church leaders; that is, the proper use of their money or possessions for the churches and their ministries. But he exhorts them to have a broader vision than the local church; do good to all men, the wicked, the lawless, the sick and suffering, the heathen. Ruskin has appraised the people who follow these orders and use their possessions for others as the richest. "That man is richest, who has personally and by use of his possessions, the widest influence over others."

SERMON OUTLINES ON GREAT TEXTS

HOW TO DEAL WITH DELINQUENT CHRISTIANS (6:1)

I. We Have Delinquent Church Members with Us Always
II. Sometimes Extreme Cases, as Here in Galatia
III. Deal with Them Gently and Humbly
Illustration: Jesus' Dealings with the Woman Taken in Adultery (John 8).

* * *

BEARING THE BURDENS OF OTHERS (6:2)

I. The Burden We Cannot Bear—Responsibility of Another (6:5)
II. The Burdens We Can Bear—those caused by circumstances, sickness, bereavement, losses, disappointment, etc.
III. Why Do So? To carry out the law of love exemplified by Christ (See Mark 5:25-42; John 11, etc.)

* * *

SOWING AND REAPING (6:6-8)

I. Sowing for Selfish Satisfaction, Reaping Decay and Destruction
II. Sowing for Spiritual Programs, Reaping Rewards to Enrich Eternal Life
III. Always Reaping *More* Than We Sow (Hos. 8:7).
V. Conclusion (6:11-18)

FINAL WARNING TO THE JUDAIZERS (6:11-18)

11 See what large letters I make, when I write to you with my own hand! 12 These men who are trying to force you to let yourselves be circumcised simply want to make a fine outward show, only to keep you from being persecuted for the cross of our Lord Jesus Christ. 13 Indeed, the very men who let themselves be circumcised do not themselves observe the law. But they simply want you to let yourselves be circumcised, so that they can boast of you as members of their party. 14 But may it never be mine to boast of anything but the cross of our Lord Jesus Christ, by which the world has been crucified to me and I to the world! 15 For neither circumcision nor the lack of it has any value, but only a new creation. 16 Now peace and mercy be on all who walk by this rule; that is, on the true Israel of God.

17 Let nobody trouble me after this, for I carry on my body the scars that mark me as Jesus' slave.

18 The spiritual blessing of our Lord Jesus Christ be with your spirit, brothers. Amen.

Key words and phrases. Verse 11. "How large letters I write." Likely this does not mean, as the Authorized Version has it, "How large a letter I have written to you." He takes the pen from the hand of his amanuensis and writes this conclusion, as his autograph, to make unquestionable the genuineness of the letter. He writes large letters (characters) because of weak eyes, either from old age or from eye trouble. But this does not prove that his thorn in the flesh was ophthalmia.

Verse 12. "The cross of Christ." This phrase is often used by the apostle to picture the death and sufferings of Christ as our Substitute. The cross was the symbol of shame, as it was the instrument used by the Romans to execute the worst criminals, murderers, traitors, etc. But to Paul it was the symbol of hope and glory and salvation by grace through faith in the crucified Christ.

Verse 13. "That they may glory in your flesh." The prime purpose of these false teachers was to "make a fair show in the flesh" (v. 12), "that they may glory in your flesh"; that is, to make proselytes to their religious party. They were hypocrites and did not love souls or yearn to see them saved.

Verse 14. "Glorying in the cross alone." These men might boast of their success in winning men to join their party and espouse their cause, but it was far from Paul to boast of achievements and success, or anything else, except the cross of Christ. This is because of what the cross has done for him. It has cut him loose from the world ("by which I have been crucified to the world and the world to me"); it has saved him from sin and made him a slave of Christ, and given him the hope of glory in the future age. Calvin, Winer, Bengel, Hoffman, Carroll, and most modern exegetes, interpret the phrase, "by which," and not "by whom" (with Meyer, *commentary*).

Verse 15. "A new creation." The Spirit creates believers over again and restores the image of God; now they are sons of God.

Verse 16. "The Israel of God." Those who boast of the cross alone as the means of salvation and their hope of eternal life, and have been made a new creation, are the true Israel of God; that is, the true people of God.

Verse 17. "The marks of the Lord Jesus." The scars he received at Lystra, Philippi, and other places where he was flogged and beaten. They are his credentials as a slave of Jesus.

Verse 18. Notice, the very last word of his closing prayer for the Galatians is "brothers." With all the soul pangs they caused him, he lovingly calls them his brothers in Christ. If we could know the results of this letter it might reveal to us that most of his readers came back "to Him who called them by the unmerited favor of Christ" (1:6).

A GREAT TEXT WITH SERMON OUTLINE (6:14)

BOASTING IN THE CROSS ALONE

I. Objects Not Worthy of Our Boasting — ancestry, ability, achievements, knowledge, one's country, family and relatives

II. The Cross Alone Is Worthy of Our Boasting—it represents Christ's love, death, and resurrection (to Paul His resurrection implied in His death)

III. Why Is It Worthy of Our Boasting? It brings atonement, salvation, sanctification, glorification (Rom. 8:29, 30).

The First Letter to the Corinthians

1. *Author, Occasion, and Date.* New Testament scholars are unanimous in ascribing this letter to the apostle Paul. It is genuinely Pauline in spirit, style, and general characteristics. He is in Ephesus conducting his third missionary campaign. It is likely about the middle of this three-year campaign, in the summer of A.D. 57. He gets information through some members of the household of Chloe that there are factions in the church there—at least four, a Paul party, an Apollos party, a Cephas (Peter) party, and a Christ party. Also three members of the church, Stephanus, Fortunatus, and Achaicus bring him a letter from the church in which he is asked to answer some questions about marriage, the status of woman in the church, eating foods offered to idols, and the grading of spiritual gifts. He also learns that gross immorality and licentiousness, common among pagans, were sapping the life out of the church, that some doubted even the resurrection of the dead.

2. *The Purpose.* The apostle's purpose was to bring about the unity of the church; to correct the moral evils in the church, litigation, improper sex relations, misuse of foods offered to idols, etc.; to stimulate their faith in the gospel of the cross, and in the resurrection of Christ and the Christian dead; to enlist the church for his world-wide evangelistic campaign.

3. *Characteristics of the Letter.* It is not a doctrinal treatise like the letter to the Romans. Only two basic doctrines, the cross and the resurrection, claim special discussion and emphasis. The letter is packed with practical wisdom for solving all social problems in accordance with the moral principles of Christianity: love, bearing the burdens of the weak, purity of heart and life, brotherhood and unity of Christians. It is characterized by reference to ideas, words, and phrases suggested by the Greek atmosphere, its customs, philosophy, and religion; by a style simple and charming, its thirteenth chapter being the most beautiful love poem ever written,

while chapter fifteen on the resurrection is a brief epic packed with keenest logic, sublimest thoughts, and sparkling rhetoric.

OUTLINE

I. Greeting (1:1-3).
II. Some Personal Matters with the Church (1:4-2:16).
   1. Thankful for their spiritual excellence (1:4-9).
   2. Rebuking them for having factions in the church (1:10-17).
   3. How the message of the cross affects different people (1:18-25).
   4. Their lowly social status (1:26-31).
   5. Paul's simple style of preaching the cross, which is the wisdom of God (2:1-5).
   6. This wisdom spiritually understood (2:6-16).
III. Correcting Evils in the Church (Chaps. 3-6).
   1. Correcting their conception of religious teachers and their function as servants of God. Building enduring materials into the temple of God (3:1-4:5).
   2. Sarcastically rebuking them for their conceit (4:6-21).
   3. Rebuking them for tolerating the incestuous man. (Chap. 5).
   4. Rebuking them for having litigation in heathen courts (Chap. 6).
IV. Answering Questions in the Letter Received from Them (Chaps. 7-14).
   1. The status of woman and marriage (Chap. 7).
   2. Eating foods offered to idols; letting love settle the problem (Chap. 8).
   3. Paul giving up his rights to become a servant to all to win some to Christ (Chap. 9).
   4. Warning against temptation and the abuse of their liberty (Chap. 10).
   5. Woman's status in the church; cliques in the church; disorder in observing the Lord's Supper (Chap. 11).
   6. Spiritual gifts differ for different individuals; Christians the spiritual Body of Christ (Chap. 12).
   7. Love the greatest spiritual gift (Chap. 13).

8. Prophecy (witnessing) superior to ecstatic speaking; good order to be kept in observing the Supper; woman's place in public worship (Chap. 14).

V. The Resurrection (Chap. 15).

1. The resurrection of Christ (proved as a fact) a basic doctrine of the gospel and a prophecy of the Christian's resurrection (1-34).

2. The resurrection of Christians with spiritual bodies (35-57).

3. This hope a high motive to toil for Christ (58).

VI. The Conclusion (Chap. 16).

1. Exhortation about the offering on the first day of the week (1-5).

2. Personal matters and greetings (6-23).

TEACHINGS IN FIRST CORINTHIANS

1. God is the Father—the same in all his letters.

2. Jesus Christ is the Son of God, mediate Creator, Saviour, Lord.

3. The Spirit only can reveal to man spiritual truths and realities.

4. The cross is the power and wisdom of God for saving sinners.

5. The resurrection of Jesus is the basic truth proved as a historical fact by unanswerable arguments.

6. The resurrection of Christians logically follows as a fact, which inspires present hope in Christians.

7. As Adam is the head of natural mankind, Christ is the head of spiritual mankind.

8. Personal purity is demanded in Christian living by the logic of basic Christians truths (6:13-20).

9. Marriage is the basic social institution, but should not be entered into in times of "distress."

10. Separation of believing and unbelieving wives and husbands is discouraged for the sake of the unbelieving consort and for the sake of the children.

11. Private differences among Christians should be settled, not in civil courts but in church conferences.

12. Each Christian must respect the weak conscience of his brother Christian and practice nothing that causes that brother to sin.

13. Love is the greatest spiritual gift, prophecy second to it. Our spiritual gifts vary but are given to us to profit in the development of the individual, for the care of one another, and for the unity of the Christian body.

14. Women may pray publicly and prophesy (witness), but must properly respect good social order, not doing things that would classify them with prostitutes, as shaving the head and refusing to wear the customary veil). I take it that these social customs are not binding on women today.

15. The Lord's Supper is to be observed in good order and with solemn recognition of the body and blood of the suffering Saviour.

16. The first day of the week (our Sunday) is the day of worship.

17. Systematic and proportionate giving is enjoined upon every Christian.

INTERPRETATION

Chapter I

GREETING; PAUL THANKING GOD FOR THEIR EXCELLENCY IN
SPIRITUAL GIFTS; PLEADING FOR UNITY IN THE CHURCH;
DIFFERENT EFFECTS OF THE MESSAGE OF THE CROSS;
THE LOWLY SOCIAL STATUS OF MOST CHRISTIANS
THERE; GREETING (1:1-3)

Paul, by the will of God called as an apostle of Jesus Christ, and our brother Sosthenes, ² to the church of God at Corinth, to those who are consecrated by union with Christ Jesus, and called to be God's people, in fellowship with those who anywhere call upon the name of Jesus Christ, their Lord and ours: ³ spiritual blessing and peace to you from God our Father and from our Lord Jesus Christ.

Key words and phrases. Verse 1. "Called by the will of God." This phrase states and emphasizes his authority as an apostle to preach the gospel everywhere. "Apostle" means one sent forth on a mission. Sosthenes is just a brother associated with Paul in this greeting and his missionary activity, not a co-writer of the letter.

Verse 2 "The church of God at Corinth." In Romans 16:16 he speaks of "the churches of Christ." God is the ultimate Author of the Church as an institution, while Christ is the medium through whom He founded it (Matt. 16:18). The verb to sanctify *(hagiazo)* is better translated consecrated (Williams). "Saints" means those set apart as God's people. "Those who call upon the name of our Lord Jesus Christ in every place," would give this greeting a universal application. Paul is a cosmopolitan Christian. Christ is Lord and on a par with the Father.

Verse 3. "Grace" is "spiritual blessing," while "peace" is a general blessing, health, and prosperity. Christ as well as the Father is the source of all these blessings.

THANKS TO GOD FOR THEIR EXCELLENCY IN SPIRITUAL GIFTS
(1:4-9)

⁴ I am always thanking God for you, for the spiritual blessing given you by God through union with Christ Jesus; ⁵ because you have in everything been richly blessed through union with Him, with perfect expression and fullness of knowledge. ⁶ In this way my testimony to Christ has been confirmed in your experience, ⁷ so that there is no spiritual gift in which you consciously come short, while you are waiting for the unveiling of our Lord Jesus Christ, ⁸ and to the very end He will guarantee that you are vindicated at the day of our Lord Jesus Christ. ⁹ God is entirely trustworthy, and it is He through whom you have been called into this fellowship with His Son, Jesus Christ our Lord.

Key words and phrases. Verse 4. Paul is ever thankful to God for the success of the gospel, especially in a strategic center like Corinth where paganism and its sins of immorality are rampant. Corinth was a wicked and corrupt city. The verb *corinthiazo* was coined to describe a man who was corrupt and immoral—it was to be like a Corinthian to be corrupt and vile.

Verse 5. They had been *enriched* in every spiritual gift, especially in "speech and knowledge." This is where they were naturally strong, and they consecrated their natural talents and were enriched with spiritual gifts.

Verse 6. "Testimony to Christ" means Paul's witness to Him in preaching the good news to the Corinthians. And this testimony has been confirmed by their abounding in these spiritual gifts.

Verse 7. This abounding in the spiritual gifts is accompanied by their "waiting for the revealing of our Lord Jesus Christ." The word reveal means to uncover. This likely refers to His parousia, second coming. At that time He will uncover His glory and splendor to His people who will "see Him as He is." This means that Paul had preached the doctrine of the parousia during his ministry in Corinth (a year and a half).

Verses 8, 9. Christ, he says, will sustain, keep, make strong *(bebaiosei)* until the end, the day of His coming. That is in verse 8, but in verse 9 he declares it is "God who is faithful, through whom they were called into the fellowship of His Son." This is very closely identifying "God" and "Christ." The deity of Christ is paramount in Paul's thinking. God "called," Christ "will sustain to the end" those who trust Him and abound in His spiritual gifts.

THE APOSTLE'S APPEAL FOR UNITY IN THE CHURCH (1:10-17)

10 Now I beg you all, brothers, for the sake of our Lord Jesus Christ, to be harmonious in what you say and not to have factions among you, but to be perfectly harmonious in your minds and judgments. 11 For I have been informed about you, my brothers, by Chloe's people, that there are wranglings among you. 12 I mean this, that one of you says, "I belong to Paul's party," another, "And I belong to Apollos' party," another, "And I belong to Cephas' party," another, "And I belong to Christ's party." 13 Christ has been parceled out by you! It was not Paul who was crucified for you, was it? You were not baptized in Paul's name, were you? 14 I am thankful that I baptized none of you but Crispus and Gaius, 15 so as to keep anyone from saying that you were baptized in my name. 16 Yes, I did baptize the family of Stephanas, too; I do not now recall that I baptized anyone else. 17 For Christ did not send me to baptize, but to preach the good news—but not by means of wisdom and rhetoric, so that the cross of Christ may not be emptied of its power.

Verse 10. The word *schmismata* means parties, factions. The next verses prove this, for there were three distinct parties follow-

ing human leaders. Paul, Apollos, Peter, and the rest of them, likely disgusted, claimed to follow only "Christ." What leads to factions is inharmonious thinking about leaders, as suggested by "mind" *(noi)* and "judgment" *(gnome)*. So he exhorts them to "be knit together in their minds and judgments."

Verse 13. Keen sarcasm when Paul says, "Has Christ been divided into pieces," so one party may have one piece, another, another piece?

Verses 14-16. He recalls having baptized only three, with the family of the third, so he cannot see how a Paul party should have been formed.

Verse 17. His mission from Christ was not to baptize but to evangelize. This is not to disparage baptism as of no significance. The duty of a local pastor is to baptize; it is not the duty of an evangelist.

How Different People React to the Message of the Cross (1:18-25)

[18] For the message of the cross is nonsense to those who are in the process of being destroyed, but it is the power of God to those who are in the process of being saved. [19] For the Scripture says:
   "I will destroy the wisdom of the wise,
      And I will set aside the learning of the learned."
[20] So where is your philosopher? Where is your man of letters? Where is your logician of this age? Has not God shown up the nonsense of the world's wisdom? [21] For since in accordance with the wisdom of God the world had never in reality, by means of its wisdom, come to know God, God chose through the nonsense of the message proclaimed, to save the people who put their faith in Him. [22] While Jews are demanding spectacular signs and Greeks are searching for philosophy, [23] we are preaching the Christ who was crucified—a message that is a trap-stick to the Jews and nonsense to the Greeks, [24] but to those whom God has called, both Jews and Greeks alike, the Christ who is God's power and God's wisdom. [25] It is so, because God's nonsense is wiser than men's wisdom, and God's weakness is mightier than men's might.

Key words and phrases. Verse 18. "The word" better rendered "the message." Cross is a graphic symbol of the sacrificial death of Christ. To those who are being saved this message is the power of God. So Romans 1:16—the gospel being the message of the cross. The verbs *perishing* and *saved* are both present participles denoting progressive action—the unbelieving are perishing, the believing are being saved.

Verses 19, 20. In the wisdom of God the philosopher, the man of letters, and the logician among the Greeks are all set aside so far as their efficacy is concerned in saving men from sin. That is proved by citing Isaiah 29:14.

Verse 21. Therefore, since man's wisdom had failed, God used His wisdom to save men through the message of the cross. "The foolishness of preaching" means the foolish message of the cross, not the foolish method of preaching.

Verses 22-23. The Jews, the Greeks, and Paul are pursuing different courses—Jews looking for spectacular signs of the coming of the Messiah, Greeks searching by speculation for the mysteries of philosophy, Paul preaching Christ crucified.

Verse 24. To the *"called"* of God—that is, foreordained and called by the gospel minister—the cross, Christ crucified, is "God's power and God's wisdom." It is God's wisdom in that it is an effective method of saving men, while the wisdom of philosophers failed. It is God's power in that it convicts the sinner of his sins and moves him by the aid of the Spirit to believe the gospel, accept Christ as Saviour and be saved. See Romans 1:16, "It is the power of God unto salvation to every one that believeth."

Verse 25. Paul uses an anthropomorphic figure of speech when he says "the foolishness of God is wiser than men, and the weakness of God is stronger than men." Of course there is no foolishness or weakness in God. He is all-wise and all-powerful. But man is all foolish and all weakness, so far as saving himself from sin is concerned.

THE SOCIAL STATUS OF THE CORINTHIAN CHRISTIANS (1:26-31)

26 For consider, brothers, the way God called you; that not many of you, in accordance with human standards, were wise, not many influential, not many of high birth. 27 Just the opposite: God chose what the world calls foolish to put the wise to shame,

what the world calls weak to put the strong to shame, [28] what the
world calls of low degree, yea, what it counts as nothing and what
it thinks does not exist, God chose to put a stop to what it thinks
exists, [29] so that no mortal man might ever boast in the presence of
God. [30] So you owe it all to Him through union with Christ Jesus,
whom God has made our wisdom, our means of right standing, our
consecration, and our redemption, [31] so that, as the Scripture says,
"Let him who boasts boast in the Lord."

Key words and phrases. Verse 26. "Calling" applies especially
to the effect of the gospel on people, rather than to foreordination.
The gospel appeal impressed the lower classes rather than the higher
in Corinth. This is true today in mission lands, I am told. The three
classes named by Paul are "the wise, the mighty, the noble born."
The first would include the educated and cultured; the second, those
of civic and social influence, the third, what the Virginians call,
"the first families." The latter would be the aristocracy, from the
social point of view.

Verses 27-29. God selected the uneducated, the uninfluential,
those of low birth to confound the wise, the influential, and the high
born; that is, to prove the power of the gospel to transform men and
women, independently of educational and social forces. This is not
to minimize educational and social forces; they help, but the main
power comes from God, to make men and women of high spiritual
ideals and achievements.

Verse 30. "From Him [God] are you." The preposition emphasizes God as *the source* of spiritual excellency and achievement.
But Christ is the medium through whom God works His will—
"in Christ." We must be in union with Christ to be in fellowship
with God. He names three other functions in addition to the two
mentioned in 1:18, which are due to "His cross." Righteousness is
right standing with God which is obtained by faith in Him. Sanctification, or consecration, as many modern translators put it, comes
through union with Christ, though the Holy Spirit is the direct agent
of sanctification (Rom. 8:5-27). But in the four preceding verses
Paul asserts that "the law of the Spirit of life" operates in "Christ
Jesus"; that is, through union with Him the Spirit sets the believer
free from besetting sins and produces a gradual sanctifying process

in his life. But He is also our "redemption." Why place redemption last and after sanctification? In experience it comes first, does it not? No, if it is the redemption of the body, as in Romans 8:23. This is likely what Paul means here, and not the sense in which the word is used in Romans 3:24.

Sermon Outline (1:18-25)

How Different People React to the Message of the Cross
I. The Perishing, the Lost—foolishness to them
1. To the Jews it is the trapstick that throws the trap which catches them as victims to their stubbornness
2. To the Greeks it is "nonsense"—looks unreasonable
3. To all it is not understandable—only so by the Spirit (2:11)
II. The Called, the Saved—to them "Christ crucified," the Cross, is
1. God's wisdom—devising the plan of salvation
2. God's power—bringing salvation to believers (Rom. 1:16)
3. Righteousness—medium of right standing with God (II Cor. 5:21)
4. Sanctification—medium through whom the Spirit works it (Romans 8:2)
5. Redemption—final deliverance, in the resurrection, of our bodies (Rom. 8:23)
III. We Must Preach This Message of the Cross—"Christ Crucified"
1. Salvation of sinners depends on it (Acts 4:12)
2. Consecration of the saved depends on it (Gal. 6:14)
3. World missions waiting for it (John 12:32)—The cross the magnet
4. Follow the example of great preachers and evangelists—Peter, Paul, Spurgeon, Moody, Chapman, Torrey, Truett, Scarborough, and others.

Chapter II

PAUL'S SIMPLE STYLE OF PREACHING; THE WISDOM OF THE CROSS SPIRITUALLY UNDERSTOOD
PAUL'S SIMPLE STYLE OF PREACHING (2:1-5)

Now when I came to you, brothers, I did not come and tell you

God's uncovered secret in rhetorical language or human philosophy,
² for I determined, while among you, to be unconscious of everything but Jesus Christ and Him as crucified. ³ Yes, as for myself,
it was in weakness and fear and great trembling that I came to you,
⁴ and my language and the message I preached were not adorned
with pleasing words of worldly wisdom, but they were attended
with proof and power given by the Spirit, ⁵ so that your faith might
not be in men's wisdom, but in God's power.

Key words and phrases. Verse 1. "With excellency of speech
or wisdom." Paul denies using lofty rhetoric or philosophy in proclaiming the good news. In verse 4 he says his message in a
simple style was attended with proof and power given by the Spirit
(subjective genitive). He trusted in the Spirit to carry his message
to the hearts of the people, not in rhetoric or philosophy.

Verse 2. Christ and Him crucified" was his central theme
while with them. The cross, he determined, must be his message
to lost men in a pagan city steeped in sin with many presuming
to know philosophy who did not know God.

Verse 3. He came to Corinth in weakness (physical likely)
but also in "fear and trembling." He had just been rejected by
the philosophers in Athens and now he is coming to the capital of
Greece, the chief city, notorious for its vice and corruption. He
felt his knees "tremble," in apprehension as to the outcome of his
mission. He was reviled by the Jews there and run out of the synagogue, but occupied the house of Titus Justus as his teaching and
preaching center. So God appeared to him in a vision and encouraged him to stay on and continue preaching, for "I am with you, and
no man shall attack you to harm you" (Acts 18:9, 10).

Verse 5. His purpose in preaching the cross in simple language
was to have them realize that the power to save was in Christ not
in rhetoric.

THE MESSAGE OF THE CROSS BEING SPIRITUAL MUST BE
SPIRITUALLY UNDERSTOOD (2:6-16)

⁶ Yet, when among mature believers we do set forth a wisdom,
but a wisdom that does not belong to this world or to the leaders
of this world who are passing away; ⁷ rather, we are setting forth

a wisdom that came from God, once a covered secret but now uncovered, which God marked off as His plan for bringing us to
glory. [8] Not one of this world's leaders understands it, for if they
had, they would never have crucified our glorious Lord. [9] But, as
the Scripture says, they are:

> "Things which eye has never seen and ear has never heard,
> And never have occurred to human hearts,
> Which God prepared for those who love Him."

[10] For God unveiled them to us through His Spirit, for the Spirit
by searching discovers everything, even the deepest truths about
God. [11] For what man can understand his own inner thoughts except by his own spirit within him? Just so no one but the Spirit
of God can understand the thoughts of God. [12] Now we have not
received the spirit that belongs to the world but the Spirit that
comes from God, that we may get an insight into the blessings God
has graciously given us. [13] These truths we are setting forth, not in
words that man's wisdom teaches but in words that the Spirit
teaches, in this way fitting spiritual words to spiritual truths.
[14] An unspiritual man does not accept the things that the Spirit of
God teaches, for they are nonsense to him; and he cannot understand them, because they are appreciated by spiritual insight.
[15] But the spiritual man appreciates everything, and yet he himself
is not really appreciated by anybody. [16] For who has ever known
the Lord's thoughts, so that he can instruct Him? But we now
possess Christ's thoughts.

Key words and phrases. Verses 6-7. Paul hastens to let his
readers know that he does have a wisdom to impart. But it is
for the mature; for those who are interested in higher spiritual
truths, who can appreciate it. It is not a human wisdom; does not
belong to this age or world, or even to the rulers of this world,
who are doomed to pass away. It is a wisdom of God, a wisdom
that came from God and not from man. It was once a secret but
now is made known; once covered up but now uncovered for any
and all to see and know, if they will. These words, *cover* and
uncover, give us the literal meaning of the Greek, *musteerion*,
secret, mystery. Observe, God foreordained it before the ages
to be for our glory. It is a part of His eternal purpose of redemption
for man. In paragraph 1:18-25 the cross is the wisdom of God;

so this uncovered secret, or mystery, is the sacrificial death of Christ on the cross.

Verses 8-9. None of the rulers of the world understood this spiritual wisdom. It was to them a real secret. If they had they would not have rejected the Messiah and crucified the Lord of glory. They did not know the "things that God had prepared for those who love Him," nor had they ever conceived them in their hearts.

Verse 10. But God uncovered the secret to us, who, led by the Spirit, accepted the crucified Christ as our Saviour. It was through the Spirit, not through human wisdom, He revealed these things to us, for the Spirit searches all things, even "the deep things of God," the hidden truths concerning God and His purposes of redemption. This tallies with Jesus' saying to the disciples, "He will guide you into all truth."

Verse 11 gives us a human illustration: Only the spirit in a man can know the thoughts of that man. So only the Spirit of God can know and make known to us the thoughts of God; that is, His spiritual truths; here concerning the cross as the means of redemption for the lost world.

Verses 12, 13. Paul is conscious of his authority to speak as he does to the Corinthian church. He has received, not the spirit of the world, but the Spirit from God (so has divine authority) that he might understand the gracious gifts bestowed upon us by God. These gracious gifts begin with the message of the cross, with the sacrificial death of Christ, and other gifts of grace to follow in Christian experience. In verse 13 he claims that the Spirit has directed him to speak these things, not in words that are taught by human wisdom, but in words that are taught him by the Spirit; that is, his simple style of speaking is inspired by the Spirit.

Verses 14, 15. The unspiritual man, the purely intellectual man, cannot receive or understand the "gifts of the Spirit of God." That is, the man not filled with the Spirit, not giving himself up to the leadings and movings of the Spirit, cannot have the highest spiritual experiences himself, nor can he understand them in others. The reason why he cannot is that they are spiritually understood, that is, understood by spiritual insight, which the unspiritual man does not have. The merely intellectual man cannot know God experimentally, for as Professor Deissmann used to say, "God is known by the heart rather than the head." The inner self, the heart, fired by the Spirit, responds to God's love, knows God and loves God.

Verse 16. Paul feels that though no man has ever perfectly known the mind of the Lord, yet he is sure that he now has "the mind [the thoughts] of Christ." That is, these teachings have the endorsement of Jesus the Teacher. See John 16:13 and 14:26, where He says the Spirit "will guide you into all truth": He will teach you all things."

Chapter III

CORRECTING THEIR CONCEPTION OF RELIGIOUS TEACHERS; BECAUSE THEY ARE UNSPIRITUAL THEY FAIL TO RECOGNIZE THESE TEACHERS AS GOD'S SERVANTS ONLY
(3:1-9)

So I myself, brothers, could not deal with you as spiritual persons, but as creatures of human clay, as merely baby Christians. ² I fed you with milk, not solid food, for you could not take it. Why, you cannot take it even now, ³ for you are still unspiritual. For when there are still jealousy and wrangling among you, are you not still unspiritual and living by a human standard? ⁴ For when one says, "I belong to Paul's party," and another, "I belong to Apollos' party," are you not acting as mere human creatures?

⁵ Then what is Apollos? Or what is Paul? Mere servants through whom you came to believe, as the Lord gave each of us his task. ⁶ I did the planting, Apollos did the watering, but it was God who kept the plants growing. ⁷ So neither the planter nor the waterer counts for much, but God is everything in keeping the plants growing. ⁸ The planter and the waterer are one in aim, and yet each of us will get his own pay in accordance with his own work, ⁹ for we belong to God as His fellow-workers; you belong to God as His field to be tilled, as His building to be built.

Key words and phrases. Verse 1. The readers are not spiritual but mere creatures of "flesh." The Greek word, *sarkinos*, means "made of flesh." We say it by using the word clay. Frail creatures of clay (dust). But he uses the term not in a physical but a spiritual sense. "Babes in Christ" means mere baby Christians, spiritual infants. The Greek word denotes either an unborn baby or a small infant.

Verse 2. So Paul had to feed them milk; simple, elementary teaching and not the more advanced Christian doctrines (as in Romans).

Verses 3, 4. The evidence of their spiritual infancy, "jealousy and wrangling" about their favorite religious teacher, one favoring Apollos, another, Paul. This is living on a low human plane.

Verses 5-8a. They should know that Apollos and Paul are only servants of Christ who brought them the message of the cross which led them to believe and be saved. Paul doing the evangelistic work (planting), Apollos, the cultivating (watering), both with one aim. So there should be no reason for them to boast of one above the other.

Verse 8b. He points out that each one of them (Apollos and Paul) will receive his reward (pay) in accordance with the work he does.

Verse 9. Apollos and Paul are God's co-workers, fellow-laborers. It does not mean that all Christians are co-laborers with God (so King James Version). This is a great truth taught elsewhere in the New Testament, but not here.

RELIGIOUS LEADERS (APOLLOS AND PAUL) RESPONSIBLE TO SEE THAT ENDURING MATERIALS GO INTO THE TEMPLE OF GOD
(3:10-15)

[10] As skilled architect, in accordance with God's unmerited favor given to me, I laid a foundation, and now another is building upon it. But every builder must be careful how he builds upon it; [11] for no one can lay any other foundation than the one that is laid, that is, Jesus Christ Himself. [12] And whether one puts into the building on the foundation gold or silver or costly stones, or wood or hay or straw, [13] the character of each one's work will come to light, for the judgment day will show it up. This is so, because that day will show itself in fire, and the fire will test the character of each one's work. [14] If the structure which one builds upon it stands the

test, he will get his pay. ¹⁵ If the structure which one builds is burned up, he will get no pay; and yet he himself will be saved; but just as one who goes through a fire.

Key words and phrases. Verse 10. *Architekton,* a skilled builder, one who knows his business, an architect. Such is Paul in spiritual affairs—building the kingdom of God, the temple of God, carrying out literally the figure. He is laying a foundation, Christ Jesus, wherever He preaches; in this case in Corinth (v. 16). He did the evangelistic work by preaching the cross and organizing the church. Apollos comes later and "waters" the field. "According to the grace given to me" expresses his sense of authority from God to do so.

Verse 11 states his inspired conviction that Christ alone is the foundation for faith and hope, for the gospel and the church.

Verses 12, 13. Two kinds of materials may be built upon this foundation—the imperishable and the perishable; the former symbolized by gold, silver, and precious stones; the latter by wood, hay, straw. The materials may be individuals received as members of the church by the religious leaders. If they are genuinely regenerated, they are imperishable like gold and silver; if they make spurious professions, they are perishable wood, hay, or straw. The lives and deeds of Christians may also be considered materials placed into the temple in building. But particularly this context limits the application to ministers like Apollos and Paul. They must be careful what materials they allow to slip by them into the church.

Verse 14, 15. The character of one's works or materials placed into the building will be tested by the judgment fires. If they are burned up like wood or hay or straw, the individual will receive no reward, but he himself will be saved; just will be saved, like a man in a burning building, who escapes through the flames with all his clothes burned off him, barely escaping with his life. So will it be with the minister or private Christian whose works are spurious—temporary and perishing. Such will receive no reward but "by grace" will be saved.

CHRISTIANS GOD'S TEMPLE AND POSSESSORS OF SPIRITUAL WEALTH
(3:16-23)

¹⁶ Are you not conscious that you are God's temple, and that the Spirit of God has His permanent home in you? ¹⁷ If anyone destroys God's temple, God will destroy him. For God's temple is sacred to Him, and you are that temple.

¹⁸ Let no one deceive himself. If any one of you supposes that he is wise in this world's wisdom, as compared with the rest of you, to become really wise he must become a fool. ¹⁹ For this world's wisdom is mere nonsense to God. For the Scripture says, "He who catches the wise with their own cunning," ²⁰ and again, "The Lord knows that the arguings of the wise are useless." ²¹ So let no one boast in men. For everything belongs to you—²² Paul, Apollos, Cephas, the world, life, death, the present, the future— they all belong to you. ²³ Yes, you belong to Christ, and Christ belongs to God.

Key words and phrases. Verse 16. Christians are God's spiritual personal temple. He dwells in us more really than He dwelt in the Temple of Solomon or the temple of Zerubbabel. It is through the Spirit of God, who has His permanent home in us. The verb is present tense of continuous action, so He permanently lives in us. His home is in us. Blessed thought!

Verse 17. This means responsibility on each one not to corrupt or defile the temple and thus destroy it. The Greek verb means both *defile* and *destroy*. God cannot destroy this temple except as we defile it. It does not mean that the Christian himself is lost, but that this temple is "holy." It is set apart to God's worship and praise.

Verses 18-20. A warning against the conceit of some Corinthians who supposed they were "wise." Belonged to the group called philosophers, "the wise." This world's wisdom, or philosophy, is folly, nonsense, to God. He sees Scripture endorsing this view of earthly wisdom: Job 5:13; Psalm 94:11. Indeed, Scripture is "profitable" to Paul (II Tim. 3:16). So, if a man desires to be really wise in God's wisdom, he must "become a fool"; that is, he must become conscious that this earthly wisdom is mere foolishness in the sight of God, and humbly accept the wisdom of God— the message of the cross and all the truths akin to it.

Verses 21-23. Boasting in one man instead of another is excluded by the great fact that all religious leaders belong to each Christian, one as much as another. Paul, Apollos, and Cephas, all three of them, belonged to every Christian in Corinth. So why pick out one and claim he is my man? All are my men, my religious teachers. More than that, all other things belong to you Christians: the world, its resources to use for your own welfare and with it to serve God and your fellowmen; life with all its opportunities and privileges; death, your release from suffering and the gateway to Heaven; the present with all its circumstances, pleasant or unpleasant; the future with all its prospects and enrichment from the past—"all these are yours." You are spiritual millionaires. And yet, you belong to Christ, and Christ belongs to God. What a consummate reciprocal ownership! We belong to God and Christ belong to us, and God and Christ, with the world, life, death, and all religious leaders, belong to us!

SERMON OUTLINES FROM CHAPTER III
CO-WORKERS WITH ONE ANOTHER AND WITH GOD (3:9)

I. Christians God's Property — *Theou*, possessive genitive — "God's co-workers"
  1. His by Creation (Ps. 100:3; I Cor. 8:6)
  2. By providence (Matt. 6:30-33)
  3. By redemption (I Cor. 6:19, 20)

II. Ministers Should Co-operate with One Another—Paul, Apollos
  1. Pastors with pastors
  2. Evangelists with pastors
  3. Directors of religious education with pastors
  4. Bible school teachers with pastors
  5. Pastors with missionaries at home and abroad

III. Lay Members Co-workers with One Another and with Pastors
  1. The Church the Body of Christ, all members working together like the parts of the body for strength, health, beauty
  2. Deacons with pastor co-operating
  3. Choir with pastor co-operating
  4. Private members co-operating with all officials
  5. All the church co-operating with denominational program

IV. All Co-operating with God

    1. God the one essential Partner—Paul plants, Apollos waters, God gives the increase (3:6). So in nature—farmer, gardener, scientist (to make synthetic gasoline must have natural gas or coal or coke, God's creation)

    2. But God depends on us to help Him—in nature and in grace. Land without man's cultivating it makes poor crops; with it produces abundant crops

    3. Salvation completed only by man's co-operating with God "Work out your own salvation with fear and trembling, for it is God who worketh in you" (Phil. 2:12-13).

SERMON OUTLINE ON I CORINTHIANS 3:21-23

ALL CHRISTIANS IMMENSELY WEALTHY

I. Many Poor in Earthly Goods but Rich in Heavenly Possessions

    1. Most Corinthian Christians of the lowly classes (1:26-29)

    2. Early disciples fishermen, farmers, tax collectors, etc.

    3. Christian Jews in the Dispersion (James 2:5)

    4. Today true on a great scale

II. Potentially Wealthy in Spiritual Possessions

In addition to "eternal life" and deeds to "crowns of righteousness, . . . all things are yours."

    1. "The world"—with its resources for our welfare and joy and to use for serving God and men

    2. All religious leaders and teachers—Paul, Apollos, Cephas

    3. Life—with all its privileges and opportunities

    4. Death—our release from physical frailty and all suffering and the gateway to Heaven

    5. The present—with its circumstances challenging us to heroic consecration and service

    6. The future—with its enrichment from the past merging into eternity

III. Made Rich by the Poverty of Jesus Christ (II Cor. 8:9)

    1. Became poor by becoming incarnate in human flesh (Phil. 2:7)

    2. Actually poor in earthly goods—"nowhere to lay His head"

3. Poor in death and burial—buried in another's tomb (Luke 23:52, 53)

Chapter IV

MINISTERS TRUSTEES OF GOD'S TRUTH; PAUL CUTS WITH IRONY, THEN PLEADS WITH A FATHER'S LOVE

MINISTERS TRUSTEES OF GOD'S TRUTH (4:1-5)

As for us apostles, men ought to think of us as ministers of Christ and trustees to handle God's uncovered truths. ² Now in this matter of trustees the first and final requirement is that they should prove to be trustworthy. ³ As for me, myself, it is of very little concern to me to be examined by you or any human court; in fact, I do not even examine myself. ⁴ For although my conscience does not accuse me, yet I am not entirely vindicated by that. It is the Lord Himself who must examine me. ⁵ So you must stop forming any premature judgments, but wait until the Lord shall come again; for He will bring to light the secrets hidden in the dark and will make known the motives of men's hearts, and the proper praise will be awarded each of us.

Key words and phrases. Verse 1. "Servants of Christ." Servant here is *attendant,* not the regular word, *diakonos,* for minister. It has a lower significance and expresses Paul's humility in estimating his rank as a minister of Christ. *Steward* is our modern term trustee, one to whom the business of another, institution or individual, is entrusted. "The mysteries of God" are committed to the apostles, Paul and Apollos, and other ministers of Christ. What are the mysteries of God? The basic truths of the gospel, His love and grace in redemption through Christ the Son; meaning something covered up in former ages but now uncovered (revealed) through Christ and the Spirit.

Verse 2. "Trustworthy." Worthy of having something valuable entrusted to one. Institutions look for men of character to be trustees of their affairs; so God looks for men of the highest character to be stewards, or trustees, of the gospel (See I Tim. 3:2-7).

Verses 3-5. Here Paul adroitly tells the Corinthians that the Lord is the final judge of the trustworthiness of His ministers. Not even he himself is sufficient to pass judgment on himself as Christ's minister. That is the privilege and function of the Lord, when

He comes. This will be a searching and perfect judgment, for He will bring to light things that were hidden in the dark and will make known the inner motives of men's hearts. So the readers must not pass judgment on God's ministers.

He Cuts with Sarcasm and Irony at Their Boasted Superiority, Contrasting with It His Privations and Persecutions (4:6-13)

⁶ Now, brothers, for your sakes I have applied all this to Apollos and myself, that from us as illustrations you might learn the lesson, "Never go beyond what is written," so that you might stop boasting in favor of one teacher against another. ⁷ For who makes you superior? And what do you have that you did not get from someone? But if you got it from someone, why do you boast as though you had not? ⁸ Are you satisfied already? Have you grown rich already? Have you ascended your thrones without us to join you? Yes, I could wish that you had ascended your thrones, that we too might join you on them! ⁹ For it seems to me that God has put us apostles on exhibition at the disgraced end of the procession, as they do with men who are doomed to die in the arena. ¹⁰ For we have become a spectacle to the universe, to angels as well as men. For Christ's sake we are held as fools, while you through union with Christ are men of wisdom. We are weak; you are strong. You are held in honor; we in dishonor. ¹¹ To this very hour we have gone hungry, thirsty, poorly clad; we have been roughly knocked around, we have had no home, ¹² we have worked hard with our own hands for a living. When abused by people we bless them, when persecuted we patiently bear it, ¹³ when we are slandered by them we try to conciliate them. To this very hour we have been made the filth of the world, the scum of the universe!

Key words and phrases. Verse 6. "I have applied all this to Apollos and me." That is, we are stewards, or trustees, of God's mysteries of the gospel, both of us faithful to our trusteeship. In saying this I make us apostles an example to you "to live according to Scripture," which is against conceit. "Be not wise in your own conceit."

Verse 7. "For who sees anything different in you?" Sarcastic! You are not so superior as you think you are, as others see what you are. If you are superior, you received it from an external source (God). So why boast as though you did not so receive it?

Verse 8. "Filled, rich, kings." That is the way they felt about themselves—intellectually and spiritually. "I could wish you were." This is an unrealized wish (in Greek). He could make such a wish if it would do any good. Since it would do no good, he does not actually make it. (So Robertson, *Grammar, in loc.*) The verse is the climax of cutting sarcasm.

Verse 9. A picture of a Roman general's triumphal march into the city of Rome with his captives in battle marching at "the end of the procession." The apostles are presented as a shameful spectacle before men and angels, not as "rich and kings!"

Verses 10-13. In the tenth verse he paints a striking contrast between him and his readers—he a "fool for Christ's sake," weak, in disrepute; they "strong, wise, held in honor." In the next three verses he enumerates some of his privations and persecutions, and he "endures it all and tries to conciliate the enemies of the cross." The very depths of humiliation are reached in being "the refuse of the world, the offscouring of all things." What a sarcastic rebuke to the haughty pride of the Corinthians!

THE APOSTLE ADMONISHES WITH A FATHER'S LOVE (4:14-21)

[14] I do not write this to make you blush with shame but to give you counsel as my dear children. [15] For though you have ten thousand teachers in the Christian life, you certainly could not have many fathers. For it was I myself who became your father through your union with Christ Jesus, which resulted from my telling you the good news. [16] So I beg you, make it your habit to follow my example. [17] This is why I have sent Timothy to you. He is a dear child of mine and trustworthy in the Lord's work; he will call to your minds my methods in the work of Christ Jesus, just as I teach them everywhere in every church.

[18] But some of you have gotten conceited over the thought that I am not coming to see you. [19] But I am coming, and coming soon, if the Lord is willing, and then I will find out, not only what those conceited fellows say but what they can do, [20] for the kingdom of God does not consist in talking but in doing. [21] Which do you prefer? My coming to you with a club, or in a gentle, loving spirit?

Key words and phrases. Verses 14-15. "As my beloved children." Paul was not brusque and hardhearted, as the preceding paragraph seems to indicate. He had a big heart. He held these haughty Corinthians in his big heart as a loving father. For it was he who evangelized them on his second missionary journey (Acts 18:5-11). His sarcasm and irony were but tools to prepare the way for this tender admonition of a father. He is dealing with them as a wise and loving father—with discipline guided by love.

Verse 16. "Be imitators of me." As a father I have set you an example. As dear children, follow it. Be loving, humble and give the glory of Christ.

Verses 17-20. He sends Timothy, another dear son and trustworthy, to explain to them his methods in the churches, so they may intelligently follow his instructions—and example. Because he sent Timothy, some haughty men claimed that Paul himself was not coming to them. He assures them he is coming, if the Lord permits. This even furnishes him the occasion to insert a great truth about the kingdom: it does not consist in talking but doing; it is not prating but power in action.

Verse 21. Questions that answer themselves. Of course, they preferred love to a club. And in love he means to come to them.

A SERMON OUTLINE FROM CHAPTER IV
STEWARDS OF THE MYSTERIES OF GOD (4:1, 2)

I. Meaning of the Term Steward
   1. Not an owner of the business or institution or other affairs
   2. Only an employee who is appointed to conduct the affairs of the owner
   3. Modern trustee, or business manager, its equivalent

II. Meaning of "the Mysteries of God"
   1. Not the wondrous secrets of Nature—its vegetable, animal or mineral kingdoms; their laws, forces, workings
   2. Not the wonders of man's body, mind and soul. "Fearfully and wonderfully made." Psychologists have not fathomed the depths of the mind.
   3. Not the harmonious blending of the divine attributes in the personality of God. An inscrutable wonder, but not Paul's mystery.

4. Mysteries of God are His love and grace contriving and consummating redemption's scheme (Eph. 3:9-11). Love and grace based on His eternal purpose (Col. 1:26, 27). Christ is the mystery.
5. Once concealed but now revealed. See Thayer's *Lexicon*.
   a. Partially to the prophets; Moses (Deut. 18:15); Isaiah (chaps. 9, 11 and 53)
   b. By Christ to the apostles (Matt. 13:11; see Col. 1:26, 27)
   c. By the Spirit to "apostolic men" (writers of the N.T.) and to any and all of us (see I Cor. 2:10-16).

III. The Character of Stewards
   1. Must be of the highest moral character—honest, truthful, dependable, etc.
   2. Trustworthy (I Cor. 4:2) This is the prime quality.
   3. Wise managers. Placed in charge of important business of owners. Must know how to run that business. So are God's stewards placed in charge of the kingdom's affairs

IV. The extent of Stewardship. Who are stewards?
   1. The apostles—the Twelve, Paul, Barnabas, Apollos
   2. All ministers of the gospel
   3. Then in general, all Christians (Luke 16:1-9; I Peter 4:10). All Christians are trustees of God's "manifold wisdom," which constitutes the "mysteries of God."

Chapter V

PAUL REBUKES THE CHURCH FOR TOLERATING A CASE OF GROSSEST IMMORALITY (INCEST), BECAUSE THEY HAD DISREGARDED PREVIOUS WARNING

THE CASE STATED AND HIS REACTION TO IT AND WHY (5:1-8)

A case of immorality is reported as actually existing among you, an immorality unheard of even among the heathen—that a man co-habits with his father's wife. ²And yet, you are proud of it, instead of being sorry for it, and seeing to it that the man who has done this be removed from your membership! For my part, though I have been absent from you in person, I have been present with you in spirit, and so as really present, by the authority of our

Lord Jesus, I have already passed judgment upon the man who has done this—⁴ for when you met I too met with you in spirit by the power of our Lord Jesus—⁵ to turn such a man as this over to Satan for the destruction of his lower nature, in order this his spirit may be saved on the day of the Lord. ⁶ Your ground for boasting about such a case is not good. Are you not aware that a little yeast will change the whole lump of dough? ⁷ You must clean out the old yeast, that you may be a fresh lump, as you are to be free from the old yeast. For our Passover Lamb, Christ, has already been sacrificed. ⁸ So let us keep our feast, not with old yeast nor with the yeast of vice and wickedness, but with the bread of purity and truth without the yeast.

Key words and phrases. Verse 1. *Porneia* is used here to designate the sin of this man. It usually means illicit sexual intercourse between unmarried persons. The son is unmarried (likely) but the father's wife is married. The word sometimes means any case of sexual intercourse outside lawful marriage by the two parties—both may be unmarried, or only one and the other married, as in this case. "A man is living with his father's wife." Cohabiting with his stepmother. Such is scarcely ever practiced by pagans. So it is unthinkable by a man claiming to be a Christian! Paul is horrified over such a sin in the church.

Verse 2. And you are *"arrogant . . . proud of it,"* literally *"puffed up."* The man must have been "an influential" citizen. His friends in the church felt they must stand by him and retain him, instead of being grieved over such a sin and taking steps to remove him from their membership.

Verses 3-5. "Absent in body but present in spirit," a universal expression to denote one's deepest interest in persons when not actually present with them—thinking about them and doing for them what he would do if present. "In the name of our Lord Jesus," means on the authority and in accordance with the will of the Lord Jesus, Paul thus feeling that his judgment on the man committing this grievous sin is not his personal decision but the judgment of Christ Himself upon such a man. "Deliver this man to Satan," means let him follow the line of conduct Satan has led him to adopt, but out of the church. His expulsion from the church ought to bring about his penitence and so "destroy his lower nature [flesh]." That is, it ought to cause him, if a regenerated man, to give up his sin and thus save his spirit on the day of the Lord Jesus. Paul believed that proper church discipline, administered in the right spirit, has a corrective influence on the subjects of such discipline.

Verses 6-8. In these verses he shows that for two reasons it is inconsistent for a church to retain in its membership such persons: first, such persons have a corrupting influence on the church. These act like leaven (yeast), fermenting and corrupting the whole. A modern adage is, "A rotten apple in a barrel will rot the whole barrel of apples." Therefore, it is not good to retain such and risk polluting the whole church. Second, Christ, our Passover Lamb, has made the sacrifice to cleanse us so as to have a church "without spot or wrinkle" (Eph. 5:27). So his conclusion is, "Let us keep the feast with the unleavened bread of purity and truth, not with the old leaven of vice and wickedness." These last terms describe how horrible Paul deems the sin of this incestuous man!

IN A PREVIOUS LETTER HE HAD GIVEN THEM WARNING (5:9-13)

⁹ I wrote you in my letter to stop associating with sexually immoral people—¹⁰ not that you are to stop all dealings with sexually immoral people of this world, any more than with its greedy graspers, or its idolaters, for then you would have to get clear out of the world. ¹¹ Now what I really meant was for you to stop associating with any so-called brother, if he is sexually immoral, a greedy grasper, an idolater, a slanderer, a drunkard, or a swindler—with such a person you must even stop eating. ¹² For what right have I to judge outsiders? Is it not for you to judge those who are inside the church, ¹³ but for God to judge those who are outside? You must expel that wicked person from your membership.

Key words and phrases. Verses 9-10. In a previous letter (now lost) Paul had written the Corinthians not to associate with sexually immoral persons; but he did not mean they should have no dealings at all with such. He did not forbid the ordinary social or economic dealings with such. If that were the case one would have to isolate himself from human society altogether, the same as getting out of the world.

Verses 11-12. What he does mean is not to have intimate fellowship (eat) with such persons *in the church*. And here he adds to the sexually immoral, greedy graspers (covetous), idolaters, slanderers, drunkards, swindlers. Notice how Paul classes with the sexually immoral the covetous man (one who is grasping for more), the idolater, the slanderer, the drunkard, the swindler (the one who snatches from others what belongs to them). The latter is a robber of the deepest dye. What bad company is this for the slanderer!

Verse 13. "Expel, or drive out, that wicked person." Paul believes and teaches church discipline for those guilty of extreme immorality.

Chapter VI

CHRISTIANS NOT TO GO TO LAW IN HEATHEN COURTS OR WITH ONE ANOTHER; PAGAN VICES INCOMPATIBLE WITH CHRISTIAN LIVING; LIBERTY NO LICENSE TO SENSUALITY; REASONS FOR PERSONAL PURITY

CHRISTIANS NOT TO GO TO LAW IN HEATHEN COURTS OR WITH ONE ANOTHER (6:1-8)

When one of you has a grievance against his neighbor, does he dare to go to law before a heathen court, instead of laying the case before God's people? ² Do you not know that God's people are to judge the world? And if the world is to be judged before you, are you unfit to try such petty cases? ³ Do you not know that we Christians are to sit in judgment on angels, to say nothing of the ordinary cases of life? ⁴ So if you have the ordinary cases of life for settlement, do you set up as judges the very men in the church who have no standing? ⁵ I ask this to make you blush with shame. Has it come to this, that there is not a single wise man among you who could settle a grievance of one brother against another, ⁶ but one brother has to go to law with another, and that before unbelieving judges? ⁷ To say no more, it is a mark of moral failure among you to have lawsuits at all with one another. Why not rather suffer being wronged? Why not suffer being robbed? ⁸ On the contrary, you practice wronging and robbing others, and that your brothers.

Key words and phrases. Verse 1. "Unrighteous" denotes non-Christians, pagans holding court in Corinth. "Saints," a general term denoting God's people, here Christians; not here used in its narrow theological sense. The word dare suggests how irrational it is for Christians to go to law in a heathen court. ..

Verses 2-3. "The saints judging the world and angels." What does it mean? Christ is the Judge on the great day of judgment (Matt. 25:31-41). Here He says the Son of Man will come "with all His holy angels with Him." It seems that the angels themselves join with Him in "judging the world." But see Revelation 3:21, where He promises that believers who conquer in the world's conflict shall "sit with Him on His throne." That is, the conquering Christian will join Him and the holy angels in passing final judgment on the world of lost sinners and the fallen angels whom the lost will join in Hades (Matt. 25:41).

Verses 4-6. Such a course reflects on their wisdom. "Is there no man in the church wise enough to try trivial matters?" That is, is there no man with sufficient judicial knowledge to act as judge in these trivial cases? If not, "shame" on you. The greater shame is that even a Christian goes to law with another Christian in a heathen court!

Verses 7, 8. Litigation between Christians and that in a heathen court suggests their moral deficiency. It is defeat in the moral realm. Your moral sense is weak. You ought to suffer wrong rather than do wrong to your brother. That is, winning a case in court against your brother is losing moral strength. It is better to be morally strong and lose a few dollars(if you have to) than to win the suit and money and lose your moral strength and influence.

PAGAN VICES INCOMPATIBLE WITH CHRISTIAN LIVING (6:9-11)

9 Do you not know that wrongdoers will not have a share in the kingdom of God? Stop being misled; people who are sexually immoral or idolaters or adulterers or sensual or guilty of unnatural sexual vice 10 or thieves or greedy graspers for more or drunkards or slanderers or swindlers will not have a share in the kingdom of God. 11 And these are just the characters some of you used to be. But now you have washed yourselves clean, you have been conse-

crated, you are now in right standing with God, by the name of our Lord Jesus Christ and by the Spirit of God.

Key words and phrases. Verses 9-10. "The kingdom of God" is a phrase used in two senses in the New Testament: a present spiritual domain in which believers in Christ are members with social and moral obligations to one another, in which the will of God is the standard of thinking and living; in brief, it is God's rule in the hearts and lives of Christians. Second, a future stage of this same kingdom, the eschatological rule of Christ at and after the second coming; the kingdom of glory in Heaven. What does it mean here? Likely the whole realm of the kingdom is in Paul's mind, but judging from the context, preceding and succeeding, he is emphasizing its present stage, especially its social and moral aspects. It is litigation in the former verses, personal purity of its members in the succeeding verses. Since that is his thought, he means that those guilty of these grievous offenses, against oneself and against his brother, cannot participate in the spiritual and moral duties and privileges and blessings of the present kingdom life. Those that practice these sins cannot at the same time be doing the will of God.

Notice, to the list in 5:11 he has added adulterers, homosexuals, thieves. He uses three terms, adulterers, sexually immoral (fornicators), and homosexuals, to comprehend the whole gamut of sexual sins. The last term includes those males who commit the unnatural sin of burning passion for one another instead of passion for females. These sex sins were so dominant in the social life of the ancients, but they were condemned by Christ (partially) as contrary to the laws of God, and by Paul as absolutely incompatible with the character and life of the members of the kingdom of God.

Verse 11. "And such were some of you." Before they became Christians some of these Corinthians (likely most of them) were guilty of these heinous sexual sins, but they "washed themselves" (middle voice in Greek) in the blood of Christ, symbolized in their baptism. The apostle is not contradicting himself when he says later we "are saved by grace" (Eph. 2:8). The verbs following in the context, "consecrate, justify," are in the passive. They were consecrated, were justified. Paul is not trying to give the chronological order of these transactions in the Christian's experience. He is emphasizing the fact that the readers once were deep-dyed sinners but they responded to the call of the good news, "washed themselves" in the fountain opened for sin, and Christ did the rest.

It is evident from this statement of Paul in verse 11 that men guilty of these heinous sins can repent and believe in Christ and become real Christians, washed clean, in right standing with God, and consecrated to Christ and His kingdom. Then this statement makes it more probable that he is emphasizing the present stage of the kingdom rather than the future eschatological state.

Reasons for Personal Purity (6:12-20)

[12] Everything is permissible for me, but not everything is good for me. Everything is permissible for me, but I will not become a slave to anything. [13] Foods are intended for the stomach, and the stomach for foods, but God will finally put a stop to both of them. The body is not intended for sexual immorality but for the service of the Lord, and the Lord is for the body to serve. [14] And as God by His power raised the Lord to life, so He will raise us too.

[15] Do you not know that your bodies are parts of Christ Himself? Then may I take away parts of Christ and make them parts of a prostitute? Never! Never! [16] Or, are you not aware that a man who has to do with a prostitute makes his body one with hers? for God says, "The two shall be physically one." [17] But the man who is in union with the Lord is spiritually one with Him. [18] Keep on running from sexual immorality! Any other sin that a man commits is one outside his body, but the man who commits the sexual sin is sinning against his own body. [19] Or, are you not conscious that your body is a temple of the Holy Spirit that is in you, whom you have as a gift from God? Furthermore, you are not your own, [20] for you have been bought and actually paid for. So you must honor God with your bodies.

Key words and phrases. Verse 12. "All things are lawful for me." The word *panta* (all things) must be taken as a hyperbole. Of course, not all things literally and absolutely are lawful for anyone. He means that most things are permissible for him if he chooses to do them. But he is careful not to bring himself under the authority (literally) of anything. His policy is to stay clean by refraining from anything that might tarnish his character or reputation. Many of the sins listed above are permitted by the social customs of Corinth, but Christians must not yield to such customs and cannot afford to tarnish their character and reputation by committing such sins.

Verses 13-20. Reasons for keeping the body pure from sexual pollution. 13b. God made the human body not to indulge in sexual immorality but to serve Him. He made sex for the propagation and preservation of the race, but He intended the body to serve Him, even in its sexual functions. To do so, sexual relations are limited to marriage and the family as the proper means for the propagation of the race.

Verse 14. The body is to be raised at last and transformed into a spiritual body. He raised Christ's body, so He will raise our bodies. Therefore, we should keep our bodies clean as Christ kept His pure.

Verses 15, 16. The bodies of Christians are members of Christ. It is irrational and incompatible to "join them to a prostitute and make them members of a prostitute." He seems to think that sexual intercourse of an immoral man with a prostitute makes them one flesh, as he quotes Genesis 2:24, referring to the matrimonial union of man and wife.

Verse 17. The Christian is united to the Lord and spiritually one with Him, so he must not have physical union with a prostitute.

Verse 18. Sexual sin is a sin against the body because it is a sin inside the body. Modern scientists confirm this conclusion. How fatal is promiscuous sexual intercourse and how destructive to the strength and health of the body is continuous sexual intercourse with any and all kinds of immoral men and women! The same fatal consequences consume the bodies of prostitutes.

Verse 19a. The Christian's body is "a temple of the Holy Spirit." Of course, this sanctuary of the Lord must be kept pure and holy.

Verses 19b-20. The Christian's body has been redeemed and paid for with the price of Christ's own blood. Therefore, "you are not your own." Christians, all they are and all they have, belong to Christ who paid for them when He redeemed them by His death.

This means our bodies are not our own to abuse and contaminate in sexual indulgence. They belong to Christ the Lord. We are His slaves, and so must glorify Him with our bodies. We cannot do so if we are fornicators, adulterers, and prostitutes.

SERMON OUTLINE FROM CHAPTER VI

THE BASIS OF CHRISTIAN STEWARDSHIP (6:19, 20)

I. We Christians Not Our Own

As Americans we boast of freedom. Are we really free?

  1. Are free from despots, dictators, and foreign rule
  2. Not free from obligations to God our Creator, Benefactor
  3. Not free from obligations to Christ who bought us
  4. All we are and have belongs to God:
    a. Our personality His
    b. Our property His. If no property, our salary, wages, His
    c. Our talents His
    d. Our bodies His
    e. Our time His

II. His Because Christ Paid for Us with the Price of His Blood.

  1. The price Himself (Gal. 2:20; Heb. 7:27)
  2. The price His death (Phil. 2:8a)
  3. The price the Cross of shame (Phil. 2:8b; Gal. 3:13; I Peter 2:24). The cross was a Roman method of punishing criminals of the deepest dye, murderers, traitors, etc.

III. Christians under Obligation to Christ to Glorify Him

  1. With our *bodies* as well as our minds and souls.
  2. With our hands — their fruits, labor — farmers, miners, blacksmiths, wage-earners, and others.
  3. With our brains, noblest part of the body—includes our talents, knowledge, skill, influence, etc.
  4. With our time. Service. His "bond-servants." As a slave's time belongs to his master, so our time belongs to Christ our Lord. The Lord's day? Seven days are the Lord's.
  5. With our children the fruit of our bodies. Hannah gave Samuel to the Lord—before he was born. All Christians should give their children to God and train them for Him. General illustrations: Paul recognized the ownership of

Christ (Rom. 1:1; Phil. 1:1). Though called to be an apostle, he felt that he was really Christ's slave; Christ was Lord. African chief who had been sold into slavery was bought by a wealthy Englishman and by him set free. But the freed chief stayed in London to say: "I am yours; I'll do anything you wish because you gave me my freedom." His benefactor answered, "Go back to your people in Africa and give them Christ as Saviour. That's why I bought you and freed you." He did.

Chapter VII

THE UNMARRIED STATE PREFERABLE TO THE MARRIED STATE; HUSBANDS AND WIVES URGED NOT TO SEPARATE; CHRISTIANS TO REMAIN IN PRESENT SOCIAL STATE; A FATHER'S DUTY TO A VIRGIN DAUGHTER; WIDOWS MAY MARRY

THE UNMARRIED STATE NOW PREFERABLE; HUSBANDS AND WIVES NOT TO SEPARATE (7:1-11)

Now I take up the matters about which you wrote me. It may be a good thing for a man to remain unmarried; ² but because of so much sexual immorality every man should have a wife of his own, and every woman a husband of her own. ³ The husband must always give his wife what is due her, and the wife too must do so for her husband. ⁴ The wife does not have the right to do as she pleases with her own body; the husband has his right to it. In the same way the husband does not have the right to do as he pleases with his own body; the wife has her right to it. ⁵ You husbands and wives must stop refusing each other what is due, unless you agree to do so just for awhile, so as to have plenty of time for prayer, and then to be together again, so as to keep Satan from tempting you because of your lack of self-control. ⁶ But I say this by way of concession, not by way of command. ⁷ However, I should like for everyone to be just as I am myself, yet each of us has his own special gift from God, one for one way, another for another.

⁸ To unmarried people and to widows I would say this: It would be a fine thing for them to remain single, as I am. ⁹ But if they do not practice self-control, let them marry. For it is better to marry than to be burning in the fire of passion. ¹⁰ To the people already

married I give this instruction—no, not I but the Lord—that a wife is not to leave her husband. ¹¹ But if she does leave him, she must remain single, or better, be reconciled to her husband. I instruct the husband too not to divorce his wife.

Key words and phrases. Verses 1, 2. Prevalence of sex immoralities. The word is in the plural to indicate the prevalence of sex sins—especially among unmarried people. The city of Corinth had a special goddess of sex with her temple prominently located; in it were a thousand beautiful maidens for men to indulge their passions as an act of worship. Oh, the depths of sex sins to which the profligate may sink! Because of this sex immorality so prevalent and so powerful in Corinth, Paul concludes that it is better for each man to have a wife and each woman a husband.

Verses 3, 4. Husbands and wives belong to each other and should respect the rights each has to the other's body—referring to the duty of sex relations. Neither one's body belongs absolutely to himself. So neither should willfully deprive the other of his or her sex functions. Each has a right to the other's sex functions.

Verse 5. Husbands and wives may have an agreement to live apart for prayer; that is, for special devotions. But this period must not be so long that Satan can tempt them through lack of self-control. Paul recognizes the sexual weakness of men and women.

Verse 7. Paul also recognizes that men and women are of different sex constitutions. So each must settle this question for himself.

Verses 8, 9. People who cannot practice self-control in sex matters should marry, for it is better to marry than to be aflame with passion. This is not to place marriage on a low basis, just to avoid sex indulgence. It is only a concession for extreme cases.

Verses 10, 11. Paul's view of the sanctity of marriage. The wife must not leave her husband; or if she does, she must remain unmarried. The husband must not divorce his wife. In Paul's view there is an absolute sanctity in the marriage relation. He does not deal with the question of adultery on a wife's part and the man's right to a divorce. (Matt. 5:32).

BELIEVING AND UNBELIEVING HUSBANDS AND WIVES TO
CONTINUE LIVING TOGETHER (7:12-16)

12 To the rest of the people I myself would say—though the Lord Himself has said nothing about it—if a Christian has a wife that is not a believer and she consents to live with him, he must not divorce her; 13 and a woman who has a husband that is not a believer, but he consents to live with her, must not divorce her husband. 14 For the unbelieving husband is consecrated by union with his wife and the unbelieving wife by union with her Christian husband; for otherwise your children would be unblessed, but in this way they are consecrated. 15 But if the unbelieving consort actually leaves, let the separation stand. In such cases the Christian husband or wife is not morally bound; God has called us to live in peace. 16 For how do you know, wife, whether you will save your husband? Or, how do you know, husband, whether you will save your wife?

Key words and phrases. Verses 12, 13. "I say, not the Lord." That is, Jesus in person did not have anything to say about the divided family—one consort a believer, the other an unbeliever—nothing as to whether they should continue to live together or separate. Paul feels that the Spirit leads him to say that they should continue to live together, if the unbelieving partner wishes to do so.

Verse 14. The reason for this is the good influence of the Christian partner on the non-Christian partner, and also on the children. The Christian should, and often does, shed a saving influence on the unbelieving husband or wife, and also on the children. This is the meaning of *sanctify* as here used.

Verse 15. If the unbelieving partner desires to leave his or her Christian partner, and give up the children, let it be so, for the Christian partner has no authority or obligation to keep the home intact under such circumstances. "Peace" is the happy goal which God sets for the home, and this is Paul's reason for the Christian partner's passive consent to separation.

Verse 16. An appeal to the Christian husband or wife to realize his or her obligation to save the unbelieving consort, and the children, by demonstrating the spirit of Christ in the home.

ALL CHRISTIANS TO REMAIN IN THE SOCIAL STATUS WHICH GOD ASSIGNS TO THEM (7:17-24)

[17] Only, everybody must continue to live in the station which the Lord assigned to him, in that in which God called him. These are my orders in all the churches. [18] Has a man been called after he was circumcised? He must not try to change it. Has a man been called without being circumcised? He must not be circumcised. [19] Being circumcised or not being circumcised has no value, but keeping God's commands is important. [20] Everybody must remain in the station in which he was called. [21] Were you called while a slave? Stop letting that annoy you. Yet, if you can win your freedom, take advantage of such an opportunity. [22] For the slave who has been called to union with the Lord is the Lord's freedman; in the same way the freeman who has been called is a slave of Christ. [23] You have been bought and actually paid for; stop becoming slaves to men. [24] Brothers, each one must continue close to God in the very station in which he was called.

Key words and phrases. Verse 17. Paul thinks that the Providence of God has much to do with one's social boundaries. "In which God has called him," refers to the social station in which God calls one to be saved by trusting Christ.

Verses 18, 19. Here Paul asserts that circumcision has no value for Christians.

Verse 20. Let everyone be contented with his social lot.

Verses 21-23. He enjoins the same contentment as to slavery and freedom.

Verse 24. Repeats the thought of verse 20—contentment with one's lot.

THE DISTRESSING TIMES SUGGEST IF NOT DEMAND NO CHANGE IN ONE'S SOCIAL STATION (7:25-31)

[25] About unmarried women I have no command from the Lord, but I will give you my opinion as of one who is trustworthy, since I have had mercy shown me by the Lord. [26] Now this is my opinion in the light of the present distress: That it is a good thing for a man to remain as he is. [27] Are you married? Stop trying to get a divorce. Are you unmarried? Stop looking for a wife. [28] But if you do get married, you have not sinned in doing so. And if a

girl gets married, she has not sinned in doing so. But those who do will have trouble in their earthly life, and I am trying to spare you this.

²⁹ I mean this, brothers. The time has been cut short. For the future, men who have wives should live as though they had none, ³⁰ and those that mourn as though they did not mourn, and those who are glad as though they were not glad, and those who buy as though they did not own a thing, ³¹ and those who are enjoying the world as though they were not entirely absorbed in it. For the outward order of this world is passing away.

Key words and phrases. Verse 25. "Virgins." Here this word seems to include unmarried men as well as girls. The whole context includes both sexes. Though the Lord Jesus has no command for such cases, Paul, as an apostle having received mercy from the Lord, has a conviction that his utterance on the matter is trustworthy. Therefore it should be accepted as valid.

Verses 26, 27. Paul has a deep feeling, if not a strong conviction, that the Lord Jesus is coming soon, so the married should not be seeking divorce, the unmarried should not be seeking to be married. Verse 29 confirms this view: "The appointed time has grown very short."

Verses 28, 29. However, if a man or a girl marries, sin has not been committed by either. Yet, it would have saved them worldly trouble to remain unmarried.

Verses 30, 31. In the light of the impending doom of the present world order he warns people to avoid extremes. Those with social and economic advantages, good wives and happy homes, should live as temperately as those who do not have these social privileges. Again he warns that "The outward show of this world is passing away." The third time he gives this warning in this paragraph.

The Unmarried Freer from the Worries of the World to Serve the Lord with Undivided Devotion (7:32-35)

³² I want you to be free from worldly worries. An unmarried man is concerned about the affairs of the Lord. ³³ A married man is concerned about the affairs of the world, and how he can please his wife, and so his devotion is divided. ³⁴ An unmarried woman or a girl is concerned about the affairs of the Lord, so as to be con-

secrated in body and spirit, but a married woman is concerned about the affairs of the world, and how she can please her husband. ³⁵ It is for your welfare that I am saying this, not to put restraint on you, but to foster good order and to help you to an undivided devotion to the Lord.

Key words and phrases. Verses 32-34. "Please." True husbands want to please their wives, and some are so devoted that they forget God, or give Him very little attention and service. The same is true of some wives who are wrapped up in their husbands. Paul has observed this and so feels that the unmarried can, and often do, render the Lord the most undivided service. Some old maids are often the most consecrated Christians in the community. Many bachelors and widowers, give Christ the most undivided devotion. For example, Dock Pegues, of Texas, after his wife died and all his children were married, gave himself unreservedly to the winning of souls, so that in the last seven years of his life (as shown in his diary) he won seven thousand people to Christ—many of them "hard cases." Undivided devotion to the Lord is the high goal that Paul sets for a consecrated Christian.

MAY A FATHER RESTRAIN HIS VIRGIN DAUGHTER FROM MARRYING?
WIVES FREED FROM THE MARRIAGE TIE ON THE DEATH OF
THEIR HUSBANDS AND MAY REMARRY (7:36-40)

³⁶ Now if a father thinks that he is not doing the proper thing regarding his single daughter, if she is past the bloom of her youth, and she ought to do so, let him do what she desires; he commits no sin. Let the daughter and her suitor marry. ³⁷ But the father who stands firm in his purpose, without having any necessity for doing so, and he has made the decision in his own heart to keep her single, will do what is right. ³⁸ And so the man who gives his daughter in marriage does what is right, and yet the man who does not do so does even better.

³⁹ A wife is bound to her husband as long as he lives. If her husband dies, she is free to marry anyone she pleases, except that he must be a Christian. ⁴⁰ But in my opinion she will be happier, if she remains as she is, and I think too that I have God's Spirit.

Key words and phrases. Verses 36-37. Perhaps the hardest exegetical nut to crack in all the New Testament. The language is ambiguous; the most ambiguous sentences in all Paul's letters. Some exegetes (and translators) regard a suitor and sweetheart (perhaps planning to marry) as the two leading characters in these verses. This may be what Paul has in mind; but what could it mean when he says the suitor is "behaving unseemly toward his virgin" (A.S.V. marg.)? Has he gone too far in sexual advances? If so, what could Paul mean when he says of the suitor, "Let him do what he will, he does not sin; let them marry"? This would commit Paul to advising immorality on his (suitor's) part, or at least, condoning it. That is unthinkable in Paul the inspired apostle. The other interpretation regards the two leading characters as a father and his virgin daughter (the last word implied). This view is demanded by the meaning of *gamizo* (v. 38) which means "to give [a daughter] in marriage." So it would read, "And so the man [father] who gives his virgin [daughter] in marriage," etc. This would make "let him [father] do what he wills," simply mean either restrain her from marrying or consent to her marrying. See Williams' New Testament *in loco*.

Verses 39-40. Paul regards the marriage tie is unbreakable except by death. He does not discuss the question of adultery as an adequate ground for divorce, which Jesus permitted on this ground (Matt. 5:32).

Chapter VIII

MAY CHRISTIANS EAT FOODS SACRIFICED TO IDOLS? (8:1-6)

Now about the foods that have been sacrificed to idols: We know that every one of us has some knowledge of the matter. Knowledge puffs up, but love builds up. ² If a man supposes that he has already gotten some true knowledge, as yet he has not learned it as he ought to know it. ³ But if a man loves God, God is known by him. ⁴ So, as to eating things that have been sacrificed to idols, we are sure that an idol is nothing in the world, and that there is no God but One. ⁵ For even if there are so-called gods in heaven or on earth—as there are, indeed, a vast number of gods and lords—⁶ yet for us there is but one God, the Father, who is the source of all things and the goal of our living, and but one Lord, Jesus Christ, through whom everything was made and through whom we live.

Key words and phrases. Verses 1-3. He begins to answer their question, May Christians eat foods that have been offered to idols? First he compares knowledge and love. Knowledge makes one proud (puffs up); love purifies and perfects character (builds up). Love is the quality that elevates and enriches personality. It makes one humble and gentle and altruistic, while knowledge makes one haughty and boastful and egoistic. Love is the beginning of the highest form of knowledge, knowledge of God. "If a man loves God [this one, God] God is known by him." As the late Professor Deissmann used to say, "God is better known by the heart than by the mind." The mind (intellect) gives us only an incomplete knowledge of God, like that of philosophers, Socrates, Plato, Aristotle, and others, and that of natural scientists. But the heart lays hold of God by experience of His presence and love, of His care and forgiveness.

Verses 4-6. Paul's conclusion: We know that an idol is nothing at all; does not really exist, except in imagination. In this way there are many so-called gods, but in reality there is only one God, the Father, the Source of life and all things; and only one Lord, Jesus Christ, who is the medium (through whom) of man's life (both physical and spiritual).

LOVE ANSWERS THE QUESTION (8:7-13)

⁷ But is it not in all of you that such knowledge is found. Some, because of their past habits with idols, even down to the present moment, still eat such food as was really sacrificed to an idol, and so their consciences, because they are overscrupulous, are contaminated. ⁸ Food will never bring us near to God. We are no worse if we do not eat it; we are no better if we do. ⁹ But you must see to it that this right of yours does not become a stumbling block to overscrupulous people. ¹⁰ For if somebody sees you, who have an intelligent view of this matter, partaking of a meal in an idol's temple, will he not be emboldened, with his overscrupulous conscience, to eat the food which has been sacrificed to an idol? ¹¹ Yes, the overscrupulous brother, for whom Christ died, is ruined by your so-called knowledge. ¹² Now if in such a way you sin against your brothers and wound their overscrupulous consciences, you are actually sinning against Christ. ¹³ So then, if food can

make my brother fall, I will never, no, never, eat meat again, in order to keep my brother from falling.

Key words and phrases. Verses 7, 8. "It is not in all of you that such knowledge is found." That is, an intelligent view of the real nature of an idol. They are overscrupulous, believing that an idol is real, and so to them food which has been offered to an idol is contaminated and if eaten by a Christian contaminates his conscience. Paul says this is not a fact. That eating food neither brings God nearer nor cuts off one's fellowship with Him. Eating or not eating has no real power one way or the other. That is, has no real spiritual significance.

Verses 9-13. But an intelligent, consecrated Christian must respect the weak (overscrupulous) conscience of his brother and not eat foods that have been sacrificed to idols. If he does, this emboldens the weak brother to eat them too and thus he would violate and contaminate his conscience. He has a right to eat such foods, but the law of brotherly love says *No.* If he does in this way offend the conscience of his weak brother, he is really "sinning against Christ," for He died for the weak brother as well as for the strong one (v. 12). Verse 13 gives us Paul's universal law of brotherly love: Never, no never, eat or do anything that causes another to fall and sin.

Chapter IX

PAUL'S APOSTLESHIP DENIED AND DEFENDED; THOSE PREACHING
THE GOOD NEWS TO BE SUPPORTED BY THOSE MINISTERED TO;
PAUL FEELS CALLED OF GOD TO PREACH THE GOOD NEWS
BUT REFUSES SUPPORT FOR IT; ADJUSTS HIMSELF
TO ALL CLASSES TO WIN THEM TO CHRIST

HIS APOSTLESHIP DENIED AND DEFENDED (9:1-12)

Am I not free? Am I not an apostle? Have I not seen Jesus our Lord? Are you not the product of my work for the Lord? ² If I am not an apostle to other people, I certainly am one to you, for you yourselves, by virtue of your union with the Lord, are the proof of my apostleship.

³ My vindication of myself to those who are investigating me is this: ⁴ It cannot be that we have no right to our food and drink, can it? ⁵ It cannot be that we have no right to take a Christian

wife about with us, can it, as well as the rest of the apostles and the Lord's brothers, and Cephas? ⁶ Or is it Barnabas and I alone who have no right to refrain from working for a living? ⁷ What soldier ever goes to war at his own expense? Who plants a vineyard and does not eat any of its grapes? Who shepherds a flock and does not drink any of the milk the flock produces? ⁸ I am not saying this only by way of human illustrations, am I? Does not the law say so too? ⁹ For in the law of Moses it is written, You must not muzzle an ox that is treading out your grain. Is it that God is concerned about oxen only? ¹⁰ Is He not really speaking on our behalf? Yes, indeed, this law was written on our behalf, because the plowman ought to plow and the thresher ought to thresh, in the hope of sharing in the crop. ¹¹ If we have sown the spiritual seed for you, is it too great for us to reap a material support from you? ¹² If others share this right with you, have we not a stronger claim? Yet, we have never used this right; no, we keep on bearing everything, to keep from hindering the progress of the good news of Christ.

Key words and phrases. Verses 1, 2. He raises the question which they had raised, Am I an apostle? He urges two reasons for accepting him as a genuine apostle: He had seen the Lord—referring to the wonderful vision of the risen Christ miraculously given him near Damascus (Acts 9:4-9). To have seen the Lord was a requirement of a genuine apostle, according to Acts 1:21. The second argument was an induction from the success of his work with the Corinthians themselves. He had evangelized them (Acts 18:5-11) and so they are his spiritual work. These divine results prove a divine cause, an apostle and preacher who had a call from God; a divine commission to be an apostle, a preacher, and a teacher (I Tim. 2:7). The seal (v. 2) on a letter or legal document proves that it is genuine. So Paul claims that the spiritual results of his preaching in Corinth prove the genuineness of his apostleship.

Verses 3-7. He here lists arguments from everyday human life. He maintains that he has the same right to material support and to marry a Christian wife as the rest of the apostles—even Peter—and the Lord's brothers, giving as human illustrations the fact that a soldier has the right to be supported by his government for which he fights; a planter of a vineyard has the right to support from the fruit of his vineyard; and a shepherd expects to be supported from the milk products of his flock. So he argues an apostle or a preacher of the good news has the right to be supported by those to whom he ministers.

Notice, Paul speaks of Peter as having the right to marry and have a wife accompany him on his preaching tours. This is quite different from the contention of the Roman Church as to the marital status of Peter's successors (as they claim). Paul does not endorse celibacy for the ministry.

Verses 8-10. He clinches his argument for the material support of an apostle or a minister by quoting what God says about it through Moses. "It is written in the law of Moses, You must not muzzle an ox that is treading out your grain" (Deut. 25:4). He then asserts that God said this, not so much because of His concern for oxen as for the sake of men; that is, it is applicable to ministers and apostles.

Verses 11, 12. It is reasonable that if we apostles have sown spiritual seed for you, you should see that we reap material benefits from you. This is good argument for the maintenance of pastors by modern churches. And Paul claims that Barnabas and he have still more right to claim this from them than others whom they recognize (as Peter and Apollos).

ALTHOUGH PAUL HAD A DEEP CONVICTION THAT GOD HAD CALLED HIM TO PREACH THE GOOD NEWS AND THAT HE HAD THE RIGHT TO BE SUPPORTED BY THOSE TO WHOM HE MINISTERED, NEVERTHELESS HE CHOSE TO SUPPORT HIMSELF AND MAKE THE GOSPEL FREE (9:15-18)

15 But I myself have never used any of these rights. And I am not writing this just to make it so in my case, for I had rather die than do that. No one shall rob me of this ground of boasting. 16 For if I do preach the good news, I have no ground for boasting of it, for I cannot help doing it. Yes, indeed, I am accursed if I do not preach the good news. 17 For if I do it of my own accord, I get my pay; but if I am unwilling to do it, I still am entrusted with trusteeship. 18 Then what is the pay that I am getting? To be able to preach the good news without expense to anybody, and so never to make full use of my rights in preaching the good news.

Key words and phrases. Verses 13, 14. Material support for those who preach the good news has scriptural and divine authority. Priests and their assistants in the temple were to be supported from the tithe paid into the temple. And the Lord Jesus said, "The laborer is worthy of his hire" (see Luke 10:7). This is said of the seventy special ministers of the kingdom whom Jesus sent forth, in addition to the preaching that He and the Twelve were doing. This furnishes divine authority for churches to support their ministers.

Verses 15-18. But Paul relinquished his right to material support from the churches he founded. He preferred to live by the work of his own hands, making tents (Acts 18:3). While in Corinth he stayed with Aquila and Priscilla, fellow tentmakers, so as to join them in tentmaking and thus support himself, and not burden the Corinthians with his support. This was the only ground of boasting he had—preaching the good news of his own accord and without expense to anybody. Just to preach it and be paid for it robbed him of any reason for boasting that he was a preacher of the good news, for necessity was laid upon him to preach it, and a curse was upon him if he did not preach it. If he was unwilling to preach it, he could not shirk his responsibility laid upon him by the Lord. He had received this trusteeship from the Lord and could not evade his personal responsibility to preach the good news. Every minister of today should feel the same responsibility.

"What is my reward?" He felt that he was worthy of no compensation from the Lord, unless he preached the good news free of charge to anyone. What a noble, altruistic soul!

PAUL ACCOMMODATES HIMSELF TO PEOPLE OF ALL CONDITIONS, AND YET PRACTICES RIGID SELF-CONTROL (9:19-27)

[19] Yes, indeed, though I am free from any human power, I have made myself a slave to everybody, to win as many as possible. [20] To the Jews I have become like a Jew for the winning of Jews; to men under the law, like one under the law, though I am not under the law myself, to win the men under the law; [21] to men who have no written law, like one without any law, though I am not without God's law but specially under Christ's

law, to win the men who have no written law. ²² To the over-scrupulous I have become overscrupulous, to win the overscrupu-lous; yes, I have become everything to everybody, in order by all means to save some of them. ²³ And I do it all for the sake of the good news, so as to share with others in its blessings.

²⁴ Do you not know that in a race the runners all run, but only one can get the prize? You must run in such a way that you can get the prize. ²⁵ Any man who enters an athletic contest practices rigid self-control in training, only to win a wreath that withers, but we are in to win a wreath that never withers. ²⁶ So that is the way I run, with no uncertainty as to winning. That is the way I box, not like one that punches the air. ²⁷ But I keep on beating and bruising my body and making it my slave, so that I, after I have summoned others to the race, may not myself become unfit to run.

Key words and phrases. Verse 19. Here is the lofty motive that stirred the heart of the apostle to preach and suffer as he did: to win as many as possible. The way he adopted to do it was to accommodate himself to the position and even the prejudices of others. "I made myself a slave to all." This word means to act as a bond-slave. He volunteered to be a slave to all kinds of people, in order to win them to Christ.

Verses 20-23. He itemizes by mentioning four classes: the Jews, those under the law, those outside the law, and the weak. The first two terms merely describe Jews, though a few Jews were not such sticklers for the law as were the Judaizers (Paul's bitter opponents). Those outside the law include all Gentiles who do not have the written law of Moses; the weak are overscrupulous people about nonessentials, like eating foods once offered to idols (discussed above).

Verse 23 likely means "that I might share its blessings with others." The Greek verb means literally "share with." Something must be supplied to complete the sense. Probably in this paragraph of altruistic motives and service to others he means "share the blessings of the good news with others," not "that I might be par-taker thereof with you" (A.V.). This closes the paragraph of altruistic thought with a selfish, egoistic motive.

Verses 24-27. Paul was familiar with the Grecian games as to how they were conducted. He compares himself to a contestant in the games—a runner in verses 24-26a, a boxer in 26b-27. He knows that the contestant must prepare for the contest by practicing self-discipline which develops self-control. Those contestants run with uncertainty as to the issue. Only one wins, though many engage in the game. In the Christian contest, all may win if they practice proper self-discipline. Athletes contest to win a wreath that withers; the Christian, a wreath that never withers. Verse 27 offers difficulty in interpretation if we follow the Authorized Version: "I myself should be a castaway." Some have pressed the last word to mean "be lost." But he means merely "disqualified for the game."

SERMON OUTLINE FROM CHAPTER IX
A MASTER SOUL-WINNER'S MAJOR METHOD (9:19-23)
PAUL A MASTER SOUL-WINNER

I. Paul Deeply Interested in the Salvation of People
   1. Interested in Jews his kinsmen (Rom. 10:1). Usually first went to the synagogue to preach (See Acts 13:17, 27; 14:1)
   2. Interested in Gentiles (Acts 13:46-48; Rom. 10:12, 13) and apostle to the gentiles
   3. Interested in governors and kings (Acts 9:15; 13:7-12; 24:25; 26:25-29)—preaching to Felix and King Agrippa.
   4. Interested in all men (I Cor. 9:22—all things to all men)

II. Because He Loved All People
   1. Christ his Saviour he loved supremely (Gal. 2:20; Phil. 3:7-11)
   2. His love for Christ constrained him to love lost sinners (See II Cor. 5:14; I Thess. 2:8)
   3. He knew immortal souls are lost in sin (Rom. 1:18-3:20)
   4. He knew the value of immortal souls (Rom. 9:3)

III. His Major Method of Winning People—"All Things to All Men"
   1. Lovingly accommodated himself to the conditions of others
   2. Not pretense, but genuine sympathy for others
   3. Spiritual diplomacy — diplomacy for spiritual service; means a sympathetic, intelligent approach to people in any social and moral situation

4. Must be backed by deep consecration to Christ and the winning of the lost

Chapter X

EXAMPLES OF SINNING ISRAEL IN THE DESERT WHO MISSED CANAAN; GOD PROVIDES WAYS OF ESCAPE FROM TEMPTATIONS; BROTHERLY LOVE LIMITS THE USE OF OUR PERSONAL FREEDOM

EXAMPLES OF SINNING ISRAEL; THEIR PUNISHMENT; GOD HELPING THE TEMPTED (10:1-13)

For I would not have you, brothers, to be ignorant of the fact that though our forefathers were all made safe by the cloud, and all went securely through the sea, and in the cloud and the sea ² they all allowed themselves to be baptized as followers of Moses, ³ and all ate the same spiritual food, ⁴ and all drank the same spiritual drink—for they continued to drink the water from the spiritual Rock which accompanied them, and that Rock was the Christ—⁵ still with the most of them God was not at all satisfied, for He allowed them to be laid low in the desert.

⁶ Now all these things occurred as warnings to us, to keep us from hankering after what is evil, in the ways they did. ⁷ Now stop being idolaters, as some of them were, for the Scripture says, "The people sat down to eat and drink and got up to dance." ⁸ Let us stop practicing immorality, as some of them did, and on one day twenty-three thousand fell dead. ⁹ Let us stop trying the Lord's patience, as some of them did, and for it were destroyed by the snakes. ¹⁰ You must stop grumbling, as some of them did, and for it were destroyed by the destroying angel. ¹¹ These things continued to befall them as warnings to others, and they were written down for the purpose of instructing us, in whose lives the climax of the ages has been reached.

² So the man who thinks he stands securely must be on the lookout not to fall. ¹³ No temptation has taken hold of you but what is common to human nature. And God is to be trusted not to let you be tempted beyond your strength, but when temptation comes, to make a way out of it, so that you can bear up under it.

Key words and phrases. Verses 1-4. He enumerates several privileges enjoyed by the Iraelites while passing through the desert: God had the cloud stand at the rear of Israel to make them invisible

to the Egyptians, so protecting them; had Moses smite the Red
Sea to roll back its waters so they could march over on dry land;
in the cloud and sea the people dedicated themselves to Moses as
their leader (baptism being a symbol of separation and dedication);
all were given supernatural manna and quails to eat, furnished fresh
each day by the Lord; all drank the supernatural drink, water
from the Rock, the Rock being the Christ. That is, they were the
objects of God's special providence and protection; and yet they
were grievous sinners instead of being grateful and devoted to God
their liberator.

Verse 5. Because of these grievous sins, God was displeased.
He let them wander 'round and 'round and leave their carcasses
in the desert, thus keeping them out of the Promised Land.

Verses 6-10. Examples of their wickedness: worshiping idols;
practicing sexual immorality; presumption on the goodness of God;
murmuring against Him and their leaders. He quotes Exodus 32:6,
which gives the account of Aaron's fashioning a golden calf for the
people to worship, while Moses was on the mount to receive the
law from Jehovah. When Moses came down, he found them dancing
around the calf. In his anger he dashed the tablet of law to the
ground and smashed it. He called for those loyal to him to stand
with him. The children of Levi stood with him. In the name of
Jehovah he commanded every son of Levi to put on his sword and
slay the idolaters—about three thousand men. This was done to
show God's abomination of idolatry. The second sin was sexual
immorality (Num. 25:6-9), where grievous punishment is visited
upon an Israelite who had committed this sin with a Midianitish
woman. Paul is warning the Corinthians against these two sins,
especially because they were their besetting sins. It was said in
those days that it "was easier in Athens to find a god than a man."
Perhaps, the same could have been said about Corinth. At any
rate, in Corinth adultery and fornication were glaringly common.
In the temple of one goddess there were kept one thousand beautiful young women, sixteen to twenty-five, for men who were worshiping in the temple. See chapter 5 for the low sexual ideals held
by the members of the church in Corinth. See chapter 8 for their
hankering after idols.

The other two sins were presuming on the goodness of God—trying His patience—and murmuring against Moses and the Lord (Num. 21:5-6; 16:41-46). This is a hint to the Corinthians not to take sides against God's leaders.

Verse 11. Paul asserts positively that God meant, in having these events recorded, that we in the later centuries might be instructed by them not to follow their examples in committing such grievous sins.

Verses 12, 13. He warns against being cocksure about our strength to resist temptation. Let such a one "take heed lest he fall." We have seen such overconfident Christians commit most heinous sins. They were caught off guard. Paul exhorts us to take heed. We must be on guard all the time, lest Satan catch us napping. But then he assures his readers that God is graciously providing a way of escape if we depend on Him and stay on guard. His grace is sufficient if we trust Him and not ourselves. What a gracious thought is this: "He will not let you be tempted beyond your strength."

Special Warning against Idolatry Enforced by the Significance of the Memorial Supper (10:14-22)

¹⁴ So then, my dearly beloved, keep on running from idolatry. ¹⁵ I am speaking to sensible men; decide for yourselves about what I say. ¹⁶ Is not the consecrated cup which we consecrate a sign of our sharing in the blood of Christ? Is not the loaf which we break a sign of our sharing in the body of Christ? ¹⁷ Because there is only one loaf, so we, though many, are only one body, for we all partake of one loaf. ¹⁸ Look at the Israelites in their practices. Are not those who eat the sacrifices in spiritual fellowship with the altar? ¹⁹ Then what do I mean? That the sacrifice to an idol is a reality, or that an idol itself is a reality? Of course not! ²⁰ I mean that what the heathen sacrifice they sacrifice to demons, not to God, and I do not want you to be in fellowship with demons. ²¹ You cannot drink the cup of the Lord and the cup of demons. You cannot eat at the table of the Lord and at the table of demons. ²² Or, are we trying to incite the Lord to jealousy? We are not stronger than He, are we?

Key words and phrases. Verse 14. "Keep on running [fleeing] from idolatry." It was a sore temptation to the Corinthians, who had been brought up in the atmosphere of idol worship, to feel that an idol is a reality and that idol worship is real worship of God. So Paul is exhorting them to keep on running from it as often as the temptation presents itself. He appeals to them as sensible men who ought to see the merits (superiority) of the spiritual worship of the one God as compared with the non-spiritual worship of idols.

Verses 15-17. The significance of the Memorial Supper makes it incompatible to try to partake of idol worship and the Lord's Supper by the same worshipers. What do the loaf and cup signify? That the partaker is sharing in the blood and body of Christ. So the one partaking of the sacrifice offered to idols may be regarded as entering into fellowship with demons (which idols are). And it is inconceivable that one can be in fellowship with Christ the Lord and with demons at the same time. Hence the exhortation to "keep on fleeing from idol worship."

Verse 18. The example of the priests (O.T.) who eat the meats offered to Jehovah teaches the same truth. They are "partakers in the altar." They are in fellowship with the God of the altar.

Verses 19-20. Paul must not be misunderstood here. He is using the formal offering of foods to idols as an illustration or analogy with our eating the bread and drinking the wine in the Lord's Supper; not that idol sacrifices are a reality or that the idol itself is a reality. They are only demon worship, so must not be practiced by Christians who are in fellowship with Christ the Lord.

Verse 21. It is inconceivable and impossible to be in fellowship with idols (demons) and Christ. "You cannot drink the cup of the Lord and the cup of demons."

Verse 22. A rhetorical question expecting the answer *No*. We must not incite the Lord to jealousy by trying to partake of idol worship; we are not stronger than He; we must submit to Him alone.

BROTHERLY LOVE SETS LIMITS FOR THE EXERCISE OF PERSONAL LIBERTY (10:23-11:1)

23 Everything is permissible for people, but not everything is good for them. Everything is permissible for people, but not

everything builds up their personality. ²⁴ No one should always be looking after his own welfare, but also that of his neighbor.

²⁵ As a rule eat anything that is sold in the meat market without raising any question about it for conscience' sake, ²⁶ for the earth and everything that it contains belong to the Lord. ²⁷ If some unbelieving heathen invites you to his house, and you wish to go, eat whatever is set before you without raising any question for conscience' sake. ²⁸ But if someone says to you, "This meat has been offered as a heathen sacrifice," make it your rule not to eat it, for the sake of the man who warned you and for conscience' sake; ²⁹ I mean his conscience, not yours. Why then should my personal freedom be limited by another's conscience? ³⁰ If I give thanks and thus partake of food, why am I to be blamed for that for which I give thanks?

³¹ So if you eat or drink or do anything else, do everything to honor God. ³² Stop being stumbling blocks to Jews or Greeks or to the church of God, ³³ just as I myself am in the habit of pleasing everybody in everything, not aiming at my own welfare but at that of many people as possible, in order that they may be saved. ¹¹ ⁻¹ You must follow my example, just as I myself am following Christ's.

Key words and phrases. Verse 23. Largely a repetition of 6:12, which see for explanation. He substitutes here, "but not all things build up," for "but I will not be enslaved by anything." "Build up" refers to one's neighbor, the other man, for he adds, "Let no one seek his own welfare, but the welfare of his neighbor." So he means here that many things are permissible for him to do, but some of them do not build up one's neighbor. Paul practiced building up others, and he is exhorting the Christians in Corinth to imitate him.

Verses 25, 26. Christians must not quibble over nonessentials. They may buy meat from the heathen meat market without raising any conscientious questions. *Makello* is a meat market kept by a heathen, not a Christian. The reason assigned is Psalm 24:1; all the earth contains is the Lord's and His people have a right to any of it if needed for food.

Verse 27-30. The same principle holds if a Christian is being entertained in the home of a non-Christian. He must not raise any conscientious question about the dishes served, unless someone tells him that a certain food has been sacrificed to an idol. In such a case the Christian must not eat that food, out of deference to the conscience of the informer. The Christian would be denounced by his informer if he were to disregard his information, and possibly the latter would be led to do wrong. Paul would emphasize this principle: Leave off doing anything, though your own conscience may approve it, if it hurts the conscience of others and might lead them to sin.

Verses 31-11:1. He repeats his emphasis of the same principle, and gives as his supreme motive, "that others may be saved" (33). Paul was a master soul-winner. It was a mighty motive of his big heart. (See Rom. 9:3; 10:1.)

Chapter XI

WOMEN'S STATUS AND SERVICE IN THE CHURCH; CLIQUES IN THE CHURCH; DISORDERS IN OBSERVING THE LORD'S SUPPER; THE ORIGIN AND SIGNIFICANCE OF THE LORD'S SUPPER
WOMEN'S STATUS AND SERVICE IN THE CHURCH (11:2-16)

² I prize and praise you for always remembering me and for firmly standing by the teachings as I passed them on to you. ³ But I want you to realize the fact that Christ is the Head of every man, that the husband is the head of the wife, and that God is the Head of Christ. ⁴ Any man who prays or preaches with anything on his head dishonors his head, ⁵ and any woman who prays or prophesies bareheaded dishonors her head, for it is one and the same thing with having her head shaved. ⁶ For if a woman will not wear a veil, let her have her hair cut off too. Now if it is a dishonor for a woman to have her hair cut off, or her head shaved, let her wear a veil. ⁷ For a man ought not to wear anything on his head, because he is the image and reflected glory of God, but woman is man's reflected glory. ⁸ For man did not originate from woman, but woman did from man, ⁹ and man was not created for woman's sake, but woman was for man's sake. ¹⁰ This is why woman ought to wear upon her head a symbol of man's authority, especially out of respect to the angels. ¹¹ But from the Lord's point of view woman is not independent of man nor man of woman. ¹² For just as woman originated from man, so man is born of woman, and both, with everything else, originated from God. ¹³ You must judge for yourselves in this matter. Is it proper

for a woman to pray to God with nothing on her head? [14] Does
not nature itself teach you that it is degrading for a man to wear
long hair, [15] but that it is a woman's glory to do so? For her hair
is given her for a covering. [16] But if anyone is inclined to be
contentious about it, I for my part prescribe no other practice
than this, and neither do the churches of God.

Key words and phrases. Verse 2. The word praise has the sense
of appreciate. Paul was appreciative of the faithful adherence of
the Corinthians to the teachings that he had given them; that is,
as far as they had been faithful in following those teachings.

Verse 3. The three headships. Christ is the head of every man;
He ought to be the director and leader of every man. The husband
is the head of his wife, not in the sense of being a hard master
over a slave, but as being the first piece of God's handiwork in the
creation of the human race, and consequently the head of the
family. Likewise, God is the head of Christ, not that His deity
is superior to that of the Son, but in the sense that the Father is
superior in station to the Son, the latter being subordinate to the
Father. (See I Cor. 15:28.) The Son is subordinate in relationship
and in activity. The will of the Father is the law of life for Christ
the Son. (See John 4:34.)

Verses 4-10. In their religious activities in the church Paul
thinks this headship of the man ought to be respected. The veil
and long hair are the symbol (as Paul sees it) of woman's inferior
rank to man. So a man should not wear long hair nor a woman a
shaven head or short hair. This is all based on the social customs
then in existence—especially among the Jews. Only lewd women
shaved the head and went without the veil. Christian women must
not put themselves in this category. As social ideals and customs
have changed through the centuries, we today need not be slavishly
bound by these ancient customs (though recorded in the Bible).
Fine Christian women now do wear short hair and no one classifies
them with prostitutes. A man need not stickle over the length of
his hair. One of the most consecrated Christians, a missionary in
China for years, wore long hair while at college with me, and ever
afterward. The college boys called him "sister," but all revered

him, for he was one of the purest and noblest Christians we ever knew.

The reason given by Paul for the fitness of these customs is that "man is the glory of God, but woman is the glory of man." What does this mean? He is referring to the Genesis account that Adam was made in the image of God (Gen. 1:26, 27). And it is the glory of man that he is made in the image of God, and so he is "the glory of God." This is the highest honor conferred by God on any creature of His. Likewise, woman is "the glory of man," because she was made from a part (rib) of man. And Eve was made after the pattern of Adam except the sexual differences, and so is "the reflected glory of man."

The eighth verse gives a striking reason for woman's subordination to man. "Man was not made from woman" (Williams' Translation). Man was made first out of dust and the breath of God. Woman was made from Adam's rib (Gen. 2:21). She was made to "be a help meet for man." In verse 10 we have a different motive for woman's wearing the veil—"because of the angels." If she wears the veil because she is subordinate to man, there is a still stronger reason—her subordination to angels, who were regarded as of a higher rank than man. This reference to angels also shows the apostle's conception that angels are acquainted with the activities of men and women, and interested and emotionally affected by them. Of course, human activities do not affect the angels volitionally—have no influence on their actions.

Verses 12, 13. At the same time, man and woman cannot be independent of each other. If woman was made from man, man is born of woman. Without a woman you cannot have a human child. Nor could it happen without a man.

Verses 13, 14. He appeals to nature to show the fitness of these distinctions—the woman's head to be covered, either with long hair or with a veil, and the man's to be uncovered with either. It is proper to have it so. Why? Largely because custom in those days made it so. It does not affect people in the twentieth century that way. "If a woman has long hair it is her pride." She used to glory in her long hair, but nowadays she glories in her permanents and other hair fashions.

CLIQUES IN THE CHURCH; DISORDERS IN THE OBSERVANCE
OF THE LORD'S SUPPER (11:17-22)

17 But as I am giving you these instructions I cannot approve of
your meetings, because they do not turn out for the better but for
the worse. 18 For, in the first place, when you meet as a congregation, I hear that there are cliques among you, and I partly believe it. 19 Yes, indeed, there must be parties among you, in order
that people of approved fitness may come to the front among you.
20 So when you hold your meetings, it is not to eat the Lord's
Supper, 21 for each of you is in a rush to eat his own supper, and
one goes hungry while another gets drunk. 22 It is not that you
have no houses to eat and drink in, is it? Or, are you trying to
show your contempt for the church of God and trying to humiliate those who have no houses? What shall I say to you? Shall I
praise you? No, I cannot praise you for this.

Key words and phrases. Verse 17. Paul is perfectly candid. He
cannot command people when they deserve criticism. He has commended the Corinthians for following his instructions in some
things, but they have failed as to the observance of the Lord's
Supper. So he now proceeds to criticize them.

Verses 18, 19. He makes a distinction between schisms and
divisions (the word from which we get our word heresy). They
have schisms, cliques. The first word means splits in the church;
the latter, differences in opinion which may not lead to a schism or
split in the church. We must have differences of opinion, in order
to determine "the approved." This latter sentence may be ironical,
Paul merely giving their view of the matter, to justify their divisions. And yet heresies in a church or community do make it
possible for the genuine, orthodox believers to be easily recognized.

Verses 20, 21. One clique of worldly, perhaps the better-to-do
class in the church, make a social feasting occasion out of the Lord's
Supper. "One is hungry, another is drunk." Some eat all the bread,
others drink all the wine (which evidently is intoxicating, fer-
mented). That means that still others are left without any bread
to eat or any wine to drink that they might properly observe the
Memorial Supper. What a travesty at such a holy ceremony sym-
bolizing the most solemn event in the life of our Saviour!

Verse 22 gives expression to Paul's critical amazement at such conduct by those claiming to be Christians. The Greek negatives express the thought that they must have houses of their own in which to eat and drink; so their conduct must be understood to express their contempt for the church of God and their humiliation of the poor who do not have the social and economic standing to engage with them in such disorderly conduct in observing the sacred supper.

ORIGIN AND SIGNIFICANCE OF THE SUPPER; THE RIGHT WAY TO OBSERVE IT (11:23-34)

²³ For the account that I passed on to you I myself received from the Lord Himself, that the Lord Jesus on the night He was betrayed took a loaf of bread ²⁴ and gave thanks for it and broke it and said, "This is my body which is given for you. Do this in memory of me." ²⁵ In the same way, after supper, He took the cup of wine, saying, "This cup is the new covenant ratified by my blood. Whenever you drink it, do so in memory of me."
²⁶ For every time you eat this bread and drink from this cup, you proclaim the Lord's death until He comes again. ²⁷ So whoever eats the bread and drinks from the Lord's cup in an unworthy way is guilty of sinning against the Lord's body and blood. ²⁸ A man, then, must examine himself, and only in this way should he eat any of the bread and drink from the cup. ²⁹ For whoever eats and drinks without recognizing His body, eats and drinks a judgment on himself. ³⁰ This is why many of you are sick and feeble, and a considerable number are falling asleep. ³¹ But if we properly saw ourselves, we would not bring down upon us this judgment. ³² But since we do bring down upon us this judgment, we are being disciplined by the Lord, so that finally we may not be condemned along with the world. ³³ So, my brothers, when you meet to eat, wait for one another. ³⁴ If anyone is hungry, let him eat at home, so that your meetings may not bring on you judgment. I will settle in detail the matters that remain, when I come.

Key words and phrases. Verse 23. Paul received the significance of the Supper from the Lord Himself. Jesus instituted it the night on which He was betrayed. There are two views as to how Paul received his knowledge of its origin. First, very conservative interpreters think it was by a special revelation to Paul. The second view is that he received the account of it from eyewitnesses; perhaps, from Peter, during the fifteen days he spent with Peter in Jerusalem (Gal. 1:18). The latter is likely what he meant. The Lord is economical in His use of miracles. Not needed here.

Verses 24-26. The significance of the Memorial Supper. The loaf broken represents the body of Christ broken for us. The wine represents His blood shed (that is, His death) to atone for our sin (John 1:29; I John 2:2). The Greek says, "This [bread] is my body; . . . this cup is the new covenant in my blood." The Roman Catholics interpret it literally, claiming that a miracle changes the bread into the body of Christ, and the wine into His blood, before the worshipers partake of them, or as they partake. This is the doctrine of transubstantiation. The Lutherans hold to consubstantiation, which they interpret to mean that the bread *and* body, the wine *and* blood are partaken of *together*. Baptists and most Protestant scholars interpret it as a strong figure of speech, meaning that the bread *symbolizes* the body of Christ, the wine *symbolizes* the blood of Christ shed for us, the shedding of His blood signifying His death and suffering for us.

Verses 25 and 26 express the purpose of observing the Supper: "To proclaim His death until He comes again." So the fundamental doctrines of Christ's work for saving the world are visually proclaimed in the observing of the Supper.

Verses 27-34. His instruction as to how to observe the Supper. The phrase, "in an unworthy manner," is explained in the phrase, "without recognizing the body [of Christ]." That is, if we do not see and recognize the truth that the bread represents the body and the wine represents the blood of Christ as a sacrifice for our sins, we eat "in an unworthy manner." By faith we realize this great truth and thus appropriate to ourselves the saving significance of Christ's death and sufferings. "Judgment upon himself" (v. 29) means punishment here, not necessarily the condemnation of the soul to perdition. Verse 30 uses figurative expressions to describe what this judgment is—spiritual weakness, illness, and drowsiness. Sleep is sometimes used to mean death (Mark 5:39; I Thess. 4:13). Verse 31 shows how if we properly judged ourselves, it would not be necessary for the Lord to judge us; that is, punish us here. Verse 32 expresses the thought that our present punishment for our errors and misconduct means that the Lord is chastening us, so that we may not be condemned at last with the world. Verses 33 and 34 state two special orders to the church at Corinth: if one is hungry, let him eat at home before coming to the meeting for the Supper. Let the church members wait for one another. The early comers must not go ahead and partake before all are present.

Chapter XII

The Church a Unit, As the Human Body Is, with a Variety of Spiritual Gifts

Spiritual Insight Essential; the Variety of Spiritual Gifts Emphasized (12:1-13)

About spiritual gifts, brothers, I do not want you to be without information. ² You know that when you were heathen you were in the habit of going off, wherever you might be led, after idols that could not speak. ³ So I want to inform you that no one speaking under the power of the Spirit of God can say, "Jesus is accursed!" and no one except one under the power of the Holy Spirit can really say, "Jesus is Lord!"

⁴ There are varieties of gifts, but the Spirit is the same in all; ⁵ there are varieties of service, but the Lord to be served is the same; ⁶ there are varieties of activities, but it is the same God who does all things by putting energy in us all. ⁷ To each of us is given a special spiritual illumination for the common good. ⁸ To one, wise speech is given by the Spirit; to another, by the same Spirit, intelligent speech is given; ⁹ to another, through union with the same Spirit, faith, to another, by one and the same Spirit, power to cure the sick; ¹⁰ to another, power for working wonders; to another, prophetic insight; to another, the power to discriminate between the true Spirit and false spirits; to another, various ecstatic utterances; and to another, the power to explain them. ¹¹ But the one and same Spirit accomplishes all these achievements, and apportions power to each of us as He chooses.

¹² For just as the human body is one and yet has many parts, and all the parts of the body, many as they are, constitute but one body, so it is with Christ. ¹³ For by one Spirit all of us, Jews or Greeks, slaves or free men, have been baptized into one body, and were all imbued with one Spirit.

Key words and phrases. Verses 1-3. Christianity is positively spiritual, while idolatry was indifferent to spiritual process. As Gentiles the Corinthians were led by various motives to worship an idol. But now as Christians the motive must be purely spiritual. Jesus cannot be flippantly cursed as a demon, which Paul says an idol is. On the other hand, if we claim Him as our Lord, it must be done under the power of the Holy Spirit. It is only by the Spirit's power that we can make Jesus our real Lord.

Verses 4-7. The various gifts are manifestations of the same Holy Spirit. It is the same Lord (Jesus) that they serve. It is the same God the Father who energizes all the gifts in all of us. So there is a beautiful unity in the variety. The Greek word for gifts, *charismata,* denotes grace gifts; that is, these special gifts originate in God's grace, or unmerited favor, which here means God's unmerited favor. This is the root meaning of this beautiful word *(charis).* It is the divine source of salvation (Eph. 2:8), and also the source of all spiritual gifts bestowed upon Christians.

Verses 8-11. The various spiritual gifts enumerated: wise speech, the word of wisdom (A.S.V.); that is, some are gifted as spiritual advisers for those who need advice for practical living; then comes speech, imparting knowledge; that is, aptness to teach (I Tim. 3:2); then follows faith—the spiritual gift that makes one optimistic, believing all things (I Cor. 13:7). Then power to cure the sick (Williams). This is the miraculous power given to one who prays in faith (James 5:15). The author of this volume has seen men of such strong faith that their prayer brought healing to the sick. Again, the power for working wonders. This is another form of miraculous power. Another receives prophetic insight, spiritual acumen to grasp the hidden truths of God's Word. Another is gifted with power to discriminate between the true Spirit of God and false spirits. Another has the gift of ecstatic utterance (speaking with tongues). This last gift is later minimized by Paul (14:9-19). Last of all is named the power to explain these ecstatic utterances, which do not edify others unless explained.

In verse 11 Paul tells us that "one and the same Spirit accomplishes all these achievements." That is, the spiritual gifts originate with God—with His unmerited favor, but the Holy Spirit is the divine Agent who operates them after bestowing them upon Christians.

Verses 12-13. There is a beautiful unity in this spiritual variety. Christians are all baptized into one Body. Though they may be Jews or Greeks, slaves or freemen, they are all made to drink of one Spirit. So we are one.

With the Human Body He Illustrates These Truths (12:14-26)

14 For the body does not consist of one part but of many. 15 If the foot says, "Since I am not a hand, I am not a part of the body," that does not make it any less a part of the body. If the ear says, "Since I am not an eye, I am not a part of the body," that does not make it any less a part of the body. 17 If all the body were an eye, how could we hear? If all the body were an ear, how could we smell? 18 But as it now is, God has placed the parts, every one of them, in the body just as He wanted them to be. 19 If they were all one part, how could it be a body? 20 But as it now is, there are many parts, but one body. 21 The eye cannot say to the hand, "I do not need you," or the hand to the feet, "I do not need you." 22 No, on the contrary, even those parts of the body that seem to be most delicate are indispensable, 23 and the parts of it we deem devoid of honor we dress with special honor, and our ill-shaped parts receive more careful attention, 24 while our well-shaped parts do not want for anything. Yes, God has perfectly adjusted the body, giving great honor to its apparently inferior parts, 25 so that there is no disharmony in the body, but all the parts have a common care for one another. 26 If one part suffers, all the parts suffer with it. If one part receives an honor, all the parts can share its joy.

Key words and phrases. Verses 14-17. "One body, many members." The human body enjoys a multiplicity of members and organs but rejoices in being a harmonious unit. Paul sees in a healthy human body a striking picture of a divinely built, Spirit-filled, smoothly operated Church. It should be like a healthy human body, strong, beautiful, and efficient for all the work it has to do. One of the minor members of it should not feel, because he is not a major member, a pastor, teacher, deacon, that he is not important in the work of the Church.

Verses 18-21. God is the Author of both the human body and
the Church. He made the body and perfectly adjusted the hundreds
of minor parts so that, if healthy, they function in harmony for
the greatest efficiency. Just as the auto builder has ingeniously devised and adjusted the two to three thousand parts in a commodious,
comfortable automobile, so that these parts work together for rapid
movement and smooth riding, so God devised a real automobile—
a self-moving machine—when He made a human body and put
within it an immortal soul to make it go. "God arranged the organs
in the body, each one of them, as He chose" (v. 18).

Verses 22-26. Even the smallest, most inconspicuous parts of
the body are essential for the proper performance of the body.
Example: invisible brains, blood vessels, intestines, kidneys, blad-
der, sex organs. Without all of these organs there could be no
proper functioning of the body. So it is in the Church. Weak and
inconspicuous members are important.

Verse 26. The unity of the human body makes it possible, even
inevitable, that whatever happens to one part affects all other parts.
The stomach suffers with indigestion, all the body is affected. If
the liver fails to function as it should, the whole body suffers the
ill consequences. So if one member of the church sins a grievous
sin, the whole church suffers.

A Few Notable Functionaries in the Church (12:27-31)

27 So you are Christ's body, and individually parts of it. 28 And
God has placed people in the church, first as apostles, second as
prophets, third as teachers, then wonder-workers; then people
with power to cure the sick, helpers, managers, ecstatic speakers.
29 Not all are apostles, are they? Not all are prophets, are they?
Not all are teachers, are they? Not all are wonder-workers, are
they? 30 Not all are people with power to cure the sick, are they?
Not all are ecstatic speakers, are they? Not all can explain ecstatic
speaking, can they? 31 But you must earnestly continue to cultivate your higher spiritual gifts.

Key words and phrases. Verse 27. The Church is an organic
body—"the body of Christ." Paul is using the human body to
represent the Church, which is the Body of Christ. The counterpart

of this doctrine is developed by Paul in his letters to the Ephesians and Colossians. (See Eph. 1:22-23, etc., Col. 1:18f, etc.) This is the Church as "an institution." (See B. H. Carroll, *Interpretation of the English Bible.)* It is reproduced in each New Testament local church.

Verses 28-30. Eight functionaries in the church are named: apostles, prophets, teachers, workers of miracles, healers, helpers, administrators, divers kinds of tongues (A.S.V.). Notice, he did not mention pastors or bishops or deacons (as in Phil. 1:1 and I Tim. 3). In this list he is emphasizing functions rather than officials. In this letter he is discussing the variety of functions in the church. Pastors and deacons are probably in his mind when he says administrators (28).

There is no hint here as to grades of position in officials, as pope, archbishop, bishop, prelates, etc. It is quality of service not rank of officials he is discussing in this letter. This is positively asserted in 31 in the phrase, "the higher gifts." "Higher" emphasizes the quality of the gifts, not the rank of the possessors of the gifts.

Chapter XIII

A POEM ON LOVE; THE CLIMAX OF SPIRITUAL GIFTS, THE QUEEN
OF SPIRITUAL GRACES; LOVE ESSENTIAL IN THE HIGHER
GIFTS AND GRACES (13:1-3)

If I could speak the languages of men, of angels too,
And have no love,
I am only a rattling pan or a clashing cymbal.
² If I should have the gift of prophecy,
And know all secret truths, and knowledge in its every form
And have such perfect faith that I could move mountains,
But have no love, I am nothing.
³ If I should dole out everything I have for charity,
And give my body up to torture in mere boasting pride,
But have no love, I get from it no good at all.
⁴ Love is so patient and so kind;
Love never boils with jealousy;
It never boasts, is never puffed with pride;

5 It does not act with rudeness, or insist upon its rights;
It never gets provoked, it never harbors evil thoughts;
6 Is never glad when wrong is done,
But always glad when truth prevails;
7 It bears up under anything,
It exercises faith in everything,
It keeps up hope in everything,
It gives us power to endure in anything.

LOVE LASTS FOREVER (8-13)

8 Love never fails;
If there are prophecies, they will be set aside;
If now exist ecstatic speakings, they will cease;
If there is knowledge, it will soon be set aside;
9 For what we know is incomplete and what we prophesy is incomplete.
10 But when perfection comes, what is imperfect will be set aside.
11 When I was a child, I talked like a child,
I thought like a child, I reasoned like a child.
When I became a man, I laid aside my childish ways.
12 For now we see a dim reflection in a looking-glass
But then we shall see face to face;
Now what I know is imperfect,
But then I shall know perfectly, as God knows me.
13 And so these three, faith, hope, and love endure,
But the greatest of them is love.

Key words and phrases. Verse 1. The word for love, *agape* in Greek, expresses the highest form of love, not simply an emotional outburst of feeling toward another, as mother, child, brother, sister; but an intelligent, voluntary placement of deep affection on another. (See Thayer, *Lexicon, sub voce;* Bishop Trench, *Synonyms of the New Testament.*) It is this type of love that Paul is describing in this chapter. The chapter is a real poem of high rank, dealing with the sublimest theme of mortal mind and heart. It covers every phase of the theme—its quality, its achievements, its superiority over every other grace or gift of man or woman, its supremacy in the heavenly triplet of Christian graces, and its eternal persistence as the wholesome, holy atmosphere of Heaven itself.

It is so essential in character and conduct that one may possess all the other graces and gifts from God, but without love in the heart crowning these graces and using these gifts, he is nothing. He may exist, but he does not live; he may appear to be somebody, but he is nothing. All his achievements are no profit to him.

Verse 2. "Prophecy . . . all mysteries . . . all knowledge," to Paul covering the whole field of possible human comprehension. A man might know all that Socrates, Plato, Aristotle, Kant, Hegel, Jonathan Edwards, and Albert Einstein have known; but if he had no love in his heart he would be nothing. Nothing so far as his relation to God and eternal destiny are concerned. Could language be more forceful? A hyperbole which pays the highest price to love ever paid by human brain and heart, even under the spell of inspiration. Greater than all John, the apostle of love, said about love.

Verse 3 explained under the word *nothing* in verse 1.

Verses 4-7. The negative achievements of love: never jealous (literally, boiling over emotionally), or boastful; never haughty or rude or selfish; never gets provoked or harbors evil thoughts; never rejoicing at wrong but always rejoicing over truth and right. Positive achievements: always patient, full of faith and hope, and enduring whatever befalls it.

Verse 8. Three highly prized gifts only transitory: prophecy passes when fulfilled; ecstatic speaking will cease; knowledge incomplete is ever giving place to fuller knowledge. In science and education this fact is every day illustrated before our eyes.

Verses 9 and 10. Our knowledge on earth is imperfect; in Heaven it will be perfect.

Verses 11 and 12. Our earthly state compared to that of a child *(nepios,* a very small child) with childish thoughts and ways, our heavenly state to that of a full-grown man, with perfect vision and knowledge. Here we see things and persons in a mirror dimly; in eternity, face to face. This last phrase means there will be no mist on our eyes and no veil over real things and truths and persons. Nothing between us and reality. What a glorious prospect!

Verse 13. Love is eternal like faith and hope, but love surpasses both in quality, power, and achievements; surpasses faith, the first step in salvation; continued medium for appropriating

spiritual power and blessings, surpassing hope; the guiding star
in prosperity and adversity. While faith and hope still persist in
Heaven, their mission will be minimized while love will furnish the
very atmosphere of Heaven and be the eternal link that binds
together the heavenly hosts and makes Heaven beautiful and
glorious and happy forever.

What makes love superior to all other gifts and graces? First,
it is unselfish—pure love is altruistic, crucifying self. Second, it
gives quality to all other gifts and graces (1-3). Third, it is the
most potent motive to sacrifice and service. Its wonder-works are
numerous and beneficent.

Brother minister, find some good illustrations and preach three
expository sermons on chapter 13. One on 1-3: Love Gives Quality
to All Other Gifts and Graces. Another on 4:7: Love's Superior
Achievements. The third on 8:13: Love Makes Heaven Perfect.

Chapter XIV

PROPHECY SUPERIOR TO ECSTATIC SPEAKING; GOOD ORDER IN
USING THESE GIFTS; WOMAN'S PLACE IN PUBLIC
WORSHIP; PAUL'S AUTHORITY
PROPHECY SUPERIOR TO ECSTATIC SPEAKING (14:1-12)

Keep on pursuing love, but still keep cultivating your spiritual
gifts, especially the gift of prophesying. ² For whoever speaks in
ecstasy is speaking not to men but to God, for no one understands him, and yet by the Spirit he is speaking secret truths.
³ But whoever prophesies is speaking to men for their upbuilding,
encouragement, and comfort. ⁴ Whoever speaks in ecstasy builds
up himself alone, but whoever prophesies builds up the congregation too. ⁵ I would like for all of you to speak in ecstasy, but I
would rather that you prophesy. The man who speaks with real
prophetic insight renders greater service than the man who speaks
in ecstasy, unless the latter explains it, so the congregation may
receive an uplift.

⁶ But as it now is, brothers, if I do come back to you speaking
in ecstasy, what good shall I do you, unless my speech contains a
revelation or new knowledge or a prophetic message or some
teaching? ⁷ Even inanimate things, like the flute or the harp, may
give out sounds, but if there is no difference in the notes, how

can the tune that is played on the flute or the harp be told?
[8] Again, indeed, if the bugle does not sound a call distinct and
clear, who will prepare for battle? [9] So it is with you; unless in
your ecstatic speaking you speak a message that is clearly intelligible, how can the message spoken by you be understood? You
might just as well be talking to the air! [10] There are, supposedly,
ever so many languages in the world, and not one is without its
own meaning. [11] So if I do not know the meaning of the language, I should be a foreigner to the man who speaks it, and he
would be a foreigner to me. [12] So, as you are ambitious for spiritual gifts, you must keep trying to excel for the upbuilding of the
church.

Key words and phrases. Verse 1. While you should all make
love your chief aim, still keep cultivating whatever spiritual gift
you have; but especially the gift of prophesying, which is a spiritual insight into some new spiritual truth and then expressing it in
speech intelligible to others.

Verses 2-5. Prophecy is superior to ecstatic speaking, because
it builds up others and edifies the church, while ecstatic speaking
benefits only the speaker. He may speak mysteries, that is, new
truths once unknown, just as the prophet does; but if the hearer
does not understand them, he is not edified. A new truth properly
spoken (by the prophet) has three results on others: upbuilding,
encouragement, and consolation. "Whoever prophesies is greater
than he who utters ecstatic speech—unless the latter explains his
speech."

Verse 6. He uses himself as an illustration of one speaking in
ecstasy: Even if I should come to you speaking in ecstasy, how
could I benefit you unless I brought you a revelation [a new truth]
or knowledge [old truth] or prophecy [practically the same as
revelation above] or some teaching [unfolding an old truth].

Verses 7-9. He illustrates with the flute and harp and bugle.
No one can know what is played on the flute or harp, unless it
gives forth distinct notes. No one would prepare for battle, unless
the bugle sounds a clear, intelligible call to soldiers. So no one
responds to ecstatic speaking unless it is explained. Otherwise,
the ecstatic speaker is "speaking into the air."

Verses 10-12. Another illustration: There are many languages, but one must know a specific language when another is speaking to him, or else he would be a foreigner to the speaker and the speaker a foreigner to him. If one is speaking French to another who does not know French, each would be a foreigner to the other. So are the hearers and the ecstatic speaker. In verse 12 he exhorts to "excel in building up the church."

PRAYING AND SINGING WITH THE MIND AS WELL AS WITH THE SPIRIT (14:13-19)

13 Therefore, the man who speaks in ecstasy must pray for power to explain what he says. 14 For if I pray in ecstasy, my spirit is praying, but my mind produces no results for anyone. 15 What is my conclusion then? I will certainly pray with my spirit, but I will pray with my mind in action too. I will certainly sing with my spirit, but I will sing with my mind in action too. For if you give thanks with your spirit only, 16 how is the man who occupies the place of the illiterate to say "Amen" to your thanksgiving? For he does not know what you are saying. 17 You are, indeed, doing right to give thanks, but your neighbor is not built up. 18 Thank God, I speak in ecstasy more than any of you. 19 But in the public congregation I would rather speak five words with my mind in action, in order to instruct the people too, than ten thousand words in ecstasy.

Key words and phrases. Verse 13. He who speaks in ecstasy ought to pray for power to interpret what he says, so the hearers may be built up by knowing what he says.

Verses 14-15. Praying and singing should be intelligent and intelligible. It is better to pray and sing so that others may understand the spiritual message of our prayers and songs and thus be built up. Paul puts no premium on ignorance in worship, but magnifies knowledge. What rebuke to sensational, emotional worship without intelligence! Frenzied, dervish worship is not of the highest order, as Paul sees it.

Verses 16-17. Public worship ought to be edifying to all, not just to a few who are ecstatic but not intelligible in praying and singing.

Verses 18-19. Paul could speak in ecstasy, in fact, excelled any of them who gloried in ecstatic speaking. But he prefers to speak "five words with his mind" (intelligible to all) than "ten thousand in ecstasy," but not intelligible to others.

PUBLIC WORSHIP SHOULD BE CONDUCTED INTELLIGENTLY AND IN AN ORDERLY WAY (14:20-25)

[20] Brothers, stop being children in intelligence, but as to evil keep on being babies; and yet as to intelligence be men of maturity. [21] In the law it is written, "By men of foreign languages and by the lips of foreigners I will speak to this people, but even then they will not listen to me, says the Lord." [22] So speaking in ecstasy is meant as a sign, not for believers but for unbelievers, while prophecy is meant, not for unbelievers but for believers. [23] Hence, if the whole church has met and everybody speaks in ecstasy, and illiterate people or unbelievers come in, will they not say that you are crazy? [24] But if everybody prophesies, and some unbeliever or illiterate man comes in, he is convinced of his sins by all, he is closely questioned by all, [25] the secrets of his heart are laid bare, he falls upon his face and worships God, declaring, "God is really among you."

Key words and phrases. Verse 20. The exhortation not to be children in thinking means not to play small children (from one to three years old); that is, do not be thoughtless. As to evil, play babies *(nepiazo)*. These are only a few weeks or months old. That is, be little babies and do not think evil (about these gifts of prophesying and speaking in ecstasy).

Verse 21. He quotes Isaiah 28:11 to show that Israel would not listen to God's commands, if He spoke in foreign languages.

Verses 22-25. So if an outsider or unbeliever enters a congregation and finds everybody speaking in ecstasy, he would think that they are all crazy (gone mad). But if he comes in and finds them prophesying, he would be convinced of his sins, he is closely questioned by all, and falls upon his face and worships God, because he is convinced that "God is among them" and speaking through them to him. So prophecy is far superior to speaking in ecstasy, because it brings good results to others.

PROPHETS AND ECSTATIC SPEAKERS SHOULD OBSERVE ORDER IN
THEIR PUBLIC SPEAKING; WOMEN SHOULD KEEP SILENCE
IN THE CHURCHES (14:26-36)

26 Then what is our conclusion, brothers? When you meet together, everybody has a song, something to teach, a revelation, an
ecstatic utterance, or an explanation of one. It must all be for the
upbuilding of all. 27 If anybody speaks in ecstasy, there must be
only two, or three at most, and let one speak at a time, and someone explain what he says. 28 But if there is no one to explain it,
let him keep quiet in the church and speak to himself and God
alone. 29 Let two or three prophets speak, and the rest consider
carefully what is said; 30 and if anything is revealed to another
who is seated, let the speaker stop. 31 For in this way you can all,
one after another, speak your prophetic message, so that all may
learn and be encouraged, 32 for the spirits of prophets yield to
prophets; 33 for God is not a God of disorder but of order, as it
is in all the churches of God's people.

34 Women must keep quiet in the churches, for no permission is
given them to speak. On the contrary, they must take a subordinate place, just as the law says. 35 If they want to find out about
something, they should ask their own husbands at home, for it is
disgraceful for a woman to speak in church. 36 Did the message of
God begin with you Corinthians? Or, are you the only people it
has reached?

Key words and phrases. Verse 26. Every Corinthian church
member seemed to want to be conspicuous in the public worship.
Paul reminds them that the edification of all is the aim of these
public meetings, not the exhibition of their special gifts. One wished
to exhibit his gift of singing (a hymn), another, a teaching (in-
culcating an old truth or doctrine), another, a revelation (uttering
a new truth), another an ecstatic utterance or explaining one.

Verses 27-28. The ecstatic speakers must observe good order
in their speaking—only one at a time, and never more than three
at a session. Not one should speak if there is no one to explain
the utterances.

Verses 29-33. Prophets should observe the same rule. Only
two or three should speak at one session of the church. True

prophets yield to one another, for God is the God of order and peace, not of confusion.

Verses 34-36. The women in Corinth were taking to themselves too much publicity and authority over men in the church. This seems to be the occasion of this strange teaching of Paul, "The women should keep silence in the churches." Paul himself interprets his position on this issue in I Timothy 2:12: "I permit no woman to teach or to have authority over men." Mere teaching in the spirit of humility and subordination is not prohibited by Paul. Likely, he would not object to modern women preaching in the churches, if they maintain the spirit of subordination. Example given, Mrs. J. M. Dawson, Washington, D.C., who has been for several years an eloquent and effective speaker in Baptist churches, conventions, and conferences.

PAUL HAS THE AUTHORITY OF THE LORD FOR GIVING THESE COMMANDS (14:37-40)

[37] If anyone claims to have the prophetic spirit, or any other spiritual gift, let him recognize that what I now am writing is the Lord's command. [38] If anyone ignores it, let him ignore it. [39] So, my brothers, cultivate the gift of prophetic speaking, but stop preventing others from speaking in ecstasy. [40] Everything must always be done in a proper and orderly way.

Key words and phrases. To be a prophet is to have the highest spiritual gift. So he exhorts them to desire earnestly to prophesy. To prophesy means to utter spiritual truths for edifying the people of God. Yet he warns them to be charitable toward those speaking in ecstasy, and so maintain decency and order. Especially does he claim to have the authority of the Lord's command to give these orders. He is inspired by the Lord's Spirit.

Chapter XV

THE RESURRECTION OF JESUS A FIRST PRINCIPLE IN THE GOOD NEWS; A FACT PROVED BY APPEARANCES TO COMPETENT EYE-WITNESSES; GREEKS ANSWERED FOR DENYING THE RESURRECTION; CHRIST'S RESURRECTION GUARAN-TEES THE BELIEVER'S RESURRECTION

The Resurrection of Jesus a First Principle in the Good News; Proved by the Appearances (15:1-19)

Now let me remind you, brothers, of the essence of the good news which I proclaimed to you, which you accepted, on which you now are standing, ² and through which you are to be saved, unless your faith at first was spurious. ³ For I passed on to you, among the primary principles of the good news, what I had received, that Christ died for our sins, in accordance with the Scriptures, ⁴ that He was buried, that on the third day He was raised from the dead, in accordance with the Scriptures, ⁵ and that He was seen by Cephas, and then by the Twelve. ⁶ After that, at one time He was seen by more than five hundred brothers, most of whom are still living, though some of them have fallen asleep. ⁷ Then He was seen by James, then by all the apostles, and finally ⁸ He was seen by me, too, as though I were born out of time. ⁹ For I belong to the lowest rank of the apostles, and am not fit to bear the title, apostle, because I once persecuted the church of God. ¹⁰ But by God's unmerited favor I have become what I am, and His unmerited favor shown to me was not bestowed for nothing; for I have toiled more extensively than any of them, and yet it was not I but God's unmerited favor working with me. ¹¹ But whether it was I or they, this is what we preach, and this is what you believed.

¹² Now if we preach that Christ has been raised from the dead, how is it that some of you are saying that there is no such thing as a resurrection of the dead? ¹³ If there is no resurrection of the dead, then Christ has not been raised, ¹⁴ and if Christ was not raised, the message which we preach has nothing in it; there is nothing in our faith either, ¹⁵ and we are found guilty of lying about God, for we have testified that He raised Christ, whom He did not raise, if indeed the dead are never raised. ¹⁶ For if the dead are never raised, Christ has not been raised; ¹⁷ and if Christ has not been raised, your faith is a mere delusion; you are still under the penalty of your sins. ¹⁸ Yes, even those who have fallen asleep, though in union with Christ, have perished. ¹⁹ If for this life only we Christians have set our hopes on Christ, we are the most pitiable people in the world.

Key words and phrases. Verses 1-2. The good news Paul preached to the Corinthians. Good news is the meaning of the word gospel, as translated in the Authorized and American Standard

Versions. The Greek *euaggelion* is glad tidings, good news. Here it is the good news of God's love and His gift of Christ to be our Saviour, His death, resurrection, ascension, and promise to save all who believe in Him. The Corinthians received it; strong term, welcomed it wholeheartedly; now they are standing on it or in it; by means of it they are to be saved from condemnation and at last to be saved completely at the parousia and the resurrection; *"if* you hold it fast." To Paul faith that is genuine is of such quality as to persevere to the end.

Verses 3-4. Here he names two of the first principles of the good news: the death and resurrection of Christ. Christ died for our sins and was raised from the dead for our justification (Rom. 4:25). The resurrection of Christ was necessary to make the atonement effective (v. 17). Both events were in accordance with the Scriptures. See Psalm 2 and Isaiah 53 for Scriptures on His death in prophecy. For His predicted resurrection see Psalm 16:10, 11.

Verses 5-7. Proofs of His resurrection are the appearances to the early disciples. He mentions four instances: first to Cephas, or Peter [the former, his Aramaic name, the latter, the Greek for it. Both mean stone or rock, a name for a character of strength (John 1:42)]. Paul heard Peter tell about this vision of the Lord while in Jerusalem those fifteen days (Gal. 1:18f). Then to the Twelve; that is, to all the original apostles (except Judas). Then to "more than five hundred brethren." This may be at the ascension from the Mount of Olives (Luke 24:50, 51). Or, it may be an occasion prior to this. Then He appeared again "to all the apostles," and "to James." This is the half-brother of Jesus, who did not accept Jesus as the Messiah till after He rose from the dead. Paul believes these are all credible witnesses whose testimony ought to convince anyone that the resurrection of Jesus is a historical fact. He adds that "most of the five hundred are still living," so that if the readers wished to interview the witnesses, they could.

Verses 8-11. His own testimony climaxes that of the early disciples and the Twelve. "Last of all" to me, as one born out of time, the "least" and lowest of the apostles, not even worthy to bear the name of an apostle, "because I once persecuted the church of God."

Though he knew that God had forgiven him for this wicked persecution of saints, it still lingered in his consciousness, and perhaps in his conscience. He could not forget it. But he glorifies the grace of God for forgiving him and saving him and making him an apostle who had "toiled more extensively" than all the other apostles. He is here ascribing all his missionary successes to the unmerited favor of God. He holds that his conversion and extensive works are evidence for the resurrection of Christ.

Verse 12. The non-Christian Greeks did not believe in the resurrection of the body. This is the conclusion of rationalism. Plato, the philosopher, held that the body is a hindrance, not a help, to man's highest attainments. So he thought that when man gets rid of his body at death he could rise higher and faster, unfettered, unshackled; a resurrection of the body would be a curse and not a blessing. Many Greeks in Corinth shared this view. Christ's resurrection is a rebuttal of this view of Plato.

Verses 13, 14. The tragic results if Christ was not raised: The good news we preach is an empty thing. It is a vessel with no bottom, and so cannot hold the truth. It takes the resurrection of Christ to make the gospel a sound vessel holding all essential truths. The second consequence is "your faith is an empty thing." There is nothing to our faith if we have no living Christ for it to rest on.

Verses 15, 16. Another awful consequence is a personal reflection on Paul and every preacher of the good news—we are false witnesses concerning God. We have asserted that He has raised Christ, but if He has not raised Him, we have misrepresented God. We are false witnesses. For if there is no resurrection at all, then Christ has not been raised. This shows Paul the keen logician, appealing to Greeks noted for their keen minds and perfect logic.

Verses 17-19. Other tragic consequences if Christ has not been raised: Your faith is a mere delusion. You were too credulous, believing in something that is incredible. He uses both Greek adjectives for vain, *kenos*, empty, *mataios*, futile. But the more tragic consequence is that you are still under the penalty of your sins. If Christ has not been raised, no atonement has been made, no salvation is possible. Tragic! Unbelievable that God should leave His sinful creatures in such a dilemma! Argumentum ad absurdum. This chapter is one of the finest pieces of logic in the New Testament.

Another conclusion to which logic drives us: Those who died in faith in Christ have perished. Christ is no Saviour if not raised from the dead. Only a living Christ can save sinners. Therefore, Christians who have hope only for this life are the most pitiable people in the world—deluded, deceived!

THE RISEN CHRIST TRIUMPHANT OVER THE LAST ENEMY (15:20-28)

20 But in reality Christ has been raised from the dead, the first to be raised of those who have fallen asleep. 21 For since it was through a man that death resulted, it was also through a man that the resurrection of the dead resulted. 22 For just as all men die by virtue of their descent from Adam, so all such as are in union with Christ will be made to live again. 23 But each in his proper order; Christ first, then at His coming those who belong to Christ. 24 After that comes the end, when He will turn the kingdom over to God His Father, when He will put an end to all other government, authority, and power; 25 for He must continue to be king until He puts all His enemies under His feet. 26 Death is the last enemy to be stopped, 27 for He has put everything in subjection under His feet. But when He says that everything has been put in subjection to Him, He Himself is evidently excepted who put it all in subjection to Him. 28 And when everything has been put in subjection to Him, then the Son Himself will also become subject to Him who has put everything in subjection to Him, so that God may be everything to everybody.

Key words and phrases. Verse 20. "Firstfruits" referring to the ancient Jewish custom of bringing in a sheaf at the beginning of harvest to show the prospects of the coming yield. So Christ in His resurrection becomes the first sheaf of the final resurrection harvest. *Sleep* is again euphemistically used for death.

Verses 21, 22. Paul's doctrine of the parallel headship of Adam and Christ, Adam the head of the natural race, Christ the Head of spiritual humanity. All the natural race die because connected by the law of heredity with Adam as its head. All in union with Christ by faith will be made alive at the resurrection. This last assertion does not mean universal salvation, as claimed by the Universalists. Christ is the Head of the spiritual race, not of the whole race. Notice, it is by Christ as a Man that He became Head of the spiritual race (v. 21). Paul is careful to place Christ as the Head of the spiritual race. "Each in his proper order" (Williams). First Christ, "the firstfruits," then at the parousia "those who belong to Christ."

Verses 24-27. "Then comes the end"—end of the present age. The parousia ushers in another age, in the economy of God (Jewish point of view). Christ will then be completing His reign of grace on earth. He will have destroyed, or put an end to, all other government, authority, and power (including Satan's) and at that time He will smash the authority and power of death, "the last enemy." In verses 54 and 55 he sings the paean of praise over death. "O death, where is your victory?" In verse 27 "God", which refers to the Father, has given Christ the victory. The Father is supreme by virtue of His relation in the Trinity.

Verse 28. Therefore, at the parousia Christ hands over to the Father the kingdom, that the Father "may be everything to everybody"; that is, supreme in all things. This does not mean that Christ has lost His deity. He will still be equal to the Father in personality and character. But He has completed the establishment of the messianic kingdom, which is now absorbed in the general kingdom of God.

Our Sense of Immortality and of Future Rewards for Doing and Suffering for the Right as Evidence for the Resurrection of the Righteous (15:29-34)

29 Otherwise, what do those people mean who submit to being baptized on behalf of their dead? If the dead are never raised at all, why do they submit to being baptized on their behalf? 30 Why too do we ourselves run such risks every hour? 31 I protest, by the boasting which I do about you, my brothers, through our union with Christ Jesus our Lord, I myself run the risk of dying every single day! 32 If from merely human motives I have fought wild

beasts here in Ephesus, what profit will it be to me? If the dead are never raised at all, "Let us eat and drink, for tomorrow we shall be dead." [33] Do not be so misled: "Evil companionships corrupt good character." [34] Sober up, as is right, and stop sinning, for some of you—to your shame I say so—are without any true knowledge of God.

Key words and phrases. Verse 29. Some Christians of that time at Corinth submitted to baptism on behalf of or due to the influence of their dead loved ones. Paul argues that this means they believe in the resurrection of the dead, or otherwise this would be silly. These people have a sense of immortality, which prompts them thus to try to help their dead loved ones. Of course, Paul does not endorse substitutional baptism. He is simply arguing from the fact that they believe in it, and so they must believe in a future life.

Verses 30-32a. He here argues from his own bitter contests with opponents, fighting with wild beasts at Ephesus and suffering other perils, so that his very life is risked every day. Perhaps, the beasts he fought with at Ephesus were fierce men, not literally beasts. See II Timothy 4:17, where he refers to Nero as a lion. His argument is that it is useless to endure suffering and risks of life itself, if there is no resurrection and so no rewards for such sacrificial suffering.

Verses 32b-34. The Epicureans, who said "Let us eat and drink, for tomorrow we die," have an argument in their favor, if "the dead are not raised." If we are not to be punished or rewarded for the deeds done in the body, we might as well revel and "have a good time." Of course, Paul is not turning Epicurean; he is merely arguing that there is not the same motivation to high living and sacrificial serving if there is no resurrection of the dead.

In verse 33 he quotes another ancient Greek maxim: "Evil companionships corrupt good character." The Corinthians are being corrupted by associating too intimately with their Greek moralists and philosophers. So he exhorts them "to sober up and sin no more." He is addressing some who have no true knowledge of God. They have no adequate conception of God's power and love, or else they could believe in His power to raise the dead.

THE NATURE OF THE RESURRECTION BODY (15:35-57)

35 But someone will ask, "How can the dead rise? With what kind of body do they come back?" 36 You foolish man! the seed that you sow never comes to life unless it dies first; 37 and what you sow does not have the body that it is going to have, but is a naked grain, of wheat (it may be) or something else; 38 but God gives it just the body He sees fit, even each kind of seed its own body. 39 Every kind of flesh is different. One kind belongs to men, another to cattle, another to birds, another to fish. 40 There are heavenly bodies, and earthly bodies, but the splendor of the heavenly bodies is of one kind, and the splendor of the earthly bodies is of another. 41 One kind of splendor belongs to the sun, another to the moon, and another to the stars; yes, one star differs from another in splendor. 42 It is just like this with the resurrection of the dead. 43 The body is sown in decay, it is raised without decay; it is sown in humiliation, it is raised in splendor; it is sown in weakness, it is raised in strength; 44 it is sown a physical body, it is raised a spiritual body. If there is a physical body, there is a spiritual body too. 45 This is the way the Scripture puts it too, "The first man Adam became a living creature." The last Adam has become a life-giving Spirit. 46 But it is not the spiritual that comes first; it is the physical, and then the spiritual. 47 The first man was made of the dust of the earth; the second man is from heaven. 48 Now those who are made of the dust are just like him who was first made of dust, and those who are heavenly are like Him who is from heaven, 49 and as we reflected the likeness of him who was made of dust, let us also reflect the likeness of the Man from heaven.

50 But this I tell you, brothers: Our physical bodies cannot take part in the kingdom of God; what is decaying will never take part in what is immortal. 51 Let me tell you a secret. We shall not all fall asleep, but we shall all be changed, 52 in a moment, in the twinkling of an eye, at the sound of the last trumpet. For the trumpet will sound, and the dead will be raised with bodies not subject to decay, and we shall be changed. 53 For this decaying part of us must put on the body that can never decay, and this part once capable of dying must put on the body that can never die. 54 And when this part once capable of dying puts on the body that can never die, then what the Scripture says will come true, "Death has been swallowed up in victory. 55 O Death, where is

your victory now? O Death, where is your sting?" ⁵⁶ Now sin gives death its sting, and the law gives sin its power. ⁵⁷ But thank God! He gives us victory through our Lord Jesus Christ.

Key words and phrases. Verses 35-38. He illustrates with a grain of wheat (or some other) how the dead body can be raised. The wheat grain has to die before it lives in a wheatfield. God gives it a body through the powers of nature, chemicals in the soil, sunshine, and moisture. Different grains reproduce different bodies but bodies like the original seed—"as God has chosen", fixed it in nature. To Paul God is the Author of nature and the Giver of all its forces. He makes the corn and wheat sprout and grow and produce the harvests to feed men and women and children, and the animals.

Verses 39-41. Paul has observed the varieties of bodies in nature—of men and animals and birds and fish; different heavenly bodies and also earthly bodies. What he observes is the difference characterizing all of them. Sun and moon and stars are different in their splendor, just as the earthly bodies differ in class and species. He reminds the objector of these differences to use it in describing resurrection bodies.

Verses 42-46. The present body is physical and psychical; that is, man in the present state is a soul with a material body. After the resurrection he is a spirit with a body adapted to his spirit. Just as he now has a body with a nature suitable for the use of his soul (psuche), so in the resurrection he will be given a body perfectly adapted to this spiritual nature. Then he has lost his physical body altogether, and so God gives him another body for appropriate use of the spirit in a spiritual world.

Notice the characteristics of these two bodies, physical and spiritual. The physical body is subject to decay, perishable; lowly or in humiliation; weak. The spiritual body is incapable of decaying; splendid, glorious, powerful, clothed in lasting strength. What does Paul mean by calling it a spiritual body? Is it the material of which the body is made, or is it the delicate nature and the high functions of the body to suit the spirit in its eternal sphere? Undoubtedly it is the latter, for he calls the heavenly body psychical and not physical. Our bodies here are made of matter;

that is, are physical. But Paul shuns the word *phusikon* and uses *psuchikon* (psychical). That is, he sees the body we now have as one fitted to serve our souls *(psuchai)* in this present sphere, and the body we are to get at the resurrection as one fitted to serve our spirits in the lofty eternal sphere of spirits.

Observe further that this spiritual body is to be "like Christ's glorious body" (Phil. 3:20). His body was a spiritual body, the firstfruits of all that shall sleep in death. "We shall also bear the image of the man from heaven [Christ]." We shall have spiritual bodies like His, resplendent in glory.

Then Paul emphasizes the fact that this spiritual body comes after the physical. We must bear the image of the man of dust, and then at the resurrection take on the glorious image of the Man from Heaven.

Verses 47-50. He follows up the parallel between Adam and Christ: we shall bear the image of the man of dust (Adam) while on earth; after the resurrection we shall bear the glorious image of the Christ in His glory. Flesh and blood in verse 50 means a physical body, which cannot possibly share in the glorious kingdom of glory. It is so because the earthly body is decaying, and the kingdom of glory is imperishable. The nature of our bodies must be compatible with the glorious nature of the kingdom.

Verses 51-57. He climaxes the discussion with his thought that Christ's parousia (second coming) is imminent and may take place in that generation. "We shall not all sleep." That is, we shall not all be dead when He comes. But these physical bodies shall be changed. That is, God will miraculously transform the bodies of the living Christians at that time, so that they will have spiritual bodies, just as those raised from the dead (see I Thess. 4:16, 17). In verses 54 and 55 he repeats the paean of victory. He sees sin to be the sting that death contains; that is, sin makes death sting the soul and cause the pain and anguish accompanying it. The law gives sin its power to sting. But Paul rises to the lofty peaks of praise when he shouts, "Thanks be to God, who gives us the victory through our Lord Jesus Christ!" Christ conquered the grave and came out of it the third morning. In that victory He made possible the victory of all Christians over death and the grave. Adam lost paradise for mankind; Christ regained it, not merely by His conquest of Satan in the wilderness and elsewhere (emphasized by Milton, *Paradise Regained*), but by His triumphant resurrection from the dead.

FINAL APPEAL TO CHRISTIANS FOR ABUNDANT LIVING (58)

[58] So, my dear brothers, continue to be firm, incapable of being moved, always letting the cup run over in the work of the Lord, because you know that your labor in the service of the Lord is never thrown away.

"My dear brothers." How tenderly he feels toward these wavering, wandering disciples of the Lord in Corinth! "Continue to be firm." Present imperative has this meaning. Let life overflow in your labors for Christ. This is the meaning of *perisseuo* (abound). Your labor for the Lord is never lost (not in vain). In the resurrection we shall be rewarded in accordance with the deeds done in the body (I Cor. 3:13-15).

SERMON OUTLINE FROM CHAPTER XV
THE RESURRECTION MAKES A PUNGENT APPEAL FOR
THE OVERFLOWING LIFE (58)

"Therefore." For this reason—Christ has been raised; Christians will be raised.

I. The Resurrection of Christ Proof of the Immortality of Man
   1. The soul the center and kernel of man's personality
   2. So if a human body (that of Jesus) can be raised, the soul must be immortal; the greater must be greater than the lesser
   3. Therefore, the soul must be immortal. So accepted by Socrates, Plato, Aristotle, many modern scientists and philosophers. Taken for granted in Old Testament and New Testament.

II. The Resurrection of Christ Guarantees the Resurrection of Christians (15:22)
   1. Believers in union with Christ, He is the Head, they His Body (12:27)
   2. Raised with Him spiritually (Eph. 2:5), so will be raised with Him at last (15:48, 49)

III. The Glorious Future of Our Dual Personality a High Motive
     to Our Living the Overflowing Life. "Therefore"
     1. The risen Christ presages for us victory over death (54, 55)
     2. The risen Christ guarantees rich rewards to Christians for
        all service rendered (Rom. 2:10-11; I Cor. 3:14, 15)
     3. No good work for Christ ever lost (15:58c—"our labor
        not in vain.")

Chapter XVI

INSTRUCTIONS CONCERNING THE OFFERING FOR THE FAMINE-
STRICKEN IN JUDEA: PRINCIPLES OF GIVING; TIMOTHY,
APOLLOS, AND PAUL TO VISIT CORINTH; PAUL CHEERED
    BY THE REPORT OF STEPHANAS' COMMITTEE;
                      GREETINGS

INSTRUCTIONS CONCERNING THE OFFERING WITH PRINCIPLES
                 FOR GIVING (16:1-4)

Now about the contribution for God's people. I want you to do
as I directed the churches of Galatia to do. ² On the first day of
every week each of you must put aside and store up something
in proportion as he is prospered, so that no contributions need
be made when I come back. ³ When I get there, I will send on,
with credentials, the persons whom you approve, to carry your
gift of charity to Jerusalem. ⁴ And if it seems proper for me to
go too, they shall go as my companions.

Agabus, the Christian prophet, showed that there was to be a
severe famine over all the Roman world, which came in the reign of
Claudius (about A.D. 44 or 45). It was very severe in Judea, and so
Paul led all the churches he had founded to contribute an offering
for these suffering Jewish Christians. He is urging the Church at
Corinth to join the churches of Galatia and Macedonia in making
a love offering for these suffering Christians.

Key words and phrases. Verses 1-4 give us the principles to
guide the givers in making their contributions. "On the first day
of the week." This is the Lord's day, our modern Sunday. This
had become the day of worship, even in the latter half of the first
century. See Acts 20:7, where Paul met the saints at Troas on the
first day of the week, as they had met for worship. It was the day

on which Jesus was raised from the dead, and in honor of Him worship was changed from the Sabbath (seventh day) to the first day of the week.

This is the day on which Paul exhorts them to lay aside their contributions for the suffering; so giving is a part of worship. We worship in giving, as well as in singing and praying. This is a basic principle in church offerings. They are a part, a sacred part, of the worship. "As he may prosper." "In proportion as he is prospered." Our material success or receipts during the week are to determine how much we give. He does not stipulate the tithe. But the tithe ought to be the minimum of Christian offerings (so Dr. B. H. Carroll, *Interpretation of the English Bible*). The third principle is that everyone should have a part in the contributions. Even those who can give only two mites. These offerings should be handled by accredited persons (3). "I will send on with letters the persons whom you approve." Letters constitute credentials carried by persons approved for handling these offerings. If they demand it, Paul himself would accompany these accredited persons. How careful Paul is in handling the Lord's money!

EXPLANATION OF PAUL'S DELAY; TIMOTHY ON THE WAY
(16:5-12)

5 I will come to see you after I pass through Macedonia—for I am to pass through Macedonia—6 and I shall likely stay over with you some time, or may be, spend the winter with you, so that you may help me on to whatever points I may visit. 7 I do not want to see you right now in a mere stop-over visit, for later I hope to spend some time with you, if the Lord permits me. 8 But I shall stay on in Ephesus until the time for Harvest Feast. 9 For I have an opportunity here that is great and calls for work, and it has many opponents.

10 If Timothy gets there, see that he is at ease among you, for he is devotedly doing the work of the Lord, just as I am. 11 So no one must slight him at all. But send him on with your good-by, that he may come back to me, for I am expecting him with the other brothers.

12 As for our brother Apollos, I have earnestly urged him to go to see you, but he is not at all inclined to come just now; yet he is coming when he has a good opportunity.

Key words and phrases. Verses 5-12. Timothy, Apollos, and Paul to visit Corinth. Paul is to stay on in Ephesus (where he writes) till Pentecost. He specially commends Timothy as one who is doing the work of the Lord as he was. High compliment (see Gal. 2:19-23). Apollos is coming later, not at once. Paul defers his visit, so that he can spend the winter, possibly, with them. Paul defers his visit especially because he now has a great opportunity in Ephesus to meet many opponents of the good news and probably win a tremendous triumph for the Master (v. 9).

BE EXEMPLARY CHRISTIANS; FOLLOW AND HONOR YOUR LEADERS
(16:13-24)

¹³ Be always on your guard; stand firm in your faith; keep on acting like men; continue to grow in strength; ¹⁴ let everything be done in love.

¹⁵ Now I beg you, brothers—you know that the family of Stephanas were the first converts in Greece, and that they have devoted themselves to the service of God's people—¹⁶ I beg you to put yourselves under leaders like these, and under anyone who co-operates with you, and labors hard. ¹⁷ And I am glad that Stephanas, Fortunatus, and Achaicus have come to see me, because they have supplied what you lacked. ¹⁸ Yes, they have cheered my spirit, and yours too. You must deeply appreciate such men.

¹⁹ The churches of Asia wish to be remembered to you. Aquila and Prisca, with the church that meets at their house, send you their cordial Christian greetings. ²⁰ All the brothers wish to be remembered to you. Greet one another with a sacred kiss.

²¹ The final greeting is mine—Paul's—with my own hand. ²² A curse upon anyone who does not love the Lord! Our Lord is coming. ²³ The spiritual blessings of the Lord Jesus be with you! ²⁴ My love be with you all in union with Christ Jesus.

Key words and phrases. Verses 13, 14. Five important exhortations: "Always be on your guard." Practice watchfulness; never be caught off guard. "Stand firm in your faith." Believe something; believe the truth and stand by it at all hazards. "Keep on acting like men." That is, be courageous in resisting evils and championing the truth. "Continue to grow in strength." That is, increase your spiritual strength through the indwelling Spirit (see Acts

1:8). The imperative means continue to grow, etc. "Let everything be done in love." He makes love the climax of Christian character (see chap. 13).

These exhortations in verses 13, 14 may be used as the outline for a series of sermons on Christian character.

Verses 15-18. Stephanus and his household were the first converts in Corinth (in all Greece). Paul was proud of them as his converts. Stephanus and Fortunatus and Achaicus visited Paul in Ephesus, bringing with them a letter from the church in Corinth asking Paul questions about marriage, women in the church, eating foods offered to idols, spiritual gifts and their grading (7-14). They were leaders in the church, so Paul exhorts them "to put themselves under leaders such as these." They are leaders who "co-operate and labor hard." This committee from the church "refreshed Paul's spirit" by giving him all the news concerning the church, likely emphasizing all the excellences.

Verses 19, 20. "The churches of Asia send greetings." Notice, there is no national church; it is "the churches of Asia." "The church that meets in their house," means that a congregation of Christians regularly worshiped at the house of Aquila and Prisca, who graciously threw upon their doors to the saints to meet at their house. The sacred kiss given on meeting and parting was common in those days; showing the finest spirit of brotherhood.

Verses 21-24. Paul sends greeting with his own hand. He likely dictated the letter—the body of it—to his amanuensis. Here he in closing the letter pronounces a curse upon anyone who does not love the Lord. This means Jesus Christ, who is Lord to Paul. Christ is so divine and so lovable in all the attributes of Deity that no one is excusable for not loving the Lord Jesus. Then he exclaims in Aramaic (his native tongue), *Maranatha*, meaning, "The Lord is coming," or it may also mean, "Our Lord, come." The verb may be indicative or imperative.

"The grace of the Lord" means "the spiritual blessing of the Lord be with you."

"My love be with you all." Paul has a big heart, and it is extended for these wayward converts of his in Corinth.

The Second Letter to the Corinthians

INTRODUCTION

1. *The Writer.* Generally thought to be Paul the apostle. However, there are still some followers of Baur, the German radical critic, who deny the Pauline authorship.

2. *The Occasion.* Paul was closing his third missionary journey at Ephesus. He had just learned that his opponents in Corinth, were bitterly attacking his message, his authority as an apostle, his speech and his style, and even his character. Titus, a Greek himself and a skillful diplomat, was sent to put the church in order, but he stayed so long that it put Paul in suspense; so he went down to Troas and crossed to Macedonia, and there they met—probably in Philippi. Titus reported Paul's triumph in Corinth. The majority had endorsed his message and vindicated him, but a minority, the Judaizing party, were unwilling to surrender, and theatened to continue their fight on him. So Paul wrote this letter, probably in A.D. 57.

3. *The Purpose.* To express his joy over the victory of his message—the good news—in the capital of Greece; to show his deep interest in the church there, even his abiding love for them; to defend his authority as an apostle and his personal character; if possible, to silence his critics; also to urge the church to complete the contribution to the famine-stricken Christians in Judea.

The letter is intensely personal and emotional, in the style of the ordinary common Greek *(Koine)*, but marked with a boundless variety of stylistic characteristics, because of the many topics discussed. His logic is keen, cutting and convincing. It is one of his four greatest letters.

Chapter I

HE GREETS THEM; GIVES THANKS TO GOD FOR COMFORTING HIM IN HIS DISTRESS AND ALMOST DESPAIR (1:1-11)

Paul, by the will of God and apostle of Christ Jesus, and Timothy our brother, to the church of God that is at Corinth, with all God's people all over Greece: ² spiritual blessing and peace to you from God our Father and the Lord Jesus Christ.

³ Blessed be the God and Father of our Lord Jesus Christ, the merciful Father and the all-comforting God, ⁴ who comforts me in every sorrow I have, so that I can comfort people who are in sorrow with the comfort with which I am comforted by God. ⁵ For just as my sufferings for Christ are running over the cup, so through Christ my comfort is running over too. ⁶ If I am in sorrow, it is on behalf of your comfort and salvation; if I am comforted, it is for the comfort that is experienced by you in your patient endurance of the same sort of sufferings that I am enduring too. ⁷ My hope for you is well founded; because I know that just as you, brothers, are sharers of my sufferings, so you will be sharers of my comfort too. ⁸ For I do not want you to be uninformed about the sorrow that I suffered in Asia, because I was so crushed beyond any power to endure that I was in dire despair of life itself. ⁹ Yes, I felt within my very self the sentence of death, to keep me from depending on myself instead of God who raises the dead. ¹⁰ He saved me from a death so horrible, and He will save me again! He it is on whom I have set my hope that He will still save me, ¹¹ because you are helping me by your prayers for me, so that thanks to God will be given by many on my behalf for God's gracious gift to me in answer to the prayers of many.

Key words and phrases. Verses 1-2. The greeting is the same as in the first letter; except he substitutes Timothy here for Sosthenes; he limits the extent of the greeting to "saints in Greece," while it was "saints in every place" in the first letter. The key words and phrases are the same. See I Corinthians 1:1, 2 for explanations.

Verses 3-7. In this short paragraph he refers to the excruciating sorrow that he experienced at Troas while waiting for Titus to return from Corinth with news as to how the church had settled the problem of his apostolic authority. He uses the editorial *we*. But there is no question but that he is referring specifically to his own sorrow for the issue in Corinth. However, it is a general truth. He feels and knows that the comfort with which God comforted him in the coming of Titus with good news of his triumph in Corinth, is given him by God Himself in order that he may be able to com-

fort others who are in similar crushing sorrows. This is a great
truth established by the experience of thousands of Christians. So
our sufferings are converted into sympathy for others whom we
can comfort more successfully than if we had never suffered. The
pastor who has never lost a child and felt the comforting grace
of God in his heart cannot sympathize fully with a mother who
has just lost a son or daughter. Job who had lost all his children
could fully sympathize with a neighbor in similar circumstances.
In verse 5, "sufferings of Christ" means Paul's sufferings *for* Christ,
not Christ's sufferings for Paul, so suggests the context (see Williams' Translation).

Verse 7 expresses Paul's unshakable hope that the Corinthians
will share his comforts, when they know how he suffered for them,
just as they now share his sufferings. The majority in the church
had been in agony over the issue involved in these problems. But
Paul feels that as soon as they read this letter, they will share his
comfort and be happy.

Verses 8-11. These are the darkest days of Paul's missionary experiences. He is waiting at Troas and crossing to Macedonia, awaiting the coming of Titus from Corinth with news of the issue in
Corinth. He was experiencing heart-rending suspense as to how
the church would settle the question of his apostolic authority and
the genuineness of his gospel message. But God delivered him (the
meaning of *save* in this connection) from the deadly suspense. It
was so biting that he felt the sentence of death within him. But
Paul feels that his "suffering" and God's deliverance from it had
a divine purpose, in order that he might be led to rely on God
instead of self, and to soften his heart so that he might sympathize
with those experiencing similar sorrows. His faith is so great that
he feels that God can "raise the dead." This is faith like Abraham
had when he offered up Isaac. Paul now feels that the church
at Corinth is praying for him, since it has endorsed his message and
vindicated him.

HE AFFIRMS HIS SINCERITY IN HIS BEHAVIOR TOWARD
THE CORINTHIANS (1:12-24)

¹² For my boast is this, to which my conscience testifies, that

before the world, but especially before you, I have acted from pure motives and in sincerity before God, not depending on worldly wisdom but on God's unmerited favor. ¹³ For what I am writing you is nothing more than what you can read and understand, and I hope that you will understand it perfectly, just as some of you have come to understand me partially; ¹⁴ that is, to understand that you have grounds for boasting of me just as I have for boasting of you, on the day of our Lord Jesus.

¹⁵ It was because of this confidence that first I planned to visit you, to give you a double delight; ¹⁶ that is, to go by you on my way to Macedonia, and then to come back to you from Macedonia, and have you send me on to Judea. ¹⁷ Now I did not resort to fickleness, did I, in planning that? Or, do I make my plans in accordance with worldly notions, to have my "Yes" mean "No," if I want it so? ¹⁸ As certainly as God is to be trusted, my message to you has not been a "Yes" that might mean "No." ¹⁹ For God's Son, Christ Jesus, who was preached among you by us, Silvanus, Timothy, and me, did not become a "Yes" that might mean "No." ²⁰ But with Him it is always "Yes," for, as many as the promises of God may be, through Him they are always "Yes." This is why our "Amen" through Him is for the glory of God when spoken by us. ²¹ But it is God who makes us as well as you secure through union with Christ, and has anointed us, ²² and put His seal upon us, and given us His Spirit in our hearts as a first installment of future rewards.

²³ But upon my soul I call God to witness that it was to spare you pain that I gave up my visit to Corinth. ²⁴ Not that we are trying to lord it over your faith, but we are workers with you to promote your joy, for in your faith you are standing firm.

Key words and phrases. Verses 12-14. He is answering the charge that he works with them not sincerely but with the use of worldly wisdom. He answers that he is doing and saying all in pure motives and godly sincerity and is behaving under the sway of God's unmerited favor (grace). What he writes to them is understandable; some there do understand in part, and he hopes they will understand it perfectly. He wants them to be as proud of him as he is of them (14). If not before, when Jesus comes.

Verses 15-20. He answers the charge of being fickle. Think of it! Such a staunch and stable character to be charged with fickle-

ness! They said he would say *Yes* but mean *No*, or at a moment
change his view of the matter in hand, or the visit to be made. He
had changed his plan to visit them, which caused them to accuse
him of fickleness. He had a good reason for changing his plan. He
asserts that his message, which was "Jesus Christ, the Son of God,"
was not *Yes* and *No*, but a changeless *Yes*. It was an affirmative
message with no negations attached to it. It was Christ crucified
(I Cor. 2:2), the one foundation of faith and of the church (I Cor.
3:11), and the guarantee of believers' resurrection at last (I Cor.
15:20ff). Yes, "All the promises of God find their *Yes* in Christ.
"And so Paul can say Amen," so be it, "through Christ." No
fickleness in his preaching. It is positive preaching, the message
heading up in Christ, the Son of God.

Verses 21-22. God the Father is given the glory for his apostolic commission and equipment for it. *Anointed* refers to the
ancient custom of anointing kings and prophets when they were
inducted into office. It was an act of consecration to a specific
office and task. (See I Sam. 10:1; 16:12; etc.) God had consecrated Paul to the office and work of an apostle. More, "He has
put His seal upon me." The seal is the sign of ownership and security. God owns him and makes him secure. "He has given me
His Spirit." Not only to give him power (Acts 1:8) but to be the
first installment (Williams' Trans.) of future blessings.

Verses 23, 24. Paul takes an oath that he gave up his visit to
Corinth in order "to spare them pain." It is not "to lord it over
your faith." This means not to dictate to them what to believe and
what not to believe. He is co-operating with them for their joy. "You
stand in your faith." In spite of their shortcomings in other respects,
the Corinthians maintained their faith and stood firm in it. This
was the main ground of Paul's confidence in and hope for them.

Chapter II

HE WRITES IN TENDER LOVE FOR THEM; HE BEGS THE CHURCH
TO FORGIVE THE PENITENT OFFENDER; TELLS OF HIS
SORROW AND SUCCESS (2:1-4)

For I have definitely decided not to pay you another painful visit. ² For if I make you sad, who is there to make me glad but the very man who has been made sad by me? ³ This is the very thing I wrote you, that when I did come I might not be made sad by the very people who ought to make me glad, for I had confidence in you all that my gladness would be gladness to you all. ⁴ For out of great sorrow and distress of heart, yes, while shedding many tears, I wrote you, not to make you sad but to make you realize that my love for you continues running over.

Key words and phrases. Verses 1-4. There is little need for comments on these verses. They explain themselves. Paul's overflowing love for the readers kept him from making another painful visit to Corinth. He had written them—in a letter now lost—to forgive the penitent offender. Who was he? Possibly the incestuous man (I Cor. 5), but not very probably. And yet, if a man is penitent of his great and grievous sins, he must be forgiven by the church. Penitent means that he has forsaken those sins. Paul assures them that it was in "great sorrow and distress of heart" that he wrote this appeal to them. He was distressed over the offender himself, but especially over the character of the church. It must be kept clean and commanding the respect and confidence of outsiders.

He Begs the Church to Forgive the Penitent Offender (2:5-11)

⁵ But if anyone has made anyone sad, it is not I, but you that he has made sad, at least, some of you, not to be severe on all of you. ⁶ To a man like that, this censure by the majority has been sufficient punishment, ⁷ so you must do the opposite, freely forgive and comfort him, to keep him from being overwhelmed by his excessive sadness. ⁸ So I beg you in your love to reinstate him entirely. ⁹ For this is why I wrote you, to see if you would stand the test, to see if you would obedient in everything. ¹⁰ The man that you forgive I too forgive. For if I have forgiven him anything, it is what I have forgiven him in the very presence of Christ for your sake, ¹¹ to keep us from being worsted by Satan, for we know what his intentions are.

Key words and phrases. Verses 5-8. A penitent offender must be forgiven and reinstated by the church. Otherwise, he might be overwhelmed by excessive sorrow. He must first receive discipline

from the church, but on repenting and forsaking his sin, he must
be forgiven.

Verses 9-11. He sets forth a great principle on the independence
and authority of the local church. "The one whom you forgive, I
also forgive." The outside adviser, even an apostle, has no right
to reinstate the penitent offender. Only the church has the authority
to do that. Only they could discipline. Paul could advise, but the
church must act.

PAUL A GOD-SENT APOSTLE SPREADING THE PERFUME OF THE GOOD NEWS (2:12-17)

12 When I went to Troas to preach the good news of Christ, although I had an opportunity in the service of the Lord, 13 I had
no rest of spirit, because I did not find my brother Titus there.
So I said good-by to them and left for Macedonia. 14 But thanks
to God, for He always leads me in His triumphal train, through
union with Christ, and everywhere through me keeps spreading
the perfume of the knowledge of Him. 15 Indeed, I am the fra-
grance of Christ to God, alike for those who are being saved and
for those who are perishing; 16 to the one a deadly perfume that
leads to death, to the other a living perfume that leads to life.
17 Now who is qualified for such a task? I am, for I am not a ped-
dler of God's message, like the most of them, but like a man of
sincerity, like a man that is sent from God and living in His
presence, in union with Christ I speak His message.

Key words and phrases. Verses 12, 13. His restlessness at
Troas. He left Ephesus for Troas, hoping to find Titus there with
news from Corinth. But no Titus appeared, and the great apostle
was almost frantic. The doors opened wide for him to preach the
good news there; but his spirit was troubled, his mind was disturbed, about the issue in Corinth. No Titus! No news from them!
Had they voted to reject his message, to condemn him, and were
his eighteen months of toiling in Corinth all lost and scattered to
the winds? So he set sail for Macedonia, and probably in Philippi
he landed, and there was Titus to welcome him! And to welcome
him with good news from the church in Corinth!

Verses 14-16a and b. "Thank God!" he exclaims. "He has
delivered me." More than that, "He always leads me as a victor

in His triumphal procession." The picture of a general entering Rome in triumph. Childlike faith and praise! His great soul is relieved of bitter suspense and flooded with thanks and praise to God. Yes, through him God was spreading everywhere the perfume of the good news of the knowledge of Christ. That is so, because Paul is "the perfume of Christ to God." What a beautiful expression! It magnifies his apostolic preaching. It carries a sweet odor to all. It becomes a living perfume for those "who are being saved," but a "deadly perfume to those who are perishing." These verbs may express a general truth or continuous action. That is, continuous state of being. Likely the latter here.

Verses 16c, 17. Paul's sufficiency for such a sublime task. Not in himself, but as a God-sent apostle. So many preachers are mere peddlers of God's Word, but Paul is a man of sincerity and commissioned by God to preach the good news. The verb *kapeleuo* is used in common Greek to mean peddle cheap wares from house to house. Many of the Judaizing preachers, Paul thinks, are mere peddlers of a cheap gospel.

Chapter III

His Converts at Corinth Proof That God Called Him to Be an Apostle; the Surpassing Splendor of This Ministry

His Converts at Corinth Proof that God Called Him to Be an Apostle (3:1-6)

Am I beginning to recommend myself again? I do not, like some people, do I, need letters of recommendation to you or from you? ² You are my letter of recommendation, written on my heart, read and understood by everybody, ³ for you are always showing that you are a letter of Christ, produced by my service, written not in ink but by the Spirit of the living God, not on tablets of stone, but on human hearts.

⁴ Such is the confidence I have through Christ in the presence of God. ⁵ Not that I am myself qualified to consider anything as coming from me myself. No; my qualification comes from God, for ⁶ He has qualified even me as a minister of the new covenant, which is not a written but a spiritual covenant. For the letter kills, but the Spirit gives life.

Key words and phrases. Verses 1-3. What he has just said about being "a God-sent apostle" and being "the perfume of Christ to God," appears to be a self-recommendation. He denies that he is beginning to "recommend himself"; denies that he "needs a letter of recommendation," since they, his converts, the fruit of his apostolic labors, are "his letter of recommendation, not written in ink but by the Spirit of the living God"; not on tablets of stone, but on tablets of human hearts. What he is saying is that the Corinthian converts themselves are proof of his apostleship, bestowed upon him by God Himself. And this human document, a saved, Christian personality as a product of his apostleship is a far more logical and convincing argument and evidence for his divine commission as an apostle than any written letter on a tablet of stone (the most enduring material for writing in those days). Note how he links this letter up with Christ and the "living Spirit of God." It is a "letter from Christ," "written with or by the Spirit of the living God." This must have been a great consolation to Paul the aged to reflect that these early converts of his preaching stand out as a logical, unimpeachable evidence of the genuineness of his divine commission to preach the good news.

Verses 4-6. He hastens to assert that this sublime mission committed to him was not a success because of his own personal qualifications, but because God had made him sufficient, or had qualified him for achieving this success. This sublime mission means the ministry of a new covenant; namely, the spiritual covenant. Paul is apparently proud of his position but in reality he is as humble as a little child, giving all the glory to God, who has qualified him for such a position.

THE SURPASSING SPLENDOR OF SERVICE UNDER THE SPIRITUAL COVENANT (3:7-11)

⁷ Now if the old religious service which resulted in death, although its law was carved in letters of stone, was introduced with a splendor so great that the Israelites could not keep their eyes fixed on Moses' face because of the splendor that was fading from it, ⁸ why should not this spiritual service be attended with much greater splendor? ⁹ For if the service connected with condemna-

tion had such splendor, the service resulting in right standing with God will surely far surpass it in splendor. ¹⁰ For on account of its surpassing splendor, what was once so splendid has now no splendor at all. ¹¹ For if what passed away was introduced with splendor, with how much greater splendor must what is permanent be attended?

Key words and phrases. The key phrases are: "dispensation of death . . . dispensation of condemnation . . . dispensation of the Spirit," which is the "dispensation of righteousness [right standing with God]." With these key phrases he makes what the logicians call, an argument *a fortiori,* from the greater to the smaller; that is, if a greater thing is true, a smaller, included in the greater, must be true. So he argues that if the old service of death and condemnation was attended with brilliant splendor, the service connected with life and righteousness and the Spirit must be attended with a surpassing glory. In the last verse (11) he asserts that what is permanent must surely be attended with a splendor far surpassing the glory of that which passes away. With this argument the apostle vindicates himself in magnifying his apostolic ministry.

THE SUPREME GLORY OF THIS SPIRITUAL MINISTRY IS THE CONTINUOUS TRANSFORMATION OF THOSE BEHOLDING THE SPLENDOR OF THE LORD (3:12-18)

¹² So, as I have such a hope, I speak with the greatest boldness, ¹³ not as Moses did, who used to wear a veil over his face, to keep the Israelites from gazing at the end of what was passing away. ¹⁴ Besides, their minds were made dull; for to this day that same veil remains unlifted, whenever they read the Old Covenant; because it is only through union with Christ that it is removed. ¹⁵ Indeed, to this very day, whenever Moses is read, a veil hangs over their hearts, ¹⁶ but whenever anybody turns to the Lord, the veil is removed. ¹⁷ Now the Lord means the Spirit, and wherever the Spirit of the Lord is, there is freedom. ¹⁸ And all of us, with faces uncovered, because we continue to reflect like mirrors the splendor of the Lord, are being transformed into likeness to Him, from one degree of splendor to another, since it comes from the Lord who is the Spirit.

Key words and phrases. Verses 12-15. Paul compares himself with Moses as a speaker for God. Moses had to put a veil over his face, not because the glory of the Lord was too bright for the people to look upon, but "to keep them from seeing the end of what was passing away"—the old regime of law. But Paul claims to have no veil on his face because it is lifted through his union with Christ. This gives him conquering hope and boldness in speaking the good news of the new covenant. Because of this veil on the Israelites their minds were dulled (hardened) so that even to this day they cannot see its spiritual meaning when the Old Covenant is read. Paul does not state who hardened the minds of the Israelites. Of course, it was they themselves, permitted by God.

Verses 16-18. The Lord Christ frees us from the veil so that we can see the splendor of the Lord. So we Christians have our faces (minds) unveiled, and continue to behold the splendor of the Lord, and reflect it as in a mirror (Williams); and this vision of Christ transforms us from one degree of glory to another; produces a gradual, continuous transformation into the likeness of Christ. A beautiful illustration with the figure of the reflecting mirror. Christians are mirrors reflecting on the world about them the glory of Christ.

Chapter IV

PAUL FAITHFULLY PREACHES THE GOOD NEWS; GOD STRENGTHENS HIM TO BEAR HIS SUFFERINGS; HIS BODY TO BE RAISED AND HIS SUFFERINGS TO INCREASE HIS ETERNAL GLORY (4:1-6)

So, because I hold a place in this ministry and that because I have had God's mercy shown me, I never give up. ² On the other hand, I have renounced all underhanded, disgraceful methods; I neither practice cunning nor do I tamper with God's message, but by clear and candid statements of truth I try to commend myself to every human conscience in God's sight. ³ If the meaning of the good news I preach is covered up at all, it is so only in the case of those who are on the way to destruction. ⁴ In their case, the god of this world has blinded the eyes of the unbelievers, to keep the glorious light of the good news of Christ, who is the likeness of God, from dawning upon them. ⁵ For I am not proclaiming myself but Christ Jesus as Lord, and myself a slave of yours for Jesus' sake. [6] For God who said, "Let light shine out of darkness," is the One who has shone in my heart, to give me the light of the knowledge of God's glory reflected on the face of Christ.

Key words and phrases. Verses 1, 2. Answers the charge that he uses disgraceful, underhanded methods in preaching and also that he tampers with the Word of God. He positively asserts that he has renounced all cunning and does not tamper with the Word of God. He says he preaches by the open statement of the truth. This means no hedging or dodging, but making clear, unambiguous statements of truth, so that every man's conscience can and will recognize his sincerity and honesty in handling the Word of God. Notice, he has been put into this ministry "by the mercy of God." Mercy saved him from sin and called him to service.

Verses 3, 4. Answers the charge that his gospel is hidden so people cannot understand it. He replies that it is hidden only to those who are perishing (pres. part. of continuous action); that is, those "on the way to destruction" (Williams). Those under the influence of the Spirit can understand it and be saved, if they will repent and trust Christ as Saviour and Lord. The reason they cannot understand it is that the god of this world—Satan—has blinded their minds so that they cannot see the glory of Christ as Saviour. He inserts here a profound theological truth: "Christ is the image of God." According to Thayer, *Lexicon,* and Trench, *Synonyms,* this Greek word *(eikon)* means the exact, inner likeness of God. It goes down to the essence of His being and nature. The other word for likeness *(schema)* denotes outward likeness. Christ is the real likeness of God.

Verses 5, 6. The essence of Paul's message, "Jesus Christ as Lord." He does not preach himself, as his enemies accused him of doing. He presents himself as a servant of the Corinthians. He preaches Jesus Christ as Lord, because God had "shone in his heart to give him the light of the knowledge of God's glory reflected on the face of Christ." God Himself had revealed Christ to Him and through Christ's glorious face shining on him he had seen the glory of God. His message is divine in origin and essence. It is not self-centered.

THIS JEWEL, THE MINISTRY OF THE NEW COVENANT, KEPT IN AN EARTHEN JAR, THE APOSTLE'S SUFFERING SELF (4:7-12)

7 But I am keeping this jewel in an earthen jar, to prove that its surpassing power is God's, not mine. 8 On every side I am ever hard-pressed, but never hemmed in; always perplexed, but never to the point of despair; 9 always being persecuted, but not deserted; always getting a knockdown, but never a knockout; 10 always being exposed to death as Jesus was, so that in my body the life of Jesus may be clearly shown. 11 For all the time I continue to live I am being given up to death for Jesus' sake, so that in my mortal lower nature the life of Jesus may be clearly shown. 12 So it is death that works in me, but it is life that works in you.

Key words and phrases. Verse 7. *"Earthen vessels."* Hs is using the editorial *we* in this paragraph, as in most of this letter. The earthen vessel is his own frail body. The divine purpose of this suffering on the part of God's minister is to show that the surpassing power of the good news message is God's, not man's. When God takes a frail and suffering human like Paul and accomplishes such wonders through his instrumentality, it proves that God must be in and beneath and behind the aims and actions, the purposes and pursuits, of such a man. "God made me sufficient for these things . . . By the grace of God I am what I am." When Paganini took an old violin with only the G-string left on it and made music for the waiting audience, it showed that the music was in Paganini and not in the violin.

Verses 8-12. A category of sufferings with five items given. In 11:23-27, he gives a far more extensive list—about twenty-one items of specific sufferings he had endured for Jesus' sake, as he journeyed far and wide preaching the good news. He here mentions only five items to show that the jewel of good news is being kept in a clay jar, a frail, lowly vessel—his suffering self. In the notes on chapter 11 we shall give a more detailed discussion of Paul's sufferings for Christ's sake.

PAUL NEVER GIVES UP, ASSURED THAT HIS SUFFERINGS FOR CHRIST ON EARTH WILL INCREASE HIS GLORIES IN HEAVEN (4:13-18)

13 Now since I have the same spirit of faith as he who said in

the Scriptures, "I believed, and so I spoke," I too believe, and so I speak, [14] because I know that He who raised the Lord Jesus from the dead will raise me too in fellowship with you. [15] For everything is for your sakes, in order that His favor by multiplying the thanksgiving of many may make the cup run over to the praise of God.

[16] So I never give up; instead, although my outer nature is wasting away, my inner nature is constantly renewed from day to day. [17] For this slight and momentary sorrow continues to accumulate for me a solid and eternal glory far beyond any comparison, [18] because I do not keep my eyes on things that are seen but things that are unseen. For things that are seen are temporary, but things that are unseen are eternal.

Verses 13-15. In all this suffering Paul is stimulated to unswerving faith, which he has fed on an Old Testament text (Ps. 116:10): "I believed, and so I spoke." This is a messianic Psalm, especially referring to the resurrection of Messiah. So quoted in Acts by both Peter and Paul (Acts 2:23-28; 13:35). Paul unswervingly believed in the power of God to raise the dead, and so he felt that all his sufferings would be rewarded in the resurrection and afterward. He knows that God raised the Lord Jesus and will also raise us at last. This sublime faith on his part all results for their sake; that is, for the stimulation of the Corinthians to greater faith and hope in the future resurrection and subsequent rewards for service to Christ.

Verses 16-18. "So I do not lose heart." I do not give up hope. I just suffer on in faith and hope that God will make it all right. So out of his sufferings for Christ's sake he writes these two wonderful sentences: "For this slight momentary suffering continues to accumulate for me a solid and eternal glory far beyond any comparison, because I do not keep my eyes on things that are seen but on things that are unseen. For things that are seen are temporary, but things that are unseen are eternal." Out of his experience of being hated and persecuted, beaten and flogged and imprisoned, grew this spiritual consciousness that our sufferings here, if borne with resignation to God's will, are accumulating for us a solid and eternal glory in the hereafter. Henry Ward Beecher said of this text: "Manhood is the greatest fruit of trouble." Yes, the highest type of manhood, spiritual, is the finest fruit the tree of suffering bears. Paul reached this conclusion because he kept his eyes on the "things that are unseen." That is, on God, on Christ the Son and Saviour and Lord, on the final resurrection and the rewards of grace for service rendered; on that far-off event when "we shall see face to face, when we shall know perfectly, as God knows us." That is, it was faith and hope that empowered him to suffer on and "never lose heart."

We must notice one strong phrase, "a far more exceeding" (King James); "far beyond any comparison" (Williams). The Greek is a double phrase, "in superfluity to superfluity." Paul is straining language to the utmost to express the truth that our glory in Heaven will be all out of proportion to the slight suffering we had to endure on earth for Him. The word glory has several meanings in Scripture. Etymologically it denotes a thought, then a good thought of someone; then praise or honor; then splendor, then the summation of all God's splendor of attributes (Sanday, Romans 6:4); then the glorious presence of God, the climax of reward to the saints forever. The latter is the meaning here. Our sufferings here are piling up for us that climactic, consummate reward, enjoyment, face to face, of that splendid presence of God forever and ever.

SERMON OUTLINE

CHRISTIAN SUFFERINGS RICHLY COMPENSATED (II Cor. 4:7)

I. Various Forms of Suffering

1. Physical—diseases; Paul, "thorn in the flesh."
2. Mental or psychical—anxiety, care, suspense, disappointment. Paul had his care for the churches. Disappointed with the Galatians (1:6). Parents over children; businessmen, etc.
3. Hated and persecuted. Paul by Judaizers (4:9). Martyrs, Huss, and others.
4. Beaten and flogged. Paul several times. Martyrs.
5. Imprisoned, later beheaded, burned, etc. Peter, Paul, Justin, Polycarp, Huss, Wycliffe, and others.

II. Our Sufferings "Working for Us" — Compound Interest in Spiritual Blessings

   1. Increasing our faith. Paul an example.

   2. Making us heavenly minded (see II Cor. 4:7-18).

   3. Refining character. Invalid of twenty-five years so sweet-tempered, patient, loving, altruistic; Kohinoor diamond must be cut to be shaped and bring out perfect luster for British crown.

   4. Making us more useful to the suffering (I Cor. 13:4)

III. Copious, Incalculable Compensation in Heaven. "Glory far beyond any comparison"

   1. Our sufferings here insignificant compared with glory there.

   2. Our happiness there "solid," "weighty"; real, satisfying.

   3. Our happiness there "eternal."

   Illustration: Paul suffered only four years in prison; thirty years hated and persecuted; only a few minutes dying on block; all eternity he is shouting, singing, enjoying glory.

Chapter V

PAUL HAS ASSURANCE OF HAVING AT LAST A SPIRITUAL BODY, BUILT BY GOD'S OWN HANDS, TO BE HIS HOME FOREVER; INSPIRED BY THIS HOPE AND CHRIST'S LOVE, HE PERSUADES MEN TO BE RECONCILED TO GOD

ASSURANCE OF HAVING A SPIRITUAL BODY AT LAST (5:1-10)

For I know that if this earthly tent in which I live is taken down, I have a building in heaven which comes from God, a house not built by human hands but eternal. ² For in this one I am sighing, because I long to put on, like a robe, my heavenly body, my future home, ³ and if I do put it on, I shall not find myself to be disembodied. ⁴ For I who am still in my tent am sighing beneath my burdens, because I do not want it to be put off but to put on the other over it, so that my dying body may be absorbed in life. ⁵ Now it is God Himself who has put the finishing touches on me for this change, because He has given me the Spirit as the first installment of future bliss.

⁶ So I am always cheerful and confident, although I know that as long as I am at home in the body I am away from home and the Lord ⁷ (for here I live by what I believe and not by what I

see), [8] and yet I am cheerful and confident, but really I prefer to be away from home in the body and to be at home with the Lord. [9] So whether I am at home or away from home, it is my constant ambition to please Him. [10] For we must all appear before the judgment-bar of Christ, that each may get his pay for what he has done, whether it be good or bad.

Key words and phrases. Verses 1-3. He compares the two bodies, one to a temporary tent, the other to a building, a house from God, in Heaven. In I Corinthians he calls the earthly body psychical, made for the soul to inhabit, the resurrection body spiritual, fitted for the spirit to inhabit. Our physical body is a tent, meaning something not permanent but a temporary place to stay. This one is destructible, the heavenly body is eternal. In this body we sigh, groan, but in the heavenly house (spiritual body) we shall be with the Lord and at home; which will be eternal bliss.

Verse 4 is a riddle. Paul seems to be horrified to lose this body and have to remain disembodied awhile before he puts on the heavenly body. He longs for a resurrection body to put on over this one.

Verse 5. Again Paul ascribes all the glory to God. It is God who has put the finishing touch on me for this change. To guarantee my faith and hope as well-founded He has given me the Spirit as the first installment of bliss in my house eternal in Heaven.

Verses 6, 7. So Paul keeps on walking by faith. In the main, here it is faith in God's provision for the future care of His children; providing in a glorious resurrection a heavenly, spiritual body, not subject to decay, not destructible but eternal. This makes him cheerful and confident in the midst of all his sufferings.

Verses 8, 9. His resignation to consequences, whether they leave him in the tent body to suffer or transport him to the heavenly house to be with the Lord. His sufferings have refined his spirit into a childlike trust in His heavenly Father.

Verse 10. Christ is the Judge. In harmony with what Jesus says in Matthew 25:31-46a. All must appear before that Supreme Judge, and He will deal out justice to all—the compensation of acceptance to His own and full compensation for what each has done, whether it be good or bad.

INSPIRED BY HOPE AND CHRIST'S LOVE HE LIVES TO PERSUADE MEN TO BE RECONCILED TO GOD (5:11-21)

[11] So, since I know what the fear of God can do, I am trying to win them. My inner self is perfectly known to God, and I hope, to your consciences too. [12] I am not trying to recommend myself to you again. I am giving you ground for speaking well of me, that you may have something to say to those who are constantly prating about external privileges and not concerned about the state of the heart. [13] For if I did go crazy, it was for God's glory; and if I am keeping my head cool, it is for your good. [14] For the love of Christ continuously constrains me, because I am convinced that as One died for all, all have died, [15] and He died for all, that those who live might live no longer for themselves, but for Him who died for them and rose again.

[16] So from this moment on, I do not estimate anybody by the standard of outward appearances. Although I once did estimate Christ by this standard, I do not do so any longer. [17] For if anybody is in union with Christ, he is the work of a new creation; the old condition has passed away, a new condition has come. [18] This has all originated with God, for He through Christ has reconciled me to Himself and has given me the ministry of reconciliation. [19] For it was through Christ that God was reconciling the world to Himself instead of debiting men's offenses against them, and He has committeed to me the message of this reconciliation.

[20] So I am an envoy to represent Christ, because, it is through me that God is making His appeal. As one representing Christ I beg you, be reconciled to God. [21] He made Him who personally knew nothing of sin to be a sin-offering for us, so that through union with Him we might come into right standing with God.

Key words and phrases. Verses 11, 14, 15. "Knowing the fear of the Lord." The verb *know* does not express experimental knowledge but perceptive knowledge. He knows by observation how the fear of God moves men in general. So he is trying to win men. Trying to persuade them to trust Christ and be saved from God's wrath. In Verses 14 and 15 a higher motive moves him to be a constant winner of men to Christ—namely, Christ's love for him and for all men. He assures his readers that God knows his inner self and knows that his intense longing of soul is for lost men.

Verse 12. He denies that he is commending himself, as they had accused him of doing. He is merely trying to show them that he is a true apostle, a representative of Christ, trying to win men to Him, so as to make them proud of him as their leader and have good grounds for boasting of him to others.

Verse 15. A favorite thought form with Paul, mystic realism, is employed here. When Christ died, all died with Him; that is, all believers, by virtue of union with Him through faith. He died and rose again to a new life. So believers rise with Him to a new life (see Rom. 6:3-11). Then he appeals to Christ's love and sacrifice as a high motive for living a new life, a life "lived for Him who died for us and rose again." We belong to Him; even our bodies, and all we have—talents, treasure, time, etc. (I Cor. 6:19, 20).

Verses 16, 17. Paul estimates people, not by external appearances but by internal reality, by the condition of the heart. Even Christ he once judged by external appearances; that is, he saw in Him only a human being, until the risen Christ appeared to him. Then he estimated Him as the Son of God with power (Rom. 1:4), because he knew that He had been raised from the dead. He now sees men from this realistic point of view, not from that of external appearances *(kata sarka,* v. 16). This is the way he regards one in union with Christ, a new creation. A believer must not be estimated by his external looks but by the new heart he has which has made him a new creation of God.

Verses 18, 19. The work of renewing sinners and making them new creations is based on the work of reconciliation wrought by Christ. "All this is from God, who through Christ reconciled us to Himself." The word reconciliation is used in two senses, subjective and objective. It is likely used objectively in this text; that is, Christ in becoming a sin-offering (21) did something which brought about a way of reconciliation between God and sinful man. Christ died in the place of lost sinners, bore their penalty, so God could "be just and justify the sinner who trusted Christ" (Rom. 3:24-26). This is objective reconciliation. When the sinner actually accepts Christ as his substitute, the reconciliation is subjective; the individual subject has become reconciled to God. But what does that mean? Is it that God is angry with the sinner and now has relented and become friendly to him? Or, is it that the sinner hated God but now gives up his hate and loves God? Or, does it mean that both God and the sinner were estranged from each other, but now are on good terms, friendly? See I Corinthians 7:11, where Paul speaks of a wife who has left her husband, saying she ought to "be reconciled to her husband." What does he mean here? She ought to change her mind with a grievance against her husband and come back with the right attitude toward him. So the sinner has a wrong attitude toward God but by faith he changes it and now loves Him and trusts Him and Christ; he is now reconciled to God subjectively.

Verses 20, 21. Paul is an envoy, or an ambassador for Christ, to persuade men to be reconciled to God. It may be used literally, so that *we* means all Christians. In a true sense all Christians are envoys to represent Christ before men. Verse 21 contains a basic theological principle, one of the fundamental doctrines of the plan of salvation. Christ, who personally knew no sin, God made to be a sin-offering for us. The word sin, *hamartia,* is so used in the Septuagint. Paul is familiar with his Septuagint Bible, and this is probably the sense in which he uses the word here. Of course, God could not literally make His innocent, sinless Son *sin.* But He is the sin-offering for the lost world, and this sacrifice of Himself as a sin-offering is the basis of reconciliation of man with God. In no other way could God "be just and the justifier of him who believes in Jesus," except by His Son becoming the sin-offering for the lost world. Righteousness in verse 21, as an antithesis to sin-offering, must not be translated literally; but as right standing with God.

Sermon Outline from Chapter 5

The Sinless Christ the Sinner's Substitute (5:21)

I. The Sinless Christ
  1. In His pre-existence, God (John 1:1)—so sinless
  2. In the incarnation became flesh—"in the likeness of sinful flesh" (Rom. 8:3)
  3. Sinful mother (as a descendant of Adam) "Immaculate conception" (so Catholics). Exegetes differ.

4. Tempted but never sinned (Heb. 2:18); "Who knew no sin." He knew sin by observation but not by experience. (a) Neither in thought, (b) or word, (c) or act. His life sinless. Even Pilate conceded, "I find no fault at all in Him." Renan, French critic, calls it "The most beautful life, that will never be surpassed, but not sinless."

II. The Sinner's substitute—"Made Him to Be Sin"—"Sin-offering"
1. Treated as a sinner—so by scribes, Pharisees, Sadducees
2. Arrested and tried as a sinner. How much He must have suffered in this role! As a cultured, pure woman would among cursing, cruel criminals.
3. Died as a sinner; in the sinner's place—bore his penalty, a "sin-offering." Even the Father forsook Him as our Substitute. (See Isa. 53:4-6; I Peter 2:24)
4. His death secured reconciliation between God and man (5:18, 19)

III. Purpose: Sinners to Be Saved, Made "the Righteousness of God"
1. Into right standing with God—justified, treated as righteous
2. Become children of God (Rom. 8:14-16; Gal. 4:4, 5)
3. Becoming sanctified, with perfect righteousness of God
4. Heirs of God, joint-heirs with Christ (Rom. 8:17)

Chapter VI

As Christ's Envoy Pleading with Them; Gives His Credentials; Pours Out His Affection (6:1-13)

As God's fellow-worker I beg you too not to accept God's favor and throw it away. [2] For He says:
"At a welcome time I have listened to you,
And on a day of salvation I have helped you."
Right now the time of welcome is here; right now it is the day of salvation. [3] To keep my ministry from being found fault with, I am trying not to put a single hindrance in anybody's way. [4] On the contrary, I am trying in everything to prove to people that I am a true servant of God: by my tremendous endurance in sorrows, distresses, difficulties; in floggings, imprisonments, riots,

labors, sleepless nights, and hunger; ⁶ through my personal purity, my knowledge, my patience, my kindness; through the Holy Spirit, my genuine love, ⁷ my message of truth, and the power of God; with the weapons of right-doing in my right hand and my left; ⁸ in honor or dishonor, in slander or praise; considered a deceiver and yet true, ⁹ obscure and yet well-known, on the point of dying and yet I go on living, punished and yet not put to death, ¹⁰ sad but always glad, poor but making many people rich, penniless but really possessing everything.

¹¹ O Corinthians, my tongue is telling you everything; my heart is stretched with love for you. ¹² You are not squeezed into a tiny corner in my heart, but you are in your own affections. ¹³ To pay me back, I tell you, my children, you too must stretch your hearts with love for me.

Key words and phrases. Verses 1, 2. Warns them not to play with God's favors and blessings. He quotes Isaiah 49:8 to show them that God has given them a "day of salvation; a day for help-ing them." Paul makes the application; it is "right now" He wants to save and help. Salvation is used in the sense of progressive un-folding of the inner spiritual life, as in Philippians 2:12, 13. This type of salvation we must work out, or work down to the finishing point. God is ready to help by working in the believer (Phil. 2:13). So Paul is warning them to lay hold of God's help and work down to the finishing point their salvation.

Verses 3-10. Another list of his sufferings as a servant of God, which he presents as his credentials to prove his divine apostolic ministry. In 3-8a he lists physical and mental sufferings along with moral and spiritual graces (purity, patience, kindness, genuine love). Along with these he lists "the Holy Spirit . . . the power of God." He is not boasting of his personal excellence and superiority. He gives God and the Holy Spirit special glory for keeping him and using him as a true servant of God. In 8-10 he pours forth another list of antitheses (see II Cor. 4:8-10). He is rich in anti-theses. This sentence (4-10) is one of finest sentences in all litera-ture on one's defense; a grand period comparable to the finest in Cicero.

Why should Paul three times in this letter (again in 11:23-27) undertake to defend himself? Not only his message and apostolic authority, but also his moral and spiritual character were being impugned. It is because some in Corinth had attacked his character, and this was stinging in his innocent heart. He answers by listing the opposite virtues and graces. He lists his sufferings and achievements as evidence of God's favor and so of God's having appointed him an apostle and preacher of the Word. We must notice how clear of egotism he is in all these lists. He claims nothing for himself but traces all his graces and virtues and successes to God.

Verses 11-13. A revelation of Paul's big heart! He loves these wayward Corinthian Christians. So he is opening up his mouth and telling them all he feels for them. Love must express itself; sometimes in words as well as in actions. He tells them that his heart is stretched; its walls are pushed back so there can be a large place for the Corinthians to occupy. How graphic! Then in pathos he appeals to them to return his love; they must push back the walls of their hearts with a greater love for him. The pathos is felt in the address, "my children." They are his spiritual children, his converts to Christ (Acts 18:8).

He Warns against Intimate Relations with Unbelievers (6:14-7:1)

14 Stop forming intimate and inconsistent relations with unbelievers. What partnership can right-doing have with law-breaking, or how can light participate with darkness? 15 What harmony exists between Christ and Belial, or what is common between a believer and an unbeliever? 16 And what agreement can a temple of God make with idols? For we are the temple of the living God, just as God said:

"I will live in them and walk in them,
And I will be their God and they will be my people."
17 Therefore:
" 'Come out of company with them,
And separate from them,' the Lord has said,
'And stop touching what is unclean;
Then I will welcome you,
18 I will be a Father to you,
And you will be sons and daughters of mine,'
The Lord Almighty said."
7:1 So, since we have such promises as these, dearly beloved, let

us cleanse ourselves from everything that defiles our bodies and spirits, and in reverence to God carry on our consecration to completeness.

Key words and phrases. Verse 14a. "Be not unequally yoked together with unbelievers" (A.V.). "Stop forming intimate and inconsistent relations with unbelievers" (Williams). The present imperative with negative means *stop.* They were practicing what he warns them against—"mismating with unbelievers . . . forming intimate and inconsistent relations with unbelievers." Likely the social relations which they were forming were "intimate," and so marriage may be included. Believers must stop intermarrying with unbelievers; and other intimate social relations must be avoided as inconsistent. This idea is suggested by the pronoun *heteron,* another which is different. In this case the opposite, as light and darkness, etc.

Verses 14b-16a. A string of questions expecting the answer *No* or *None.* There can be no harmony or agreement between light and darkness, a believer and an unbeliever, Christ and Belial (from Hebrew word, meaning "worthlessness," so a worthless idol), the temple of God and an idol. Hence, the warning, stop forming such relations, marriage and other intimate social ties, which are absolutely inconsistent and irrational.

Verses 16b-18. He first quotes a passage from Leviticus and Ezekiel telling us that God's people are the temple of God. This furnishes the basis of his warning. "For" we are God's temple. Then he draws his conclusion, "Therefore, come out from them [the unbelievers]." He is not asking Christians to separate from Christians.

The first verse of chapter 7 belongs to this paragraph. It gives the conclusion in Paul's words. Since God has made such promises as to dwell with us as His temple, and be a Father to us and own us as His sons and daughters, we should "cleanse ourselves from everything that defiles our bodies and souls," and complete our consecration by living lives separate from the world of darkness and unbelievers and idolatry, and all in reverence to God, who is holy and demands from us devotion to clean living.

Chapter VII

CONTINUES TO TELL OF HIS LOVE FOR THE CORINTHIANS; TITUS REPORTS TRUE REPENTANCE AT CORINTH; PAUL'S HOPE REALIZED; HIS CUP OF JOY RUNS OVER

CONTINUES TO TELL OF HIS LOVE FOR THEM (7:2-4)

² Make room for me in your hearts. I have not wronged or harmed or taken advantage of a single one of you. ³ I do not mean this for your condemnation, because, as I have said before, you have such a place in my heart that I would live with you or die with you. ⁴ I have the greatest confidence in you; I speak most highly of you. I am fully comforted; in the face of all my sorrow my cup is running over with joy.

Key words and phrases. Verse 2. He assures them again that he is not guilty of any of the things of which he is charged by a few—wronging them or taking advantage of a single person.

Verse 3. He has repeatedly told them they are in his heart; that is, he loves them so devotedly that he would die or live with them, whatever might happen.

Verse 4. In the midst of all his sorrows and afflictions "his joy is overflowing." This is the meaning of the Greek verb *perisseuo.* A favorite term of his.

IN MACEDONIA GOD COMFORTS HIM WITH THE GOOD REPORT BY TITUS THAT HIS FORMER LETTER CAUSED THEM GRIEF THAT LED TO REPENTANCE (7:5-12)

⁵ For even after I had gotten to Macedonia, my frail, human nature could find no relief; I was crushed with sorrow at every turn—fightings without and fears within. ⁶ But God, who comforts the downhearted, comforted me by the coming of Titus, ⁷ and not only by his coming but by the comfort he had gotten from you, because he kept on telling me how you were longing to see me, how sorry you were, and how loyal you were to me, so that I was gladder still.

⁸ For, although I did cause you sorrow by that letter, I do not now regret it; although I did regret it then. I see that the letter caused you sorrow only for a time. ⁹ I am glad of it now, not because you had such sorrow, but because your sorrow led you to repentance, for you took your sorrow in accordance with the will

of God, so that you should not suffer any loss at all from me. [10] For the sorrow that comes in accordance with the will of God results in repentance that leads to salvation and leaves no regrets; but the sorrow the world produces results in death. [11] For see what this very sorrow, suffered in accordance with the will of God, has done for you! How earnest it has made you, how concerned to clear yourselves, how indignant, how alarmed, how much it made you long to see me, how loyal to me, how determined to punish the offender! At every point you have cleared yourselves in the matter. [12] So, although I did write to you, it was not for the offender's sake, nor for the offended party's sake, but in the sight of God for the sake of having your enthusiasm for me made perfectly clear to you. This is why I am so comforted.

Key words and phrases. Verse 5. We must remember the situation in order to appreciate Paul's overflowing joy in this chapter. He had left Ephesus and reached Macedonia (perhaps Philippi) and there Titus met him, just back from Corinth, where Paul had sent him to iron out the difficulties in the church there. In Ephesus he had "fightings without and fears within." The conflicts were with Demetrius the silversmith and his employees. A great uproar had occurred and Paul's life was endangered; perhaps saved by the Roman officials who kept him out of the angry mob in the theater (Acts 19:30, 31). His fears within were caused by his anxiety over the issue in the church at Corinth. Now Titus has come from Corinth and gives him the good news that the church had definitely decided in favor of Paul's apostolic authority and his message as the true gospel. That is, the majority had done so, leaving only a small minority opposing him, which fact called forth this letter. See introduction to this letter above.

Verses 6, 7. Paul's joy was enhanced and made to overflow, not so much by the bare fact that the majority of the church had decided in his favor, but by the overwhelming expression of their endorsement which they gave Titus. After the vote they kept on talking of their "longing to see Paul, how sorry they were (over the affair with the offender), how loyal they were to him."

Verses 8, 9. He had ceased to regret that he had written the letter recommending such harsh dealing with the offender (perhaps the lost letter, not our first Letter to Corinthians, so say most

scholars. He is now rejoicing that he wrote the letter, because of
its salutary effect on the church—they took it "in accordance with
the will of God." Then it resulted in genuine repentance on their
part. They changed their mind from showing a favor to the sinning
one to removing him from their fellowship. This increased Paul's
joy. They were loyal to him. They saw it was essential to keep
the church of Christ free from corruption—"they cleansed themselves from everything that defiles the body and mind" (7:1).

Verse 10. The incident leads Paul to describe the nature of
repentance. It is a "godly sorrow that leads to salvation and brings
no regret."

Verses 11, 12. He enumerates the effects of the letter on them
and gives them as an illustration of how genuine repentance works
and what results it produces: Indignation and alarm at the gross-
ness of the offender's sin, and actual punishment of him; longing
to see Paul and clear themselves of guilt in the matter. The last
sentence gives Paul's broad purpose in writing the scathing letter,
to "make their enthusiasm for Paul perfectly clear to them"; to
show them how loyal they were to him but did not know it until
this test was made.

PAUL SHARES THE OVERFLOWING JOY OF TITUS OVER THE FAVOR-
ABLE RESPONSE THE CORINTHIANS MADE TO HIS PEACE
MISSION (7:13-16)

13 In addition to my own comfort, I was made so glad that my
cup ran over at the gladness Titus felt, because his spirit has been
set at rest by you. 14 Indeed, if I have been doing some boasting
of you to him, I have never been ashamed of it; but just as all I
said to him was true, so now my boasting before Titus has been
shown to be true. 15 Yes, his heart is running over toward you,
as he continues recalling how you all obeyed him, with what
reverence and trembling you welcomed him. 16 I am glad that I
have perfect confidence in you now.

Key words and phrases. Verse 13. Paul's greatness is seen as
to his emotional capacity. His intellect was gigantic, the peer of
Plato, Socrates, or Aristotle. But his heart is bigger than his intellect. He was capable of the deepest grief, the keenest distress of

mind; but at the same time he could rise on wings of ecstasy to the heavenly heights of exultant joy. At Troas he sank to the depths of sorrow, at Philippi (Macedonia) he rose to the highest peaks of altruistic joy. He could rejoice with them who rejoice. Titus' joy lifted his soul to still greater thrills of ecstasy.

Verse 14. Paul was proud of the Corinthian church. It was in the chief city of Greece, the home of philosophy. The Greeks were a noble people and Paul was proud of having planted a church in their capital.

Verse 15. Titus must have been a diplomat in handling a church problem. Timothy had been sent by Paul, but he failed to get results. Titus succeeded. He was a great peacemaker. Such men are valuable in ironing out church difficulties. All pastors ought to be spiritual diplomats, tactful peacemakers.

Verse 16. Paul now has perfect confidence in the Corinthians, and that gives him the greatest joy. Confidence in those we love always makes us happy. Little confidence makes us miserable.

Chapter VIII

CHURCHES IN MACEDONIA EXAMPLES OF GENEROUS GIVING; JESUS GAVE HIMSELF, SO DID THEY; TITUS AND ANOTHER BROTHER ROUND UP THE CONTRIBUTION IN CORINTH

HE URGES AND APPEALS TO THE EXAMPLES OF THE CHURCHES IN MACEDONIA (8:1-7)

Now I am going to tell you, brothers, of God's spiritual blessing which was given in the churches of Macedonia, ² because in spite of a terrible test of trouble, the mighty flood of their gladness mingling with the depths of their poverty has overflowed and resulted in the abundance of their liberality. ³ For they have given, I can testify, to the utmost of their ability, and even beyond their ability. Of their own accord, ⁴ with earnest entreaty, they kept on begging me for the favor of sharing in this service that is being rendered to God's people. ⁵ They did not do as I expected but even more; they first by God's will gave themselves to the Lord, and then to me; ⁶ so that I insisted that Titus, as he had formerly commenced it, should bring to completion this gracious contribution among you too. ⁷ Yes, just as you are grow-

ing rich in everything else, in faith, expression, knowledge, perfect
enthusiasm, and the love inspired in you by us, you must see to
it that you grow rich in this gracious contribution too.

Key words and phrases. Verses 1-4. One of Paul's key words
(charis) is used four times in this first paragraph (1-7), and with
three of its five different meanings. In verse 1 it means spiritual
blessing; in verse 4 it has its original, root meaning, favor, and
in 6 and 7 it means gift, contribution—this gracious contribution.
In verses 1-4 he is urging the Corinthian church to follow the example of the churches in Macedonia, who "gave to the utmost of
their ability, and even beyond their ability"—to help the suffering
Christians in Judea. Verse 2 expresses a great truth that poverty,
even extreme poverty, if it is accompanied by abundant joy, may
result in abundant liberality. Through the years we have seen
some very poor Christians (poor in this world's goods) practice a
most beautiful liberality, giving not only a tenth, but often beyond
the tithe and beyond their economic ability. But this spirit of
sacrifice produced the hightest type of a Christian, happy, useful,
ready for every good work. The word *diakonia,* used to denote the
office of a minister (pastor) and that of a deacon, is here used as
service of a private Christian (4). *Koinonia* has its root meaning,
sharing, in verse 4.

Verses 5-7. He first gives us the great truth that liberal giving
roots itself in giving of self to Christ the Lord. Because most
Christians have not "given themselves to the Lord" unreservedly
and completely, they do not give of their means to relieve the poor
and to carry on the work of the church and the kingdom. It also
follows that if Christians fully surrender themselves to the Lord
they also give themselves to the minister to follow his leadership
in the movements of the church, charity, missions, etc. This must
be done "by the will of God." Christians who make the will of God
their standard of living are usually generous with their means.
Verse 6 tells us that Titus had commenced this great contribution
in the church in Corinth, and so Paul is sending him to complete it.

Verse 7 shows that the church there was excelling in many basic
Christian virtues and graces, and Paul exhorts them to "excel
in this gracious work also"; "grow rich in this gracious contribu-

tion too." They excel in faith, utterance, knowledge, perfect enthusiasm, and in love—why not in generosity with their means?

THE MIGHTIEST MOTIVES TO GIVING—LOVE AND THANKS TO THE SACRIFICING CHRIST; THE VOLUNTARY PRINCIPLE; EQUALITY AND CHRISTIAN BROTHERHOOD (8:8-15)

⁸ I am not saying this in the spirit of a command, but I am simply trying to test the genuineness of your love by the enthusiasm of others. ⁹ For by experience you know the unmerited favor shown by our Lord Jesus Christ; that although He was rich, yet for your sakes He became poor, in order that by His poverty you might become rich. ¹⁰ Now I will give you my opinion on this matter. For this is for your interest, because you were not only the first to do anything about it, but the first to want to do so; you started it a year ago. ¹¹ Now finish doing it too, so that your readiness to finish it may be just like your readiness to start it, in accordance with what you have. ¹² If a man is ready and willing to give, his gift is acceptable in accordance with what he has, not with what he does not have. ¹³ For I do not want it to be a relief for others and a burden on you, ¹⁴ but through an equalizing of matters in the present crisis I do want your abundance to relieve their need, that some day their abundance may relieve your need, so that equality may exist—¹⁵ just as the Scripture says, "The man who gathered much did not have too much, and the man who gathered little did not have too little."

Key words and phrases. Verses 8, 9. He appeals, not to obedience to his command, but to love and thanks to the sacrificing Christ, as the highest motives to sacrificial giving. He appeals to their experimental knowledge of Christ; how He, although rich in glory in the pre-existent state, became poor by incarnation in a human form, in order that they might become rich—rich in the blessings of salvation and the new spiritual life, culminating in the glorious inheritance as fellow heirs with Christ. Christ loved them and sacrificed Himself for them; now gratitude and love should prompt them to "give themselves to the Lord," as they did, and to make a sacrificial offering for the relief of the needy Jewish Christians.

Verses 10, 11. The voluntary principle is urged for church action. He as an outsider does not presume, though an apostle, to command them to give so much as their part in the great offering. He merely advises or gives his opinion as to what they should do. He compliments them for desiring to commence this offering a year ago, and first of all the churches. So it is reasonable for them now to complete it in the same voluntary and altruistic manner. When a boy I knew Baptist churches that assessed members how much they were to give on church expenses. This method of giving is not scriptural. It is not in accordance with the genius of Christianity. "Whosoever will . . . if any man wills to do," is the spirit of action in Christian circles.

Verse 12. Our giving must be measured by what we have. A man's responsibility to contribute is not measured by some other man's ability to give, but by his own.

Verses 13-15. Paul urges equality as a great principle in our relation as Christians—not that some should be burdened and others should be in ease. Those who have much should help those who have little, if they are in need. This is brotherhood of Christians, one of the most beautiful doctrines of our religion. God is our common Father and all Christians are brothers, and should, therefore, love and sacrifice for one another. So Jesus in the Gospel of John, and John in his first Letter.

TITUS AND TWO OTHER WELL-KNOWN BROTHERS TO ROUND UP
AND HANDLE THE CONTRIBUTION FOR THE SUFFERERS
(8:16-24)

16 But thanks be to God, who kindles in the heart of Titus the same enthusiasm for you that I have, 17 because he has acceded to my request, or rather, because he is so enthusiastic for you, of his own accord he is off to visit you. 18 I am sending with him the well-known brother whose praise for spreading the good news is ringing through all the churches. 19 Not only that, but he has been selected by the churches to travel with me for this gracious contribution which is being raised by me, so that it may turn out for the glory of the Lord and a proof of my readiness to serve. 20 I am arranging it so that no one can blame me in the matter of this munificent fund that is being handled by me. 21 For I am taking the precaution to do what is right, not only in the sight of the Lord but also in the eyes of men. 22 I send with them another

brother of ours, whom I have often in many ways tested and found to be enthusiastic, but now he is more enthusiastic than ever, because of his great confidence in you.

²³ As for Titus, he is my partner and comrade in the work for you, while these brothers of ours, the representatives of the churches, will bring glory to Christ. ²⁴ So you must furnish them, before all the churches, proof of your love and ground for my praising you so highly.

Key words and phrases. Verses 16, 17. He thanks God for Titus' concern for the Corinthians, a concern equal to that of Paul himself. Titus, we must remember, is a native Greek (Gal. 2:3). His congenital relation to the Corinthians and his superb diplomacy fitted him for successful peacemaking with the Corinthian church. Timothy had been sent to undertake the job, but had failed, although he was half Greek (Acts 16:1, 2) and enjoyed a fine reputation in his home town. Titus was a fine altruistic, diplomatic Christian, and Paul loved him, admired him, and used him to great advantage where troubles infested a church, as in Corinth.

Verses 18-22. He appointed two other distinguished, efficient brothers to join Titus as a special delegation to Corinth to round up and handle the gracious contribution of that church and see that all things were done decently and in order. One of these other men was a great evangelistic preacher of the gospel (18), the other had been tested and found enthusiastic (22). How we wish he had named these two eminent preachers and workers! Why did Paul send this committee of three eminent Christians, of honorable and unquestionable character and well known to the churches, to administer this great offering? Why did he not take care of it himself? He was being attacked by a minority in the church, so he is practicing diplomacy, safeguarding his reputation and handling the Lord's money safely and above board. A fine example for modern churches and mission boards.

Verse 23. Another special compliment to Titus; he is "my partner and comrade in your service." The other two are "messengers of the churches, the glory of Christ." It is a great honor to any man to represent a church and Christ Himself; to do so makes us His glory. Christ is proud of us and we are increasing His glory.

Verse 24. In this verse he appeals to his readers "to give proof, before the churches, of their love," and ground "for his boasting of them." They must not fall down on such a marvelous situation; they must measure up to the splendid opportunity. They must make an offering worthy of so great a church and commensurate with the cause for which it is made—a love-offering for their suffering Jewish brothers.

SERMON OUTLINE FROM CHAPTER 8

THE SACRIFICING LOVE OF CHRIST A MIGHTY MOTIVE TO SACRIFICIAL SERVICE (8:9)

I. In His Pre-existence He Was Rich
  1. In His Person—Deity, equal with the Father (Phil. 2:6-8)
  2. In praise and adoration of angels
  3. In love and glory of the Father (John 17:5)

II. For the Lost World He Became Poor
  1. Came "in the likeness of sinful flesh" (Rom. 8:3) Incarnated in human flesh was poverty compared to Deity
  2. Poor in material possessions. "Not where to lay His head" Born of a poor mother in a stable; no cradle but a manger.
  3. Dependent on others for food and drink—traveling missionary
  4. Buried in another's tomb (Luke 23:50-56)

III. The Purpose of His Becoming Poor—to Make Sinners Rich
  1. In salvation from sin—from its guilt, power and penalty (Matt. 1:2)
  2. In being sons and daughters of God (Gal. 4:4, 5; Rom. 8:14-16)
  3. In fellowship and universal brotherhood. Gentiles now helping Jewish Christians with love-offering (see Eph. 2:11, ff).
  4. In becoming heirs of God and fellow heirs of Christ (Rom. 8:17). Sharing with Christ Heaven, glory, association with angels, etc. "I'm the child of a King! With Jesus my Savior, I'm the child of a King!" Yes, the child of the King of the universe. Prince Charles, child of the British Queen, and heir to British Empire.

IV. A Mighty Motive to Sacrificial Service. "For you know"—
the basis of his appeal to their generosity.

   1. The powerful appeal comes through experimental knowledge of Christ *(ginoskete)*. "Heart-felt religion" creates the
appeal.

   2. Moves us to give ourselves (v. 5). So it did the Macedonians.

   3. Moves us to give our talents. So it did Paul—his learning,
logic, etc.

   4. Our means.

Chapter IX

The Contribution to Be Ready When Paul Arrives; Laws
Governing Christian Giving; Generous Blessings
Bestowed on Generous Givers

The Three Brothers Sent Ahead to Have the Contribution
Ready When Paul Arrives (9:1-5)

It is really superfluous for me to write to you about this service
which is being rendered to God's people, ² for I know your readiness
to help in it. I am boasting of you about it to the Macedonians,
reminding them that Greece has been ready since last year, and
your enthusiasm has stimulated the most of them. ³ But I send the
brothers that in this matter my boasting of you may not turn out
to be an idle boasting, that you all may be ready, as I have told
them you will be, ⁴ to keep me—not to mention you—from being
humiliated for having such confidence in you, if some Macedonians come with me and find that you are not ready. ⁵ So I have
thought it necessary to urge these brothers to visit you ahead of
me and get your promised love-offering ready beforehand, so as
to have it ready as a real love-offering, not as one grasped and
grudgingly given.

Key words and phrases. Verse 1. "Superfluous for me to write."
Not necessary for him to be so careful in sending these brothers
and having everything so arranged that the contribution cannot be
a failure. But he feels it is safer to take these precautions.

Verses 2-5. Two motives urge him to adopt this plan: first, to
keep him and them from being humiliated, if some Macedonians

should come down and find the offering not ready. Second, to have the contribution made as a real love-offering and not as a high-pressure collection pulled out of grasping givers. He calls the offering a blessing, this word suggesting love as the motive prompting it; so a love-offering.

LAWS GOVERNING CHRISTIAN GIVING (9:6-15)

⁶ Now this is the way it is: Whoever sows sparingly will reap sparingly too, but whoever sows bountifully will reap bountifully too. ⁷ Each must give what he has purposed in his heart to give, not sorrowfully or under compulsion, for it is the happy giver that God loves. ⁸ And God is able to make your every spiritual blessing overflow for you, so that you will always have in every situation an entire sufficiency and so overflow for every good cause; ⁹ as the Scripture says:

"He has generously given to the poor,
His deeds of charity go on forever."

¹⁰ He who always supplies the sower with seed and the eater with bread will supply you with seed and multiply it and enlarge the harvest which your deeds of charity yield. ¹¹ In every way you will grow richer and richer so as to give with perfect liberality, which will through me result in thanksgiving to God for it. ¹² Because the service rendered by this sacred offering is not only fully supplying the needs of God's people, but it is also running over with many thanks to God for it. ¹³ For through the test you get by doing this service you will continue praising God for your fidelity to your confession of the good news of Christ, and for the liberality of your contributions to them and all others; ¹⁴ and so in their prayers for you they will continue longing for you, because of God's surpassing favor shown you. ¹⁵ Thank God for His unspeakable gift!

Key words and phrases. In this paragraph Paul gives some laws governing Christian giving: Verse 6. The amount reaped depends on the amount sown. "Whoever sows sparingly will reap sparingly, whoever sows bountifully will reap bountifully." The harvest is mainly spiritual, but see verse 8.

Verse 7. Giving is a voluntary matter. "Each one must do as he has made up his mind." Assessing church members for expenses, charity, missions, is not scriptural.

Verse 7. Cheerful givers are objects of God's love. The word cheerful literally means hilarious *(hilaros)*. God does not care for our gifts if given grudgingly. His heart leaps with joy to see a poor peasant give his last dollar for missions and then shout "Hallelujah! bless the Lord, O my soul!" That's what the word means.

Verse 8. God is able to reward the cheerful, bountiful giver.

Verse 9. God actually prospers the generous giver by "increasing the harvest of his good deeds." So He did W. H. Wolfe, Dallas, when he vowed on his deathbed to give God a tenth if He would deliver him from death. He prospered as a cotton broker and gave hundreds of thousands to education, charity, missions.

Verses 11-13. Liberal giving inspires Christians to give God thanks and praise. Both the benefactors and the beneficiaries are made more spiritual and worshipful. So it was with the Corinthian benefactors and Jewish beneficiaries.

Verse 14. It creates and cultivates fine fellowship and a beautiful brotherhood between people of different races. Here it is Greeks and Jews.

Verse 15. Paul's big heart bursts forth with thanks and praise to "God for His indescribable gift!" It is the gift of His dear Son and with Him the gift of salvation, including everything He gives us, from forgiveness to Heaven and all its riches and glory! The word unspeakable literally means untraceable. The boundaries of the gift have never yet been traced by any surveyor, nor can they be. Sublime thought!

This paragraph on The Laws Governing Christian Giving, may be expanded into a useful expository sermon for a missionary occasion, or any occasion for inspiring the people to liberal giving.

Chapter X

PAUL PROVES HIS APOSTLESHIP; ANSWERS CHARGES AGAINST HIS
PERSONAL APPEARANCE AND SPEECH; CORINTH IN
HIS APOSTOLIC TERRITORY

IN DEFENDING HIS APOSTOLIC AUTHORITY HE ANSWERS CHARGES
AGAINST HIS PERSONAL APPEARANCE AND SPEECH (10:1-11)

Now I appeal to you in person, by the gentleness and fairness
of Christ, I, Paul, who am so "condescending when face to face

with you, but so courageous toward you when far away!" ² I beg you not to make me too courageous in that confidence in which I think to take a daring stand against some people who try to think that I am acting from the lowest human motives. ³ For though I do still live the life of a physical human creature, I am not waging this war in accordance with physical human standards, ⁴ for the weapons used in my warfare are not mere human ones, but through my God are mighty for demolishing fortresses. ⁵ For I am demolishing arguments and every barrier that is raised against the genuine knowledge of God, taking captive every thought to make it obedient to Christ, ⁶ and am prepared to punish any disobedience, when your obedience is made complete.

⁷ You look at me and measure me by outward appearances. If anyone is confident in himself that he belongs to Christ, let him have another thought about himself, that just as he belongs to Christ, so do I. ⁸ For if I do boast a little too much about my authority, which the Lord gave me for building you up and not for tearing you down, I shall never have to blush for doing so. ⁹ I do not want to seem to be frightening you with my letters. ¹⁰ For they say, "His letters are impressive and forceful, but his physical personality is unimpressive, and his delivery is perfectly contemptible." ¹¹ Such people should consider this: When I arrive for action I shall do exactly what I said I would in my letters when far away.

Key words and phrases. Verse 1. "By the meekness and gentleness of Christ" (A.S.V.). "Gentleness and fairness that Christ gives me" (Williams). The genitive with Christ is subjective, and so Paul is reminding them that when he comes to Corinth he is going to be governed, in his dealing with the minority, by the gentleness and fairness which he knows Christ gives him for such a task. The latter part of this verse states their charge against him as a moral coward: "Condescending when face to face with you, but so courageous toward you when far away."

Verse 2. He refers to another charge against him, "acting from the lowest motives." He urges them not to act so as to incite him to show too great boldness and courage when he is face to face with them.

Verses 3, 4. He answers the latter charge. Though he is living as a human creature in the physical sense, he is not using worldly weapons in this warfare for truth; he uses God-given weapons to demolish fortresses of evil.

Verses 5, 6. These fortresses are the arguments of men and their barriers raised against the genuine knowledge of God. He refers to the arguments used by the Judaizers and their sympathizers (minority in Corinthian church). He uses military terms and says that he "takes every thought captive to obey Christ." It is Christ he wants to glorify in this victory for his apostleship and the genuineness of his gospel. Not Paul but Christ is the goal of his personal defense in these chapters (10-12).

Verse 7. His opponents in Corinth judge him by outward appearances; by what they see face to face. Paul appeals to a deeper look at him. He knows that he is not prepossessing in physical appearance, but he also knows what he has experienced; how Christ appeared to him and saved him and called him to be a "chosen vessel," an apostle to the Gentiles. So he appeals to the objector to his apostleship that he have another thought, to remind himself that as he calls himself Christ's, so is he, Paul.

Verse 8. He denies that if he does boast a little too much of his authority (as an apostle), he will ever be put to shame on that score. He will never be made to blush on account of his boasting. He claims that this apostolic authority was given him by the Lord for the purpose of building up people and not for tearing them down. So he is trying to use that authority to build up the Corinthian church, and for that he is not, and will never be, ashamed. His boasting is only apparent, not real. When he magnifies his authority it is only to build them up.

Verses 9-11. He answers their charge that "His letters are impressive and forceful, but his physical personality is unimpressive and his delivery is perfectly contemptible." That is, his opponents see only the outward physical Paul, which is not the real Paul. According to the oldest picture of Paul he is little of stature, weighing about one hundred and twenty-five pounds, red-headed, and freckle-faced. Such a physique did not favorably compare with an athletic Greek with muscular arms, mauling fists, and mighty legs, standing six feet tall and weighing two hundred pounds. But that puny physique which his opponents gazed at was not the great and mighty apostle Paul. On him God had bestowed a brilliant brain bigger than that of Socrates; a majestic mind with towering thoughts profounder than Plato's; a scintillating logic superior to Aristotle's; a celestial soul surpassing that of Seneca. To them "his physical personality was not impressive, and his delivery was despicable [contemptible]." He simply reminds such opponents that what he says in letters that he is going to do when he reaches Corinth. He is conscious of his "authority which the Lord gave him." He must not bury it but use it for building them up.

CORINTH BELONGS TO HIS APOSTOLIC TERRITORY. SO HE MUST USE HIS AUTHORITY THERE (10:12-18)

¹² Indeed, I do not dare to count or compare myself with certain men who are always recommending themselves. ¹³ But they do not show good sense, because they do continue measuring themselves with one another and comparing themselves with one another. ¹⁴ But I shall never go too far in my boasting; no, I shall stay within the limits of the sphere which God apportioned me, so as to reach even you. For I am not overstepping my authority, as though I should not reach you, for I was the very first to reach as far as you with the good news of Christ. ¹⁵ I am not going too far in my boasting, and actually boasting of other men's labors, but I am cherishing the hope that your faith may so continue to grow that through you my work within my sphere may be so enlarged as to run over, ¹⁶ so that I can preach the good news in the regions beyond you, without boasting in another man's sphere of work already done by him. ¹⁷ "But the man who boasts must boast in the Lord." ¹⁸ For it is not the man who keeps on recommending himself who is really approved, but it is the man whom the Lord recommends.

Key words and phrases. Verse 12. Men who measure themselves by other men act without understanding. Our only true standard for measuring ourselves is the Lord Himself (Matt. 5:48). God is the absolute, invariable standard of conduct and character.

Verses 13, 14. Paul is boasting only inside the territory of his apostolic authority. But that includes Corinth (part of the Gentile world). He was the first to reach Corinth with the good news of Christ (on second missionary journey). So he is not overstepping himself when he boasts to the Corinthians of his authority which the Lord gave him.

Verses 15, 16. He will not boast of other men's labors in their territory, but it is his hope that the Christians in Corinth so continue to grow in faith and spiritual power that through them he may be able to preach the good news in the regions beyond Corinth. He loves to be on the ground floor—a pioneer.

Verses 17, 18. Self-commendation does not give a man approval, either with God or men. It is only the man whom God commends that is approved.

Chapter XI

LOVE MOVES PAUL TO DEFEND HIS AUTHORITY; TELLS WHY HE SURRENDERS HIS RIGHT TO FINANCIAL SUPPORT; CALLS HIS CRITICS SHAM APOSTLES; IRONICALLY DEFENDS HIS SANITY IN BOASTING; CLAIMS HIS SUFFERINGS ARE THE CREDENTIALS OF HIS APOSTLESHIP

LOVE MOVES HIM TO DEFEND HIS AUTHORITY (11:1-10)

I wish you would now listen to a little folly of mine. Please do listen to me! ² For I feel a divine jealousy for you, as I betrothed you to Christ, to present you as a pure bride to her one husband. ³ But I am apprehensive that, somehow or other, as the serpent by his cunning deceived Eve, your thoughts may be turned aside from single-hearted devotion to Christ. ⁴ For if anybody comes along and preaches another Jesus than the one I preached, or you receive another spirit different from the one you did receive or a glad message different from the one you did accept, you listen to it all right! ⁵ For I consider myself not a single bit inferior to those surpassingly superior apostles of yours! ⁶ Although I am untrained as an orator, yet I am not so in the field of knowledge. Surely, I have always made that perfectly clear to you.

⁷ Did I do wrong in taking a lowly place to let you have an exalted one, in that I preached the good news about God to you without accepting any pay? ⁸ I sponged on other churches by taking pay from them to render service to you, ⁹ and when I was with you and needed money, I never burdened a single one of you for a cent, for the brothers came from Macedonia and supplied what I needed. And so I kept myself, as I shall always do, from being a

burden to you in any way. ¹⁰ By the truth of Christ in me, this boasting of mine shall never be stopped in the boundaries of Greece. ¹¹ Why? Because I do not love you? God knows I do.

Key words and phrases. Verse 1. Paul feels that boasting of his apostolic authority smacks of "foolishness." Yet, he feels just as strongly that it is his duty to emphasize it before these critics and opponents of his in Corinth. So he begs them to bear with him in a little foolishness. He does not voluntarily boast; they have driven him to it.

Verse 2. His excuse for doing so is his "spiritual jealousy for you, for I betrothed you to Christ to present you as a pure bride to her one husband." They were his converts on the second missionary journey (Acts 18:8-11).

Verses 3, 4. He is "afraid of them"; he knows that some of them are fickle. A new teacher comes and preaches a new message; they fall for it. They are as easily deceived as Eve in the Garden by the serpent who cunningly takes advantage of his victims.

Verses 5, 6. Here one of his most cutting sentences of sarcasm slips from his pen. "For I consider myself not a single bit inferior to those surpassingly superior apostles of yours! I am untrained as an orator, yet I am not so in the field of knowledge." He is answering their charges that he is no apostle at all; that his delivery is despicable; that he is an ignoramus in comparison with their philosophers. Their favorite apostles were likely Peter and John, so highly praised by those Judaizing influences.

Verces 7-11. This whole paragraph is used to tell why he preached to them "without accepting any pay." Notice his description of the good news: the gospel of God. This genitive may be either subjective or objective, or perhaps including elements of both. It is the gospel which God gave to the world; it is the gospel about God, His grace and love and purpose of redemption. "I sponged on other churches." This phrase in verse 8 is expressive. The Greek verb means exactly what our word "sponge on" denotes—to receive benefits without giving anything in return. The church at Philippi often sent him money while he was preaching elsewhere (9). Another expressive verb occurs in verse 9: "I never stuck [lit.] a single one of you." The picture is of a lower animal which sticks his bill into his victim depositing a fluid that benumbs it as he enjoys his meal. We use the term when we say, "That horse trader stuck me in the trade." Paul was not guilty of feeding on the Corinthians like this.

Verse 10 assures them that Paul is going to continue this policy of preaching without taking any pay; that is, "in the regions of Greece." Then his critics cannot say that he is preaching for money.

Verse 11 gives a higher motive for this policy in Corinth; he loves this church and all its members. He takes oath to this effect: "God knows."

HE WILL CONTINUE THIS POLICY OF NONSUPPORT FROM THE CORINTHIANS TO SILENCE HIS OPPONENTS WHOM HE CALLS SHAM APOSTLES; DEFENDS HIS SANITY IN BOASTING (11:12-21)

¹² And I shall keep on doing as I am, in order to cut the ground from under the feet of those who want an opportunity to show themselves on a level with me in the matters of which they boast. ¹³ For such men are sham apostles, dishonest workmen, masquerading as apostles of Christ. ¹⁴ And no wonder, for even Satan himself masquerades as an angel of light. ¹⁵ So it is no surprise if his servants also masquerade as ministers for doing right, whose doom shall be in accordance with what they do.

¹⁶ Let me say again that no one must think that I am a fool; but if you do, please treat me like a fool and let me do a little boasting too, as other fools do. ¹⁷ But when I talk in this boastful confidence, I am not talking in accordance with the way the Lord talked, but just as a fool talks. ¹⁸ Since many boast in accordance with their human nature, I will do it too. ¹⁹ For you who are so wise yourselves are glad to listen to fools! ²⁰ For you listen to a man, if he makes you his slave, or spends your money for his living, or cheats you, or puts on airs, or slaps you in the face.

²¹ I am ashamed to say that I was, as it were, so weak in the matter. And yet in whatever respect anyone else is daring to boast—I am talking like a fool—I too will dare to boast.

Key words and phrases. Verse 12. His immediate purpose in nonsupport of his ministry is to undermine the wicked claim of the sham apostles, his critics, that they are working under the same terms as he; that he was getting his living from preaching, as they are. He would silence this claim and not take any pay.

Verse 13. A drastic charge against them he makes: they are sham, or false apostles, just "masquerading as apostles of Christ."

Verses 14, 15. It is no wonder that they do this, for Satan masquerades as an angel of light. Surely, his servants can do the same.

Verses 16-21. Paul says in effect: "I repeat it, no man should think me a fool, and yet I am forced by the minority, opposing me in the church, to act as a fool, for the spirit of boasting is not that of the Lord. But as they boast of their rank and authority, so will I. For you are listening to them, so why not listen to me, acting as a fool like them? They make slaves of you [to their views], prey upon you, take advantage of you, put on airs, and still you bear with them and follow them [that is, the minority do]. It was to my shame that I could not do as they did."

He Boasts of His Sufferings As the Credentials for His Apostleship (11:22-33)

22 Are they Hebrews? So am I. Are they Israelites? So am I. Are they descendants of Abraham? So am I. 23 Are they ministers of Christ? So am I. I am talking like a man that has gone crazy— as such I am superior!—serving Him with labors greater by far, with far more imprisonments, with floggings vastly worse, and often at the point of death. 24 Five times I have taken thirty-nine lashes from the Jews, 25 three times I have been beaten by the Romans, once I was pelted with stones; three times I have been shipwrecked, and once I have spent a day and a night adrift at sea. 26 I have served Him on frequent journeys, in dangers from rivers, dangers from robbers, dangers from my own people, dangers from the heathen, dangers in the city, dangers in the desert, dangers at sea, dangers from false brothers, 27 through toil and hardship, through many a sleepless night, through hunger and thirst, through many a fasting season, poorly clad and exposed to cold. 28 Besides all other things, there is my concern for all the churches. 29 Who is weak without my being weak too? Who is caused to fall without my being fired with indignation? 30 If I must boast, I will

boast of the things that show my weakness! [31] The God and Father of the Lord Jesus, who is blessed forever, knows that I am telling the truth. [32] At Damascus the governor under King Aretas kept guards watching the city gates to capture me, [33] but through a hole in the wall I was lowered in a basket, and so escaped from his clutches.

Key words and phrases. Verse 22. As his critics do, he boasts of his lineage—descended from Abraham, so a Hebrew and an Israelite. Abraham was the first to be called a Hebrew; that is, the one from beyond the river (from Hebrew preposition for *beyond*). Israelite, the title given Jacob, a prince, a prince of God. Paul was proud of this lineage. Well might he be.

Verses 23-29. He lists some of his greatest sufferings as Christ's minister, as His apostle sent to proclaim the good news. First he lists his greater toils. He made more journeys and reached more cities than any other apostle.

His sufferings may be grouped under three heads: First, forms of persecution—imprisonments, beatings, five times with thirty-nine lashes by Jews; three times by Romans; once stoned at Lystra and left for dead. His attempted capture at Damascus by the city officials was likely a form of persecution instigated by Jews. Second, sufferings from travel and climatic conditions—three times shipwrecked, once with a night and day adrift on the sea, dangers from rivers (swollen) and robbers (on road from Perga to Pisidian Antioch on first missionary journey), dangers from Jews and Gentiles (Demetrius and his laborers examples of the latter), with sleepless nights and many a fasting season, poorly clad and exposed to cold. Third, his care and consuming concern for all the churches he had founded. Especially had he suffered for the church at Corinth—perhaps, more for their divisions and opposition to him and his message and apostleship than for all the other churches. These sufferings, which God has permitted, but delivered him out of them all, are proofs that God had appointed him an apostle and a preacher of the good news to the Gentiles.

Chapter XII

PAUL'S VISIONS ARE SUBLIME BUT HIS SUFFERINGS ARE MORE
VALUABLE AS CREDENTIALS OF A TRUE APOSTLE; HIS MO-
TIVES UNSELFISH, STILL HE IS UNEASY AS TO HIS
EXPECTED VISIT

HIS SUFFERINGS MORE VALUABLE AS CREDENTIALS THAN HIS
SUBLIME VISIONS (12:1-10)

I have to keep on boasting. There is no good to be gotten from
it, but I will go on to visions and revelations which the Lord has
given me. ²I know a man in union with Christ fourteen years
ago—whether in the body or out of it, I do not know, but God
knows—who was caught up to the third heaven. ³Yes, I know that
this man—whether in or out of the body, I do not know, but God
knows—⁴was actually caught up into paradise, and heard things
that must not be told, which no man has a right even to mention.
⁵On behalf of this man with such an experience I will boast,
but on behalf of myself personally I will boast only about my
weaknesses. ⁶However, if I want to boast, I will not play the fool,
for it will be nothing but the truth that I will tell. But I refrain
from doing so, to keep anybody, on account of the superiority of
the revelations, from giving me a higher rating than my actions
and teachings deserve. ⁷So, to keep me from being overelated,
there was sent upon me a physical disease, sharp as a piercing
stake, a messenger of Satan, to continue afflicting me, and so to
keep me, I repeat, from being overelated. ⁸Three times I begged
the Lord about this to make it go away and leave me, ⁹but He
said to me, "My spiritual strength is sufficient, for it is only by
means of conscious weakness that perfect power is developed."

¹⁰So I most happily boast about my weaknesses, so that the
strength of Christ may overshadow me. That is why I take such
pleasure in weaknesses, insults, distresses, persecution, and difficulties, which I endure for Christ's sake, for it is when I am consciously weak that I am really strong.

Key words and phrases. Verses 1-4. He tells of a man who
fourteen years ago was caught up to the third heaven, or paradise,
and had visions and revelations the contents of which must not
be told; in fact, no man has a right even to mention them (in

aorist tense with negative, not even once to mention). He refers to them here just to boast of the glorious visions God gave him as a proof of his apostleship. But he makes the nice distinction that he will not boast of himself personally. It is only this exalted man caught up by the Lord of whom he will now boast. Note, he first said he was caught up "to the third heaven," and next time he said he was caught up "into paradise." So the third heaven is synonymous with paradise. The Jews had developed in their thinking seven heavens. The first starts with the aerial regions just above our earthly atmosphere (of which Satan is prince) up to the seventh, the most glorious sphere where God and archangels dwell and reign. The third heaven is the first domain where God's special presence is glorious. So Paul was not favored with the highest visions; or with visions of the highest and most glorious possessions of the heavens. Yet, the essence of his visions must not be mentioned by any man.

Verses 5-11. He magnifies his weaknesses as superior credentials to his apostleship. Yet, he still holds that if he should boast of these visions, he would not act the fool, for he would tell only the truth (about these visions). He modestly claims that he refrains from boasting of these visions, to keep anyone from rating him above his deserts. He wanted no honor for Paul; he wanted no ranking of him above what he really was, truly honest and sincere.

To keep him from being overelated about these celestial visions there was sent upon him a thorn in the flesh, a messenger of Satan. It was undoubtedly a physical (flesh) disease. Lightfoot thinks it was eye trouble; some German critics, epilepsy; Ramsay, chronic malaria. It is immaterial as to which disease it was, or whether it was something other than any one of these. How did it come upon him? Did God send it, or did Satan send it? Or, was it a natural consequence of Paul's sins? Likely each of these three causes played a part in developing this disease in Paul's body. God permitted it with a gracious purpose. Satan played a part in tempting Paul to do some things that he ought not to have done. Paul yielded to the temptations. Paul emphasizes Satan's part, and the gracious purpose of God in permitting it.

Three times Paul prayed for the removal of the thorn. God refused to grant it, but He promised to give him His spiritual strength to help him endure it; to keep it from overcoming him. It is to be noticed that God did not grant him the request of his prayers, but He gave him greater blessings—spiritual blessings with divine power to make him the greatest apostle of the Church, the profoundest theologian of the first century and the mightiest missionary of the centuries. He is the Job of the New Testament. He says, "I am content with weaknesses, insults, hardships, persecutions, and calamities." Well might he be content, with a patience equal to that of Job, for his conscious weakness was developing in him spiritual strength surpassing all human power.

THE SIGNS OF A TRUE APOSTLE SHOWN AMONG THEM (12:11-13)

> 11 I have made a fool of myself, but you have forced me to do it, for I am the man who ought to have been constantly approved by you. For I am not a single bit inferior to your surpassingly superior apostles, though really I am "nobody." 12 The marks that signify the genuine apostle were exhibited among you in my perfect patience, in signs, wonders, and wonder-works. 13 In what respect, then, were you inferior to the rest of the churches, except for the fact that I, and I only, never received from you any financial support? Please forgive me this wrong.

Key words and phrases. Verse 11. He puts the blame upon them for his having to boast of his apostolic authority. What he was to them in their conversion and the founding of their church put them under obligation to recognize him as an authorized apostle. He says that he was not a whit inferior to their boasted surpassingly superior apostles (likely Peter and John). Yet he humbly asserts, "I am nobody." His deep humility is always latent beneath his boasting. However, there is a note of sarcasm in this word *nobody.* This was the charge the minority made against him.

Verse 13. The miracles he wrought among them were unanswerable arguments for his authority as an apostle. In addition to his perfect patience with all their strife and divisions and accusations, he performed signs, which are miracles from the point of view of being an evidence for the divine authority of the one who works the miracles. He performed wonders, miracles that aroused terror and wonder; also wonder-works, miracles that emphasize the divine power *(dunamis)*. So they had no excuse for doubting his apostolic authority.

Verse 14. He lacked only one thing of acting as the other apostles did; he preached without cost to them. They were denied the favor of supporting the preacher of the good news to them. He begs their pardon for this wrong. Mild sarcasm! Notice, he feels that it was a wrong to deny them the privilege of supporting the preacher.

LOVE AND SERVICE TO THEM, NOT PERSONAL ADVANTAGE, HIS RULING MOTIVE FOR HIS COURSE (12:14-21)

¹⁴ It is now the third time that I have been ready to come to see you, and I will never ask you for financial support, for it is not your money but you yourselves that I want; for children are not by duty bound to lay up money for their parents, but parents for their children. ¹⁵ So in my own case, I will most happily spend my money and myself for your sakes. If I love you much more than I love others, am I to be loved less by you? ¹⁶ But let it be granted, you say, that I never received from you financial support, yet, you say, being a trickster I cheated you by my cunning. ¹⁷ I did not make any money out of you through anybody that I sent to you, did I? ¹⁸ I actually begged Titus to go, and sent the well-known brother with him. Titus did not make any money out of you, did he? Did not he and I act in the same spirit, and take the very same steps?

¹⁹ Are you thinking all this time that I am defending myself to you? It is in the very presence of God and as one who is in union with Christ that I am speaking. And it is all for building you up, beloved, for I am apprehensive that, somehow or other, when I come I shall find you not as I want to find you, and that you may find me not as you want to find me. ²⁰ I repeat it, I am apprehensive that, somehow or other, there may be quarreling, jealousy, anger, rivalries, slanders, gossiping, haughty pride, and disorders, ²¹ and that when I come back my God may humiliate me before you, and I may have to mourn over some of those who formerly have committed shocking sins, and have not repented for them—their impurity, sexual immorality, and sensuality, which once they practiced.

Key words and phrases. Verses 14, 15. His policy of nonsupport for his services to them he asserts he will still carry out, he is "seeking not their money" but it is their souls, their hearts, their lives, and only for the Lord Jesus. What a model of unselfishness for all preachers of the good news! He is acting like loving parents who lay up for their children. In the same spirit of sacrifice he says, "I will most gladly spend my money and myself for your souls." That is what thousands of sacrificing parents are doing for their children. It is what Paul is doing for the Corinthians.

Verses 16-18. This is exactly the way Titus, whom he sent to work with them, and the well-known brother, behaved among them. They took nothing from them for their services. They took no advantage of them.

Verses 19-21. He asserts again that this is not written simply to defend himself, but for their building up. Love has been the ruling motive that has moved him to say all he has said. Yet, he does not refrain from letting them know that he has some fear that some of them will not find him as they wish, when he comes on this third visit. If the minority have not relented in their opposition, and some guilty of grievous sins, impurity, sexual sins, and sensuality, have not repented, he will have to reprove and condemn, instead of being gentle and loving with them all.

SERMON OUTLINE FROM CHAPTER 12

PAUL'S UNANSWERED PRAYERS (12:8-10)

I. The Nature of These Prayers
1. Not for spiritual blessings or guidance
2. Not for others, as in Romans 10:1, where he prays for the lost
3. For himself; and for a physical blessing, for removal of the thorn in the flesh; that is, a physical disease. Ophthalmia (Lightfoot); epilepsy (some German critics); chronic malaria (Ramsay). The disease not fatal; only an annoyance.

II. Not Answered Directly
1. God did hear them and consider them. He always considers every prayer.

2. Did not give him the request asked—removal of the disease.
3. Gave him something better—His grace; that is, spiritual strength to endure the disease. He always does this if the prayer is offered in faith; father refusing ten-year-old son a pony, but gave him a university education; now a famous university professor.

III. Why Not Answered Directly

1. Perhaps not sufficient faith by Paul. Old woman praying for hill in front of window to be removed. "Just like I expected," she said next morning, as she looked out and saw the hill.
2. God wanted to test his faith, as He did Job (Job 1)
3. God knew that suffering perfected character and polished personality (II Cor. 4:17). Miss Wright, an invalid for twenty-five years, a model Christian.
4. He knew it would increase Paul's usefulness; more sympathetic, more dependent on God. Jesus made perfect by suffering (Heb. 2:10, 18).

IV. Conclusion: Our Prayers Today Not Answered Because

1. We pray for the wrong objects: physical, material, for self.
2. We pray the wrong way.
3. Not submissive for God's time to answer.

> Oh for a faith that will not shrink,
> Tho' pressed by every foe;
> That will not tremble on the brink
> Of any earthly woe.

Chapter XIII

He Asks That Offenders Be Examined and, If Found Guilty, Punished; His Farewell Greetings; Benediction

How to Deal with Offenders (13:1-10)

This is my third visit to you. Any charge preferred must be sustained by the evidence of two or three witnesses. [2] I have already warned those who formerly committed shocking sins, and all the rest, and though so far away I warn them now, as I did on my second visit, that if I come back I will not spare them, [3] since you demand a proof that Christ is speaking through me. For

Christ is not exhibiting weakness toward you but power in you.
⁴ For though He was crucified in weakness, yet by the power of
God He goes on living. We too, indeed, show weakness through
our union with Him, yet by the power of God we too shall be
alive toward you through fellowship with Him. ⁵ You yourselves
must continue testing yourselves to see whether you are continuing in the faith. You must continue standing the test. Do you
not know by a growing experience that Jesus Christ is in you?—
provided you stand the test.

⁶ Now I hope that you will learn that I am standing the test.
⁷ But I am praying God that you may never do anything wrong,
not to show that I am standing the test, but that you should continue doing right, though I should fail to stand the test. ⁸ For I
cannot do anything against the truth, but only for it. ⁹ I am glad
to be consciously weak, if you are really strong. This is my con-
tinual prayer, the perfecting of your characters. ¹⁰ This is why I
am writing this while far away from you, that when I do come,
I may not have to deal harshly with you in accordance with the
authority which the Lord has given me, for building you up, not
for tearing you down.

Key words and phrases. Verses 1-4. He asks them to deal fairly
with the accused; they must not be condemned except by the
testimony of two or three witnesses. This is the requirement of the
Mosaic law, which is just and fair. He warns them to deal with
these cases before he comes, so he will not have to show his authority from Christ, for he will not be weak then but strong with the
strength of the risen Christ who lives in him. He feels that he is
weak by virtue of his union with the crucified Christ, but he will
be powerful through his union with the risen Christ, when he comes
to deal with those offenders (if he has to do so).

Verses 5-8. He exhorts them to test themselves, to see if they
are continuing in the faith. This may be subjective or objective
faith; that is, their personal trust in Christ, or the doctrines to be
believed. It seems that here he is emphasizing the subjective faith,
as there is no hint at their defection in doctrine. Examine themselves to see if they are personally and really holding on to the
crucified and risen Christ. The next sentence seems to bear out
this interpretation: "Do you not by experience know that Jesus is

in you? Provided you stand the test." This teaches perseverance of the saints. The believer must persevere and stand the test to prove that he is a genuine believer. Then he expresses the hope that they will learn that he is standing the test. The second verb used *(dokimazo)* means to be successful in standing the test; the former simply testing *(peirazo)*. Then he assures them that he is praying for them that they may be approved in standing the test. He knows that he is approved, for he "cannot do anything against the truth but only for it." What a stalwart character!

Verses 9, 10. He is glad to be consciously weak, if they can be really strong. How unselfish! He is "praying continually for the perfecting of their characters." Then he tells them he is giving these warnings so that the disagreeable work may be done before he arrives, that he may not be forced to deal harshly with the offenders when he comes. If they do not have these matters out of the way before he arrives, he will have to assert his "authority which the Lord gives him."

Final Exhortations; Greetings; Benediction (13:11-14)

¹¹ Finally, brothers, good-by! Practice the perfecting of your characters, keep listening to my appeals, continue thinking in harmony and living in peace, and the loving, peace-giving God will be with you. ¹² Greet one another with a sacred kiss. ¹³ All God's people wish to be remembered to you.

¹⁴ The spiritual blessing of the Lord Jesus Christ, the love of God, and the common sharing of the Holy Spirit be with you all.

Key words and phrases. Verse 11. His final exhortations are personal and appealing and tender. The imperatives are in the present; they are to continue in these fine thoughts and behavior. Continue piecing together the broken joints so as to have a whole, perfect body (the church body). The verb *(katartizo)* is a physiological term; the joints of the body have been torn apart and must be knit together again. The second appeal is to keep listening to these loving appeals which their spiritual father has made to them. The third is continue thinking in harmony; do not have so many opinions that differ, try to think yourselves together (important exhortation for any church). The fourth is to live in peace; this will naturally follow if they piece together the torn joints and think in harmony. The blessed result of these four activities will be the presence of the loving, peace-giving God with the church as a whole and with the individual Christian. It is true that God who loves us so and who gives "peace" cannot be pleased with a bickering, divided church.

Verses 12, 13. The sacred kiss is again to be used to express their unity. All God's people (saints) with Paul send greetings to Corinth.

Verse 14. The full form of Paul's benediction: Grace of the Lord Jesus Christ; grace here means spiritual blessings. The love of God here means the love of the Father God. The common sharing of the Holy Spirit; "fellowship" means common sharing; each Christian has a share in the Holy Spirit, if he claims it and lays hold of it. It teaches the doctrine of the Trinity, the Triune God—Father, Son, and Spirit.

The Letter to the Romans

INTRODUCTION

1. *The Church in Rome.* It is not certain who founded the church in Rome, the capital of the Roman Empire. There is no record of its origin. It is quite certain that the apostle Peter did not found it (Gal. 2:9; Rom. 15:20). See the Introduction to Carroll's *Notes on Romans,* for positive proofs that Peter did not found it. It is just as certain that Paul did not found it (Rom. 1:9-13). It is possible but not probable that the proselytes converted at Pentecost (Acts 2:10) organized it on their return home. What is sure about its origin is that missionaries preaching the Pauline type of the good news founded it, because he does not have a criticism, in all his letter, of the doctrine held in it.

2. *Its Constitutent Members.* Baur and his school of extreme radicals held that the majority were Jewish Christians, the minority Gentiles. Most scholars hold the opposite view—that the majority were Gentiles. So especially the Commentaries of Godet, Meyer, and Denney. Compare Romans 1:5, 6, 13, 14; 11:25; 15:15, 16.

3. *Author of Romans.* Even the extreme critics concede that Paul is the author. There is no doctrine in the church to occasion a letter of rebuke, as is the case with writing Galatians; no schism in the church or a letter of request from them, as is the case with the first Letter to the Corinthians. Paul is on the third missionary journey, still in Corinth, in the winter of A.D. 58, when Phoebe, a deaconess of the church at Cenchreae, near Corinth, is planning a trip to Rome. Paul hears of it and writes this letter for her to take to the church at Rome (A.D. 58.)

4. *Purpose.* Why did he write it? Renan held that his purpose was to write a compend of all Christian theology; Godet, a compend of Pauline theology. It is more probable that he did not think of producing a logical system of theology, but to set forth the fundamental teachings of the gospel as he preached it—the universality of sin, justification by faith without the works of the law, re-

demption by the vicarious death of Christ which was rendered efficacious by the resurrection from the dead (4:25), and so on. He had also a second purpose: to show that Christianity is a universal religion, for all nations as well as for Jews. A third purpose was to enlist the influence of this mighty church in the capital for the evangelization of Spain and other nations (15:19, 24, 28).

GENERAL CHARACTERISTICS

Four characteristics stand out prominently: its originality of thought, through apparently an elaboration of the Letter to the Galatians; its logical presentation; its quotations from the Old Testament (74); the deep and tender emotions of Paul (9:3; 10:1). Juelicher says, "Here the entire Paul presents himself. He shows himself the greatest thinker of the first century, at the same time having the biggest heart filled with love for all men. He is a logician equal to Aristotle. If you would master Romans, you must master Paul's *gar's* and *oun's*. *Gar* means for, *oun* means therefore. Usually in the first eight chapters you can trace the line of thought with his *gar's* and *oun's.*"

ITS INTEGRITY

Do all sixteen chapters in our English Bible belong to this letter? Marcion, about A.D. 145, was the first to make a canon of the New Testament, and he closed the letter with chapter 14:1. He rejected chapter 15 and 16. McGiffert, church historian, thinks 16:1-20 belongs to the Letter to the Ephesians. Most scholars, however, regard the letter as a whole was written to the church at Rome.

GENERAL OUTLINE

I. Introduction (1:1-17)
   1. Greeting (1:1-7)
   2. Paul's relation to the church (1:8-15)
   3. Theme (1:16, 17)
II. Sin a Universal Fact (1:18—3:20)
III. Justification Universal on Condition of Faith (3:21—5:21)
IV. Sanctification a Vital Part of Justification (Chaps. 6-8)
V. Justification by Grace through Faith in Harmony with God's Purpose and Program in History (Chaps. 9-11)

MAIN TEACHINGS IN ROMANS

1. God, though absolute in power, is the Father of Christ and Christians. He loves all men, Jews and Gentiles (2:11).

2. Jesus Christ is the Son of God, the Saviour, Lord, and even God (9:5).

3. Sin is universal, and so all men are under condemnation (3:19, 21).

4. Salvation includes the whole process of man's deliverance from sin, from justification to the resurrection (5:10; 13:11).

5. Salvation rests on election which is according to God's foreknowledge.

6. Yet, men are free and so are responsible for sin and their destiny.

7. Justification, or right standing with God, is the initial stage of the saving process, simultaneous with the new birth (5:17); it is secured by grace through trust in Christ (3:24).

8. Justification depends on redemption through Christ's death (3:24).

9. Redemption is secured through the death of Christ and is stamped as acceptable to God by the resurrection of Christ (3:24, 25).

10. Redemption secures reconciliation with God for those accepting Christ as personal Saviour.

11. The death of Christ is an expression of both the righteousness and love of God (3:26; 5:8).

12. Faith as the condition of justification is a personal committal of oneself to Christ as Saviour and Lord (10:9, 10).

13. Sanctification, the process of unfolding the new life in character and conduct, rests on and grows out of justification (chap. 7).

14. The believer in Christ is secure and safe for his final glorification, through election by the Father, redemption by Christ, and sanctfication by the Spirit (chap. 8).

15. God has a program of grace that is being worked out in history, not to be frustrated by the sins of individuals or the failure of nations (chaps. 9-11).

16. Christians are the Body of Christ and members of one another.

17. Love is the queen of graces and virtues, forgives our enemies, and is the fulfillment of the whole law.

18. Our spiritual gifts differ, and each is responsible to use his gifts for others and for God.

19. The state is a divine institution to punish evildoers and to promote the good; so Christians should be loyal citizens.

20. The Jews must be evangelized before a universal turning of the nations to Christ takes place (chap. 11).

21. The parousia, resurrection of Christians, and their bliss in Heaven are implied though not stressed as in his other letters.

EXEGESIS

INTRODUCTION

Chapter I

GREETING; INTRODUCTION; DESCRIPTION OF
UNIVERSAL SIN BEGUN
GREETING (1:1-7)

Paul, a slave of Jesus Christ, called as an apostle, set apart to preach God's good news, ² which long ago He promised through His prophets in the holy Scriptures, ³ about His Son, who on the physical side became a descendant of David, and on the holy spiritual side ⁴ proved to be God's Son in power by the resurrection from the dead—I mean, Jesus Christ our Lord, ⁵ through whom we have received God's favor and a commission as an apostle in His name to urge upon all the heathen obedience inspired by faith, ⁶ among whom you too as called ones belong to Jesus Christ—⁷ to all those in Rome who are God's loved ones, called to be His people: spiritual blessing and peace be yours from God our Father and from our Lord Jesus Christ.

Key words and phrases. Verse 1. "Slave of Jesus Christ." Paul delights in emphasizing this lowly title of his to express his lowly relation to Jesus Christ as His devoted slave to serve Him. "Called an apostle," one sent forth, which also includes his being set apart to preach the good news of justification by faith in Christ the Son.

Verse 2. "Long ago . . . promised." As in Galatians, he traces the good news back to God's promises by His prophets; though not going clear back to Abraham, as in Galatians. "Holy Scriptures." To Paul the writings of the Old Testament were holy, set apart by God as His own revelation.

Verse 3. "His Son . . . Jesus Christ our Lord." He is regarded by Paul as the central theme of the Old Testament Scriptures.

Verse 3. "On the holy spiritual side," or "according to the Spirit of holiness" (A.V.). That is, Jesus is not only human as a descendant of David, but He is also the Son of God, proved to be such by His perfect holiness in character and life; but especially powerfully proved to be such "by the resurrection from the dead." This manifestation of divine power in the resurrection of Christ convinced Paul, beyond the shadow of a doubt, that He was the promised Messiah. See Acts 9 for Paul's surrender to the risen Christ.

Verse 5. "Through whom we have received favor and a commission as an apostle." The *we* is editorial for I (Paul). Grace means unmerited favor of God, which prompted Him to call him to be saved by trusting Jesus Christ as Saviour and Lord. Notice he says it was by or through Christ that he received this grace and apostleship (see Acts 9:15, 16).

Verse 6. "Called ones [of] Jesus Christ." As called of God they belong to Jesus Christ—possessive genitive.

Verse 7. As in Galatians, he emphasizes the equality of our Lord Jesus Christ with the Father as the source of spiritual blessing (grace) and general prosperity (peace). The *and* connects Father and Christ as equal givers of these blessings. So Robertson, *Grammar, in loco.*

PAUL'S RELATION TO THE CHURCH IN ROME (1:8-15)

⁸ First through Jesus Christ I thank my God for you all, because the report of your faith is spreading all over the world.
⁹ Indeed, my witness is God, whom I serve in my spirit by telling
the good news about His Son, that I never fail to mention you
every time I pray, ¹⁰ always entreating God that somehow by His
will I may some day at last succeed in getting to see you. ¹¹ For I
am longing to see you, to impart to you some spiritual gift, that
you may be strengthened; ¹² in other words, that we may be
mutually encouraged, while I am with you, by one another's faith,
yours and mine. ¹³ Furthermore, I want you to know, brothers,
that I have often planned to come to see you (though until now
I have been prevented), in order that I may gather some fruit
among you too, as I have among the rest of the heathen. ¹⁴ To
Greeks and to all the other nations, to cultured and to uncultured people alike, I owe a duty. ¹⁵ So, as far as I can, I am eager
to preach the good news to you at Rome, too.

Key words and phrases. Verse 8. "I thank my God through
Jesus Christ." Praise and thanks to God the Father are due by and
through Jesus Christ the Intermediary. The ground of this thanks
to God is the spread of faith of the Roman Christians all over the
world; of course, he means the Roman world. Surely, it had not
reached India, China, and Japan.

Verse 9. "Serve in my spirit by telling the good news about
His Son." The phrase, in my spirit, means in his heart, with all
his heart and soul. He serves the Son by preaching the good news
of His love and mercy, but especially he preaches it with all his
heart, or inner being. He takes an oath that he mentions them in
his prayers always; that is, every time he prays. Paul must have
been a man of constant prayer; praying even for a church that he
had never seen; most of whose members he had never seen or
known. He lived in prayer.

Verse 10. "A prosperous journey by the will of God" (A.V.).
He longed to see them, but it must be the will of God, or he did not
want it so. The will of God was his will; his measuring rod for
all his actions.

Verse 11. "Impart . . . some spiritual gift." To help others spiritually was his consuming ambition; to stimulate their faith, to comfort their hearts, and to encourage them to greater achievements in Christ.

Verse 12. "By the mutual faith both of you and me" (A.V.). Paul was a perfect gentleman. How adroitly and courteously he suggests that he does not presume to be superior to them and impart some miraculous blessing to them without including himself on a plane of equality! "Both . . . you and me."

Verse 14. The four words in the Authorized Version—Greeks, barbarians, wise and unwise—to Paul's mind included all classes. He feels that he is debtor to all races and nations and classes, to everybody. No racial or cultural boundaries circumscribed Paul's field of service. "The world is his field."

Verse 15. So he is ready and eager to preach the good news at Rome, too.

THE THEME OF THE LETTER (1:16, 17)

16. For I am not ashamed of the good news, for it is God's power for the salvation of everyone who trusts, of the Jew first and then of the Greek. 17 For in the good news God's Way of man's right standing with Him is uncovered, the Way of faith that leads to greater faith, just as the Scripture says, "The upright man must live by faith."

Key words and phrases. Verse 16. "God's power for salvation." The word for *power* is *dunamis*, from which we get our word dynamite. As dynamite is one of nature's mightiest forces, so the good news of God's love and grace and Christ's readiness to save is God's spiritual dynamite which blasts open the hearts of sinners and opens them to receive Christ as Saviour and Lord. "For salvation." The purpose of the good news is to lead to the salvation of sinners. "Of everyone who trusts, of the Jew first and then of the Greek." Faith as the condition of salvation makes it possible for salvation to be for all men regardless of racial or social status. And yet Paul says it is to the Jew first. As God's chosen people the Jews must have the first opportunity to receive the gospel. Paul went to the synagogue first to preach it.

Verse 17. "God's way of right standing . . . is uncovered." Here the word translated in the Authorized Version *righteousness* likely means God's method of bringing men into right standing with Himself. See Sanday, *Commentary on Romans*. Also God's attribute of righteousness is also revealed in the good news.

A GREAT TEXT WITH SERMON OUTLINE (1:16)

I. The Christian's Attitude toward It—Not Ashamed of It
1. To believe it
2. To live it
3. To preach it or tell it
4. To die for it

II. Why? It Is God's Power (Spiritual Dynamite)
1. To convict of sin
2. To lead to faith in Christ
3. To lift life to higher levels
4. To help the Christian die in triumph (e.g., Paul as martyr)

III. Its Extent—for All Men
1. For the Jew
2. For the nations
3. On condition of faith to all

SIN A UNIVERSAL FACT (1:18—3-20)
NATURAL RELIGION LEADS TO IDOLATRY (1:18-23)

[18] For God's anger from heaven is being uncovered against all the impiety and wickedness of the men who in their wickedness are suppressing the truth; [19] because what can be known of God is clear to their inner moral sense; for in this way God Himself has shown it to them. [20] For ever since the creation of the world, His invisible characteristics—His eternal power and divine nature—have been made intelligible and clearly visible by His works. So they are without excuse, [21] because, although they once knew God, they did not honor Him as God, or give Him thanks, but became silly in their senseless speculations, and so their insensible hearts have been shrouded in darkness. [22] Though claiming to be wise, they made fools of themselves, [23] and have transformed the splendor of the immortal God into images in the form of mortal man, birds, beasts, and reptiles.

Key words and phrases. Verse 19. "God's anger." This is the revulsion of His holy nature against sin. It is not sudden, temporary anger, but a constant righteous revulsion of His holiness against sin. The Greek word is *orge*. The verb *revealed* (uncovered) is in the present of continuous action; His revulsion against sin is ceaseless. Impiety is sin against God; wickedness, sin against man. Truth is reality about God and man and the world; sinful men suppress—literally, hold down—truth in or with their unrighteousness.

Verses 19, 20. God has made known to pagan peoples His truth. He has given them only a partial, imperfect knowledge of Himself. "His eternal power and divine nature." These attributes have been clearly perceived in His works that are so evident to ordinary intelligence, and of course to the Greek philosophers. That is, man's moral sense—conscience—and his constant contact with external nature have given pagans a knowledge of these attributes. Deity is something the pagan sees above himself in the world about him. God has power and it is eternal; He existed before the world and its creatures. But we observe that Paul does not say that nature gives man a knowledge of God's love and mercy in salvation. Pagans can get only a dim conception of God's love in providence. But nature and conscience furnish man enough knowledge of God and his relation to Him to make him responsible for his thoughts and actions and destiny. "They are without excuse." They have no excuse for failing to honor God as God, and for making images and worshiping them instead of the true God.

Verses 21-23. But this revelation of nature led only to idolatry. "A little knowledge is a dangerous thing." They had some knowledge of the true God, but they did not honor Him as God; they were not thankful to Him for all the blessings He daily bestowed upon them. Instead, they glorified their knowledge. They claimed to be wise and gave their minds up to speculation about God and the world. They knew so little they made themselves fools in the silly conclusions they reached with their logic. The real result was that they exchanged the splendor of the true, immortal God for images in the likeness of mortal men, birds, beasts, and reptiles.

Idolatry Plunges the Pagans into the Grossest Sensuality
(1:24-32)

24 So God has given them up to sexual impurity, in the evil trend of their heart's desires, so that they degrade their own bodies with one another, 25 for they had utterly transformed the reality of God into what was unreal, and worshiped and served the creature rather than the Creator, who is blessed forever! Amen. 26 This is why God has given them up to degrading passions. For their females have exchanged their natural function for one that is unnatural, 27 and males too have forsaken the natural function of females and been consumed by flaming passion for one another, males practicing shameful vice with other males, and continuing to suffer in their persons the inevitable penalty for doing what is improper. 28 And so, as they did not approve of fully recognizing God any longer, God gave them up to minds that He did not approve, to practices that were improper; 29 because they overflow with every sort of evil-doing, wickedness, greed, and malice; they are full of envy, murder, quarreling, deceit, ill-will; 30 they are secret backbiters, open slanderers, hateful to God, insolent, haughty, boastful; inventors of new forms of evil, undutiful to parents, 31 conscienceless, treacherous, with no human love or pity. 32 Although they know full well God's sentence that those who practice such things deserve to die, yet they not only practice them but even applaud others who do them.

Key words and phrases. Verses 24, 25. Notice the *so* in verse 24 and the *for* in verse 25. Because they exchanged the splendor of the immortal God for images of men, birds, beasts and reptiles, God gave them up to immorality. God was not responsible for their immorality; He only permitted them to follow their depraved tendency (a Hebrism). In verse 25 Paul changes the expression of their idolatry to "utterly transformed the reality of God into what was unreal, and worshiped and served the creature rather than the Creator." That is, an idol (image) is a lie. It is not a god but presumes to be. They had some truth about God learned from conscience and nature, but they exchanged it for idols and worshiped a lie; unreality instead of the true, real God. At the close of verse 25 Paul breaks forth in a doxology in praise of the true God, "who is blessed forever! Amen." God is so real to him that he cannot refrain, even while discussing this disagreeable idolatry, from blessing and praising Him who is the only true God.

Verses 26, 27. The awful sin of sodomy, unnatural sex copulation. Practiced even by women, called females, the sex instinct predominating. Men too called *males* for the same reason. Sodomy still practiced in heathen lands (say missionaries). In America, too, I am told. Returned missionaries say pagans accuse them of writing Romans after reaching their land.

Verses 28-31. This catalog of twenty-one sins is headed by a causal conjunction, *since (kathos)*. The same thought is continued as above—idolatry leads to immorality and sensuality. "And so, as they did not approve of fully recognizing God any longer, God gave them up to minds that He did not approve, to practices that were improper." Notice, a base mind precedes this improper conduct. "As one thinks so is he." If men entertain low thoughts, they will do mean and debasing things. God gave them up to this unapproved mind (a play on words in Greek), but He did so because they forgot Him and worshiped and served idols. Then the awful category of selfish, disgraceful sins follows. Notice the strong verb *overflow* (filled, A.V.), filled up to the brim and overflowing with these twenty-one black sins. Three types of sins are committed: *sins against God*—haters of God, failing to worship and serve Him; *personal sins retroacting on the individual sinner*—wickedness, malice, deceit, malignity, insolence, haughtiness, boastfulness, and so on; *social sins especially harming others*—covetousness (greed), envy, murder, quarreling, secret backbiting, slandering, inventing new forms of evil, disobedience to parents, being unmerciful and without love or pity. In verse 32 he seems to add another sin to this catalog—that of backing and applauding the ones who do dirty things. This is what Paul did when Stephen was stoned to death. He did not throw a stone, but he held the clothes of those who murdered the first Christian martyr. Such a man or woman, who is a passive accomplice in crimes or atrocious sins, sins against knowledge. He knows it is wrong and yet he approves and applauds the criminals who do the dirty work. Such sinners are worse than Pilate, for he did not approve of crucifying Christ, although he

permitted the Jews and Romans to do so, when he had the authority
to prevent it.

Chapter II

THE JEWS ARE SINNERS, SO SIN IS UNIVERSAL (2:1—3:20)
GOD'S STANDARD OF JUDGMENT TOO HIGH FOR
MAN TO MEASURE UP TO (2:1-5)

Therefore, you have no excuse, whoever you are, who pose as
a judge of others, for when you pass judgment on another, you
condemn yourself, for you who pose as a judge are practicing the
very same sins yourself. ² Now we know that God's judgment
justly falls on those who practice such sins as these. ³ And you,
who pose as a judge of those who practice such sins and yet continue doing the same yourself, do you for once suppose that you
are going to escape the judgment of God? ⁴ Do you think so
little of the riches of God's kindness, forbearance, and patience,
not conscious that His kindness is meant to lead you to repentance? ⁵ But in your stubbornness and impenitence of heart
you are storing up wrath for yourself on the day of wrath, when
the justice of God's judgments will be uncovered.

Key words and phrases. Verses 1-5. God's judgment is according to truth, according to reality. The facts in each case determine what God's judgment is for each individual. The Greek
aletheia literally means that which is uncovered, not hidden, so
it comes to mean what is seen to be so, truth. The Jew judges
(krino) the Gentile for his sins, but because he is practicing the
same things he at the same time condemns *(katakrino)* or passes
judgment against himself. Paul being a Jew himself and living
all his life among them knew they were practicing *(prasso* from
which our word practice is derived) the same things Gentiles were,
cataloged above (21). In verse 2 he intimates how silly it is for
this Jew to think that he will be privileged to escape *(ekpheugo,*
flee from) the judgment of God. In verse 4 he gives God's purpose
in being so lenient with the sinner now; it is all His kindness, forbearance, and patience in punishing and delaying the judgment in
full, to lead him to repentance. How often we have seen how God's
gentle dealing with a wicked man has finally melted his heart to
penitence and led him to Christ! In verse 5 he shows how this

Jew, or any man, by being stubborn and hardhearted is laying up a tremendous store of divine wrath to be visited on him in the judgment.

GOD'S JUDGMENT IMPARTIAL (2:6-16)

⁶ For when He finally judges, He will pay everyone with exactness for what he has done, ⁷ eternal life to those who patiently continue doing good and striving for glory, honor, and immortality; ⁸ but wrath and fury, crushing suffering and awful anguish, to the self-willed who are always resisting the right and yielding to the wrong, ⁹ to every human soul who practices doing evil, the Jew first and then the Greek. ¹⁰ But glory, honor, and peace will come to everyone who practices doing good, the Jew first and then the Greek; ¹¹ for there is no partiality in God's dealings.

¹² All who sin without having the law will also perish apart from the law, and all who sin under the law will be judged by the law. ¹³ For merely hearing the law read does not make men upright with God; but men who practice the law will be recognized as upright. ¹⁴ Indeed, when heathen people who have no law instinctively do what the law demands, although they have no law they are a law to themselves, ¹⁵ for they show that the deeds the law demands are written on their hearts, because their consciences will testify for them, and their inner thoughts will either accuse or defend them, ¹⁶ on the day when God through Jesus Christ, in accordance with the good news I preach, will judge the secrets people have kept.

Key words and phrases. Verses 6-11. God's judgment will be according to one's works. This means that God shows no partiality. God has no special friends who will be spared His punishment when they do evil. He will be fair with everybody, but will show no special favors to anyone. The rich and the poor are to be treated on the same level of justice, according to their actions. Of course, motives will be considered, which Paul does not take time to emphasize, but which is emphasized by Jesus in the Sermon on the Mount.

The portion coming to evildoers will be wrath and fury. The first word *(orge)* is the *natural revulsion of God's holiness against sin,* the latter the culmination and outburst of that revulsion. There will be tribulation and distress for all evildoers. These come in this life, the former to be visited on them at the last day. The portion of those who patiently do good will be eternal life, which starts at regeneration but continues through eternity. Also glory and honor and peace, starting in this life but continuing to a greater degree in eternity. It is to be observed that Paul is not teaching here that eternal life with glory and honor and peace are purchased by the good works of the righteous. We must not forget that in this chapter he is discussing how God judges and punishes and rewards men, and not how men are justified and saved.

Verses 12-16. In this paragraph Paul is elaborating the thought that God shows no partiality. Jews live under the written law, enjoying all the privileges and blessings which that means, whereas Gentiles are living without the privileges and blessings the written law brings. But privileges mean greater responsibility. So the Jew who enjoys more light from God will be judged more severely than the Gentile who is deprived of this superior light. The greater light we have the heavier punishment we shall receive, if we do not live up to that light. Verse 15 refers to the work of the law written on their hearts. This means that Gentiles who do not possess the written law have a law written in their hearts and consciences. This is the moral law, the natural man's sense of right, imparted to him by the Creator and rendered keener by the increase of his knowledge of his social relations and general culture. Verse 16 shows how God's judgment is to be according to Paul's gospel. That is, according to the good news of God's love and mercy to save men. God is just, but He leans toward mercy in dealing with men. He must preserve His moral government, but in doing so He is merciful even when His wrath and fury are visited on wrongdoers. Notice, the judgment of God is by Jesus Christ. This again emphasizes His mercy, for Christ came to extend mercy to the sinner. But it also makes it hard for the Gentiles who do not know Christ and have never heard His name. Can God save a Gentile who keeps the moral law written in his heart? Paul says they will perish, but apart from the severity of the written law (v. 12).

Jews, Like Gentiles, Fail to Measure up to This Standard; Their Privileges Increase Their Guilt (2:17-29)

[17] Now if you call yourself a Jew, and rely upon the law, and boast about God, [18] and understand His will, and by being instructed in the law can know the things that excel, [19] and if you are sure that you are a guide to the blind, a light to those in darkness, [20] a tutor of the foolish, a teacher of the young, since you have a knowledge of the truth as formulated in the law—[21] you who teach others, do you not teach yourself, too? You who preach that men should not steal, do you steal? [22] You who warn men to stop committing adultery, do you practice it yourself? You who shrink in horror from idols, do you rob their temples? [23] You who boast about the law, do you by breaking it dishonor God? [24] For, as the Scripture says, the name of God is blasphemed among the heathen because of you.

Key words and phrases. Verses 17-20 list the extraordinary privileges the Jews enjoy by living under the law. They are "the praised ones," literal meaning of the Hebrew word from which the Greek comes; and also the English word *Jew*. As the specially honored and praised by God, he relies upon the law and boasts of his relation to God as belonging to His chosen people, who know His will and approve what is excellent by being instructed in the law. This makes him a guide and teacher of others, an exalted position and one of responsibility. Paul lists these privileges and honors of the Jew to show how they increase his guilt. He has sinned against superior light and knowledge. He has sinned against the God who has loved him and exalted him as no other people.

Verses 21-24 list some particular sins of which the Jew is guilty: stealing, adultery, robbing pagan temples (Josephus substantiates this as a fact), blaspheming the name of God by breaking the law—thus making the name of God a byword among the heathen. This is in addition to asserting that they practice such things (2:1b), the sins listed in 1:26-32, and so, with the superior privileges and brighter light of the written law, they are worse than the pagans. This is a picture of the Jewish world as shocking as the picture drawn of the heathen world in 1:26-32.

THE REAL CIRCUMCISION AND THE REAL JEW (2:25-29)

25 Now circumcision benefits you only if you practice the law; but if you break the law, your circumcision is no better than uncircumcision. 26 So if the uncircumcised heathen man observes the just demands of the law, will he not be counted as though he were a Jew? 27 And shall not the heathen man who is physically uncircumcised, and yet observes the law, condemn you who have the letter of the law and are physically circumcised, and yet break the law? 28 For the real Jew is not the man who is a Jew on the outside, and real circumcision is not outward physical circumcision. 29 The real Jew is the man who is a Jew on the inside, and real circumcision is heart-circumcision, a spiritual, not a literal, affair. This man's praise originates, not with men, but with God.

Verses 25-27. Circumcision has no value to one unless he keeps the law (all of it). It is an act of obedience to the law, and unless that end is achieved it has no spiritual value. If you Jews are transgressors of the law, your circumcision has become uncircumcision; that is, it has been a complete failure. But if a Gentile keeps the law, his lack of circumcision has all the value to him that circumcision was intended to have. Paul feels that the pagan who is not physically circumcised but keeps the law, actually condemns the Jew who has been circumcised but breaks the law.

Verses 28, 29. The real Jew is not the man who has been physically circumcised, but the one who is a Jew inside (in the hidden part); that is, has a circumcised heart. The heart is the "seat of the soul" (Thayer), the source giving out all motives, thought, and actions. Physical circumcision has no spiritual value except as a sign, or seal, or an inward reality. So the man who has a circumcised heart enjoys the praise of God. He is a real Jew—a praised one (literal meaning of Hebrew word, Greek *Joudaios*, English *Jew*).

Chapter III

FOUR OBJECTIONS TO THIS CONCLUSION ANSWERED (3:1-8)

What special privilege, then, has a Jew? Or, what benefit does circumcision confer? 2 They are great from every point of view.

In the first place, the Jews are entrusted with the utterances of God. ³ What then, if some of them have proved unfaithful? Can their unfaithfulness make null and void God's faithfulness? ⁴ Not at all. Let God prove true, though every man be false! As the Scripture says,

"That you may prove yourself upright in words you speak,
And win your case when you go into court" (Ps. 51:4).

⁵ But if our wrongdoing brings to light the uprightness of God, what shall we infer? Is it wrong (I am using everyday human terms) for God to inflict punishment? ⁶ Not at all! If that were so, how could He judge the world? ⁷ But, as you say, if the truthfulness of God has redounded to His glory because of my falsehood, why am I still condemned as a sinner? ⁸ Why should we not say, as people abusively say of us, and charge us with actually saying, 'Let us do the evil that good may come from it'? Their condemnation is just.

Key words and phrases. Verses 1, 2. "What advantage then has a Jew?" the objector asks. The word translated advantage literally mean overflowing. So the idea is, what superfluity of honor and privileges and station has the Jew? Paul answers that the primary superiority of the Jew over other people is that he was entrusted with the special revelations of God to men. To Abraham He gave the grace covenant; to Moses the codes of the law; to the various prophets, special revelations to mankind in particular situations, and the promises of the Messiah. All of these were Jews. Not a single Gentile was honored by God to receive and transmit to mankind a special revelation. The Jew is honored by God as His human mediator between God and man.

Verses 3, 4. The words *apistia* and *pistis* in verse 3 are not unfaith and faith, but unfaithfulness and faithfulness. They are often used in this secondary sense. Of course, the unfaithfulness of a few Jews cannot nullify the faithfulness of God, any more than the unfaithfulness of a small group of citizens could nullify the faithfulness of the President of the United States to abide by the oath he took to be faithful to the Constitution of the United States. The word for *without effect* literally means to be idle, inactive, inoperative, so to annul or nullify a promise or agreement.

Verses 5, 6. A third objection is raised, "Is God unjust because

He shows His wrath for sin and punishes sinners? Of course not. How could He judge the world at all if He were unjust? Paul argues that God really shows that He is righteous because His nature revolts against sin (has wrath) and punishes sinners. Notice, he really quotes, or refers to, the saying of Abraham, "Shall not the Judge of all the earth do right?" (Gen. 18:25).

Verses 7, 8. Paul's enemies, the Judaizers, accused him of saying, "Let us do evil that good may come." They said this because he magnified, or emphasized, the sins of Gentiles and Jews alike, and then concluded that God is merciful and saves sinners, not by their obedience to the law, but by merely believing in Jesus Christ. They call this message of Paul's a lie or falsehood; but Paul feels that this "falsehood" of his has redounded to the glory of God, and that God's just condemnation is on those who thus accuse him.

UNIVERSALITY OF SIN PROVED BY QUOTATIONS FROM THE OLD TESTAMENT (3:9-20)

⁹ What is our conclusion then? Is it that we Jews are better than Gentiles? Not at all. For we have already charged that Jews and Gentiles alike are all under the sway of sin, ¹⁰ as the Scriptures say:

"Not a single human creature is upright,
¹¹ No one understands, no one is searching for God;
¹² They all have turned aside, all have become corrupt,
No one does good, not even one!
¹³ Their throats are just like open graves,
With their tongues they have spoken treachery;
The poison of asps is under their lips,
¹⁴ Their mouths are full of bitter cursing.
¹⁵ Their feet are swift for shedding blood,
¹⁶ Ruin and wretchedness are on their paths,
¹⁷ They do not know the way of peace.
¹⁸ There is no reverence for God before their eyes."

¹⁹ Now we know that everything the law says is spoken to those who are under its authority [to Jews], that every mouth may be stopped [from making any excuse for sin] and the whole world held responsible to God. ²⁰ Because no human creature

can be brought into right standing with God by observing the law. For all the law can do is to make men conscious of sin.

Key words and phrases. Verse 2. The verb *proechometha* literally means to hold ourselves before or ahead of others in sinning; that is, worse than they, as the King James translates it. The context favors the former. Paul replies, Not at all do we Jews regard ourselves as better than the Gentiles, for we have above charged that Gentiles are horrible sinners (1:18-32), and Jews likewise (2:1-24).

Verses 10-18 give us quotations from Psalm 14:1f, or Psalm 53:1f; Psalm 140:3; 10:7; 36:1; Isaiah 59:7. Notice, these passages are all from either the second or third division of the Old Testament, as the Jews divided it—the Psalms or the Prophets, not a single quotation from the Law, or first division. Paul believes in the inspiration of the Old Testament (II Tim. 3:16). So he is claiming that these quotations give the divine confirmation to his conclusion that all the world is guilty before God; that Jews as well as Gentiles are under the wrath of God and exposed to eternal condemnation, and if saved at all, it must not be by the works of the law, but by the mercy of God. "None is righteous" (v. 10); that is, no one measures up to the law.

Verse 11. No one understands, that is, spiritually.

Verse 12. Not one, literally, not even up to one. Most emphatic.

Verses 13, 14. The mouth is completely contaminated, from the throat up to the lips.

Verses 15-17. Their feet led them to murder and miseries, but never to peace.

Verses 18, 19 give the cause of this complete moral depravity: they have no reverence for God.

III. JUSTIFICATION UNIVERSAL ON CONDITION OF FAITH (3:21— 5:21) THE METHOD STATED WITH TWO IMPLICATIONS (3:21-30)

21 But now God's way of giving men right standing with Himself has come to light; a way without connection with the law, and yet a way to which the law and prophets testify. 22 God's own way of giving men right standing with Himself is through

faith in Jesus Christ. It is for everybody who has faith, for no distinction at all is made. [23] For everybody has sinned and everybody continues to come short of God's glory, [24] but anybody may have right standing with God as a free gift of His undeserved favor, through the ransom provided in the death of Christ Jesus. [25] For God once publicly offered Him in His death as a sacrifice of reconciliation [or propitiation] through faith, to demonstrate His justice (for in His forbearance, God had passed over men's former sins); [26] yes, to demonstrate His justice at the present time, to prove that He is right Himself, and that He considers right with Himself the man who has faith in Jesus.

[27] So where has human boasting gone? It was completely shut out. On what principle? On that of doing something? No, but on the principle of faith. [28] For we hold that a man is brought into right standing with God by faith, that observance of the law has no connection with it. [29] Or, is He the God of Jews alone? Is He not the God of heathen peoples too? Of course, He is the God of the heathen peoples too, [30] since there is but one God, who will consider the Jews in right standing with Himself, only on condition of their faith, and the heathen peoples on the same condition.

Key words and phrases. Verses 21-22. The phrase *righteousness of God* in these verses has a peculiar meaning. It includes God's attribute of righteousness but means also the way, or method, God has provided for giving sinful men right standing with Himself. It is the righteous attribute of God moved by His attribute of love (5:9) reaching down to sinful men to lift them up to Him, not as sinners but as righteous.

Four characteristics of this method are stated: (1) It has no causal connection with the law, Mosaic or moral—"without (or apart from) . . . the law." (2) Yet under the Old Testament system of law it received witness from the law books and the prophets; it was taken for granted and foretold. (3) The sinner's right standing with God is obtained on condition of faith in Jesus Christ. (4) It is of universal application; it is for all classes and nations and races.

Verse 23 states the need of such a method, if it is to be effective; all men are sinners—have sinned and continue to fall short of the standard set by God's glorious character. We must notice that the verb *have sinned* is not a perfect but an aorist tense in Greek. This tense expresses an act done in the past once for all and does not have any connection with the present. All sinned some time in the past and all together. That was when Adam and Eve sinned in the garden. So it is possible that Paul is here emphasizing the fact that all the race in Adam and all sinned in him. That is, from the scientific point of view, Adam transmitted to all his descendants the sin-principle. All are sinners by nature or heredity. See 5:12 and following, where this thought is elaborated.

The phrase, *God's glory* has a unique meaning here. Glory is likely used as in 6:4, Christ was raised by the glory of the Father; that is, by the glorious character of the Father, all His attributes combining to complete the plan of redemption in the raising of Christ. So here *glory of God* means the standard set by His glorious character, and all men continue to fall short of measuring up to that glorious standard.

Verses 24-25a tell us that Christ's death is the paying of the price that ransoms the world of sinners who are locked up in the prison of depravity (Gal. 3:23)—"through the redemption which is in Christ Jesus, whom God publicly offered up in His death as a propitiatory offering." The word *redemption, apolutrosis,* suggests the idea of paying a ransom to set prisoners free. Blood is a symbol for death—"in His blood . . . in His death." The word *hilasterion,* propitiatory offering (see Thayer, *Lexicon)* expresses the purpose of paying the ransom, to make atonement for sins and satisfy God's law. It had said, "The soul that sinneth shall die." "In the day ye eat thereof ye shall die." Christ's death satisfied the law in that He paid the penalty of the broken law; broken by all men, as shown above. We must not think of Paul as saying that Christ's death placated God, or made Him willing to save men. He was already willing when He "gave His only begotten Son." God was willing all the time, but something had to be done to prove that He is righteous and punishes sinners, and so satisfy the demands of His holy and righteous character. This Christ's death accomplished.

Verses 25b, 26. The last thought is elaborated in these verses.

Righteousness of God here is His attribute of justice. The prime purpose of Christ's death was to demonstrate the justice of God. In past centuries He, in forbearance, had passed over any outburst of His wrath in punishing sinners. So now it is necessary to convince the transgressing world that He is just and does punish transgressors. The *ultimata* purpose *(eis to einai)* was to show that God can maintain His righteous character and at the same time, according to His method of grace (unmerited favor), grant right standing with Himself to every lost man who trusts in Christ as his ransoming Saviour. This is what Paul means when he says "justified . . . by His grace" (A.V.).

Verses 27, 28 state an implication of this grace-faith method of justification; all boasting by any man is completely shut out. If a man's works have nothing to do with securing his right standing with God, then he has no ground for boasting. Notice, it is shut out by the law (or principle) of faith. Law is here used in the sense of a way of operation, or a principle, as in Galatians 6:2; Romans 8:2, and a few other passages.

Verses 29, 30 give us another implication from this method; namely, that God is a universal God; not only the God of Jews but also the God of all nations. There is only one God, the God of us all.

SIGNIFICANT TEXT WITH SERMON OUTLINE (3:23)
SIN

I. *What* Is It?
1. A reality. Mrs. Eddy's theory. Modernists.
2. The sin-principle; inherited from Adam (see 5:12, ff).
3. Sin acts. Violations of God's laws.

II. *Who* Have Sinned?
1. The Gentiles (1:18-32). Even cultured Greeks, conquering Romans.
2. The Jews (2:1-24).
3. So all races have sinned. Sin is universal.

III. *What Is Its Penalty?*
1. Physical death   3. Moral death
2. Spiritual death   4. Eternal death

Chapter IV

THIS METHOD OF JUSTIFICATION IN HARMONY WITH THE OLD TESTAMENT SYSTEM OF LAW (3:31-4:25)

ABRAHAM JUSTIFIED BY FAITH BEFORE HE WAS CIRCUMCISED (3:31-4:12)

[31] Do we then through faith make null and void the law? Not at all; instead, we confirm it. [1] Then what are we to say about our forefather Abraham? [2] For if he was considered in right standing with God on the condition of what he did, he has something to boast of; but not before God. [3] For what does the Scripture say? "Abraham put his faith in God, and it was credited to him as right standing with God." [4] Now when a workman gets his pay, it is not considered from the point of view of a favor but of an obligation; [5] but the man who does no work, but simply puts his faith in Him who brings the ungodly into right standing with Himself, has his faith credited to him as right standing. [6] So David, too, describes the happiness of the man to whom God credits right standing with Himself, without the things he does having anything to do with it:

[7] "Happy are they whose transgressions have been forgiven,
　　Whose sins were covered up;

[8] Happy the man whose sin the Lord does not charge against
　　him!" (Ps. 32:1, 2).

[9] Now does this happiness come to the Jews alone, or to the heathen peoples too? For we say 'Abraham's faith was credited to him as right standing.' [10] Under what circumstances was it credited to him as right standing? Was it after he was circumcised, or before? Not after but before he was circumcised. [11] Afterward he received the mark of circumcision as God's seal of his right standing with Him on condition of faith which he had before he was circumcised, that they might have their faith credited to them as right standing with God; [12] and the forefather of those Jews who not only belong to the circumcision but also follow in the footsteps of our forefather Abraham in the faith he had before he was circumcised.

Key words and phrases. Verse 1. The verb found (A.V.) is not in the oldest and best manuscripts. So the substantive *Abraham* is accusative of specification, meaning *as to* or *about* Abraham. Verse 2. The Greek has *out of works,* not *by* or *through works,* so it emphatically asserts that his justification has no causal connection with works. The word for boasting means *ground for boasting,* not the act.

Verse 3. *Righteousness* (A.V.) is right standing with God. *Credited* is a commercial term, and so his faith was credited to his account; he was considered as righteous before God.

Verses 4, 5. An illustration from the industrial world. It is the man who works for another who gets his pay as due him, but Abraham did not work for right standing, for God graciously granted it as a favor, because he had faith in God. The quotation from Genesis 15:6 proves this.

Verses 6-8. He further illustrates by quoting David in Psalm 32:1, 2. Here people are blessed, or happy, because God has graciously forgiven their transgressions, and does not charge their sins against them; all not because of works but on condition of faith.

Verses 9-12. He answers the question, How was Abraham's faith credited to him? He really means, *when* was it, *after* his circumcision or *before?* Surely it was before, for he received circumcision as a sign or seal, as stated in verses 11 and 12. Circumcision did not bring Abraham into right standing with God; it was only a symbol of what had taken place in his heart. He was right with God, because he put his trust in Him.

THE PROMISE TO ABRAHAM CONDITIONED ON JUSTIFICATION BY FAITH (4:13-25)

¹³ For the promise made to Abraham and his descendants, that he should own the world, was not conditioned on the law, but on the right standing he had with God through faith. ¹⁴ For if the law party is to possess the world, then faith has been nullified and the promise has been made null and void. ¹⁵ For the law results in wrath alone; but where there is no law, there can be no violation of it. ¹⁶ So it is conditioned on faith, that it might be in accordance with God's unmerited favor, so that the promise might be in force for all the descendants of Abraham, not only for those who belong to the law party but also for those who belong to the faith group of Abraham. He is the father of us all, ¹⁷ as the Scripture says, "I have made you the father of many

nations." That is, the promise is in force in the sight of God in whom he put his faith, the God who can bring the dead to life and call to Himself the things that do not exist as though they did. [18] Abraham, building on hope in spite of hopeless circumstances, had faith, and so he actually became the father of many nations, just as it had been told him, "So numberless shall your descendants be." [19] Because he never weakened in faith, he calmly contemplated his own vital powers as worn out (for he was about one hundred years old) and the inability of Sarah to bear a child, [20] and yet he never staggered in doubt due to the promise of God but grew powerful in faith, because he gave the glory to God [21] in full assurance that He was able to do what He had promised. [22] Therefore, his faith was credited to him as right standing with God.

[23] It was not for his sake alone that it was written, "It was credited to him"; [24] it was for our sakes too, for it is going to be credited to us who put our faith in God who raised from the dead our Lord Jesus, [25] who was given up to death because of our shortcomings and was raised again to give us right standing with God.

Key words and phrases. Verse 13. The clause, *that he should own the world,* is another way of saying that he should be the father of many nations. This promise to Abraham is based on his right standing with God by faith.

Verse 14. The verb in the phrase, *faith is made void,* means to make empty, as a bucket with no bottom that cannot hold water. The verb in *made null and void,* means that the promise is made inoperative, invalid. Paul uses these terms to show how awful would be the consequences, if, as the Judaizers claim, only those who trust in keeping the law were heirs of the promise.

Verse 15 gives the ground (for) on which he bases his conclusion that it is by faith; the law brings only wrath (of God) and then punishes its violators.

Verse 16 shows that God devised the way of faith, so that it might extend His grace (unmerited favor) to all, not only to Jews but to Gentiles who exercise the same kind of faith that Abraham did.

Verses 17-21. *Zopoiountos* ascribes to God the power to make dead objects live; He is the source of life. He can even call, or use, things that do not exist as though they did, which refers to Sarah's procreative powers which did not exist (being barren). Yet God made them alive and she did become the mother of Isaac, the child of promise. Abraham believed that God could make her the mother of the child He had promised. "In spite of hopeless circumstances" (v. 18) means that he had no hope that by nature she could ever become a mother. By such faith he became the father of many nations. This is the way God had His promise fulfilled—through Abraham's faith. *Sperma,* seed, means offspring, descendants. In verse 19 the participle *worn out* and the substantive, "inability of Sarah to hear a child" mean that Abraham's body and Sarah's sex organs were impotent for procreation. In verse 20 his faith rises to its climactic peak. Instead of weakening in faith he did not at all stagger *(diakrino)* in doubt but rather grew powerful *(endynamoed)* in faith. His faith installed a powerful dynamo in him, and this kept on generating more faith and brought it to the climax of full assurance *(plerophoretheis).*

Verses 22-25 show how Paul regards Abraham's faith as the type of Christian faith. As he believed in the God who had power to make dead things live, so the Christian believes in the same God, who raised Christ from the dead, to prove that He is the Son of God and that God accepted His death as the propitiatory offering through which we receive justification, or right standing with God. Our failings *(paraptomata)* caused Christ's death; His resurrection becomes the cause of our justification—"raised for our justification" (A.V.).

Chapter V

The Blessed (Happy) State of the Believer (5:1-11)

Since we have been given right standing with God through faith, then let us continue enjoying peace with God through our Lord Jesus Christ, ² by whom we have an introduction through faith into this state of God's favor, in which we safely stand; and let us continue exulting in the hope of enjoying the glorious presence of God. ³ And not only that, but this too: let us continue exulting in our sufferings, for we know that suffering produces endurance, ⁴ and endurance, tested character, and tested character, hope, [5] and hope never disappoints us; for through the Holy Spirit that has been given us, God's love has flooded our hearts.

[6] For when we were still helpless, Christ at the proper time died for us ungodly men. [7] Now a man will scarcely ever give his life for an upright person, though once in a while a man is brave enough to die for a generous friend. [8] But God proves His love for us by the fact that Christ died for us while we were still sinners. [9] So if we have already been brought into right standing with God by Christ's death, it is much more certain that by Him we shall be saved from God's wrath. [10] For if while we were God's enemies, we were reconciled to Him through the death of His Son, it is much more certain that since we have been reconciled we shall finally be saved through His new life. [11] And not only that, but this too: we shall continue exulting in God through our Lord Jesus Christ, through whom we have obtained our reconciliation.

Key words and phrases. Verse 1. The participle *dikaiothentes,* being justified, is causal, meaning *since* or *because,* giving the reason of the blessed state of the believer. Because he is in right standing with God he has the following blessings: peace, access to God, hope, joy, and so on. *By faith* is *ek pisteos,* out of faith, emphasizing the human source of the justification; it is faith, not works. Peace with God (A.V.), reconciliation through the redemption secured by Christ's death, appropriated by faith. But it is more than reconciliation, as the preposition *with (pros,* face to face, Robertson, *Grammar)* indicates; it means intimate fellowship with God. The justified believer stands in Heaven's court in the closest association and affiliation with the King. The verb *have* (A.V.) is more likely *let us hold to, enjoy.* Best manuscripts have subjunctive, not indicative; supported also by the internal evidence. So it must be translated, "Let us," and so on.

Verse 2. The word *access* (A.V., Gr., *prosagogeen)* means introduction. The believer has been introduced to the court in Heaven by a Friend, Christ the Son. He is the medium (pre. *dia* denotes this) of our peace, and introduction to the King. This exalted privilege is called grace, the unmerited favor of the King who grants it. The believer is enjoying the limitless favor of the heavenly King. Because of such a privilege we as believers can "exult in our hope of the glory of God." Glory *(doxa)* here may mean either "the summation of God's moral character" (Sanday's *Commentary*) or "perfect fellowship with God in His glorious presence forever" (Thayer, *Lexicon*). The latter is more probable.

Verse 3. "Glory in our tribulations" (A.V.), or rejoice in our tribulations (A.R.V.), and "exulting in our sufferings" (Williams). Here the verb is in the subjunctive, and so it means, "let us exult in our suffering." Paul was a good example of doing so. In I Thessalonians 5:16 he exhorts, "Rejoice evermore" (in prosperity or adversity). In the Philippian jail (Acts 16:25) he was singing praise to God and in the Roman prison he exhorts, "Rejoice in the Lord always" (Phil. 4:4).

The reason we should keep on exulting (present) in our sufferings is threefold: they produce endurance (increase the capacity for endurance), endurance, tested character, and tested character, hope. This thought may be illustrated with the Galveston storm wall, erected after the destructive storm of September, 1900; this wall has shown its tested character by withstanding all the storms since then. Only in a personality with sensibility the storm *increases* as well as proves the endurance and character. One's hope for the glory of God in Heaven never shines so brightly until we suffer for our faith and learn to endure in patience. Then, like Venus as evening star, it shines most brilliantly.

Verse 5. This hope "never disappoints us" (Williams) and "putteth not to shame" (A.R.V.). It prevents our sufferings from making us feel disappointed. How does this hope have such power over us in our sufferings? Because *(hoti,* causal conjunction) "God's love has been poured out into our hearts." But how does this love achieve such results? Love is the "greatest thing in the world" (Drummond); it is the mightiest force that operates in human hearts. But how does our consciousness grip the love of God? Not by an intellectual rational process. Socrates and Plato used that, but never had an adequate sense of God's limitless love; only His power and wisdom. Phidias had the keenest aesthetic sense, but by it he never was conscious of the matchless love of God. Only through the power of the Holy Spirit can we adequately respond to this unspeakable love.

Verse 6. *Kata kairon,* literally, *according to time;* that is, on schedule time as planned by God's eternal purpose (Gal. 4:4), Christ died for the ungodly; that is, for those who would not worship God and actually hated Him (Rom. 1:30).

Verses 7, 8 give human illustrations to show how much greater is the love of God for us than the love of man for man. Scarcely ever does any man die for another who is merely a law-abiding citizen *(dikaios)*. Only a few as Damon and Pythias, are willing to die for a good friend of tried friendship. But God loved His enemies (v. 10), and so loved them that He gave His Son to die for them.

Verses 9-11. Paul argues *a fortiori* (from the stronger to the weaker), that if God could justify us as enemies by Christ's death, the medium of reconciliation (10, 11), much more easily shall we finally be saved from the wrath of God. *In His blood* means by His death we are justified. The word *save* is used here in the eschatological sense; that is, our final deliverance at the end of the age. Usually it includes only justification and regeneration. A few times it includes sanctification, the process of spiritual development into the likeness of Christ (Phil. 2:12, 13). *Saved by His life,* means by His resurrection life, not His earthly life. "Christ lives in me," says Paul; that is, by His resurrection life and power He lives in believers (Gal. 2:20). Notice the strong argument: Christ's death secures for the believers reconciliation and justification, but his final deliverance and the sanctifying process of development preparing for that final stage are secured by His resurrection life.

Notice again, the word in verses 10 and 11 translated *atonement* in the King James Version is *reconciliation* (Thayer, *Lexicon* and most commentators). The idea of atonement is in the word *redemption (apolutrosis)* and the word *hilasterion, propitiatory offering* (3:24, 25). Here reconciliation between God and man is accomplished because the ransom has been paid and the propitiatory offering has been made.

The Blessed State of the Justified Believer Enhanced As It Is Silhouetted against His Baneful State of Sin in Adam (5:12-21)

¹² So here is the comparison: As through one man sin came into the world, and death as the consequence of sin, and death

spread to all men, because all men sinned. ¹³ Certainly sin was in the world before the law was given, but it is not charged to men's account where there is no law. ¹⁴ And yet death reigned from Adam to Moses, even over those who had not sinned in the way Adam had, against a positive command. For Adam was a figure of Him who was to come. ¹⁵ But God's free gift is not at all to be compared with the offense. For if by one man's offense the whole race of men have died, to a much greater degree God's favor and His gift imparted by His favor through the one man Jesus Christ, has overflowed for the whole race of men. ¹⁶ And the gift is not at all to be compared with the results of that one man's sin. For that sentence resulted from the offense of one man, and it meant condemnation; but the free gift resulted from the offenses of many, and it meant right standing. ¹⁷ For if by one man's offense death reigned through that one, to a much greater degree will those who continue to receive the overflow of His unmerited favor and His gift of right standing with Himself, reign in real life through One, Jesus Christ.

¹⁸ So, as through one offense there resulted condemnation for all men, just so through one act of uprightness there resulted right standing involving life for all men. ¹⁹ For just as by that man's disobedience the whole race of men were constituted sinners, so by this One's obedience the whole race of men may be brought into right standing with God. ²⁰ Then law crept in to multiply the offense. Though sin has multiplied, yet God's favor has surpassed it and overflowed, ²¹ so that just as sin had reigned by death, so His favor too might reign in right standing with God which issues in eternal life through Jesus Christ our Lord.

Key words and phrases. Verses 12-14. In these verses Paul states a parallel between Adam and Christ, who represent the states of mankind. Adam heads the natural race of mankind; Christ heads spiritual mankind. The former includes man in a state of sin precipitated upon the race by the fall of Adam. The latter includes all believers in Christ who are living in Him, and because of Him and His death and resurrection. In tracing this parallel he adopts the thought form called "mystic realism." He uses it in Galatians 2:20. By this method of thinking he regards the head of each race as so vitally and causally connected with all the members of the respective race that what the head does all the members do. What he experiences the members experience. That is, Adam sins, all the race sin. Christ dies, all His believers die with Him. He rises to a new life, they do likewise. It is not mere fiction, it is fact.

So in verse 12, he goes back to the previous arguments to prove the universality of sin in the human race; but also the justification of believers in Christ, whose death secures for them redemption, reconciliation, and justification by faith. One man—Adam, named in verse 14. "Because all men sinned and death spread to all men." Sin is the cause, death is the consequence, the penalty. All sinned, so all died. Again we have the aorist, a historical tense expressing a definite act in the past. Undoubtedly Paul conceives of all men as sinning in Adam; that is, when Adam sinned, all men sinned. How? Not personally and in act, but as each man in the race was seminally in Adam, when he sinned all sinned. Scientifically this means that Adam as the father of the natural race by heredity transmitted the sin-principle to all his descendants. The sin-principle was in the world before Moses gave the law. Men sinned in acts and died. Death reigned from Adam to Moses. The moral law was in operation and the sin-principle led men to transgress it. The type *(tupos)*, or figure, of Him who was to come; that is, the Anointed One, the Christ. Adam headed the natural race; Christ was to head the spiritual race of believers. This is Paul's thought.

Verses 15-17. Here is given a contrast between the two states, the state in Adam, the state in Christ. The parallel breaks down, and Paul adroitly uses the contrast in thought. The antitheses magnify the grace of God and the work of Christ. Adam had a trespass, or fall; Christ makes believers a free gift *(charisma)*, which means a gift of grace or God's unmerited favor. Many died because of that one man's offense; much more, to a far greater degree, God's favor and the free gift by that favor abounded, or literally overflowed, to many. The effects of Adam's one act and that of Christ are so different. The one fall brought condemnation, but the free gift in spite of many failures (of many men) brought justification, or right standing with God. Death reigned because of Adam's one fall, but to a much greater degree believers in Christ who receive the overflow of God's favor and the free gift of right standing with Him, will reign in life (here and hereafter) through one, Jesus Christ. The one is the reign of an impersonal force (death); the other is redeemed personalities, believers, who become kings that will reign forever.

Verses 18-21. Here is a kind of résumé. One man's fall led to condemnation of all. So Christ's one righteous act (dying) leads to right standing with God and life for all believers. This result is based on *(gar,* for) the fact that by Adam's disobedience many (all) were made sinners, and by Christ's obedience many will be made righteous—first brought into right standing with God and in life ethically righteous through the indwelling of the living Christ. According to verse 20 the soteriological function of the law was to increase or to multiply the Fall; to show the power of the sin-principle in men so as to increase the baneful effects of it, thus driving sinners in despair to Christ for help and forgiveness. (See Rom. 7:24, 25, Paul's experience.) In verse 21 two things are contrasted: sin—the sin-principle—reigns, wielding the black scepter of death; grace, or God's unmerited favor, reigns through Jesus Christ in righteousness for eternal life.

A GREAT TEXT FOR AN EXPOSITORY SERMON (5:1-11)
THE BLESSEDNESS OF THE BELIEVER

    I. He Is Justified by Faith—in Right Standing with God (v. 1)
   II. He Has Peace—Reconciliation with God, and Peace of Mind (1)
  III. He Enjoys the Special Favor of God (Grace, v. 2)
  IV. He Rejoices in the Hope of the Glory of God (2)
   V. He Rejoices Even in His Sufferings—They Develop Character (3)
  VI. Christ by His Death Secured These Blessings (6-11)
 VII. God's Excelling Love Made the Gift of His Son to Die (8)
VIII. Result, the Higher Resurrection Life of the Believer—Saved by His Life (Resurrection Life). Life and Personality Saved by the Indwelling of the Risen Christ (Gal. 2:20; Phil. 1:21)

GREAT TEXT FOR A TOPICAL SERMON (5:8)
GOD'S EXCELLING LOVE

    I. His Love Excelling Human Love—(Illustrated in v. 7)

II. Why He Loves Us So—His Creatures; His Potential Children; Our Intrinsic Worth—in His Image, Rational, Immortal; Love the Essence of His Nature (I John 4:8)

III. The Proof of His Excelling Love—Gives His Best, His Son; for Sinners, for His Enemies (8; 10). Damon and Pythias, Jonathan and David.

IV. Santification a Vital Part of Justification; the Process of Unfolding Righteousness in the Believer's Life (chaps. 6-8)

Chapter VI

THE BELIEVER'S UNION WITH CHRIST INVOLVES HIS PASSING
FROM THE STATE OF SIN (6:1-14)

What is our conclusion then? Are we to continue to sin for His unmerited favor to multiply? ² Not at all! Since we have ended our relation to sin, how can we live in it any longer? ³ Or, do you not know that all of us who have been baptized into union with Christ Jesus have been baptized into His death? ⁴ So through baptism we have been buried with Him in death, so that just as Christ was raised from the dead by the Father's glorious power, so we too should live an entirely new life. ⁵ For if we have grown into fellowship with Him by sharing a death like His, surely we shall share a resurrection life like His, ⁶ for we know that our former self was crucified with Him, to make our body that is liable to sin inactive, so that we might not a moment longer continue to be slaves to sin. ⁷ For when a man is dead, he is freed from the claims of sin. ⁸ So if we died with Christ, we believe that we shall also live with Him, ⁹ for we know that Christ, who once was raised from the dead, will never die again; death has no more power over Him. ¹⁰ For by the death He died He once for all ended His relation to sin, and by the life He now is living He lives in unbroken relation to God. ¹¹ So you too must consider yourselves as having ended your relation to sin but living in unbroken relation to God.

¹² Accordingly sin must not continue to reign over your mortal bodies, so as to make you continue to obey their evil desires, ¹³ and you must stop offering to sin the parts of your bodies as instruments for wrongdoing, but you must once for all offer yourselves to God as persons raised from the dead to live on perpetually, and once for all offer the parts of your bodies to God

as instruments for right-doing. [14] For sin must not any longer
exert its mastery over you, for now you are not living as slaves
to law but as subjects to God's favor.

Key words and phrases. Verse 1. "What shall we say then?"
(A.V.) means, What is our conclusion then? To all the preceding
propositions established: the universality of sin with God's holy
nature revolting against it; but His love and grace providing a
method for man's redemption and salvation through the death of His
Son, on condition of simple faith in Him as Saviour and Lord, without having to keep the law as a condition of justification and salvation. The objector would ask, If God is so free with His favor
on sinners, is it not a logical conclusion that we should continue to
sin that His unmerited favor might all the more abound?

Observe, Paul introduces this section on sanctification with an
inferential particle *(oun,* therefore, then), which shows that sanctification is closely linked with justification, a real part of it, the
logical fruiting of the principle of righteousness implanted in the
believer by his faith.

Verse 2 answers the objection with an emphatic "Not at all!"
The reason for the answer is given in a causal relative clause, "Since
we have ended our relation to sin." This means, we died with
Christ on the cross (again he uses the thought-form of mystic
realism); that is, Christ did something when He died that causes us
to end the sin state (be dead to it), when by faith we surrendered
to Him as our Saviour and Lord. Godet *(Commentary on Romans)*
gives an apt illustration of what this dying to sin means. A Bechu-
ana convert (African) answers the missionary by saying, "When
my flock of sheep feed over my grave, we shall be dead to each
other; we shall have ended our relation to each other." This is
exactly what Paul means. (See Gal. 6:14, "I died to the world and
the world to me.")

Verses 3-4. Here he argues that our very baptism symbolically
teaches this basic truth. We were baptized into Christ, that is,
into union with Christ, and so baptized into His death. But he does
not mean that actually we were baptized into union with Christ or
into His death. He is fond of symbolical language. The acts of
the minister in baptizing a believer picture a death, burial and

resurrection. When he submerges him into the water it symbolizes a burial of one that is dead, and when he lifts him out of the watery grave it pictures a resurrection. It is not baptismal regeneration; it is symbolical teaching that the believer has died to sin, is now buried to that past life of sin, and rises to walk in the newness of life, that is, in a new resurrection life. The abstract noun *newness* is used to emphasize the fact of the *new life* the believer must live. Of course, this teaching implies that only immersion is Christian baptism. Even John Wesley, in his notes on Romans (*Explanatory Notes on the New Testament*), concedes this.

Verses 5-11. Here Paul is arguing and pleading for the resurrection life of the believer. His justification implies that he will go on to sanctification, living a new life of right-doing far above the old life of wrongdoing. *Sumphuta* (6), a biological term, literally means *planted together with Him* in a death like His, and predicates a vital, living relationship of the believer with Christ—in real union with Him as the graft is in vital union with the stock onto which it is grafted. Faith grafts the believer onto the same stock with Christ and they died together. The next clause states the logical conclusion to this truth: "We certainly shall be planted together with Him in a resurrection life like His." That is, in a new life separated from the old life of sin. Verse 6 speaks of our old man, the old self of sin, the unregenerate self, which was crucified with Christ, and so it is dead.

The logical conclusion then is that the body of sin is destroyed; literally, rendered inactive. Body of sin means a body easily yielding to sin, not teaching the essential sinfulness of matter, as claimed by some. He closes verse 6 with the conclusion that we should not be slaves to sin (the sin-principle).

Verse 7 gives an illustration from the natural life. When a man dies he is freed from sin, does not sin any more. Verse 8 states that Paul believes that believers will also live in union with Christ, because they have died in union with Him. Verses 9-11 show that Christ's resurrection life is one separated from any relation to sin, a brand new life. So the believer's resurrection life should be a new life. "Death now has no more mastery over Christ." It did master Him at Calvary, but now He lives an exalted life devoted to God.

Therefore, the believer, vitally grafted with Him, should live this higher resurrection life devoted to God. The believer draws his vitalizing vigor from the indwelling Christ, who is the risen Christ Himself living a higher life.

In verse 9 he appeals to his readers to consider themselves dead to sin (as having passed out of the sin state) and alive to God in union with Christ Jesus. This appeal is to intelligence and reason by the Christian. How important it is for the Christian to know these basic truths, so that he may be able to consider himself dead to sin and alive to God, and so be fitted to live the resurrection life in union with Christ! The ministers have on them the responsibility to teach and re-teach these basic truths to their people so that they may reach up and out for this higher life with Christ.

Verses 12-14 contain an elliptical exhortation (hortatory portion supposed to begin at 12:1). But Paul is on fire with this doctrine of the new life of sanctification, which is the process of unfolding the principle of righteousness in a growing character and personality toward the likeness of Christ Himself. So he inserts here this exhortation. In verse 12 the present imperatives with negative means, You must stop letting the sin-principle rule in and over your mortal bodies, as you did before your conversion. In verse 13 he uses an aorist imperative which means you must once for all, now, definitely, dedicate yourselves to God as persons risen from the dead and now living a higher resurrection life. Likewise a definite once-for-all dedication of your bodies, their parts, you must make.

Verse 14 gives a higher motive to live this higher life. Believers are no longer slaves to law but subjects to God's unmerited favor, and this loving favor of God should motivate them to rise above the slave state to realize their spiritual liberty; it should dynamize them with spiritual power to consider themselves dead to sin and alive to God and so live a life compatible and commensurate with the dignity implied in enjoying the special favor of God.

UNION WITH CHRIST IN THIS NEW LIFE ILLUSTRATED BY SLAVERY AND EMANCIPATION (6:15-23)

15 What is our conclusion? Are we to keep on sinning, because we are not living as slaves to law but as subjects of God's favor?

Never! ¹⁶ Do you not know that when you habitually offer yourselves to anyone for obedience to him, you are slaves to that one
whom you are in the habit of obeying, whether it is slavery to sin
whose end is death or to obedience whose end is right-doing?
¹⁷ But, thank God! that though you once were slaves of sin, you
became obedient from your hearts to that form of teaching in
which you have been instructed, ¹⁸ and since you have been freed
from sin, you have become the slaves of right-doing. ¹⁹ I am
speaking in familiar human terms because of the frailty of your
nature. For just as you formerly offered the parts of your bodies
in slavery to impurity and to ever increasing lawlessness, so now
you must once for all offer them in slavery to right-doing, which
leads to consecration. ²⁰ For when you were slaves of sin, you were
free so far as doing right was concerned. ²¹ What benefit did you
then derive from doing the things of which you are now ashamed?
None, for they end in death. ²² But now, since you have been freed
from sin and have become the slaves of God, the immediate result is
consecration, and the final destiny is eternal life. ²³ For the wages
paid by sin is death, but the gracious gift of God is eternal life
through union with Christ Jesus our Lord.

Key words and phrases. Verse 15. The same old objection is
raised—are we to continue sinning because we are not slaves to
law but subjects of God's special favor? By no means!

Verses 16-19 give a human illustration of two masters, Sin and
Righteousness, personified. He argues from a general premise accepted in social life, that one is a slave to anyone whom he habitually obeys. Men in the sin state, before being justified by faith
in Christ, yielded themselves to Sin as their master, to obey his
impulses and passions. But there is also a servitude to Righteousness, too. Believers, being set free from the chains of sin's slavery,
are in servitude to a new master, Righteousness, the principle of
righteousness planted in them by faith and their union with Christ,
and the practice of doing right. Paul thanks God that his readers,
though once slaves of the cruel master Sin, have now become obedient from the heart to the Christian standard of teaching, and so are
now slaves of Righteousness. In verse 19 he exhorts them that just
as they had once yielded the parts of their bodies to impurity and
excessive lawlessness, now they must yield them to righteousness for

sanctification. The Greek word *hagiasmos* (sanctification) here means the process of becoming holy, or like Christ, by doing right as slaves of Righteousnes. Sometimes it means the goal reached, holiness or the likeness of Christ. This is the ideal of every noble Christian. See Philippians 3:9-14, where Paul is striving to attain the goal but disclaims having already reached it.

Verses 20-23 state the compensation paid by the two masters. In verse 20 it is stated that the servants of Sin were free as to Righteousness; that is, they were expected to serve Sin only without any regard to Righteousness. In verse 21 it is stated that the result of slavery to Sin is death—in all its phases, from physical to eternal death. The apostle reminds his readers that they are now ashamed of the shady things they did while slaves of Sin. In verse 22 he gives the rewards of the slaves of God, the slaves of Righteousness. These are of two kinds: the immediate result is sanctification, which is progress in right-doing and doing good; the ultimate result, eternal life *(zoe aionios)*, which begins here at regeneration and continues through time into eternity. It is both qualitative and quantitative. In essence it is fellowship with God through union with Christ (John 17:3).

Verse 23 gives a summary of the results or rewards of the two classes. Servants of Sin receive death as their wages (a military term for the pay a soldier receives for his services). But the servants of Righteousness receive "eternal life" as the "free gift" of God; not as pay or reward for their service in right-doing and doing good. God in His grace steps in to supplement the pay that right-doing has already bestowed upon the servants of God. Eternal life is a bonus—eternal life with all the blessedness and glory belonging to it, Heaven, happy associations, inspiring environment forever, enjoyment of God the Father, God the Son, and God the Spirit, basking in their love, peace, and smiles.

Outlined Message for New Converts (6:4); What Our Baptism Teaches Us

I. That Christ Died, Was Buried, and Rose Again
  1. That He died for our sins (v. 10)
  2. That He was buried. Joseph and Nicodemus.

3. That He rose again (6:4). See 8:34, His intercession

II. The Believer's Death, Burial, and Resurrection

  1. That he died to sin—separated himself from it

  2. That he is buried with Christ in baptism

  3. That he rises with Him to live a new life

III. To Teach These Basic Truths, Baptism Must Be Immersion of Believers

  1. Only believers could die to sin

  2. Only immersion can picture these basic truths

THE TWO GREATEST PAYMASTERS (6:23)

I. Sin the Paymaster of Sinning, Unregenerate People (23a)

  1. Every one of his servants receives pay (Gal. 6:7b)

  2. In diseases, failing health, losses, failures, etc.

  3. Finally death—physical, eternal (Matt. 25:34; John 3:36)

II. God the Good Paymaster for Righteousness

  1. Righteousness the master of those who do right and good

  2. Righteousness rewards his servants here and hereafter—health, success, friends, good conscience, satisfaction (Mark 10:29, 30)

III. Eternal Life God's Free Gift, Not Compensation (23b)

  1. Eternal life not earned (3:24; Eph. 2:5, 8)

  2. Part of its blessing received in this life

  3. Full payment in the after life—eternal fellowship with God and the good.

Chapter VII

BELIEVERS MARRIED TO CHRIST FURTHER ILLUSTRATE SANCTIFICATION (7:1-6)

Do you not know, brothers—for I speak to those who are acquainted with the law—that the law can press its claim over a man only so long as he lives? ² For a married woman is bound by law to her husband while he lives, but if her husband dies, she is freed from the marriage bond. ³ So if she marries another man while her husband is living, she is called an adulteress; but if he dies, she is free from that marriage bond, so that she will not be an adultress though later married to another man. ⁴ So, my brothers, you too in the body of Christ have ended your relation to the law, so that you may be married to another husband, to Him who was raised from the dead, in order that we might bear fruit for God. ⁵ For when we were living in accordance with our lower nature, the sinful passions that were aroused by the law were operating in the parts of our bodies to make us bear fruit that leads to death. ⁶ But now we have been freed from our relation to the law; we have ended our relation to that by which we once were held in bonds, so that we may serve in a new spiritual way and not in the old literalistic way.

Key words and phrases. In verses 1-6 the apostle used a legitimate second marriage to illustrate and enforce sanctification. The sinner is married to the law as his first husband. But by faith in Christ he dies to the law and is freed from his relation to the law and is married to Christ. The law is the first husband (of the sinner); Christ becomes the second husband (of the believer). It is the same individual, but he changes states. In verse 1 likely the word *law* is used in the civil sense, as he is speaking to Romans who were acquainted with their civil laws. Roman law became the forerunner of British and American law.

In verse 2 he illustrates with a woman who is bound by law to her husband as long as he lives, but if he dies she is free from that marriage bond.

In verse 3 he shows how she would be an adulteress if she lived with, or was married to, another man while her husband still lives. He preserves the distinction between adultery (the sin of illicit sex relations between married persons) and fornication (that between unmarried persons).

In verse 4 he again resorts to mystic realism to state his teaching on the two marriages. You believers died with Christ on the cross, and thus ended your relation to the law, and by your faith you have been married to the risen Christ. Notice how he then changes from second person to *we*. You ended your old marriage relation to the law and entered into a new one with Christ, "in order that *we* might bear fruit for God." That is, Paul here includes himself with his readers as married to Christ to mean that he and they together are now bearing the fruit of sanctification to the glory of God. As children are the fruit of a natural marriage, the spiritual marriage to Christ is thought of as bearing the fruit of sanctification—growing in right-doing and in doing good.

Verse 5. Death is the fruit of the first marriage to sin and law, because it is a life according to the lower nature (flesh). This is a common meaning of this word with Paul. It feeds on the appetites and passions of our bodies.

Verse 6. We believers are dead to the law (as the first husband), so that we do not have to serve and work to save ourselves by obedience to the law, but we serve in a spiritual manner to bear the fruit of righteousness and sanctification for the glory of God.

The Christological Function of the Law (7:7-13)

[7] What are we then to conclude? Is the law sin? Of course not! Yet, if it had not been for the law, I should not have learned what sin was, for I should not have known what an evil desire was, if the law had not said, 'You must not have an evil desire.' [8] Sin found it rallying point in that command and stirred within me every sort of evil desire, for without law sin is lifeless. [9] I was once alive when I had no connection with the law, but when the command came, sin revived, and then I died; [10] and so, in my case, the command which should have meant life turned out to mean death. [11] For sin found its rallying point in that command and through it deceived me and killed me. [12] So the law itself is holy, and its specific commands are holy, right, and good.

[13] Did that which is good, then, result in death to me? Of course not! It was sin that did it, so that it might show itself as sin, for by means of that good thing it brought about my death, so that through the command sin might appear surpassingly sinful.

Key words and phrases. Before taking up a verse-by-verse exegesis we must notice two views of this section (7:7-25). Augustine and all the hyper-Calvinists and a few milder Calvinists regard it as a description of a Christian living on the borderline of the lower life, who allows sin to deceive him and dominate his life for the most part, instead of living the growing spiritual life of sanctification. Most modern New Testament scholars regard it as the experience of an awakened sinner with his struggles for the light until he finally finds Christ as his only hope. So hold Stevens,

Sanday, Denny, Meyer, and others. The internal evidence is in favor of the latter view, for 8:1 fits perfectly with 7:7, leaving this section as a parenthesis. In 7:7 he states that we believers are dead to the law and now free to serve in a spiritual way. In 8:1 the apostle shouts, "There is therefore now no condemnation for those who are in Christ Jesus" (i.e., in union with Him), which, to carry out his illustration of a second marriage, are married to Him (as he states it in 7:4).

The whole paragraph (as Westcott and Hort Greek Text) 7:7-13 refutes the idea that the law is an evil or sinful thing. On the contrary, it is a holy and good thing, even in the salvation of the believer. It has a Christological function. It helps prepare the sinner for Christ to save him. Verse 7 tells us that it is by the law that the sinner gets his first knowledge of what sin is—a violation of a positive command of God. This is illustrated by the Tenth Commandment, which says, "You must not have an evil desire." Paul says, "I did have evil desires, and so I came to know that I was a sinner, one that missed the mark set by God." *Covet* is too weak a translation of the Greek verb *(epithumeo)*. It expresses all sorts of evil desires, of appetite, power, fame, money, property of others, sex impulses, and so on.

Verse 8 states that the real cause of evil-doing is not the law but the sin-principle *(hamartia)*, which is the meaning of sin throughout chapters 6 and 7. The sin principle merely used the Tenth Commandment as a rallying point (a military term denoting a favorable position seized by an ingenious general for attacking the opposing army). Sin is personified as intelligent. Of course, it is the Devil who has the intelligence and directs the sin-principle to seize the Tenth Commandment as an easy point for attacking and tempting the man who is depraved and weak. He did just that thing in Eden when he said to Eve, "You shall not surely die," though that was just what God had said to her. He told her the fruit was desirable to make one wise, and he deceived her. Sin has no power if there is no law to break.

Verse 9-10. Paul thought he was alive—doing God's service while he was persecuting saints who followed the Nazarene, *before* the Tenth Commandment faced him. But when it did thunder into his conscience, "You must not have an evil desire," he knew he was a dead sinner: "Sin revived and I died." So the very commandment which "should have meant life turned out to mean death." "I died" means that Paul saw that he was spiritually dead; not right with God, thus paving the way for his conversion.

Verse 11 gives a description of the power of sin to deceive and destroy the morally weak man or woman. Of course, it is the Devil, the father of lies, the father of sin on earth, who deceives, as he did in Eden (I Tim. 2:14). Sin also kills its victim; separates him from God, as it did Adam and Eve who tried to hide from God as soon as they had sinned.

Verses 12, 13 give the apostle's estimate of the law. It is holy; that is, it expresses the holy character of God. Its specific commands are holy, each expressing some phase of God's character; they are right, and so set moral standards for conduct; they are good, that is, useful for serving the welfare of men and the glory of God. So the law is only the rallying point, or occasion, which the sin-principle seizes to attack and tempt depraved men and women. The law itself is not responsible for man's wickedness and lawlessness; it is the sin-principle that works havoc in human hearts and lives.

THE INNER CONFLICT OF THE AWAKENED SINNER (7:14-25)

14 For we know that the law is spiritual, but I am made of flesh that is frail, sold into slavery to sin. 15 Indeed, I do not understand what I do, for I do not practice what I want to do, but I am always doing what I hate. 16 But if I am always doing what I do not want to do, I agree that the law is right. 17 Now really it is not I that am doing these things, but it is sin which has its home within me. 18 For I know that nothing good has its home in me; that is, in my lower self; I have the will but not the power to do what is right. 19 Indeed, I do not do the good things that I want to do, but I do practice the evil things that I do not want to do. 20 But if I do the things that I do not want to do, it is really not I that am doing these things, but it is sin which has its home within me. 21 So I find this law: When I want to do right, the wrong is always in my way. 22 For in accordance with my better inner nature I approve God's law, 23 but I see another power operating in my lower nature in conflict with the power oper-

ated by my reason, which makes me a prisoner to the power of sin which is operating in my lower nature. ²⁴ Wretched man that I am! Who can save me from this deadly lower nature? ²⁵ Thank God! it has been done through Jesus Christ our Lord! So in my higher nature I am a slave to the law of God, but in my lower nature, to the law of sin.

Key words and phrases. Verse 14. A repetition of the apostle's high estimate of the law. It is spiritual. That is, it deals with spiritual and ethical principles, and if properly evaluated and obeyed it contributes to man's spiritual welfare. "I am made of flesh that is frail" *(sarkinos)*. This is the meaning of this adjective, while *sarkikos* means fleshly, pertaining to flesh. Paul feels that his very moral constitution is frail and impotent. The word is both physical and ethical as used here. In all other passages in chapters 7 and 8, it means man's lower nature contrasted with his higher nature *(pneuma)*.

Verse 15. The apostle says he does not understand his own actions. They are a puzzle to him. He practices the things he hates, and not the things he loves and longs to do. The result of his slavery to the sin-principle.

Verse 16. This conflict between his actions and desires (between *poio and thelo)*, his doing and willing, does not implicate the law. "I agree that the law is right and good." It is even spiritual.

Verses 17-21. The blame is placed upon the sin-principle which has its permanent home within him. The Greek verb *oikeo* means to dwell permanently. In verse 17 he apparently exculpates himself. "It is no longer I that do these things." It is the sin-principle that does them. He does not mean to deny his personal responsibility, but it is his way of emphasizing the complete enslavement to which he is subjected by the sin-principle. In 18-20 he emphasizes the fact that sin has robbed him of moral ability to follow up his choices with actions. In 20 he again emphasizes the fact that the blame is on the sin-principle which has its permanent home within him and has enslaved him.

Verses 21-23 describe the conflict as one between two laws operating in him. In 21 the word *law* means a way of operating. "The law of God" in 22 means the law of Moses and the moral law in his moral constitution. In 23 "another law in my members," a way of operation in my lower nature. "The law of my mind" has the same sense. These two laws, forces, operate against each other and make him a captive to the sin-principle; "sold under sin."

Verses 24, 25. The conflict drives him to despair, and he cries, "Wretched man that I am! Who can save me? Thank God! It has been done through Jesus Christ our Lord!" This seems to be a vivid recapitulation of his conflict in those weeks and months as an awakened sinner culminating in the happy experience near the Damascus gate, his glorious conversion in accepting the risen Christ as his Saviour and Lord. During that time he thought he was serving "the law of God with his mind" (reason) but really he was "with his lower nature serving the law of the sin-principle."

Chapter VIII

The Glorification of the Believer; the Indwelling Holy Spirit the Causal Agent of His Sanctification and Glorification (8:1-30)

The Indwelling Holy Spirit Sets the Standard for the Higher Life (1-11)

So then there is no condemnation at all for those who are in union with Christ Jesus. ² For the life-giving power of the Spirit through union with Christ Jesus has set me free from the power of sin and death. ³ For though the law could not do it, because it was made helpless through our lower nature, yet God, by sending His own Son in a body similar to that of our lower nature, and as a sacrifice for sin, passed sentence upon sin through His body, ⁴ so that the requirement of the law might be fully met 'in us who do not live by the standard set by our lower nature, but by the standard set by the Spirit. ⁵ For people who live by the standard set by their lower nature are usually thinking the things suggested by that nature, and people who live by the standard set by the Spirit are usually thinking the things suggested by the Spirit. ⁶ For to be thinking the things suggested by the lower nature means death, but to be thinking the things suggested by the Spirit means life and peace. ⁷ Because one's thinking the things suggested by the lower nature means enmity to God, for it does not subject itself to God's law, nor indeed can it. [8] The people who live on the plane of the lower nature cannot please God. [9] But you are not living on the plane of the lower nature, but on the spiritual plane, if the Spirit of God has His home within you. Unless a man has the Spirit of Christ he does not belong to Him. [10] But if Christ lives in you, although your bodies must die because of sin, your spirits are now enjoying life because of right standing with God. [11] If the Spirit of Him who raised Jesus from the dead has His home within you, He who raised Christ Jesus from the dead will also give your mortal bodies life through His Spirit that has His home within you.

Key words and phrases. Verse 1. The particle *nun* means "now," not "then" or "therefore." The word *no* heads the sentence for emphasis—"no condemnation at all." This happy state is for "those who are in union with Christ Jesus." Those who are "married" to Him (7:4).

Verse 2. The particle *for* gives the reason why they are not under condemnation any more: the life-giving Spirit set them free. We observe that Paul says, "set me free." He is still thinking of his personal experience as given in 7:25, but the *me* represents all believers. This refers to his conversion, for he uses the aorist, the historical tense.

The word *law* in this verse means a way of operating, but approaches the meaning of *power* or *force*. "The power of the Spirit set me free from the power of sin and death." We must notice that the Spirit co-operates with Christ in doing so—"in union with Christ Jesus." Christ is absolutely essential for saving a soul; not even the Spirit can do so without Christ.

Verse 3. It was impossible *(adunaton)* for the law to set the sinner free. Its impotency was caused by man's lower nature *(sarx);* man could not perfectly obey it. So God sent His Son to do so. He came in the likeness of sinful flesh, not incarnated in sinful flesh. He had a sinless not a sinful body. It was a miracle, for though He had a divine Father for His incarnate body, He had a human mother who was not sinless. And sons usually inherit more from their mothers than from their fathers (a scientific demonstration). The earthly Jesus was God-Man, and as such had a sinless body. "He condemned sin in the flesh." In dying in His incarnate body He passed sentence on sin as the cause of death. Sin is the criminal guilty of death.

Verse 4. *Dikaioma* means what the law requires, a "righteous requirement," and the purpose or result of His condemning sin on the cross is that believers might or may receive the benefit of this righteous requirement of the law. The preposition *kata,* according to, sets the standards men live by, that of the lower nature, and that of the Spirit.

Verses 5-9 picture the lives of those following the two standards, that of the lower nature, and that of the Holy Spirit. What they think is basic in characterizing them. Those following the lower standard habitually (present) think the things of the lower nature, vile, immoral, wicked thoughts. Those following the standard of the Holy Spirit think the things of the Spirit, high, pure, spiritual, elevating thoughts (see Phil. 4:8). In verse 6 the former thinking leads to death, moral and spiritual death. The latter thinking means life, the higher life of the Spirit, and peace—fellowship with God and serenity of mind. This is all true because the thinking of the lower nature is enmity to God and not at all subject to the law of God. Of course it cannot please God.

Verse 9. The phrases, in the flesh (A.V.), and in the Spirit, mean living on these planes respectively. The man in the flesh is living on the plane of the lower nature; the man in the Spirit is living on the high plane of the Spirit. And if one does not have the Spirit of Christ, that is, the Holy Spirit, dwelling in him, he does not belong to Christ at all.

Verses 10-11. In the first verse Christ is dwelling in believers; and because of this indwelling of the Christ, though the body is going to die (so Sanday, Godet, and many other exegetes), yet the spirits of believers are now enjoying the higher life of the Spirit, "because of being in right standing with God." Verse 11 emphasizes the fact that it is the indwelling Holy Spirit who is the causal Agent of this higher life, in which our mortal bodies are made to join in living this higher life. "Shall make alive our mortal bodies." Sanday thinks this clause refers to the ethical and spiritual life here, and not to the final resurrection. The context makes it clear that the apostle is thinking of our material bodies being brought into subjection so as to contribute to the higher life of sanctification. The final clause of 11 should read "on account of His Spirit who dwells in you," which makes the Holy Spirit the direct causal Agent of this higher life of sanctification. The higher life is the life empowered and sponsored by the Holy Spirit.

As Children of God We Enjoy the Indwelling Spirit of God (8:12-17)

12 So, brothers, we are under obligations but not to our lower nature to live by the standard set by it; 13 for if you live by such a standard, you are going to die, but if by the Spirit you put a stop to the doings of your lower nature, you will live. 14 For all who are guided by God's Spirit are God's sons. 15 For you do not have a sense of servitude to fill you with dread again, but the consciousness of adopted sons by which we cry, "Abba," that is, "Father." 16 The Spirit Himself bears witness with our spirits that we are God's children; 17 and if children, then also heirs, heirs of God and fellow-heirs with Christ—if in reality we share His sufferings, so that we may share His glory too.

Key words and phrases. Verse 13. If we should live this higher spiritual life we must crucify the practices of the body inclined to sinning. This is done by the power of the Spirit (*pneumati*, instrumental).

Verse 14 extends this thought to show that the children of God are guided, which includes controlled, by the Spirit of God, the Holy Spirit. Believers who are not controlled by the Holy Spirit are either not children of God or they are disobedient ones. He uses the word sons which is often employed to include sisters, so children.

Verses 15-17 continue the idea that the believer with the indwelling Spirit is a child of God. "For you did not receive the consciousness of servitude which leads to dread, but you received the consciousness of adoption by which you cry, 'Abba' [Aramaic], Father." Notice, the word spirit (*pneuma*) is used in the sense of consciousness or feeling or disposition—twice in this sense in this verse. The consciousness of the believer is not one of slavish dread but that of an adopted son of God. This is so, for the Spirit Himself bears witness with the believer's spirit that he is a child of God. In this verse 16 we have the great doctrine of assurance. The Christian can know, and ought to know, that he is a child of God. This shows how closely akin are God and believers, both spiritual personalities, so their spirits can intermingle in personal fellowship, and God's Holy Spirit can tell the believer's spirit that he is a child of the heavenly King. Notice he uses both words, sons and children *(huios* and *teknon)*, interchangeably. The word *son* emphasizes the dignity and heirship of the child; the word *child* emphasizes the origin of his sonship, a begotten one. We must observe that this exalted station of the believer, a son and an heir (17), has a condition attached—"if indeed we share His sufferings, so that we may share His glory too." Later in life Paul emphasizes this same thought (Phil. 3:10, 11). This sentence introduces the next paragraph.

SUFFERINGS PURIFY THE BELIEVER AND PAVE HIS ROAD TO GLORY (8:18-25)

[18] For I consider all that we suffer in this present life is nothing to be compared with the glory which by-and-by is to be uncovered for us. [19] For all nature is expectantly waiting for the unveiling of the sons of God. [20] For nature did not of its own accord give up to failure; it was for the sake of Him who let it thus be given up, in the hope [21] that even nature itself might finally be set free from its bondage to decay, so as to share the glorious freedom of God's children. [22] Yes, we know that all nature has gone on groaning in agony together till the present moment. [23] Not only that but this too, we ourselves who enjoy the Spirit as a foretaste of the future, even we ourselves, keep up our inner groanings while we wait to enter upon our adoption as God's sons at the redemption [resurrection] of our bodies. [24] For we were saved [brought into right standing with God and made His children] in such a hope. [25] But a hope that is seen is not real hope. For who hopes for what he actually sees? But if we hope for something we do not see, we keep on patiently waiting for it [the glory to be uncovered after the resurrection of our bodies and when we begin to enjoy the privileges of our adoption as sons of God].

Key words and phrases. Verse 18. The *for* gives the reason why Paul says our future glorification is conditioned on our present suffering with Christ. All nature as well as man is the victim of suffering because of man's sin. But it is his deliberate calculation *(logizomai)* that all we suffer here is nothing to be compared with the glory we shall enjoy hereafter. What is Paul's conception of glory that awaits the believer as his reward for all his toils and sufferings? In Philippians 1:23 he says when he dies he departs to be with Christ. In II Timothy 4:8 he speaks of "the crown of righteousness" which the Lord is to give him on that Day. So the glory is something personal—not golden streets, jasper walls, white robes, music of harps and hallelujah choruses, but face-to-face fellowship with Christ the Son and God the Father. It is to wear a crown of righteousness; to be a king upon the throne beside the King of kings who was his Saviour and Lord when he was lost in sin. That rapture far transcends the light affliction suffered here. The splendor of such intimate fellowship with God forever far outweighs the petty sorrows in the fleeting years of life.

Verses 19-22. In these verses he uses the word creation *(ktisis)* in the sense of nature. In harmony with the Hebrew idea he regards all nature as cursed by man's sin and has gone on groaning in agony up to the present moment. But he personifies nature and thinks of it as "expectantly waiting for the unveiling of the sons of God," and some day to "share the glorious freedom of the children of God." He does not tell us definitely when that is to take place, but apparently at the end of this age when Christ's parousia ushers in the new era. Then will occur the unveiling of the sons of God.

Verse 20 shows that nature did not voluntarily give up to this state of failure, but that God let it occur in hope that deliverance would finally come for nature as well as for believers.

Verse 23 contains great thoughts. Even we believers are not exempt from this law of suffering. Even we believers must keep on groaning within ourselves and suffering agony in this state of preparation for the glory state by-and-by. But we are enjoying the foretaste (firstfruits) of the Spirit's glory in expectancy of two great events in the future: our final entrance on our adoption as sons of God, and the resurrection of our bodies (called redemption).

Notice, these two words adoption *(huiothesia)* and redemption *(apolutrosis)* are used in the eschatological sense, elsewhere in Paul not so used. In Galatians 4:5, adoption is used in a present sense, and in Romans 3:24 redemption is something secured by Christ through His death, and already achieved. But in Romans 8:23 both words refer to the end of the age.

Verses 24, 25. In these verses he exalts hope as a grace. In our sufferings hope is the star that shines the brightest. "We were saved in hope" (not "by hope," as translated by the King James Version). It is a locative and not an instrumental case *(elipidi)*. It is nowhere hinted that hope is a condition to salvation; it is an attendant grace. Hope helps the Christian "patiently wait for the things not seen"; the glory and the reward for all his toils and sufferings. Hope inspired Paul to write II Corinthians 4:17, where he sees by hope that our light affliction is contributing to a far more exceeding and eternal weight of glory.

THE HOLY SPIRIT HELPS THE BELIEVER BEAR HIS SUFFERINGS (8:26, 27)

[26] In the same way, too, the Holy Spirit is helping us in our weakness, for we do not know how to pray as we should, but the Spirit Himself pleads for us with upspeakable yearnings, [27] and He who searches our hearts knows what the Spirit thinks, for He pleads for His people in accordance with the will of God.

Key words and phrases. Verse 26. The word *help* is graphic. It literally means the Spirit "takes hold with us in turn." We bear up as long as we can, then the Spirit takes hold of our burden and relieves our weakness. We take turns in carrying the sorrows and bearing the sufferings. The Spirit intercedes for us within our hearts. He helps us pray since we do not know how to pray when crushed by our sufferings. What a friend we have in the Spirit as well as in Jesus! Jesus ascended intercedes for us in Heaven; the Spirit indwelling intercedes in our hearts to make us strong to bear our sufferings, and patient and hopeful to pray as we ought. The believer has two Intercessors to help him, so as to assure his sanctification and glorification.

THE BELIEVER'S GLORIFICATION BASED ON THE FIVE-LINKED
CHAIN OF GOD'S ETERNAL PURPOSE (8:28-30)

28 Yes, we know that all things go on working together [though
apparently in chaos] for the good of those who keep on loving
God, who are called in accordance with God's purpose. 29 For those
on whom He set His heart beforehand He marked off as His own
to be made like His Son, that He might be the eldest among many
brothers; 30 and those whom He marked off as His own He also
calls; and those whom He calls He also brings into right standing
with Himself; and those whom He brings into right standing with
Himself He also glorifies.

Key words and phrases. Verse 28. A general conclusion based
on the apostle's knowledge. "We know." This word does not mean
to know by experience, but to know by what one observes in life
and history. This is Paul's mature conclusion from his observation
of what takes place in the lives of those who love God. All things
seem to be in chaos and confusion, if we take a close-up view and
draw a quick conclusion. If we take a long perspective of successive
events and carefully note results for the people who love God, we
see that there is a real harmony for the good of the righteous. It
may not always be for his physical and material good, but if all advantages are added up—material, social, moral and spiritual—we
find that it is true that "all things are working together for his
good." The condition laid down is twofold: called in accordance
with God's purpose, and loving God. This is the effectual call of
the Spirit and the gospel, but based on God's eternal purpose, as
the next verse positively states. I am sure that Paul also felt sure
that this general conclusion of his is verified by his own experience
of persecution and suffering. All is working for his good.

Verses 29, 30 list the five links in the chain of God's eternal
purpose: God's foreknowledge, His foreordination, the effectual
call, justification and glorification. The word foreknowledge is not
mere knowledge in advance; it is knowledge in the heart and soul
of God, God in past eternity setting His heart on prospective believers. He fell in love with them millions of years before they were
born. See Psalm 1:6, "He knoweth the way of the righteous."
Not only intellectually but emotionally and volitionally—approv-

ingly and lovingly. So they "stand in the judgment." The second link is foreordination or predestination. This means literally "He marks off as His own." The verb *elect* means to pick out for His own; so synonymous. He discusses this doctrine more elaborately in the next chapter. There we shall explain more in detail. *He calls* explained above. Fourth link, *He justifies*. Explained many times in previous chapters. The fifth link is *He glorified*. Observe the past tense. This is "the dramatic aorist" (Robertson, *Big Grammar, in loc.*). That is, Paul dramatically describes the believer's glorification as already having taken place. It is so certain that it will take place that he conceives of it as already a historical fact.

The Security of the Believer; or, the Certainty of His Glorification (8:31-39)

³¹ What are we then to say to facts like these? If God is for us, who can be against us? ³² Since He did not spare His own Son but gave Him up for us all, will He not with Him graciously give us everything else? ³³ Who can bring any charge against those whom God has chosen? It is God who declared them in right standing; ³⁴ who can condemn them? Christ Jesus who died, or rather, who was raised from the dead, is now at God's right hand, and is actually pleading for us. ³⁵ Who can separate us from Christ's love for us? Can suffering or misfortune or persecution or hunger or destitution or danger or the sword? ³⁶ As the Scripture says,

"For your sake we are being put to death the livelong day,
We are treated like sheep to be slaughtered" [Ps. 44:22].

³⁷ And yet in all these things we keep on gloriously conquering through Him who loved us. ³⁸ For I have full assurance that neither death nor life nor angels nor principalities [the highest angels] nor the present nor the future, ³⁹ nor evil forces above or beneath, nor anything else in all creation, will be able to separate us from the love of God as shown in Christ Jesus our Lord.

Key words and phrases. Verse 31. "If God be for us," in the King James Version should be, "If God is for us." There is no doubt in Paul's mind as to God's being for us.

Verse 32 presents the *a fortiori* argument for the security of the believer. If God gave the supreme gift, His Son, when we were enemies (as put in 5:10), surely He will now, when we are His adopted children enjoying His favor, gives us "all other things" we may need to sustain us and keep us.

Verse 33 gives us the judicial argument for it. No one can bring further indictments against God's elect whom He has pronounced innocent and in right standing with Himself. Their case is settled in the supreme court of the universe—God's court in Heaven.

Verse 34 presents the argument of the supreme Advocate, or Attorney, Christ, who died for us, rose from the dead, and now pleads our cause at Heaven's court. This is a strong argument. The Advocate is the King's Son, who is the Judge of the supreme court; He has already proved His love for us by dying for us. Surely He will keep our case secure forever.

Verses 35-37 present the conquest argument. Believers are victorious over all the forces of evil on earth, in the skies, and in the bottomless abyss. He lists seven things as harassing and disturbing as can be conceived (35) and then asserts, "in all these things we are more than conquerors through Him that loved us." Not only conquerors but "more." Conquering believers conquer all these hostile powers and persecutions and afflictions and then have power over and beyond victory (*huper*, over and beyond, in the compound verb). They are unconquerable. Napoleon conquered till he reached Waterloo but he was not "more than a conqueror" and went down to defeat before the armies of the Duke of Wellington.

Verses 38, 39. This is the grandest sentence in Greek literature. Nothing in Demosthenes surpasses it in grandeur of thought and diction. The tie of love that binds God the Father to His children cannot be broken by any power on earth, by death or life or things present or things future; or by any power in the heavens or in Hell, angels or principalities (the highest angelic dignitaries) or powers above or beneath. Then in 39 he adds a phrase, "Nor any other creature," which excludes even the Devil as having power to break the tie of love between God and His children.

EXPOSITORY SERMON OUTLINES ON ROMANS VIII

THE GLORIFICATION OF THE BELIEVER (8:1-27)

I. The Indwelling Spirit Co-operates with Christ to Set Him Free (1-4)
   1. The law could not do so (2)
   2. The Spirit through Christ could and did (3, 4)
II. The Indwelling Spirit Sets the High Standard for Sanctification (5-9)
   1. The two standards, that of the lower nature (flesh), that of the Spirit
   2. The former leads to death, the latter means the higher life life of sanctification
III. The Indwelling Spirit the Agent of the Higher Life (10-13)
   1. The indwelling Christ essential as the medium (10)
   2. The same power that raised Christ gives the higher life (11)
   3. Believers debtors to live the higher life (12-13)
IV. The Higher Life Peculiar to the Children of God (14-17)
   1. They are guided and controlled by the Spirit (14)
   2. They have assurance not dread (15-16)
   3. They are heirs of God and fellow-heirs of Christ (17)
V. Sufferings Pave the Believer's Path to Glory (18-27)
   1. Nature suffers because of man's sin (19-22)
   2. Believers not exempt from the law of suffering (23)
   3. They are saved in hope of final deliverance—at the resurrection of their bodies (24-25)
   4. The glory by-and-by far transcends the sufferings of to-day (18)
   5. The Spirit helps them bear their sufferings (26-27)

THE SECURITY OF THE BELIEVER; OR, THE CERTAINTY OF
HIS GLORIFICATION (28-39)

I. The Basis of Security, the Five-linked Chain of God's Eternal Purpose (28-30)
   1. Foreknowledge—God setting His heart on them in past eternity (29). Compare Psalm 1:6: "The Lord knows the way of the righteous."

    2. Foreordination, or predestination—God marking them off as His own (29b)

    3. He called them effectually—by the gospel preached and lived, and by the Spirit (30)

    4. He justified them—brought them into right standing with Himself (30)

    5. He glorifies them (30)

    6. His providence overrules all things for their good (28)

II. The A Priori Argument for Security (31-32). If God made the supreme gift of His Son, surely He will give all other blessings needed for their security.

III. They Have Been Declared Innocent by the Judge in the Supreme Court (32a). "It is God who declares righteous."

IV. They Have the Supreme Advocate, or Attorney, to Plead Their Cause (33b)

V. They Enjoy the Supreme Love of God the Father and Judge (35-39)

    1. All forms of suffering combined cannot break the tie (35-37)

    2. They are more than conquerors over them (37)

VI. The Triune God Is for Them

    1. The Father loves and made the supreme gift, His Son (5:8; 8:32)

    2. The Son died, rose and pleads their cause in Heaven (34)

    3. The Spirit sanctifies and intercedes in their sufferings (10-13; 27)

V. Justification by Grace through Faith in Harmony with God's Purpose and Program in History (chaps. 9—11)

Chapter IX

GOD'S FAITHFULNESS AND JUSTICE IN SPITE OF ISRAEL'S REJECTION (9:1-29)

PAUL'S PASSIONATE GRIEF OVER ISRAEL'S REJECTION (9:1-5)

I am telling the truth, as a Christian man, I am telling no lie, because my conscience, enlightened by the Holy Spirit is bearing me witness to this fact, ² that I have deep grief and constant anguish in my heart; ³ for I could wish myself accursed, even cut off from Christ, for the sake of my brothers, my natural kinsmen. ⁴ For they are Israelites; to them belong the privileges of sonship, God's glorious presence [the skekinah over the mercy seat], the special covenants [with Abraham, Isaac, and Jacob], the giving of the law [through Moses], the temple service [and worship], the promises [of protection and deliverance], ⁵ the patriarchs, and from them by natural descent the Christ has come, who is exalted over all, God blessed forever. Amen!

Key words and phrases. Verse 1. The solemn assertion of his consuming sorrow for Israel's rejection is threefold: I assert in Christ, by union with Christ I swear, I am not falsifying, the Holy Spirit bears witness with my enlightened conscience.

Verse 2 expresses the quality of the grief—great and ceaseless— and like the mother's child-bearing anguish *(odune)*—similar to his anguish over the defection of the Galatians (4:19). This anguish is in his heart (the seat of his soul).

Verse 3 is a hard text to explain—to some who do not understand the genius of the Hebrew mind and the Greek language. "I could wish that I myself were accursed, even cut off from Christ for my brethren, my kinsmen by race." The suggestion of Professor Davis (Louisville Seminary) is not in harmony with the context— "an extraordinary life-devotion *(anathema)* by *(apo)* Christ, not *anathema from* Christ." He is out of line with famed Greek exegetes (Meyer, Sanday, Burton, Robertson, and others). The wish that Paul made is *not* in the tense that asserts an *actual wish* but a tense which expresses an *unrealized wish*. (See Robertson, *Big Grammar, in loco*). He did not say, "I now wish," but "I could wish if . . . " So it is merely a linguistic method of expressing his consuming soul-anguish for his racial kinsmen. He knows he could not save the Jewish nation by himself dying for it and condemning his own soul to perdition. That is not what he means.

Verses 4, 5 list the outstanding privileges possessed by the Israelites which increase the heartbreaking grief of Paul for them. The adoption refers to God's making Israel as a nation His sons and Himself loving them and caring for them as a Father. The glory is the Shekinah, the glorious presence of Jehovah over the mercy seat.

The covenants are those with Abraham and the other patriarchs. Moses was an Israelite through whom Jehovah gave the law. The promises are those to Moses, Joshua, David, Solomon, and the prophets, for the nation. The fathers are the ancient dignitaries like Abraham, and others. But the climax of their privileges was their giving to the world, as to natural descent, the Christ. Jesus the Messiah on the human side was a Jew. How could they reject their own flesh, the greatest mission God ever planned, to save a sinning world of God's own creatures! Perhaps, this element in their exalted privileges is the one that broke Paul's heart. But in consuming sorrow he rises to the peaks of praise to the Christ "who is God over all, blessed forever. Amen!" This is the interpretation of all the ancient exegetes, while a minority of scholars, the Modernists, follow Tischendorf, the German textual critic, in punctuating it so it reads, "The God who is over all be blessed forever," closing the former sentence with Christ according to the flesh. Westcott and Hort, authoritative textual critics, followed by most of the exegetes today, punctuate it with a comma, not a period, after *flesh*.

ISRAEL'S REJECTION NOT INCONSISTENT WITH GOD'S PROMISES (9:6-13)

⁶ But it is not that God's word has failed. For not everybody that is descended from Israel really belongs to Israel, ⁷ nor are they all children of Abraham, because they are his descendants, but the promise was "In the line of Isaac your descendants will be counted." ⁸ That is, it is not Abraham's natural descendants who are God's children, but those who are made children by the promise are counted his true descendants. ⁹ For this is the language of the promise, "About this time next year I will come back, and Sarah will have a son." ¹⁰ Not only that but this too: there was Rebecca who was impregnated by our forefather Isaac. ¹¹ For even before the twin sons were born, and though they had done nothing either good or bad, that God's purpose in accordance with His choice might continue to stand, conditioned not on men's actions but on God's calling them, ¹² she was told, "The elder will be a slave to the younger." ¹³ As the Scripture says, "Jacob I have loved, but Esau I have hated."

Key words and phrases. Verses 6-9. He shows from Scripture that not all of Abraham's natural descendants are children of promise or children of God. The descendants of Ishmael are not Israelites; only the descendants of Isaac, the sons of promise, are. This is based on the promise in Genesis 21:12: "Your descendants will be reckoned through Isaac." Also on Genesis 18:10.

Verses 10:13. Here the apostle begins to magnify his doctrine of the sovereignty of God. Rebecca, wife of Isaac, became mother of twins, Esau and Jacob. But before the boys were born and before they had done anything good or bad, God told her that "the elder will serve the younger." That is, Esau, born with the birthright and to be the heir should yield these privileges to Jacob his younger brother. Paul further bolsters his doctrine from Scripture by quoting Malachi 1:2, 3, "Jacob I loved, Esau I hated." But we must remember that Esau bartered away his birthright for a mess of pottage. He failed to put first things first. He lived for the lower instead of the higher things. Jacob was ever looking for advancement and the higher things for his future. After God met him at Bethel, he became a new man and his wicked name, Jacob, Supplanter, was changed to Israel, Prince of God (Gen. 28:16-22).

The crucial statement in this paragraph is in verse 11b: "that the purpose of God according to election might stand" (A.R.V.). Literally the Greek reads, "that God's purpose according to election might continue." God's election *(ekloge,* His picking out, His selecting) sets the standard *(kata* with accusative means this) for His dealings with men in individual lives and in history. This is a turning point in the lives of these two boys; also in the history of Chosen People. God settled the issue as to who should be the father of the twelve tribes and also as to whether they should be called Israelites or Esauites. Verse 12 further explains this sovereignty of God by asserting that the issue was not determined because of works but because of His call. According to Malachi, God settled it this way because Jacob He loved and Esau He hated. *Why* did He love Jacob and hate Esau? It is not said. It is a secret of God. We may surmise that He foresaw the superior potentialities of virtue and achievement in Jacob. Paul places God's foreknowledge at the basis of His eternal purpose (Rom. 8:29). That would help us see *why* He loved Jacob more than He loved Esau, which is all the antithetic sentence means. Not that God actually hated Esau. He loves all in spite of their sins. He loved Esau, but He loved Jacob more.

Israel's Rejection Not Inconsistent with God's Justice (9:14-29)

[14] What are we then to conclude? It is not that there is injustice in God, is it? Of course not! [15] For He says to Moses, "I will have mercy on any man that I choose to have mercy on, and take pity on any man that I choose to take pity on." [16] So one's destiny does not depend on his own willing or strenuous actions but on God's having mercy on him. [17] For the Scripture says to Pharaoh, "I have raised you to your position for this very purpose of displaying my power in dealing with you, of announcing my name all over the earth." [18] So He has mercy on any man that He chooses to, and He hardens any man that He chooses to harden.

[19] So you will ask me, "Why does He still find fault? For who can resist His will? [20] On the contrary, friend, who are you anyway that you would answer back to God? Can the clay that is molded ask the man who molds it, "Why did you make me like this?" [21] Has not the potter the right with his clay to make of the same lump one vessel for ornamental purposes, another for degrading service? [22] And what if God, though wishing to display His anger and make known His power, yet has most patiently borne with the objects of His anger already ripe for destruction, [23] so as to make known the riches of His glory for the objects of His mercy, whom He prepared in ages past to share His glory—[24] even us whom He has called, not only from among the Jews but from among the heathen too? [25] Just as He says in Hosea:

"I will call a people that was not mine, my people,
And her who was not beloved, my beloved,
[26] And in the place where it was said, 'You are no people of mine,'
They shall be called sons of the living God."

[27] And Isaiah cries out about Israel, "Although the sons of Israel are as numberless as the sands of the sea, only a remnant of them will be saved, [28] for the Lord will completely and quickly execute His sentence on the earth." [29] As Isaiah again has foretold,

"Unless the Lord of hosts had left us some descendants,
we would have fared as Sodom did and would have been
like Gomorrah."

Key words and phrases. Verse 14. If God seems to be so arbitrary in His dealings with individuals and nations, am I to conclude that He is unjust? Away with such a thought! Of course not. He is absolutely just with all men.

Verses 15-17. He predicates God's justice in dealing with men and nations on His freedom of will. He is sovereign and free to use His sovereignty as He chooses. But He never chooses to be unjust or unfair with anyone. He illustrates with Pharaoh. God tells him that He has raised him to his station of power, in order (as translated in the King James) to "show my power in your case and in order to proclaim my name to all the earth." On first glance it would seem that God had a grudge against Pharaoh and He is now going to get even with him. That is an unfair interpretation of the sentence. The purpose particle *(hopos)* may be *result* as well as purpose. Then it would read *so that* instead of *in order that*. So Burton, *Moods and Tenses;* Robertson, *Big Grammar*. This would soften the meaning and harmonize with the statements in Exodus (chap. 9) that Pharaoh "hardened his heart." God hardened Pharaoh's heart only in the sense that He allowed Pharaoh to exercise his freedom of will and harden his own heart.

Verse 19 makes an objector ask, "Why does God still find fault? For who can resist His will?" This is a play on the double meaning of *resist*. Pharaoh *did* resist God's will and refused to let God's people go, but he could *not* resist God's will in the sense of *frustrating* that will. No man can do that. God goes right on and carries out His purpose, if Pharaoh or anyone else fails to do His will.

Verses 20, 21. The illustration of the potter and two kinds of vessels, those for ornamental purposes and those of menial service. The vase for a king and the slop jar for the peasant would illustrate in the concrete. Of course, the potter has the right to select one part of a big lump of clay and make out of it a beautiful vase for the king. Then he may take another part of the same lump and make out of it a slop jar for the peasant. If the clay could talk, it would not have the right to say to the potter, "Why did you make a slop jar out of me instead of a vase?" As the potter is sovereign over his piles of clay, so God is sovereign over His creatures and has the right to exercise His freedom of will in dealing with all of them.

Verses 22-24. God's dealings with the vessels of wrath and the vessels of mercy. The vessels of wrath represent the wicked exposed to the wrath of God in perdition; the vessels of mercy represent the believers who are in right standing with God, who are in the process of sanctification and awaiting their glorification. Paul says that God with much patience bore with them. He did not want them to be lost at last. With His goodness He tried to lead them to repentance and to salvation through His Son (Rom. 2:4). The difficult phrase is *prepared for perdition (kateertismena eis apoleian).* What does it mean? *Who* prepared them for perdition? *When* and *how* were they prepared? It is not said that God prepared them for it. It is nowhere said that God elects some to perdition. The Presbyterian Assembly a few years ago deleted from their catechism the expression, "infants a span long in Hell." The hyper-Calvinists once believed that God predestined some infants for Hell and others for Heaven. No, God has made sufficient preparation in the universal atonement made by Christ on the cross to save all the infants, all children up to the age of responsibility for their personal sins.

It must be noticed that the perfect participle, *prepared,* is either middle or passive voice in Greek, and so may be translated, *"having prepared themselves* for perdition," instead of just "prepared." That is, Paul's idea may have been that these vessels of wrath prepared themselves for perdition. They alone were responsible for their being lost, not God. Certainly it is not stated that God was at all responsible for it. In the next verse he positively asserts that "He [God] beforehand prepared for glory the vessels of mercy." Surely there is not hyper-Calvinism, no predestination of some to perdition, in this passage. His election and predestination refer in Paul only to the vessels of mercy to whom He makes known the riches of His glory. What a wonderful phrase, riches of glory! He has for them not only glory, but glory that is opulent, abundant, in spiritual possessions for the saved.

Verses 25-29. Paul again proves his doctrine by quoting the Old

Testament as suggesting centuries ago these wonderful teachings. The two passages from Hosea are to prove that God's election included Gentiles as well as Jews (v. 24). "Even us whom he also called, not from the Jews only, but also from the Gentiles" (A.R. V.). Hosea says, "Those who were not my people I will call my people . . . They will be called sons of the living God." This means people from outside the Jewish nation, Gentiles. He quotes from Isaiah 11:11 to prove that God by His election has a remnant from the Jews, in spite of the general rejection of Israel. In all, Paul has used ten quotations from the Old Testament in this chapter, to prove his teaching on God's purpose of election.

Chapter X

ISRAEL ITSELF TO BLAME FOR ITS REJECTION (9:30-10:13)

³⁰ What are we then to conclude? That heathen peoples who were not in search for right standing with God have obtained it, and that a right standing conditioned on faith; ³¹ while Israel, though ever in persuit of a law that would bring right standing, did not attain to it. ³² Why? Because they did not try through faith but through what they could do. They have stumbled over the stone that causes people to stumble, ³³ as the Scripture says:

"See, I put on Zion a stone for causing people to stumble,
    a rock to trip them on,

But no one who puts his faith in it will ever be put to
    shame." [Isa. 8:14; 28:16]

10. THE FAITH METHOD OF RIGHT STANDING WITH GOD INTENDED FOR ALL; SO THE GOOD NEWS MUST BE PROCLAIMED TO ALL

Brothers, my heart's good will goes out for them, and my prayer to God is that they may be saved. ² For I can testify that they are zealous for God, but they are not intelligently so. ³ For they were ignorant of God's way of right standing and were trying to set up one of their own, and so would not surrender to God's way of right standing. ⁴ For Christ has put an end to law as a way to right standing for everyone who puts his trust in Him. ⁵ For Moses says of the law-way to right standing with God that whoever can perform the law will live by it. ⁶ But here is what the faith-way to right standing says, "Do not say to yourself, 'Who will go up to heaven?' " that is, to bring Christ down; [7] or " 'Who will go down into the depths?' " that is, to bring Christ up from the dead. [8] But what does it say? "God's message is close to you, on your very lips and in your heart"; that is, the message about faith which we preach. [9] For if with your lips you acknowledge the fact that Jesus is Lord, and in your hearts you believe that God raised Him from the dead, you will be saved. [10] For in their hearts people exercise the faith that leads to right standing, and with their lips they make the acknowledgment which means salvation. [11] For the Scripture says, "No one who puts his faith in Him will ever be put to shame." [12] But there is no distinction between Jew and Greek, for the same Lord is over them all, because He is infinitely kind to all who call upon Him. [13] For everyone who calls upon the name of the Lord will be saved.

Key words and phrases. Verses 30-33 present the different attitudes of the two, Jews and Gentiles, toward God's way of righteousness, or right standing with Himself. Gentiles generally were not in pursuit of any way of righteousness, while Jews were in diligent pursuit of a law of righteousness; that is, in pursuit of a law-method of attaining right standing with God. The result was that Gentiles, many of them, obtained right standing with God, but Jews did not attain to it. Paul asks, "Why?" The answer is clear. Gentiles sought it by faith, Jews sought it by their own works. Paul uses the preposition *ek* with faith and works, which emphasizes the fact that the source of justification on *man's* part is faith, and not his obedience to the law. Notice, Paul confirms his doctrine of faith as the source of justification for man by quoting Isiah 28:16, "No one who puts his faith in it [the rock on Zion] will ever be put to shame."

Chapter 10, verse 1. Here the apostle's heart-power shows itself, as we saw also in 9:3. His head was full of sense and knowledge. But his heart was full of love and sympathy. He was one of the most symmetrical men in all history; great in intellect, heart (emotions), and will power for action. He was a perfect combination of an introvert-extrovert. His heart's good-will went out in love and tenderness to his Jewish kinsmen who were rejecting his and their Messiah and Saviour. His prayer to God was ceaseless for them to be saved.

Verses 2-4. Here he shows how the Jews clung to their own law-way of righteousness which kept them ignorant of God's way of righteousness, which is the faith-way. They were so interested in a law of righteousness that they were blind to the faith-way. They were more interested in the law than in righteousness. Undoubtedly the word righteousness in these verses mean "God's way of bringing men into right standing with Himself," not His attribute of justice. In verse 4 he says that "Christ is the end of the law for righteousness to everyone that believes." What is the meaning of *end of the law?* Not that Christ has fulfilled the law in His character and living, as many ministers and interpreters formerly claimed, so that He could impute His righteousness (He having kept the law perfectly) to the believer. Imputed righteousness is taught in other passages, but not in this one. Paul means to say here that Christ has put an end to the law as a system to be relied on by anyone who believes in Him. Its principles are *not* ended. They are eternal and binding on everyone, Christian and non-Christian. This interpretation is endorsed by many leading exegetes (Sanday, Godet, Denny and others; and by modern writers of New Testament theology, as Weiss, Stevens, Sheldon, Adeney, and others).

Verses 5-10. Paul describes the two ways, the law-way and the faith-way. Moses himself tells us what the law-way requires: that one must *do* the law if he would live by it. But no one can perfectly keep the law, and therefore no one can live by it, or be saved by obedience to it. Paul had proved this by his own experience. By the same method he knew that a sinner who trusts in Christ as his Saviour and Lord is brought into right standing with God; is saved. The faith-way urges the sinner not to look for the place, either to Heaven or to the abyss, to find Christ the Saviour. He has already come down and has already been raised from the dead. And the faith-way says, The message of faith is in your mouth and in your heart, and what you have to do is accept it. This is done by two steps: confess with your mouth that Jesus is Lord, and believe in your heart that God raised Him from the dead, and you will be saved. This means, your sins will be forgiven and you will be brought into right standing with God. But verse 10 asserts that the faith that saves must be believing with the heart. No intellectual

belief or mere credal subscription is sufficient. The heart is the
seat of the soul. So it comes to mean a complete personal surrender
of the whole self to the risen Christ is essential to this faith that
saves, Christ must be accepted as Lord as well as Saviour, a fact
which is often overlooked by revivalists. Then it is no light thing
to believe as Paul stipulated one must believe with the heart that
Jesus is Lord.

Verses 11-13. This faith-way makes salvation universal in its
offer. No one of any race or class need be put to shame, for there
is no social or racial distinction in the mind of God. He is ready
to forgive and save Jew and Greek, American and European, Asi-
atic and African, on the same footing. This is so because whoever
calls upon the name of the Lord will be saved. This latter sentence
is an echo of Joel 2:32. Paul is again proving his faith-method of
justification by recourse to the Old Testament. And also the universality of the offer God makes to men: "Whoever calls . . . No
distinction."

ISRAEL'S UNBELIEF NOT EXCUSED BY WANT OF OPPORTUNITY (10:14-21)

14 But how can people call upon One in whom they have not
believed? And how can they believe in One about whom they
have not heard? And how can people hear without someone to
preach to them? 15 And how can men preach unless they are
sent to do so? As the Scripture says, "How beautiful are the feet
of men who bring the glad news of His good things!" [Isa. 52:7].

16 However, they have not all given heed to the good news,
for Isaiah says, "Lord, who has put faith in what we told?" 17 So
faith comes from hearing what is told, and hearing through the
message about Christ. 18 But may I ask, They had no chance
to hear, did they? Yes, indeed:

"All over the earth their voices have gone,
To the ends of the world their words" [Ps. 19:4].

19 But again I ask, Israel did not understand, did they? For
in the first place Moses says:
"I will make you jealous of a nation that is no nation;
I will provoke you to anger at a senseless nation" [Deut.
32:21].

²⁰ Then Isaiah was bold enough to say:

"I have been found by a people who were searching for me,
I have made known myself to people who were not asking to know me [Isa. 65:1].

²¹ But of Israel he said:

"All day long I have held out my hands to a people that is
disobedient and obstinate" [Isa. 65:2].

Key words and phrases. Verses 14, 15 give expression to the missionary heart of Paul. For people to be able to hear the message about Christ, preachers must be sent to tell them the story of the good news. The first sentence in 14 shows that the calling on the name of the Lord which brings salvation must be calling in faith, for how can they call upon Christ unless they believe in Him? In order to have a chance to believe they must hear the glad news, and to hear there must be preachers sent to tell that news. This means a missionary program similar to that in which Paul has been engaged for several years since he first went out from Antioch.

Verses 16, 17. But the Jews did not all heed the good news when they heard it, and this was the experience Isaiah had when he preached to them, for he asked, "Lord, who has believed what we told them?" Many in some places stoned Paul for preaching the good news, instead of believing the message about Christ. As in Lystra.

Verses 18, 19. These verses make it clear that Israel both heard the message and understood it. Again he quotes from Psalm 19:4 to prove that the message went out into all the earth, so they had an opportunity to hear. He quotes from Deuteronomy 32:21 to prove they understood it. He ascribes Deuteronomy to Moses.

Verses 20, 21 make it clear that the Messianic message was intended to be universal; for Gentiles as well as for Israel. Isaiah foresaw this great truth. So Paul has cited all three divisions of the Old Testament, the Law, the Psalms, and the Prophets (Isaiah) to prove that Israel had an opportunity to hear and heed the good news, but that God all the time intended it for Gentiles also.

A GREAT TEXT WITH SERMON OUTLINE (9:3 and 10:1)
BURNING AND YEARNING FOR THE LOST TO BE SAVED

I. The Normal Desire of the Christian—for the Lost to Be Saved
1. He knows the worth of souls (Mark 8:36)
2. He knows they are lost (John 3:18; Rom. 1:28)
3. He loves souls. Jesus, Peter, John, Paul.
II. Burning and Yearning for Them to Be Saved
1. Only Consecrated Christians have this passion (9:3). Paul said, "I could wish myself accursed from Christ."
2. Such feel their responsibility for their salvation. Ezekiel a watchman on the wall to warn.
III. Putting Forth Efforts to Win Them
1. Praying—"My prayer to God for them . . . "
2. Preaching to win them. Peter and the three thousand at Pentecost.
3. Teaching to win them. Baylor professor teaching in Sunday school and winning Baylor boys to Christ.
4. Sacrificing self. So Paul. Henry Martyn in India. "Now let me burn out for God!" Burning and yearning for souls, as Paul did.

Chapter XI

GOD'S PROGRAM OF HISTORY BEING FULFILLED IN THE REJECTION
OF ISRAEL; THE REJECTION OF ISRAEL NOT TOTAL (11:1-10)

I ask then, God has not disowned His people [Israel], has He? Of course not! Why, I am an Israelite myself, a descendant of Abraham, a member of the tribe of Benjamin. ²No, God has not disowned His people, on whom He set His heart beforehand. Do you know what the Scripture says in Elijah's case, how he pleaded with God against Israel? ³"Lord, they have killed your prophets, they have demolished your altars; I alone have been left, and they are trying to kill me" [I Kings 19:10]. ⁴But how did God reply to him? "I have reserved for myself seven thousand men who have never bent their knees to Baal." ⁵So it is at the present time; a remnant remains, in accordance with God's unmerited favor. ⁶But if it is by His unmerited favor, it is not at all conditioned on what they have done. If that were so, His favor would not be favor at all. ⁷What are we then to conclude? Israel has failed to obtain what it is still in search for, but His chosen ones have obtained it [salvation through the Messiah]. The rest have become insensible to it, [8] as the Scripture says, "God has given them over to an attitude of insensibility, so that their eyes cannot see and their ears cannot hear, down to this very day" [Isa. 29:10; Deut. 29:4]. [9] And David said:

"Let their food become a snare and a trap to them,
Their pitfall and retribution;
[10] Let their eyes be darkened, so that they cannot see,
And forever bend their backs beneath the load"

[Ps. 69:22, 23].

Key words and phrases. Verse 1. God has not abandoned His chosen people Israel. The Greek verb *aposato* describes a custom in ancient times when parents often abandoned their own children, threw them out to be devoured by the wild beasts. Of course God has not thrown out His chosen children, Israel. No, Paul says, for I myself am an Israelite, and He has not abandoned me. That could have been said of hundreds of believing Jews and of Peter, James and John, and all the early apostles; of Stephen, Barnabas, Silas, and others. Another reason given by Sanday and other modern exegetes is, Of course as I myself am an Israelite I would not dare to assert such a thing of God about His chosen children.

Verse 2a. The great reason why Paul knows God has not disowned His chosen people is that He set His heart on them in former ages. Here is the word *foreknew*. He foreknew them in past ages. He fell in love with them, so to speak. He used it in Romans 8:29, and made foreknowledge the first link in the chain of God's eternal purpose of redemption.

Verses 2b-4. He proves from God's reply to Elijah's complaint against Israel (I Kings 19:10) that He had seven thousand as a faithful remnant who never bent their knees to Baal; that God has not been completely forsaken by His chosen people Israel. Verses 5 and 6 show that this remnant of them remaining faithful to His Messiah are the elect of His grace. That is, God's unmerited favor has selected this remnant, and they have by faith selected Christ as the Messiah. He again emphasizes the fact that this selection by God was not on the basis of works. If so, it could not have been on the basis of unmerited favor.

Verses 7-10 show how Israel (most of them) failed, proving it by citing Old Testament Scripture—Deuteronomy, Isaiah, and Psalm 69:22, 23. Again, Paul emphasizes the divine election but not minimizing man's freedom and responsibility. These passages must not be interpreted literally. God merely gave these unbelieving Jews over to their personal beliefs and behavior. "God gave them a spirit of stupor" (A.S.V.), or "an attitude of insensibility" (Williams). No, God did not positively and personally give them this stupor or insensibility, so that they could not see or hear. This is a Hebraic thought-mode, ascribing to God what He merely permits man to do in his freedom of will, where the results are produced according to God's moral laws. So the Jew thought of God *as actually doing* what He *permitted* to result according to His laws. The vast majority of Jews were hardened; that is, like Pharaoh they hardened their own hearts and would not submit to God's way of bringing men into right standing with Himself, but were seeking to establish their own way (the law-way). That is, they rejected Christ as the Messiah and would not trust Him to save them by faith. But the election obtained it. God chose those who accepted Jesus as their Messiah and their Saviour by faith (v. 8), Paul, Silas, Barnabas, Stephen, and a host of faithful Jews in those days.

REJECTION OF ISRAEL NOT FINAL (11:11-24)

[11] I say then, they did not stumble so as to fall in utter ruin, did they? Of course not! On the contrary, because of their stumbling, salvation has come to heathen peoples, to make the Israelites jealous. [12] But if their stumbling has resulted in the enrichment of the world, and their overthrow becomes the enrichment of heathen peoples, how much richer the result will be when the full quota of Jews comes in!

[13] Yes, I now am speaking to you who are a part of the heathen peoples. As I am an apostle to the heathen peoples, I am making the most of my ministry to them, to see [14] if I can make my fellow-countrymen jealous, and so save some of them. [15] For if the rejection of them has resulted in the reconciling of the world, what will the result be of the final reception of them but life from the dead? [16] If the first handful of dough is consecrated, so is the whole mass; if the tree's root is consecrated, so are the branches.

[17] If some of the branches have been broken off, and yet you although you were wild olive suckers, have been grafted in among the native branches, and been made to share the rich sap of the native olive's root, [18] you must not be boasting against the natural branches. And if you do, just consider, you do not support the root, but the root supports you. [19] Then you will say, "Branches have been broken off for us to be grafted in." [20] Very well; but it was for lack of faith that they were broken off, and it is through your faith that you now stand where you are. Stop your haughty thinking; rather continue to be reverent, [21] for if God did not spare the natural branches, certainly He will not spare you. [22] So take a look at the goodness and the severity of God; severity to those who have fallen, but goodness to you, on condition that you continue to live by His goodness; otherwise, you too will be pruned away. [23] And they too, if they do not continue to live by their unbelief, will be grafted in, for God is amply able to graft them in. [24] For if you were cut off from an olive wild by nature, and contrary to nature were grafted on to a fine olive stock, how much easier will it be for the natural branches to be grafted on to their own olive stock?

Key words and phrases. Verses 11, 12. Paul plays upon the words *stumble* and *fall*. Israel stumbled over the Messiah who had come in the person of Jesus. But this stumbling is not to result in their utter fall, or ruin. The fall is temporary. Evidently the particle *hina* is *result* and *not purpose*, as in the King James Version. *Result* is the translation of all modern translators; so of Sanday, Denney, and most modern exegetes. Neither the Jews nor God had any specific purpose in their stumbling. But the result was a temporary fall. This fall meant salvation to the Gentiles. That is, the missionaries, Barnabas and Paul and Silas, on having their message rejected by the Jews, turned to the Gentiles and offered them salvation by faith in Christ. In verse 12 he shows that this partial rejection by Jews has meant the enrichment of Gentiles and the world. He thinks this enrichment of the nations will move the Jews to jealousy and after a time it will result in the full quota of Jews (*plerome auton*) accepting Jesus as their Messiah and Saviour.

Verses 13, 14. Paul begins his appeal to the Gentile Christians in Rome. A large majority of the membership in the Roman church was doubtless Gentile. So in this paragraph he is addressing them with a personal appeal not to be too proud of their election by God to carry out His purpose of redemption, in spite of the failure of Israel, His chosen nation. He calls himself an apostle to the Gentiles, and as such is magnifying his office, as the King James Version translates it. This is not the real idea he has in mind; not to magnify or honor his ministry as an apostle, but to *make the most of his ministry* as an apostle to the Gentiles, is what he has in mind, as indicated by the next sentence, "in order to make my fellow-countrymen jealous." That is, he is trying to make his apostolic ministry to the Gentiles count for the most in winning all the Gentiles he can and helping to develop among them as strong churches as possible. That is one great reason why he is writing to this church at Rome, to enlist its sympathy and co-operation in his world missionary campaigns. See 15:28, where he states that he is coming by Rome on his way to Spain.

Verse 15. The expression, *life from the dead,* must be understood in a spiritual sense—a spiritual quickening among the churches. "Reconciliation of the world" also is used in a spiritual sense; the rejection of Israel opened the way for preaching the gospel to the nations so that Gentiles might find reconciliation with God through redemption in Christ.

Verse 16 expresses a general truth that the portion of dough offered as first fruits to God, being holy, makes holy the whole lump of dough. Also if the root of a tree is holy, sound, so are the branches. This is introductory to the following discussion of the olive tree, native (Israel) and wild (Gentiles).

Verses 17-24 contain the discussion of Israel's being broken off from the native olive stock; that is, a large number of branches have broken off so that Gentiles, as believers in Christ, may be grafted on to the native stock of Israel. Bear in mind, he is addressing directly the Gentile members of the Roman church and reminds them that they were wild olive branches, but God, in His kindness (*chrestoteta,* 22), has grafted them on to the cultivated olive stock; that is, He has given them the place occupied by His chosen Israel. But he reminds them that they must not boast against Israel because they have supplanted the Jews in the favor of God; He has thus favored the Gentiles because of their simple faith in Christ; He has rejected the Jews because of their unbelief. Furthermore, if the Jews cease to be unbelieving and accept Christ, they will be grafted back on to their native stock. He warns the Gentile Christians that their faith must continue, or they will be branches broken off, just as Israel was. We must observe that this illustration from the orchard and grove reverses the natural way of grafting. The orchardist grafts a superior tree (peach, apple, orange) on to an old inferior stock, and expects the grafted shoot not to be like the old inferior stock but to produce the fruit of the superior shoot. But in Paul's grafting, the Gentile, the inferior shoot, is grafted on to the superior stock, Israel, and is expected to be God's genuine olive tree. That is, it is a supernatural process, contrary to nature (24).

MERCY TO ALL IS THE ULTIMATE PURPOSE OF GOD (11:25-36)

25 For to keep you from being self-conceited, brothers, I do not want to have a misunderstanding of this uncovered secret, that only temporary insensibility has come upon Israel until the full quota of the heathen peoples comes in, 26 and so in that way all Israel will be saved [I mean, the most of them], just as the Scripture says,

"From Zion the Deliverer will come;
He will remove ungodliness from Jacob;
27 And this my covenant I make with them,
When I shall take away their sins" [Isa. 59:20, 21].

28 As measured by the good news the Jews are God's enemies for your sakes, but as measured by God's choice they are His beloved because of their forefathers, 29 for the gracious gifts and call of God are never taken back. 30 For, just as you once disobeyed God, but now have had mercy shown you because of their disobedience, 31 so they too are now disobedient because of the mercy shown you, that they too may now have mercy shown them. 32 For God has locked up all mankind in the prison of disobedience so as to have mercy on them all.

33 How fathomless the depths of God's resources, wisdom, and knowledge! How unsearchable His decisions, and how mysterious His methods! 34 For who has ever understood the thoughts of the

Lord, or has ever been His adviser? [35] Or who has ever advanced
God anything to have Him pay him back? [36] For from Him
everything comes, through Him everything lives, and for Him
everything exists. Glory to Him forever! Amen.

Key words and phrases. Verses 25. Paul announces the mystery
that this hardening of Israel, this spiritual insensibility, is only
partial and temporary. The word *mystery* in the New Testament
means that what was once a secret has now been made known, uncovered. He wants them to know this historical fact that they
might not be puffed up over their exaltation by God's election of
them to a place in the true olive tree. Israel will come back to his
own place as God's chosen nation. Not as a nation, to be sure, but
in the spiritual sense.

Verse 26. So he emphatically announces to the Gentile Christians, "All Israel will be saved," and he bases this conclusion on a
prophecy of Isaiah (59:20, 21). The Deliverer, the Messiah, will
come and take away ungodliness from Jacob (Israel). He further
buttresses his statement by a quotation from Jeremiah concerning
the new covenant God will make with Israel (31:33).

What does Paul mean when he says, "All Israel will be saved?"
It is a hyperbole, a common figure of speech in the New Testament,
especially in Paul. It means that vast hosts of Israel at some time
will accept Jesus as their Messiah and Saviour (Deliverer). Surely,
he is not saying that Israel will all be restored to the Holy Land in a
physical and political sense. But when will it come to pass that
vast hosts of Jews will be flocking into the kingdom of Christ and
joining hands and hearts with Gentile Christians as one brotherhood? Will it be when the Lord comes back to earth personally at
the parousia? Most probably it must be when the Christian world
has put on a world-wide Jewish missionary program and united
heartily and lovingly to win the Jews to Christ, their promised
Messiah. I think that is what Paul means in verse 15: "For if the
rejection of them has resulted in the reconciliation of the world
[Gentiles reconciled to God], what will the result be of the final
reception of them but life from the dead?" Two reactions are
predicted by Paul: Gentile Christians will become more interested
in Jews and send hundreds of missionaries among them to win them

to Christ. Then the Deliverer will come to them and take away their sin of disobedience to their Messiah, and hundreds of thousands of them will become Christians. Then will follow the greatest revival since Pentecost, and the greatest missionary prosperity ever witnessed on earth, to the uttermost part of the earth; in all the nations, east and west, north and south; and the isles of the sea will find Him for whom they have waited for centuries. The modern Christian world needs to reverse its missionary order and send more missionaries among the Jews. We Gentiles are debtors to them. Their Christian missionaries, Paul and Silas, first evangelized our ancestors in Europe and planted the first church on European soil, the church in the city of Philippi. Let us throw overboard our prejudice and persecution of them, and love them and win them; then we can take the world for Christ. We are debtors to the Jews who gave us the Christ, and now we must give Him to them, in loving earnestness. As R. B. Jones says in his recent book, "We should live to lead them [the Jews] to Jesus. This is their only hope for the present or the future." It is not only their only hope but ours for taking the world for Christ.

Verses 28-32. This paragraph emphasizes mercy for all, Jews and Gentiles, as God's eternal purpose. In verse 28 though God has at present to treat the Jews as enemies, yet they are His beloved for the sake of Abraham, Isaac, and Jacob (the fathers). Verse 29 gives the reason for this: God's gracious gifts and call are not to be taken back; literally, not to be regretted. God does not do one a favor and later regret it. If that one is at all worthy, God still makes His gift and call good. So He continues to love Israel (his descendants) and His gracious call to them is still in force.

Verses 30, 31 extol the mercy of God, both to Jews and Gentiles. He has been compelled to withdraw His mercy temporarily from the Jews because of their unbelief and disobedience; but He is showing mercy to the Gentiles, so that they in turn may win their Jewish friends to Christ to receive the mercy of God. Verse 32 again emphasizes the universality of sin. Because of unbelief and disobedience, God has locked up all mankind, Jews and Gentiles, in the prisonhouse of sin, so that He may have mercy on all.

Verses 33-36. A paean of praise to the unsearchable and incomprehensible purposes and methods of God. *Bathos,* depth, expresses the apostle's conception of how deep are God's thoughts and ways; so deep that man cannot fathom them. The word for riches does not refer to the material resources of the universe, all of which belong to God, but to His character and personality—His grace and greatness, His glory and goodness, His holiness and mercy, as well as His wisdom and knowledge. His knowledge is original and too high for man to understand. His ways or methods of carrying out His purpose are literally untraceable; so, incomprehensible to man. We must accept them by faith in His goodness and grace. He accepts two passages from Isaiah and Job as expressing the final word on this subject.

Verse 36 gives the apostle's paean of praise to such a Supreme Being. To Him be praise forever, for He is the Creator of all things; He is the Preserver of all things; He is the Goal for which all things exist.

A LIFE OF DEVOTION TO GOD AND SERVICE TO OUR FELLOW MEN
THE LOGICAL RESULT OF SALVATION BY GRACE AND
JUSTIFICATION BY FAITH (12:1—15:13)

Chapter XII

PRACTICAL MORAL LIVING OF THE JUSTIFIED MAN

DEVOTION TO GOD AND THE RIGHT USE OF SPIRITUAL GIFTS
(12:1-8)

I beg you, therefore, brothers, through these mercies God has shown you, to make a decisive dedication of your bodies as a living sacrifice, devoted and well-pleasing to God, which is your reasonable service. ² Stop living in accordance with the customs of this world, but by the new ideals that mold your minds continue to transform yourselves, so as to find and follow God's will; that is, what is good, well-pleasing to Him, and perfect.

³ Now through the unmerited favor God has shown me I would say to every one of you not to estimate himself above his real value, but to make a sober rating of himself, in accordance with the degree of faith which God has apportioned to him. ⁴ For just as we have many parts united in our physical bodies, and the parts do not all have the same function, ⁵ so we, though many, are united

in one body through union with Christ, and we are individually parts of one another. ⁶ As we have gifts that differ in accordance with the favor God has shown us, if it is that of preaching, let it be done in proportion to our faith; ⁷ or of practical service, in the field of service; or of a teacher, in the field of teaching; ⁸ or of one who encourages others, in the field of encouragement; or one who gives his money, with liberality; or one who leads others, with earnestness; or one who does deeds of charity, with cheerfulness.

Key words and phrases. Verse 1. This practical section begins with *therefore.* For this reason, or rather, for these reasons: because God has elected you to salvation and to glorification; because Christ has redeemed you; because God by grace has brought you into right standing with Himself and made you His children; because He is keeping you secure in all life's struggles for your final glorification; because the Spirit is dwelling in you and helping you transform yourselves to be like Christ; for all these reasons I appeal to you to offer your bodies at once as living sacrifices to God. What a fine piece of logic! Spiritual logic that ought to move every Christian to immediate consecration to God and higher living! The Christian sacrifice is a living sacrifice. Jewish sacrifices were dead animals. Christian sacrifices are bodies with living souls dominating them, so living personalities. To offer these to God is our logical devotion to Him. Many modern versions translate it "spiritual worship." But the word in Greek is *logiken,* from which we derive our words logic, logical and logician. Then the context demands the translation *reasonable,* or *rational,* or some word akin to these. The verse begins with *therefore,* giving the conclusion of a logical argument. The word service is better translated devotion or worship, as it means something rendered to God.

Verse 2. "Be not fashioned" is really better than "be not conformed" to this world. The word refers to *outward* conformity; that is, to the wicked ways of the age. Of course, Christians should not be conformed to its principles of wickedness, shrewdness and trickery. The positive appeal is to "be transformed by the renewing of your minds." Moral and spiritual transformation is also a mental process. The character and personality are transformed by renewing, renovating ideas and ideals which the mind reaches by the study of spiritual truths—reading the Scriptures, religious books and papers, and by meditation. This is why the transformation of most Christians is so slow. They study and meditate on spiritual things *so seldom* and *so spasmodically*.

The goal and standard of this moral transformation is the will of God. It is the highest law in the universe; it is good, leads to the good of those who live up to it; it is perfect, because the highest law.

Verses 3-8. Paul names the spiritual gifts and how to use them. He has authority to give instructions about Christian living because of the grace given him. God conferred His special favor upon him as an authoritative apostle. His first injunction is to think soberly about our spiritual gifts; not to overrate ourselves but to rate ourselves according to the measure of faith we have. In verses 4-8 he compares a local church, or Christian community, to a human physical body. As it has many parts and organs and yet is one organism functioning harmoniously, if in normal condition, so a church, or Christian community, is a complex body with various parts with different spiritual functions, but all working in harmony for doing the glorious work for which it stands. The grace gifts *(charismata)* are: preaching (prophecy); general service; teaching; exhortation or encouraging others; giving or contributing money; leading or ruling others; showing mercy to the needy.

Notice in verse 6 these gifts of ours differ according to the grace given us. It is in harmony with the blessed laws of God that we are born different, and so our spiritual gifts differ according to the same gracious laws of God. Each is exhorted to practice his gifts according to the proportion of faith he has; that is, each must do his best in the field of service for which he is fitted. The spirit of hilarity and cheerfulness is to characterize us in all these services.

MORAL MAXIMS FOR THE CHRISTIAN LIFE (12:9-21)

9 Your love must be true. You must always turn in horror from what is wrong, but keep on holding to what is right. 10 In brotherly love be affectionate to one another, in personal honors put one another to the fore, 11 never slack in earnestness, always on fire with the Spirit, always serving the Lord, 12 ever happy in hope, always patient in suffering, ever persistent in prayer, 13 always supplying

the needs of God's people, ever practicing hospitality. ¹⁴ Keep on blessing your persecutors; keep on blessing and stop cursing them. ¹⁵ Practice rejoicing with people who rejoice, and weeping with people who weep. ¹⁶ Keep on thinking in harmony with one another. Stop being high-minded but keep on associating with lowly people. Stop being conceited. ¹⁷ Stop returning evil for evil to anyone. Always see to it that your affairs are right in the sight of everybody. ¹⁸ If possible, so far as it depends on you, live in peace with everybody. ¹⁹ Stop taking revenge on one another, beloved, but leave a place for God's anger, for the Scripture says, Vengeance belongs to me; I will pay them back, says the Lord. ²⁰ Do the opposite. If your enemy is hungry, give him something to eat. If he is thirsty, give him something to drink. For if you act in this way, you will heap burning coals upon his head! ²¹ Stop being conquered by evil, but keep on conquering evil with good."

Key words and phrases. These verses, 9-21, need few comments to clarify them. The moral maxims here given are of the highest ethical quality. If all of us would read these verses every day and practice these lofty virtues, our lives would be approaching perfection in our social relations. Love is queen of all these virtues; first, last, and all the time is love in various forms of expression. But it must be true love. It must not be merely "acted on the stage." This was the original meaning of the Greek word (anupokritos). Noticeable is the word *cleave,* in the phrase, "cleave to that which is good." It means to glue yourself to the good; stick tight to it. What a noble quality is expressed in verse 10—for the first honors prefer the other fellow and not yourself! There is a graphic word in 11, fervent. Literally it is *boiling.* So hot in our enthusiasm we are boiling, "on fire with the Spirit." In 12 he puts great emphasis on the prayer life, "continuing to hold on to prayer." These moral maxims cannot be practiced without divine aid. In 13, two great social qualities are stressed, sharing our bounty with the needs of the needy and practicing hospitality. The world has recently practiced to a wonderful degree the first of these, but the last is almost a lost art in modern life. The sufferings of the war-torn peoples of Europe and Asia have touched the hearts and opened the purses of us Americans, even non-Christians. But hospitality is almost a historic relic of the past—even old-fashioned Southern hospitality is passing away. Of course there is not now the same necessity for it as in the days of Paul. Then there were no hotels and few inns to entertain travelers. Now the country is full of hotels, cafés, restaurants, and cafeterias, for the lodging and feeding of travelers and tourists. Then people raised most of their food, now only country people even approach that happy economic condition.

Verse 14 urges us to bless our persecutors. Paul illustrated this in his life, working and praying for the Judaizers, just as Jesus and Stephen did when dying at the hands of their persecutors.

Verse 15 encourages Christian sympathy with others in success or in sorrow. Perhaps it is harder to rejoice with others in success than to weep with others in sorrow. Jealousy might prevent the former.

Verse 16 has a triplet of maxims: Practice uniformity of thinking; stop proud thinking, but practice associating with the lowly; stop being conceited. As to the first Paul is merely urging unity in the church by cultivating uniform thinking on the basic principles and truths, but is not forbidding freedom of thought (in reason) or urging the practice of Sovietism (compelling the masses to follow the thinking of the Kremlin).

Verses 17-21. He urges Christians to live in peace with one another by forgiving offenders and feeding enemies. He must have been familiar with the Sermon on the Mount—loving our enemies and praying for them. This last statement in 20 reflects his acquaintance with the Book of Proverbs (see 25:21, 22). Verse 21 lays down the best rule in the world for conquering evildoers: to do good to them heaps burning coals upon their heads and wins them to be friends. If this does not work, they are hardly worth winning.

A GREAT TEXT WITH SERMON OUTLINE (12:1, 2)

CONSECRATION

I. The Appeal for Consecration: "Therefore . . . By the mercies of God"
   1. Elected and foreordained by God (8:29; 9:11, 19, 23)
   2. Redeemed by Christ's death (3:24-25; 5:9-11)
   3. Justified by God's grace (3:24)
   4. Sanctified by the Spirit (8:10-26)

    5. Kept by the Triune God (8:31-39)

    6. Glorified (8:30)

II. The Standard and Goal of Consecration—"The Will of God"

    1. Perfect standard—highest law in the universe

    2. Good—leads to good for all concerned, if followed

    3. Acceptable—to God and man

    4. Proving and approving it (so Greek, *dokimazein*)

III. The Essence of Consecration—"Sacrifice and Service"

    1. Sacrifice of self—body, mind, soul—body living only if mind and soul are in it

    2. Service or devotion (*latreia*) to God (1b, c)

    3. Service to men

        a. Winning their souls (9:3; 10:1)

        b. Ministering to their bodies—the defective, dependent, the sick and suffering

        c. Ministering to their minds—Christian colleges, universities, seminaries, etc.

Chapter XIII

CIVIC AND SOCIAL DUTIES OF CHRISTIANS

CIVIC DUTIES OF CHRISTIANS (13:1-7)

Everybody must obey the civil authorities that are over him, for no authority exists except by God's permission; the existing authorities have been established by Him, ² so that anyone who resists the authorities sets himself against what God has established, and those who set themselves against Him will get the penalty due them. ³ For civil authorities are not a terror to the man who does right, but they are to the man who does wrong. Do you want to have no dread of the civil authorities? Then practice doing right and you will be commended for it. ⁴ For the civil authorities are God's servants to do you good. But if you practice doing wrong, you should dread them, for they do not wield the sword for nothing. Indeed, they are God's servants to inflict punishment upon people who do wrong. ⁵ Therefore, you must obey them, not only for the sake of escaping punishment, but also for conscience sake; ⁶ for this is the reason why you pay your taxes, for the civil authorities are God's official servants faithfully devoting themselves to this very end. Pay all of them what is due them—tribute to the officer to receive it, taxes to the officer to receive them, respect to the man entitled to it, and honor to the man entitled to it.

Key words and phrases. Verse 1. The context shows that authorities are civic officials. That is, Paul is asserting that civic government is of divine origin—instituted by God. Many modern sociologists (Small, Giddings, Ross, and others,) teach it is the product of evolution under the influence of natural forces in human society. Paul teaches that *God* is back of all these social forces and it is by divine authority that civic government is established among men. God has given man three institutions set up by His authority: the home with monogamous marriage, the state, and the church, each to be dominant in its own sphere.

Verse 2 shows that he who resists the civic authorities resists God.

Verses 3 and 4. These civic officials are servants of God to punish those who do wrong (who break the laws) and to guarantee good, public welfare, for the interests of individuals and for society at large.

Verse 5 adds the idea that we should obey civic laws for conscience sake. It is a matter of moral obligation to be a law-abiding citizen.

Verses 6, 7 lists four duties due different civic officials: tribute (paid by a subject people to a foreign power, as Jews to Romans), taxes, respect, honor. The representatives of government should receive from loyal citizens the respect and honor due the government.

LOVE THE FULFILLMENT OF THE LAW (13:8-10)

8 Stop owing anybody anything, except the obligation to love one another, for whoever practices loving others has perfectly satisfied the law. 9 For the commandments, "You must not commit adultery, You must not murder, You must not steal, You must not have an evil desire," and any other commandment if there is any, are summed up in this command, "You must love your neighbor as you do yourself." 10 Love never does a wrong to one's neighbor; so love is the perfect satisfaction of the law."

Key words and phrases. Verse 8. The verb *fulfilled* is interesting; it means to fill up to the brim. All the law contains is contained in love. Love keeps the law inviolate. Love is the law's best friend. Men who hate will not keep the law, either of God or of man. Paul is true to his motto in I Corinthians 13:13, "The greatest of these is love."

Verses 9, 10 make the moral command, "You must love your neighbor as you do yourself," the embodiment of the law; that is, of the whole moral code involving all our social duties. This is so because genuine love never wrongs a neighbor; it does him good and shows him favor.

THE ESCHATOLOGICAL APPEAL FOR MORAL LIVING (13:11-14)

"Do this in particular because you know the present crisis, that it is high time for you to wake up out of your sleep, for our salvation is now nearer to us than when we first believed. ¹²The night has almost passed; the day is at hand. So let us put aside the deeds of darkness, and put on the weapons of light. ¹³Let us live becomingly for people who are in the light of day, not in carousing and drunkenness, nor in sexual immorality and licentiousness, nor in quarreling and jealousy. ¹⁴Instead, put on the Lord Jesus Christ, and put a stop to gratifying the evil desires that lurk in your lower nature.

Key words and phrases. Verse 11. The expressions, *the time, the hour,* show that Paul is thinking of the parousia, the coming of the Lord Jesus, which he hopes is near. About seven years before this he wrote his letters to the church at Thessalonica and stressed the parousia. He seems not to be stressing it so much in his Roman letter, but now he makes this eschatological appeal to the Roman Christians to wake up out of sleep, that it is full time for them to begin living in the light of that great day. "For our salvation is nearer . . . than when we first believed." The word salvation is here used in its eschatological sense; that is, our final deliverance from all evil and suffering at the second coming of Jesus. It has three meanings: saved at justification and regeneration; saved progressively by the process of sanctification; and this last sense. The first is illustrated with Ephesians 2:5, 8; the second with

Philippians 2:12. The first sense may be called its spiritual sense, the second the ethical, and the last the eschatological.

Verses 12, 13 use the terms night and darkness, day and light, figuratively. Darkness and night stand for sins men are ashamed to be seen in in the light of day. Under cover of night's darkness men and women sink to the blackest depths of sensual sins, carousing and drunkenness, sexual immorality and licentiousness, and so on. He exhorts his readers, in the dazzling light of that great day of His coming, to put off the deeds of darkness and put on the weapons of light. Live in the open, under the noonday sun, not ashamed for all to see what they are doing.

Verse 14 exhorts to put on the Lord Jesus Christ; it is the figure of putting on a shining new garment; put on His character of purity and His life of holiness and devotion to God and your fellow men. Augustine, the noted Latin father, who in youth led a licentious and dissolute life and broke the heart of his consecrated mother, was awakened by reading this paragraph and converted to the Lord Jesus. He put on Christ and finally wrote the Christian classic, *The City of God*. The eschatological appeal aroused his cultured mind and woke up his sleeping conscience.

Chapter XIV

THE LAW OF LOVE IN OPERATION TOWARD THE WEAK; CHRIST THE LORD OF ALL, STRONG AND WEAK, LIVING AND DEAD (14:1-12)

Make it your practice to receive into full Christian fellowship people who are overscrupulous, but not to criticize their views. ² One man believes that he can eat anything, another who is overscrupulous eats nothing but vegetables. ³ The man who eats anything must not look down on the man who does not do so, nor must the man who does not do so condemn the man who does, for God has fully accepted him. ⁴ Who are you to criticize another man's servant? It is his own master's business whether he stands or falls, and he will stand, for the Lord has power to make him stand. ⁵ One man rates one day above another, another rates them all alike. Let every man be fully convinced in his own mind. ⁶ The man who keeps a certain day keeps it for the Lord. The man who eats anything does it for the Lord too, for he gives God thanks. The man who refuses to eat anything does it for the Lord too, and gives God thanks.

[7] For none of us can live alone by himself, and none of us can die alone by himself; [8] indeed, if we live, we always live in relation to the Lord, and if we die, we always die in relation to the Lord. So whether we live or die we belong to the Lord. [9] For Christ died and lived again for the very purpose of being Lord of both the dead and the living. [10] Then why should you criticize your brother? Or, why should you look down on your brother? Surely, we shall all stand before God to be judged, [11] for the Scripture says:

"As surely as I live," says the Lord, "every knee shall bend before me,
And every tongue shall make acknowledgment to God."
[12] So each of us must give an account of himself to God.

Key words and phrases. Verse 1. "Weak in faith" does not mean faltering faith but it characterizes one who is overscrupulous about eating certain meats or observing certain days as sacred. The verb *receive* is a compound with a cumulative significance; welcome him or receive him into full fellowship.

Verse 2. The man strong in faith eats meats as well as vegetables, the overscrupulous eats only vegetables.

Verses 3, 4 contain the exhortation to be charitable toward each other, the nonscrupulous and the overscrupulous, for God has welcomed both and they both give God thanks. Verse 4a gives an illustration from the household. An outsider has no right to criticize the house-servant of his neighbor. That is his neighbor's affair. So we should not criticize God's servants who are overscrupulous or nonscrupulous.

Verses 5, 6 bring in the element of observing days as sacred. The same principle holds good here as with the question of eating. This may refer to the issue between the Jewish Sabbath or the Lord's day, the first day of the week, which Christians early began to observe as a memorial of Christ's resurrection. Most likely it refers rather to certain feast days which were observed as sacred— by some and not by others.

Verse 7 teaches that there is no moral or spiritual isolation. Not a single human being can bottle up his life so that it has no signi-

ficance for others and for the Lord. The influence of human beings
is as universal as sin and the offer of salvation. All, great and small,
strong and weak, are living with respect to others and the Lord.
If not Christians, their influence is against the Lord and is leading
others to be against Him. *No one* is a compound pronoun meaning
literally *not one*.

Verse 8. Our living and our dying are both related to the Lord;
we belong to Christ whether living or dead. It is a glorious, hope-
inspiring thought that we are as much the Lord's when we die as
when we are living. Verse 9 gives the reason for this: Christ died and
lived again so as to be the Lord of the dead as well as the living.

Verses 10-12. Here Paul shows why we should not pass judgment on one another: all of us must stand before God and give an
account of ourselves. He only has the right to pass judgment on
any of us. So we should not presume to take to ourselves this privilege which belongs only to God.

THE STRONG MUST PRACTICE THE LAW OF LOVE
TOWARD THE WEAK (14:13-23)

13 Then let us stop criticizing one another; instead, do this,
determine to stop putting stumbling blocks or hindrances in your
brother's way. 14 I know, and through my union with the Lord
Jesus I have a clear conviction, that nothing is unclean in itself;
that a thing is unclean only to the person who thinks it unclean.
15 For if your brother is hurt because of the food you eat, you are
not living by the standard of love. Stop ruining, by what you eat,
the man for whom Christ died. 16 Then stop abusing your rights.
17 For the kingdom of God does not consist in what we eat and
drink, but in doing right, in peace and joy through the Holy Spirit;
18 whoever in this way continues serving Christ is well-pleasing to
God and approved by men. 19 So let us keep on pursuing the things
that make for peace and our mutual upbuilding. 20 Stop undoing
the work of God just for the sake of food. Everything is clean,
but it is wrong for a man to eat anything when it makes another
stumble. 21 The right thing to do is not to eat meat, or drink wine,
or do anything else, that makes your brother stumble. 22 On your
part, you must exercise your faith by the standard of yourself
in the sight of God. Happy is the man who need not condemn

himself for doing the thing that he approves. ²³ But the man who has misgivings about eating, if he then eats, has already condemned himself by so doing, because he did not follow his faith, and any action that does not follow one's faith is a sin.

Key words and phrases. Verse 13. The only judgment a Christian may pass is on himself as not a stumbling block or hindrance to a brother. That is, no one has a right, according to the law of love, to practice anything that puts a stumbling block across the path of another.

Verse 14. "Nothing is unclean in itself." This does not apply to fundamental principles. Of course adultery is unclean, and murder is unclean. But Paul refers to personal views about these nonessentials, like eating certain meats, observing certain days as sacred, etc. It is not a moral issue that is at stake in these things; that is what he means. He has reached this conviction because of his union with the Lord Jesus; it is a firm Christian conviction.

Verse 15. You are not conducting yourself by the law of love if you eat meat and by this act grieve your brother—hurt his conscience.

Verse 16. Because Christ died for that brother you must not ruin his spiritual life.

Verse 17. "Kingdom of God" here is not the ethico-spiritual or eschatological kingdom of which Jesus so often spoke. It is the practical doing of the will of God—obeying your King. In this sense it is not meat and drink, but it is doing right (righteousness), and peace (with your brothers, especially with the weak), and joy which the Holy Spirit inspires. This puts practical religion on a high plane.

Verse 18. Such a practical life as a Christian pleases God and is approved by men—even unsaved and wicked men.

Verse 19. An exhortation to pursue that course in eating meats and observing days that will promote peace in the church and among brothers, and contribute to the upbuilding of individual Christians and the church. Peace and edification are high ideals for Christians and churches.

Verse 20. Appeals to them not to destroy the work of God because of food. That is, the work of building up the church and

Christian character would be destroyed if they did not follow this law of love toward the weak.

Verse 21. The right thing for all is not to eat meat or drink wine, or do anything else, that makes your brother stumble. A high and basic principle in Christian living. All should practice it.

Verses 22, 23. A man's faith must give him a conviction as to what is right. He must decide this matter in the sight of God; he must have an enlightened conscience on these nonessential matters, and then duty demands that he follow these convictions (his faith). If he does, he is happy because he does not condemn himself in what he does. But if he does not follow his convictions (faith), it is a sin. To Daniel it would have been a sin if he had eaten the king's meat and drunk his wine. So he purposed in his heart not to defile himself.

SERMON OUTLINE FROM A GREAT TEXT (14:9):

OUR INFLUENCE; OR LIVING IN THE LIVES OF OTHERS

"None of us lives to himself." None lives without some relation to God and to others. *Influence,* literally, *flowing in.*

I. All of Us Have Influence. "Not one lives to himself." No Isolationists.
   1. The great, the learned, the rich. Eisenhower, Rockefeller, Paul.
   2. The lowly, the poor, the illiterate. Mary, Martha, widow and mite (story of her told around the world in nineteen centuries).

II. Our Influence Either Good or Bad
   1. No neutrality in morals and religion (Matt. 12:30)
   2. So with parents' influence over children. Saloon-keeper converted at forty. Eldest son delayed till he was forty.
   3. So with youth and influence on pals. Girl climbing Alpine peak fell, dragging another down to the bottom. Lost. All are lifters or sinkers. Dryden:
       "He raised a mortal to the skies,
       She drew an angel down."

III. All Responsible to Make Influence Good

1. God expects it. Made us; redeemed us; providence over us.
2. Capable of it. God endowed us with wills to choose good.
3. Good influence God's most popular book. Three books by God: Bible, nature, good influence. Few read Bible and nature; all read influence every day.
4. Influence all we can leave to posterity. Not lands, bonds, etc.
5. Influence inevitable and eternal. Cannot stop it. Tom Payne dying asked friend to burn all copies of his *Age of Reason*. That did not stop its baneful influence already done. Good influence eternal. Paul through his thirteen letters still preaching and winning the lost.

Ruskin: "That man is richest who has the widest influence, both personally and by means of his possessions, over the lives of others."

George Eliot: "Oh, may I join the choir invisible
　　　　Of those immortal dead who live again
　　　　In minds made better by their presence."

Chapter XV

THE ATTITUDE OF THE STRONG TOWARD THE WEAK; PAUL'S APOLOGY FOR ADMONITIONS TO THE ROMANS; HIS FUTURE PLANS

THE ATTITUDE OF THE STRONG TOWARD THE WEAK (15:1-7)

It is the duty of us who are strong to bear with the weaknesses of those who are not strong, and not merely to please ourselves. ² Each one of us must practice pleasing his neighbor, to help in his immediate upbuilding for his eternal good. ³ Christ certainly did not please Himself; instead, as the Scripture says, "The reproaches of those who reproach you have fallen upon me." ⁴ For everything that was written in the earlier times was written for our instruction, so that by our patient endurance and through the encouragement the Scriptures bring we might continuously cherish our hope. ⁵ May God, who gives men patient endurance and encouragement, grant you such harmony with one another, in accordance with the standard which Christ Jesus sets, ⁶ that with united hearts and lips you may praise the God and Father of our Lord Jesus Christ.

7 Therefore, practice receiving one another into full Christian fellowship, just as Christ has so received you to Himself.

Key words and phrases. Verses 1-2. It is the duty of the strong to please his neighbor, even if he is weak. The purpose is to give help for his immediate upbuilding for his ultimate good. The Greek preposition with upbuilding denotes *immediate* purpose, the one with *good* expresses ultimate, permanent purpose. The present upbuilding is to result in permanent good.

Verse 3 gives Christ's example for not pleasing ourselves but our neighbor. Christ even bore the reproaches of others. Proved by citing Psalm 69:9.

Verse 4 states the benefits bestowed upon us by the Scriptures—they encourage us in our patient endurance and inspire hope for the future.

Verses 5-6. The apostle prays for their harmonious thinking about these minor issues (eating meat and observing days) so that with united hearts and mouths they may glorify the God and Father of our Lord Jesus Christ. He feels that unity in the church is essential to secure the greatest glory to God.

Verse 7 merely repeats the exhortation to unity for the glory of God.

THE LARGER BROTHERHOOD (15:8-13)

8 Yes, I mean that Christ has become a servant to Israel to prove God's truthfulness, to make valid His promises to our forefathers, 9 and for the heathen peoples to praise God for His mercy, as the Scripture says:

"For this I will give thanks to you among the heathen,
And will sing praises to your name."

10 And again:

"Rejoice, you heathen peoples, with His people!"

11 And again:

"All you heathen peoples, praise the Lord,
Yea, let all peoples sing His praise."

12 And again Isaiah says:

"The noted Son of Jesse will come,
Even He who rises to rule the heathen;
On Him the heathen will set their hope."

[13] May the hope-inspiring God so fill you with perfect joy and peace through your continuing faith, that you may bubble over with hope by the power of the Holy Spirit.

Key words and phrases. Verses 8-9a. Christ a servant to Israel means that He limited His public ministry to the Jews and the purpose was to prove God's faithfulness in keeping His promises to our forefathers, from Abraham to the prophets and psalmists. These promises are especially the Messianic prophecies. A larger purpose was to prepare the way for the Gentiles to glorify God for His mercy. That is, that Christ later might be preached to the Gentiles (as Paul did) that they might be included in the fulfillment of the messianic promises.

Verses 9b-12 cite messianic promises from Deuteronomy, two Psalms, and from Isaiah, to prove that the heathen are included in the redemptive program of the promised Messiah. God intended all the time that the pagan peoples should receive His mercy and glorify His name. That includes Romans, the mighty people then holding supremacy over the world.

Verse 13 is a prayer that Paul prays for this great and influential church. He addresses the God of hope. The genitive, of hope, may be descriptive: the hopeful, optimistic God; or it may be subjective: the God who inspires hope in His people. He would have to be the optimistic God in order to inspire hope in His people. What he prays for is interesting: "all joy and all peace," perfect joy and perfect peace; that they be jubilant, peaceful, and united Christians. The means for producing these qualities, continuous faith and the power of the Holy Spirit. The result to be attained by his readers is to be overflowing and bubbling over with hope—hopeful, optimistic, conquering Christians.

VII. CONCLUSION—PERSONAL MATTERS, GREETINGS, ETC. (15:14-16:27)

APOLOGY FOR ADMONISHING THEM; PLANS FOR THE FUTURE (15:14-33)

MOTIVE FOR WRITING—THE APOLOGY (15:14-21)

[14] As far as I am concerned about you, my brothers, I am con-

vinced that you especially are abounding in the highest goodness, richly supplied with perfect knowledge and competent to counsel one another. ¹⁵ And yet, to refresh your memories, I have written you rather freely on some details, because of the unmerited favor shown me by God ¹⁶ in making me a minister of Christ Jesus to the heathen peoples, to have me act as a sacrificing minister of the good news, in order that my offering of the heathen peoples to God may be acceptable, consecrated by the Holy Spirit. ¹⁷ So, as a Christian, I am proud of the things that I have done for God. ¹⁸ For I would venture to mention only what Christ has accomplished through me in bringing the heathen peoples to obedience, by word and by work, ¹⁹ by the power of signs and wonders, by the power of the Holy Spirit. So I have completed the telling of the good news of Christ all the way from Jerusalem around to Illyricum. ²⁰ In this matter it has ever been my ambition to tell the good news where Christ's name had never been mentioned, so as not to build upon foundations laid by other men, ²¹ but, as the Scripture says:

> "They will see who were never told of Him,
> And they will understand who have not heard."

Key words and phrases. Verse 14. Paul is a real gentleman. He is considerate of other people's feelings. He is here complimenting the Roman Christians on their virtues—to keep them from thinking he is trying to impose upon them his personal notions about social and ethical matters. They are "full of goodness, abounding in all sorts of knowledge, competent to counsel one another." He is not just patting them on the back. Nor is he trying to make them think they are already perfect. As a gentleman and a good psychologist he is making his admonitions stick and stay with them.

Verses 15-17. Here is the main thing he wanted to say: God has given me grace and appointed me a "priestly minister of Christ to offer the good news to pagan peoples, to be acceptable to God and to man, consecrated by the Holy Spirit." Here he gives his divine authority to say to them what he has written. In verse 16 are two Greek words that suggest the priestly idea in Paul's mission as a minister of the good news. He is not only a minister *(diakonos)* but a *leitourgos,* working at holy things *(hierourgon).* This is a high and holy conception of preaching the good news. He uses another word, offering, which tallies with this holy, priestly characteristic of a gospel minister.

Verse 18. He is conscientious and dares not include a single thing that Christ has not done through him. His humility is seen in that he gives Christ the glory for doing these things through him as an instrument. Also he says it is by the power of the Holy Spirit (19a).

Verses 19b-21. He has preached the good news from Jerusalem all the way to Illyricum (a large territory northeast of the Adriatic stretching on the east to Macedonia). That is, he has evangelized western Asia (continent) and eastern Europe. So now he is ready to visit Rome and lands farther west to carry the good news. Verse 20 gives his missionary policy, to tell the good news where Christ has not been mentioned before; to evangelize where others have not laid the foundation. He says this is scriptural, citing Isaiah 52:15.

His Delayed Visit; Asks Their Prayers for Protection in Judea (15:22-33)

22 This is the reason why I have so often been prevented from coming to see you. 23 But now, as there are no more places for me to occupy in this part of the world, and as I have for many years been longing to come to see you, 24 when I make my trip to Spain, I certainly hope to see you on my way there and to be helped forward by you, after I have enjoyed being with you awhile. 25 But just now I am on my way to Jerusalem to help God's people. 26 For Macedonia and Greece were delighted to make a contribution to the poor among God's people in Jerusalem. 27 They certainly were delighted to do it, and they really are under obligation to them, for if the heathen peoples have shared in their spiritual blessings, they ought to serve them in material blessings. 28 So, after I have finished this matter and made sure of the results of this contribution for them, I shall come by you on my way to Spain. 29 And I feel sure that when I do come to you, I shall come with Christ's abundant blessing on me.

30 Now I beg you, brothers, for the sake of our Lord Jesus Christ and by the love that the Spirit inspires, to wrestle with me in prayers to God on my behalf, 31 that I may be delivered from

those in Judea who are disobedient, and that the help which I am taking to Jerusalem may be well received by God's people there, [32] so that, if it is God's will, I may come with a happy heart to see you and have a refreshing rest while with you. [33] The peace-giving God be with you all! Amen.

Key words and phrases. Verses 22-23. For many years he has been longing to come to Rome, but he assures his readers that he has been prevented because he has been so busy preaching the good news where God seemed to be calling him—in western Asia (continent) and in eastern Europe.

Verse 24 tells of a planned visit to Spain and his hope to see them in passing. The key expression in this verse is "to be sent forward by you." What does he mean? Is he expecting the church in Rome to sponsor his mission to Spain? Possibly so. It is almost a sure thing that Paul is planning a mission campaign in Spain. He has preached the good news in western Asia and in eastern Europe, and there is left western Europe; Spain lies on the Atlantic to the west, the utmost southwestern limit of the Roman world. Paul set out at first to evangelize the Roman world; now he wants to reach the western boundary, Spain. What a world missionary! No scrap of history is left us to prove that he ever visited Spain and preached the good news there; but internal evidence points to a fourth missionary journey not recorded in Acts. Many places are visited, as recorded in his letters, not included in or fitting into the narrative given by Luke.

Verses 25-28. He tells them that he is now on his way to Jerusalem with the contribution from the churches of Macedonia and Greece, to relieve the suffering Christians in Jerusalem. A great famine has been on some time, and hundreds of Jewish Christians were in want. Paul urged these Gentile Christians to make this contribution; and now he in person is taking the offerings, hoping that better feeling will be fostered between Jewish and Gentile Christians. He feels that the Gentile Christians are debtors to the Jewish Christians, because the latter have sent the good news with its spiritual blessings for the Gentile Christians to enjoy. So now in turn the Gentile Christians ought to minister to them in material blessings. He promises that when he has finished this piece of work he is coming by them on his way to Spain.

Verse 29 expresses his optimism about the prospective visit; it is to be in the fullness of blessing from Christ. Both to them and to him. See 1:11, 12 where he says he longs to see them "to impart some spiritual gift to strengthen you; that is, that we may be mutually encouraged by each other's faith."

Verses 30-32. He begs his readers to agonize with him in prayers to God on his behalf, for his protection from the disobedient Jews, the Judaizers who have hated and hunted him for years; and that this contribution for the saints in Jerusalem might be acceptable, so that he might come to Rome in joy and be refreshed with rest among them. This is intercessory prayer; praying for one another. Paul is humble enough, though an apostle, to beg these Christians to pray for him. He asks for prayer on his behalf many times.

Verse 33 is a benediction from the God of peace. Perhaps he thinks of God as the One who gives peace to His people.

OUTLINE OF A GREAT TEXT (15:13)

WANTED! OPTIMISTIC CHRISTIANS

I. A Prayer to the Optimistic God—"the God of Hope"
  1. God optimistic as to His redemptive program (11; 15:1-12)
  2. God optimistic for His people (8:28-30)—guarantees their security and glorification (8:31-39)
  3. He inspires hope in His people; hope of salvation, victory, etc.

II. Essentials to Being Optimistic Christians
  1. Perfect joy (all joy, Phil. 4:4; I Thes. 5:16)
  2. Perfect peace (all peace); peace in the heart; with all
  3. Continuing faith; in God; in Christ; in the triumph of righteuosness (John 14:1)

III. The Result—Hopeful, Optimistic Christians
  1. Overflowing with hope—hope like the Nile overflowing its banks; bubbling over
  2. Optimistic as to one's own salvation and security (8:28-39)

3. Optimistic as to the success of the right and the supremacy of Christianity (John 16:13)

Chapter XVI

COMMENDATION OF PHOEBE; GREETINGS TO FRIENDS; BENEDICTION

As there is no consecutive line of thought, we vary our usual procedure.

Verses 1, 2 are devoted to commending "our sister Phoebe" to the Christians at Rome. She is a deaconess in the church at Cenchreae (a small town near Corinth where Paul is writing). There were women deacons in many churches in the early times. Many scholars think that the women mentioned in I Timothy 3:11 are deaconesses, not deacons' wives. She has been a useful Christian, giving help, protection to many, including Paul. So Paul asks the church to welcome her in a manner becoming God's people. Also to help her in whatever she requires of them. This is beautiful Christian fellowship of Christians in different countries (Greece and Italy).

Verses 3-5a. Asks especially to be remembered to Prisca and Aquila, his fellow workers in the work of Christ Jesus. Salute So-and-so means in modern parlance, Remember me to So-and-so, or Give my love to So-and-so. This fine couple were fellow workers with Paul in Corinth (Acts 18:2, 18) and Ephesus. They had risked their lives for Paul, possibly in Ephesus in the uproar created by Demetrius (Acts 19). Not only was Paul thankful for them but all the churches among the heathen. They must have been tireless workers and so, influential Christians. They were so open-hearted that there was a church in their house. That is, they opened their doors to all Christians in the neighborhood, and their home became the regular meeting place for worship and fellowship and planning for the Lord's work. There were no church houses, and so this was necessary, gracious service of Priscilla and Aquila.

Verses 5b-16. Paul's personal greetings to twenty-five fellow Christians and workers. What a galaxy of distinguished friends of Christ and of the apostle! Six of these are women: Mary, Julia, Tryphaena, Tryphosa, the mother of Rufus, the sister of Nereus (names not given). Counting Phoebe and Priscilla, we have a list of eight distinguished women co-workers and sympathizers. Paul, although unmarried, was not a woman-hater, as some have claimed. Women had a significant place in church work and world missions, he knew, and he recognized them as worthy of mention for a special honor.

Of the others, four are his kinsmen, Andronicus, Junias, Herodion and Sosipater. Several had been fellow prisoners of Paul. Many were fellow workers in different places. Some are called beloved, special personal friends. Paul must have been a true friend to have so many friends, a Christian of the finest social qualities. What a personality! A titanic thinker, a profound theologian, an illustrious logician, a ceaseless soul-winner, a world missionary, a loving friend!

The holy kiss mentioned in verse 16 was an expression of Christian brotherhood and was practiced by most early Christians. In 16 all the churches of Christ send greetings to the church in Rome. Notice, Paul emphasizes the local church and knows no national or federal church. They are the churches of Christ. Christ is the Founder (I Cor. 3:11; Matt. 16:18). See Ephesians 5:25: "Christ loved the church [as an institution] and gave Himself up for her." He redeemed the Church, and so it is His possession.

WARNING AGAINST FALSE TEACHERS (16:17-20)

He does not indicate who they are or what they teach, as in Galatians they are Judaizers, and in Colossians, Gnostics. Perhaps, as there is a large minority of Jews in the church at Rome, there are some inside the church who create division and difficulty; more likely, however, they are traveling teachers, and naturally they would try to get a foothold in a great church like that in Rome. He describes them as "not serving our Lord Christ but their own base appetites, and by their fair and flattering talk are deceiving the hearts of unsuspecting people." This is the policy of false teachers; they have plausible and persuasive appeals to make to catch unsuspecting people who are off their guard as to doctrines. Unsuspecting. He intimates they are living on a low moral level, yielding to the satisfaction of their lower nature (belly). They teach one thing, they live another. In the latter part of the verse (19) he intimates that they are emissaries of Satan, asserting that God will soon crush Satan under their feet. He assures them that it is not because they are already yielding to these false teachings that he is warning them, but because he wants them to be wise about what is good and innocent about what is bad. He is warning them because he wants them to remain loyal to the teachings they had learned. Then he pronounces a benediction on them, "The grace [spiritual blessing] of our Lord Jesus be with you."

HIS FELLOW WORKERS SEND GREETING (21-23)

These are Timothy, Lucius, Jason, Sosipater; also Tertius the amanuensis who writes the letter for him; Gaius, his host in Corinth, and Erastus, the treasurer of the city, and also Quartus a layman. So the gospel in Corinth had reached a few noted men, although most of the converts there were from the lower and middle classes (I Cor. 1:26, 27).

DOXOLOGY (16:25-27)

25 To Him who can make you strong in accordance with the good news I bring and in accordance with the message preached about Jesus Christ, in accordance with the uncovering of the secret which for ages past had not been told, 26 but now has been fully brought to light by means of the prophetic Scriptures, and in accordance with the command of the eternal God has been made known to all the heathen, to win them to obedience inspired by faith—27 to the one wise God be glory forever through Jesus Christ. Amen.

A few key words and phrases in this the lengthiest doxology in the Bible demand an explanation. In his salutation (1:1) occurs the word gospel (*euaggelion,* good news or glad tidings). There he is set apart to preach the gospel; here the gospel he has preached is the standard for making strong those who believe it. *Preaching of Jesus Christ* means what is preached about Jesus Christ. *Mystery* means something that once was unknown but now is uncovered and fully known; it is the gospel of grace and faith kept in silence for ages in past eternity; but through the prophetic Scriptures it began to be uncovered and fully made known by Jesus and His apostles, the Twelve and Paul. God is alluded to as the eternal God, the only wise God. He has always existed, an uncreated Being, and the only God, who knows all things, even things that have not come to pass but are to. His command in verse 26 is that of a military commander with supreme authority over his soldiers. The mystery has not yet been made known to all the nations. It is a hyperbole; it is God's command that it should be done and is sure to be done. *Glory* in 27 is *praise* to God for His eternity, His all power and all wisdom, and for revealing His eternal secret of grace through the writings of the prophets. He is commanding it to be made known to all the nations. He honored Jesus Christ as the medium through whom this praise is given God.

The Letter to the Philippians

INTRODUCTION

1. *Author*. The writer is Paul; so held by all New Testament scholars. Paul was in prison at Rome, and the church at Philippi had sent, by Epaphroditus, a member of their church and probably a minister, a gift expressive of their love and devotion to him. Epaphroditus also told Paul about the dangers threatening the church from an attack of the Judaizers and the Antinomians—two groups holding opposite views of the law; the former strong advocates of legalism, the latter belittling the importance of the law. The date was A.D. 62.

2. *Purpose*. The purpose was to pour out his feelings and affections for the Christians at Philippi; to warn them against the false teachers named above, to show how his sufferings and imprisonment has contributed to his own Christian development and to the progress of the good news in Rome; to show his optimism and joy in spite of imprisonment and impending death.

It is a personal letter; a love letter; a joy letter. Nine times he uses the words *joy* and *rejoice*. It is written in the easy style of the everyday, common Greek, though containing a few terms, in 2:6-11, found in classical and later literary Greek. In the Greek it is an excellent specimen of a beautiful Christian letter to special friends. The church at Philippi was Paul's favorite church. It was born in his sufferings in prison (Acts 16:19-34).

OUTLINE

I. Introduction (1:1-11)
  1. Greeting (1:1, 2)
  2. Thanksgiving and prayer (1:3-11)
II. Personal Matters and Exhortations (1:12-2:18)
  1. Some personal matters (1:12-26)
  2. Exhortation to live worthily amid persecutions (1:27-30)
  3. To live humbly and live after the example of Christ (2:1-11)

Chapter I

HE GREETS THEM AND PRAYS FOR THEM; THANKS GOD AND RE-
JOICES OVER THEIR CO-OPERATION; THAT CHRIST IS
PREACHED; HIS FEELINGS CLASH AS TO WHICH
IS BETTER, TO LIVE OR DIE; CHRISTIAN
LIFE ONE OF SELF-SACRIFICE

THE GREETING (1:1, 2)

Verse 1. "Paul and Timothy." The latter is closely attached to Paul in the missionary work, but Paul is the exclusive author of the letter. Timothy is soon to come to them to let them know about Paul's condition (see 2:19-23). Servants; rather, bondslaves *(douloi)*. Christ Jesus is their Master whom they serve. Bishops and deacons are only two church officers.

Verse 2. "Grace and peace." The usual words of his greetings to the churches. Former means spiritual blessing, the latter, the ordinary greeting of health and happiness. "From God our Father and the Lord Jesus Christ." The Father and the Son on equal basis are the source of these blessings. The co-ordinate conjunction *kai* puts Christ on an equal footing with the Father; certainly a hint at His deity.

IN THANKS TO GOD, HE REJOICES IN THEIR CO-OPERATION;
PRAYS FOR THEM (1:3-11)

³ Every time I remember you I thank my God, ⁴ and always do it with joy in every entreaty I make for all of you, ⁵ for your co-operation in spreading the good news, from the first day you heard it until now. ⁶ For I am certain of this very thing, that He who began the good work in you will go on until the day of Jesus Christ to complete it. ⁷ And I have a right to think this way about you, because I always have you in my heart, whether shut up in prison or out defending and vindicating the good news, for you are sharers with me of God's favor. ⁸ For God is my witness how I never stop yearning for all of you with the affection Christ Jesus inspires.

⁹ And it is my prayer that your love may overflow still more and more, directed by fuller knowledge and keener insight, ¹⁰ so that you may always approve the better things, and be men of transparent character and blameless life, ¹¹ men that are abounding in the fruits of right-doing with the help of Jesus Christ, to the honor and praise of God.

Some key words and phrases. Verses 3-5. His prayer is with thanksgiving to God. Prime element in true prayer. It is also entreaty, prayer in conscious need *(deesis)*. It is also with joy. And yet he is in chains.

Verse 6. "I am sure that He who began a good work in you will continue it and complete it at the day of Jesus Christ." It is God who begins the work of grace at regeneration, and through the process of sanctification by the Spirit will continue that work until Christ comes. This is the divine guarantee for the preservation of the saints. Perseverance is secured by God through the Holy Spirit. So the Christian perseveres. God preserves, the believer perseveres.

Verses 7, 8. Paul's deep affection for the Philippian Christians. He holds them in his heart; the affection is inspired by the heart of Christ. Greek *splagchna,* seven vital organs, means the seat of affection, which we call the heart. His love for the Philippians is divinely inspired.

Verses 9-11. He prays for them to be enriched in these spiritual blessings: First, overflowing love—to God and one another and to all men; growing experimental knowledge and spiritual insight; so that they may always approve what is better (excellent)—always approve the higher spiritual blessings rather than material and worldly goods; to be transparent in character and blameless living; always overflowing in the fruits of doing right and good; it is all achieved through union with Christ Jesus; the aim, to glorify God. What an outline for an expository sermon! Love is of the highest order *(agape)*; not natural affection of kin, but voluntary, elective love, even of unworthy people. The knowledge is experimental coupled with spiritual insight into spiritual realities. The better things approved; not only approved but practiced. Character and life must be transparent, not hidden but clear as crystal, so all can see through them and see God in their character and conduct. Abounding in the fruits of doing right and doing good, doing church work and kingdom work. Paul was abounding in the fruits of doing good as he proclaimed the good news far and wide. The Philippians were co-operating with him in doing this work (v. 5). The supreme helper is Christ; the ultimate aim is to glorify God.

II. Personal Matters and Exhortation (1:12-2:18)

Paul's Sufferings Have Resulted in More Extensive Preaching of Christ (1:12-18)

¹² Now I want you to rest assured, brothers, that those things which have befallen me have actually resulted in the progress of the good news; ¹³ in this way it has become well known throughout the Imperial Guard and to all the rest here that I am a prisoner in the service of Christ, ¹⁴ and that most of the Christian brothers have grown confident enough because of my imprisonment, to dare to tell God's message without being afraid.

¹⁵ Some, indeed, are actually preaching Christ because they are moved by jealously and partisanship, but others are doing so from the motive of good-will; ¹⁶ the latter, indeed, are doing so from love to me, for they know that I am providentially put here to defend the good news; ¹⁷ the former are preaching Christ from the motive of rivalry, not in sincerity, supposing that this is making it harder for me to bear my imprisonment.

¹⁸ What difference then does it make? In one way or another, whether in pretense or in sincerity, Christ is being preached, and that is the thing that makes me glad; yes, more too, I will continue to be glad of it.

Key words and phrases. Verses 12-14. "The things that have befallen me" means his persecution by the Judaizers and his consequent imprisonment. "Have resulted in the progress of the good news" means have emboldened many to preach Christ without fear; Paul's bold sacrifice for Christ has impressed them that the gospel is the power of God for salvation (Rom. 1:16). The Imperial Guard was made up of noble Roman soldiers appointed to keep guard over the Emperor and the palace. Even these soldiers of the Emperor have been reached with the gospel. "The rest" refers to others in Rome, and perhaps beyond the limits of the capital.

Verses 15-18. In those days as now, some preached the gospel out of partisan motives; they belonged to a party opposing Paul, leaning toward the Judaizers; perhaps not out-and-out Judaizers, and really preaching Christ as the only Saviour, though not in sympathy with Paul's whole gospel of grace. But Paul rejoices that Christ, his Saviour, is preached even by his opponents. He believed in religious liberty and was charitable toward all his opponents.

CHRIST LIVING IN PAUL GIVES HIM A VICTORIOUS LIFE IN THE FACE OF PERSECUTION AND DEATH (1:19-26)

19 For I know that through your prayers and a bountiful supply of the Spirit of Jesus Christ this will turn out for my spiritual welfare, 20 in accordance with my eager expectation and hope that I shall never disgrace myself, but that now as always hitherto, by my all-conquering courage, whether by living or dying, Christ will be honored in me.

21 For to me living means Christ and dying brings gain. 22 But if to keep on living here means fruit from my labor, I cannot tell which to choose. 23 I am hesitating between two desires, for I long to depart and to be with Christ, for that is far, far better. 24 And yet for your sakes it is very necessary for me to stay on here. 25 Now since I am certain of this, I know that I shall stay on and stay by you all to promote the progress of your faith, 26 which will result in your joy; so that, through union with Christ Jesus, you may have more than sufficient ground for boasting about me, through my being with you again.

Key words and phrases. Verses 19, 20. "For I know that . . . this will turn out for my spiritual welfare." The *this* refers to his imprisonment and the consequent preaching of Christ by both friends and foes to him. "Spiritual welfare" is likely what he means and not "my deliverance" (A.V.). The context points to his spiritual welfare in that this preaching of Christ because of his imprisonment and his patient endurance of it for Christ's sake, are developing in him an "all-conquering courage." And this spiritual courage is secured to him through their prayers and the bountiful supply of the Spirit of Jesus Christ. See how the divine and the human co-operate—the divine Spirit of Christ and the human prayers of the readers. The phrase, "I shall not be disgraced or ashamed" (v. 20), makes it evident that he is talking about spiritual welfare and not personal deliverance. This word *soteeria*, salvation, has both meanings, and only the context can decide for us which it means.

Verse 21. A great thought. "To me to live means Christ and dying brings gain." Christ revealed in Paul was the origin of this spiritual life he now lives (Gal. 1:16, "chose to unveil His Son in me"). Christ continued to live in him (Gal. 2:20, "It is no longer I who live, but Christ who lives in me"). And the indwelling Christ is the source of Paul's power for conquests and achievements (Phil. 4:13). "I can do anything through Him [Christ] who gives me strength." "For Christ's sake" is the personal slogan of Paul's living.

"And to die is gain." A brand-new thought on dying. Jesus and Paul taught us to look upon death as a sleep. Now Paul advances and asserts that dying is gain. To him it will mean deliverance from persecution and all suffering and also to be with Christ. The latter is the consummate gain; to be and live in closest fellowship with the glorified Christ is the climax of this spiritual gain. After death Paul and all Christians collect the profits of their life investments in suffering, sacrifice, and toiling for Him and others.

Verses 22-26. He is in a dilemma, hard-pressed between two desires, "to sail away and be with Christ," and to live on and bear fruitful labor. One desire is far, far better, the other is more necessary for helping others. He does not know at first thought which he will choose, but after reflection he says, "I know that I shall stay on—to promote the progress of your faith." He is sure of his deliverance, not because the Philippians are praying for him, but because he is conscious of being able to bear more fruitful labor for Christ by being delivered. He may be contemplating the further missionary journey to Spain (Rom. 15:24, 28). "My desire is to depart" (22). The verb means to set sail, or sail away. The picture in the word is that dying is to lift anchor and set sail from time to eternity, from earth across the sea to the heavenly harbor.

HE REMINDS HIS READERS THAT IN GOD'S GRACIOUS PLAN CLIMACTIC CHRISTIAN LIVING IS SECURED IN SUFFERING FOR CHRIST'S SAKE (1:27-30)

27 Only you must practice living lives that are worthy of the good news, so that whether I come and see you or stay away, I may hear of you that you are standing firm in one spirit, and that with one purpose you are continuing to co-operate in the fight for faith in the good news. 28 Never in the slightest degree be frightened by your opponents, for such fearlessness will be strong evidence to them of their impending destruction, but to you a sure sign, and that from God, of your salvation. 29 For it has been graciously granted to you for Christ's sake, not only to trust in Him but also to suffer for Him, 30 since you are having the same struggle that you once saw me have and which you hear that I am still having.

Key words and phrases. Verses 27, 28. Living worthily of the gospel so as to maintain a solid front for the faith of the gospel. Notice, living worthily is the condition for maintaining one spirit and one mind in the church. Loose living in a church is the cause of a divided church. Worldly Christians are a prey to false doctrines. If all members of a church will walk worthily of the gospel ideals of pure character and conduct, they can easily maintain spiritual unity in the church and successfully resist all inroads of false teaching. Paul exhorts the readers to strive for the faith of the gospel, not fearing their opponents who would introduce false doctrines. They must not fear in the least degree these opposing teachers. This boldness drives back the opponents and keeps them from trying so hard to pervert the faith of true Christians. The timid, timorous Christians are easy prey to these opponents of the faith of the gospel. Faith here is a system of truths to be believed. Destruction is the end awaiting those opponents; salvation means the spiritual changes at the beginning of the Christian life, regeneration, justification, adoption, which guarantee the sanctification process, if unity and a firm stand for the truth are maintained.

Verses 29, 30. These orders should be carried out for the reason (*gar*) that God has graciously granted to Christians, not only to believe on Christ but also to suffer for His sake. Believing starts the new life, but suffering for Christ's sake in championing and proclaiming the truth lifts it to an incredible climax capable of reaching a happy completion.

This higher life of suffering for Christ's sake is the gracious gift of God. *Charizomai*, from *charis*, grace, has this meaning. It is God's grace, not His wrath, that permits His children to suffer for Him. A glorious reward will be given at last for all the sufferings (II Cor. 4:17).

Sermon Outline for Chapter I

Christ Living in and Through the Christian (1:21)

I. Christ the Source of the Spiritual Life (see John 1:4; 14:6; Gal. 1:16)
1. The Holy Spirit in regeneration imparts the life (John 3:3, 5)
2. Christ mediates the imparting of this life
3. Faith ties the believer on to Christ the life. The Holy Spirit renews the nature of the believer (Titus 3:5)

II. Christ Continues to Live in the Believer to Enrich His Life (see Gal. 2:20; Eph. 3:17; and this text, Phil. 1:21)

III. Christ the Standard of the Spiritual Life
1. In love to one Another and to enemies (Eph. 4:32-5:2)
2. In sacrificial service (II Cor. 8:9; Eph. 5:2)

IV. Christ the Conquering Power in the Christian Life (Phil. 4:13)
1. Paul says he conquered by this power (Phil. 4:13)
2. So can we (I Cor. 15:58; see John 16:33)

V. Christ the Glorious Goal of the Christian Life (Phil. 1:18)
1. So it was with Paul (II Cor. 5:14, 15); "Live for Him who died for us."
2. Should be our highest aim in living (See I Cor. 15:58).

Chapter II

AN APPEAL TO LOVE AND TENDERHEARTED SYMPATHY; URGES
CHRIST'S EXAMPLE OF HUMILITY AND SELF-SACRIFICE;
TELLS OF SALVATION AS A PROCESS TOWARD PER-
FECTION; TIMOTHY SENT TO THEM; EPA-
PHRODITUS SENT BACK

THE APPEAL TO LOVE AND CHRIST'S EXAMPLE OF HUMILITY AND SELF-SACRIFICE (2:1-11)

So, if there is any appeal in our union with Christ, if there is
any persuasive power in love, if we have any common share in
the Spirit, if you have any tenderheartedness and sympathy, ² fill
up my cup of joy by living in harmony, by fostering the same disposition of love, your hearts beating in unison, your minds set on
one purpose. ³ Stop acting from motives of selfish strife or petty
ambition, but in humility practice treating one another as your
superiors. ⁴ Stop looking after your own interests only but practice
looking out for the interests of others too.

⁵ Keep on fostering the same disposition that Christ Jesus had.
⁶ Though He was existing in the nature of God, He did not think
His being on an equality with God a thing to be selfishly grasped,
⁷ but He laid it aside as He took on the nature of a slave and became like other men. ⁸ Because He was recognized as a man in
reality as well as in outward form, He finally humiliated Himself
in obedience so as to die, even to die on a cross. ⁹ This is why God
has highly exalted Him, and given Him the name that is above
every other name, ¹⁰ so that in the name of Jesus everyone should
kneel, in heaven, on earth, and in the underworld, ¹¹ and everyone
should confess that Jesus Christ is Lord to the praise of God the
Father.

Key words and phrases. This paragraph is the only purely theological (or christological) paragraph in Philippians. So we must
carefully and thoroughly sift its every word and phrase.

Verse 1. The conditional particle *if* used four times in this verse
expresses a logical condition, one expressed as a fact. It is almost
equal to *since.* "If there is any encouragement in our union with
Christ." Of course there is. "If any incentive in love"; of course,
love is the mightiest incentive that moves the heart. "If any com-

mon sharing in the Spirit." All Christians may have a common share with all others in the Holy Spirit. "If there is any tender-heartedness and sympathy." The ancients regarded *splagchna*—seven organs, the heart, lungs, liver, spleen, pancreas, kidneys and stomach, according to Philo, the seat of the affections and emotions. The modern word tenderheartedness expresses what the ancient *splagchna* denoted. He is sure that the readers fulfill thse conditions.

Verse 2. The strongest appeal for spiritual unity: "Fill up my cup of joy [by] being of the same mind, having the same love with yours souls knit together *(sunpsuchoi)*, and of one mind." This would be perfect unity and harmony in the church and in their social relations. That is what Christianity can do for a people.

Verses 3, 4. The way to accomplish this ideal state is through selflessness, humility, and consideration for others. "Stop acting from motives of selfish strife or petty ambition [vain glory], but in humility practice treating one another as superiors" (Williams' Translation). "Not looking each of you to his own things, but each of you also to the things of others" (A.R.V.). This fourth verse might better be translated, "Stop looking after your own interests," etc. They are usually doing that. He exhorts them to practice utter unselfishness and altruistic consideration of others' interests. What a world we should have if this were practiced everywhere! Heaven on earth! But this is the way to live in peace and harmony and stop all wars, national and international. Paul says this would complete his joy, fill up the cup of his joy.

Verses 5-8. Humility and personal humiliation are enforced by the example of the pre-existent Christ Jesus. "Have the mind that was in Christ Jesus . . . Keep on fostering the same disposition that Christ Jesus had." Mind means disposition; disposition to humiliate Himself by being incarnated as a human being; and that for the sake of others. Notice, this exquisite christological dissertation (5-11) is primarily not to teach christology but to enforce practical humility and unselfish consideration of others by Christians. "Though He was existing in the exact image of God [in His pre-existence], He did not think His being on an equality with God a thing to be selfishly grasped, but He laid it [equality with God] aside as He took on the exact likeness of a slave and became like other men." The key words in this sentence are: *morphe; huparchon; isa theo; harpagmon; heauton ekenosen; morphen doulou; homoiomati; anthropon; schemati hos anthropos.* "In the image of God." This is the strongest word in Greek to denote likeness: the exact image, the inner image, image in being and essence. *Huparchon,* being, is stronger than *eimi,* am; it is not simply *being* but *existing. Isa theo,* equality with God, confirms the strong meaning of *morphe* above. He must have been *Deity in essence,* is what Paul is saying. He was on equality with the Supreme Being. Yet see what He did. He did not think this equality with God a thing to be selfishly grasped, held on to, for His own pleasure and glory. "He emptied Himself." This is the literal translation. Emptied Himself of what? Undoubtedly it was this equality with God. For He took on the exact likeness of a slave *(doulou)* and was born like other men (of course, minus sin).

It is to be observed that in His humiliation He took on the exact image of a slave, but was born like other men, *en homoiomati,* as a man, and was found to be merely in the external fashion *(schemati)* like a man. This is not to deny the real humanity of Jesus (see II Cor. 5:21, a Man without sin). The distinction above between the words for likeness, image, fashion, is based on Trench, *Synonyms.* See Lightfoot, *Commentary on Philippians,* for the above interpretation of equality with God *(isa theo).*

To show how complete was His humility and humiliation Paul says, "He humiliated Himself in obedience so as to die on a cross." He made Himself not only a man but a slave, and even put Himself on a plane with human criminals and died on a cross, the death of the worst of criminals.

Verses 9-11. His consequent exaltation. Paul must have been familiar with Jesus' laconic maxim, "He that exalts himself shall be abased, but he that humbles himself shall be exalted." *Therefore,* for this reason—His humiliation in incarnation and dying on a cross like a criminal—God highly exalted Him and gave Him a name that is above every other name." His humiliation lifted Him to the highest lordship. To Him every knee shall bow, His name every tongue shall confess. *Every* here includes rational, moral beings in all the universe, earth, Heaven, and the underworld. This does not mean universal salvation for men, whether now living on earth or dead in the underworld. He is merely extolling the exalted Christ to the highest degree. Even the lost must ascribe to Him universal lordship.

Their Salvation Is a Process to Be Worked Down to the Finishing Point (2:12-18)

¹² So, my dearly loved friends, as you have always been obedient, so now with reverence and awe keep on working clear down to the finishing point your salvation, not only as though I were with you but much more because I am away; ¹³ for it is God Himself who is at work in you to help you desire it as well as do it. ¹⁴ Practice doing everything without grumbling and disputing, ¹⁵ so that you may prove to be blameless and spotless, faultless children of God in a crooked and perverted age, in which you shine as light-bearers in the world as you continue ¹⁶ to hold up the message of life. That will give me ground for boasting on the day of Christ, because neither my career nor my labor has been a failure. ¹⁷ Yes, even if I am pouring out my life as a libation on the sacrifice and service your faith is rendering, I am glad to do so and congratulate you upon it; ¹⁸ you too must do likewise, be glad of it, and congratulate me.

Key words and phrases. Verses 12, 13. The struggle stage of salvation. This stage of salvation is a process, extending from the moment of conversion to the day of death. It is characterized by struggle, temptation, conquests, achievements, all the way from regeneration to the resurrection. The first stage is given in Ephesians 2:5, 8 (which see in our comments); the spiritual stage when the believer is saved by grace through faith; when he is born again. The new spiritual life imparted to the believer helps him save his character and conduct, his personality and life career. This is what Paul exhorts the readers to do: "Keep on working down to the finishing point your salvation, for it is God Himself who is at work in you to help you desire it as well as do it." The finishing point will not be reached until the last day the believer can consciously act and react to the Spirit's promptings. The preposition *kata*, down, gives us this conception of the believer's part in his salvation. He had nothing to do with his new birth, except to believe on Christ as the human condition of it. Now he must work and work down to a point of completion. (See Robertson, *Grammar*, p. 606, *kata* in composition. Here it is *katergazesthe*, keep on working down to perfection, etc. Robertson calls it perfective action.)

It must be observed that God is at work in this process of salvation. He is the prime worker, "working in you to help you desire it and do it." The believer could not even desire the higher life of conquest over self and sin, and the sanctification of character and conduct, except as God through the Spirit works and helps him both to will and to work, to desire and do. So this process of salvation is still salvation by grace and not by works. For this reason the believer should work in the spirit of reverence and awe, of fear and trembling, not in the spirit of the haughty Pharisee who thanked God that he was not as other men or as this tax-collector.

Verses 14-16. How the readers are to make effective this process of salvation: "Practice doing everything without grumbling and questioning." Present imperative makes it continuous action. No stopping, but keeping on and on till the night comes. We must show the right spirit and disposition—no grumbling about hard situations or questioning God's leading or the motives of others. "Keep sweet." This disposition accelerates the development of character, so that we may become "blameless and spotless, children of God without blemish in a crooked and perverted age." *Spotless* is stronger than *blameless;* and *without blemish* is the strongest of the three terms. Paul is not teaching sinless perfection. But he is urging the readers to save their characters; they must be spotless and without blemish. The ancient lamb for sacrifice must be without blemish as to his body. The believer as he offers himself to God must be so morally. In life believers are to be light-bearers. This word, *phosteres,* literally means those who bear the light as torch bearers. They are not merely lights, but torch-bearers, holding up the Word (message) of life. The picture is that of a procession at night, in a crooked and perverted age, in which torch-bearers are going ahead and holding on high their blazing torches, so that the marchers can see how to walk in the dark. This is a graphic picture of what believers are in this sin-darkened world. Paul must have been familiar with Jesus' teaching as recorded in Matthew 5:14-16.

Notice, the light is in the Word of life, the Bible truths, especially the good news. But the moral precepts must accompany it.

Verses 17, 18. Paul is glad to sacrifice himself for his friends the Philippians. Libation is a term used in a form of heathen sacrifice; but Paul gives it a sacred, Christian meaning. He is pouring out his life, himself, as a sacrifice to the faith of the Philippians, so that their faith may be more active and effective in the transformation of character and life. It is highly figurative language and must not be pressed literally. He rejoices that he can make this sacrifice for them, to help and inspire them. They should join him and rejoice in it.

III. CONCERNING TIMOTHY, EPAPHRODITUS, AND PAUL'S HOPE TO VISIT THEM (2:19-3:1)

TIMOTHY, THE SELFLESS MINISTER, SENT TO PHILIPPI; EPAPHRODITUS, THE CHURCH'S MESSENGER BEARING THEIR GIFT TO PAUL, AFTER RISKING HIS LIFE FOR THE GOSPEL, SENT BACK TO PHILIPPI (2:19-30)

[19] I hope, with the approval of the Lord Jesus, soon to send Timothy to you, so that I too may be cheered on getting the news about you. [20] For I have no one else with a heart like his who would take such genuine interest in you, [21] for most people are looking out for their own interests, not for the interests of Jesus Christ. [22] But you know his tested character, how like a son in fellowship with his father he has toiled with me like a slave in preaching the good news. [23] So I hope to send him to you just as soon as I can see how my case is going to turn out. [24] Really, I am trusting that by the help of the Lord I soon shall come myself.

[25] But I think it proper now to send back to you Epaphroditus, my brother, fellow-laborer, and fellow-soldier, but your messenger to minister to my needs. [26] for he has been longing to see you and has been homesick because you have heard that he was sick. [27] For he was so sick that he was on the point of dying, but God took pity on him, and not only on him but on me too, to keep me from having one sorrow after another. [28] I very eagerly send him, so that when you see him you may be glad of it, and I may be less sorrowful. [29] So give him a hearty Christian welcome and hold in honor men like him, [30] because he came near dying for the sake

of the Lord's work and risked his life to make up for your lack of
opportunity to minister to me.

Key words and phrases. Verses 19-22. The selfless character of
Timothy, Paul's messenger to the church. With only a few pen
strokes the apostle draws a character sketch of this spiritual son of
his (Acts 16:1-3). His character has been tested by Paul. Like a
son as to his personal relation he has "toiled like a slave with me
in preaching the good news." He knows him and his worth. "He
will care truly for your state" (A.R.V.). He is not like "most men
who look after their own interests, not the interests of Jesus Christ."
Timothy looks after the interests of Christ and of the churches.
He is genuinely anxious for others, especially for the Philippian
church. He is a selfless personality; self is crucified and Christ is
crowned in his life. A model for all ministers.

Verses 23, 24. Paul hopes to be set free at his trial before Nero
and at once come to Philippi. Timothy is to precede him as soon
as he sees any good prospects of his being released by Nero. As
soon as released he plans to go to Philippi himself.

Verses 25-30. Epaphroditus, who risked his life for the work
of the Lord, to be sent back to Philippi. He was Paul's "brother,
fellow worker, and fellow soldier." Paul emphasized Christian
brotherhood; the brotherhood of different social classes (Philem.
16). In relationship he was his brother, in service to Christ and
others, he was his fellow worker and fellow soldier. Paul thinks
of the Christian life as that of a real soldier (Eph. 6). Epaphroditus
was their messenger and minister to Paul's need. The word *apostolos* here used in its literal sense, one sent on a mission; here
to bear the gift from the church to Paul in prison. *Minister* also
used in its literal sense, not official for preacher or deacon. And
yet Epaphroditus may have been a minister officially—a preacher.

He was sick and sick almost to death, and that for the work of
the Lord. Perhaps this work was the bearing of the church's gift
to Paul—a real work of the Lord as it comforted and helped the
Lord's servant, Paul. However, if he was a minister officially, he
may have risked his life by preaching in Rome while waiting to
return to Philippi. But probably he became sick on the way to

Rome, perhaps shortly after leaving home; but he would not give
up the task, and went on getting worse and worse until he arrived
in Rome and had to go to bed, and came near dying. But God took
pity on him; that is, God intervened for His servant and helped
him to recover. In the meantime, the Philippians had heard of his
being sick and were troubled about it. So Paul felt that it was
necessary and proper to send him back at once. He may have carried this letter; at any rate, he took back Paul's love and thanks
for the love gift he had brought to Rome for him. Paul's motive
in sending him so early was twofold: to relieve the anxiety of the
readers and to let them rejoice to see their faithful messenger again.
Also to lessen his own sorrow. God had raised him from the bed
and kept Paul from having sorrow upon sorrow, and so to complete
the process he must send the sick man, now well, back to his friends.

Sermon Outline from Chapter II
The Mind of Christ the Christian's Motive (2:5)

I. His Mind Was Not to Grasp Things for Self; "Thought it not
a thing to be grasped."
  1. Not even His equality with God
  2. Not even the glory He had with the Father (John 17:5)
  3. Not even the joyous fellowships of Heaven, with the Father
  and the angels (II Cor. 8:9)
II. The Mind to Humble Himself and Even to Humiliate Himself
  1. Emptied Himself—laid aside His deity and its glory; if not
  entirely, partially; shone out once on the Mount (Matt.
  17:2)
  2. To be incarnated—take on human form (2:6-7); from
  Deity to humanity (a real man minus sin)
  3. To sacrifice Himself, even to die on a cross, the death of
  the most degraded criminal (2:8)
III. He Had the Mind to Save and Serve
  1. To save sinners, even the chief of sinners (I Tim. 1:15)
  2. To serve His people (John 13:1-16)
  3. To sacrifice Himself, not only in death but in life (John
  14:6). So all great Christians, with this "mind of Christ"
  sacrifice themselves to serve God, their fellow-Christians,

and all men. Examples: Paul; Judson, Carey, David Livingstone, and others.

IV. Warning against the Judaizers and the Antinomians (3:2-4:1)

Chapter III

EXTERNAL PRIVILEGES WORTHLESS AS MEANS OF RIGHT STANDING WITH GOD; PAUL COUNTS HIS PRIVILEGES BUT REFUSE COMPARED WITH HIS PERSONAL EXPERIENCE IN TRUSTING CHRIST; ASPIRES TO BEING LIKE CHRIST

PAUL'S GIVING UP OF ALL PERSONAL PRIVILEGES (IN CONVERSION) FOR EXPERIMENTAL KNOWLEDGE OF CHRIST AS HIS JUSTIFIER AND SAVIOUR (3:1-11)

Finally, my brothers, continue to be glad that you are in union with the Lord. I am not tired of writing you the same things over and over: it means your safety.

2 Look out for those dogs, those mischief-makers, those self-mutilators! 3 For we are the true circumcision, who by the Spirit of God worship Him, who take pride in Christ Jesus only, and do not rely on outward privileges, 4 though I too might rely on these. If anyone thinks that he can rely on outward privileges, far more might I do so: 5 circumcised when I was a week old; a descendant of Israel; a member of the tribe of Benjamin; a Hebrew, a son of Hebrews. Measured by the standard set by the law, I was a Pharisee; 6 by the standard set by zeal, I was a persecutor of the church, and measured by the uprightness reached by keeping the law, I was faultless. 7 But for Christ's sake I have counted all that was gain to me as loss. 8 Yes, indeed, I certainly do count everything as loss compared with the priceless privilege of knowing Christ Jesus my Lord. For His sake I have lost everything, and value it all as mere refuse, in order to gain Christ 9 and be actually in union with Him, not having a supposed right standing with God which depends on my doing what the law commands, but one that comes through faith in Christ, the real right standing with God which originates from Him and rests on faith. 10 Yes, I long to come to know Him; that is, the power of His resurrection and so to share with Him His sufferings as to be continuously transformed by His death, 11 in the hope of attaining, in some measure, the resurrection that lifts me out from among the dead.

Key words and phrases. Verse 1. "Finally." He seems to be concluding his letter. The same *rejoice* occurs in 4:1. This is characteristic of Paul's style—"going off at a word," as grammarians call it. "To you it is safe." These words remind him of the Judaizers who are threatening to make an inroad into Macedonia, especially into Philippi. It is not irksome to Paul to write the same things. He never gets tired of warning his churches of the dangers lurking all about them—false teachings.

Verses 2, 3. His warning against the Judaizers. "Look out for the dogs, look out for the mischief-makers, look out for those who mutilate their flesh!" These three descriptions, dogs, mischief-makers, self-mutilators, refer to the Judaizers. *Dogs,* devourers, biting and snapping and barking to intimidate and destroy others. *Evildoers,* making mischief among the believers, disturbing their faith and peace of mind. Self-mutilators is a play on the word circumcision *(peritome).* He calls them *katatome,* down cutters, complete cutters, mutilators of the flesh. They claim to be the circumcision; that is, true Jews. No, says Paul, "we are the true circumcision [true Jews] who worship God in spirit, and glory in Christ Jesus, and put no confidence in the flesh." Paul in accepting Jesus as the Messiah and Saviour and Lord is fulfilling the Jewish Scriptures and such are the true Jews, in spirit and not merely in the letter of the law.

Verses 4-8. Paul's inherited privileges and achieved advantages renounced for Christ's sake. If he would, he could glory in the flesh, in inherited privileges and legal achievements. He was circumcised according to law; he was descended from Israel; member of the tribe of Benjamin, the only tribe that remained faithful to Judah and the kingdom in Jerusalem; born of Hebrew parents; from the law standard *(kata nomon)* a Pharisee (prime advocates of legalism); from the point of view of zeal, a persecutor of the church (the institution and also the local church in Jerusalem); judged from the law standard, faultless and blameless. A superb character from the external point of view! But with all these natural possessions he was not saved. At the gates of Damascus he felt condemned as a sinner lost. There he relinquished all these personal advantages and privileges and scooped them out of his con-

fidence and life, as he would scoop up the barnyard filth *(skubala)*
and fling it on the refuse heap. "I count everything as loss." No
gain to him to bring him into right standing with God. They were
all loss. For these he gained Christ; "the surpassing superiority of
the experiential knowledge of Christ," is the literal meaning of
the Greek: *"To huperechon tes gnoseows Christou Iesou." Knowledge is that gained by experience,* by personal contact with Christ
as Saviour and Lord. Notice, the apostle emphasizes that Jesus
becomes "my Lord." He does not use *soteer,* Saviour, but it is
implied in what follows: right standing with God, righteousness
which is by faith in Christ. He suffered the loss of all things. He
stripped himself of all he had counted dear and precious to gain
Christ and be found in Him. In Him is in union with Him by faith."

Verses 9-11. Ultimately to know the power of His death and
resurrection. "Knowing Him"; by experience of fellowship with
Christ he came to know (not surmise and speculate about), really
to know the power of His sufferings, so that he could share those
sufferings by himself suffering scurrilous criticisms, stoning, imprisonment, and at last be beheaded as a martyr for Christ's sake.
He came to know (aorist) the power of His resurrection; that is,
the power imparted to him by the indwelling, risen Christ (Gal.
2:20). This dynamic empowered him to suffer and sacrifice all
things for Christ's sake. His goal is to attain to the complete resurrection from the dead. This is not the final physical resurrection;
he does not use the regular word for resurrection. This is *anastasis;*
he uses a compound, *exanastasis,* a complete rising out from the
dead. He uses the regular word, *anastasis,* in verse 10. But he aspires to attain not the ordinary resurrection. He knows he will
have that as an immortal man. It is a spiritual resurrection from
the dead things of sin and its blighting curse. In the next verses
he describes what he is thinking about; to be like Christ, to be
"perfect." (See Rom. 6:4-6; Eph. 2:5-6, for his use of resurrection
in the spiritual sense.)

THE APOSTLE'S SPIRITUAL ASPIRATION TO BE "PERFECT"; WARN-
ING AGAINST FALSE MORALISTS; CITIZENS OF HEAVEN (3:12-21)

¹² It is not a fact that I have already secured it or already

reached perfection, but I am pressing on to see if I can capture it, the ideal for which I was captured by Christ Jesus. [13] Brothers, I do not think that I have captured it yet, but here is my one aspiration, so forgetting what is behind me and reaching out for what is ahead of me, [14] I am pressing onward toward the goal, to win the prize to which God through Jesus Christ is calling us upward. [15] So let us all who are mature have this attitude. If you have a different attitude, God will make it clear to you. [16] However, we must continue to live up to that degree of success that we have already reached.

[17] Follow my example, brothers, and keep your eyes on those who practice living by the pattern we have set you. [18] For there are many, of whom I have often told you, and now tell you in tears, who practice living as the enemies of the cross of Christ. [19] Their doom is destruction, their stomach is their god, their glory is in their shame, and their minds are feeding on earthly things. [20] But we are citizens of the republic in heaven, from which we are eagerly waiting for our Saviour, the Lord Jesus Christ. [21] He will so change the outward appearance of our lowly bodies that they will be like His glorious body, by the exertion of the power He has to subject everything to Himself.

Key words and phrases. Verses 12-14. Paul aspires to be perfect. He does not claim to have reached perfection, but he is pressing on toward it as his goal of life. "It is not a fact that I have already reached perfection." How different is his claim to that of thousands of the so-called "holiness people"! Some of them claim it as an actual possession. John Wesley said, "I preach perfection but I have not reached it." It is a glorious personal ideal for which to strive. It is taught in the New Testament as our ideal. (See Matt. 5:48; Heb. 6:1; 12:14.)

There can be little doubt in the mind of any careful student of this paragraph that Paul is discussing the highest spiritual attainment as his aspiration. "The prize of the upward calling of God" (14) is not some future reward in Heaven to be given him for his arduous toils and ceaseless sufferings. The prize is to be like Christ, to be perfect, for which he is stretching forward like a hound or horse on the race track stretching forward the head and neck and whole body to win the prize presented for victory. The Greek participle *epekteinomenos* means literally reaching, stretching up. In the spiritual realm stretching forward is stretching *up*.

Verses 15-17. Exhorts readers to follow his example and press on to perfection. "Let those of us who are mature be thus minded." He is complimenting his readers in thus appealing to them. But he realizes there may be some there who are not thus mature. Who do not have so high a spiritual ideal but are satisfied with medium or even low attainments in Christian living. Alas! Millions of Christians are satisfied with the low level of life. "If in anything ye are otherwise minded, this also God shall reveal unto you." If some are satisfied with low standards of spiritual living, God can and will show them, if they will pray and look up instead of down, that the higher life is His ideal for them and that He will help them live on that higher level. "Only whereunto we have attained by that same rule let us walk." (A.R.V.). "We must continue to live up to that degree of success that we have already reached" (Williams). This applies to all, whether on the low, medium or high level of spiritual living. Hold on to what you have and strive to go higher.

He exhorts them to follow his example and those of other noble Christians of maturity.

Verses 18-21. He gives a reason for this exhortation to nobler living: "For many are enemies of the cross of Christ." He warns against the false moralists, the Antinomians. This group of false teachers were now threatening inroads into Macedonia and especially into Philippi. They were antilegalists, as their name suggests. They taught and practiced loose living; be a law unto yourself; do whatever brings you pleasure. Really they were Hedonists, Epicureans. Pleasure, not the law, is the standard of living, first taught by the Greek philosopher Epicurus. Paul had often warned them against these fellows and now does it in tears. They are enemies of the cross of Christ. The cross means sacrifice, not only for Christ but also for the Christian; not selfish, sensual living but sacrificial, self-denying living. "Their end is destruction, their god is the belly (stomach and sex organs), and they glory in their shame." They are so low in morals that they boast of how mean they can be to satisfy their "bellies." They worship their "bellies." But their doom is destruction from the presence of the Lord (II Thess. 1:9).

"But our citizenship is in the republic in Heaven." The word translated commonwealth is used by Plato in the sense of republic; hence our translation. That is where the believer's citizenship is; in the republic, commonwealth, in Heaven. Paul was a Roman citizen (of which he was proud), but he was also a citizen of Heaven. He tells his readers that this heavenly prestige and glory should motivate us to live the resurrection life; a higher life than an ordinary citizen; higher and richer by far than the sensual, selfish, sordid life the Antinomians live.

"From Heaven we are eagerly awaiting for our Saviour, the Lord Jesus Christ." The Christian should live in eager expectancy for the coming Saviour. We do not know when He is coming; but He is surely coming, and the expectancy of it should spur us on to higher spiritual living and to greater sacrifices for Christ and the lost. That is Paul's appeal to his readers.

"He will so change the outward appearance of our lowly bodies that they will be like His glorious body." At the final resurrection that is what will take place. The outward appearance of our bodies of humiliation, their physical nature and appearance, will be changed into spiritual bodies (I Cor. 15:46-50). First we had physical bodies, but then we shall have spiritual bodies, imperishable bodies. "Flesh and blood cannot inherit the kingdom of God" (I Cor. 15:50). Jesus after His resurrection was not visible to ordinary men; only to His disciples when He showed Himself to them. His body then was such that He could go into a closed and locked room and suddenly appear to them (John 20:19, 20). His body had been changed from its natural constituency into a spiritual body, invisible to physical eyes until Jesus showed Himself to them (Acts 1:3); that is, showed Himself miraculously. As to the scene at the seashore that morning John tells us that "This was the third time that Jesus was revealed to the disciples after He was raised from the dead" (21:14). Luke's account of His revealing Himself to the two disciples at Emmaus (24:31) gives us a strong proof that His physical body in rising from the dead was wholly changed. "And their eyes were opened and they recognized Him; and He vanished out of their sight." He miraculously made their physical eyes able to see His body by changing it enough for them to recognize Him.

If He is to have this spiritual body in Heaven, as in the forty days of post-resurrection period on earth, shall we see the nail-prints in His hands? Most surely, but we shall see His glorious body, not with our physical eyes but with spiritual eyes, the eyes of the spirit matched with a spiritual body (I Cor. 15:44).

SERMON OUTLINES FROM CHAPTER III

THE POWER OF CHRIST'S RESURRECTION IN THE CHRISTIAN'S LIVING (3:10, 11)

I. This Power Mediated through a Genuine Experience in Conversion
  1. Paul renounces all personal privileges and achievements—heredity, early culture, personal morality, etc.
  2. Renounces family pride and former religion (legalism)
  3. Personal honors; being groomed for a rabbi
  4. Surrenders to Christ as Lord and Saviour (Rom. 10:9, 10)

II. This Power Obtained through Experimental Knowledge of Christ
  1. Started in penitence for his own sins. Likely prayed the publican's prayer, "God be merciful to me a sinner."
  2. In this experience he recognized Jesus as the Risen Son of God (Rom. 1:4)
  3. The Risen Christ empowers him for conquering living (Phil. 4:13)
  4. Also for suffering for Christ's sake (Phil. 1:29, 30; 1:25-30)

III. By Experiencing This Knowledge of His Resurrection He Can Reach His Own Spiritual Resurrection in the Higher Life. See comments above for interpretation of the expression, "attain the resurrection from the dead."
  1. Living the Christ life; that is, His resurrection life (Phil. 1:21)
  2. Living the life of sacrifice and service
  3. Which means the victorious life (Phil. 2:9-11)
  4. Resulting in exaltation and glory (II Tim. 4:8)
     Paul, Livingstone, Judson, and other noted missionaries, illustrations of this higher resurrection life in Christians

Paul's Spiritual Aspiration (3:13, 14)

I. Not Satisfied with His Past. "Not that I have already," etc.
  1. Not satisfied with his character and personal development
  2. Not satisfied with his labors and achievements
  3. Are you? Am I? "Woe to them that are at ease in Zion."

II. Forgetting the Past. "Forgetting what lies behind."
  1. His sufferings and sorrows
  2. His failures and disappointments
  3. His successes
  4. His joyous experiences. Victory in Corinth reported by Titus

III. His Attitude toward the Future—"Straining forward; . . . press on"
  1. Has faith in it; his own release from prison and future missionary activities
  2. His hope for its blessed experiences and richer rewards (II Tim. 4:8)
  3. Actually striving and pressing on to seize its opportunities.
    Alexander listening to astronomer Anaxagoras tell of other worlds besides earth, exclaimed, "And I have not finished conquering this one!" Said it in tears. Not satisfied, still reaching out for other worlds to conquer.

Citizens of Two Worlds (Phil. 3:20)

I. The Fact That We Christians *Are* Citizens of Two Worlds
Plato in his Republic intimates that man is not only a citizen of earth but is also a citizen of a celestial republic. Author, The Letter to Diognetus (early second century A.D.) writes, "Christians live in the world, but they are citizens of Heaven."
  1. Paul a citizen of Rome; also of Heaven.
  2. We American Christians, citizens of U.S.; also of Heaven
  3. The regular way to become a citizen of U.S. is by *birth;* so the *only* way to become a citizen of Heaven is by the *second birth*

II. Duties of the Two Citizenships
  1. Primal duty, loyalty—patriotism
  2. Specific duties: paying taxes (contributions as a heavenly

citizen); fighting for our country (Christian soldiers, Eph.
6:10-20); working for our country (Christians, God's
workers, I Cor. 3:9). Illus.: A brave wife in Texas during
World War I said to husband: "Go, and help whip the
Germans. I will stay at home and run the farm." Christians
are God's farmers as well as His soldiers.

3. We should perform the duties of our earthly citizenship in
   the spirit of heavenly citizens: love and justice to all; sacrifice and service to our country. So in World Wars I and II.
   So we do as citizens of Heaven. Paul debtor to all (Rom.
   1:14). Gave his life and talents and all he had. So did
   Livingstone for Africa.

III. Jesus the Bond of Union for the Two Citizenships
   1. Gave Himself to plant the heavenly republic on earth and
      help earthly governments succeed. Illustration: giant oak
      with boughs bending under a load of snow and sleet and
      ice lost a huge limb, falling and leaving an open scar. A
      bird dropped a mistletoe seed into the scar; germinated
      and grew and spread, fed by the sap and blood of the suf-
      fering tree, covering the giant oak and furnishing decora-
      tions for the birthday of the King.
   2. He is the Dynamic and Inspiration for sacrifice and service
      in both citizenships. It was so with Paul (Gal. 2:20).
      Browning:

> That one face far from vanish, rather grows,
> Or, decomposes but to recompose,
> Become my universe that feels and knows.

Chapter IV

VARIOUS EXHORTATIONS
POURING OUT HIS HEART TO THE READERS, HIS JOY AND CROWN
OF REWARD; INSPIRES THEM TO "BEAUTIFUL THOUGHTS AND
NOBLE DEEDS"; THANKS THEM FOR THEIR MANY
GIFTS; SENDS FAREWELL GREETINGS

So, my dearly loved brothers, whom I long to see, my joy and
crown, by the help of the Lord keep on standing firm, dearly
loved friends.

² I beg Euodia and I beg Syntyche to live in harmony by the help of the Lord. ³ And I solemnly beg you, my true comrade, keep on co-operating with those two women, because they shared with me the struggle in spreading the good news, together with Clement and the rest of my fellow-workers, whose names are in the book of life.

⁴ By the help of the Lord always keep up the glad spirit; yes, I will repeat it, keep up the glad spirit. ⁵ Let your forbearing spirit be known to everybody. The Lord is near. ⁶ Stop being worried about anything, but always, in prayer and entreaty, and with thanksgiving, keep on making your wants known to God. ⁷ Then, through your union with Christ Jesus, the peace of God, that surpasses all human thought, will keep guard over your hearts and thoughts.

⁸ Now, brothers, practice thinking on what is true, what is honorable, what is right, what is pure, what is lovable, what is high-toned, yes, on everything that is excelled or praiseworthy. ⁹ Practice the things you learned, received, and heard from me, things that you saw me do, and then the God who gives us peace will be with you.

Key words and phrases. Verse 1. "Therefore." For this reason, that perfection lies ahead of you as an ideal goal, that Christ is coming from Heaven to transform our lowly bodies and make them like His own glorious body, he exhorts to certain noble qualities and spiritual exercises. "My dearly loved and longed-for brothers." Strong epithets to express his heartfelt emotions of tenderest feelings for the Philippians. They are dearly loved and they are longed for by the aged prisoner in his loathsome, lonely room. He is homesick to see them, like a boy away from home and mother and father for the first night, longing to be there in the old home with those who love him. "My joy and crown." They are the source of greatest joy every time he thinks of them. His crown of reward, as his converts on his first visit to Philippi; some converted by the river bank, some in jail. "My dearly loved." This endearing term is repeated at the close, though used to introduce the sentence. He cannot find terms sufficient to express all his heart feels for them. How he loved them!

Verses 2-3. "I beg Euodia and I beg Syntyche to live in peace and harmony." Literally, "to think the same thing." These two leading women in the church had minds of their own and often clashed as to what to do and how to do it in the church; as to community service, as to mission work and so on. They are fine workers, but they want their ideas to prevail; do not seem to be bosses in the church; just enthusiastic leaders with strong convictions as to their being right. Paul lovingly warns them to agree; they can do that by thinking the same thing. He loves peace and harmony in a church; unity must be preserved.

"I ask you also, true yokefellow, help these two women, for they joined me in the struggle to spread the gospel." Noble missionaries they were! They had co-operated heartily in Paul's struggles, his conflicts, to spread the good news. The true yokefellow is probably the pastor of the church at Philippi (unknown). "With Clement and the rest of my fellow workers, whose names are in the book of life." Clement is not to be positively identified. He may be the Clement who later lived at Rome and wrote letters to the church at Corinth—two excellent letters appealing to the Greek church in this capital to stay united and live and work on a high spiritual plane. "Whose names are in the book of life." A reference to the Roman custom to have the names of Roman citizens recorded in a great book of citizenship. So God has recorded in a book called "the book of life," all citizens of the heavenly republic mentioned above; all who shall live on after the resurrection as citizens of Heaven.

Verse 4. Rejoicing Christians. Paul in prison talks of "rejoicing." He is a happy Christian; happy all the time (vv. 10-13). Nine times in this love letter he refers to joy or rejoicing. "Continue to rejoice in the Lord." Present imperative means continuous action. And *always*. In prisons or in palaces; in prosperity or in adversity; in health or in sickness. "In the Lord," because of your union with the Lord (Jesus); because of what He has done for you and still is doing. I repeat it, "Continue rejoicing."

Verse 5. Forbearance should be universal; Christians should be forbearing, overlooking faults and shortcomings in all men. Not only in our fellow Christians but in outsiders; be considerate and patient with all. *The Lord is at hand.* Probably refers to the second coming for which Paul so expectantly looks. Might refer to the fact that the Lord is near us all the time and watching our conduct; so be careful and live up to these noble ideals. On either interpretation this is the main thought.

Verse 6. "Stop worrying about anything." Negative with present imperative always has this meaning—stop doing something already being done. Instead of worrying, "Take it to the Lord in prayer." "In prayer and supplication with thanksgiving." The first word *prayer* is a general term for any kind of prayer; the second is to plead as a suppliant in distressful need at the feet of a superior. Thanksgiving should always accompany a prayer of petition. "In everything." In whatever situation in life we can come to the Lord in prayer and let our requests be made known to God.

Verse 7. "And the peace of God, which surpasses all human understanding, will keep guard over your hearts and minds." This is the peace of mind which God only can give a child of His when he trusts and prays. Liebman wrote a best seller on *Peace of Mind,* emphasizing the psychological phase of this wonderful peace. The spiritual phase of it is more significant than the psychological. If we can pray away the worries, God will give us the sweet peace. "Thou wilt keep him in perfect peace whose mind is stayed on thee" (Isa. 26:3). Prayer helps keep the mind stayed on God. This peace surpasses all human understanding. Its depths of sweetness and richness of solace and quiet of soul, no human mind can fathom! "In Christ Jesus." This is all done through our personal union with "Christ Jesus."

Verses 8-9. Noble thinking and a noble example to follow. As a final word of exhortation he points their minds to the loftiest thinking man can possibly do. Continue to think on these things. The thinking is not casual or superficial, but constant and logical. Our word logic and logical come from the Greek verb think, *logizomai.* "These things": the true, the honorable, the right, the pure, the lovable, the high-toned, the excellent, the praiseworthy. A list of the noblest qualities conceivable. Seven of them, the number indicating perfection to a Jew. Observe, the first quartet of qualities are truth, honor, right, and purity, the cornerstones of the noblest character and personality.

Then follows a noble example for the readers to follow, Paul himself. He modestly says, "What you have learned and received and heard and seen in me, do." The first two verbs are mental receivers, the last two, physical avenues of personal contact. They had heard Paul preach and teach, they had received the truth thus learned. They had "seen" him live and suffer for Christ. They can safely follow his example in "practice." (prasso).

JOYFULLY THANKS THE READERS FOR THEIR LOVE GIFT BROUGHT
BY EPAPHRODITUS, BUT ASSURES THEM OF HIS CONTENTED
MIND IN ANY CIRCUMSTANCES (4:10-20)

[10] I was made very happy as a Christian to have your interest in my welfare revived again after so long; because you have always had the interest but not the opportunity to show it. [11] Not that I refer to any personal want, for I have learned to be contented in whatever circumstances I am. [12] I know how to live in lowly circumstances and I know how to live in plenty. I have learned the secret, in all circumstances, of either getting a full meal or of going hungry, of living in plenty or being in want. [13] I can do anything through Him who gives me strength. [14] But you did me a kindness to share my sorrow with me. [15] And you Philippians yourselves know that immediately after the good news was first preached to you, when I left Macedonia, no church but yours went into partnership with me to open an account of credits and debits. [16] Even while I was at Thessalonica you sent money more than once for my needs. [17] It is not your gift that I want, but I do want the profits to pile up to your credit. [18] I have received your payment in full, and more too. I am amply supplied after getting the things you sent by Epaphroditus; they are like sweet incense, the kind of sacrifice that God accepts and approves. [19] My God will amply supply your every need, through Christ Jesus, from His riches in glory. [20] Glory to our God and Father forever and ever. Amen.

Key words and phrases. Verses 10-13. Constant contentment. The coming of Epaphroditus to Rome bearing the love gifts of the Philippians to their beloved spiritual father was a mountain-top experience in the aged prisoner's life. He could scarcely contain himself. It had been some time since they had sent him a gift, as suggested by the word, "at length" *(eedee)*. Had they forgotten him, he may have wondered in his chains. Now, like a peal of thunder out of a clear sky, the love-gift is dropped into his lap, and his cup of joy runs over. "I rejoice in the Lord greatly." He rejoices as a Christian (in the Lord). It is not the gift that makes him happy; it is the Christian love behind the gift and the fruit of grace in their hearts (17). He sees in them (his converts) genuine, growing Christians, and that makes his heart leap with joy inexpressible.

However, he hastens to assure them that he did not need the gift to make him contented with his lot in prison. "I have learned, in whatever state I am, to be content." What a colossal Christian poise! Content in a prison in chains! "In whatever circumstances I am." Even in want and hunger. Perhaps a few times he really suffered for something to eat! Yet contented with his lot. This Greek word content is interesting. It means self-satisfied. That is not literally what Paul means. His satisfaction is not in self, but in Christ. He had experienced the truth of God's promise, "My grace is sufficient for thee" (II Cor. 12:9). This grace, spiritual power, had been sufficient, not only for bearing the thorn in the flesh, but also for bearing chain and imprisonment, want and hunger. What he makes the Greek word mean is, my satisfaction and contentment do not depend on circumstance but on what is in me, the indwelling Christ, the indwelling Spirit, by the grace of God. Prisons and palaces do not affect my state of mind; my joy bubbles up from within and not from without!

Verses 14-18. In this paragraph he assures them that he does appreciate their gifts. "It was kind of you to share my trouble." He reminds them of the frequency of their gift-sending, "once and again." It started immediately after he first left Macedonia, shortly after his first visit to Philippi, and had continued. He uses bookkeeping terms, giving and receiving, credit, received full payment, to express vividly their dealings with him. They have been keeping books with God and with him. They have entered into partnership with him. Now he says, "I have received full payment, and more." They have more than compensated him for all he had done for them; for his imprisonment that night in Philippi and the humiliation of a Roman citizen in a Roman colony.

"I am filled"; perfect tense, "I have been filled since receiving from Epaphroditus the gifts you sent." Not his stomach but his soul has been filled. Perhaps a little of it went into his stomach; but the main emphasis is on his spiritual satisfaction which is complete. The climax is reached when he asserts that these gifts are a fragrant offering, a sacrifice acceptable and pleasing to God. Helping one another is fragrant incense and sacrifices pleasing to God. God will reward those who make such sacrifices to Him: "Will supply every need of yours according to His riches in glory in Christ Jesus." Every need, not only spiritual but all other needs—mental, social, economic, and so on. His storehouse is riches in glory. Glory here means the summation of God's attributes. His storehouse of supply then includes His power and greatness, His righteousness and holiness, His grace and mercy, all reinforced by His unchanging love.

He closes with a doxology: "To our God and Father be glory for ever and ever. Amen." *Glory* here means *praise*. God the Father is the ultimate source of salvation and all our blessings (John 3:16; Rom. 5:8). Hence he ascribes glory to Him; but it is through union with Christ Jesus.

CONCLUDING THE LETTER: GREETINGS; BENEDICTION (21-23)

Verses 21, 22. He sends greetings to every saint in Christ Jesus. No partiality with Paul. Every individual child of God is greeted, the lowest and the highest. "In Christ Jesus" likely modifies "saint"; they are saints because they are in union with Christ Jesus, not because they are sinless or are pronounced saints by some hierarchy.

"The brothers who are with me greet you." Luke and Demas are with him as he closes Colossians (4:14). They and others (possibly Timothy) may be with him now. "All the saints greet you." All Christians, all the people of God here. "Especially those of Caesar's household." He was evangelistic and had preached the good news in his prison room; many of the Imperial Guard (1:13) and others of Caesar's household had embraced the Lord Jesus as their Lord and Saviour. They join in sending greetings to their fellow Christians in this Roman colony at Philippi.

"The grace of our Lord Jesus Christ be with your spirit." A single benediction emphasizing Christ as the medium of all blessings. So in Galatians 6:18 and I Corinthians 16:23. The triune benediction occurs in II Corinthians 13:14. Grace in the benediction means spiritual blessings. Perhaps, especially it emphasized spiritual strength. See Philippians 4:13. *Spirit* in the singular emphasizes the individual saint, as in 4:21.

SERMON OUTLINES FROM CHAPTER IV
CHRISTIAN JOY (4:4)

I. What It Is Not
   1. Not rejoicing in one's country. Paul proud of being a Roman citizen, but his Christian joy was "in the Lord"; in what Christ had done for him.
   2. Not in one's home. We should be proud of our homes; home the basic social institution; civilization and Christianity depending on it.
   3. Not in good health. May be proud of our heredity and environment.
   4. Not in our outstanding education and culture. Paul repudiated it.
   5. Not in personal prosperity.

II. It Is Rejoicing in What the Lord Has Done for Us
   1. He has loved us and given Himself for us (Gal. 2:20)
   2. He has saved our souls (Acts 4:12). He is the only Saviour.
   3. He has kept us hitherto (John 10:26-28)
   4. He has called us to service in the kingdom (Mark 1:17-20) This is an honor angels would rejoice to have. (See I Cor. 3:9).

III. Rejoicing in What He Has Promised Yet to Be and Do
   1. To be with us to the end of the age (Matt. 28:20)
   2. To love us to the end of life (John 13:1)
   3. To keep us always (John 10:28)
   4. To give us Heaven and eternal life (Luke 10:20; Phil. 4:3)
   5. To give us crowns of righteousness and life (II Tim. 4:8; Rev. 3:21; 14:13; 22:12)

   Illustration: Poor brother shouting in a fashionable church. Rich brother offered him the finest pair of boots if he would quit. He answered: "Hallelujah to the Lord, boots or no boots!"

THE PEACE OF GOD OUR GRACIOUS GUARD (4:7)

I. Two Phases of This Peace
  1. Peace, or reconciliation, with God. Lost sinners at enmity with God (Rom. 8:7, 8)
  2. "Peace of mind." Liebman writes a great book on it. Jesus exhorts us to have it by trusting the Father (Matt. 6:25-33). *Surrender yourself* and *your all to God* and "all these things shall be added." Jesus calmed the minds of the disciples on the angry sea of Galilee by speaking to the storm: "Peace, be still." So to us in storms.

II. God the Giver of This Peace
  1. Through Christ Jesus He gives peace with God (II Cor. 5:19)
  2. Through Christ Jesus He gives peace of mind. So to disciples: so to Paul (II Cor. 12:9, "My grace is sufficient.")

III. The Superior Quality of This Peace of God
  1. "It surpasses all understanding"
  2. Hence it surpasses all human description. As it approaches "perfect peace" (Isa. 26:3) in anyone, he can understand it and express it. Angels and redeemed understand it, for they have it.

IV. What the Peace of God Does for Us Christians
  1. "Keeps guard over our hearts." Literal meaning of Greek verb
     (a) Keeps the heart fixed on the pure (Matt. 5:8)
     (b) Keeps the heart fixed on *God* and *spiritual things* (Isa. 26:3).
  2. "Keeps guard over our minds." Paul watching the Roman guard keep watch over him knew that God's peace in his heart was keeping guard over his "heart and mind."
     (a) Keeps the mind quiet and placid in sickness. Miss Wright, invalid of twenty-five years, happiest Christian I ever saw. "Peace of mind."
     (b) In disappointments and financial losses. George Carroll, rich man of Beaumont, Texas, lost all. Without a murmur started all over again.

The Letter to the Ephesians

INTRODUCTION

1. *Author, Date, and Occasion.* The writer is Paul the apostle, so held by all conservative, and by an increasing number of liberal scholars. The occasion is likely the fact that the Gnostics are still threatening to undermine the faith of Christians throughout the province of Asia. The date is likely A.D. 62 or 63, just before he wrote Colossians. The letter is likely addressed to all the churches in the province of Asia (Ephesus the capital). After being read by the other churches it was naturally returned to Ephesus the capital as the guardian of the letter. This is why it came to be called the Letter to the Ephesians.

2. *Purpose.* To show that salvation is obtained only in Christ; to emphasize the fellowship of believers with Christ and the oneness of all believers with one another, even suggesting international peace for mankind, and the unification of the whole universe around Christ; to magnify the Church as a divine institution; to show that a well-rounded life, moral and spiritual, flows out of salvation by grace through faith. The letter traces man's salvation back to the grace of God which flows out of His "great love" (2:4). The letter is non-personal and general in tone, even cosmopolitan and cosmic in thought. Its vocabulary is rich in new words found nowhere else in the New Testament or in Paul, and its style represents his best literary effort. Its thoughts are profound and its treatment comprehensive.

ITS MAIN TEACHINGS

1. God is the Father—emphasized.
2. Christ is the Messiah, the Son of God, the Redeemer, the Reconciler of God and man, of races, and of the universe.
3. Christ has supreme authority over the Church. He is the Head.
4. The Holy Spirit seals believers as God's own and stamps them with the image of God.

5. The church is a divine institution, built by Christ's love for men, endowed with various spiritual gifts and functionaries for the perfecting of Christian character and personality and for the propagation of the gospel to all races so as to bring about a universal brotherhood of mankind.

6. Unification and fellowship of Christians as a logical sequence of the seven unities—one God, one Lord, one Spirit, One faith, one baptism, one hope, so one Body of united Christians.

7. God's power to keep Christians safe measured by His power to raise Christ from the dead and to exalt Him far above all other rule and authority.

8. The power of prayer and inducement to the Christian to pray, namely, the Father's ability to do exceeding abundantly above all that we ask or think.

9. The home, the foundation of society and the Church.

10. The tender relation of Christ to His Church, that of a loving husband to his bride.

11. Husbands to imitate Christ in their devotion to their wives.

12. Wives to respect their husbands as heads of their homes.

13. Parents under obligation to give their children a Christian education.

14. The Christian life a campaign with the Devil and the forces of evil, but each one may be so armed as to be sure of victory.

GENERAL OUTLINE

I. Salutation (1:1, 2)

II. The Doctrinal Portion (1:3-3:21)

1. Thanksgiving to God for election by the Father, redemption in Christ, and sealing by the Holy Spirit(1:3-14)

2. Thanksgiving for the spiritual state of the readers with a prayer for their deeper spiritual knowledge (1:15-19)

3. A formal statement of God's power in Christ (1:20-2:22)

(a) As to Christ Himself, the Father brought about His resurrection, ascension, universal and ecclesiastical headship (1:20-23)

    (b) As to individuals, their spiritual resurrection and ascension in union with Christ (2:1-10)

    (c) With respect to all mankind, reconciliation and brotherhood (2:11)

  4. Paul's personal relation to his readers (3:1-21)

    (a) His authority to preach the gospel to them (3:1-13)

    (b) His prayer for their spiritual strength (3:14-21)

    (c) He closes these great teachings with a doxology (3:20-21)

III. The Practical Duties in the Church, and in All Social Relations

  1. In the Church (4:1-5:22)

    (a) To live a life worthy of the unity of the church (4:1-16)

    (b) To live a life different from the old Gentile life (4:17-24)

    (c) To practice certain virtues and avoid certain vices (4:25-5:21)

  2. In the various classes

    (a) The duties of wives and husbands (5:22-25)

    (b) The duties of children and parents (6:1-4)

    (c) The duties of slaves and masters (6:5-9)

  3. In the whole church again (6:10-20)

    (a) The Christian life a spiritual warfare (6:10-12)

    (b) The Christian soldier's armor (6:13-18)

    (c) A request that the readers pray for the apostle to preach the gospel as he ought (6:19-20)

IV. Conclusion (6:21-24)

  1. Tychicus sent to them (6:21-22)

  2. Salutation and benediction (6:23-24)

SALUTATION

Chapter I

SALUTATION; GOD'S ETERNAL PURPOSE OF LOVE; UNIVERSAL REDEMPTION BY CHRIST; THE HOLY SPIRIT STAMPS BELIEVERS AS GOD'S OWN; HIS FIRST PRAYER FOR THE READERS

THE SALUTATION (1:1, 2)

Verse 1. He gives his title, "an apostle of Christ Jesus." The last two words are in this order in the best manuscripts: "By the will of God." He is ever conscious of his divine commission as an apostle. "To the saints who are also faithful in Christ Jesus." Some very ancient authorities omit the phrase "in Ephesus." This is in accordance with the best manuscripts. As we said above in the Introduction, this letter is a circular and not a local letter. It is addressed to all the churches in the province of Asia whose capital is Ephesus. So, it came to be known as "The Letter to the Ephesians," because it was probably kept in the church library in Ephesus. The internal evidence, the general tone of the letter, the larger institutional sense in which the word church is used, corroborate this manuscript evidence.

Verse 2. "Grace and peace" generally used by Paul. Grace is spiritual blessing, peace is health and happiness.

THE DOCTRINAL PORTION

GOD'S LOVING, ETERNAL PURPOSE OF REDEMPTION BY CHRIST; THE HOLY SPIRIT SEALS THE SAVED AS GOD'S OWN (1:3-14)

³ Blessed be the God and Father of our Lord Jesus Christ, who through Christ has blessed us with every spiritual blessing in the heavenly realm. ⁴ Through Him He picked us out before the creation of the world, to be consecrated and above reproach in His sight in love. ⁵ He foreordained us to become His sons by adoption through Christ Jesus, to carry out the happy choice of His will, ⁶ so that we might praise the splendid favor which He has shown us in His beloved Son. ⁷ It is through union with Him that we have redemption by His blood and the forgiveness of our shortcomings in accordance with the generosity of His unmerited favor ⁸ which He lavished upon us. Through perfect wisdom and spiritual insight ⁹ He has made known to us the secret of His will, which is in accordance with His purpose which He planned in Christ, ¹⁰ so that, at the coming of the climax of the ages, everything in heaven and on earth should be unified through Christ, ¹¹ in union with whom we were made God's portion, since we had been foreordained in accordance with the purpose of Him who in everything carries out the plan of His will, ¹² that we who had

first put our hope in Christ might praise His glory. ¹³ You too, as you have heard the message of the truth, the good news that means your salvation, and as you have trusted in Him too, have been stamped with the seal of the promised Holy Spirit, ¹⁴ who is the first installment of our inheritance, so that we may finally come into full possession of the prize of redemption, and praise His glory for it.

Key words and phrases. Verses 3-8. This paragraph (3-14) contains the most profound thoughts in all the Bible. Paul is at his best in reproducing the thoughts of God. He is peering into the secrets of the all-wise God in contriving the plan of man's redemption. Here he traces the redemption and salvation of man back to the plan of God's will. In remote eternity God's will, acting upon the foreknowledge of His omniscient mind, purposed to redeem His disobedient, fallen creature, man.

In verse 3 his heart swells with thanks and praise to God for "blessing us in Christ with every spiritual blessing in the heavenlies." This last phrase has no substantive—"in the heavenlies." This adjective expresses quality rather than place. It is in the heavenly realm of quality and character and personality. Redemption and salvation have brought believers in union with Christ into a new world of character and life and personality. Paul praises God for these spiritual blessings in this lofty sphere of life and character.

Verse 4. He sets forth the doctrine of election. "Before the creation of the world He chose us." He elected us; He picked us out to save and make His own. To pick out is the literal meaning of the verb, *eklegomai.* When we pick out something, we usually pick the best, but God picks sinners, even the chief of sinners. But He foresees and foreknows that these sinners picked will believe on His Son, accepting Him as personal Saviour. So it is said, "He chose us in Him." This phrase signifies "in union with Him." Faith brings the trusting sinner into union with Christ and only such are chosen. Note the purpose of election, "that we should be holy and blameless before Him." The goal of election is not only Heaven at last, but it is a separated new life in this world. *Blameless* is not synonymous with *sinless,* but it means a life on a high plane striving to attain high ideals and not subject to blame.

Verse 5. Foreordination or predestination. "He foreordained us in love." It is very likely that the phrase, "in love," goes with this verb, *foreordain*, and not with the preceding clause. But what does foreordain, predestinate, mean? The verb literally means to mark off the boundaries of something. As the surveyor marks the boundaries of the lot or farm to show the owner how far his property goes, so God marks off the boundaries of His possession in us; marks off the boundaries of those who are His own possession. Which comes first, election or foreordination? Nothing in the tenses used to indicate with precision. Likely both take place simultaneously in the mind of God. Note we are foreordained "to be His sons through Jesus Christ." We are elected, chosen. "to be holy and blameless," foreordained to be His sons. Character and position in the divine family are the goal of the divine eternal purposes—"according to the purpose of His will."

Verse 6. "To the praise of His glorious unmerited favor." Literally, the glory, the splendor, of His unmerited favor. The undeserved favor which God condescended to show us is splendid, magnificent, dazzling (to the mind). Sinners on the brink of the bottomless pit were the objects of His amazing grace, His wonderful personal favor.

Notice, He bestowed this unmerited favor on us in the Beloved. The only time Christ is termed the Beloved, without the word Son. But the sense is clear. In giving His Beloved Son for lost sinners the Father proved His love to be genuine and unspeakable (see John 3:16).

Verse 7. The result achieved was redemption through His blood. The word *redemption* means deliverance by paying a ransom price, as for a prisoner for his deliverance. Christ paid the price of His blood, which is a graphic way of saying by His death (see I Cor. 6:19, 20; Rom. 3:25). This redemption secures the forgiveness of our shortcomings. And this is measured by the riches of His unmerited favor. And this grace is unlimited in riches.

Verse 8. "Which He lavished on us in all wisdom and insight." The *which* refers to grace, the unmerited favor of God. Lavish means to overflow. Like the Nile overflowing its banks to enrich all Egypt, so God's grace overflows to enrich believers in Christ. They are enriched in wisdom and insight. This is spiritual and moral perception and know-how in Christian living.

Verses 9-12. God's eternal purpose accomplished through Christ as His medium. "He has made known to us the mystery [uncovered secret] of His will." This is according to "His purpose which He set forth in Christ." "As a plan for the fullness of time." "Fullness of time" refers, according to a thought-form of the Jews, to the Messianic time. God has a plan for redeeming and saving fallen man, and this plan is to be carried out by the Messiah in the period following His coming as the Redeemer and Saviour. This plan is comprehensive. It is not only cosmopolitan but cosmic; it takes in all this world of lost sinners, but in and around Christ the Messiah all things, "in heaven and all things on earth," are to be headed up and unified. Philo, the Alexandrian philosopher, conceived of all things in the universe as unified through his Logos. Was Paul acquainted with Philo? At any rate, Paul conceives of Christ as being the unifying force of the whole universe. Christ is the hub around which the wheel of the universe turns. What a sublime conception of the exalted Christ!

Verse 11. "In Him," through Christ as the medium, God the Father accomplishes all things "in accordance with the plan of His will." That is, the Father has adopted the Son, the Christ, as the medium and the plan of His will for the accomplishing of redemption and unification of mankind on earth, and also the plan He has for unifying the whole universe. All intelligent, spiritual beings throughout the universe are somehow to be recipients of blessings from the eternal plan of God for the redemption of this world; and finally they shall all be unified into a grand brotherhood of immortal spirits. Neither Philo nor Plato, nor Socrates, nor Aristotle, ever dreamed of such a grand consolidation of worlds and unification of spiritual beings.

Verse 12. The ultimate purpose of God in redeeming those who "set their hope on Christ" is "to praise His glory." "To glorify God and enjoy Him forever," is the expression of the Presbyterian Catechism, as the ultimate aim of Christians. *First hoped* likely refers to early apostles and other Christians in those early years.

Verses 13, 14. Those who heard the gospel and believed were

sealed with the promised Holy Spirit. Here he brings in faith, the connecting link between sinful man and the redeeming Christ. So in this paragraph we have all the basic, salient doctrines of salvation—election, fore-ordination, redemption, reconciliation, faith, hope, unification, brotherhood—not only unification and brotherhood of the redeemed on earth, but also of intelligent, spiritual beings of the whole universe. "In Him," he repeats; that is, he emphasizes over and over again that this work of redemption and reconciliation, and unification of the whole universe, is to be accomplished through the medium of Christ. He is the center of the eternal plan of the Father's will.

The third Person of the Trinity seals those who have believed and set their hope on Christ. *Promised* refers to the promise of Christ that He would send the Comforter after He had ascended (John 14:16). To seal means that the Spirit ratifies the ownership of God over the believers in Christ. As the United States government sets its seal and stamp on letters to be carried by its postmen and other carriers, so God fixes the seal of the Holy Spirit on His children, and this assurance is a guarantee of our future inheritance in Heaven's glory.

His First Prayer for the Readers to Realize Their Hope and God's Power (1:15-23)

15 This is why I myself, since I have heard of your faith in the Lord Jesus and in all His people, 16 never cease to thank God for you when I mention you in my prayers, 17 that the God of our Lord Jesus Christ, the glorious Father, may grant you the Spirit to give wisdom and revelation which come through a growing knowledge of Him, 18 by having the eyes of your hearts enlightened, so that you may know what the hope is to which He calls you, how gloriously rich God's portion in His people is, 19 and how surpassingly great is His power for us who believe, measured by His tremendously mighty power 20 when He raised Christ from the dead and seated Him at His right hand in heaven, 21 far above every other government, authority, power, and dominion, yea, far above every other title that can be conferred, not only in this world but in the world to come. 22 And so He has put all things under His feet and

made Him the supreme Head of the church, [23] which is His body, that is being filled by Him who fills everything everywhere.

Key words and phrases. Verses 15-23. This is Paul's first prayer for his readers of this letter. He was a man of prayer. His great faith in God through Christ gave him intimate fellowship with God. Let us analyze this first prayer.

Verses 15, 16 show him a man of prayer. His prayers are accompanied by thanksgiving; they are ceaseless prayers. In the third chapter of this letter he offers another prayer for these readers. In several of his letters he records prayers for other churches, the church at Thessalonica, Philippi, and other places.

Verse 17a names the addressee of his prayer, the God of our Lord Jesus Christ, the Father of glory. It is the same God Jesus taught His followers to address, "our Father." He is the "Father of glory." This genitive with *doxa* (glory) may be qualitative, so "glorious Father" (Williams), or it may be a substantive and the genitive objective; that Father who bestows glory on His children. The former seems the better interpretation. Glory then would mean all those grand attributes of God, love, grace, mercy, power, holiness, righteousness, perfectly blended (so Sanday on Rom. 6:4: "Christ was raised by the glory of the Father").

The Father is "the God of our Lord Jesus Christ." This is a high conception of the Father; He loves and gives us His only Son and is perpetually the God who works through Christ as the medium of His plan of redemption and salvation. So He is the Almighty God "able to do far more exceedingly than all we ask or think" (Eph. 3:20).

Verses 17b-19a. The objects prayed for. "That He may grant you the Spirit to give wisdom and revelation which come through a growing knowledge of Him [Christ]." Paul in his second prayer for these readers prays that they may have strength through "the Spirit in the inner man." This is the indwelling Holy Spirit. So it is probable that he prays for the Spirit to give them wisdom and revelation; which means the knowledge of new spiritual truths and the know-how (wisdom) to apply these new truths to life. The next phrase, "in the knowledge of Him" (A.R.V.); or, "through a

growing experimental knowledge of Him." The word *knowledge,*
epignosis, means experimental knowledge upon knowledge, so a
growing experimental knowledge. He prays that they may day by
day be growing in a deeper and wider experience of Christ's love
and keeping power. That tallies with the entreaty of Peter, "Grow
in the grace and experimental knowledge of our Lord and Saviour
Jesus Christ" (II Peter 3:18). The Christian's life should not and
cannot be static but ought to be mobile and active and growing.

Verse 18b. "By having the eyes of your hearts enlightened."
The soul has inner eyes, the eyes of the heart. These eyes can per-
ceive the hidden secrets of God, and it is through the keen vision
of these inner eyes that the Christian grows in experimental knowledge of Christ and also in the finer traits of moral and spiritual
character, which enable him to be more useful in service to God
and his suffering fellow men.

Verse 18, b, c. The purpose of this growing experimental knowledge: "to know what is the hope to which He has called you, what
are the riches of God's glorious inheritance, or portion, in the saints,
His people." Hope is one of the three superlative virtues of Christianity (I Cor. 13:13). Only love is superior to hope as a Christian
virtue. But hope is not realized to its acme unless the individual
Christian is growing in experimental knowledge of Christ. Then
he can realize (know) what his hope embraces: perfect deliverance
at last from all sin and evil; more intimate, joyful fellowship with
God through Christ, and at last perfect enjoyment of all the riches
of God's love and glory in Heaven.

The second object of this growing experimental knowledge is
to know "what are the riches of God's glorious inheritance in the
saints." God owns the "riches" of the universe—all its gold and
silver, all its minerals and precious stones and jewels, but His most
precious "jewels" are His redeemed children of men. Malachi speaks
of God's jewels, when he says, "And they shall be mine, saith the
Lord of hosts, in that day when I make up my jewels" (see Mal.
3:17).

Verses 19-23. "The immeasurable greatness of His power in
us who believe." Where is this immeasurable power of God exhibited? Not in creating a world or a universe, but in raising Christ

from the dead and exalting Him far above all other governments and powers, authorities and rules, and making Him the supreme Head of the church. What Paul is saying here is merely the exaltation of Christ to supreme power and position and glory, but that the almighty power which God had to exert in thus raising Him from the lowest depths of a tomb to the highest pinnacle of power, measures the keeping power which God grants His saints, His own people. See Romans 8:31-39, where he sets forth his teaching on the security of the believer. He is absolutely safe and secure. God's infinite resurrection power holds him. "Head of the church." This expresses Christ's supreme authority over His Church. No pope or potentate or any other power or authority has the right to govern a church. It is the sole prerogative of Christ to direct all the affairs of a church. The pastor and deacons must be subordinate to Christ and do His will in directing the affairs of the church.

Pastors, if you desire a good subject for an expository sermon, use this paragraph, Ephesians 1:15-23, Paul's first prayer for the Ephesians. As Alexis Carrel says, "When we pray we link ourselves with the inexhaustible motive power that spins the universe."

Chapter II

JEWS AND GENTILES, LOST IN SIN, SAVED BY GOD'S UNMERITED
FAVOR THROUGH FAITH IN CHRIST; CHRIST THE BOND
OF INTERNATIONAL PEACE

JEWS AND GENTILES, DEAD IN SIN, SAVED BY GOD'S UNMERITED
FAVOR THROUGH FAITH IN CHRIST (2:1-10)

You too were dead because of the shortcomings and sins [2] in which you once lived in accordance with the spirit of this present world, and the mighty prince of the air, who is always at work in the disobedient, among whom all of us, we Jews as well as you heathen, [3] once lived while gratifying the cravings of our lower nature, as we continued to carry out the impulses of our lower nature and its thoughts, and by nature we were exposed to God's wrath, as the rest of mankind. [4] But God, who is so rich in mercy on account of the great love He has for us, [5] has made us, though dead because of our shortcomings, live again in fellowship with Christ—it is by His unmerited favor that you have been saved.

⁶ And He raised us with Him and through union with Christ Jesus He made us sit down with Him in the heavenly realm, ⁷ to show, throughout the coming ages, the boundless generosity of His unmerited favor shown us in His goodness to us through Christ Jesus. ⁸ For it is by His unmerited favor through faith that you have been saved; it is not by anything that you have done, it is the gift of God. ⁹ It is not the result of what anyone can do, so that no one can boast of it. ¹⁰ For He has made us what we are, because He has created us through our union with Christ Jesus for doing good deeds which He beforehand planned for us to do.

Key words and phrases. Verses 1-3. "Dead because of your shortcomings and sins." Paul tells his readers that this was the natural state God found them in when He saved them. What does *dead* mean? It is spiritual death, which is separation from God. When Adam and Eve sinned, they sewed fig leaves together to cover their nakedness, because their sin had separated them from God; they were conscious that they were out of fellowship with Him. They were spiritually dead. "In the day ye eat thereof ye shall surely die" (see Gen. 2:17-3:19). As descendants of this sinning pair, all of us, Jews and Gentiles, cultured and uncultured, are spiritually dead. To live again we must be made alive by God Himself (v. 1). In this state we all "gratified the cravings of our lower nature" (v. 2). Even our minds are vitiated by sin *(dianoiai,* thoughts). The inspiring spirit that prompts these sinful desires and cravings is "the mighty prince of the air." This is the Devil. "The air" is the first of the "seven heavens" in Jewish theology. So, when God banished him from Heaven, he sneaks back into the lower regions of the heavens to undo the works of God as far as he can. This puts him in close association with men and women on earth, and he becomes "the prince of this world" (John 14:30). Sinful men and women follow the mighty prince of the air. According to verse 3 we were all, even Jews with all their privileges, "children of wrath." This means, according to this Jewish thought-form, "exposed to the wrath of God." By nature all men are exposed to the wrath of God; that is, the first birth into the natural state leaves us all "children of wrath, exposed to the wrath of God."

Verses 4-8. So salvation comes from the unmerited favor of God.

But this unmerited favor of God is derived from His great love for us as shown in the gift of Christ. His love is the originating cause of salvation; this love makes God pity us, have mercy on us, and this, in turn causes Him to be willing to save us through faith in Christ. Notice, Paul says that God initiates the act of saving sinners, even when we were dead because of our shortcomings. As sinners are spiritually dead, they are helpless until God initiates the process of making us alive. In verses 5 and 6 Paul uses the preposition *sun*, with, denoting fellowship, to show how the dead sinner is made alive and saved. God raises the believer with Christ, and thus he is made alive in fellowship with Christ, then He makes the believer sit down with Christ in the heavenly realm. This is the spiritual resurrection of the believer (see Rom. 8:9-11). This is Paul's favorite thought-form, mystic realism. It is mystic in that it deals with the invisible spiritual fellowship of believers with Christ; it is realism in that the Divine Spirit is really doing His work in regenerating and exalting the believer in union with Christ, the appointed medium of salvation.

According to verse 8 the unmerited favor of God is the agent of salvation; faith in Christ is the instrument that unites the believer with Christ, the medium of salvation. This is delicate thinking and is accurately and precisely expressed in the Greek, the language of exactness and precision. So the saving of a sinner does not depend on anything he can do; it is the gift of God. The gift is made because of His great love which produces His mercy or pity for the sinner in his helpless, wretched condition, and mercy bestows the unmerited favor which actually saves the believer. Magnificent chain of divine attributes in the saving process!

Verses 9-10. Here is shown the relation to each other of divine purpose, divine action in spiritual creation, Christ, and good works. God has purposed in His gracious plan that the goal of salvation shall be good works. The sinner is saved to serve and work for God and suffering mankind. The saved sinner is the creation of God. Christ is the medium through whom the creation is made. The Christian is the masterpiece (*poiema*) of God's power and grace. "Workmanship" (*poiema*), that is, God's poem, His masterpiece, is the saved sinner. As *Paradise Lost* is Milton's greatest masterpiece, so a sinner saved by grace is God's greatest masterpiece. His greatest work is not the creation of the solar system or the sidereal systems, although "the heavens declare the glory of God and the firmament showeth His handiwork."

In the Unification of Nations and Races Christ Is the Bond of Peace (2:11-22)

11 So remember that you were once heathen in a physical sense, called the uncircumcised by those who call themselves the circumcised—though only in a physical sense, by human hands. 12 At that time you were without any connection with Christ; you were aliens to the commonwealth of Israel, strangers to the sacred compacts made by God's promise, with no hope, and no God in the world. 13 But now through your union with Christ Jesus you who were once far away have through the blood of Christ been brought near. 14 For He Himself is our peace, He is the one who has made us both into one body and has broken down the barrier that kept us apart; 15 through His human nature He has put a stop to the hostility between us, namely, the law with its commands and decrees, in order to create one new humanity out of the two parties and so make peace through union with Himself, and in one body 16 to reconcile them both to God with His cross after He had killed the hostility through it. 17 When He came, He brought the good news of peace for you who were far away and for you who were near; 18 for it is by Him through one Spirit that both of us now have an introduction to the Father. 19 So you are no longer foreigners and strangers, but you are fellow-citizens of God's people and members of His family; 20 for you are built upon the foundation of the apostles and prophets, with Christ Jesus Himself the cornerstone. 21 In union with Him the whole building is harmoniously fitted together and continues to grow into a temple, sacred through its union with the Lord, 22 and you yourselves, in union with Him, in fellowship with one another, are being built up into a dwelling for God through the Spirit.

Key words and phrases. Verses 11, 12. The lost condition of the heathen—readers not Jews. The Jews, the "circumcised so-called," dubbed them the uncircumcised. But this was only "human handmade" circumcision, so the Gentiles should not take it to heart to be thus dubbed. In that heathen state they were alienated from the commonwealth of Israel (did not belong to the theocracy of Israel, governed directly by God); "strangers to the covenants of promise" (not included for the blessings of the special promise God made to Abraham, Gen. 15:4-18); "no hope" for the future life, no deliverance from sin and its penalty, because "without God in the world." They had gods, but were without the true God of infinite love and mercy and grace. So they were in a lost state.

Verses 13-18. Their present state through Christ the medium between God and man: "Brought near"—near to God Himself and all He has promised in His unmerited favor to believers in Christ. "By the blood of Christ." Blood is the symbol of death; so it is Christ's death that tears down the partition between Gentiles and Jews, between God and man. "He is our peace." That is, He (Christ) is the great Peacemaker (see Luke 2:14). It took His incarnation (John 1:14) plus His death to make peace between God and man. He became flesh and shed His blood on the cross. The racial result of this death, He "created in union with Himself one new humanity [man] in place of two [Jews and Gentiles], so making peace." So this is the way He became our peace, our Peacemaker. "And might reconcile us both [Jews and Gentiles] to God in one body through the cross." The primary aim of His death was to make peace between God and man. The racial result is the ending of the hostility between these two wings of mankind (Jews and Gentiles). He preached peace to both and sends forth His apostles to preach the gospel to all the world. "To make disciples of all nations." All races are thus united into one body by one Spirit. The Holy Spirit co-operates with Christ and the Father for the unification of all the races and all the nations.

Verses 19-22. United humanity, saved by grace, is the temple or dwelling place of God. Gentiles become "fellow citizens with the people of God and members of His family." This temple is built upon the foundation of the apostles and prophets (N.T. prophets, I Cor. 14), with Christ Himself being the chief cornerstone. This united body of all races in union with Christ is growing into a holy temple in the Lord. It is not yet built or grown. It is in the process of building and growing by preaching the good news of God's unmerited favor and Christ's work of making peace between

God and men, men and men, nations and nations. What a grandiose conception, united humanity in Christ the Lord gradually growing into a magnificent temple for the dwelling place of Almighty God on earth!

SERMON OUTLINES FROM CHAPTER II

THE RELATION OF GRACE, FAITH, AND GOOD WORKS IN INITIAL SALVATION (2:8-10)

I. What Grace Does
  1. Love the initiating cause of the plan of salvation (Eph. 1:5; 2:4)
  2. Love resulted in mercy and grace (2:4, 5)
  3. Grace backed by love gave Christ to die for the world (John 3:16)
  4. Grace spares the sinner while going astray
  5. Grace gives the Spirit to convict and woo the sinner

II. The Function of Faith in Saving a Sinner
  1. Faith does not save. Grace saves.
  2. Personal surrender to Christ who saves
  3. Faith the means or instrument of connection between the sinner and Christ. Illustrations: The coupling pin unites the train with the locomotive which moves it. The trolley wire puts the electric car in connection with the powerhouse.
  4. Faith is the gift of God. See John 12:39, 40

III. The Place of Good Works
  1. Not the cause of initial stages of salvation (regeneration, justification)
  2. Not even a help to the initial stages (2:8, 9)
  3. By good works the Christian co-operates with God in the ethical process of salvation (sanctification). See Philippians 2:12, 13: "Work out, or, work down to finishing point, your own salvation."
  4. Good works the purpose or goal of initial stage—"for good works"

PAUL'S PLAN FOR INTERNATIONAL PEACE (2:11-20)

I. Some Man Made Plans

1. Cecil Rhodes and Oxford Scholarships. This was Rhodes' aim
2. Carnegie Peace Conferences at The Hague
3. Bryan's Arbitration Plan with a "Cooling-off Period"
4. President Harding's Disarmament Plan
5. The League of Nations. Wilson's and Smuts' dream of peace
6. The Kellogg-Briand Pact
7. United Nations Organization
   With all of these in operation (except The United Nations), World War II followed World War I in twenty-one years

II. Paul's Plan
1. Based on God's plan of redemption (Eph. 1:3-14; 2:5-10)
2. Christ is the Peacemaker (2:14). Between God and man, between man and man, nation and nation
3. Saved people (by God's grace) can keep the peace; can and do live together in peace. Jews and Gentiles then

III. Why Paul's Plan Is the Best
1. It is God's plan. Paul is inspired by the Holy Spirit (I Tim. 3:16)
2. It operates by love and not force. Napoleon: "Alexander founded an empire; Caesar organized an empire; I have established an empire. But we did it by *force*. Jesus Christ founded a kingdom on love, and now millions would die for Him."
3. Jesus Christ endorses this plan. "Love your enemies." "They that take the sword shall perish by the sword."
   Illustrations: Hitler and Mussolini built up mighty nations but on force. But where are they now?
   Canada and United States, Christian people, have lived side by side over a century without a war.
   Chile and Argentina, old enemies, had a huge statute of Christ erected on their border, and swore by the Christ "never to fight each other again." For nearly half a century they have lived in perpetual peace.

Chapter III

PAUL IS ENTRUSTED WITH THE SECRET OF THIS UNIVERSAL, PEACE-
MAKING GOSPEL; HE PRAYS FOR HIS READERS, THAT THEY
MAY BE STRENGTHENED BY THE SPIRIT, THAT CHRIST
MAY LIVE IN THEIR HEARTS, AND THEY MAY KNOW
THE BOUNDLESS LOVE OF CHRIST

PAUL IS ENTRUSTED WITH THE SECRET OF THIS UNIVERSAL, PEACE-MAKING GOSPEL (3:1-3)

This is why I, Paul, a prisoner of Christ Jesus for the sake of the heathen—² that is, if you have heard how God's favor has been entrusted to me for you, ³ and how by revelation the secret was made known to me, as I have briefly written before. ⁴ By reading this you will be able to understand my insight into the secret about the Christ—⁵ which in the earlier ages, so different from the present, was not made known to mankind as fully as now, but through the Spirit it has been revealed to His holy apostles and prophets—⁶ that the heathen through union with Christ Jesus are fellow-heirs with the Jews, are members with them of the same body, and sharers with them of the promise through the good news, ⁷ for which I was called to serve in accordance with the gift of God's unmerited favor which was bestowed on me by the exercise of His power—⁸ yes, on me, the very least of all His people, this unmerited favor was bestowed—that I might preach as good news to the heathen the boundless riches of Christ, ⁹ and to make clear how is to be carried out the trusteeship of this secret which has for ages been hidden away in God, the Creator of all things, ¹⁰ so that the many phases of God's wisdom may now through the church be made known to the rulers and authorities in heaven, ¹¹ in accordance with the eternal purpose which God executed in the gift of Christ Jesus our Lord. ¹² By union with Him and through faith in Him we have a free and confidential introduction to God. ¹³ So I beg you not to lose heart over the sorrows that I am suffering for your sake, for they bring you honor.

Key words and phrases. Verse 1. Paul has a new title—"a prisoner" *(desmios)*. As he writes this letter he is bound to a Roman soldier in a Roman prison. Suppose we catalog the titles of Paul. *Apostolos,* apostle (Rom. 1:1; I and II Cor. 1:1; Gal. 1:1, etc. *Presbeuomai,* acting as an ambassador (II Cor. 5:20); a preacher *(kerux)* and teacher, *didaskalos* (II Tim. 1:11); a minister, *diakonos* (Eph. 3:7); a bond servant, a slave (Rom. 1:1) of Christ. His official titles are apostle, minister, teacher, preacher, ambassador. His personal titles, bond servant, prisoner; in His relation to Christ he is a slave, bought by His blood and so belongs to Him. Now he is a prisoner for Christ's sake. These are voluntary relations, but He is called, appointed by God, as an apostle, a preacher, a minister, a teacher, an ambassador. Of course, the functions of these overlap at many points. He is ministering when he acts as ambassador. As an apostle he preaches, and teaches. In all of them he is Christ's slave. While serving as a prisoner he preaches, teaches, acts as an ambassador.

Verses 2-4. Paul's trusteeship (stewardship) of God's grace. God had bestowed on him this stewardship when He called him as an apostle through the revelation Christ made to him at his conversion (Acts 9:4ff). This means that he is responsible faithfully to proclaim this unmerited favor of God to Jews and Gentiles, but especially to the non-Jewish peoples (see Rom 11:13). So the readers of this letter must be told about this wonderful grace of God. He is assuming that they have heard of his having received this commission from God; so they can through reading this letter understand Paul's insight into the secret about Christ. What was this secret (mystery) about Christ? That as the Son of God Christ is God's appointed medium of communicating this grace, or unmerited favor, of God, to lost men, Gentiles as well as Jews. As explained before, let us remember that mystery is something once unknown by men but now made known, as he states in subsequent verses. It was once a secret but now is well known.

Verses 5, 6. This mystery has been revealed to His apostles and prophets. That is, to the original eleven who learned from Jesus in the flesh, and to Paul who had a special revelation at the gates of Damascus which was made clear to him in his experiences in the desert of Arabia (Gal. 1:12-17). The prophets meant here are New Testament men who by the Spirit have an insight into new truths of Christianity. The chief element in this mystery is that Gentiles have the same footing with Jews as recipients of the blessings of this grace—they are fellow heirs and partakers of the promise through union with Christ on the same conditions of faith in the gospel. There is no respect of persons with God (Rom. 2:11).

Verse 7. Paul made a "minister" by the "gift of God's grace." It was by the working of God's power; perhaps, reference is made to the miraculous resurrection of Christ by the power of God, since this convinced Paul that Jesus is the Son of God (Rom. 1:4; see Acts 9:15). "The Lord said, 'Go, for he is a chosen instrument of mine to carry my name before the Gentiles and kings and the sons of Israel.' " It is the gift of God's unmerited favor (grace) which makes him a minister to carry the name of the Lord Jesus to Gentiles and kings.

Verses 8-9. Paul's deep humility in the presence of such wonderful grace. "To me, though I am the very least of all the saints." Literally, "Unto me who am less than the least of all saints" (A.V.). It is a hyperbole, a figure of speech often used by Paul for emphasis. Of course, he could not be less than the least. Our expression, the very least, is exactly what he means. He puts himself on the bottom round of all God's people, and yet God stooped to make him "a minister to preach to the Gentiles the unsearchable riches of Christ." What are the riches of Christ? The inexhaustible bounty of His love and grace and mercy to save even the chief of sinners. Paul himself was an example of God's bountiful grace and forgiveness (I Tim. 1:15, 16). *Unsearchable* means untraceable, incapable of having any boundaries set for them. Boundless as the ocean is Christ's love and grace to forgive a sinner! The purpose of this preaching is "to make all men see what is the plan of the mystery hidden for ages in God." God had an eternal plan for redeeming man, but it was hidden in God—no one knew it but God— till Christ came and began to reveal the plan of the ages. Paul's ministry to the Gentiles is to publish it far and wide. *All men* is another hyperbole for emphasis to express the universality of the gospel.

Verse 10. The church the instrument to make known "the many-colored wisdom of God." This letter magnifies the church (see 1:22; 3:10, 20; 5:23-33). The word church in this letter is not used in a local sense but in an institutional sense. But the local body called a church represents the institution which Christ founded on this rock (confessing faith in Christ as the Son of God and Messiah to save lost men). "Principalities and powers in the heavenly places," refers to heavenly intelligencies, angels and archangels, who are interested in man's redemption. Paul seems to think there is a vital interest on the part of angels in the actions of women, as well as men (I Cor. 11:10). Peter says the angels long to look into the affairs of salvation on earth (I Pet. 1:12).

Verses 11-12. Christ is the fulfillment of God's eternal purpose in redemption, and through Him we Christians have free and confident access to God. Christ is the medium of execution of this purpose.

Verse 13. He begs them not to lose heart on account of his sufferings, for they are for their honor. He gladly suffers for the sake of others.

HIS SECOND PRAYER FOR THE READERS (3:14-21)

14 For this reason I kneel before the Father, 15 from whom every family in heaven and on earth derives its name, 16 and beg Him to grant you, in accordance with the riches of His perfect character, to be mightily strengthened by His Spirit in your inmost being, 17 and that Christ in His love, through your faith, may make His permanent home in your hearts. You must be deeply rooted, your foundations must be strong, 18 so that you with all God's people may be strong enough to grasp the idea of the breadth and length, the height and depth, 19 yes, to come at last to know the love of Christ, although it far surpasses human understanding, so that you may be filled with the perfect fullness of God. 20 To Him who by His power that is at work within us can do surpassingly more than all we ask or imagine, 21 be glory in the church and through Christ Jesus to all generations forever and ever. Amen.

Key words and phrases. Verse 14. "For this reason," refers to the long paragraph (2-13) in which Paul describes the mystery hidden for ages but now revealed by Christ and committed to him to preach to the Gentiles as "the unsearchable riches of Christ." He offers this prayer for them that they may qualify to help him to realize the eternal purpose of God in Christ. The latter part of the verse states that God is the source of all fatherhood and of every family in Heaven or earth. This is creative fatherhood, not spiritual. All groups, or families, of angels in Heaven derived their life from God. All families of men (all races) were made by Him (Acts 17:26). So the Fatherhood of God is not derived from human fatherhood, but vice versa. It is not a figure of speech but a reality.

Verse 15. The measure of God's ability to bestow blessings asked is the riches of His glory. Glory is the "summing up of His glorious attributes" (see Sanday on Rom. 6:4); His greatness and power, His love and mercy and grace, His holiness and righteousness. These all combined constitute His ability to bestow our requests in prayer. What a stimulus to prayer!

Verse 15. "Mightily strengthened by His Spirit in the inmost being." He prays for spiritual power to possess their inner being (see Acts 1:8). The indwelling Spirit is the believer's power house. Inner man means the spiritual man which responds to the Holy Spirit in the creation of spiritual power.

Verse 16. The indwelling Christ. It is by faith that Christ dwells in us. The more faith we have the more intimate is the fellowship we enjoy with the indwelling Christ. The phrase "in love" may modify Christ; then it would read, "That Christ by His love," etc. It may, as in the King James version go with *grounded* and read *grounded in love*. Either interpretation gives us a fine thought.

Verses 18-19. Having spiritual strength to grasp the love of Christ. The first verb is grasp mentally *(katalabesthai);* that is, to get a mental hold on the greatness of Christ's love. The second verb is to know experimentally. We first get a mental picture of its greatness, and by a growing experience we gradually come to know its breadth (as broad as humanity and its needs), its length (as long as eternity), its height (as high as Heaven's glory), its depth (as deep as sin can sink a sinner). Such love surpasses knowledge, of angels as well as men. It is likely that not even Gabriel or Michael can perfectly understand the infinite love of Christ for man. As we experimentally know the dimensions of Christ's love, we may be filled with all the fullness of God. This is a hyperbole. No finite man can be filled with all the fullness of God. But the more we experience Christ's love, the larger grow our souls and the more of God's fullness we can hold and enjoy.

Verses 20-21. Doxology. In contemplation of the holy truths and the heavenly triumphs possible in prayer, his soul bursts forth in this noble doxology, "To Him who, by His power working within us, can do surpassingly more than all we ask or imagine, be glory in the church and through Christ Jesus to all generations forever and ever. Amen." God must answer our best prayers inwardly, by His power working within us. This is the power the Holy Spirit generates in our souls. But that enables Him "to do surpassingly more than all we ask or imagine." He not only can do more than we ask but more than we can think or imagine. This is not a hyperbole but literal truth. He believes in God's infinite power. The church is God's appointed instrument for answering our most spiritual prayers. Church here is the institution, but each local church can be the instrument used by its members to help answer all noble, spiritual, missionary prayers. "Through Christ." He is the medium of God's redemptive operations through whom these prayers are answered. The word *glory* means praise (Luke 2:14).

SERMON (EXPOSITORY) OUTLINE FROM THIS CHAPTER

PAUL'S SECOND PRAYER FOR HIS READERS (3:14-21)
I. The Addressee of the Prayer
  1. God the Father
  2. The original Father—of groups of angels in Heaven; of all tribes and races on earth (Acts 17:26)
II. The Inexhaustible Riches of the Father to Answer the Prayer
  1. The riches of His perfect character (see comments above)
  2. His ability to do surpassingly more than we ask or think (21) Charles Spurgeon's father to him: "Charles, I always prayed God to make you a minister, but not a Baptist minister." Charles replied, "Father, God always gives us more than we ask for."
III. The Blessings Asked For
  1. To be mightily strengthened in soul by the Spirit (Acts 1:8)
  2. That Christ have a permanent home *(katoikesai)* in their hearts; not a guest but one of the home (see Gal. 2:20).

3. To be deeply rooted and solidly founded on Christ and truth (3:17)

4. To be strong enough to grasp (mentally) the four dimensions of the love of Christ. See comments above. Ultimately to come to know by experience *(ginosko)* the surpassing love of Christ.

5. Ultimately filled with all the fullness of God. To the utmost of their capacity. Illustration: floating open jug filling with the ocean's abundance. Notice, all three Persons in the Trinity have a part: the Father grants the blessings; the Spirit gives power; the Son lives in the heart as Friend and Companion.

III. The Practical Duties in the Church, and in All Social Relations (4:1-6:20)

Chapter IV

The Moral and Spiritual Life: To Be Fostered through Unity and Service Rendered by All with Varying Gifts; Vices Laid Aside, Virtues Cultivated

The Moral and Spiritual Life to Be Nourished through Unity and Service by All (4:1-16)

So I, a prisoner for the Lord's sake, entreat you to live lives worthy of the call you have received, ² with perfect humility and gentleness, with patience, lovingly bearing with one another, ³ continuing with eager earnestness to maintain the unity of the Spirit through the tie of peace. ⁴ There is but one body and one Spirit, just as there is but one hope resulting from the call you have received; ⁵ there is but one Lord, one faith, one baptism, ⁶ one God and Father of all, who is over us all, who pervades us all, and who is within us all.

⁷ But in accordance with the measure of Christ's gift, His favor has been bestowed upon each one of us. ⁸ Concerning this the Scripture says:

"He led a host of captives, when He went up on high,
   And granted gifts to men."

⁹ What does "He went up" mean except that He had first gone down into the lower regions of the earth? ¹⁰ The very One that

went down has gone up, too, far above all the heavens, to fill the universe. [11] And He has given some men to be apostles, some to be prophets, some to be evangelists, some to be pastors and teachers, [12] for the immediate equipment of God's people for the work of service, for the ultimate building up of the body of Christ, [13] until we all attain to unity in faith and to perfect knowledge of the Son of God, namely, to a mature manhood and to a perfect measure of Christ's moral stature; [14] so that we may not be babies any longer, or like sailors tossed about and driven around by every wind of doctrine, by the trickery of men through their cunning in inventing new methods of error. [15] But, on the other hand, we shall go on holding to the truth and in love growing up into perfect union with Him, that is, Christ Himself who is the Head. [16] For it is under His direction that the whole body is perfectly adjusted and united by every joint that furnishes its supplies; and by the proper functioning of each particular part there is brought about the growing of the body for its building up in love.

Key words and phrases. Verses 1-6. Exhortation to live a life worthy of the divine calling of the Christian. God has called the believer to salvation; but He means also that the call is to a noble life, rich in a beautiful character and filled with the fruits of righteousness. Basic traits are humility, gentleness, and patience. Humility is an essential element in conversion. "Except ye be converted and become as little children, ye shall not enter into the kingdom of heaven" (Matt. 18:3). Gentleness is closely akin to self-control. The Greek word was used to describe an animal that has been tamed—a wild animal now tame. We still speak of a gentle horse, one easily controlled. Patience is longsuffering. Literally, a mind or soul that endures a long time—with resignation endures whatever comes.

Then follow social qualities: lovingly bearing with one another, with a forgiving spirit, eager earnestness to maintain unity in the church and community, which is held together with the bond of peace. The word translated *bond* means a tie that fastens two or more things together. Peace, a peaceful spirit in all, is the tie that holds a church together in unity. Paul exhorts his readers to maintain the unity of the Spirit. Spirit is in the subjective genitive, so it is "unity which the Spirit inspires." It is not organic union but spiritual unity (see John 17:21). It is the same oneness that Jesus prayed for (John 17:21).

The argument for church unity, Christian unity, is the seven basic unities in the Christian system: *one body,* the Body of Christ which is the Church as an institution but to be exemplified in each local body of believers; *one Spirit,* the Holy Spirit, the source of the spiritual life for everyone, and the instrument that seals each one; *one hope,* the hope of the resurrection and Heaven with all its glory; *one Lord,* Jesus the Son; *one faith,* which is one and the same condition of salvation for everyone (hardly one system of doctrine as in Jude 3, 4); *one baptism,* probably water baptism (though many Pedobaptist scholars contend it is baptism with the Spirit); *one God and Father of us all,* who is over all and through all and in all. Does Paul teach the universality of God's Fatherhood? Or, is He the Father only of Christians? See Romans 8:14-17, which teaches the particular Fatherhood of God. And here he says, He is "the Father of us all." The *us* seems to refer to Christians and not to universal mankind.

Verses 7-13. The variety of spiritual gifts in the Church and their purpose. He mentions five in particular, "apostles, prophets, evangelists, pastors, teachers." The first class includes the Twelve, and Paul and Barnabas—especially the Twelve and Paul. Prophets in the New Testament are men or women who have a deep insight into spiritual truths, especially seeing and teaching truths only partially discerned before. Evangelists are proclaimers of the good news, traveling preachers. Pastors are shepherds of a local church or churches. Teachers are those who unfold old truths to new converts and train them in the doctrines. Pastors and teachers seem to be one class, not two. The two words have only one article, which suggests only one class (so Robertson, *Big Grammar, in loco;* so Moulton, *Prolegomena, in loco).*

The spiritual gifts are the gifts of the ascended Christ. As Head of the Church He has authority to bestow these gifts. They are grace gifts (7). By His unmerited favor to us He bestows these gifts. These are all continued except that of apostles. The gift of prophecy was practically limited to the first Christian century. The chief functionaries today are evangelists, pastors, and teachers.

Paul sees in this spiritual bestowment of the ascended Christ a fulfillment of Psalm 68:18.

The purpose of these gifts is for the immediate equipment of the saints (God's people) for the work of service, for the ultimate purpose of building up the Body of Christ (the Church). The preposition *pros* expresses immediate purpose, work in serving God and the phases of church activity, and all that is for the building up of the church, winning the lost and baptizing believers, training the members for service at home and abroad. Verse 13 gives the goal set to be reached by all this work and service and training—"till we all attain to the unity of the faith and the knowledge of the Son of God." Not a few leaders but all the members should strive for this goal. Unity of the faith means that unity which the common faith of all the members produces. Experimental knowledge *(epignosis)* co-operates with this common faith to bring about the unity desired. The negative result will be stalwart Christians able to resist false doctrines, just as a well-built boat with strong sails can safely withstand the gales and storms that beat upon it. The positive result will be a growing church, growing in fellowship with Christ the Head of the Church, every joint and member perfectly fitting into its place under the direction of Christ the Head. Paul had a fine conception of the physiology and anatomy of the human body, which furnishes him with the illustration of how Christ's Body, the Church, should grow. He still mixes figures of speech, the architectural and biological view of the Church. Love is magnified in this growth; they are "speaking the truth in love" (if a warning is needed it must be given in brotherly love). Then the whole church is to "be built up in love," brotherly love, which makes for peace and unity.

VICES TO BE LAID ASIDE; VIRTUES TO BE CULTIVATED (4:17-32)

17 So I mean this and now testify to it in the name of the Lord: You must now stop living as the heathen usually do, in the frivolity of their minds, 18 with darkened understanding, estranged from the life of God because of the ignorance that exists among them and because of the stubborness of their hearts: 19 for in their recklessness they have abandoned themselves to sensuality which leads to excessive practices of all sorts of immorality. 20 But this is not the way you have learned what Christ means, 21 if, as I take it,

you have heard Him and in union with Him have been taught the truth as it is seen in Jesus, [22] to lay aside, with your former way of living, your old self which is on the way to destruction in accordance with its deceptive impulses; [23] and to have a new attitude of mind [24] and put on the new self which has been created in the likeness of God, which fruits in right and holy living inspired by the truth.

[25] So you must lay aside falsehood and each of you practice telling the truth to his neighbor, for we are parts of one another. [26] If you do get angry, you must stop sinning in your anger. Do not ever let the sun go down on your anger; [27] stop giving the devil a chance. [28] The man who used to steal must now stop stealing; rather, he must keep on working and toiling with his own hands at some honest vocation, so as to have something to contribute to the needy. [29] You must stop letting any bad word pass your lips, but only words that are good for building up as the occasion demands, so that they will result in spiritual blessing to the hearers. [30] You must stop offending the Holy Spirit of God by whom you have been stamped for the day of redemption. [31] You must remove all bitterness, rage, anger, loud threats, and insults, with all malice. [32] You must practice being kind to one another, tender-hearted, forgiving one another, just as God through Christ has graciously forgiven you.

Key words and phrases. Verses 17-19. The Gentile way of life to be given up by the readers. This way of life grew out of frivolous minds and darkened understanding, and these resulted from their alienation from God, which is, in turn, caused by their natural hardness of heart. Sin had hardened their hearts; benumbed them so as not to be sensitive to the presence of God or to His truth and requirements. They had become entirely indifferent to moral principles and practices. So they "abandoned themselves to sensuality and excessive practices of all sorts of immorality." This sounds like a reflection of Romans 1:24-27. Now Paul solemnly affirms in the name of the Lord that his Christian readers must not any longer live this kind of life.

Verses 20, 21. As his readers had been taught about Christ and His way of life, they must have learned that the truth as Jesus taught and practiced it was directly opposite to this kind of life.

He taught that the mind and heart must be pure to guarantee clean and pure conduct and living. Adultery and murder rooted themselves in the heart. Hate and and lust are heart-sins that flood the world with actual scenes of sexual immorality and murder.

Verses 22-24. So they must put off, lay aside, the old corrupt nature and put on the new nature by being renewed in the spirit of their minds. They must be sure that they have been genuinely regenerated. (See Gal. 6:15). A "new creation" is absolutely essential. Nothing else "avails" to save the soul and produce a clean, pure life. The "new nature is created in God's likeness and fruits in right and holy living inspired by the truth." This is a positive, simple, understandable statement.

Verses 25-29. Four common sins to be laid aside: lying, anger, stealing, evil speech. We should lay aside the principle of falsehood and practice telling the truth to our neighbors. No duplicity and deception to be practiced with our neighbors, whether they are Christians or not. If you get angry you must stop the habit of sinning with it; get cooled off before the sun sets. Occasionally it is not sin to be indignant at some gross injustice done us or done someone else. But temper must be controlled, or else it is sin to "get mad." If we fail to control our temper, we give the Devil a chance at us, to lead us into sinning. The man who used to steal before conversion must stop it and work and toil with his hands to care for himself and family, and also have something to contribute to the needy. No place for dishonesty in Christian dealing. "An honest man is a noble work of God," though not the noblest unless he is a Christian also. Christians must guard their tongues and never allow evil talk to pass their lips; but practice speaking good things so as to be a spiritual blessing to all who hear them.

Verse 30. Grieving the Holy Spirit. The present imperative with a negative is still used and means *stop* doing the thing forbidden. It is already being done, but must be *stopped*. The verb *lupeo*, to grieve, offend, means that the Holy Spirit is a person, and capable of being grieved and offended. It is He who seals or stamps the Christian for the day of redemption—the day when we shall be raised from the dead, our old physical bodies being then transformed into spiritual bodies; our redemption, deliverance from the last stage of sin, will be completed. See Romans 8:23, where Paul speaks of the redemption of our bodies. This is what is called the eschatological stage of redemption *(apolutrosis)*. There are two ways in which we grieve the Holy Spirit; positively, by going on in these various sins Paul has just enumerated, and others named in 31; negatively, by failing to follow His leading into all truth and into active service to God, His Church and kingdom; failing to help the needy, win the lost, and send the gospel to every creature.

Verses 31, 32. We must lay aside all bitterness (a grudge or hard feeling), anger, threats and insults to others out of rage, with all malice. Malice is a heart sin, the bad seed which grows the rest of these sins. A man may carry malice in his heart for years before it breaks out in one or more of these heinous sins. Just the opposite must be practiced by the Christians—"being kind, tenderhearted, forgiving one another." Tenderheartedness is the root grace, and kindness and forgiveness are the fruits of it. If our hearts are right and tender, we will be kind to others and forgiving. The measure of our forgiving one another is the example of God in forgiving us for Christ's sake. He forgives and forgets. He throws our sins over His back, and buries them in the depths of oblivion. God treats us as though we had never wronged Him and grieved Him. So must we Christians treat others.

SERMON OUTLINE FROM CHAPTER IV
GRIEVING THE HOLY SPIRIT (4:30)

I. The Holy Spirit a Person Susceptible to Being Grieved
1. In Ephesians 1:3-14, the three Persons of the Trinity co-operated in the redemption process—the Father foreordains and elects, the Son pays the ransom price, the Spirit seals the saved.
2. In Genesis 1:2, 3, 26, the Spirit functions in creation. "Let *us*."
3. On the Day of Pentecost the Holy Spirit inaugurated His special dispensation (Acts 2)

II. The Special Functions of the Holy Spirit
1. To convict the world of sin, righteousness, and judgment (John 16:8-11)

2. To regenerate the believer in the name of the Son (John 3:3, 5)
3. To guide Christians into all truth (John 16:13) and in service (Rom. 8:14; I Cor. 2:7-13)
4. To assure Christians of their divine sonship (Rom. 8:16)
5. To empower Christians for service (Acts 1:8; Eph. 3:16)

III. How We Grieve the Spirit
1. By being guilty of the sins named by Paul in context, or any other sins, race prejudice, covetousness, sex immoralities, etc.
2. By failing to follow His guidance. Illustration: President of United States grieved when the Congress fails to follow his suggestions for the welfare of the country. Husbands and wives grieved when either one fails to listen to the other's loving suggestions.

IV. Why Should We Not Grieve Him
1. He is our loving, sacrificing Friend. The Holy Spirit loves us as tenderly as the Father and the Son. Paul appeals to Roman Christians "by the love of the Spirit" (15:30). The Father loved and gave His Son; the Son loved and gave Himself to die for us; the Spirit loves us ceaselessly and gives Himself perpetually to guide, inspire, and empower for service. "His work is never done."
2. Our sins cause Him ceaseless sorrow. A prodigal son grieves his mother and father. A faithless husband grieves a faithful wife.
3. For us to refuse to respond to His guidance breaks His heart.

Chapter V

AGAIN WARNS THEM AGAINST LIVING IN SUCH VICES; EXHORTS
TO LIVE IN THE LIGHT, BE ALERT, SPIRITUAL, EVER SINGING;
NAMES HUSBANDS' AND WIVES' DUTIES

CONTINUES WARNING AGAINST LIVING IN SIN; AS CHILDREN OF
THE LIGHT THEY MUST LIVE (5:1-13)

So you must keep on following God's example, as dearly loved

children of His, ² and practice living in love, just as Christ loved
you too and gave Himself for you as a fragrant offering and
sacrifice to God.

³ But sexual vice and any form of immorality or sensual greed
must not so much as be mentioned among you, as that is the only
course becoming in God's pepole; ⁴ there must be no indecency,
silly talk or suggestive jesting, for they are unbecoming. There
should be thanksgiving instead. ⁵ For you may be absolutely sure
that no one who is sexually impure, immoral or greedy for gain
(for that is idolatry) can have a part in the kingdom of Christ
and God.

⁶ Stop letting anyone deceive you with groundless arguments
about these things, for it is because of these very sins that God's
anger comes down upon the disobedient. ⁷ So you must stop having
anything to do with them. ⁸ For at one time you were darkness
itself, but now in union with the Lord you are light itself. You
must live like children of light, ⁹ for the product of light consists
in practicing everything that is good and right and true; ¹⁰ you
must approve what is pleasing to the Lord. ¹¹ Stop having anything
to do with the profitless doings of darkness; instead you must
continue to expose them. ¹² For it is disgraceful even to mention
the vices practiced in secret by them; ¹³ and yet anything that is
exposed by the light is made clear to them, for anything that is
made clear is light.

Key words and phrases. Verses 1, 2. Again he appeals to the
love of the Father; as dearly loved children they must walk in
love. He also appeals to the sacrificial love of Christ, who loved
us and gave Himself up for us, a fragrant offering and sacrifice to
God." The first word, offering, refers to the sweet incense going
up to God; the second word, sacrifice, refers to the animals slain
and offered to God. So Christ is both a slain sacrifice and an offering to God for us. The *for* may express substitution, so Christ is
our Substitute who bore the penalty of death for us.

Verses 3-5. Again he warns against sexual sins, "immorality
and impurity." These sins were the disgrace of the pagan world.
They must not be brought over into the church. Covetousness is
placed in company with these heinous sexual sins and dubbed idolatry. The covetous man usually makes money his god, and so is

an idolater. These things are not becoming God's people. They are incompatible with the pure religion of Christ which seeks to save the whole man, soul, mind, and body. He also denounces filthiness, silly talk, levity (jesting) as not becoming God's people. Instead of this silly jesting and levity there should be thanksgiving. Our tongues which God made can be better employed giving thanks and singing praise to God.

Observe, he attaches a severe penalty to the sexual sins and covetousness; no one who commits these sins has any share in the kingdom of Christ and God. The kingdom is the Father's in that it is His will which is the standard of character and conduct and life in that kingdom. It is the kingdom of Christ in that He came to set it up on earth with saved men and women as its citizens (see Matt. 5:2-12).

Verse 6. He warns against being deceived with empty words. This seems to allude to the Gnostic teachers who are exerting great influence in the province of Asia. This is seen specially in the letter to the Colossians, which is written about the same time as Ephesians. This letter, we saw above, was addressed to the churches of the whole province but kept in Ephesus, the capital. "These things," the sins above denounced. "Sons of disobedience" is a Hebraism meaning simply the disobedient.

Verses 7-14. Christians must not associate with those guilty of these heinous sins. The reason (*gar*, for) they once were darkness but now through union with the Lord are light. He quotes from an early Christian hymn (so Expositor's Greek Testament):

"Awake thou that sleepest and arise from the dead,
    and Christ shall shine upon you." (A.R.V.)

If they are real Christians, Christ has given them light. So they must awake out of their temporary sleep (moral and spiritual) and Christ will continue to "make the day dawn on them" (Williams). They must walk as children of light and bring forth the fruit of light, which is practicing the things that are good and right and true. They can do this, if they try to learn what is pleasing to the Lord. This is to make the will of God as expressed in Jesus the Lord, the standard of life and conduct.

EXHORTS TO ALERTNESS AS TO THE USE OF TIME AND WINE; TO BE
SINGING SPIRITUAL SONGS AND PRAISING GOD (5:15-21)

> 15 So you must be very careful how you live, not thoughtlessly
> but thoughtfully, 16 and continue to make the most of your oppor-
> tunities, for the times are evil. 17 So stop becoming senseless, but
> understand what the Lord's will is. 18 Stop getting drunk on wine,
> for that means profligacy, but ever be filled with the Spirit, 19 and
> always be speaking to one another in psalms, hymns, and spiritual
> songs. Keep on praying and praising the Lord with all your heart;
> 20 continue giving thanks for everything to God our Father; 21 keep
> on living in subordination to one another out of reverence to Christ.

Key words and phrases. Verses 15-18. Careful and thoughtful
living. Even the times are evil, so that a Christian must always be
alert as to how to use time so as to have opportunity to do good
and understand what the will of the Lord is. Christ is meant as
our Lord. He does the will of the Father, so doing His will is doing
the will of the Father. He warns against debauchery, getting drunk
with wine. A common sin then; more so than now. Instead of being
filled with wine, they must be filled with the Holy Spirit. This means
to be dominated by the Spirit of Christ, which is the Holy Spirit.

Verses 19, 20. A positive, beautiful fellowship of Christians is
enjoined: "Speaking to one another in psalms, hymns, and spiritual
songs." Instead of criticizing one another, believers should be singing
to one another and be happy with each other. Biblical psalms, as in
the Old Testament Psalter; hymns, such as were being composed
and used in the early churches; spiritual songs, not silly, secular
songs with no spiritual significance, worldly and carnal, distracting
the mind and disturbing the soul in its fellowship with God. "Always and in everything giving thanks in the name of our Lord Jesus
Christ to God the Father." Yes, Christians must give thanks to
God for everything, for sickness and calamity as well as health and
prosperity; and *always*. What an ideal Paul paints for the Christian life! Singing perpetually to one another in spiritual, soul-
inspiring songs, and giving thanks to God incessantly, whatever be-
tide! How useful and happy we all could be if we only approximated
this lofty ideal!

THE IDEAL CHRISTIAN HOME (5:22-33)

[22] You married women must continue to live in subordination to your husbands, as you do to the Lord, [23] for a husband is the head of his wife, just as Christ is the Head of the church, His body, and Saviour of it. [24] Just as the church is subject to Christ, so the married women in everything must be subject to their husbands. [25] You married men must love your wives, just as Christ loved the church and gave Himself for her, [26] to consecrate her, after cleansing her through His word, as pictured in the water bath, [27] that He might present the church to Himself as a splendid bride without a blot or wrinkle or anything like it, but to be consecrated and faultless. [28] This is the way married men ought to love their wives, as they do their own bodies. The married man who loves his wife is really loving himself, [29] for no one ever hates his own physical person, but he feeds and fosters it, just as Christ does the church; [30] because we are parts of His body. [31] Therefore, a man must leave his father and mother and so perfectly unite himself to his wife that the two shall be one. [32] This is a great secret; I mean this about Christ and the church. [33] But each one of you married men must love his wife as he loves himself, and the married woman, too, must respect her husband.

Key words and phrases. Verses 21-24. Many modern women regard this paragraph as antique. Paul was an old fogy, they say; he hated women and sought to lower their dignity. The facts are against this evaluation of Paul. In Roman 16 Paul commends seven women whom he knew as great servants of the Lord. He tenderly greets them as noble Christians; he appreciates them for their personal worth and for their sacrificial service to the Lord. In Philippians 4:3 he writes, "And I ask you also, true yokefellow, help these women, for they have labored *side by side with me* in the gospel together with Clement and the rest of my fellow workers, whose names are in the book of life." Those women include women like Lydia, Phoebe, Priscilla, and many others in the early churches. No, Paul is not a woman-hater; he is merely showing us how we may build beautiful, harmonious, happy Christian homes by having one head, the husband, and both partners in the married life so loving and respecting one another that they can fulfill the Scripture which says, "And they shall be one."

The subordination, the submission, which the wife is to yield to the husband is not servile, enslaving, but only respectful recognition of the husband as head of the home. See I Timothy 2:13-15, where he gives the priority to Adam, because God had done so by creating him first, and Eve afterward.

Verses 25-33. Paul's teaching in these verses is overlooked by those who would relegate Paul to antiquity and disregard his teaching concerning the relation of husbands and wives to one another. He makes the duty of the husband to the wife even harder than that of the wife to the husband. He is "to love his wife as Christ loved the Church and gave Himself up for her." The husband's love is to be deathless, and sacrificial of self. This is as high a standard as can be imagined. The husband in his relation to his wife is required to stand with Christ in His love and sacrifice of Himself for the Church as His Bride. The husband must so love his wife as he loves himself and so perfectly love her that he would die for her.

"This is a great mystery." Not the relation of husband and wife, but the relation of Christ to His Church as His Bride. It was once a mystery hidden from man, but now it is an open secret, that Christ so loved the Church that He gave Himself up for her as His Bride to be made holy and without blemish, starting with regeneration (the washing of water by the Word) through the process of sanctification to the last stage of salvation, the final resurrection (Rom. 8:23).

Sermon Outline from Chapter V

The Sacrificial Love of Christ for the Church (25-27)

I. The Object of His Love—the Church
  1. Before the foundation of the world He loved her (John 17:5)
  2. He loved the very institution of the Church. So used in Ephesians and Colossians. Elsewhere usually a local body of believers. Hebrews 12:23, "Church triumphant."
  3. He loved all the individual members of all local churches. He loved them individually (Gal. 2:20), "Love *me*." Catholics hold to a general church, which is "The Holy Roman

Catholic Church." Many Protestants think of a general
church including all who are or will be saved.

II. The Expression of His Love—"Gave Himself Up"

   1. To humiliation in Incarnation; from God to a man (Rom.
8:3); from glory to shame (Isa. 53); from riches to poverty
(II Cor. 8:9)

   2. To vilifying criticism (John 8:48-54; 18:40, 41)

   3. To crucifixion, the most shameful death (John 19:5, 6;
Luke 23:32-46; see also Phil. 2:8)

III. The End to Be Achieved by His Sacrificial Love

   1. To cleanse and save sinners to be suitable members of the
Church, His spiritual Body (v. 26; see also I Tim. 1:15).

   2. To consecrate her to the service of God and man (v. 27)

   3. To sanctify her to the point of perfection—"without spot
or wrinkle"; "holy and without blemish" (a pure and beautiful and perfect Bride). This is to be achieved when the
Church militant becomes the Church triumphant (see Rev.
19:7; 21:9). Here she becomes the wife of the Lamb
after the marriage of the Lamb in Heaven.

Chapter VI

IDEAL CHRISTIAN HOME CONTINUED; SPIRITUAL WEAPONS FOR
MEETING SPIRITUAL FOES; TYCHICUS TO REPORT PAUL'S
CONDITION; FAREWELL

DUTIES OF CHILDREN AND PARENTS; DUTIES OF SLAVES AND MASTERS (4:1-9)

Children, obey your parents, for this is right. [2] "You must
honor your father and mother"—this is the first commandment,
with a promise to make it good—[3] "so that you may prosper and
live a long life on earth." [4] You parents, too, must stop exasperating your children, but continue to bring them up with the
sort of education and counsel the Lord approves.

[5] You slaves must practice obedience to your earthly masters,
with reverence and awe, with sincerity of heart, as you would
obey Christ, [6] not serving them as though they were watching you,
but as true slaves of Christ, trying to carry out the will of God.
[7] Heartily and cheerfully keep on working as slaves, as though it

were for the Lord and not for men, [8] for you know that everyone, slave or free, will get his reward from the Lord for anything good he has done. [9] You slaveowners, too, must maintain the same attitude toward your slaves, and stop threatening them for you know that their real Lord and yours is in heaven, and that He never shows partiality.

Key words and phrases. Verses 1-3. Duties of children: to obey, literally, to listen to, give attention to what father and mother say, and do it. They are both teachers and guides to their children. The first school on earth was the home, with mother and father as teachers. The second duty of children is to honor father and mother. This verb means not only to respect them but to reverence them as the origin of life for them, as their supreme authority for control of their conduct and life. Paul reminds us that this is the first commandment with a promise; that is, it is the first one where God assures us that He will make good the blessings promised. *Fathers* (A.V.) should be translated *parents*. Paul is not exempting mothers from his exhortation. They can exasperate their children as well as fathers. Moulton and Milligan in their scholarly study of the vocabulary of the papyri find that the word *pateres,* fathers, often means *parents,* including mothers with fathers. So it is likely that Paul means that parents must not exasperate their children. This word exasperate, provoke to anger, is easily understood. They must not rub the child the wrong way. Every parent ought to be a good practical psychologist—ought to know how to approach a child with a command or a prohibition. The right way is not to be abrupt or peremptory or angry. Love and gentleness win obedience and leave the child sweet in temper.

"Bring them up in the nurture and admonition of the Lord." Better, "Bring them up with the right sort of education and instruction." The first word is used by Plato in the sense of education. The second word means counsel or instruction. These two words give the positive duties of parents to their children: they are teachers to start their children in the process of true education by giving them such counsel or instruction as the Lord approves (subjective genitive).

Verses 5-9. Duties of slaves and masters. You slaves must not shirk your duties but continue to obey your earthly masters, with sincerity of heart, as though you were directly serving the Lord Christ; work as faithfully when your masters are not looking as when their eyes are on you. In serving this way you will be "doing the will of God from the heart." He urges the motive that the Lord will reward all good deeds done whether by a slave or by a freeman. He is no respecter of persons. Masters are likewise to deal kindly and fairly with their slaves, not hectoring over them and threatening them with punishment, because slaves and masters have the "same Master in heaven, and that there is no partiality with Him."

Observe, following the example of Jesus Himself as a teacher, Paul did not attack slavery as a social and political system. But like Jesus he taught moral and spiritual principles that undermine slavery and have gradually exterminated it from human society. He taught that masters and slaves have "one and the same Master in heaven"; that is, Christ is Master of both. He is teaching the brotherhood of men of differing social classes. In the letter to Philemon he expressly orders Philemon to "receive Onesimus as a beloved brother." Although Onesimus his slave had run away, repudiating his master, now when he is converted in Rome under Paul's preaching, Paul sends the converted slave back to his master with this personal letter requesting the master to receive the runaway slave with open arms, "as a beloved brother." Not as a slave but as a brother. Brotherhood, Christian brotherhood, of master and slave, is what Paul teaches in Ephesians as well as in Philemon.

THE SPIRITUAL WAR AND THE CHRISTIAN'S WEAPONS TO MEET THE ENEMY (6:10-20)

[10] From now on you must grow stronger through union with the Lord and through His mighty power. [11] You must put on God's full armor, so as to be able to stand up against the devil's stratagems. [12] For our contest is not with human foes alone, but with the rulers, authorities, and cosmic powers of this dark world; that is, with the spirit-forces of evil challenging us in the heavenly contest. [13] So you must take on God's full armor, so as to be able to take a stand in the day when evil attacks you, and, after having completely finished the contest, to hold your own. [14] Hold your

position, then, with your waist encircled with the belt of truth, put on right-doing as a coat of mail, [15] and put on your feet the preparation the good news of peace supplies. [16] Besides all these, take on the shield which faith provides, for with it you will be able to put out all the fire-tipped arrows shot by the evil one, [17] take the helmet salvation provides, and take the sword the Spirit wields, which is the word of God. [18] Keep on praying in the Spirit, with every kind of prayer and entreaty, at every opportunity, be ever on the alert with perfect devotion and entreaty for all God's people, [19] and for me that a message may be given me when I open my lips, so that I may boldly make known the open secret of the good news, [20] for the sake of which I am an envoy in prison; so that, when I tell it, I may speak as courageously as I ought.

Key words and phrases. Verses 10-12. The spiritual war. It is not fought with human personalities, but with Satan's hosts of evil. Paul exhorts them to "be strong through union with the Lord, in His mighty strength." We cannot overcome the mighty, cunning hosts of evil in our own strength; it takes the mighty strength of the Lord to re-enforce us to be able to withstand in the evil day; to measure swords with the cunning stratagems of the Devil. The enemy to be met is "the principalities and the powers," which are evil dynasties under the generalissimo Satan, further described as "world rulers of this present darkness and spiritual hosts of wickedness in the heavenly places." The last two terms are in apposition with the first two. They are associated with Satan, the prince of the power of the air (2:2), which are called spiritual hosts of wickedness in the heavenly places. That is, following the thought-forms of Jewish theology, Paul thinks of these mighty rulers of evil under Satan as his cohorts, as located in the lower heavens next to earth which are ruled by Satan as the prince of the power of the air (the lower heaven).

Verses 13-20. "The whole armor of God." This is the equipment of the Christian warriors. There are seven pieces of armor— a complete and perfect armor provided by the Lord. The girdle of truth is the whole truth, revealed in the Bible from Genesis to Revelation. More particularly, it is the gospel truth, the special revelation by Christ and the apostles through the guidance of the Spirit.

Second piece is the breastplace of righteousness. Is it Christ's "imputed righteousness"? The old theologians and expositors said so. But more likely, it also includes practical righteousness in character and conduct. Being and doing right count for more in vanquishing Satan and his hosts with their deceiving, destructive methods of attack, than the objective imputed righteousness, although that is absolutely essential for our justification and salvation in its first stages. Notice, this piece of armor protects the breast where the heart is located. The third piece is the foot protector—likely corresponding to the ancient piece of armor called greaves, reaching from the knees down to the feet. Spiritually this piece is the gospel of peace. The feet of the Christian walk the paths of peace. He is fighting spiritually, not mentally and physically and socially. He is a man of peace. He does not fight with material and military weapons. Quakers press this literally and so are pacifists. They never go to war. This is too literal. If the Christian does go to war it must be for moral and spiritual ends—protection of one's country, its life and liberty, its government and its highest religious good. This was the motive urging the Allies, representing Christian countries, to wage and win World Wars I and II.

The fourth piece is the shield of faith. The ancient shield was a huge piece of metal (sometimes wood) worn on the arms of the soldier, or held by a handle, in front of him to shield him from the flying darts hurled by the enemy. It covers nearly all the body above all other pieces of armor. Faith is that all-protecting piece of armor, faith in God, in Christ, in the cause you fight for, the religion of Christ and the salvation of the whole world. Such a faith makes the Christian soldier invincible and leads the hosts of Christ to victory. The helmet of salvation is the fifth piece. In I Thessalonians 5:8 Paul calls the helmet "the hope of salvation." It is not the salvation itself which is the helmet, but the hope the Christian has as a saved man that protects his head, his mind and thoughts; keeps down doubts and depression and makes him optimistic and conquering. This hope nerves him for any conflict, for any sacrifice, for any emergency.

The sixth piece is the sword of the Spirit, which is the Word of God. This is almost identical with the first piece, the girdle of truth. This is an offensive piece of armor. In the first piece, truth protects; here the soldier wields the sword of truth to conquer the Devil and his hosts. It is the only piece of offensive armor. We must master the use of the Word; it is our only sword with which to slay the hosts of sin. Jesus used this sword to route Satan (Matt. 4:4, 7, 10). The seventh piece is all prayer. Every phase of prayer must be used to route the enemy: confession, adoration, thanksgiving, petition, intercession. Especially does Paul ask for intercessory prayer—"for all the saints," but especially for him the preacher, that he might open his mouth in boldness so as to declare the "mystery of the gospel, as he ought to speak." Mystery is now an open secret.

CONCLUSION: SENDS TYCHICUS TO INFORM THEM OF HIS CONDITION; FAREWELL (6:21-24)

Verses 21, 22. He knows they are solicitous of his situation in prison. So he sends Tychicus, "a dearly loved brother and a faithful minister in the Lord's service." He is a fine character and a noble worker—likely a preacher and evangelist. He is beloved by all, and especially by Paul. As a minister he is faithful, the highest compliment paid to a preacher of the gospel. He is to tell the Ephesians how Paul is and to cheer their hearts. Paul was a consummate gentleman as well as a superb Christian. He was considerate of others' feelings. He must relieve the anxiety of the readers as to his health, environment, etc.

Verses 23, 24. His usual farewell greeting: grace, spiritual blessing, be yours from the Father and the Lord Jesus Christ. Peace, health and happiness, to the brethren—usual farewell greeting. "And love with faith." Love to all and to one another keeping up faith and optimism.

Pastors may preach a good expository sermon from 6:10-20, The Spiritual War; or, they may preach a series of seven or eight on first, The Foes to Be Met—the Devil as Generalissimo; the Allies under Him, Principalities and Powers in the Lower Heaven (Air); Earthly Forces of Evil—Liquor Traffic, Gambling, White Slave Traffic, Materialism, etc. Then a sermon on each of the seven pieces of armor.

The Letter to the Colossians

1. *The origin of the church at Colossae.* Colossae was a small town in the Lycus valley, Hierapolis being a holy city and Laodicea the metropolis of the valley. Epaphras and Philemon were members of the church there, the former a minister and possibly pastor, Philemon a slave owner and apparently a layman of great influence. Both may have visited Rome and been converted under Paul's preaching; if not, likely under the preaching of someone in Paul's missionary party. So Paul is deeply interested in the church as one in sympathy with his "gospel."

2. *Occasion and date.* Epaphras had come from Colossae to Rome and told Paul of the love of the Colossians for him. Very probably he told him of the threat by false teachings and is expecting Paul to intercede on behalf of the church. What were these false teachings threatening Colossae? Zahn *(Introduction)* thinks it is an extreme Judaistic heresy similar to that earlier threatening the Galatians. Lightfoot *(Commentary)* thinks it might be Essenism. So do some German scholars. But we, with most modern scholars, think it was Gnosticism, with its theory of aeons, imaginary intermediaries between God and man. This Gnostic theory of aeons as intermediaries between God and man was a serious threat to the doctrine of Christ as the only intermediary between God and man. The fact that Paul emphasizes the person and work of Christ in this letter as nowhere else in his writings, is strong evidence that Gnosticism is the heresy to be combated there.

The date was simultanous with that of Philemon (cf. Philem. 10, 13; Col. 4:7-9; probably A.D. 63).

3. *The purpose.* Three lines of purpose are discernible: (a) To express his personal interest in the Colossian Christians. Though he had never visited them (2:5), he feels they are converts of his missionary party and that he is spiritually responsible for their doctrinal safety. (b) The main purpose was to warn them against

Gnosticism and its undermining influence on the doctrine of the person and work of Christ. So he expands his views on Christology. In Colossians we find the most thorough presentation of Christology in the New Testament. He emphasizes the deity and pre-existence of Christ; His work in creation and the upholding of the universe; His headship over the Church, etc. (c) He wants to show how a well-rounded Christian life is based on one's true relation to Christ. This purpose is in common with one line of his purpose in writing Ephesians.

4. *The Pauline authorship.* A few radical critics of the New Testament—mostly in Germany, The Netherlands, and France—have denied the Pauline authorship of Colossians. Their argument is threefold: (a) The heresy implied is post-apostolic. But Harnack, noted German church historian, has shown that there was a Jewish Gnosticism before so-called Christian Gnosticism existed (See *History of Dogma,* I) There is little doubt that incipient Gnosticism was in its stride before the Letter to the Colossians was written. (b) They urge differences in vocabulary and general phraseology. But we saw above that Paul is discussing Christology in this letter as he nowhere else did. This would necessitate new words, a different vocabulary; exactly what we find, and some of these different terms are taken from the Gnostic vocabulary, as "fullness, mystery, knowledge, treasures of wisdom," etc. (c) Differences in style between Colossians and Paul's recognized letters, Galatians, Romans, I Corinthians, etc. In reply it may be said that Paul is now in prison and has more leisure to write these rather stilted sentences found in Colossians, instead of the short, jerky, abrupt sentences characteristic of his style in the earlier letters, when he was in the thick of the fight and on the go here and yonder. He is now doing his most profound thinking, which helps account for the style.

On the other hand, the external evidence for the Pauline authorship is overwhelming. It is mentioned in the Muratorian canon and by Irenaeus; seems to be quoted by Justin and Theophilus, and even by the apostolic Fathers (early in the second century). So we are convinced that Colossians belongs to the letters of Paul. So were this array of New Testament scholars: Germans—Hilgenfeld, Juelicher, Weiss, Belser, Zahn, Beyschlag, Weinel; French—Jacquier, Godet, Bovon; British and American—Sanday, Salmon, Abbott, W. B. Hill, Ropes, and others.

5. *Main Teachings.* (a) God is the Father. (b) Jesus Christ is the Son of God, the fullness of Deity permantly dwelling in Him; the mediate Creator of the cosmos, having existed before anything was made; the Saviour, the Redeemer, by means of His death; the Reconciler of all rational, moral beings into an eternal cosmic fellowship; Head over all things to the Church, which is His Body and instrument for redeeming and ruling the world. (c) The gospel is the mystery of God's love now made known to men by Christ. (d) Morality roots itself in spiritual religion which consists in union with God by faith in the Son, not by ascetic practices (so the Gnostics). (e) The home is the bedrock of society and the church, so all its members are called upon to practice the principles of the Christ-life in the home. (f) The husband is the head of the family. (g) Even slaves can serve the Lord by faithfully doing the daily duties of life. (h) Kind words are the salt of life. (i) Prayer for self and others enjoined.

OUTLINE

I. Salutation (1:1, 2)
II. Personal Portion (1:3-2:5)
  1. Thanksgiving for their faith and love and hope (1:3-8)
  2. His prayer for them (1:9-12)
  3. His prayer passing into a description of the person and work of Christ (1:13-23): as Creator; as Redeemer; as Upholder of the Universe; as Head of the Church
  4. Paul's suffering, preaching, and toiling (1:24-29)
  5. His interest in the Colossians (2:1-5)
III. Monitory Portion (2:6-3:4)
  1. Warning against various false teachings (2:6-19)
  2. Warning based on union with the death and resurrection of Christ (2:20-3:4)
IV. Hortatory Portion (3:5-4:6)
  1. Put away the sins of the old nature (3:5-11)
  2. Put on the graces of the new man (3:12-17)
  3. Domestic relations (3:13-4:1)

    (a) Husbands and wives (3:18, 19)
    (b) Parents and children (3:20, 21)
    (c) Masters and slaves (3:22-4:1)
  4. Various exhortations: To prayer, watching, thanksgiving, proper use of time, right talking, etc. (4:2-6)
V. Conclusion (4:7-18)
  1. Sends Tychicus and Onesimus to Colossae (4:7-9)
  2. Greetings from those with him (4:10-14)
  3. Greetings to brothers at Colossae and instructions as to the reading of his letters (4:15-17)
  4. Signature and benediction (4:18)

SALUTATION (1:1, 2)

Chapter I

SALUTATION; THANKSGIVING AND PRAYER FOR THE READERS;
HIS SUFFERINGS AND PREACHING

SALUTATION AND THANKSGIVING FOR THEIR FAITH AND
LOVE AND HOPE (1:1-8)

Paul, by God's will an apostle of Christ Jesus, and our brother Timothy, ² to the consecrated and faithful brothers at Colossae who are in union with Christ; spiritual blessing and peace to you from God our Father.

³ Every time we pray for you we thank God the Father of our Lord Jesus Christ, ⁴ because we have heard of your faith in Christ Jesus and of your love for all God's people, ⁵ because of your hope of what is laid up for you in heaven. Long ago you heard of this hope through the word of truth, the message of the good news ⁶ which reached you, and since it is bearing fruit and growing among you, just as it is all over the world, from the day you first heard of God's favor and in reality came to know it, ⁷ as you learned it from Epaphras, our dearly loved fellow-slave. As a faithful minister of Christ for me, ⁸ he is the very one who told me of the love awakened in you by the Spirit.

Key words and phrases. Verses 1-2. In the salutation he includes Timothy, as in II Corinthians and Philippians. Of course, Paul does the writing; Timothy sends greeting through Paul. He addresses them as saints and faithful brothers in Christ. Saints include all God's people, separated to Him and His service. "Faithful brothers." Quite a compliment. He knows of their fidelity through Epaphras, the minister at Colossae, who has come to Rome to inform Paul of the spiritual condition of the church and the perils threatening it.

See notes on other letters for meaning of grace and peace.

Verses 3-5a. He thanks God in his prayers for the readers' faith and love and hope. Here we have the trio of Christian graces and virtues, as in I Corinthians 13:13; only the order is changed, hope forming the climax here, while love is the greatest in Corinthians; more emphasis being put on hope here, more on love in the former letter. It is to be noticed that their love is for all the saints, for all the people of God. They are not isolationists, but cosmopolitan in spirit. The hope is laid up for them in Heaven. According to Thayer, *Lexicon, in loco,* hope in this sense refers to what we hope for, the reward and blessings we hope for are laid up in Heaven; the hope itself is in our hearts.

Verses 5b-8. Of this hope they had heard "in the word of truth, the . . . good news which reached you," probably through Epaphras, their minister. *Truth* is possibly in apposition with *the word,* and *good news* is in apposition with both; that is, they all refer to the good news, which is truth and which is the Word (of God). "It is bearing fruit . . . in the whole world." Paul's world was the Roman Empire, and he and his fellow workers had preached the good news in nearly all the provinces they could reach at that time. He was an enthusiastic world missionary. Epaphras is a "faithful minister of Christ on our behalf, or on your behalf." Westcott and Hort Text gives preference to *our,* as based on the older manuscripts.

PAUL'S PRAYER FOR THE READERS (1:9-14)

⁹ For this cause, ever since we heard these things about you, we have not ceased to pray that you may have, by experience, a deeper insight into spiritual truths; ¹⁰ that you, by means of the spiritual power in you, may live worthily of the Lord, ¹¹ and bear the fruits of endurance, long-suffering, and joy; ¹² especially giving thanks for what God has done for us through the Son of His love, ¹³ who delivered us from the power of darkness and trans-

ferred us to the kingdom of His beloved Son, [14] who purchased us
from the bondage of sin and made possible the forgiveness of our
sins.

Key words and phrases. Verse 9a. "We have not ceased to pray
for you." Paul was a man of ceaseless prayer. He prayed especially
for all the churches established by him or his fellow workers. Hence
his constant prayers for the church at Colossae.

Verses 9b-14. Experimental knowledge of God's will. *Epignosis*
is knowledge gained by experience; it is growing knowledge upon
knowledge; it is "all [complete] spiritual wisdom and understanding." It is not theoretical, intellectual knowledge, such as is
acquired by physicists and astronomers prying into the secrets of
the universe. It is that knowledge which we acquire from day to
day as to God's ways with us and His will concerning our lives. The
word translated *understanding* denotes inner perception. Paul feels
and knows that personal experience of God and His will is the basic
element in Christian growth and progress. See Ephesians 1:16, 17,
where he prays that the Ephesian Christians should first of all have
this experimental knowledge. See also Philippians 1:9b for the
same thought.

Verse 10. Living worthily and bearing good fruit. "Living
worthily of the Lord." Living a life that is worthy of Jesus who
gave His life for us. Living a life of service and sacrifice. "Fully
pleasing to Him." "I am satisfied with Christ, but is He satisfied
with me?" Paul's high aim was to please Christ; he prayed for his
readers to do likewise. "Bearing fruit in every good work." The
church has many fields of good works—Sunday school, training
unions or other young people's organizations; women's missionary
societies; brotherhoods, and many ramifications of these main organizations. A growing Christian should be at work in some phase
of the general work, yes, as many as his talents and time warrant.
This fruitbearing is positive proof of our discipleship, says Jesus
(John 15:8). "Increasing in the knowledge of God." The experience is to be "increasing"; it is to be knowledge of God Himself, of
His love, power, purposes, and His will for our lives.

Verse 11. Spiritual power. "May you be strengthened with all
power, according to His glorious might." This is spiritual power.

See Ephesians 3:16, where He names the Spirit as the Source of this power. This power is measured by God's glorious might. The power of God in raising Christ from the dead is at the command of the Christian, if he surrenders to the will of God. The practical results of this power are endurance, patience, and joy. An empowered Christian can endure suffering; he is patient with all persons and in all circumstances, and his soul is flooded with joy.

Verses 12-14. Giving thanks to the Father for redemption and salvation. This is a part of the prayer for the readers. He has delivered us from the dominion of darkness and transferred us to the kingdom of His beloved Son. Darkness the symbol of sin and its reign over men; light the symbol of righteousness and the "kingdom of His beloved Son. Literally, Christ is here called "the Son of His love." Descriptive genitive, so *beloved*. "In whom we have redemption, the forgiveness of sins." Redemption means literally deliverance by payment of a ransom price. Christ paid the ransom with His life (Mark 10:45) on the cross. "Forgiveness of sins," the result achieved because of His payment of the ransom. Our sins are sent away (literal meaning of forgive) because Christ bore our sins on the tree (Col. 2:14; I Peter 1:19).

THE PERSON AND WORK OF CHRIST: IMAGE OF THE INVISIBLE GOD, THE FULLNESS OF GOD, PRE-EXISTENT; HELPING CREATOR, UPHOLDER OF THE UNIVERSE, HEAD OF THE CHURCH (1:15-20)

[15] Yes, He is the exact likeness of the unseen God, His first-born Son who existed before any created thing, [16] for it was through Him that everything was created in Heaven and on earth, the seen and the unseen, thrones, dominions, principalities, authorities; all things have been created through Him and for Him. [17] So He existed before all things, and through Him all things are held together. [18] Yes, He is the Head of the church as His body. For He is the beginning, the first-born among the dead, so that He alone should stand first in everything. [19] It is so because it was the divine choice that all the divine fullness should dwell in Him, [20] and that through Him He might reconcile to Himself all things on earth or in Heaven, making this peace through the blood He shed on His cross.

Key words and phrases. Verse 15. "The exact likeness of the unseen God, His first-born Son, who existed before any created thing. *Likeness* means the exact, inner, essential, likeness of God (so Thayer, *Lexicon*, Trench *Synonyms of the N.T.*). It is synonymous with *the fullness* (2:9), "all the fullness of Deity" (2:9). The essence of Deity was Christ even in His bodily form *(somatikos)*. In His incarnate state He was Deity covered with humanity; Deity under human limitations—as to power and knowledge. He prayed to the Father before raising Lazarus; He did not know the day or hour of His parousia (see comments on Phil. 2:6-9). "The first-born of all creation." In verse 18 He is called "the first-born among the dead." In 17 "He is the beginning." This likely refers to "In the beginning" (Gen. 1:1; John 1:1). He existed before anything was created. "First-born among the dead" must mean He rose before others rose. "Birth" used figuratively—He took on a new form of life.

Verses 16-17. He is mediate Creator and Upholder of the universe. Paul does not claim that Christ is the direct or ultimate Creator of all things. If that were his claim, he would have used the preposition *hupo,* by. "By Him all things were created." Instead he wrote, "Through Him as a medium [*dia*] all things were created." The Father is the direct Creator, the Son is the medium through whom the Father created. The Son is the Mediator, not only of redemption but also of creation. He is the Mediator between the Father and "all things." "And for Him." All creation was to witness for Him and co-operate in spreading His kingdom to "the uttermost part of the earth" (Acts 1:8). Christ must reign until after the resurrection, but then He will "deliver the kingdom to God the Father . . . that God may be everything to everyone" (I Cor. 15:24-28). "Through Him all things are held together." Literally, all things stand together. He is the mediate Upholder of the universe; He helps the Father hold it together. The preposition *dia* is used here too, not *hupo.*

Verses 18-20. He is the Head of the Church as His body. *Church* used in the institutional sense, as in Ephesians. But what is true here is also true of the local church; He is its Head. That is, He is the supreme authority of a local body of Christians. He has given it its laws for government and operation. The church is to execute those laws locally and to the ends of the earth. It has no authority to make new laws. The church is His Body. If He is the Head it must be His Body; He must operate in the world through His Church, a divinely established institution to be His instrument for carrying out His will in the world.

And through Him He might reconcile to Himself all things on earth or in Heaven, making this peace by the blood He shed on His cross. This gives us Paul's cosmic sweep of thought as he contemplates God's work of redemption. He includes all things in Heaven as well as on earth. He cannot mean that unfallen angels are subject to redemption in the same sense as fallen men. In some real sense, however, the cross of Christ has unified the inhabitants of Heaven and earth; we of earth are saved and prepared to join them as brothers; they are mentally prepared to welcome us as fellow creatures of the common Father in the great family in Heaven; and so in a real sense God, through the cross of His Son, reconciles, or brings into peaceful relations, all things; that is, all unfallen angels and all men redeemed from earth. This thought helps make Heaven a real home for saved men and welcoming angels.

THE PAGAN READERS, THOUGH ONCE HOSTILE TO GOD IN EVIL DEEDS, NOW THROUGH UNION WITH CHRIST ARE AT PEACE WITH THE FATHER; PAUL REJOICES THAT HE CAN SUFFER AND TOIL FOR HIS READERS AND OTHERS LIKE THEM (1:21-29)

[21] So you, who were once estranged from Him, and hostile in disposition as shown by your wrongdoings, He has now reconciled [22] by His death in His human body, so as to present you consecrated, faultless, and blameless in His presence, [23] if indeed you continue well grounded and firm in faith and never shift from the hope inspired by the good news you heard, which has been preached all over the world, and of which I, Paul, have been made a minister.

[24] I am now glad to be suffering for you, and in my own person I am filling in what is lacking in Christ's sufferings for His body, that is, the church. [25] In it I have been made a minister in accord-

ance with the trusteeship God entrusted to me for you, that I
might prove among you the universal message of God, [26] the open
secret, covered up from the people of former ages and generations,
but now uncovered to God's people, [27] to whom God has chosen to
make known how glorious are the riches of this open secret among
the heathen, namely, Christ in you the hope of your glorification.
[28] We are proclaiming Him, warning everyone and teaching everyone with ample wisdom, in order to present to God everyone
mature through union with Christ. [29] For this I am toiling and
struggling by His active energy which is mightily working in me.

Key words and phrases. Verses 21-23. The former and present
states of the readers compared. Before believing in Christ they were
"estranged . . . and hostile in disposition." Of course, they were estranged from God and hostile in their minds toward the true God
(see Rom. 8:7-8). "You . . . He has now reconciled by His death."
This is a basic teaching of the apostle (II Cor. 5:19). Simple in-
finitive, to "present," expressing ultimate purpose of God and conceived result. Namely, "that you may be consecrated, faultless, and
blameless in His presence." This presentation occurs at the final
assize when Christ comes back. "If indeed you continue well
grounded and firm in faith, and never shift from the hope inspired
by the good news you heard." "Perseverance of the saints." Believers prove the genuineness of their faith in Christ by being stable
and steadfast; by not shifting from the good news of salvation by
simple faith in Christ to false teaching that simple faith must be
supplemented by something else, good works or knowledge of a
false philosophy (as the Gnostics taught).

"The good news [which] you heard, which has been preached
all over the world." A strong hyperbole to say that the gospel had
been preached by Paul and his missionary party all over the Roman
world.

Verses 24-26. Paul's rejoicing in his sufferings to preach to the
Gentiles the mystery of Christ, the good news, to which God has
called him. He is rejoicing to wear chains in a Roman prison, in
order to preach the good news to the Colossians and other Gentiles.
"I fill up what is lacking in Christ's sufferings for His body, that is,
the church." Paul is not hinting at the insufficiency of Christ's

sufferings for the atonement of "the sin of the world" (John 1:29). They are all-sufficient to make Him "the expiation for the sins of the whole world" (I John 2:2). He merely means that his sufferings for Christ's sake are helping sinners and believers to see how powerful are the sufferings of Christ to transform sinners into saints and saints into sacrificing martyrs for the sake of His Body, the Church.

"In it I have been made a minister in accordance with the trusteeship God entrusted to me for you." The office of preaching the good news is a divine office; one to which God calls men. The message of the minister is the mystery hidden for ages and generations but now made manifest to His saints. It is the Word of God. The root idea of mystery in the New Testament is something formerly hidden from man but now revealed to God's people by Christ and His apostles, including Paul. So Thayer's *Lexicon*.

Verses 27-29. "The riches of this open secret . . . Christ in you, the hope of your glorification." The mystery is the Word of God, but the heart of God's Word, Old Testament and New, is "Christ in you, the hope of glory" (A.V.) So He is the mystery. But the mystery now, by personal faith in Christ, becomes the hope of glory in the believer.

He is answering the Gnostic heresy without mentioning it. The mystery of wisdom and knowledge was the essence of Gnostic philosophy. The votary of Gnosticism attained perfection through a series of initiations, usually as many as sixteen, often as many as thirty-two. Paul says he teaches every man that he may present every man mature (perfect) in Christ. With Paul, maturity, or perfection is attained through union with Christ, which is by faith. This perfection involves, or includes the hope of glory. Glory here means the enjoyment by the saints of the splendid presence of God in Heaven (see Thayer, *Lexicon*). As Christ is the mystery, Paul says, "Him I proclaim." This has been his theme for years (I Cor. 2:2; Acts 9:20).

"With all the energy which He mightily inspires within me." Paul toiled and preached with a holy enthusiasm, "with all his might," with all the energy which God inspired within him. What an example of toiling and sacrificing for Christ's sake and for the salvation of men!

There is a good textual sermon in Paul's prayer for the Colossian church. See notes and outline above (9-14).

MONITORY PORTION (2:6-3:4)

Chapter II

PAUL'S DEEP INTEREST IN GENTILES NOT PERSONALLY KNOWN TO HIM; WARNINGS AGAINST GNOSTICISM; SETTING FORTH THE FULLNESS OF CHRIST'S DEITY; DENOUNCING ASCETICISM AND FALSE WORSHIP

PAUL'S DEEP INTEREST IN GENTILES, LIKE THE COLOSSIANS AND LAODICEANS (1-7)

I want you to know what a battle I am fighting for you and for those in Laodicea, yes, for all who have never known me personally, ² that their hearts may be encouraged, by having been knit together in love and by having attained to the full assurance of understanding, so that they may finally reach the fullest knowledge of the open secret, Christ Himself, ³ in whom all the treasures of wisdom and knowledge are stored up. ⁴ I am saying this to keep anyone from misleading you by persuasive arguments. ⁵ For though I am far away in person, still I am with you in spirit, and I am glad to note your fine order and the firmness of your faith in Christ.

⁶ So, just as you once accepted Christ Jesus as your Lord, you must continue living in vital union with Him, ⁷ with your roots deeply planted in Him, being continuously built up in Him, and growing stronger in faith, just as you were taught to do, overflowing through it in your gratitude.

Key words and phrases. Verse 1. All who have not seen my face." Meaning those who have not known him personally. Paul seems to have stayed in Ephesus and sent his evangelistic helpers out to Colossae, Laodicea, and other cities.

Verse 2. "That their hearts may be encouraged by being knit together in love." "Knit together," a beautiful figure. All their hearts united as the stitches of a vast coat made by knitting needles. All the stitches by being united as one make the coat. Such union and brotherhood among believers brings encouragement to their hearts, "to have all the riches of assured understanding and the knowledge of God's mystery, which is Christ." Riches means full, complete abundance. "Assured understanding." Gnostics made much of this full understanding of the mysteries. Paul is getting ready to assert that this full understanding is reached only by faith in Christ, not by a process of taking degrees, each time rising a little higher up the ladder of intellectual knowledge. Christ is God's mystery, His secret of the ages, in the fullness of time manifested and made known in His incarnate form (see Gal. 4:4). God's mystery—only little by little did He unfold His eternal purpose of redemption through the prophets of the Old Testament; finally fully revealed by Christ Himself and His apostles (including Paul) reaching the climax.

"In whom are hidden all the treasures of wisdom and knowledge." This positive assertion knocks all the props from under Gnosticism. The Gnostics would admit that Christ might be one of aeons (rungs) in the ladder up to perfect knowledge. But Paul knows and states that all the treasures of wisdom and knowledge are hidden in Him. You cannot find any treasures of wisdom and knowledge outside of Him, apart from Him.

Verses 4-5. "I say this." I am telling you what Christ is: the mystery of God, an eternal secret now revealed, with all the treasures of true wisdom and knowledge hidden in Him, "that no one may delude [deceive] you with beguiling speech." The Gnostics could shrewdly advertise their system of philosophy with beguiling speech; with specious talk, propositions that look plausible, that seemed to be the exact truth. Paul tries so to present Christ in all the fullness of His Deity, which would surely include all wisdom and knowledge, that no ambassador of Gnosticism could possibly unsettle them in their firm faith in Christ. "Rejoicing to see your good order and firm faith in Christ." He had this report from Epaphras, the minister from Colossae, that they were maintaining good order and a firm faith in Christ. But Paul knows the power of heresy; the insidiousness of false teachings, and so he strives to reinforce their faith in the person of Christ.

Verse 6-7. An exhortation to "continue to live through union with Christ, rooted and built up in Him and established in the faith." In the faith they had in Him. Mixed figures, but it is clear

what he means. *Rooted,* a biological term. They must send the roots
of the new life down deep into the fullness of Christ as God's
mystery. *Built up,* an architectural term; with Christ as the sure
foundation keep on building character, life and personality. "Just
as you were taught." Epaphras and others of the Pauline group had
properly taught them. "Abounding in thanksgiving." That Christ
is such a complete Saviour and giver of wisdom and knowledge.

He Warns Them against the False Teachers Whose Philosophy and Practices Are Undermining and Detracting from the Deity of Christ (2:8-15)

⁸ Take care that nobody captures you by the idle fancies of his
so-called philosophy, following human tradition and the world's
crude notions instead of Christ. ⁹ For it is in Him that all the fullness of Deity continues to live embodied, ¹⁰ and through union
with Him you too are filled with it. He is the Head of all principalities and dominions. ¹¹ And through your union with Him
you once received, not a hand-performed circumcision but one
performed by Christ, in stripping you of your lower nature, ¹² for
you were buried with Him in baptism and raised to life with Him
through your faith in the power of God who raised Him from the
dead. ¹³ Yes, although you were dead through your shortcomings
and were physically uncircumcised, God made you live again
through fellowship with Christ. He graciously forgave us all our
shortcomings, ¹⁴ canceled the note that stood against us, with its
requirements, and has put it out of our way by nailing it to the
cross. ¹⁵ He thus stripped the principalities and dominions of
power and made a public display of them, triumphing over them
by the cross.

Key words and phrases. Verse 8. "Makes a prey of you by
philosophy." This undoubtedly refers to Gnostic philosophy.
Makes a prey is the picture of a wild animal dragging off a smaller
animal to devour. So the Gnostics lead astray and devour their
victims by deceiving propositions of their philosophy. "According to
the *a b c's* of the natural world *(kosmos)* . . . not according to Christ."
That is, their system of philosophy belongs to the natural world and
not to the spiritual which is communicated to men by Christ.

Verses 9, 10. These are the key verses of Colossians. "For in

Him permanently dwells the whole fullness of Deity bodily." Paul commits himself to faith in the full Deity of Christ. *Fullness* is a Gnostic term; they claiming that the fullness of wisdom is acquired through their system of aeons (degrees or steps taken upward). No, says Paul. Christ possesses in Himself the fullness of Deity, and so He can communicate to one who believes in Him the fullness of life. Christ is the whole ladder of aeons up from man to God, from earth to Heaven. See 3:11, where he asserts "Christ is all." *Bodily* may have one of three interpretations: (1) substantially, really, contrasted with "shadow." (See 2:17 for the contrast of rules as a shadow, but to Christ "belongs the substance.") (2) Symmetrically as a whole. (3) In the bodily state, in His incarnation. The last seems likely what Paul is thinking. Even in His lowly form as a human being He has lying permanently at the base of His personality the whole fullness of Deity. Does this seem to conflict with Philippians 2:7, where Paul says, "He emptied Himself"? That is not a categorically absolute emptying of Himself. It means He put limitations on Himself by becoming a man. He was not as a man omnipotent, omniscient, or omnipresent. His divine attributes were limited, so that He prayed to the Father when raising Lazarus (John 11:41, 42).

"The Head of every principality and power." This may mean that Christ exercises authority over all good angels, or, He is superior to all the evil angels, the hierarchy of the air, the first heaven where dwell the evil spirits (Jewish theology). At any rate, it is His superior authority that Paul is emphasizing.

Verse 11. You have received spiritual circumcision from Christ, which helps you put off the body of the flesh; that is, helps crucify the lower nature (flesh). Physical circumcision, demanded by the Judaizers, cannot accomplish this. Here it seems that Judaizers, as well as Gnostics, are threatening the Colossians.

Verse 12-14. By using the figure of mystic realism he pictures the symbolic significance of baptism. In baptism as a symbol, you were buried in fellowship with Him; and also in fellowship with Him, you were raised from the dead. But it is through faith in the mighty working of God, who raised Him from the dead. Faith is the belt which unites the believer with Christ, in intimate fellowship (so prep. *sun*) with Christ so that what Christ suffered in dying causes the believer to die to sin and the world and, by virtue of the resurrection life of Christ, to rise from the dead past of sin. This is called "the power of His resurrection" in Philippians 2:9. The risen Christ lives in the believer the new life of righteousness (Gal. 2:20). "Dead in trespasses and the uncircumcision of your flesh." Before being buried they were dead in and because of trespasses. "In the day ye eat thereof ye shall die." Sin brought death upon all men (Rom. 5:12). Their uncircumcision did not cause death; it was a sign of their death in sin. "God made alive in fellowship with Him [Christ]." A repetition of the thought expressed in the clause, "who were also raised in fellowship with Him." The new life follows the raising from the dead. This is the spiritual resurrection so prominent in Paul's doctrinal letters. It is the result of Christ's resurrection and the believer's faith in the risen Christ. Faith in Him brings about the intimate fellowship with Christ, and this fellowship is the cause of the spiritual resurrection of the believer (see again Gal. 2:20).

"Having forgiven us all our trespasses." Because Chriest died for us as our Substitute, God graciously (literal meaning) forgives us all our trespasses. That precedes the spiritual resurrection. As we receive God's gracious forgiveness we die to our sins and are ready for God to make us alive through fellowship with Christ. Christ's death canceled the bond which stood against us with its legal demands. This bond we could not redeem except by death. Christ redeemed us from its legal demands, by paying off the bond in our place. He did it by nailing it to the cross. How graphic! Today we burn the note and the bond after paying it. Another result of His death: He stripped the principalities and powers. These powers of evil were stripped of their power to conquer believers in Christ. He was victor over them when He rose from the dead. By faith we rise with Him and become victorious over all evil powers. In His resurrection Christ made a "public example of the principalities and powers," leading them in His triumphal procession from the tomb to the right hand of the Father. The picture of a Roman conquerer (as Pompey) marching into Rome in triumph with his captives trailing his chariot.

WARNING AGAINST ASCETIC PRACTICES AND FALSE WORSHIP (2:16-23)

[16] Stop letting anyone pass judgment on you in matters of eating and drinking, or in the matter of annual or monthly feasts or sabbaths. [17] These were but the shadow of what was coming; the reality belongs to Christ. [18] Stop letting anyone, in gratuitous humility and worship of angels, defraud you as an umpire, for such a one is taking his stand on the mere visions he has seen, and is groundlessly conceited over his sensuous mind. [19] Such a person is not continuing in connection with the Head, from which the whole body, when supplied and united through its joints and sinews, grows with a growth that God produces.

[20] If once through fellowship with Christ you died and were separated from the world's crude notions, why do you live as though you belonged to the world? Why submit to rules such as, [21] "You must not handle," "You must not taste," "You must not touch," [22] which refer to things that perish in the using, in accordance with human rules and teachings? [23] Such practices have the outward expression of wisdom, with their self-imposed devotions, their self-humiliation, their torturings of the body, but they are of no value; they really satisfy the lower nature.

Key words and phrases. Verses 16-17. Forbidding certain foods and drinks and fixing days of worship are tenets and practices of both the Essenes and Gnostics. Both set up external rites and days of worship and religious festivals. Paul denounces such ceremonies as only a shadow of things to come, while "to Christ belongs the reality of things to come" (See Romans 14:17, where Paul gives his opinion of "food and drinks" as related to "the kingdom of God."

Verses 18-19. These false teachers rob their disciples of the real prize of the spiritual life, giving up the Head who supplies nourishment and keeps it a unit, and furnishes strength for its spiritual growth. If these readers should fail to hold fast to the fullness of Christ's deity, they would not receive from Him the fullness of the spiritual life (2:9-10). A complete faith in a complete Christ, and that only, can produce the fullness of the spiritual life. In verse 19 Paul shows a good knowledge of human physiology—"whole body . . . joints and ligaments . . . nourished and knit together." A description of a healthy body governed by a wise head. Christians submitting to these false teachings constitute an unhealthy body with no normal growth.

Verses 20-22. These false teachings belong to the cosmos, the natural world, not the spiritual. So why live as if you still belonged to this natural order? Did you not rise in fellowship with Christ to the spiritual realm? Why not live in that higher realm by holding fast to Christ, the Head? Why "submit to regulations [rites], Do not handle, Do not taste, Do not touch?" These false teachers emphasized this sort of living. But Christians are living on a higher plane, in fellowship (in preposition *sun*) with Christ the fullness of Deity. It is not logical to stoop from this higher life to their lower life. It is only human commands and teachings that govern this lower life. It is heavenly and divine principles that govern the higher spiritual life (3:1).

Verse 23. External rites are deceiving; they have the appearance of wisdom. Really they are powerless to promote self-denial and self-sacrifice, especially to prevent free indulgence of the lower nature (the flesh). Mere external rites cannot keep a man from indulging the baser appetites of his lower nature. Example given, the appetite for liquors, the passion for sex indulgence.

SERMON OUTLINE FROM CHAPTER II

THE FULLNESS OF DEITY DWELLING IN CHRIST (2:9, 10)
I. Gnostics and Other Heretics Deny It
  1. Gnostics held to a system of aeons or emanations from God; these mediated between God and man, between Heaven and earth; Christ only an emanation, only a rung in a ladder
  2. Judaizers with legalism and extreme monotheism denied the deity of Christ; only a good man, a human prophet
  3. The Essenes with their emphasis on asceticism and personal purity through ascetic practices
  4. Modernists with their emphasis on the dignity and achievements of man, moral as well as scientific
II. Paul Posits the Deity of Christ. "In Him dwells permanently and bodily the whole fullness of Deity."

1. In His personality; in His pre-existence; in His incarnate state; in His exaltation, God and man, the God-Man

2. Deity exerted in creation. "Through Him all things were created." Only Co-Creator; the Father created all things through the co-operation of the Son and Spirit. This thought rests on Paul's use of preposition *dia*, through, not *hupo*, by (1:16)

3. Deity exerted in upholding the universe. "In Him all things hold together" (1:16b)

4. His deity in action as the medium of redemption for man (2:14). In 2:9 we see His deity; in 2:14 He nails the law with its demands to the cross, thus canceling it on our behalf.

5. His deity in action as Reconciler of the spiritual universe. In Ephesians 1:10 Paul sees that it is God's purpose to "unite all things in Him, things in Heaven and things on earth."

III. Our Response to His Deity
1. Should accept it by faith
2. In fellowship with Him live new life
3. Champion and proclaim it. So did Paul.

Chapter III

Urging Them to Be Heavenly Minded, Since Their Life Is Hidden with Christ in God; To Put Away the Sins of the Old Nature and Put on the Graces of the New; How to Live in the Home

Heavenly Mindedness Based on Union with Christ in His Resurrection Life (3:1-4)

So if you have been raised to life in fellowship with Christ, keep on seeking the things above, where Christ is seated at the right hand of God. ² Practice occupying your minds with the things above, not with the things on earth; ³ for you have died, and your life is now hidden in God through your fellowship with Christ. ⁴ When Christ, who is our life, appears, you too will appear to be glorified in fellowship with Him.

Key words and phrases. Verses 1-2. The preceding paragraph
(2:20-23) gives a negative conclusion; in this one he urges a positive conclusion: "Seek the things above, set your minds on things
above—where Christ is seated at the right hand of God." Christianity is a positive religion and demands a positive life of positive
morality based on heavenly mindedness. The present imperatives
(zeteite and *phroneite)* demand continuous seeking and thinking
on heavenly things.

Verses 3-4. The reason for such a demand, Christ is at the right
hand of God and is our life. More than that, this new life is hidden
in God. It is a heavenly life, a divine life. It must not trail in the
dust and filth of earth. This sets before the Christian a lofty, inspiring hope: "When Christ, who is our life, appears, then you
also will appear with Him in glory." This is the second coming, so
enthusiastically cherished by Paul and other first century Christians. When Christ appears on that day, those in fellowship with
Him will appear shining in splendor like the sun (Matt. 13:43).
This hope is urged as a motive to higher, heavenly living *(gar)*.

HORTATORY PORTION (3:5—4:6)

THIS MEANS PUTTING OFF THE OLD NATURE AND LAYING ASIDE ITS SINS (3:5-11)

[5] So once for all put to death your lower, earthly nature with
respect to sexual immorality, impurity, passion, evil desire, and
greed, which is real idolatry. [6] It is on account of these very sins
that God's anger is coming. [7] You too used to practice these sins,
when you used to live that sort of life. [8] But now you too must
once for all put them all aside—anger, rage, malice, and abusive,
filthy talk from your lips. [9] Stop lying to one another, for you
have stripped off the old self with its practices, [10] and have put on
the new self which is in the process of being made new in the likeness of its Creator, so that you may attain a perfect knowledge
of Him. [11] In this new relation there is no Greek and Jew, no
circumcised and uncircumcised, no barbarian, Scythian, slave and
freeman, but Christ is everything and in us all.

Key words and phrases. Verses 5-7. "Put to death your lower,
earthly nature." Literally, "The members [of the body] upon

earth." These are practically synonymous with *sarx*, flesh (Rom. 8:7, 8; Gal. 5:17-19). This is the practical, ethical application of the theoretical dying in fellowship with Christ on Calvary (Gal. 2:20). The besetting sins are identified with the lower nature *(sarx):* "immorality (fornication), impurity, passion, evil desire, and covetousness, which is idolatry." The first is a sex sin; the second is closely connected with sex uncleanness; the third, passion, is also a sex impulse out of control. These sex sins enslaved the pagan world. They must be put to death, and so put out of action in Christian living. Covetousness is placed in the worst of company in this category of sins, with sex sins on one side and idolatry on the other. Literally it is grasping for more. More land, more houses, more money, more power to dominate others. This makes money a god, and so such a man is an idolater. Idolaters and adulterers are in the same class with the basest of sinners. Evil desire is placed in the same company. It may be desire for sex indulgence or for property or power, or anything that we should not have. "Among whom you also once walked . . . and lived in these things." As unregenerated heathen the Colossians were enmeshed in these sins, "lived in and under the power of these things." What a picture of sin's slavery! "He that committeth sin is a slave of sin" (see John 8:34).

Verses 8-10. "But now put away all these: anger, wrath, malice, slander, foul talk [indecent speech], lying, inasmuch as you have put off the old nature [man] and have put on the new nature [man], which is continuously renewed after the image of its Creator." The *now* is likely temporal with a touch of the logical in it. "Put away" once for all; a definite stripping off of the old nature and tossing it to the garbage heap. It is a definite act of surrender and consecration to the new life. See Romans 6:13, for a definite, once-for-all dedication of ourselves to God.

These sins are both personal and social: anger is a continuous feeling of hate against someone; wrath is a sudden outburst of it. Malice is ill-will in the heart, the cause of the anger. Slander (blasphemy) is saying evil things about others, usually false. Lying is speaking falsely to injure others; usually grows out of malice. "Stop lying," negative with present imperative expresses this.

"Which is being renewed." The new nature must daily be re-newed, just as the physical body must be daily renewed by food and exercise. The pattern for the new creature in Christ is the image of its Creator (God). We lost that image in Adam; in Christ, through our fellowship with Him, we regain it. But it is a process of renewal.

Verse 11. National and social differences abolished in Chris-tianity. The Jew with all his religious privileges, the Greek with all his intellectual and cultural advantages, are on the same footing before God as the Scythian and the barbarian. The free man stands on a level with his slave. Christ is the same to all of them, Saviour, Friend, Lord. "Christ is all, and in all." By faith the barbarian has the same intimate fellowship with Him as the cultured Greek.

HE URGES THEM TO PUT ON THE ROBE OF PRACTICAL RIGHTEOUS-NESS AND STRIVE FOR PERFECTION (3:12-17)

12 So as God's own chosen people, consecrated and dearly loved, you must once for all clothe yourselves with tenderheartedness, kindness, humility, gentleness, patience; you must keep on 13 for-bearing one another and freely forgiving one another, if anyone has a complaint against another; just as the Lord has freely for-given you, so must you also do. 14 And over all these qualities put on love, which is the tie of perfection that binds together. 15 Let the peace that Christ can give keep on acting as umpire in your hearts, for you were called to this state as members of one body. And practice being thankful. 16 Let the message of Christ continue to live in you in all its wealth of wisdom; keep on teaching it to one another and training one another in it with thankfulness, in your hearts singing praise to God with psalms, hymns, and spiritual songs. 17 And whatever you say or do, let it all be done with reference to the Lord Jesus, and through Him continue to give thanks to God the Father.

Key words and phrases. Verses 12-14. "Put on therefore." For this reason *(oun)* namely, you have risen in fellowship with Christ to a new life (3:1). "Put on." "Once for all" at a definite dedica-tion of yourselves (aorist imperative). Here is the robe of practical righteousness: for God's chosen ones *(eklektoi)*. See Ephesians 1:4-6, where he elaborates the doctrine of predestination and election. The elect are holy, separated (from the world to God) and beloved (by Him). The robe they should wear consists of: compassion (literally, heartfelt sympathy), kindness (love in action), humility (a grace unknown to the heathen), gentleness (used of a once wild horse now tamed, broken), patience, and the spirit of forgiveness. And the clasp *(sundesmos)* that fastens all these graces into a unit is love. He magnifies love as the queen of graces, as he does in I Corinthians (13:13). It is the crowning grace that brings perfection. It is the clasp of perfection. Last word is in the genitive, in the objective sense; love conduces to and brings perfection.

Observe, the standard for the Christian's forgiving the other fellow is "as the Lord [Jesus] graciously forgave you." This is the literal meaning of *chorizomai*. Even if our offender does not merit our love and forgiveness, we must freely forgive him and forget the offense.

Verses 15-17. "And let the peace of Christ rule in your hearts." The verb *rule* literally means to be an arbiter, or referee in the Greek games. Here, "Let the peace which Christ gives be referee in the game of life." Let that peace settle the points of difference or disagreement. The reason, "To peace you were called." Peace is a basic, key principle in Christianity. The sinner makes peace with God by trusting Christ as Saviour and Lord. God is the God of peace. Christians must be peacemakers. They must live in peace with one another. "Let the word of Christ live in you permanently and richly." Present imperative denotes permanently. *Richly* means in fullness and completeness. Christians ought to be rich in knowledge of the Word. It is the food that nourishes the soul. It is the sword of the Spirit with which we put to rout the Devil. It is the standard by which we ought to live. It is the lamp unto our feet and the light to our path (Ps. 119:105). Versed in the Word of Christ we can teach and admonish one another in the perfect wisdom Christ gives. More Christians ought to know the Bible so well that they can be teachers of the Word; not in classes, but in our daily concourse and conduct. It must be teaching that fits us to admonish one another as to the pitfalls and perils of the race track of life. With peace as the referee and the Word as our guidebook, we can cross the goal line and make the touchdown. And we can be singing as we run. See Ephesians 5:19, 20 for an exposition of these verses, which are almost an exact copy of Colossians 3:16, 17. These two letters were likely written in the same year. In Colossians he does not warn against drunkenness or urge to be filled with the Spirit, as he does in Ephesians 5:18. Probably Colossae, a smaller city, was not so steeped in drunkenness as was Ephesus, a large city and the capital of the province. The general exhortation to lay aside common heathen sins and put on the graces of the new nature is the same, though the verbiage differs slightly.

DUTIES OF WIVES AND HUSBANDS, OF CHILDREN AND PARENTS AND SLAVES (3:18-25)

¹⁸ You married women must continue to live in subordination to your husbands, for this is your Christian duty. ¹⁹ You husbands must continue to love your wives and stop being harsh with them. ²⁰ Children, practice obedience to your parents in everything, for this is acceptable in Christians. ²¹ Fathers, stop exasperating your children, so as to keep them from losing heart. ²² Slaves, practice obedience to your earthly master in everything, not as though they were watching you and as though you were merely pleasing men, but with sincerity of heart, because you fear the Lord. ²³ Whatever you do, do it with all your heart, as work for the Lord and not for men, ²⁴ for you know that it is from the Lord that you are going to get your pay in the form of an inheritance; so keep on serving Christ the Lord. ²⁵ For the man who wrongs another will be paid back the wrong he has done; and there are no exceptions.

Keys words and phrases. Verses 18-22. Duties of wives and husbands, of parents and children, to each other. In Ephesians 5:22-25 we find a little different statement of these duties, but the main thought is identical. Wives must be submissive to their husbands, husbands must love their wives. In Ephesians he adds, "your own" *(idiois)*, and "it is fitting" for wives to be submissive. As to husbands, in Ephesians he adds, "as Christ loved the church and gave Himself up for her." We observe that more stringent orders are given to the Ephesians than to the Colossians. This is probably so as hinted above, because moral conditions were worse in the capital city Ephesus. In Ephesians he emphasized the fact that the husband is the head of the wife, but not in Colossians. Children are to "obey your parents *in everything*," as given in Ephesians, but in Colossians "in everything" is omitted. In Ephesians he gives the Hebrew form, "Honor your father and mother," etc. But Paul adds his interpretation, "which is the first commandment with a promise." It is only different phrasing for expressing the same ethical demands in all these domestic relations.

Verses 23-25. The duties of slaves to their earthly masters given in almost the same phrasing as in Ephesians 6:5-8. Of course, in those days slaves were regarded as a part of the household. So the duties of slaves and masters are given in connection with other domestic duties.

HEAVENLY MINDED CHRISTIANS (3:1-4)

I. The Grounds for Such a Lofty Ideal ("therefore")
1. Believers died and rose again in fellowship with Christ (3:1)
2. The resurrection life of Christ the source of our new life (3:3)
3. His exalted life at God's right hand unites with His resurrection life as the source of our new life (3:1b). See Galatians 2:20; Philippians 1:21 as proof texts for these points.

II. The Exercise of Heavenly Mindedness
1. "Thinking on the things above"
2. "Seeking the things above"
3. These exercises to be habitual, continuous (in present imperative which expresses continuous action). Daily, hourly
4. What are the things above? Kingdom of God (of Heaven); joys of angels (Luke 15:7); winning souls to Christ; growing in grace; our treasures or rewards in Heaven; our loved ones up there

III. Rewards for Heavenly Minded Christians
1. Spiritual joys; such Christians the happiest people on earth. So was Paul in spite of chains in Rome (joy used nine times in the Letter to the Philippians)
2. Such Christians most useful; greater influence over others

3. At last they "appear with Christ in glory" (3:4; II Tim. 4:8), and reign with Him (Rev. 3:21)

Illustration: Stephen a heavenly minded Christian; the first Christian martyr; though dying under a storm of pelting stones, he died gazing into Heaven with a vision of Christ standing to welcome him to glory. So was Paul as he faced martyrdom (II Tim. 4:6-8).

Chapter IV

DUTIES OF MASTERS; CONCLUDING EXHORTATIONS; TYCHICUS AND ONESIMUS SENT TO COLOSSAE; VARIOUS GREETINGS; PAUL'S AUTOGRAPH

DUTIES OF MASTERS; CONCLUDING EXHORTATIONS (4:1-6)

¹ Masters, you must practice doing the right and square things by your slaves, for you know that you have a Master in heaven.

² You must persevere in prayer and by this means stay wide awake when you give thanks. ³ At the same time keep on praying for me too, that God may open the door of opportunity for the message, so that I may tell the open secret about Christ, for the sake of which I am held a prisoner, ⁴ in order to make it evident why I have to tell it. ⁵ Practice living prudently in your relations with outsiders, making the most of your opportunities. ⁶ Always let your conversation be seasoned with salt, that is, with winsomeness, so that you may know how to make a fitting answer to everyone.

Key words and phrases. Verse 1 belongs to chapter 3. Paul abbreviates his appeal to masters which occurs in Ephesians 6:9. Omits the appeal, "forbear threatening," and the statement, "there in no partiality with Him" (the Lord).

Verses 2-4. See Ephesians 6:18-20 and our comments there on his request for their prayers for him to preach the open secret as he ought, as well as his expression, "all prayer" there used.

Verses 5-6. Christians warned to conduct themselves prudently before outsiders—those not Christians. We must watch our influence on them. "Buy up time." It means turn time into opportunity for doing good to those outside. "Let your speech be salted with graciousness." Cultivate softness and kindness of speech, "so as to know how to answer each one." Failing to do this robs our religion of its influence on outsiders.

CONCLUSION

TYCHICUS AND ONESIMUS SENT TO COLOSSAE; GREETINGS FROM COMRADES; PAUL'S AUTOGRAPH (4:7-19)

Verses 7-9. Tychicus sent as a messenger to inform the readers about Paul's affairs, especially how he is faring in prison, Onesimus, a runaway slave from Colossae, is returned as a beloved brother to his master, Philemon, a member of the church there. Tychicus, a beloved brother, a faithful minister, and a fellow slave (of Christ) with Paul, seems to be Paul's messenger boy (Eph. 6:21; II Tim. 4:12; Titus 3:1; Col. 4:12). He must have been a persuasive personality, a successful go-between for Paul and his churches. Titus had performed this duty between Paul and the Corinthian church (II Cor. 7:6-7). Tychicus is not a prisoner, and so is free to go on errands to the churches for Paul.

Onesimus is a beloved and faithful brother, although he is a slave of Philemon. Paul is now sending him back to his master both as a slave and a brother (Christian). See Philemon 16 for our comments.

Verses 10-18. He names a few of his fellow workers and intimate comrades. There were only three men of the circumcision, only three of Jewish stock, now staying with him and co-operating with him in preaching the good news of salvation by grace to all the Gentiles: Aristarchus (a Jew from Thessalonica, Acts 20:4), Mark, the cousin of Barnabas, and Justus. These three seem to have been intimate friends of Paul, for he writes, "They have been a comfort to me." Next he extols Epaphras, "one of yourselves, a bondslave of Christ Jesus, always remembering you especially in his prayers, that you may stand mature and fully assured in all the will of God." He was probably a minister who had preached at Colossae, Laodicea, and Hierapolis (12-13), and so he was deeply concerned for them and worked hard for them. The goal he sought for them was to be "mature and fully assured in all the will of God." These two words are prime terms in the Gnostic vocabulary, but Paul is using them *(teleios* and *plerophoreo)* in a spiritual sense; never doubting what the will of God is for them. An ideal state to reach in Christian experience.

Paul has special commendation for Mark, although once he had deserted the apostle (Acts 13:13), and asks them to "welcome him." He is now one of the three Jews who stick closest to Paul in his sufferings and sacrifices to give the good news to the Roman world.

Verse 14. "Luke the beloved physician." He had been with Paul ever since the first days of the second missionary journey (Acts 16:10). The evidence for this is that Luke in his narrative changes from "they" to "we." That is, he was one of the missionary party after that. "The physician." Some have thought that Paul took him with him as his private physician. Perhaps so. But he was beloved especially by Paul, because he was so devoted and attentive to him. He remained with him in the Caesarean imprisonment and now in the Roman prison with him. He embraces in toto the Pauline gospel (Rom. 2:16), as evidenced by the inclusion in his gospel much of the universal gospel of grace (see Luke chaps. 14-18).

"And Demas." He seems still to be devoted to Paul and a loyal disciple, but afterward he fell in love with the world and deserted Paul (II Tim. 4:9). When the apostle was closing his letter to the Colossians, Demas joined Luke in sending greetings.

Verse 15. Paul sends greetings to "the brethren at Laodicea and to Nympha and the church in her house." She is likely a leader loyal to Paul.

Verse 16. Instructs them to send this letter to the Laodiceans to be read in their church. Also to get the letter of the Laodiceans and read it. Did Paul write also to the Laodiceans, and the letter got lost, or did it not get into the canon? Some scholars claim that the so-called Ephesian letter was addressed to the Laodiceans. This is only a guess. But Paul probably did write a letter to the Laodiceans.

Verse 17. Archippus is exhorted to make the most of his ministry. He may be the present pastor of the church at Colossae; or, he may be a minister who is a member of the church there but preaches elsewhere in the province of Asia; or he may be an evangelist with headquarters at Colossae. At any rate, he has an important ministry received in the Lord. He must fulfill that ministry; he must fill it with service to the church and to individual Christians and lost men.

Verse 18. Here he gives his autograph. Only twice elsewhere does the Apostle give his autograph (Gal. 6:11; II Thess. 3:17). Extreme radical critics have urged that this is evidence against the Pauline authorship of II Thessalonians and of Colossians. Why not urge it against the Pauline authorship of Galatians? But no one dares do that; it is so evident that Paul wrote Galatians. But II Thessalonians and Colossians are just as Pauline in spirit and teaching, except that in II Thessalonians he stresses the second coming of Christ. But why? It is the one crucial problem of the church at Thessalonica, founded by Paul and loved by him. He may have given his autograph there because of much opposition to him there (Acts 17:5-9) and because of the gravity of the situation in the church over this question (II Thess. 2:1-7): See also I Thessalonians 4:13-18. It would be natural for him to give his autograph in closing this letter to the Colossians, since he has never visited Colossae and was personally unknown to the Colossian Christians.

"Remember my bonds [fetters]." A pathetic appeal! An old man in fetters, not for anything wrong he has done, but for Christ's sake. "Grace be with you." "Spiritual strength be with you all [you in pl.]."

The Letter to Philemon

INTRODUCTION

1. *Occasion and date.* Philemon was a slave owner in Colossae, a member of the church there. Onesimus, a slave of his, ran away, went to Rome, heard Paul preach the good news of Christ's love. He was converted and was so appreciative of what Paul had done for him that he wanted to remain with Paul and minister to him as a prisoner of the Lord. Paul in turn appreciated Onesimus' love, but would not retain him from his master without his consent. So he writes this letter, explaining the change that Onesimus had experienced and his own love for and faith in Philemon, and pleading with him for love's sake to take Onesimus back, not only as a slave but much more, a beloved brother.

It is almost certain that Paul wrote this personal letter at the same time he wrote Colossians, A.D. 63.

2. *Purpose.* Two distinct designs are evident: (a) To ask Philemon to forgive Onesimus and take him back as a brother in the Lord. He knew that Philemon felt mistreated by his runaway slave, and so pleads with him to recognize the change in his heart and life and relationship, and freely forgive him and take him back. He advocates the highest form of Christian brotherhood, that of masters and slaves, of the wealthy and the poor. (b) To engage a room in Philemon's house for himself on a visit he is contemplating—likely the missionary journey to Spain and other points (Rom. 15:24, 28). (c) Its genuineness and characteristics. Marcion the heretic, who made the first canon of the New Testament, includes it as Paul's. So did the Muratoian Fragment; the oldest version in the West, the Itala; the oldest in the East, the Peshitto.

Its characteristics are simplicity and elegance of style, just like Paul in his off moments; directness of statement, a purely personal, private letter; expressive of the finest courtesy and gentlemanliness; breathing the spirit of love and brotherhood which led Erasmus to say of it, "Cicero never wrote with greater elegance."

INTERPRETATION

Verses 1-3. The Greeting. "Paul a prisoner of Christ Jesus." He has been a prisoner so long that it bears down upon his mind; but he does not complain. He belongs to Christ and is a prisoner for His sake. "And Timothy our brother." Timothy was a great comfort to Paul in these late years of suffering. He includes him in the greeting to Philemon.

"To Philemon our beloved brother." He may be a convert of Paul's; may have visited him several times in Rome and so he loved him. "And Apphia our sister." Not definitely known who she was; maybe wife of Philemon; at any rate, a leader in the church. "Archippus our fellow soldier." See notes on Colossians 4:17. "Grace to you and peace," etc. (see Eph. 1:2, exactly the same greeting.) See our comments on Galatians 1:3, where he uses the same greeting.

Verses 4-7. He thanks God for Philemon's love and faith. The two basic graces out of which flows a selfless, sacrificial life. His faith is "toward the Lord Jesus and all the saints." He has confidence in his fellow Christians, a fine spirit for the larger service in the church. Paul prays that "the sharing of his faith may promote the knowledge of all the good that is ours in Christ." Strong faith in Christ and our fellow Christians can promote the highest good that Christ bestows on His people. "For I have derived much joy and comfort from your love." Paul is sensitively responsive to the love and brotherhood of Christians. He gets joy and comfort out of this beautiful brotherhood.

Verses 8-14. For "love's sake" Paul appeals to Philemon for Onesimus. As an ambassador of Christ he has authority to command him, but he prefers to appeal for love's sake. There must have been an intimate friendship between Paul and Philemon. His appeal is for his spiritual child. Onesimus had listened to his story of Christ's love for sinners and had accepted Him as Saviour and Master. "In my imprisonment." The apostle seems to be proud of the opportunity, even in prison, to win a soul to Christ, and that of a slave. In a parenthesis he plays on the meaning of Onesimus' name; "formerly he was useless, but now he is indeed useful to you and me." This is a favorite usage of words with Paul. See Romans 1:28 for a fine illustration of it. He means to magnify the new Onesimus, with a new heart and a new outlook on life; with Christ as his Saviour and spiritual Master he is "more beneficial" (see v. 20). He will be a better slave because a better man, now a Christian.

"I am sending him back to you, sending my very heart." The apostle fell in love with the converted slave; he was so devoted to Paul; he wanted to remain in Rome and minister to his spiritual father. But Paul was a Chesterfieldian gentleman and would not rob his friend Philemon of a slave, as much as he needed someone to minister to him in his old age and imprisonment.

Verses 15-20. A beautiful Christian brotherhood, even of the utmost extremes of society, master and slave. "That you might have him back forever, no longer as a slave but more than a slave, as a beloved brother." He is a brother, "especially to me but how much more to you, both in the flesh and in the Lord." Even from the natural point of view he is now much more than a slave to you, Philemon; he is a brother because of his union with the Lord (the Master in Heaven).

Paul is not trying to establish the universal brotherhood of man, regardless of relationship to Christ. It is universal brotherhood of Christians that is emphasized. Social differences must not separate Christians into distinct classes. They are one through union with Christ (Col. 3:11).

"If he has wronged you at all, or owes you anything, charge that to my account. I, Paul, write this with my own hand, I will repay it." He gives his autograph as a guarantee that he will pay whatever debt Onesimus may owe his master. An expression of his love for and his faith in Onesimus.

"Yes, brother, I want some benefit from you in the Lord [i.e., some spiritual benefit]. Refresh my heart in Christ." Again, he plays on the meaning of Onesimus' name, "beneficial, useful." I cannot keep the personal Onesimus, so you just let me have a spiritual benefit (Onesimus).

Verses 21, 22. In supreme confidence in Philemon to do even more than he says, he engages a guest room at Philemon's. He is optimistic as to his trial, feeling sure of being released through Philemon's prayers. Others, too, were praying for his release. Paul believes in the efficacy of prayer.

Verses 23, 24. Epaphras is now a fellow prisoner for Christ's sake; for preaching the gospel of grace. The same fellow workers, barring Justus, that sent greetings to the Colossians (4:12-14) send greetings to Philemon.

Verse 25. Benediction. "Grace [means spiritual blessing] of the Lord Jesus Christ be with your spirit."

Paul and the Pastoral Epistles

INTRODUCTION

DID PAUL WRITE THE PASTORAL EPISTLES?

These are I Timothy, II Timothy, and Titus. In modern times there are three theories held as to the authorship of these letters. These are (1) The view that they are completely genuine; that is, that Paul wrote them in exactly the form in which they have been transmitted to us. This is the position taken by such eminent scholars as Conybeare and Howson, Farrar, Dods, Gloag, Godet, Lightfoot, Salmon, Weiss, Zahn, Alford, Adeney, Hort, Humphreys, Huther, Findlay, Gilbert, Fairbairn, Knowling, Plummer, Plumptre, Ramsay, Sanday, Wace, Barth, Baumgarten, Berk, Hertzog, Hoffman, Lange, Shaff, Spitta, Wieseler, Van Oosterzee, Schlatter, Belser, Headlam, Shaw, Rutherford, White, Lilley, James, Hill, D. Smith (E.G.T.), Hayes, and others. (2) The view that they are not genuine; that is, they are not Paul's production at all. There is not so large a number holding this view. They are extreme radicals. This view was and is championed by Schmidt, Schleiermacher, Baur, Beyschlag, Hilgenfeld, Holtzmann, Jülicher, Meyer, Shenkel, Schwegler, Davidson, Hatch, Robert Scott, and a few others. This view is so radical and unfair to the facts that it has few followers outside of Germany. (3) Then there is what may be called the mediating view: namely, denying that they are entirely genuine, admitting that they do contain a kernel of genuine Pauline matter, but that a second century writer (some would place the date in the last decade of the first century) used this Pauline material in composing the epistles in the form in which we have them. This is a very popular view today and is apparently gaining in its appeal to young New Testament scholars. It has been held by such noted scholars as Clemen, Credner, Harnack, Hausrath, Hesse, Hitzig, Pfleiderer, Krenkel, Immer, Knoke, Lemme.

PAUL'S RELEASE FROM THE ROMAN IMPRISONMENT AND A FOURTH MISSIONARY JOURNEY

Many New Testament scholars, including Alford, Ellicott, Farrar, Findlay, Salmon, Godet, Neander, Renan, Zahn, Shaw, Burton, Ramsay, Weiss (with reserve), and many others of equal reputation, hold that the apostle was released from his Roman imprisonment at the end of two years. He then went on a fourth missionary journey, perhaps realizing his dream to evangelize Spain (Rom. 15:28).

Although there is no account given of this supposed fourth missionary journey, there are sufficient references to his journeys not mentioned in Acts, from which we can construct its itinerary. It is as follows. He first visited Asia and Macedonia, according to Philemon 22 and Philippians 2:24. It is probable that he then went on to Spain to evangelize that most western province of the empire (Rom. 15:24-28). On his return from Spain he would revisit Ephesus, where it is almost certain he left Timothy, according to I Timothy 1:3. After spending a short time in this eastern capital, he returned to Macedonia, and most probably at Philippi he wrote the first letter to Timothy. On leaving Macedonia he visited Miletus and Troas, according to II Timothy 4:20. He then probably went on to Crete, where he left Titus, according to Titus 1:5. After remaining on the island for a short time, he proceeded next to Corinth, where he left Erastus, according to II Timothy 4:20. On leaving Corinth he probably visited Nicopolis, according to Titus 3:12, where he was arrested and sent to Rome for the second and final imprisonment there. Although these visits to these places are not mentioned by Luke in Acts, yet with Paul's own purpose expressed for further visits (Rom. 15) this journey was probably made by him.

EARLY HISTORY OF TIMOTHY AND HIS POSITION IN EPHESUS

His father was a Greek, but his mother, Eunice, was a faithful Jewess and reared her son Timothy according to the strictest traditions for a Jewish mother. She was faithfully aided by her mother Lois. So he was well trained in the Scriptures from childhood (II Tim. 1:5). When Paul came back to Lystra on the second missionary journey, Timothy was so gifted and so well trained in the Scriptures, that Paul felt he was fitted for being a member of their missionary party. He was ordained by the laying on of the hands of the elders (pastors) and joined the mission company headed by Paul and Silas. With them he went to Philippi, Thessalonica, Berea, to Corinth and Troas. He later joined Paul in Rome, but the apostle felt that he was needed in Ephesus, so he gave him up and sent him on to Ephesus to assume leadership there and throughout the province (Asia).

There is some difference of opinion as to what position Timothy filled at Ephesus. Eusebius, early church historian, generally reliable, says he was the first bishop (pastor) of the church at Ephesus. And he was said to have remained here until he was martyred for interfering with a pagan feast. (See Hayes, *The Synoptic Gospels and Acts,* page 169.) At first it is very probable that his labors were limited to the church at Ephesus. But as he grew in experience and wisdom and power in living and laboring in the capital city, he became the superintendent of missions for all the state of Asia, heading up in Ephesus as the capital. On no other supposition is it easy to explain why Paul should charge Timothy so stringently and minutely as to the moral character, the administrative ability, and the didactic gifts of pastors to be placed over the church in the province of Asia (see I Tim. 3:1-7).

The First Letter to Timothy

Occasion, Purpose, and Date. Paul left Timothy in Ephesus to perfect the organization of the churches in Asia (province) while he went on to Macedonia—likely he stopped in Philippi, to rest and see how the church there was prospering. First of all he writes to encourage Timothy. He was timid and had to meet many opponents to the genuine gospel. Morals generally were low. So the morals of ministers and deacons must be kept on a high grade. He wants to impress young Timothy that in a world of loose and low morals the churches must be led by men of high ideals and pure character, who must be good teachers and administrators. Date likely about A.D. 65.

GENERAL OUTLINE

THE MAIN TEACHINGS

1. God is the Father, the happy God, the eternal, immortal, invisible, King and Saviour of all men. No special emphasis on the Fatherhood of God.

2. Christ is a "man," the Saviour of sinners through His sacrificial death, but also the only Potentate, the King of kings, the Lord of Lords.

3. The Spirit is not emphasized at all but implied.

4. The church is made prominent, a central theme. It is to be properly organized with pastors, deacons, and deaconesses.

5. Pastors must be competent teachers, good administrators, and above all of unquestioned character, and with a good reputation with outsiders and all the people.

6. Deacons must be of the same excellent moral character, and also with a good reputation with all the people, good administrators, conscientious men of convictions.

7. Deaconesses must be of excellent moral character.

8. Pastors should be respected and loved and supported by the churches.

9. Aged widows (sixty years old or upward), if they do not have relatives able to care for them, should be cared for by the church.

10. Young widows should marry, be mothers, and homemakers.

11. Christians should always pray for all civil officers, that good government may make conditions favorable to right living and the progress of Christianity.

12. The purpose of the law is to restrain from evil-doing.

13. Christians are to live piously and righteously; the rich especially are to be charged to do good with their riches, to be rich in good works.

14. Christ is to appear at the fitting time and all should so live as to be ready any time for His appearing.

BIBLIOGRAPHY

Bible dictionaries: International Standard Bible Encyclopedia, Hastings'

Introductions: Hayes, Moffatt, Peake, Shaw, Williams, Zahn

Commentaries: Expositor's Bible, Englishman's Greek Testament, Carroll, Interpretation of the English Bible.

EXEGESIS

Chapter I

I. THE GREETING (1:1, 2)

Paul, an apostle of Christ Jesus by command of God our Saviour and of Christ Jesus our hope, 2 to Timothy my genuine child in faith; spiritual blessing, mercy, and peace be with you from God our Father and Christ Jesus our Lord.

Key words and phrases. Verse 1. "Paul an apostle." The word apostle means one sent forth. Same as missionary. Apostle is from Greek and denotes that special class of men called by Christ to be with Him and represent Him in the world. Paul was not of the original group of apostles, but he was also the recipient of a special call from Christ (Acts 9:15). "By command of God." Jesus is executing the command of His Father. "God our Saviour." It is peculiar to the pastoral letters to call God *Saviour*. This expression cuts two ways: it shows that Christ is God (Rom. 9:5) and that the Father as well as the Son is Saviour. It is implied, however, that the Father is Saviour. Even John 3:16 traces salvation back to the Father and makes Him ultimately the Saviour, the giver of eternal life. "Jesus our hope." Nowhere else in Scripture. The aged Paul now feels the reality that our hope hangs on Christ Jesus alone. While the word occurs nowhere else in Paul's letters, the thought permeates them.

Verse 2. "My true child in faith." True not in a physical sense but in the spiritual sense. Paul preached the good news to him, Timothy received it by faith, and he became Paul's true child—his spiritual child. Faith is subjective not objective. Timothy's trust in Christ Jesus made him a child of God in reality, but instrumentally the spiritual child of Paul who won him to Christ.

The greeting is couched in three terms, grace, mercy and peace; whereas in the early letters he uses only two, grace and peace. Mercy is grace, or God's unmerited favor, at work forgiving sins and beginning the work of grace in the heart. The older Paul grows the more conscious he becomes of God's merciful forgiveness of his many enormous sins. The first two terms deal with the spiritual process, while *eirene* is the ordinary greeting, wishing one health and happiness.

Two Specific Missions of Timothy: to Correct Legalism and Point Out the Moral Function of the Law (1:3-11)

³ As I begged you to do when I was on my way to Macedonia, I still beg you to stay on in Ephesus to warn certain teachers to ⁴ stop devoting themselves to myths and never-ending pedigrees, for such things lead to controversies rather than stimulate our trusteeship to God through faith. ⁵ But the aim of your instruction is to be love that flows out of a pure heart, a good conscience, and a sincere faith. ⁶ Some people have stepped aside from these things and turned to fruitless talking. ⁷ They want to be teachers of the law, although they do not understand the words they use or the things about which they make such confident assertions.

⁸ Indeed, I know that the law is an excellent thing, if a man makes a lawful use of it; ⁹ that is, if he understands that law is not enacted for upright people but for the lawless and disorderly, the godless and sinful, the ignorant and profane, people who kill their fathers or mothers, murderers, ¹⁰ the immoral, men who practice sodomy, men who make other men their slaves, liars, perjurers, or anything else that is contrary to sound teaching, ¹¹ as measured by the glorious good news of the blessed God, with which I have been entrusted.

Key words and phrases Verse 3. "Not to teach any different doctrine." After the Jerusalem Conference and Paul and Barnabas, on the one hand, and Peter and James, on the other, came to an agreement (Gal. 1:11-24); the good news had slightly crystallized and it was understood that all believers, Gentiles or Jews, had a sort of common faith—certainly as to God's character, who the Christ is, how to be saved by faith apart from works, the nature of the kingdom and the Church, demands of Christian living, and so on.

So teachers must not teach any different doctrine. The good news was recognized as having a common mold in which it was cast. Especially must myths be rejected. It comes from a Greek word which means *word*. At first it means something just verbal with no reality. Applied to stories without historic basis. "Unending pedigrees." Perhaps alluding to the emanations in the Gnostic system. All these fanciful ideas generate controversies and do not stimulate our loyalty to God by faith. These false teachers, in the main, seem to be Gentiles, though a small percentage of Judaizers (at least there is some legalism with a false slant).

Verses 5-7. Love is the true motive to obedience to law. "Love out of a pure heart." Was Paul acquainted with the Sermon on the Mount? "Blessed are the pure in heart." "A good conscience." Paul is not analyzing the personality. Heart and conscience likely overlap, if we take into consideration the Jewish view of heart; in some sense a knowing organ, if the knowledge is true ethically. And the word conscience has the word know as its chief component part.

Verse 6 merely alludes to these men as certain teachers. He then says they turned to fruitless talking. What a volume is expressed in these words—fruitless talking! Just talking but doing nothing! Just talking but saying nothing! If we bring forth fruit we must do something!

Verses 7, 8. These teachers are placed on the lowest level by Paul. They desired to be teachers, but they neither knew the things which they were trying to teach nor did they understand the words they used to explain the teaching. "Ignoramuses." Ignoramuses in the top story of the profession of teaching. This is true of most false teachers. If they had a clear understanding of the doctrine at issue, they would not be false teachers.

Verses 8-11. In these lines he shows that the real function of law is negative—to restrain people from sinning. "Not for the righteous," but for "the lawless and disorderly"—for lawbreakers. "For the ungodly and sinners, the unholy and profane" (all these special sinners against God). The remainder are guilty of social sins, sins against our fellow men, some of the most heinous sinners in the world—killers of fathers or mothers, murderers, sodomites, guilty of burning out in sex passion, male for male, forsaking the natural use of the female (see Rom. 1:27). Even women (females) did so (Rom. 1:26). "Made slaves of their fellowmen; liars, perjurers." If Paul wrote Romans 1, could he not write I Timothy 1?

All other sins are included in the expression, "and whatever else is contrary to sound doctrine," as "measured by the glorious good news of the blessed [happy] God." With this phrase he makes a net that catches every false doctrine. If anything taught is not in accordance with "the glorious good news of the happy God," it is ranked with the worst sins of the race.

Paul's Conversion an Example of Saving Grace for the Foremost Sinner (1:12-17)

¹² I am always thanking Christ Jesus our Lord who has given me strength for it, for thinking me trustworthy and putting me into the ministry, ¹³ though I once used to abuse, persecute, and insult Him. But mercy was shown me by Him, because I did it in ignorance and unbelief, ¹⁴ and the spiritual blessing of our Lord in increasing floods has come upon me, accompanied by faith and love inspired by union with Christ Jesus. ¹⁵ It is a saying to be trusted and deserves our fullest acceptance, that Christ Jesus came into the world to save sinners; and I am the foremost of them. ¹⁶ Yet, mercy was shown me for the very purpose that in my case as the foremost of sinners Jesus might display His perfect patience, to make me an example to those who in the future might believe on Him to obtain eternal life. ¹⁷ To the King eternal, immortal, invisible, the only God, be honor and glory forever and ever! Amen.

Key words and phrases. Verses 12-13. He never ceases to be thankful to Christ Jesus for forgiving his persecutions of His people, for he now feels he was really persecuting Christ. His ignorance and unbelief in Jesus at that time do not condone his sins. He changed his mind about Jesus and He showed him mercy, although the foremost among sinners.

Verse 14 has a beautiful thought expressed in the Greek words: "The unmerited favor of our Lord overflowed for me with the faith and love inspired by union with Christ." Grace overflowed and Christ saved the foremost sinner of that age.

Verse 15, 16. Paul feels that this one example of his being saved as the object of Christ's patient mercy, in spite of being the foremost sinner of his age, is sufficient to make true the saying that Christ came into the world to save sinners.

Verse 17. A charge and warning to Timothy. "Prophetic utterances," referring to those messages given Timothy by Paul and the elders when they set him apart to the ministry and to missions

(Acts 16:1-5). "Fight the good fight of faith." To be a positive leader for Christ one must fight. It is a good warfare because it fights for truth, for Christ and His kingdom, for lost souls, and for the edification of believers. "By holding on to faith and a good conscience." Subjective faith; a conscience is good when it follows the will of God. Paul's conscience was not good while he was persecuting Christ and His followers. Observe, we must successfully wage the good warfare "by conquering faith" and with a good conscience. Observe further that Hymenaeus and Alexander ceased to be conscientious when they forsook faith. It is possible that Paul is using the word in its double sense, objective as well as subjective. That is, Hymenaeus and Alexander turned aside from conscience because they gave up the faith, the elementary doctrines of the good news. "Alexander the coppersmith did me great harm" (II Tim. 4:14). Possibly the same man. Both Hymenaeus and Alexander were false teachers and strenuously opposed Paul's teaching—Alexander being the more pugnacious.

EXHORTATION TO PRAYER AND PUBLIC WORSHIP

Chapter II

PUBLIC PRAYERS FOR ALL MEN LED BY CHRISTIAN MEN (2:1-8)

First of all, then, I urge that entreaties, prayers, and thanksgiving be offered for all men, ² for kings and all who are in authority, so that we may lead peaceful, quiet lives in perfect piety and seriousness. ³ This is the right thing to do and it pleases God our Saviour, ⁴ who is ever willing for all mankind to be saved and to come to an increasing knowledge of the truth. ⁵ For there is but one God and one intermediary between God and men, the man Christ Jesus ⁶ who gave Himself as a ransom for all, a fact that was testified to at the proper time, ⁷ and for which purpose I was appointed a preacher and an apostle—I am telling the truth, I am not lying,—a teacher of the heathen in the realm of faith and truth.

⁸ So I want the men everywhere to offer prayer, lifting to heaven holy hands which are kept unstained by anger and dissensions.

Verse 1. "First of all." This may mean first in order of presentation, but it is likely first in importance. Prayer lies right at the threshold of the Christian life; it lies at the door of each day. Christians must pray for all men. All races, all nations, all classes, all individuals. But especially for kings (v. 2) and for all who are in high position. Would not Paul have prayer offered for the poor and needy, the sick and suffering? Of course, but environment demands the other way around. Nero is on the throne—or soon will be—and Christians must now rule the world by way of the throne of grace. God can change the hearts and lives of kings, and that means better government for Christians to "lead peaceful, quiet lives in perfect piety and seriousness." If the king is a good Christian, all Christians in his kingdom have a better opportunity to live better and more influential lives.

"Supplications." Earnest pleadings for God's mercy for self and others, emphatically for self. "Prayers." The general term including all phases of prayer. "Intercessions." For others alone. "Thanksgiving," for self and others. How comprehensive these prayers must be!

Verse 3. Universal prayer is good. Good in spirit and brings good results. It is acceptable to God. He loves all men. He loves even wicked kings like Nero.

Verse 4. "One God who desires all mankind to be saved." This is not contrary to the election taught in Romans 11, and not contrary to Romans 9:23, "vessels of wrath made for destruction." See our notes on this passage. As Paul sees it, Christ died for all, and so all might be saved, if they accepted God's simple condition. God not only loves all but He desires that all be saved.

Verse 5. "One God, one Mediator." Is he meaning the Father as "the one God"? Or, does he think of the Father, the Son, and the Spirit as one God? The "one God," to Paul, includes the Father, the Son, and the Spirit. See his benediction (II Cor. 13:14, etc). But in this letter to Timothy he is stressing the Father and the Son, especially the Son as intermediary between God and men. If the Son and the Spirit are Deity, there is just as much necessity for atonement to be made with the Son and the Spirit as with the Father. So one God is the Triune God, three Persons, one in essence, purpose, and redemptive aim. Christ is the intermediary between the Deity (the shocked Deity in the Godhead) and men.

Christ is all the Intermediary we need; all we have. He has made it right for the Deity to forgive the trusting sinner. In this way each person in the Deity is Saviour: the Father calls and forgives; the Son forgives and selects for service; the Spirit regenerates and seals as children of God. What a grand display of co-operation in the Deity of the "One God!"

Verses 5-6. "One intermediary . . . the man Christ Jesus." Every word here is packed with theological and christological meaning. Paul teaches one Intermediary between God and men. And that Intermediary is the man Christ Jesus. Is not the God Christ Jesus also associated with this high office of bringing about reconciliation between the Deity and His creature man? The Son of God must become a man in order to understand and sympathize with sinful, suffering men. He knew, as a man, all about our temptations, although He never yielded to those temptations. He was Deity at first, then He became a man (II Cor. 8:9). While in human flesh He gave Himself as a ransom for all. This word was used as a military term or as an ordinary economic term. The price paid by an owner who had lost a precious, almost priceless jewel, which had been found by another and sold to a jeweler. The original owner spies his jewel in the jewelry shop, and asks the price of it. When told he informs the shop man that the jewel is his, but was stolen by someone and, it seems, sold to this jeweler. "That's my price. I paid a heavy price for it, and I must have my money back and a good profit." There is another idea in *lutron*, ransom, that of appeasing or propitiating the person to whom the ransom is given. See Thayer, Cremer, Greek lexicons. In the case of God and the ransom paid, God has been offended, His law has been smashed, so Christ is paying a ransom which propitiates the Deity for the insults heaped upon Him. See Romans 3:24-25, where Paul elaborates more than here.

"A ransom for all." We have just been told that God desires all mankind to be saved. In harmony with that desire He gave the Son as a ransom for all. But this does not mean universalism. Only those who accept and comply with God's plan of redemption can be saved. They must come to the knowledge of the truth—repentance and faith at first, later knowledge of the will of God and service to

Him. See Hebrews 9:28; I John 2:2, "for the sins of the whole world." To this, testimony was borne when Christ rose and ascended.

Verse 7. To make known to the Gentiles this plan of God, Paul was appointed "a preacher and apostle . . . a teacher of the Gentiles in faith and truth." *Apostle* emphasizes authority given him to represent Christ. *Teacher* emphasizes the inculcation of known truths to the world; *preacher* emphasizes the public presentation of the truth so as to secure men's acceptance of it and obedience to it. Paul was appointed as apostle to the Gentiles.

Verse 8. "In every place." Prayer is to be offered everywhere—in all places. "Men should pray." Men, not women, are to lead the public prayers for kings, governors, lawmakers, judges, and others. This is not union of church and state. It is the duty of the churches to pray for the officials and leaders of civil affairs. In this way better laws can be made and executed, so that Christians may have peace and quiet.

"Lifting holy hands without anger and dissensions." If the leaders of the public prayers tolerate anger and dissensions, they and their prayers are stained. May not be answered.

PLACE AND DUTIES OF WOMEN IN THE CHURCHES (2:9-15)

⁹ I want the women, on their part, to dress becomingly, that is, modestly and sensibly, not adorning themselves with braided hair and gold or pearls or expensive dresses, ¹⁰ but with good deeds; for this is appropriate for women who profess to be pious.

¹¹ A married woman must learn in quiet and in perfect submission. ¹² I do not permit a married woman to practice teaching or domineering over a husband; she must keep quiet. ¹³ For Adam was formed first, and then Eve; ¹⁴ and it was not Adam who was deceived, but it was the woman who was utterly deceived and fell into transgression. ¹⁵ But women will be saved through motherhood, if they continue to live in faith, love, and purity, blended with good sense.

Key words and phrases. Verses 9, 10. A Christian Woman's Fitting Adornment. Not glittering gold and flashing gems; not expensive dresses and costly supplements for hands and feet, but with good deeds. Handsome is as handsome does. The most beautiful woman is a consecrated Christian woman, simply clad but dressed in taste and utterly unconscious of her beauty or her dress.

There are three chief reasons for this: First, most people whom she goes out to help and serve are poor and not well-dressed. Secondly, gaudy dressing does not show good taste. Thirdly, if the serving Christian woman goes in simple dress, her religion and her Saviour have a better chance to get proper recognition by those she would serve.

Verse 13. See I Corinthians 14:34, 35 for a discussion of woman's work in the church and her relation to a husband. See William's New Testament. The American Standard Version thinks Paul applies this language to all women; Williams translates so as to limit the discussion to wives. Wives must not domineer over their husbands. The teaching forbidden is likely teaching men. He would not forbid a wife or woman to teach boys or girls or other women. Does not this shed light upon Paul's attitude toward women's, or wives', relation to men or husbands, at home or in church?

Verses 13-14. Why he gives man the priority. First, "Adam was formed first." Secondly, not Adam but Eve was deceived by Satan and plunged the whole human race into the gulf of sin and mortality. So as Paul sees it, the priority of man over woman is natural; God made it so by forming Adam first. Eve made herself responsible for the race's sin by allowing Satan to deceive her and lead her to commit the first human sin.

Verse 15. "Woman saved through motherhood." But a tremendous condition is attached: "If they continue to live in faith, love, and purity blended with good sense." But what kind of salvation does Paul mean? Of course, it is not spiritual salvation, including regeneration and justification. She is saved by faith, in this sense, just as a man is. But Paul uses the word in an ethical and social sense, and that is what it means here. See Philippians 2:12, 13. "Work out your own salvation" (A.R.V.); or, better, "keep on working clear down to the finishing point of your salvation." This is evidently the ethical and social phase of our salvation, which is not finished till life is over. We can help God put the finishing touches on by seeking to do His will each day. In this way wives may help God save themselves and society. Faith conditions her spiritual salvation, but love, purity, and good sense make it complete in social and ethical salvation—the building of character, and growing beautiful personalities to grace the world and to adorn the kingdom of Christ.

VI. Qualifications of Pastors, Deacons, and Deaconesses (3:1-13)

This is a saying to be trusted: "Whoever aspires to the office of pastor desires an excellent work." [2] So the pastor must be a man above reproach, must have only one wife, must be temperate, sensible, well-behaved, hospitable, skillful in teaching; [3] not addicted to strong drink, not pugnacious, gentle and not contentious, not avaricious, [4] managing his own house well, with perfect seriousness keeping his children under control [5] (if a man does not know how to manage his own house, how can he take care of a church of God?). [6] He must not be a new convert, or else becoming conceited he may incur the doom the devil met. [7] He must also have a good reputation with outsiders, or else he may incur reproach and fall into the devil's trap.

[8] Deacons, too, must be serious, sincere in their talk, not addicted to strong drink or dishonest gain, [9] but they must continue to hold the open secret of faith with a clear conscience. [10] They, too, should first be tested till approved, and then, if they are found above reproach, they should serve as deacons. [11] The deaconesses too must be serious, not gossips; they must be temperate and perfectly trustworthy. [12] A deacon too must have only one wife, and manage his children and household well. [13] For those who render good service win a good standing for themselves in their faith in Christ Jesus.

Key words and phrases. Verse 1. "The office of pastor." This is the highest office in the local church. The Greek word *episkope* means looking over, overseeing, as a shepherd oversees his flock of sheep, so the local head of a church keeps watch over his flock (church members). It is an excellent work (Williams). We have heard many great ministers affirm that they would rather be a pastor of a local New Testament church than to be President of the United States. Paul feels that it is an office so high in its services and aims that it demands men to fill it who have the purest and noblest characters and the strongest and most varied talents. He proceeds to give the component elements in such a character and personality.

Verse 2. "Above reproach," not exactly blameless, flawless, but so close to it that it is very hard to find anything in his character to reproach him for. So many pastors cannot leap that bar clear-footed. "Must have only one wife." He must not be a bigamist, as many men were in those early times. Even the men of the Old Testament—Abraham, Jacob, and much later David, Solomon and others. Jesus taught monogamy. Paul deems it a requisite for both pastors and deacons (12).

Some versions translate it "married only once." The historical setting and early practices do not warrant this interpretation of "one wife." If the first wife has died, Paul does not say the preacher husband should not marry again. "Temperate." Controlling one-self—in drinks, foods, temper, tongue, passion, etc. "Sensible." Having good horse sense. "Well-behaved." Paul is more concerned about good behavior than about dignity. His actions conform to the best standards. "Hospitable." A choice quality in early Christianity. Hotels and inns were few and hospitality was a necessity to the comfort of travelers. "Skillful in teaching." Most New Testament preaching was didactic. It should be more so today. If the pastor is a skillful teacher he can make the Bible live again before the eyes of his people and make it attractive and desirable to follow.

Verse 3. "Not addicted to strong drink" (Williams). The thought is that the pastor should not be a habitual drinker, moderately or excessively. "Not pugnacious." Not easily yielding to anger and actually fighting with his fists. But "gentle and not contentious." The two ideas are equal to each other. Gentle means self-controlled and so not contentious. "No lover of money." Either millions or thousands. Love of money dries up one's spiritual nature; by degrees at first, but finally dries it up, as the hot winds dry up the branch.

Verses 4-5. "He must manage his household and have his children under control." If he cannot do this, he cannot manage a local church.

Verses 6-7. "Not a recent convert . . . a good reputation with outsiders." Why? If too recently converted he might become conceited—think too much of himself—and incur the doom of the Devil (be cast out). If no reputation with outsiders (non-Christians) he might incur reproach and fall into the snare the Devil sets for such preachers.

Verses 8-13. Deacons and deaconesses. "Deacons must be serious." To them life is purposeful and they must live for a wise and good purpose. If full of humor it must be restrained to serve serious purposes—the aims of redeemed men, winning the lost and doing good to all. "Not double tonged"—truthful. "Not given to much wine" (A.R.V.); "not addicted to strong drink" (Williams). Two expressions mean almost the same thing, as strong drink is more intoxicating than wine. "Not addicted to dishonest gain." Must not love money so much as to seek it dishonestly. Be on the square in business. "Must hold the mystery of the faith [basic doctrines] with a clear conscience." Must conscientiously believe the basic doctrines of the good news. "Mystery of the faith." As explained in Romans and elsewhere, mystery means a once-concealed truth now openly known by revelation. "Let them first be tested; if found blameless, let them serve as deacons." Blameless does not mean perfect but so near it that it is hard to pick flaws in their characters and blame them for something.

Verse 11 is a battleground. The King James Version translates, "The women likewise must be serious, no slanderers," etc. Many modern versions translate "deaconesses." We think it should be "deaconesses." "Must be serious." Like the male deacons, they must be calm judges of life's real aims and face its problems with grim purpose, not aimless and flippant with life's opportunities. See Romans 16:1 for Phoebe the deaconess. "Not gossips. Temperate." Self-controlled as to temper, tongue, foods, drinks, etc. "Faithful, in all things." Faithfulness placed at the top of all the virtues.

"Have only one wife." This may mean that a pastor should not re-marry, if his wife dies. But see Romans 7:1-3. "A deacon too must have only one wife" (Williams). If a woman may re-marry, surely a man may under the same circumstances. So Paul is likely warning against plurality of wives so common in those times. This was common even among Jews. The same requirement is made of deacons as of pastors in managing their homes and keeping their children under control. The deacon is a helper to the pastor in administration, so should be a good administrator at home before he is put into a position demanding it in the church. Success as a deacon has two results, one on the public: gives the successful deacon good standing with other churches; gives him "great confidence in the faith which is in Christ Jesus." He develops in faith and spiritual living.

Two Specific Purposes: To Announce His Visit and Encourage Timothy (3:14-16)
The Letter

Key words and phrases. Verses 14-15a. Two purposes of writing are given: a) To announce a forthcoming visit of the apostle. If the visit is delayed, if unforeseen causes prevent his coming soon, b) he aims to give information how people ought to conduct themselves in the house of God. This letter deals specifically with church affairs. Timothy was likely (Eusebius) pastor of the church at Ephesus in the early years of his stay there, but later became a sort of superintendent of missions for the whole province of Asia (Ephesus the capital).

Verse 15b. "The house of God." The word house also means home. Perhaps Paul is thinking of that holy and heavenly relation between God and His spiritual children. The church is God's earthly home with His spiritual children on earth. The word means called out; the thought is that God calls His people out from among the world and sets them apart as His own children. He lives with them. He walks with them. They constitute His church, His separated ones.

The word has two uses as referring to God's people on earth: a) A local body of believers in Christ united for worship and work. Worship is primary. It gives power to go to work in the kingdom. Worship includes reading the Scriptures and preaching from them, praying and singing praise to God. This furnishes opportunity for fellowship with one another, as well as giving spiritual touch with God and thus enduing them with power from on high.

Religious work was undoubtedly a primary purpose of the Early Church—teaching, preaching, winning the lost among them, giving their means to help the helpless and otherwise promote the work of the church. Even the women became great workers in early churches, in spite of the prejudice against them in social life. See Romans 16:1, the case of Phoebe, the deaconess. See Philippians 4:2, 3: "Help those women, for they labored side by side with me in the gospel." See Acts 13:1-3: the church at Antioch had a missionary spirit and sent out the first foreign missionaries.

b) The word church is also used in an institutional sense. In an abstract sense it is used, just as state, home, school are used. The state deals with political and civic matters, the school deals with education of the children, and the home deals with the early training of the child preparing him for citizenship and for membership in the church (partially). The latter is imperfectly done even in Christian homes. So the word church has this general sense. The church deals with the religious and spiritual life and problems of the people.

As an institution the church is "the pillar and foundation of the truth" (Williams). "The pillar and stay of the truth" (A.R.V.). The word bulwark puts a supreme emphasis on the defensive as the chief mission of the church. This is not the case. The chief function of the church is to proclaim the truth until the knowledge of the Lord covers the earth as the waters cover the sea. The word pillar corresponds to underpinning in modern architecture; the pillar rests on the general foundation. Christ is the foundation (I Cor. 3:11).

Verse 16. The Great Wonders of Christianity. In very early times these were succinctly packed into a six line hymn. We know nothing as to who wrote it or where it was first sung. Perhaps in some great Christian center, Antioch or Ephesus or Corinth or Rome or Philippi. Likely the hymn grew slowly for years before it reached the form we now have. However that may be, it puts in a nutshell the six basic doctrines of our religion.

a) The incarnation. God is a great pedagogue. He knew we could learn vastly more about God if He took on a human form, "became flesh" (John 1:14). So the pre-existent Son became a human Baby, miraculously born of a virgin. He lived a natural life till He was thirty years old. Then He came to John to be baptized; then He began His public ministry. He called the apostles to "be with Him," and taught them, committing to them His gospel to transmit to the world and the future centuries. No other way of introducing Him could have been so impressive and effective.

b) The vindication of the Spirit. The Holy Spirit came down at Pentecost, as He said, and proved Him to be all He had said of Himself before His crucifixion. His mission to earth was vindicated by the Spirit's conviction and conversion of three thousand on the day of Pentecost. For nineteen hundred years the Spirit has been vindicating Him by regenerating thousands of souls.

c) Seen by angels. Possibly at His baptism, His transfiguration, at His resurrection (Luke 24:23). Possibly at other times. All this is given to prove the certainty of the reality of His personality and His existence in the incarnate state.

d) Proclaimed among the nations. Before He finished His earthly career and ascended to the Father, He had been proclaimed to the Syrians, the Greeks, the Romans, the Phoenicians, the Samaritans, the Ethiopians, not to mention the list named who had the gospel preached to them on the day of Pentecost (Acts 2:8, ff). In other words, Christianity was recognized as a missionary religion, and that from the beginning. The Book of Acts is a history of missions in the early churches. Christ Himself was the first great missionary (I Tim. 1:15). Philip (Acts 8); Barnabas and Paul (Acts 13 ff); Paul and Silas, all foreign missionaries.

e) Trusted as Saviour. The early hymn emphasized the power of the good news as "the power of God" (Rom. 1:16) to save both Jews and Gentiles.

f) In triumph He ascended to the throne of glory at the Father's right hand. "Taken up in glory," or "Taken up to glory." The preposition *en* may have the double use of *en* and *eis*, motion to and rest in a place (Robertson, *Grammar*). The six are an outline of basic spiritual truths, not all truth, physical, civic, philosophical, etc.

Chapter IV

WARNING AGAINST HERESIES (4:1-5)

Now the Spirit distinctly declares that in later times some will turn away from the faith, because they continuously give their attention to deceiving spirits and the things that demons teach

² through the pretensions of false teachers, men with seared consciences, ³ who forbid people to marry and teach them to abstain
from certain sorts of food which God created for the grateful enjoyment of those who have faith and a clear knowledge of the
truth. ⁴ For everything in God's creation is good, and nothing is to
be refused, provided it is accepted with thanksgiving; ⁵ for in this
way it is consecrated by the word of God and prayer.

Key words and phrases. Verses 1-2. The Spirit has warned the
minister that "some will turn away from the faith." *Faith* here used
in the objective sense, the true doctrines to be accepted. "They turn
away"; reject these doctrines. "Deceitful spirits . . . doctrines of
demons" (A.R.V.). Better translated, "The things the demons teach
through the pretensions of false teachers." That is, demons originate
the false doctrines; false teachers are their human instruments to
spread them. "Men with seared consciences." The false teachers
have had their consciences burned with the white hot iron of doubt,
and so they cannot distinguish between the true and the false
doctrines.

Verse 3. "Who forbid people to marry and teach them to abstain
from certain sorts of food." The legalists and Gnostics were usually
ascetic in living habits. Paul feels that God created all edible objects
in nature for His people to enjoy; that is, to use for promoting
strength and health.

Verses 4-5. "Everything in God's creation is good." That is,
there is no religious uncleanness attached to anything in nature per
se. All edible objects may be eaten if accepted with thanksgiving,
for "in this way it is consecrated by the word of God and prayer"
(see John 17:17). Consecrate means to set apart to God's special
service, also with the idea of being separated from the world. "And
prayer." Prayer enlists the believer in the process of consecration,
while the Word of God is the divine agent to secure it.

TIMOTHY TO REBUKE THESE ERRORS AND TRAIN HIMSELF FOR
PURE LIVING AND PATIENT PREACHING AND TEACHING (4:6-16)

⁶ If you continue to put these things before the brothers, you
will be a good minister of Christ Jesus, ever feeding your own
soul on the truths of the faith and of the fine teaching which you

have followed. ⁷ But make it your habit to let worldly and old women's stories alone. Continue training yourself for the religious life. ⁸ Physical training, indeed, is of some service, but religion is of service for everything, for it contains a promise for the present life as well as the future. ⁹ This is a saying to be trusted and deserves to be accepted by all. ¹⁰ To this end we are toiling and struggling, because we have fixed our hope on the living God, who is the Saviour of all mankind, especially of believers.

¹¹ Continue to give these orders and to teach these truths. ¹² Let no one think little of you because you are young, but always set an example for believers, in speech, conduct, love, faith, and purity. ¹³ Until I come, devote yourself to the public reading of the Scriptures, and to preaching and teaching. ¹⁴ Stop neglecting the gift you received, which was given you through prophetic utterance when the elders laid their hands upon you. ¹⁵ Continue cultivating these things; be devoted to them, so that everybody will see your progress. ¹⁶ Make it your habit to pay close attention to yourself and your teaching. Persevere in these things, for if you do you will save both yourself and those who listen to you.

Key words and phrases. Verse 6. "A good minister of Christ Jesus." What must a pastor do in order to be a good minister of Christ Jesus? "If you continue to put these things before the brothers." If he continues to warn his people of the false views of truth and life and continuously seeks to keep them following in the footsteps of the Master and holding tenaciously to the teachings of the faith; the basic truths of Christ's person and work of atonement and salvation; and the life of service and sacrifice. "Feeding your own soul on the truths of the faith." The preacher must feed his own soul, if he would be a good minister. If he has applied the truths he preaches to his own soul, and they work, and make him strong and a good servant of the Lord, he may know that it will also feed the sheep.

Verse 7. "Have nothing to do with godless and silly old women's sayings" (myths). The atmosphere, in ancient times, was saturated with such silly things. To some people they sounded like philosophy, and they fell for them. Paul told the young minister to let them alone. Keep the people's minds on the great teachings of the good news.

Verses 7b-8. Religious training versus physical training. "Continue training yourself for the religious life [literally, in godliness]." Good instruction for all young ministers; good for all Christians. All Christians should be members of Training Unions and faithfully continue to train. "For it [godliness, or religious training] contains a promise for the present life as well as the future." The spiritual exercise to which Paul submitted himself for over a quarter of a century made him a colossal saint in Heaven. Heaven is sweeter now to him, and the future life with its enrichments of his soul which he obtained from his continuous spiritual exercises, is larger and more lustrous.

Verse 9. "The saying is sure and worthy of full acceptance." The saying as to the value of godliness, or religious training—valuable here and hereafter. Give it full credence.

Verse 10. "The living God, who is the Saviour of all men." He reached this lofty thought by way of saying, "We have set our hope on the living God." Because God is the object of substantial and eternal hope, he inspired Paul to think of the universal plan of salvation God has prepared in and by His Son, Christ Jesus. He is not asserting that God actually saves all men. He desires to. He loves the world (John 3:16); that is, He loves the last dark-skinned African and the last sin-shriveled soul on the isles of the Pacific. He is big enough to save all; His heart is big enough to save all men, if they would bow to Christ Jesus as the Saviour.

Verses 11, 12. Teaching by example too. The apostle tells Timothy not only to teach by word of mouth but also by example. Because he was a young man some would make little of his youth, if he did not live above reproach and live a completely exemplary life. So Paul specifies five points for him to consider: "Speech, conduct, love, faith, and purity." Two of these are basic doctrines: Love and faith. There is no ministerial activity and success without faith and love. Faith keeps the young minister lashed to the Redeemer, keeps him filled with the Holy Spirit, so that he possesses power from on high. Love must be the motive back of all the minister's movements—love to God, to the Bible and its truth, to the church and all its members, to the lost and all the nations. To his enemies (if he has any); yea, even to enemy nations. This was the spirit

of the Master and of Stephen. The other three are ethical qualities—speech, conduct, purity. Speech must be chaste and considerate, not ever spotted with the world. Conduct must be measured
by the highest standards, the Golden Rule and Jesus Himself.
Purity must start in the heart. "Blessed are the pure in heart."
Timothy in all five of these spheres of living must set an example
for believers in Ephesus and Asia. The preacher must walk the
rope while all the world looks on.

Verse 13. Timothy's three principal tasks: "public reading of
the Scriptures, preaching, and teaching." The masses did not have
the Scriptures in their homes, so the pastor must be reader of the
Scriptures to and for his people. A primary duty of pastor. Preaching from the Scriptures (as Peter did on Pentecost, Acts 2). Preaching is the public proclamation of the Word, teaching is unfolding it
so as to bring out the exact meaning, without trying to enforce it in
conduct (as preaching does).

Verse 14. The minister's gift must not be neglected. "Which
was given you when the elders laid their hands upon you." The
basis of the gift was in Timothy before these hands were laid upon
him; but that time was the climactic moment when the prophetic
utterance of the elders brought the gift to its climax. "Stop neglecting the gift" (Williams). Before the warning he was neglecting
it. Stop, says the apostle. Too much at stake. Oh, ministers everywhere, heed the voice of the apostle!

Verse 15. "Practice these duties." Public reading of the Scriptures, preaching, and teaching. "So that all may see your progress."
The pastor is like the flag of the United States, on top of a flag
pole for everybody to see. He should be so living and acting that
they may see his progress. Yes, the minister is the great example
of progress for all his people—progress in consecrated character and
life, progress in church work and kingdom movements (education
and missions). He can have progress if he practices these things.
That is, the three things mentioned in verse 13.

Verse 16. "Take heed to yourself and your teaching." Of the
highest importance is keeping watch over self—physical, mental,
social, moral, spiritual. First of all the pastor is pastor of Self;
he must keep watch over himself, keep clean, keep safe. Then he

must guard his teaching (doctrine). He must walk the Bible rope, though narrow. Another thrust at false teachings.

Some have stumbled over these last words. "For by so doing you will save both yourself and your hearers." Does the pastor save himself? No, Christ saves him in the sense that his sins are forgiven and he is regenerated by the Spirit. Saved like any of his people. But socially and morally he saves himself. He keeps growing a finer personality, he keeps on making progress in using his gift. This is the salvation all should "work down to the finishing point of salvation" (Phil. 2:12, 13).

Chapter V

THE CHURCH'S ATTITUDE TOWARD THE DIFFERENT CLASSES IN THE CHURCH: THE YOUNG, THE OLD, WIDOWS, AND ELDERS, OR PASTORS

A GENERAL DISCUSSION (5:1-8)

Never reprove an older man, but always appeal to him as a father. Treat younger men like brothers, ² older women like mothers, younger women like sisters, with perfect purity. ³ Always care for widows who are really dependent. ⁴ But if a widow has children or grandchildren, they must first learn to practice piety in the treatment of their own families, and to pay the debt they owe their parents or grandparents, for this is acceptable to God. ⁵ But a woman who is really a widow and lives alone has fixed her hope on God, and night and day devotes herself to prayers and entreaties, ⁶ while a widow who gives herself up to luxury is really dead though still alive. ⁷ Continue to give these directions so that the people may be without reproach. ⁸ Whoever fails to provide for his own relatives, and especially for those of his immediate family, has disowned the faith and is worse than an unbeliever.

Key words and phrases. Verses 1, 2. General social relations. There is no difficult exegesis in this chapter; just good practical sense is all that needs to be applied to understand how to treat each class in the church. Treat the older men as fathers and the older women as mothers—in love and the deepest respect. Treat the younger men as brothers and the younger women as sisters, taking care not to let the sex motive enter in association with younger women.

Verses 3-8. Christian sons and daughters to care for their own widows. A widow over sixty years of age, who led a devoted Christian life with only one husband (at a time), who has been devoted to prayers, has fixed her hope on God, is a real widow and worthy of a place on the church charity roll. Any son or daughter, grandson or granddaughter, who fails to care for his or her own widowed mother or grandmother, has disowned the faith (the loving genius of Christianity) and is worse than an unbeliever. Not infidel. Timothy is again urged to give these orders and instructions, so that "the people may be without reproach."

DEVOTED, DEPENDENT WIDOWS TO BE CARED FOR BY THE CHURCH (5:9-16)

⁹ No widow under sixty years of age should be put on this roll. A widow must have had but one husband, ¹⁰ must have a reputation for doing good deeds, as bringing up children, being hospitable to strangers, washing the feet of God's people, helping people in distress, or devoting herself to any sort of doing good.

¹¹ But you, as a man of God, must be fleeing always from these things; you must constantly strive for uprightness, godliness, faith, love, steadfastness, gentleness. ¹² Keep up the good fight for the faith. Keep your hold on eternal life, to which God called you, when before many witnesses you made the good profession of faith. ¹³ Before God who preserves the life of all His creatures and before Christ Jesus who in testifying before Pontius Pilate made His good profession, I solemnly charge you ¹⁴ to keep His command stainless and irreproachable until the appearance of our Lord Jesus Christ, ¹⁵ which will be brought about in His own time by the blessed, only Sovereign, the King of kings, the Lord of lords, ¹⁶ who alone possesses immortality and dwells in unapproachable light, whom no man has ever seen or can see. To Him be honor and eternal dominion. Amen.

Key words and phrases. Verse 9. Paul charges that no one under sixty years of age should be enrolled on the widow charity list. And only one who has been "the wife of one man" (A.R.V.). Better, "Who has had but one husband" (Williams). That is, who has had only one husband at a time. See Romans 7:1 f, where Paul sanctions the second marriage by a wife whose husband is dead.

Verse 10. She must have been a doer of good deeds, hospitable, caring for the sick and afflicted, also has reared a family of children.

Verses 11-15. Urges younger widows to marry and rear children. They must not burden the church's charity roll. They are liable to be tempted to indulge the lower nature and give occasion for censure by outsiders. So the best thing for these younger, vivacious widows is to marry and serve the Lord by rearing good Christian children. They are liable to break the church vow they made. Some have already turned aside to follow Satan—in some well-known sin, likely. Compare Paul's teaching here about women's marrying with what he writes in I Corinthians 7. There is no contradiction. The environments in Corinth and Ephesus are different.

Verse 16. He again urges Christian sons and daughters to care for their own widowed relatives so that the church may be free to help all the really dependent widows. This is heavenly wisdom for all time in solving these social problems in the church.

How to Deal with Delinquent Pastors; Health Charge to Timothy; General Truth (5:17-25)

17 Elders who do their duties well should be considered as deserving twice the salary they get, especially those who keep on toiling in preaching and teaching. 18 For the Scripture says, "You must not muzzle an ox when he is treading out the grain," and, "The workman deserves his pay." 19 Make it a rule not to consider a charge preferred against an elder, unless it is supported by two or three witnesses. 20 Those who are guilty reprove in public, so that others may be warned. 21 I solemnly charge you before God and Christ Jesus and the chosen angels, to carry out these instructions without prejudice and with perfect impartiality. 22 Make it a rule not to ordain anyone in haste and not to be responsible for the sins of others; keep yourself pure. 23 Stop drinking water only, but take a little wine to strengthen your stomach and relieve its frequent attacks. 24 Some men's sins are very evident and clearly lead them on to judgment, but the sins of others lag behind. 25 Good deeds, too, are usually very evident, and if they are not, they cannot be completely concealed.

Key words and phrases. Verses 17, 18. A church should recognize the excellent service rendered by an elder—here used for pastor, who is said to be ruling well. The honor given him should be double. Perhaps the salary should be doubled, if not increased considerably, to show the church's appreciation of him and his work. An appreciated preacher works better and he is more capable of rendering the best service. Paul quotes Deuteronomy 25:4 to give scriptural ground for thus treating the elder (pastor). He quotes it again in I Corinthians 9:9. He also quotes the words of Jesus, afterward recorded in the Gospel of Matthew. "The workman deserves his pay."

Verse 19. "Do not consider a charge against an elder [pastor], unless it is supported by two or three witnesses." This is following the old Jewish law; a safe law to protect an official.

Verse 20. "Those who are guilty reprove before them all, so that others may be warned." This is hard on the culprit, but "The way of the transgressor is hard." Criminal law has been operated on this principle for centuries.

Verse 21. He puts Timothy under a most solemn oath—before God and Christ Jesus and the elect angels—to "keep these rules." And "without partiality."

Verse 22. Warns him not to be "hasty in setting aside a man to the ministry." If he does he is liable to "participate in another man's sins [have to suffer for sins done by such a man]." Following this rule he will "keep himself pure"—free from other men's sins.

Verse 23. Advises him "to take a little wine" to relieve his stomach when it so frequently suffers attacks. Notice, it is a "little." We must remember that medicine was in its infancy at that time, and a little wine was the best people could do as a simple remedy for small ailments. This is no encouragement to drinking intoxicating liquors.

Verses 24-25. A general statement, relating to dealing with officials who have sinned. The sins of some "lag behind . . . appear later." You have to wait, sometimes, to see if a man is really sinning; so we must not be hasty in setting men apart to the ministry. The same rule holds in regard to good deeds. Sometimes you must wait to see if a man is really doing good, or playing the hypocrite.

So to pass a sane judgment on a bad man or a good man, you must wait awhile.

XI. FINAL EXHORTATIONS: TO SERVANTS; AS TO FALSE TEACHINGS; WARNING AGAINST RICHES; HOW A CHRISTIAN MAY USE RICHES FOR GOOD (Chapter 6)

DUTIES OF SLAVES TO THEIR MASTERS (6:1, 2)

All who are under the yoke of slavery must esteem their masters to be deserving the highest respect, so that the name of God and our teaching may not be abused. 2 Those who have Christian masters must not pay them less respect because they are brothers; they must serve them all the better, because those who get the benefit of their service are believers and so are dear to them.

These are the things that you must continue to teach and urge them to do.

Key words and phrases. Verse 1. The word yoke was applied to a slave, as well as an ox. Sometimes slaves in their drudgery as slaves were not treated much better than the ox. The word yoke was also used by Jesus to connote the relation between a pupil and his teacher. (See Matt. 11:29, 30.)

Paul urges two reasons for slaves rendering faithful service to their masters, though not Christians and maybe not kind to their slaves: a) So that the name of God may not be defamed; b) So that the accepted Christian doctrines may not be defamed. That is, the slave will be adorning the doctrines of Christ (Titus 2:10).

Verse 2. If the masters are Christians, their slaves must serve them all the better, because their masters are believers and beloved by their slaves. This is beautiful Christian idealism as taught by Paul. The two classes farthest apart in human society must love each other—"be dear to each other." Christian brotherhood magnified as in Philemon. See our notes on Ephesians 6:5-8, where Paul has more to say on the relation of slaves and masters. Our comments are more copious.

GODLINESS (TRUE RELIGION) WITH CONTENTMENT IS GREAT GAIN (6:3-10)

3 If anyone teaches different doctrines and refuses to agree with

the wholesome messages of our Lord Jesus Christ, the teaching that is in accordance with true religion, ⁴ he is a conceited ignoramus with a morbid appetite for discussions and controversies which lead to envy, quarreling, abuse, base suspicions, ⁵ and perpetual friction between people who are depraved in mind and deprived of truth, who imagine that religion is only a means of gain. ⁶ Now the fact is, religion with contentment is a means of great gain. ⁷ For we bring nothing into the world and surely we can take nothing out of it. ⁸ If we have food and clothes we will be satisfied. ⁹ But men who keep planning to get rich fall into temptations and snares and many foolish, hurtful desires which plunge people into destruction and ruin. ¹⁰ For the love of money is the root of all sorts of evil, and some men in reaching after riches have wandered from the faith and pierced their hearts with many a pang.

Key words and phrases. Verses 3-5. False teachers characterized. "Teach different doctrines." After the Jerusalem conference (Acts 15) there was a sort of mold into which Christian doctrines were cast. They must agree "with the sound words of our Lord Jesus Christ and the teaching which accords with godliness." We see that the teaching of Jesus became the absolute standard of true teaching (doctrine). If a teacher rejected this standard and followed his own thought, Paul says he "is a conceited ignoramus with a morbid appetite for discussions and controversies which lead to envy, quarreling, abuse, base suspicions and perpetual friction between people who are depraved in mind and deprived of truth, who imagine that religion is only a means of gain."

In verse 3 we have translated the Greek, "puffed up, knowing nothing," with the vernacular expression, "conceited ignoramus." This is not original with me. I have heard men in mediocre circles of life use the expression to describe a man who is superbly conceited who knows little but thinks he knows it all. That fits these men Paul is describing. Such men have a morbid appetite for discussions and controversies. They are depraved in mind and destitute of truth. Their trouble is both moral and mental. Dr. Scarborough, the noted and successful evangelist, used to say that men of false doctrines usually had loose morals at some point. Paul places the moral state ahead of the intellectual. Perhaps loose morals are the greater cause of the false doctrines held by these men.

"Imagining that godliness is a means of gain." These men are not only immoral in mind but avaricious, greedy for gain and follow religion to secure the gains attached to it. Roughly speaking, being godly is being religious (literally, to try to be like God).

Verses 6-10. True religion is great gain. Paul seizes their phrase and swings it into use. Of course, real godliness, being like God by worshiping and serving Him, is tremendous gain. He does not mean it brings millions of money. But being godly bestows physical, mental, social, moral, and spiritual gain. A man can be healthier by being truly religious; also mentally more vigorous (Paul, Jonathan Edwards, and others). Of course, he is a superior social and moral personality.

Verses 7-9. To pursue riches a dangerous course. Contentment with food and clothes is conducive to a happy and useful life. "But they that are minded to be rich fall into a temptation, and a snare, and many foolish and hurtful lusts, such as drown men in destruction and ruin" (A.R.V.). They are tempted to lie and cheat, to take the short cut to success; tempted to rob the other man, or take small advantages of him which result in robbing him of full justice in the deal. "Into a snare." The Devil is ever setting traps for such men and they walk into them. "Foolish and hurtful desires." The man who has money and wants to make more by the thousands and millions is full of desires, many of which are foolish; many of which are hurtful, to him and his family, and hurtful to the community or country (often). The man who wants to be rich is miserable compared with the man who is contented with his lot.

Verse 10. "The love of money is the root of all sorts of evil." This is the most laconic statement of the power of money over men. Notice, however, it is not money itself that brings so many evils upon human society. It is man's corrupt nature so easily appealed to by money and what it enables a man to do. A good preacher and pastor, a friend of mine, a few years ago, preached on this text and applied it to each one of the Ten Commandments, and showed conclusively from Biblical and practical illustrations how the love of money has broken every single one of the Ten Commandments.

FURTHER CHARGES TO TIMOTHY (6:11-16)

But you as a man of God must always be fleeing from these things; you must constantly strive for uprightness, godliness, faith, love, steadfastness, gentleness. ¹² Keep up the good fight for the faith. Keep your hold on eternal life, to which God called you, when before many witnesses you made the good profession of faith. ¹³ Before God who preserves the life of all His creatures and before Christ Jesus who in testifying before Pontius Pilate made His good profession, I solemnly charge you to ¹⁴ keep His command stainless and irreproachable until the appearance of our Lord Jesus Christ, ¹⁵ which will be brought about in His own time by the blessed, only Sovereign, the King of kings, the Lord of lords, ¹⁶ who alone possesses immortality and dwells in unapproachable light, whom no man has ever seen or can see. To Him be honor and eternal dominion. Amen.

Verse 11. The minister must not allow himself to be entangled in the net of financial embarrassments—must not show himself anxious about his own compensation, increase of salary, or even stickle for his money rights. President Weston (Crozer Seminary) used to say to his ministerial class, "The minister has no rights." He claimed the minister's rights are wrapped up in those of others. He is the champion of everybody but not of himself. "Strive for," or "aim at" uprightness (the quality of being on the square with one's fellowmen); godliness (worshiping and serving God); faith (basic or doctrine quality); love (strongest motive and queen of graces); steadfastness (enduring till one can endure anything); gentleness (self-control). If Timothy attained these qualities, what a man he was!

Verses 12, 13. "Keep up the good fight for the faith." This is undoubtedly the objective meaning of faith. Continue [present] to fight for the basic doctrines of Christianity. This is one of the aged apostle's consuming concerns—to have the young ministers continue to fight for the things he had lived for and championed through persecutions, and now is facing death for the maintenance of and defense of these basic doctrines. "Keep your hold on eternal life." This looks as though he might let it slip out of his hands and lose it. So the anti-Calvinists contend. "Lose it today, regain it tomorrow." That is not what Paul is saying to Timothy. "Keep a tight grip on eternal life," not for fear that you will lose it, but that it may grow bigger to you and in you. The more we put into our religion, the more we shall get out of it. Eternal life is everlasting life; but more, it starts here, at regeneration; and the more we work at it the more we enjoy it here; when we enter the long stretch on eternal life—through the ceaseless ages of future eternity, it will be life indeed; all joy in the very presence of God the Father, the Son, and the Spirit; eternal life is living with the eternal God and enjoying Him now and forever.

Verses 14-16. "Keep His command stainless and irreproachable." He has just appealed to Timothy with the *example of Christ* before Pilate, how firm He stood, and yielded not a hair's breadth (v. 13). So Timothy is to stand firm before all enemies of the good news, before all false teachers; in this way there will be no stain or blot on the command, and thus it will not be worthy of reproach, so "irreproachable." "The blessed, only Sovereign, the King of kings, the Lord of lords, who alone possesses immortality and dwells in unapproachable light, whom no man has ever seen or can see. To Him be honor and eternal dominion. Amen." Is this benediction addressed to the Father only, or to the Son only, or to Them both? Surely the Father is included because he said, "He alone possesses immortality and dwells in unapproachable light." He has just put Timothy under a most solemn oath, in the presence of God "who preserves the life of all His creatures," which undoubtedly refers to the Father. But he goes on to put him in the presence of "Christ Jesus who in testifying before Pontius Pilate made His good confession." In the benediction He is primarily thinking of God the Father, but in his adoration of Christ as King of kings and Lord of lords he unmistakably is ascribing "honor and eternal dominion" to Him, also.

A CHARGE TO THE RICH IN MATERIAL THINGS (6:17-19)

[17] Continue charging the rich in this world to stop being haughty and not to fix their hope on a thing so uncertain as riches, but on God who richly and ceaselessly provides us with everything for our enjoyment; [18] charge them to continue doing good and being rich

in good deeds, open-handed and generous-hearted, ¹⁹ in this way amassing for themselves the riches that forever endure in the life to come, so that at last they may grasp the life that is life indeed.

Key words and phrases. Verse 17. "Not to be haughty." The tendency is for rich men to be haughty. They feel that they have something the other fellows do not have. But the truth is, riches do not make men great. If the rich man masters his riches, and does not allow his riches to master him, they furnish him golden opportunities for doing good, and this makes him a greater man, if he seizes these opportunities. "Set their hope not on uncertain riches but on God who richly and ceaselessly provides us with everything for our enjoyment." Riches in farms and pasture lands are uncertain, for fires and floods may sweep over them without a warning. Riches in bonds and stocks are uncertain, for a rich man at sunrise may be a pauper at sunset. So Paul exhorts Timothy to exhort rich men to be rich in good deeds. Like Dorcas with her needlework, Barnabas with his selling his property and laying the money at the apostles' feet; industrialists who have given millions to missions, Christian colleges, and general benevolences; others who are giving millions to educate young ministers, to support evangelistic campaigns, and for missions around the world. Yea, if we have only one hundred dollars to give, we are starting to be "rich in good deeds."

"Fix our hope on God." If riches are not worthy of having our hope fixed on them, God is supremely worthy, for He "richly and ceaselessly provides us with everything for our enjoyment." He is so good in His providential gifts, which come regularly for our use and enjoyment. Then He is not "uncertain." He is "unchangeable" (see James 1:17). Then He is all-powerful and vastly rich; the owner of all things. These gifts come ceaselessly (expressed by the present of the verb *provide*). "So that at last they may grasp the life that is life indeed." The rich who continue to go good and be rich in good deeds, at last may "grasp the life that is life indeed." That is, by doing good with their riches they are making investments in Heaven's bank which enrich their spiritual life, so that when at last they go up higher to the heavenly stage of life, they can grasp, enter into full possession of, that eternal life which started at regeneration, and has been growing in its riches all the time. It has endured and increased.

Verses 20, 21. The two things uppermost in the apostle's mind are left with Timothy as the last charge. "Guard what has been entrusted to you." What is it? The good news with all its precious doctrines, the faith. He must keep guard over the doctrines of the early churches in Asia. The second charge is to turn away from what is falsely called knowledge. A keen cut at the heart of Gnosticism. They claim to have the knowledge of God and His universe. But it is falsely called knowledge. Timothy has the true knowledge in the faith.

"Grace"—spiritual blessing—be with you and all. You is plural in Greek; so it means Timothy and the churches.

CHRIST'S MISSION TO SAVE SINNERS (I Tim. 1:16)
PAUL'S EXPERIENCE TAUGHT HIM THIS SAYING
WORTHY OF FULL ACCEPTANCE

I. The Grand Person Who Came
  1. "Christ." Means anointed. So kings, prophets, priests
  2. "Jesus." His historical name. Incarnated (John 1:14). To save sinners, the Anointed in Heaven must become man (Gal. 4:4)

II. The Humble Manner of His Coming
  1. As a human Babe (Gal. 4:4; Phil. 2:6-8). "He humbled Himself."
  2. By being tempted in all points as we are (Heb. 4:15)
  3. By being obedient to the death of the cross (Phil. 2:8)

III. The Noble Purpose of His Coming
  1. To save sinners from sin's guilt, power, consequences
  2. To save sinners to divine sonship (Gal. 4:5-7)
  3. To save sinners to service to God and man. Peter, John, Paul, Polycarp, Carey, Judson, Livingstone, and others.

IV. To Save Even the Foremost among Sinners
  1. Paul, Augustine, John Newton, John Bunyan, and others.
  2. Paul not an immoral man. An attractive personality from the external point of view. Zealous for the law of God.

A missionary (before conversion) for legal Judaism (see Phil. 3:4-7).

3. So we judge Paul as deeply religious before converted.

4. An example of Christ's omnipotent power to save even the foremost sinners. Newton's hymn,

> In evil long I took delight,
> Unawed by shame or fear,
> Till a new object struck my sight,
> And stopped my wild career.
>
> I saw One hanging on a tree,
> In agonies and blood,
> Who fixed His languid eyes on me,
> As near His cross I stood.
>
> Sure, never till my latest breath
> Can I forget that look;
> It seemed to charge me with His death,
> Though not a word He spoke.

SERMON OUTLINE FROM I TIMOTHY (2:4-6)

OUR GOD WISHES ALL MEN TO BE SAVED
HE IS THE ONE GOD

I. One God—who is He?

1. The Trinity—the Father, Son, and Holy Spirit
2. One in essence, Deity
3. One in love and redemptive aim. Milton, *Paradise Lost,* has Father, Son, and Spirit holding a council to plan how to defeat Satan. Milton's time, after; Paul's, before, the Fall (Eph. 1:3-10)
4. He desires all men to be saved (John 3:16; Rom. 5:8) His heart as big as His kosmos.

II. "One Mediator, the Man Christ Jesus"

1. Definition: One who intercedes between two hostile parties. God and men at enmity (Rom. 1:30, "haters of God"). Also II Cor. 5:19.
2. Who? The Man Christ Jesus.

    a. Christ the Anointed by the Father. So kings, priests, prophets.

    b. "Jesus," His human name (Matt. 1:21)

  3. "Man." Incarnation necessary (see Gal. 4:4)

III. The Ransom and Reconciliation (6)

  1. Definition: Ransom is the price to release and reclaim a valuable object or distinguished person. E.g., engagement ring lost and now in jewelry store to be ransomed. Huge price. So we.

  2. Christ the Son gave Himself. Greatest price God could pay. Abraham called upon to give his son of promise; figure of "Only begotten Son" (John 3:16). On the cross most horrible death. Bleeding to death.

  3. Gave Himself as a Substitute. Exchange of prisoners illustrates it. See Thayer, *Lexicon, anti, huper,* for, in place of. Damon and Pythias, willing to die for each other, illustrates it.

SERMON OUTLINE (3:16)

THE CHURCH THE PILLAR OF THE TRUTH
PAUL AND EARLY CHURCH POEM (SIX LINES)

I. Christ the Pillar and Foundation of the Church (Matt. 16:18)

  1. Not Peter.

  2. Not Wesley, Calvin or Campbell (see I Cor. 3:11)

II. Christ the Builder of the Church (Matt. 16:18) "I will build."

  1. Lays the foundation with His own death (I Cor. 3:11)

  2. Uses ministers (and others) as builders with Him (I Cor. 3:10) Sir Christopher Wrenn and St. Paul's Cathedral, London

  3. Ministers must be careful to build on Christ and build enduring materials (I Cor. 3:12ff). Eddystone Lighthouse destroyed several times until built on huge, deep, and solid rock.

III. The Church the Pillar of the Truth

  1. The ultimate mission of the Church:

    a. To evangelize the world and win the lost to Christ (John 20:21)

        b. To be God's instrument in establishing the kingdom of God

  2. The immediate mission—to support (pillar) the truth.

        a. Not all truth—not physical, scientific, philosophical, etc.

        b. But spiritual, evangelical truth—ethical and spiritual.

  3. Early outline in early Christian poem (I Tim. 3:16)

        a. Truth of the Incarnation—"He was made visible"

        b. "Vindicated." By the resurrection proved to be Son (Rom. 1:4)

        c. Seen by angels at resurrection (Matt. 28:3-6)

        d. Proclaimed in the world (Roman Empire)

        e. Trusted as Saviour

        f. Taken up to glory (ascension). Early Church creed, all built around Christ, from incarnation to ascension. Resurrection stressed more than death. So Paul. So Acts throughout

IV. Church Organizations to Support the Truth

  1. Sunday School

  2. Training Union or Young People's Societies

  3. Missionary Societies.

The Letter to Titus

INTRODUCTION

TITUS

Titus is not mentioned in Acts. Paul tells us he was a Greek (Gal. 2:3). He was converted under the preaching of Paul (Gal. 2:3). He was living at Antioch in A.D. 50. Paul took him to the Jerusalem conference as an example of a good Greek Christian who had not been circumcised (Gal. 2:1). The conference did not compel him to be circumcised (Acts 15).

Titus was a diplomat. Although Timothy failed to unify the church at Corinth, Titus succeeded (II Cor. 7:5f). Like Paul he never married. He died at ninety-four, still at his post in Crete and was buried at Cortyna.

OCCASION AND DATE OF THE LETTER TO TITUS

Just before his visit to Corinth (his last) Paul remained a short time on the island of Crete helping Titus in the organization of churches there. Titus remained for the task. After going on to Corinth Paul wrote back to Titus not long after writing the first letter to Timothy, likely A.D. 65.

PURPOSE OF THE LETTER TO TITUS

1. To certify to Titus' authority as an apostolic representative.
2. To give further directions to Titus as to the organization of the churches and the character of men selected as pastors.
3. To urge Titus to stand for sound teaching in all the churches and urge the election of men of fine moral character as examples to pure moral living by all Christians.

MAIN TEACHINGS

1. God is the Father and the Saviour.
2. Election and grace are the sources of salvation.
3. Christ is the Saviour who gave Himself to redeem us.
4. The Holy Spirit is the agent of regeneration.
5. We are justified by grace.
6. Pastors of blameless character.

GENERAL OUTLINE

I. Introduction (1:1-4)

II. Titus' Mission on the Island of Crete (1:5-9)
1. To perfect the organization of churches (1:5)
2. To insist upon proper qualifications of pastors (1:6-9)

III. Sins of the Cretans (1:10-16)
1. Unruly, vain talkers, deceivers, false teachers for the sake of gain (1:10-11)
2. Confirmed by the testimony of a Cretan writer (1:12)
3. Titus to reprove them severely for such sins (1:13-16)

IV. Instructions on What Titus Shall Teach (2:1-3:11)
1. Sober living by both old and young, by men and women, by servants and by Titius himself as an example of all (2:1-10)
2. The first and second coming of Christ urged as a motive for such living (2:11-15)
3. Christian citizenship and general benevolence (3:1-8)
4. The factious spirit to be condemned (3:9-11)

V. Conclusion (3:12-15)
1. Personal instructions to Titus about his own movements and those of Zenas and Apollos (3:12-14)
2. Greetings and benediction (3:15)

EXEGESIS
Chapter I

INTRODUCTION (1:1-4)
THE GREETING

Paul, a slave of God, and an apostle of Jesus Christ, to stimulate faith in God's chosen people, and to lead them on to a full knowledge of religious truth, ² in the hope of eternal life which God, who never lies, promised ages ago ³ but at the proper time made known as His message through the message that I preach with which I have been entrusted by the command of God our Saviour; ⁴ to Titus, my genuine child in our common faith: be spiritual blessing and peace from God our Father and Christ Jesus our Saviour.

Key words and phrases. One of the lengthiest salutations. See comments on Galatians 1:1-5; Romans 1:1-7, the longest in the New Testament.

Verse 1. To stimulate faith in God's chosen people and to lead them on to a full knowledge of religious truth. This is a peculiar thought and expression, but in perfect harmony with Paul's purpose in writing to Titus. Prevalence of false teachers made such a purpose needful.

Verses 2-3. "In hope of eternal life which God, who never lies, promised ages ago and at the proper time manifested through the preaching with which I have been entrusted by command of God our Saviour." Eternal life, one of Paul's favorite thoughts — spiritual life starting at regeneration and continuing through time into eternity. "God, who never lies." This is a strong Hebrew method of asserting a positive truth—God is always truthful. "Promised ages ago." From the promises to Abraham in Genesis to Malachi. "Manifested, or made known, in the word that I preach." Paul is not minimizing the teaching of Jesus which began to make known the meaning of "eternal life." "By command of God." (See comment on it in I Tim. 1:1.)

Verse 4. Same titles to Titus as to Timothy (see 1:1). He adds "common" to faith in Titus. Perhaps, objective, and all believers are thought of as having the same doctrines of faith.

The greeting is the same as in I Timothy, except the omission of the much discussed "mercy" *(oleos)*. It shows that Titus was not copied from I Timothy. The apostle is writing independently under the direction of the Spirit, in both cases.

Titus' Mission on the Island of Crete (1:5-9)
To Perfect Church Organization

I left you in Crete for this express purpose, to set in order the things that are lacking, and to appoint elders [pastors] in each town, as I directed you—6 each elder must be above reproach, have only one wife, and his children must not be liable to the charge of profligacy or disobedience [i.e. must be under control]. For as God's trustee a pastor must be above reproach, not stubborn or quick-tempered or addicted to strong drink or pugnacious or addicted to dishonest gain, 8 but hospitable, a lover of goodness, sen-

sible, upright, of pure life, self-controlled, [9] and a man who continues to cling to the trustworthy message as he was taught it,
so that he may be competent to encourage others with wholesome
teaching and to convict those who oppose him.

Key words and phrases. Verse 5. "Appoint elders." Was church
government democratic or oligarchic on Crete? The Greek word in
Acts 14:23 means to lift the hand in voting. So the method of ap-
pointing elders in those days was by election on the part of the
church by lifting the hand. Then how did Titus appoint elders? By
having the churches elect suitable men under his direction as led
by the Holy Spirit. The Greek verb in 1:5 *(kathistemi)* has no
suggestion as to how they were appointed.

Verse 6. The pastor, as God's steward (trustee), must be above
reproach. Just as in I Timothy 3. "Must have only one wife."
That is, he must not have a plurality of wives, as was common on
Crete at that time. We must observe that he uses in verse 6 *epis-
kopos*, overseer, pastor, while in verse 5 he uses *presbuteros*, elder.
They are synonymous and mean pastor. "Whose children are believers." The man worthy of leading a church should be able to
lead his own children to become Christians. In Timothy he describes
the children as being kept under control.

Verse 7. "Above reproach." Repeated, so it is important in a
pastor's character. He is God's steward, or trustee. God has entrusted him with His gospel for the salvation of the world. "Not
stubborn or quick-tempered." "Not addicted to strong drink or
pugnacious or addicted to dishonest gain." Most of the qualities
here are identical with those stipulated in I Timothy 3. See comments there.

Verse 8. "Hospitable, sensible," repeated (see comments in I
Tim. 3). "Of pure life." Not in I Timothy. Needed in Titus because of the immorality of the Cretans. "Self-controlled," not in I
Timothy. Likewise, "skillful in teaching," in I Timothy.) "A lover
of goodness," not in I Timothy. Surely these letters were not copied
from each other, but are independent compositions. They sound
more like the aged Paul than anyone else.

Verse 9. "A man who continues to cling to the trustworthy
message as he was taught it, so that he may be competent to en-

courage others with wholesome teaching and to refute those who
oppose him." That is, no man is fit to be pastor of a church on
Crete with its isms and many false teaching, unless he is firm in the
basic doctrines and can encourage others with wholesome (sound)
teaching, and actually refute those who persist in clinging to the
false doctrines.

THE CRETANS TO BE REPROVED FOR THEIR HEINOUS SINS
SINS OF THE CRETANS (1:10-16)

10 For there are many insubordinate people, mere talkers with
nothing to say, but deceivers of their own minds, especially those
of the circumcision party, 11 whose mouths must be stopped, for
they upset whole families by teaching things they ought not to
think, for the sake of dishonest gain. 12 One of them, a prophet of
their own countrymen, has said, "Cretans are always liars, wicked
brutes, lazy bellies." 13 Now this tendency is true. So continue correcting them severely, that they may be healthy in faith, 14 by ceas-
ing to give attention to Jewish myths and to the commands of
men who turn their backs on the truth. 15 To the pure everything
is pure, but to the impure and unbelieving nothing is pure, but
their very minds and consciences are impure. 16 They profess to
know God, but by their actions they disown Him; they are detestable, disobedient, and useless for anything good.

Key words and phrases. Verses 10, 11. "Mere talkers with
nothing to say." False teachers! They not only say nothing but
they have nothing to say. No truth in what they say. "Deceivers
of their own minds." In coming to the false conclusions they have
reached they deceived their own minds, which are corrupt. "Especially of the circumcision party." These are the Judaizers who
caused so much trouble in Galatia. See comments on the Letter
to the Galatians. See also the second Letter to the Corinthians,
where Paul defends himself and his gospel against the Judaizers.
"Their mouths must be stopped." Why? They are "upsetting whole
families." Their motives are selfish: "for dishonest gain." Lovers
of money, and teaching false doctrines for the sake of financial
gain. "Teaching what they have no right to teach." No one has
any right to teach what is false, for it harms those who are taught;
and no one has the right to harm others.

Verses 12-14. "Cretans are always liars, wicked brutes, lazy bellies [gluttons]." Two natives of Crete made similar remarks about their fellow-countrymen. But Epimenides is the better known. He was a sort of prophet of the Cretans. Paul confirms "the tendency to such lying, brutality, and gluttony." "Continue correcting them severely." This is the apostle's charge to Titus. "That they may be healthy in faith." Faith in false doctrines is sickly faith. These false teachers on Crete seem to be giving attention to Jewish myths. (See comments on I Tim. 1:4.)

Verses 15, 16. "To the pure all things are pure." That is, they are able to see things that are pure. They do not make pure things impure, nor impure things pure. They can see even God Himself (Matt. 5:8). But to "the corrupt and unbelieving nothing is pure." Even their consciences are corrupt. The conscience is the mind applying its thought to moral issues to decide whether right or wrong. Such people cannot see or know God. Their spiritual eyes are blinded. "They profess to know God but by their actions deny Him." "By their fruits you shall know them." Paul's conclusion: Such people are "detestable, disobedient, unfit for anything good."

Instructions on What Titus Shall Teach (2:1-3:11)
Sober Living (2:1-10)

You must continue telling the people what is proper for wholesome teaching: [2] the older men to be temperate, serious, and sensible, healthy in faith, in love, and in steadfastness; [3] the older women, too, to be reverent in their deportment, and not to be slanderers or slaves to heavy drinking, but to be teachers of what is right, [4] so as to train the younger women to be affectionate wives and mothers, [5] to be serious, pure, homekeepers, kind, and subordinate to their husbands, so as not to cause God's message to suffer reproach. [6] Keep urging the younger men to be sensible. [7] In everything you yourself continue to set them a worthy example of doing good; be sincere and serious in your teaching, [8] let your message be wholesome and unobjectionable, so that our opponent may be put to shame at having nothing evil to say about us. [9] Continue urging slaves to practice perfect submission to their masters and to give them perfect satisfaction, [10] to stop resisting them and stealing from them, but to show such perfect fidelity as to adorn, in everything they do, the teaching of God our Saviour.

Key words and phrases. Verse 1. "Teach what befits sound doctrine." That is, character and life must accord with wholesome
teaching (doctrine). Doctrine must be backed up with doing and
being.

Verses 2-8. The character and life that are becoming "sound
doctrine." In older men it is to be "temperate [controlling oneself],
serious [taking life seriously and with a great purpose], sensible
[looking at everything from a reasonable point of view], sound in
faith, in love, and in steadfastness [faith in objective sense]"; must
be genuine and include all classes; endurance till one can stand anything (steadfast). "The older women to be reverent [recognizing
their subordinate place in the church]; not slanderers [controlling
their tongues], not slaves to drink." By "teaching what is good,"
older women are to "train the young women to love their husbands
and children." Strengthen the domestic ties by setting a good example before the young women. "Not slaves to drink," a common
sin among heathen women. Christian women must not be "heavy
drinkers." Better not to drink intoxicating liquors at all. "Serious
[young wives must take life seriously], pure [chaste in character],
homekeepers [rearing children by the Christian standard], kind
[doing good to all], submissive to their husbands." Paul teaches
that the husband is the head of the family. The result of such living
will be that God's message will not suffer reproach. Living will tally
with the Word taught, character will accord with doctrine.

"Younger men to be sensible." Not silly and lightheaded but
soberminded.

Verses 7-10. Charge to Titus. "Continue to set them a worthy
example of doing good." The minister must be a worthy example
to young and old. That is, he must himself practice what he teaches
others to be and do. The purpose and result of such living by ministers will be that "our opponent [to Christianity] will be put to
shame at having nothing evil to say about us." "Slaves to stop
resisting their masters and stealing from them." Common practice
by non-Christian slaves. If Christian slaves heed these instructions,
they will adorn the doctrines of God our Saviour, in everything
they do. What a beautiful thought! Even a slave by doing right

and being faithful as a slave can adorn the doctrines of Christianity. God our Saviour as well as Christ the Son.

HE APPEALS TO BOTH THE FIRST AND SECOND COMING OF CHRIST (2:11-15)

> For God's favor has appeared with its offer of salvation to all mankind, [12] training us to give up godless ways and worldly cravings and live serious, upright, and godly lives in this world, [13] while we are waiting for the realization of our blessed hope at the glorious appearing of our great God and Saviour Christ Jesus, [14] who gave Himself for us to ransom us from all iniquity and purify for Himself a people to be His very own, zealous of good works. [15] You must continue teaching this, and continue exhorting and reproving people, with full authority. Let no one belittle you.

Key words and phrases. "The grace of God has appeared" (11). The unmerited favor of God. It showed itself historically at the coming of Christ in human flesh. Historical aorist indicative *(ephane)*. "Salvation for all mankind" (11). Not every individual, but all races and conditions of mankind. Yet, God's plan of salvation is all comprehensive, intended to save men of all races and nations. John has the same conception of the atonement (I John 2:2).

"Training us to give up godless ways and worldly cravings." Notice, this training to give up or renouncing of godless ways and worldly cravings (of human nature in its lowest forms) is to be continuous (present participle). The race has been in the process of training throughout history and each individual has to go through a process of training to give up these lower impulses, before they can be anything like completely given up.

"And live serious, upright, and godly lives in this world." This is the positive side of Christian living. The negative comprises renouncing "godless ways and worldly cravings." The positive life involves three relations—to self, to others, and to God. As to self, the Christian must not only give up the godless cravings of the lower self, but he must grow a better self by training himself to be sober and take life seriously, not to spend it in silly fun and sport. Secondly, as to others, it must be a life of uprightness, all his deal-

ings with others must be right (in accordance with the Golden
Rule). Thirdly, in relation to God it must be godly. That is, God
must be first in all things; we must love Him best, serve Him most
loyally.

Verse 13. "Waiting for the realization of the blessed hope at
the glorious appearing of our great God and Saviour Christ Jesus."
Hope in the New Testament often means the fulfillment or realization of the anticipated hope. Here it is the realization of the hope.
We could translate it "the glorious hope." Also, "appearing of the
glory of the great God," or the "glorious appearance of the great
God," etc. *Doxes* is descriptive genitive. "Great God and Saviour
Christ Jesus." Jesus is called God, God is called the Saviour, a doctrine emphasized in the pastoral epistles.

Verse 14. "Who gave Himself for us." That is, Jesus gave Himself to the humiliation of dying in company with sinners as a sacrifice for sin. The prepositions are used to show the relation of
Christ's death to the sinner and his salvation: *anti,* instead of, in
the place of; and *huper,* for, insead of, in the place of. See Thayer,
Lexicon, anti, huper. See also Robertson, *Grammar,* in *loco.* "Who
gave Himself" may be easily rendered, "Who gave Himself in our
stead, in our place." So claim all who advocate the substitutionary
theory of the atonement.

"To redeem us from all iniquity." To loose us from iniquity or
sin in general; to deliver us from all the consequences of sin, its
guilt, power, etc.

"To purify for Himself a people to be His very own." God is
pure and perfect in holiness. He must have a people who are finally
pure like Himself. His people must be pure for only such can see
God (Matt. 5:8). "Zealous of good works." A logical result of
pure character. Redeemed; purified; zealous of good works.

Verse 15. "Continue teaching and reproving with full authority."
He has the apostolic authority conferred upon him by Paul. So his
teaching and reproving are "with full authority." Therefore, he is
commanded, "Let no one belittle you" as God's man, as God's
apostle (sent one). He is never called an apostle but he is ordered
by an apostle to speak as an apostle, "with full authority."

TITUS TO REMIND PEOPLE TO BE OBEDIENT CITIZENS AND GENTLE
TO EVERYBODY, SINCE THEY ARE SAVED BY GOD'S
LOVINGKINDNESS (3:1-7)

Constantly remind people to submit to and obey the rulers who
have authority over them, so as to be ready for any good enterprise, ² to stop abusing anyone, to be peaceable, fairminded,
showing perfect gentleness to everybody.

³ For once we too were without understanding, disobedient, misled, habitual slaves to all sorts of passions and pleasures, spending
our lives in malice and envy. ⁴ But when the goodness and lovingkindness of God our Saviour were brought to light, ⁵ He saved us,
not for upright deeds that we had done, but in accordance with
His mercy, through the bath of regeneration and renewal of the
Holy Spirit, ⁶ which He abundantly poured out upon us through
Jesus Christ our Saviour, ⁷ so that we might come into right
standing with God through His unmerited favor and become heirs
of eternal life in accordance with our hope.

Key words and phrases. Verses 1, 2. Paul teaches that Christians
must be loyal citizens. Even if wicked Nero is the supreme ruler,
as now in Rome. Ready for any "good enterprise." Not for wicked
enterprises, as selling intoxicating drinks. "Peaceable and gentle to
everybody." Peace is one of the main marks of a Christian. "Gentleness," self-control, is another.

Verse 3. The Christians to whom Titus ministered were once
lost in sin. The same dark picture of man's original state as described in Romans 1:20-32 and Ephesians 2:1-3. To Paul the natural man was utterly sinful and corrupt. If Paul wrote Romans he
must have written Titus.

Verses 4-7. He traces the salvation of men back to God's goodness and lovingkindness *(chrestoes* and *philanthropia).* In verse
7 he uses the same word that he used in Ephesians 2:5, 8: *charis,*
grace, unmerited favor. (See the comments on Eph. 2:4-8.) He
uses another word, *eleos,* mercy. Grace is the fountain, mercy is
the stream flowing from that fountain. Salvation comes from God's
unmerited favor as its fountainhead. The stream is God's pity and
compassion for man's wretched and helpless condition. "He saved
us." The first sense emphasized here—forgave us, regenerated us.

"By the bath of regeneration and renewal in the Holy Spirit." Perhaps *bath* indirectly refers to baptism, but only as a figure. The water baptism does not save; it is the renewal of the Holy Spirit that saves. Although Paul does not use the word regeneration in Galatians and Romans, he expresses the thought in the expressions "new creature . . . new life." (See Gal. 4 and our comments there. Especially see 6:15.)

In verse 5 he emphasizes the fact that "He saved us, not for upright deeds that we had done." No salvation by ordinances or by good works, in Paul. It is by grace, by God's "goodness and lovingkindness."

"Through Jesus Christ." Although the Holy Spirit renews and regenerates, it is "through Jesus Christ our Saviour."

In verse 7 he emphasizes, as in Romans 8:17, that "we become heirs of eternal life." Of course, heirship is the logical conclusion of being children. "Children, then heirs" (Rom. 8:17).

THOSE SAVED BY GRACE MUST TAKE HEED TO LEAD IN DOING GOOD (3:8-11)

> 8 It is a message to be trusted, and I want you to be emphatic about these things, so that those who believe in God may be careful to take the lead in doing good. These things are right and render service to mankind. 9 But hold yourself aloof from foolish controversies, pedigrees, strife, and wrangles about the law, for these are fruitless and futile. 10 After one or two warnings to a man who is factious, stop having anything to do with him, 11 for you may be sure that such a man is crooked and sinful, even self-condemned.

Key words and phrases. Verse 8. "Be emphatic about these things . . . lead in doing good." The things in which Titus is to be emphatic are justification by faith and salvation by His goodness and lovingkindness (5, 6). Still he must also emphasize it as their duty and an excellent thing for people thus saved to be fruitful in "doing good." Not doing good to be saved, but doing good because saved and because it is right and because mankind needs service to relieve it of suffering.

Verse 9. "But avoid stupid constroversies, genealogies," etc.

There is a remnant of Gnosticism still in the world—some left on the island of Crete. Also some Judaizers, or, at least sticklers for law. But the apostle warns Titus to avoid these heresies.

Verse 10. He must avoid all factious men. Whatever deviates from the faith is to be avoided. The man who is factious must be ignored. Paul is jealous of the faith, the teachings recognized as standardized by Christ and the apostles. The church in Jerusalem "continued in the apostles' teaching" (Acts 2:42). After the Jerusalem conference (Acts 15) all the churches accepted the agreement there made.

THE CONCLUSION (3:12-15)

Verse 12. Paul has decided to spend the winter at Nicopolis, not far from Corinth. It is some six years since he wrote them his last letter, one of brilliant but sarcastic defense of his apostleship and character. The Judaizers are whipped, and likely the great church at Corinth is prospering and more or less united. He wants Titus to meet him at Nicopolis. Titus had been partially instrumental in bringing the factions into harmony (II Cor. 7:5-10). Tychicus is one of Paul's supply men (II Tim. 4:12); he later sent him to Ephesus. Likely Artemas was one of Paul's supply men.

Verse 13. We know little of Zenas except that he was a lawyer, which means he was versed in the law of Moses (perhaps the Roman law), but he was not a Judaizer. He placed grace above the law. Zenas joined Apollos, the brilliant Bible scholar of Alexandria and a great orator (Acts 18:24 ff), in helping Paul in places where he could not be in person. Paul was planning to send one of these two men to Titus. He was to speed them on their way and was to co-operate so fully with the one who came that he "was to lack nothing."

Verse 14. The apostle of grace is also the apostle of good deeds. "Let our people learn to apply themselves to good deeds, so as to help cases of urgent need, and not to be unfruitful." The world is full of cases of urgent need, and God's people should be alert to see them and supply their needs. These good deeds do not save the soul but they help develop the personality and polish the character of Christians.

Verse 15. "All who are with me send greetings." How beautiful is the fellowship of Christians! "Greet those who love us in the faith." This means that there is a different feeling in one's heart for those who love him as Christians loving fellow Christians. They know and appreciate a higher relationship (brothers in Christ). What a thrill the minister often feels as he responds to the spiritual love of hundreds of his brothers and sisters in his church! "Grace be with you all." Spiritual blessing with spiritual strength be with you all.

Sermon Outline on Titus 2:11-14

Redeemed to Be God's Own People

(Textual sermon)

I. Divine Source of Salvation. "Grace of God for salvation."
  1. Not human philosophy. Socrates, Plato, Aristotle, and others
  2. Not human achievements. Prominent in Paul's writings
  3. But by God's grace
     a. Unmerited favor
     b. On His love
     c. Mercy the stream
II. Redeemed by Jesus Christ
  1. Released us from prison by paying the ransom price. Picture
  2. He gave Himself. The ransom *(lutron)* (see Mark 10:45)
  3. The price of the ransom, death on the cross (Phil. 2:8) Most horrible death; died between two thieves (Isa. 53)
III. Redeemed for a Noble Purpose—to Be God's Own People (14)
  1. Not simply to enjoy our religious lives. Shouting days.
  2. Not merely to be saved in Heaven after death. Some seem to think so.
  3. To be God's own people. So He chose Abraham and his descendants.
  4. Redeemed from "all iniquity." From all sin. We must renounce:
     a. Worldly ways—things that please self
     b. Worldly passions

    5. Positively, live noble lives
       a. Serious, for a purpose
       b. Upright; on square with others
       c. Godly; devoted to God and His Church and kingdom
IV. A Blessed Hope for the Redeemed
    1. Hope of the second coming. Here realization of it, as well as hope for it. (See Thayer, *Lexicon, Elpis,* hope)
    2. Christ is the "great God and Saviour." Deity of Christ. In all the pastoral epistles
    3. Our hope centers in the parousia—consummation of this age

SERMON OUTLINE TITUS 3:4-7

HOW SINNERS ARE SAVED

  I. Not Saved by Personal Good Deeds (5)
    1. Not by keeping the law. Paul proved it a failure (Gal. 2-4)
    2. Not by deeds of charity (Acts 9:36-42). Dorcas and charity.
    3. Not by missionary gifts and life sacrifices. Paul, Polycarp
 II. But by God's Goodness
    1. By His goodness—including all His benevolent attributes
    2. By His love (John 3:16; Rom. 5:8; Eph. 2:4)
    3. By His kindness—goodness in action
    4. By His grace, unmerited facor (Eph. 2:5, 8; Titus 3:7)
    5. By His mercy (Eph. 2:4; Titus 3:7). J. H. Mills' founding two orphan Homes, Oxford and Thomasville, N. C., expressions of mercy.
III. Steps of Salvation
    1. Regeneration by the Spirit (John 3:3, 5). Not emphasized in Paul
    2. Justification by grace (unmerited favor, see Titus 3:7)
    3. Adoption (Gal. 4:4; also in Rom. 8)
    4. Salvation worked out in life (Phil. 2:12-13)
IV. Attendant Blessings
    1. Rich pouring out of the Holy Spirit on the saved (6). So on Pentecost; in Caesarea (Acts 10)
    2. The hope of eternal life. Begins at regeneration continues through eternity. Queen Elizabeth I to doctor when dying, "All my possessions for a moment of life."

The Second Letter to Timothy

INTRODUCTION

1. *The occasion.* The apostle, while on the fourth missionary journey, had at last come to Nicopolis (Titus 3:12), where he was arrested and sent to Rome for his final imprisonment. It was here while facing death at the hands of cruel Nero that the apostle wrote this last message to his beloved young preacher friend; his last message to the world.

2. *The purpose.* There is a double line of design: (a) To assert his personal triumph through Jesus Christ, who long years ago brought him into right relation with God the Father, has been the channel through which the divine power has nerved him for every conflict of his busy life, and now guarantees to the dying martyr the consciousness of victory though his life is suddenly cut short by the executioner's axe. There are no more beautiful words of Christian triumph than these last words from the apostle's pen: "For I am already being offered [or more literally translated, My life, indeed, is already ebbing out] and the time has come for me to sail away. I have fought the fight for the good, I have run my race, I have kept the faith. Now the crown for doing right awaits me, which the Lord, the righteous Judge, will award me on that day, and not only me but also all who have loved His appearing." (b) To encourage Timothy to keep on combating the false doctrines. See how he exhorts the young minister in 1:6-8; 2:3; 4:5, where he warns Timothy to suffer hardship for the gospel. Three times the apostle warns his young preacher friend to endure hardness caused by the persuasive appeals of the false teachers.

3. *The date.* This last letter was written in the year A.D. 65, just before Nero had him beheaded on the Ostian road just outside the city of Rome; just before the faithful and accurate interpreter of Jesus passed into the kingdom of glory (4:8).

4. *Main teachings.* (a) God is the Father. (b) Christ is the Saviour, the Conquerer of death, and the Morning Star to immor-

tality's day. (c) Salvation is not secured by works but is given according to the merciful purposes of God. (d) The Holy Spirit helps guard the believer unto the last day. (e) The Scriptures (only O.T. then) are God-inbreathed and useful for growing strong, symmetrical Christian character. (f) The noblest Christian life is one of hardship and suffering. (g) The minister should keep himself untrammeled from financial affairs. (h) The second coming of Christ preceded by times of grievous sins and distress. (i) Assurance of being kept by God's grace (spiritual power). (j) Rewards to be granted the faithful suffering Christian at the second coming of Christ.

GENERAL OUTLINE

  I. Greeting (1:1, 2)
 II. Thanksgiving and Remembrances (1:3-14)
    1. He thanks God for the religious ancestors of himself and Timothy (1:3-6)
    2. Thanks God also for salvation by grace through Jesus Christ (1:7-11)
    3. In assurance he remembers the keeping hand of God (1:12-14)
III. The Courses of Phygelus and Hermogenes Compared with That of Onesiphorus (15-18)
 IV. Exhorts Timothy to Be a Brave Soldier (Chap. 2)
    1. The apostle's solemn charge (2:1-7)
    2. The motives for the appeal, the resurrection of Christ and the persecutions of the apostle (2:8-13)
    3. Be a good workman and so an example to all (2:14-24)
  V. How Timothy Must Deal with the Coming Evils (Chap. 3)
    1. A description of moral evils in the last days (3:1-9)
    2. Timothy charged to remember the apostle's triumph over all persecutions (3:10-13)
    3. Charged to rely upon the holy Scriptures for final success (3:14-17)
 VI. Solemn Charge to Timothy and Announcement of the Apostle's Pending Death (4:1-8)
    1. The charge puts Timothy under oath (4:1-5)
    2. Announcing his own triumph in the face of death (4:6-8)

VII. Conclusion (4:9-22)

    1. Personal matters: those who have forsaken him; the cloak, the books, the parchments especially (4:9-18)
    2. Greetings (4:19-21)
    3. Benediction (22)

EXEGESIS

Chapter I

GREETING (1:1, 2)

Let us compare the greeting in the second Letter with that in the First Letter to Timothy. In the first letter Paul calls himself "an apostle of Christ Jesus by the command of God our Saviour and of Christ Jesus our hope." In the second Letter he substitutes "by the will of God" (omitting "our Saviour"); but he adds, "in accordance with the promise of the life which comes through union with Christ Jesus." In the second clause he adds, "our hope" to "Christ Jesus." In verse 2 in I Timothy he calls Timothy "my true child"; in II Timothy he calls him "my beloved child." There are two conclusions lying right on the surface: the second Letter is not a copy of the first, nor is either the copy of a common source. Again, the thought is so nearly the same that the Pauline authorship could not be asserted for one and denied for the other. Nor can it be claimed that Paul is trying to write the second Letter greeting exactly like the first.

The benediction implored in verse 2 is exactly the same in both letters. "Grace [spiritual blessing], mercy and peace be with you from God," etc. See comments on I Timothy 1:2.

THE APOSTLE'S THANKSGIVING AND SOME PLEASANT REMEMBRANCES (1:3-14)

[3] I thank God, whom I worship, as my forefathers did, with a clear conscience, as I ceaselessly remember you in my prayers. Because I remember the tears you shed for me, I am always longing night and day [4] to see you again, that I may feel the fullest joy [5] on being reminded of your genuine faith, a faith that first found a home in the heart of your grandmother Lois, then in the heart of your mother Eunice, and now in yours too, I am sure.

[6] For this reason I now remind you to rekindle and keep burn-

ing the fire of the divine gift which came upon you when I laid my hands upon you. [7] For the Spirit that God has given us does not impart timidity but power and love and self-control. [8] So you must never be ashamed of me His prisoner, but suffer for the good news in fellowship with me and by the power of God. [9] For He saved us and called us with a holy call, not in accordance with anything that we had done, but in accordance with His own purpose and unmerited favor which was shown us through union with Christ Jesus eternal ages ago, [10] but has only recently been made known through the appearance of our Saviour Christ Jesus, who through the good news has put a stop to the power of death, and brought life and immortality to light. [11] Of this good news I have been appointed a preacher, an apostle, and a teacher. [12] This is why I am suffering so, but I am not ashamed of it, for I know whom I have trusted and I am absolutely sure that He is able to guard what I have entrusted to Him until that day. [13] Continue to be an example in wholesome instructions which you learned from me, in the faith and love that come through union with Christ Jesus. [14] Guard this fine deposit of truth by the aid of the Holy Spirit who has His home in our hearts.

Key words and phrases. Verses 3-4. Timothy's tears for his spiritual father cause Paul ceaselessly, night and day, to long for him. What a beautiful tie of fellowship bound together the hearts of this father and son in the faith! Paul was an intellectual giant, but his heart was bigger than his brain. He loved everybody; he loved deeply those of kindred spirits and similar ideals. He loves Timothy so devotedly that he "ceaselessly remembers him in his prayers."

"As did my forefathers." This is the only reference to his ancestors made by Paul. Both father and mother must have been very devoted to God according to the Jewish faith; possibly Pharisees. Paul inherited the tendency toward a strict Jewish faith, and his environment nourished it. So he can appreciate, to the fullest, a similar condition for Timothy and thank God for it.

Verses 5-7. The religious chain from grandmother to grandson. "I am reminded of your sincere faith." He seems to give the grandmother and mother credit for the deep sincerity of Timothy's faith. This faith first had its home *(oikei,* present) in the heart of your grandmother Lois. Then "your mother Eunice" accepted it and cultivated it in her heart. No wonder it lives and grows in your heart too. So Paul reminds him to "rekindle the gift of God that is in you through the laying on of my hands." Has Timothy backslidden? Not necessarily. The aged friend knows how easily the young man may slip and relax his grip on the higher spiritual realities. This laying on of hands refers to the ordination of Timothy at the beginning of the second missionary journey (Acts 16:1-5). "The laying on of my hands." Paul refers to the laying on of hands rather than the circumcision. The latter was a sign of Judaism, the former of Christianity. Laying the hands of elders or apostles on one did not bestow the gift and power of the Holy Spirit; but it was a sign which if performed in faith God blessed with the bestowal of the Spirit's power.

God did not give us the spirit of timidity, but a spirit of power and love and self-control. The timidity of Timothy was not the gift of the Spirit; but his "love and self-control" were the gifts of the Spirit. (See Gal. 5:22.)

Verses 8-10. "Do not be ashamed of me His prisoner." Let us remember that it is hard to stand foursquare for a condemned prisoner. The public generally is against him; only a very small minority stand for him and consider him innocent. "Your share of suffering." Paul was not expected by God to endure all the suffering for the gospel in Rome. Timothy had a share to bear. The martyrs in all the centuries have borne sufferings that belonged to others who ought to have shared them with men like Paul and Peter and Polycarp; the Baptists of Massachusetts, Virginia, and North Carolina in the colonial period. "For the good news." This suffering Paul endured was for the promotion of the good news. "By the power of God." The omnipotent arms were underneath the feeble arms of Paul and would be holding up Timothy's too. "He saved us." Antecedent of *He is God;* primarily the Father God. As we saw in I Timothy, so in II Timothy, God the Father is called Saviour.

"Grace which He gave us in Christ Jesus eternal ages ago." In the mind and heart of God, salvation was wrought out in the past eternal ages. Grace is unmerited favor of the Father. "Eternal ages." Not to be grasped by the finite human mind, for it is an infinite concept. "Not in accordance with anything we had done." All of grace, that is Pauline doctrine. "He abolished death and brought life and immortality to light" (10). This refers to Christ's victory over death at His resurrection. Death could not hold Him, even if sealed in Joseph's new tomb. Not literally had He abolished all death. But He had His heels on death's skull and in due time (by the parousia) He would have crushed the last skull of the death monster (see I Cor. 15:54-56). "Death is swallowed up in victory . . . Brought to light." Life and immortality existed before the resurrection of Christ, but not in triumphant sway over death. Christ's resurrection sounded the death knell of death itself.

Verses 11-14. Paul absolutely sure of his final salvation. Paul reasons backward from his present state to his conversion. For the gospel that brought life and immortality to light Paul was "appointed a preacher and apostle and teacher, and therefore I suffer as I do." Apostle is the general term, one called and sent on a mission. It embraced the functions of both preaching and teaching. Preach means to proclaim truth publicly with a view to get people to practice it. Teach means to set forth truth so as to increase knowledge. Teaching leaves truth there. Preaching uses truth to induce people to live better and develop personality in harmony with the higher forms of truth. So Paul could, if appointed an apostle, and almost necessarily, be a preacher and teacher. For being a preacher and apostle and teacher he is now suffering in a Roman dungeon (11).

"I know whom I have trusted and am absolutely sure that He is able to guard what I have entrusted to Him until that day." Paul has trusted Christ with his soul. He did that because of his intellectual and rational certainty *(oida)* that Jesus was the Son of God and the Christ to set up the kingdom and to save mankind for that kingdom. Now for thirty years he has proved it by experience *(ginosko)*. Therefore, he knows from every high, exalted vantage ground of his being that Christ is able to guard what he has deposited with Him until that day (parousia). So we see that Paul is not depending only on his experience for these thirty years of Christian experience during which Christ has guarded his deposit with Him against the Judaizers and against Nero the "lion"; but before that he had summoned his higher reason and before he made the deposit of his soul with Christ he was absolutely sure that Jesus was the Son of God and Saviour of men. See Romans 1:4: "Proved to be the Son of God . . . by His resurrection from the dead." He started with rational certainty which he corroborated by personal Christian experience for thirty years. "Absolutely sure." A great doctrine resting on the Rock of ages, the pillar of intelligent reason and Christian experience corroborating each other and the Scripture assertions.

The apostle cannot leave this great doctrine without exhorting Timothy to "continue to be an example of wholesome instruction which you learned from me . . . Guard this fine deposit of truth by the aid of the Holy Spirit" (13, 14). The "fine deposit of truth" which Paul is transmitting to Timothy is burdening his heart these last days and hours. Timothy guarded the truth as long as he lived. Shall we?

Paul Forsaken by Asiatic Leaders among Whom Are Phygelus and Hermogenes; Onesiphorus Commended for Faithful Service to Paul (1:15-18)

Verse 15. "All in Asia turned away from me." Paul is in a dungeon and needs friends. Phygelus and Hermogenes "turn away from him." Such men are not friends.

Verses 16-17. Onesiphorus on getting to Rome searches for Paul. Finds him in the dungeon and ministers to him. They weep together, rejoice together. Not ashamed of his imprisoned friend.

Verse 18. His services in Ephesus well known by Timothy.

Chapter II

Timothy Charged to Be Brave as a Soldier in Meeting False Teachers (2:1-26)

So you, my son, must keep renewing your strength through the spiritual blessing that comes to you because of your union with Christ Jesus. ² The truths you learned from me before many witnesses you must commit to trustworthy men who will be competent to teach others also. ³ Take your share of hardships like a good soldier of Christ Jesus. ⁴ No soldier ever allows himself to be involved in the business affairs of life, so that he may please the officer who enrolled him. [5] No contestant in the games is crowned, unless he competes according to the rules. [6] The toiling farmer ought to be the first to share the products of the crop. [7] Keep on thinking about what I am saying. For the Lord will grant you understanding of it in all its phases. [8] Continue to remember Jesus Christ as risen from the dead, and descended from David, in accordance with the good news that I preach, [9] for the sake of which I am suffering hardships even to the extent of wearing chains as though I were a criminal. But God's message is not in chains. [10] For this reason I am bearing anything for the sake of His chosen people, so that they too may obtain the salvation that comes through Christ Jesus and with it eternal glory also.

[11] This message is to be trusted: "If we indeed have died with Him, we will live with Him too. [12] If we patiently endure, we will reign with Him too. If we disown Him, He will disown us too. [13] If we are unfaithful, He remains faithful, for He cannot prove false to Himself."

[14] Keep on reminding men of these things. Solemnly charge them before God to stop petty debating which does no good at all but brings destruction on those who hear it. [15] Do your best to present yourself to God an approved workman who has nothing to be ashamed of, who properly presents the message of truth. [16] Continue shunning worldly, futile phrases, for they lead on to greater depths of godlessness, [17] and their message will spread like a cancer; men like Hymenaeus and Philetus, [18] who have missed the truth by saying that the resurrection has already taken place, are undermining some people's faith. [19] But God's foundation stands unshaken, with these inscriptions: "The Lord knows the people who belong to Him" and "Everyone who bears the name of the Lord must abstain from evil."

[20] In any great house there are not only gold and silver articles but also wooden utensils, some for honorable uses and some for lowly uses. [21] So if a man will cleanse himself from these things, he will be an instrument for honorable uses, consecrated, useful for the Master, and ready for any good service.

[22] You must keep on fleeing from the evil impulses of youth, but ever strive for uprightness, faith, love, and peace, in association with those who call upon the Lord with pure hearts. [23] Always avoid foolish discussions with ignorant men, for you know that

they breed quarrels, [24] and a slave of the Lord must not quarrel but must be gentle to everybody; he must be a skillful teacher, and not resentful under injuries. [25] With gentleness he must correct his opponents, for God might grant them repentance that would lead them to a full knowledge of the truth, [26] and they might recover their senses and escape from the devil's trap in which they have been caught by him to do his will.

Key words and phrases. Verse 1-7. The apostle's solemn charge.

Verse 1. "Be strong in the grace that is in Christ Jesus." The only source of spiritual strength is the grace, spiritual strength, that comes through union with Christ Jesus (in Christ Jesus). Notice, Paul addresses Timothy as "my son," just as in I Timothy *(teknon)*. The word emphasizes the source of the relation, "a begotten one." Here and in I Timothy it is a spiritual begetting. Paul knew that Timothy would need spiritual strength to meet the various types of false teachers.

Verse 2. "What you have heard from me . . . entrust to faithful men." If Timothy is superintendent of missions for the state of Asia, he is the one most responsible for the kind of men who are selected as pastors and teachers *(episkopous)* in the various churches. The leaders must be faithful. Men to be trusted with the bed-rock doctrines. They must be able to teach others. "What you have heard from me." Paul is jealous of his type of doctrines. He has worked it out from experience, backing logic; he has suffered for it, and now he is facing death for it. He can but feel that it is the faith, the teaching that is to be accepted by faith. "Before many witnesses." Many had heard Paul teach these things and had seen Timothy receiving the teaching.

Verses 3, 4. A good soldier he must be. Such must not "be involved in the business affairs of life," so that he may be free "to please the officer who enlisted him." Christ enlists the minister and he must keep himself untangled from worldly affairs so that he may constantly please Christ. To be a good soldier he must "take his share of suffering."

Verse 5. An athlete must compete "according to the rules," if he would be victorious and crowned as victor. Timothy is contestant in the big game of winning the world for Christ. Therefore, he must suffer, he must endure hardships.

Verse 6. The hard-working farmer is another example; he toils and suffers hardship, but rightfully partakes of the products of his crops. God is just and does not allow His soldiers to suffer without receiving just rewards.

Verse 7. "Keep on thinking about what I am saying." Paul was a great thinker. He must have been as great a thinker as Aristotle, if you compare their writings and teachings. He knew that it took thinking to get to the bottom of great truths. So he left Timothy to think about what he had said. There are three chief ways to understand spiritual truth: give up to the Holy Spirit's leading and He will lead you into all truth; then pray yourself to a solution; all the time use your brains and do your best thinking.

Verses 8-13. The motives urged—Christ's resurrection and Paul's suffering.

Verse 8. "Remember Jesus Christ risen from the dead, descended from David." To Paul, Christ risen is the climax of His achievements for mankind. He rose to vindicate His claims to be the Son of God (Rom. 1:4). Timothy, as you face the false teachers, remember Christ is alive and all-powerful. You do not serve a dead Christ but a living Christ. This faith in the risen Christ gave power (Acts 1:8) to the Early Church and crowned them with triumph over their persecutors. Paul caught the same spirit. He believed in a conquering Christ, who conquered death as well as all earthly foes. foes.

"The message of God is not in chains." Paul was bound with galling chains which robbed him of his freedom to do what he wanted to do for Christ and lost humanity, but the Word of God, the good news of salvation, was not fettered. Not even Nero could fasten chains on the Word of God.

Verses 11-13. The four invincible truths:

1. "If we have died with Him, we shall also live with Him;
2. "If we endure, we shall also reign with Him;
3. "If we deny Him, He also will deny us;
4. "If we are unfaithful, He remains faithful, for He cannot prove false to Himself."

A Commentary on the Pauline Epistles

The first great truth in this quartet is found from Galatians on in Paul's letters, Galatians 2:20: "I have been crucified with Christ; it is no longer I that live, but Christ lives in me." Romans 6:8-11: "If we have died with Christ, we believe that we shall also live with Him." See Ephesians 2:7. Dying with Christ and living with Him, in Paul, have a unique meaning. Christ died for us. Paul conceives of future believers as united with Christ on the cross (Gal. 2:20), so that when Christ rises from the dead believers rise with Him to walk in the newness of life (Rom. 6:4).

"If we endure, we shall also reign with Him." See Romans 8:17: "If in reality we share His sufferings, so that we may share His glory too." If we suffer and endure it, we shall share His glory; we shall reign with Him. See Philippians 2:9-11, where Paul asserts that Christ's glorification depended on His humiliation in suffering on a cross. The same principle holds for all believers.

"If we deny Him, He also will deny us." Another saying from the logia of Jesus: "If any man would come after me, let him deny himself."

The fourth one, "If we are unfaithful, He remains faithful, for He cannot prove false to Himself." This is a self-evident truth logically deduced from two and three.

Verses 14-19. Timothy must avoid petty debates and discussions. They bring ruin to the hearers. Spiritual truth is not reached via debating.

Verse 15. "A workman who has no need to be ashamed, rightly handling the word of truth." When one is debating with an opponent, the temptation is to win by straining a point, by taking advantage of your opponent. Such a workman is not approved by God and ought to be ashamed. Such debating leads the people into more and more ungodliness (16), "and their talk will eat its way like gangrene" (17).

Verses 17-18. Hymenaeus and Philetus (perhaps still in Asia, "upsetting the faith of some"). They have gone so far as to teach that the resurrection is already past. They must be rationalists— with no real reason.

Verse 19. The apostle ignores their argument (if they had any) and merely quotes, "The Lord knows those who are His" (Num.

16:5). Again "Everyone who bears the name of the Lord must abstain from evil" (Isa. 26:13). He dismisses the whole subject by sarcastically saying, "God's foundation stands unshaken." "The gates of hell shall not prevail against it [the church]."

Verses 20-26. A good workman must keep clean for the Master's service.

Verse 20. In a great household there is a great variety of utensils—from those of gold and silver to those of wood and clay. So in a great church, and even in smaller churches, there are variously gifted workers—from the best-trained teachers and pastors down to janitors. A good, faithful janitor is more to be desired than a well-trained but unfaithful pastor. To run a household you must have water jars or tubs or buckets and mops and brooms, as well as fine chandeliers and electric gadgets for brilliant lights. The illustration holds good for a church.

Verses 21-22. To be the best worker the Christian must purge himself from what is unworthy; then he will "be ready for the master's use, for every good work." Yes, he will be "consecrated," that is, set apart to some noble use. Among the ignoble things Paul warns Timothy, "shun youthful passions." This includes sex, temper, all lower passions. As a Christian grows older he must feel and know that gradually, if not suddenly, he is putting all these ignoble things under his feet and being triumphant over them.

On the other hand, he must positively "keep on striving for uprightness, faithfulness, love, and peace." *Pistis* may be translated "faith," but the nature of the nouns here associated with it makes it probable that Paul uses the word in the secondary sense, "faithfulness." "Along with those who call upon the Lord from a pure heart" (22b). Good companionship is helpful in growing good character, even for leaders.

Verses 23, 24. Warns against stupid controversies. He is dead set against all petty debates and discussions about doctrines. They breed quarrels, and the Lord's servant must not be quarrelsome.

Verses 25, 26. The pastor, or any religious leader, must be gentle and deal gently with everybody, for God might grant repentance to the opponents. Gentleness wins rather than harshness; even helps win those caught in the Devil's trap, so that they at last become fellow Christians with us and no longer opponents. "A skillful teacher." In handling these opponents, he again emphasizes that pastors, or other leaders, need to be skillful teachers (I Tim. 3:2).

BEWARE OF UNGODLY MEN AND HERETICS (3:1-9)

Now you must know that in the last days there are going to be hard times. ² For people will be selfish, avaricious, boastful, haughty, abusive, disobedient to parents, ungrateful, irreverent, ³ lacking in love for kinsmen, irreconcilable, slanderers, having no self-control, savage, lacking in love for the good, ⁴ treacherous, reckless, conceited, loving pleasure more than God, ⁵ keeping up the forms of religion but not giving expression to its power. Avoid such people. ⁶ For some of them practice going into people's houses aand capturing weak and silly women who are overwhelmed with the weight of their sins, who are easily led about by all sorts of evil impulses, ⁷ who are always trying to learn but never able to come to a full knowledge of the truth. ⁸ Just as Jannes and Jambres resisted Moses, these people resist the truth, for they are depraved in mind and so counterfeits in the faith. ⁹ But they will not make any more progress, for their folly will be evident to everybody, as theirs was.

Key words and phrases. Verse 1. These verses give a description of the increasing wickedness of people in the last days. These are the days toward the close of the period just before the coming of the Son of Man—the days just before the parousia. Paul thought that the parousia was imminent. See comments on the letter to the Thessalonians, especially chapter 2 of the second Letter.

Verses 2-4. Paul does not mean to say that people in other generations or periods of history were not "lovers of self, lovers of money, boastful, haughty, railers, disobedient to parents, unthankful, unholy, without natural affection, implacable, slanderers, without self-control, fierce, no lovers of good, traitors, headstrong, puffed up, lovers of pleasure rather than lovers of God." Every period of human history has been peopled by all these classes of sinner. But some periods are worse than others. Paul means they are reaching a climax in this period preceding the parousia. In this paragraph we have followed the American Revised Version. In the line of thought above, we followed the Williams' New Testament. Different translators use different synonyms, the resultant meaning being nearly the same in a category of sinners like these.

Just a few words to connect II Thessalonians 2 with what Paul is saying to Timothy. There he says "the man of lawlessness" must be "revealed." Whatever and whoever this bold expression meant to Paul, it seems clear that he (or it) is exerting his (or its) influence and power on the period described in II Timothy 3:2-4. The period of falling away precedes the parousia. But we must take heed to that specific warning that Jesus gave us as to the day or hour of the parousia (Mark 13:32).

Verse 5. "Keeping up the forms of religion but not giving expression to its power. Avoid such people." These are polite hypocrites. They are devoid of the spiritual power of Christianity, but they punctiliously keep all the external forms of church attendance and worship. Paul exhorts, "Avoid such people." Pray for them and seek to win them to Christ, but have no common social life with them.

Verses 6-7. "Weak and silly women, always trying to learn, but never able to come to the full knowledge of the truth." They are burdened with their sins, and yet ever trying to learn something about religion. But "willing to listen to anybody." Such people are the easy prey of false teachers.

Verses 8-9. Compared to Jannes and Jambres. These were Egyptian magicians who sought to hinder Moses in his guidance of the Israelites. "These people [false teachers] resist the truth, for they are depraved in mind and so counterfeits in the faith." Jannes and Jambres were magicians; like the Pharisees in the time of Christ, they were jealous of the power of Moses to perform miracles and thus exert power over Pharaoh and continue to lead the people of Israel out of bondage. Paul calls these false teachers counterfeits in the faith. They are not good currency in Paul's realm of religion. "They are corrupted in mind." Mind to Paul is closely associated with soul *(psuche)* and heart *(kardia)*. To him their entire internal being is corrupted with sin. "But they will not make any more progress." This is to encourage Timothy. "The truth will prevail." "For their folly will be evident to everybody." Jannes' and Jambres' folly was evident to everybody; so will that of these false teachers be.

TIMOTHY'S FAMILIARITY WITH PAUL'S CAREER AND THE
SACRED SCRIPTURES (3:10-17)

¹⁰ But you, on your part, have faithfully followed my teaching, my conduct, my aim, my faith, my patience, my love, my steadfastness, ¹¹ my persecutions, my sufferings, such as befell me at Antioch, Iconium, and Lystra, such as I endured—but the Lord delivered me out of them all. ¹² Yes, indeed, everyone who wants to live a godly life as a follower of Christ Jesus will be persecuted. ¹³ But bad men and imposters will go on from bad to worse, misleading others and misled themselves. ¹⁴ But you, on your part, must continue to abide by what you have learned and been led to rely upon, because you know from whom you learned it ¹⁵ and that from childhood you have known the sacred Scriptures which can give you wisdom that leads to salvation through the faith that leans on Christ Jesus. ¹⁶ All Scripture is inspired by God and is useful for teaching, for reproof, for correction, for training in doing what is right, ¹⁷ so that the man of God may be perfectly fit, thoroughly equipped for every good enterprise.

Key words and phrases. Verses 10-11. The Christian life of Paul with its persecutions and successes. Timothy was perfectly familiar with all the persecutions the Jews inflicted upon Paul in Macedonia, and how the Lord "delivered him out of them all . . . faithfully followed." Timothy's response to the teaching, conduct, aim, faith, patience, as he saw these exemplified in Paul's life, was far more than observed. Timothy "faithfully followed" (Williams) Paul's teaching, conduct, etc. He did not literally follow his persecutions, sufferings, but he did follow the spirit of suffering which he saw exhibited in his spiritual father. What a heritage he had from such a spiritual father!

Verses 12-13. A general truth as to the righteous and the wicked. "Everyone who wants to live a godly life as a follower of Christ Jesus will be persecuted." The best Christians, those who live nearest to the ideals of Christ, who earnestly strive every day to let Christ "live in them," must be crucified with Christ. This means dying daily with Christ. That means persecution and suffering for His sake.

The second general truth: "But bad men and impostors will go on from bad to worse, misleading others and misled themselves." This is literally true until the Spirit of God lands a thunderbolt of truth in the heart, as he did in the heart of Paul at the gate of Damascus. Only God can halt such wicked men and impostors. He does it through the Holy Spirit and gospel truth.

Verses 14-15. Timothy's early religious training in a religious home. His grandmother Lois had an abiding faith in the Old Testament Scriptures and in the promise they gave to future generations, that the Messiah was coming to deliver, not only Israel, but all mankind insofar as men would believe in Him. His mother Eunice imbibed the spirit and devotion of her mother and continued instructing young Timothy. Paul seems to be happy to narrate three generations of abiding faith in God and the Messiah (II Tim. 1:5). "From childhood you have known the sacred Scriptures." From grandmother Lois, to his mother Eunice, faith in God and His promises of love and grace to mankind; now in the third generation Timothy tightens the cord of faith in the Scriptures and their promises of salvation and life. To know the Scriptures from childhood is the greatest blessing a growing child can have. These Scriptures "can give you wisdom that leads to salvation through faith in Christ Jesus."

Verses 16-17. The sacred Scriptures inspired. *Theopneustos,* literally God-breathed, God in-breathed. Paul's thought is that God's own breath through the Holy Spirit in the prophetic writers, Moses, David, Isaiah, and others, breathed into those Old Testament writers and thus made the Scriptures "sacred," that is, produced by the divine breath of God. This thought is more impressive when you remember that the same Greek word is used for spirit and breath.

Thus we see that Paul believed in the inspiration of the Old Testament. As evidence, notice that he quotes from it seventy-four times in Romans to prove the validity of his teaching.

Verse 3:16b. Because the Old Testament Scriptures are inspired they are "helpful for teaching, for reproof, for correction, for training in doing what is right." The Old Testament from Moses to Malachi is full of moral and spiritual teaching. We find here the background for nearly all of Jesus' moral and spiritual teaching.

Also useful "for reproof." It is profitable in telling one when he has done wrong and how great is the punishment he must bear, thus warning him not to repeat the sin. The first great reproof we find in Genesis 3 when Eve and Adam are reproved for partaking of the forbidden fruit. "For correction." "This word is a close synonym of reproof. It is more positive; takes up the thought where reproof leaves off. A father reproves his son for telling a lie; he corrects him as he seeks to show him the horrible consequences of lying and the blessed results of always telling the truth. The historical books of the Old Testament and Proverbs are packed with reproof and correction. "For training in doing what is right." Ruskin's mother taught her son John to memorize scores of great gems in the Bible, many from the Old Testament. He later attributes his stability of character and his attractive English style to this familiarity with the Bible. I am informed that today many teachers of English use the Old Testament especially to train their pupils in the use of pure English.

Verse 17. "The thorough equipment of the man of God." Paul was "perfectly fit and thoroughly equipped for every good work" because of his knowledge of the Old Testament. So was B. H. Carroll. So was J. B. Gambrell. So was John A. Broadus. So are all great church leaders.

After receiving these letters from his spiritual father, the apostle to the Gentiles, Timothy must have felt under weighty obligation to continue the study of these sacred Scriptures that he might be "perfectly fit, thoroughly equipped, for every good work." How should our young ministers of today feel about their obligation to "know the sacred Scriptures?" Few of them have equal opportunities with Timothy to "know them from childhood." But our college and seminary systems of schools furnish modern young ministers privileges for the study of the Scriptures that not even Timothy had. Every young minister should take at least a two-year seminary course, or better, a four-year course, so that he may "know the sacred Scriptures, and be thoroughly equipped for every good work."

"The man of God." More than likely the apostle is thinking of Timothy and men preparing themselves for the ministry. But laymen, and laywomen, today are privileged to enter our great Bible schools and study the sacred Scriptures according to more thorough methods. They have the same privileges to secure the infilling of the Holy Spirit to help them interpret these Scriptures. More and more new phases of good work are opening up for laymen and women workers. The seminaries are trying to supply these demands by offering, under specially trained teachers, courses in departments, and even schools of religious education.

Chapter IV

ANOTHER SOLEMN CHARGE TO TIMOTHY (4:1-5)

I solemnly charge you, before God and Christ Jesus who is to judge the living and the dead, and by His appearing and His kingdom, ² preach the message, stay at it in season and out of season; convince, reprove, exhort people with perfect patience as a teacher. ³ For a time will come when they will not listen to wholesome teaching, but to gratify their own evil desires will surround themselves with teachers who teach to gratify their own evil desires, because their ears are itching so to be tickled, ⁴ and they will cease to listen to the truth and will turn to listen to myths. ⁵ But you, on your part, must always keep your head cool, suffer hardship, do your work as a herald of the good news, and so fill your ministry to the brim.

Key words and phrases. Verse 1. A most solemn oath is administered to Timothy—fourfold: "Before God and Christ Jesus, the Judge of the living and the dead, by His appearing and His kingdom." He puts Christ Jesus on an equality with God the father. To make it more solemn, Christ Jesus is the Judge of the living and the dead. Then he adds, which strengthens the oath as Paul sees it, "by His appearing and His kingdom." The parousia is the climax of Christ's redemptive career, and the eschatological kingdom climaxes the whole soteriological process. To Paul this is the strongest and most solemn form of oath.

Verse 2. "Preach the message *(ton logon)*." The "word, the message," is the *euaggelion,* the good news. This includes the six line poem of the Early Church (I Tim. 3:16). "In season and out of season." Make opportunities if they do not open up to you. It also includes practical instruction: "convince [of sin], reprove [rebuke for sin committed], exhort with perfect patience as a teacher." Paul is a teacher as well as a preacher and apostle. He is laying upon Timothy especially the functions of a preacher and a teacher.

Verses 3-4. People with itching ears gather around them false teachers to tickle their ears. "A time will come." It will be worse further on, so the apostle warns the young minister to be ready. "Itching ears." An expression to describe how the people are itching to hear something new or different, and more often false. This class of people get tired of the true because it is old and gets tame. "Will turn to listen to myths" (see comments on I Tim. 1:4). Myths are more or less flashy, sensational stories with no historical basis. They appeal to the imagination. Notice, the people are more or less responsible for the work of false teachers; they have itching ears, and gather around them false teachers. However, aggressive false teachers are responsible for perverting the people and turning them away from the truth.

Verse 5 warns Timothy to do three things to overcome the false teachings: a) "Keep your head cool," b) "endure hardship," c) do the work of an evangelist. Stay in proper mental attitude; take the hard knocks as they come, and keep up the main task, telling the story of the good news and winning people to Christ.

PAUL HEROICALLY FACES MARTYRDOM (4:6-8)

My life, indeed, is already ebbing out, and the time has come for me to sail away. [7] I have fought the fight for the good, I have run my race, I have kept the faith. [8] Now the crown for doing right awaits me, which the Lord, the righteous Judge, will award me on that day, and not only me but also all who have loved His appearing.

Key words and phrases. Verse 6. Paul's view of death. "Being poured out." Referring to the heathen libation, a sacrifice made by pouring. So he feels his life is already being poured out, equivalent to our *ebbing out.* "Time to sail away." Paul had likely crossed the Mediterranean Sea several times; had also been on the Adriatic and Aegean Seas. As he sat in his dungeon meditating on how he was soon to depart from this life, he thought of his soul as sailing away from the shores of time and suffering, to the shores of eternity and endless bliss. Not sailing to Rome for trial before Nero, but sailing to the kingdom of glory to receive his rewards for work and service and sufferings.

Verse 7. His résumé of life. "Fought the fight for the good." That is what makes the fight good. Washington and his colonial troops fought for freedom and that made it a good fight. Paul fought for the good of mankind, for the glory of Christ and the Father. "I have run my race." He sees the athlete in the Grecian games fall at the end of his race, exhausted but hilarious because he has won the wreath. "I have kept the faith." Objective sense of the term. He feels that he has kept "the basic doctrines of the Christian faith." Now he is ready to die for the faith, as well as live and suffer for it.

Verse 8. Looking to the rewards for his labors and sufferings. "Crown of righteousness." This is the crown he wins for being and doing right. He got right with God at Damascus through faith in Christ as the Son of God and Saviour of sinners. After that he practiced righteousness; that is, doing right. It is for the latter that he will receive the wreath made in the shape of a crown for the winner in the Greek races. "Which the Lord, the righteous Judge, will award me." The Greeks appointed a noted dignitary to award the wreaths in the games. So Paul sees the Lord Jesus, the righteous Judge, as placing this crown upon his head by-and-by. The wreath is won by doing right; it is awarded by the Lord Jesus who is righteous. "On that day." The parousia, which includes Christ's coming and judging and awarding—separating the wicked from the righteous (Matt. 25:34-46). "Not only me but also all who have loved His appearing." The toiling, suffering ones have loved and longed for the day which marks the cessation of the suffering and the reception of the rewards from the Master.

CONCLUDING WITH SOME PERSONAL MATTERS (4:9-18)

Verse 9. He pleads with Timothy to come soon. He is lonely.
Verse 10. "Demas has deserted me, because he loves this world." Love for this world is the cause of thousands of deserting saints. "Gone to Thessalonica." Perhaps his kin or worldly friends are

there. Crescens and Titus had gone, one to Galatia, the other to Dalmatia; perhaps to preach the Word and meet the brothers.

Verse 11. "Luke alone is with me." For two reasons: professional, to administer to his physical comforts in this trying hour; to share Christian fellowship. Beautiful tie; a cultured Greek and a learned Jew bound together in ties of Christian love.

Verse 12. Sends Tychicus to Ephesus—to be with Timothy; perhaps in an emergency.

Verse 13. Needs his extra coat which he had left at Carpus' home in Troas. Asks Timothy to bring it. Also bring his ordinary books (papyri) and his Bible (parchments). He may have forgotten his own copy , or this may be a special copy which he wishes to see before his execution.

Verses 14, 15. Alexander the coppersmith, who had done Paul much harm by opposing the good news he preached, is mentioned to Timothy as one of whom he should beware. He leaves Alexander to the Lord who will requite him for his deeds. Paul avoids spite or revenge toward his opponents.

Verses 16, 17. "At my first defense no one took my part." Perhaps Dr. Luke was still with him. We know "the Lord stood by me and gave me strength, so that the message preached by me might have its full effect . . . So I was rescued from the lion's mouth." Undoubtedly this was Nero, and refers to his release at his first defense (trial).

Verse 18. "The Lord will rescue me from every wicked work and save me to His heavenly kingdom." As he faces the second trial he looks to the future for his complete vindication—"save" in eschatological sense, "to His heavenly kingdom." "To Him be glory forever and ever. Amen." Such praise just bubbles up from the great soul of Paul as his heart throbs with a sense of being saved by grace!

GREETINGS AND BENEDICTION (19-22)

Verses 19-21. Paul cannot forget Prisca and Aquila (Acts 18). Sends his best wishes to them. Also to Onesiphorus who ministered to him as a prisoner in Rome (1:16-18). Erastus and Trophimus left at important posts. Four others send their best wishes to

Timothy and to all the brothers. A cordial fellowship characterized the early Christians.

Verse 22. Benediction. "The Lord be with your spirit." "Lord" is Jesus. "Spiritual blessing [grace] be with you all" (plural).

TRUE RELIGION IN THE HOME—II TIMOTHY 1:5
PAUL A PRACTICAL TEACHER AS WELL AS A THEOLOGIAN

I. What Conditions Put True Religion in the Home?
   1. Both parents, surely one, stalwart Christians
   2. Children of responsible age Christians. Jonathan Edwards converted at six.
   3. Regular Bible reading and prayer. Noted minister: "In these times family religion has declined."
   4. All Christians daily practice the Christ life. Girl with each chore praying suitable prayer, "Washing dishes, wash me," etc.

II. Why Is Family Religion So Essential and Significant?
   Two laws:
   1. Heredity. Moses, as well as scientists, accept it: "To third and fourth generation." *Century Dictionary:* "The transmission of the qualities and character of parents to offspring." Spurgeon: "My son can inherit my gout but not my religion." Neither, only a "tendency" toward each. Tubercular child inherits only a tendency toward the disease.
   2. Environment. These forces are about 50-50 in determining character and personality. A race horse must have both to succeed. So Christians. Southey: "Live as long as you may, the first twenty years of life are the longer half." Modern scientists (some) conclude that the child in the first seven years receives into his mind all the materials for making life (to seventy or eighty). In educational process the child is reworking the materials to different forms and products. If this is so, how significant is home training the first seven years!

III. Our American Civilization and Christianity Dependent on Home Culture

1. Roman homes and women degenerated before Rome fell (476). So the soldiers degenerated; could not stop the Goths, Visigoths.

2. So German homes. Hitler taught children world supremacy and hatred of English and Americans, not love and humility; his regime fell in 1945. Daniel Webster: "If we Americans continue to hold and practice the principles of the Bible on which this Republic was founded, we go on prospering and to prosper. If not, some powers now unseen will prevail and destroy us and our civilization." If our homes are lost to the Christian religion, we shall go like Rome, Greece, Germany.

3. Let us tie up generation after generation with true religion, as we find it in the history of Timothy: "Your sincere faith, the faith that dwelt first in your grandmother Lois and your mother Eunice, and now, I am sure, dwells in you." Grandmother, mother, son and grandson. The faith not inherited but the tendency toward it. Why not make the tendency good and not evil? By maintaining true religion in all our American homes.

It is good to remember what Burns sang in "The Cotter's Saturday Night":

From scenes like these Old Scotia's grandeur springs,
Which make her loved at home, revered abroad.

Also those pungent thoughts from Charles Wagner's *Simple Life:*

"It [the home] is the germ of all those grand and simple virtues which ensure the permanence of all our institutions." State, school, church, all draw their constituents from the home, and can live and flourish only as the home maintains true religion from generation to generation.

SERMON OUTLINE FROM II TIMOTHY 4

THE APOSTLE PAUL FACING A MARTYR'S DEATH IN PERFECT PEACE (II Tim. 4:6-8)

His First Roman Imprisonment in a Private House; the Second in a Dungeon

I. New Conception of Death
 1. A sacrifice—offering (a libation). In I Thessalonians 4:13 it is "falling asleep."
 2. "Sailing away." From the shores of time to eternity. Paul had often sailed the Mediterranean, the Adriatic, the Aegean.

II. He Surveys His Life (7)
 1. He has fought the fight for good. The purpose: conquest of self; conquest of the world for Christ; for the glory of God.
 2. He has finished the race. Greek games. Life a race.
 3. He has kept the faith. Objective: basic doctrines.

III. Facing the Future in Triumphant Hope (8)
 1. The crown. Conquest and now King; Greek crowns fade.
 2. Awarded by the righteous Judge (Lord Jesus)
 3. "On that Day" (parousia). He coming to separate (Matt. 25:34-46).
 4. A crown "for all who love His appearing."

Shortly after Dr. Williams finished writing these words, he sailed away from the shores of time and disembarked on the shores of eternity (in May, 1952).